AMERICA'S TOP
RESUMES

for AMERICA'S TOP JOBS™

SECOND EDITION

Michael Farr with Louise M. Kursmark

JIST
Works

America's Top Resumes for America's Top Jobs, Second Edition

© 2002 by JIST Publishing, Inc.

Published by JIST Works, an imprint of JIST Publishing, Inc.
8902 Otis Avenue
Indianapolis, IN 46216-1033
Phone: 1-800-648-JIST   Fax: 1-800-JIST-FAX   E-mail: info@jist.com

Some Other Books by Michael Farr:

Getting the Job You Really Want
The Quick Resume & Cover Letter Book
Best Jobs for the 21st Century
Young Person's Guide to Getting and Keeping a Good Job
The Right Job for You
America's Fastest-Growing Jobs

America's Top Jobs® for College Graduates
America's Top Jobs® for People Without a Four-Year Degree
America's Top Medical, Education & Human Services Jobs
America's Top White-Collar Jobs
The Very Quick Job Search

Visit our Web site at **www.jist.com** for information on JIST, free job search information, book chapters, and ordering information on our many products!

Quantity discounts are available for JIST books. Please call our Sales Department at 1-800-648-5478 for a free catalog and more information.

Acquisitions and Development Editor: Lori Cates Hand
Interior Design and Layout: Debbie Berman
Cover Designer: Trudy Coler
Proofreaders: Jeanne Clark, Veda Dickerson, and Mary Ellen Stephenson
Indexer: Tina Trettin

Printed in the United States of America
06 05 04 03 02   9 8 7 6 5 4 3 2 1

Library of Congress Cataloging-in-Publication data is on file with the Library of Congress.

We have been careful to provide accurate information in this book, but it is possible that errors and omissions have been introduced. Please consider this in making any career plans or other important decisions. Trust your own judgment above all else and in all things.

Trademarks: All brand names and product names used in this book are trade names, service marks, trademarks, or registered trademarks of their respective owners.

ISBN 1-56370-856-6

This Is NOT Just Another Resume Book

As you have surely noticed, this is a very big resume book—perhaps the biggest ever. As far as I can tell, it is the only book that has attempted to include sample resumes for ALL major jobs. And I can tell you that doing this was not easy. Thousands of hours have been spent writing the hundreds of resumes that are included. Real people are behind each and every resume—the job seekers who "own" them and the many professional writers who crafted them. In addition, the authors and the editors at JIST have spent many more hours selecting resumes, revising the narrative sections, writing notes on the resumes, editing, designing, and completing all the other tasks required to produce a book. But I think it is all worth it.

Does the World Need Another Resume Book?

Over the years, I have written many books on job seeking, and most include a section on resumes. But, for many years, I resisted writing a "resume book" because I was not convinced that yet another one was needed. About now you might be thinking that this is an odd thing for a writer of a resume book to be telling you. My first resume book, *The Quick Resume & Cover Letter Book*, has done very well. It was selected as one of the top three business books of the year by the Publishers Marketing Association and continues to sell very well. Based on this, I decided to do a second resume book. Based on that book's success over the years, I decided to update and revise it for this new edition.

But I see my task as helping you with your life planning and job search—and not just telling you "how to write a resume." So I decided that my resume book would put the resume-writing process into the more important context of an effective job search. So *America's Top Resumes* is a resume book, yes, but it is also a book on how to best *use* your resume in your job search.

What Is Unique About This Book

In spite of what most resume book writers suggest, a good resume will *not* get you a good job, nor will a better, best, or perfect resume. At most, a well-written resume will help you get an interview. Yet, as I will gently remind you from time to time, there are better ways to get an interview than sending out resumes.

Over the years, I've seen lots of resume books, and most share two major problems:

- **Problem 1:** Most resume book writers suggest that a good/better/best/perfect resume is the most important element in getting an interview. They tell you that a great resume, sent to lots of people, will help you get a great job. I think, instead, that a well-written resume is an important *tool* to use in your job search, and that making direct contacts is a far more effective way to set up interviews. And it is during the interview where the real action is. Sending out resumes and hoping someone will call you is a passive approach with a low effectiveness rate for getting interviews.

■ **Problem 2:** Everyone is a resume expert. Most resume books suggest that there is one and only one "correct" way to write a good/better/best/perfect resume. They suggest that *their* way is the best way, and all sample resumes included in the book use that particular style. Baloney! I say that each resume is unique, just like you are, and that there is room for lots of variation.

In my books I avoid the first problem by providing you with job search advice (brief though it is in this book) that will help you put your resume into the proper job search context. My advice is, in its simplest form, to write an acceptable resume and then get on with the important work of your job search, which is getting interviews. If you want to write a better resume, do so in the evenings and on weekends—and I will even show you how to write one.

I've solved the second problem, "one-size-fits-all" resumes, by providing examples written by dozens of professional resume writers. These well-done resumes give you a wide array of writing styles, layouts, graphic designs, and other features to browse. I hope you find this combination of practical advice and many excellent resume samples helpful.

I wish you well in your job search and your life.

Mike Farr

P.S.: I want to thank all the members of the Career Masters Institute, the Professional Association of Résumé Writers and Career Coaches, and the National Résumé Writers' Association who submitted and "fictionalized" their best resumes for this book. They are true professionals who do more to help their clients than you can imagine. Thanks.

Contents

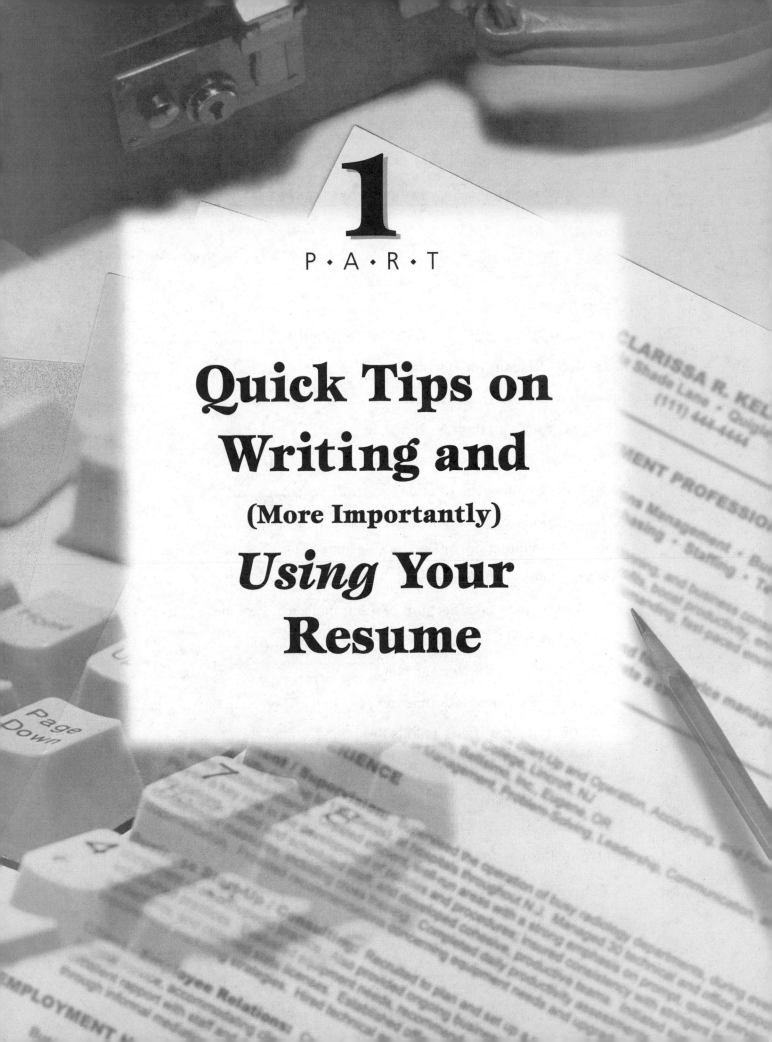

1
P·A·R·T

Quick Tips on Writing and
(More Importantly)
Using Your Resume

Major Topics in This Part

Quick Tips on Writing and
(More Importantly)
Using Your Resume

The material in this section provides a short review of how to write an acceptable resume. I say "acceptable" because I advise you to begin with a resume you can complete in a day or less. Then you can use that resume in an active campaign to get interviews and job offers. Later, you can write a better resume if you feel you need or want to.

Don't let writing a resume become a problem for you. Writing a basic one is really quite simple and shouldn't take more time than watching a movie. This section provides you with all you need to create a basic resume, as well as tips for writing more sophisticated ones. Part 2 provides hundreds of examples of well-written, well-designed resumes. I invite you to browse through them and use ideas you find there on your own resume.

As I worked on this book, it became clear that there wasn't room to include substantial job search advice. Some is provided in this section, but if you want or need more, I humbly suggest that you get it from one of my other books. Either *The Very Quick Job Search* (very thorough) or *Seven Steps to Getting a Job Fast* (shorter) will do.

Some people put entirely too much emphasis on a resume in a job search. If you are looking for a job for which an employer will expect you to have a resume, you should write one. But many people believe that a resume on its own will get them an interview or a job. That is a very old-fashioned idea.

Unfortunately, many resume and job search books provide bad advice. Too many authors hold to an outdated view of the job search, in which a job is advertised and people are screened in or out of an interview based on an application or a resume. In that context, their advice is to send out lots of great-looking resumes that will somehow stand out from the rest and get you an interview.

Although that approach makes sense from the personnel manager's point of view, it is not a helpful mind-set for you to adopt. It encourages you to be passive—completely dependent on someone else to evaluate your merits without ever meeting you. Because most people now work for smaller employers—many of which don't even have a personnel or human resources department to look at unsolicited resumes—the passive, traditional approach just does not make good sense.

Even with companies that *do* have a personnel office and a traditional interview/ screening process, you are far better off calling the person who is most likely to super-vise you and asking for an interview. How can it hurt? While others are dutifully (and passively) sending their resumes to the personnel department, you have made direct contact and have a shot at an interview.

So a legitimate question might be, "Why have a resume at all?" Later we'll look at both sides of that argument and I'll tell you my own conclusions. I'll also give you guidelines for writing your resume and tips on how to use it in your job search.

What Is a Resume?

As the first step in creating your resume, let's examine what a resume is and consider what it can and cannot do.

"Resume" is the term most often used to describe a piece of paper (or two) that summarizes your life history. The idea is to select those specific parts of your past that support your ability to do a particular job well. Most often, the paper presents you to prospective employers who, based on their response to the paper, may or may not grant you an interview. Along with the application form, the resume is the tool employers use most to screen job seekers.

So a resume is clearly a tool to use in getting a job, right? The answer to this is yes…and no. Many people confuse the purpose of a resume and put entirely too much emphasis on using it to get interviews. But before I give you my own opinions on this matter, let's look at what others say about resumes.

Some People Say You Don't Need a Resume

Trying to get an interview by sending out dozens of resumes is usually a waste of stamps. For a variety of reasons, many career professionals suggest that resumes aren't needed at all. Some of these reasons make a lot of sense:

1. **Resumes aren't good job search tools.**
   It's true: Resumes don't do a good job of getting you interviews. Used in the traditional way, your resume is far more likely to get you screened out. There are better ways to get in to see people, and we review some of these ways later in this book.

2. **Some jobs don't require resumes.**
   Employers of office, managerial, professional, and technical workers often want the details that a resume provides. But for many jobs—particularly entry-level, trade, and unskilled positions—resumes typically aren't required at all.

3. **Some job search methods don't use resumes.**
   Many people get jobs without even using a resume. In most cases, they get interviews because they are already known to the employer or are referred by someone who is. Although a resume might help in this situation, it is not required.

4. **Some resume experts call a resume by another name.**
   In his book *Who's Hiring Who?*, for example, Richard Lathrop says you shouldn't use a resume at all. Instead, he advises his readers to use his "qualifications brief." Bernard Haldane, author of *Career Satisfaction and Success,* suggests using his "professional job power report" instead of a resume. And there are other names, including "curriculum vita" and "employment proposal." In all their forms, they are really various types of resumes.

Good Reasons for Having a Resume

In my opinion, all things considered, there are stronger reasons to have a resume than not:

1. **Employers often ask for resumes.**
   This alone is reason enough to have one. If an employer asks for a resume, why have only excuses?

2. **Writing a resume can help you structure your communications.**
   Writing a resume requires you to clarify your job objective, select related skills and experiences, document your accomplishments, and get it all down in a short format. These are all worthwhile activities for job seekers and essential steps in a job search, even if you don't use a resume at all.

3. **Used properly, a resume can be an effective job search tool.**
   A well-done resume presents details of your experience efficiently, in a way an employer can access conveniently. It can also present the skills you have to support your job objective and details that are often not solicited in a preliminary interview. Used appropriately, a well-done resume can help you conduct an effective job search campaign.

How Do You Use a Resume?

"Send out your resume to lots of strangers and, if it is good enough, you will get lots of job offers." If you believe this, we've got other fairy tales for you. Your objective is to get a good job—not to do a great resume.

That's right. Contrary to the advice of many resume and job search "experts," writing a dynamite or perfect (or whatever) resume will rarely get you the job you want. A job offer comes only after *the interview,* with an occasional odd exception. So the goal of your job search is to get interviews and to do well in them. The admonition to send out lots of resumes to people you don't know—and other traditional resume advice—is a lot of baloney (or, if you prefer, bologna).

I hope this doesn't upset you. It's simply the truth. That's why I suggest you do a *simple* resume early in your job search. This allows you to get on with getting interviews rather than sitting at home working on a "better" resume.

And, for those of you who don't like to read (or are anxious to get on with your job search), following are some basic tips for *using* your resume.

At best, a resume will help you get an interview. However, there are better, more effective ways to get one. Here are four tips for using your resume to its best effect:

1. **Get the interview first.**
   Don't send an unsolicited resume. It is almost always better to contact the employer directly by phone or in person. Then send your resume, *after you schedule an interview,* so the employer can read about you before your meeting.

2. **Send your resume after an interview.**
   Send a thank-you note after an interview and enclose a JIST Card® (my preference) or a resume. Or both. A copy of a JIST Card is presented later in this section, and this unique job search tool is covered more thoroughly in part 3.

3. **Give resumes to people you know.**
   Give copies of your resume (and JIST Card) to everyone in your job search network. They can pass copies along to others who might be interested in hiring you.

Guidelines for Writing a Superior Resume

Here are some basic guidelines to follow when you develop your resume. They aren't rules exactly, but you should carefully consider each suggestion because each is based on many years of experience and, I think, makes good common sense.

Keep It Short

Opinions differ on this, but one or two pages is a good range. If you are seeking a managerial, professional, or technical position—for which most people have lots of prior experience—two pages is the norm. In most cases, a resume any longer than two pages will not be read at all by a busy employer. Shorter resumes are often more difficult to write, but they are well worth the effort because they get read.

Eliminate Errors

I am always amazed at how often an otherwise good resume has typographical, grammatical, or punctuation errors. *Don't have any!* Find someone who is good at proofreading to review yours. Then review it again.

Make It Look Good

You surely know that your resume's overall appearance will affect an employer's opinion of you. Is it well laid out? Is it "crisp" and professional looking? Does it include good use of white space?

Use Technology Tools

It is essential to use a computer to prepare your resume and create electronic files for e-mailing and pasting into online job applications. If you don't have access to a computer or high-quality printer, have someone else print or produce your resume for you. And be certain you obtain a copy on disk so that you can update, edit, and e-mail your resume throughout your job search.

Word-processing programs can create very attractive resumes because you can use bold, italics, and different sizes and styles of type while adjusting type sizes for ample white space.

You can use any word-processing program to prepare your resume. Because Microsoft Word is the most commonly used program, I recommend that you use it if possible, particularly if you plan to use the Internet and e-mail extensively during your search. You can also have your resume word processed and "designed" at local secretarial services and smaller print shops, as well as nationwide chains such as Kinko's. They will charge a modest fee for this service but can make your resume look quite professional with attractive formatting and sharp laser printing.

Use Good Photocopying and Printing

Good-quality photocopies of resumes are now widely used and accepted. If you do have your own computer and high-quality printer, individually prepared and printed resumes can present a better appearance and, of course, allow you to target your resume to a particular job. While laser printers create a crisper image, good-quality inkjet output is also perfectly acceptable.

You can also take your resume to most small print shops and have them print a few hundred copies for a reasonable price. However you produce them, it is important that you have plenty of them on hand. You can individually produce targeted resumes and cover letters for important job prospects as you need to.

Use High-Quality Paper

A good-quality paper is important. Never use cheap paper like that typically used for photocopies. Most copy machines will copy your resume onto good-quality paper, so get your own paper supply if necessary. Print shops and office-supply stores have a selection of papers, and you can usually get matching envelopes. Although most resumes are on white paper, I prefer an off-white paper. You can use other light, pastel colors such as tan, blue, or gray, but I do not recommend red, pink, or green tints.

Papers also come in different qualities, and you can see and feel the difference. Papers that include cotton fibers, for example, have a richer texture and a quality "feel" that is appropriate for the professional look you want in a resume.

Stress Accomplishments and Use Action Words

Most resumes are boring. Don't simply list what your duties were in previous jobs; emphasize what you got done! Make sure you mention the specific skills you have to do the job, as well as any related accomplishments and credentials. Even a simple resume can include some of these elements. Look over the list of "Action Words and Phrases" on page 15 and the sample resumes later in this section for ideas.

Don't Be Humble

Like an interview, your resume is no place to be humble. If you don't communicate what you can do, who will?

Make Every Word Count

Write a long rough draft and then edit, edit, edit. If a word or phrase does not support your job objective, consider dropping it.

Write It Yourself

Although I expect you to use ideas and even words or phrases from the sample resumes in this book, *it is most important that your resume represent you, not someone else*. Present your own skills in your resume and support them with your own accomplishments. If you do not have good written communication skills, it is perfectly acceptable to get help from someone who does. Just make sure your resume ends up sounding as if you wrote it. (See appendix A for a list of professional resume writers who contributed resumes to this book.)

Break Some Rules

This is *your* resume, so you can do whatever makes sense to you. There are few rules that can't be broken in putting together your own resume. In this section, you will learn about the types of resumes and see a few basic examples. Remember that it is often far more useful to simply have an acceptable resume as soon as possible—and to use it in an active job search—than to delay your job search while working on a better resume. A better resume can come later, after you have created a presentable one that you can use right away.

4.   **If all else fails, use traditional techniques.**
      If you can't make direct contact with a prospective employer—for example, if you are answering a want ad that lists only a box number for an address—send your resume in the traditional way. But if that's all you do, don't expect much to happen.

Whatever you do, remember: Honesty is the best policy. Many people lie on their resumes, claim credentials they don't have, and hope that no one will find out. Many organizations now verify this information, sometimes long after a person is hired. I have always found that it is best to avoid lying—but that doesn't mean you have to present negative information! Make sure that everything you put in your resume *supports your job objective* in some direct way! If you really can do the job you want, someone will probably hire you because you can. And you will sleep better.

Everyone's an Expert

A resume is one of those things that almost everyone seems to know more about than you do. If you show your resume to any three people, you will probably get three different suggestions on how to improve it. One person might tell you that you really need only a one-page resume. ("And how come no references are listed?") Another might tell you that you should have listed all your hobbies, plus the fact that you won the spelling bee in sixth grade. And the third might tell you that your resume is boring—that the way to grab attention is to print your resume in red ink on a brown paper bag.

So, one of the problems with resumes is that everyone is an expert but few agree on anything. This means that *you* will have to make some decisions on how you do your resume. Fortunately, I'm here to help.

The Different Types of Resumes

To keep this simple, I will discuss only three types of resumes. There are other, more specialized types, but these three are generally the most useful and the most common.

The Chronological Resume

The word "chronology" refers to a sequence of events in time, and the primary feature of this resume is the listing of jobs you've held, from the most recent backwards. This is the simplest of resumes, and it is a useful format if used properly. This type of resume works best when you've had a long, steady work history and promotions that you want to showcase.

The Skills, or Functional, Resume

Instead of listing your experience under each job, the skills resume clusters your experiences under major skill areas. For example, if you are strong in communication skills, under that major heading you would list a variety of supportive experiences from different jobs, school, or volunteer situations. Several other major skill areas would also be presented.

This approach would make little sense, of course, unless you had a job objective *that required these skills.* For this reason and others, a skills resume is harder to write than a simple chronological resume. If you have limited paid work experience, are changing careers, or have not worked for a while, a skills resume can be a clearly superior approach to help you present your strengths and avoid displaying your weaknesses.

The Combination, or Creative, Resume

Elements of chronological and skills resumes can be combined in various ways to improve the clarity or presentation of a resume. For example, if you have a good work history that supports your current job objective, you could start with a Skills section that supports the skills needed in the job you want, and then include a shorter chronological Work Experience section that presents the essential elements of your work history. Or you could begin with a summary of your work history, in chronological order, followed by a review of the key skills you have to do the job, or some other creative combination that presents you well.

There are also creative resume formats that defy any category, but which are clever and have worked for some people. I've seen handwritten resumes (usually *not* a good idea); unusual paper colors, sizes, and shapes; resumes with tasteful drawings and borders; and lots of other ideas. Some were well done and well received; others were not.

Write a Chronological Resume in an Hour

Keeping things simple has its advantages. This section shows you how to create a basic chronological resume in about an hour. Although the resulting resume can certainly be improved, it has the distinct advantage of letting you get on with your job search right away. Later, as time permits, you can do a better one.

The biggest advantage of a chronological resume is that it's easy to do. This format works best for those who have several years of experience in the same type of job they are seeking now, because a chronological resume clearly displays their recent work experience. If you are changing careers, have been out of the workforce, or do not have much paid work experience related to the job you want, a skills resume, presented later in this section, might be a better choice.

Most employers prefer chronological resumes—even those that are basic and lack excitement—provided that they are neat and error free. You can use one early in your job search while you work on a more sophisticated resume. The goal here is to put together an acceptable resume quickly so that you won't be sitting at home worrying about your resume instead of out looking for a job.

Following are two examples of chronological resumes. The information and format of the first are quite basic, but the approach works well enough because Matthew is looking for a job in a field where he has experience and long-time interest. The Instant Resume Worksheet on page 17 will help you write the content for this kind of basic resume in about an hour.

In the second example, Matthew's basic resume is improved, with a number of added features. Note especially the more descriptive job objective, the Skills and Qualifications section, and the added details of his accomplishments and skills in both the Education and Work Experience sections. Although the improved resume would take most people longer than an hour to create, it uses the basic chronological approach and could be completed by most people in just a few hours.

A basic chronological resume

Matthew Taylor

115 South Hawthorne Avenue
Chicago, IL 46204
(317) 653-9217 (home)
(317) 272-7608 (message)
matthewtaylor@yahoo.com

OBJECTIVE

Sales position in the sports industry.

EDUCATION

Bachelor of Science in Psychology, 2002
Loyola University, Chicago, IL

WORK EXPERIENCE

Windy City Sporting Goods, Chicago, IL, January 2000–Present
Sales Representative
Sell soccer equipment and uniforms to teams and individuals. Requires organization and problem-solving to put together best package of equipment in appropriate sizes and prices.

Chicago Soccer Festival, Chicago, IL, 1999–2002
Co-chair
Played a key role in organizing and running highly successful soccer festival sponsored by Windy City Sporting Goods and designed to build visibility for the store and recognition for the sport. Organize festival details including field rental, recruitment of officials, and vendor licensing. Develop informational and marketing campaigns.

Oak Park High School, Oak Park, IL, 2000–2002
Assistant Coach, Varsity Boys' Soccer (2001–2002)
Coached defense and goalie squads; worked with high school boys 2 hours a day, 6 days a week to help develop athletic and life skills.

Head Coach, Freshman Girls' Soccer (2000–2001)
Managed 50 high school girls and 2 assistant coaches. Scheduled games and officials for the season. Worked to develop soccer skills for beginners.

ATHLETICS

Soccer   Chicagoland Men's Club team, 1997–Present
Oak Park High School, 1993–1997

Football   Oak Park High School, 1993–1997

An "improved" chronological resume

Matthew Taylor

115 South Hawthorne Avenue, Chicago, IL 46204
(317) 653-9217 (home)   (317) 272-7608 (message)
matthewtaylor@yahoo.com

OBJECTIVE

Sales position in the sports industry using skills gained through experience in sporting goods sales, sports event management, coaching, and team play.

SKILLS AND QUALIFICATIONS

- Two years of successful sales experience with a track record of increasing sales and effectively solving customer problems.
- Strong leadership abilities—demonstrated through coaching positions, sports leadership roles, and organizational leadership activities.
- Communication and presentation skills—comfortable and experienced speaking before groups and interacting with diverse individuals in sales, coaching, and competitive situations.
- Computer skills—proficient in MS Excel, Word, and PowerPoint.

EDUCATION

Bachelor of Science in Psychology, Loyola University, Chicago, IL, 2002
- Elected Vice President of Adventure Travel Club. Organized and ran meetings of club involved in planning and carrying out trips to various parts of the United States.

WORK EXPERIENCE

Sales Representative, Windy City Sporting Goods, Chicago, IL, January 2000–Present
Sell soccer equipment and uniforms to teams and individuals. Requires organization and problem-solving to put together best package of equipment in appropriate sizes and prices.
- Increased sales 25% annually.
- Serve as an expert resource to customers, including coaches and officials. Focus on developing long-term customer relationships by finding solutions to customer problems.

Co-chair, Chicago Soccer Festival, 1999–2002
Played a key role in organizing and running highly successful soccer festival sponsored by Windy City Sporting Goods and designed to build visibility for the store and recognition for the sport. Organize festival details including field rental, recruitment of officials, and vendor licensing. Develop informational and marketing campaigns.
- Festival has grown from a small, 5-team program in the late 1990s to a well-regarded regional event attracting 30–40 teams from throughout the Midwest.
- Began planning to launch similar festival for women's club teams (fall 2002).

Assistant Coach, Varsity Boys' Soccer, Oak Park High School, Oak Park, IL, 2001–2002
Coached defense and goalie squads; worked with high school boys 2 hours a day, 6 days a week to help develop athletic and life skills.
- Chicago Region II Soccer Champions, 2002

Head Coach, Freshman Girls' Soccer, Oak Park High School, Oak Park, IL, 2000–2001
Managed 50 high school girls and 2 assistant coaches. Scheduled games and officials for the season. Worked to develop soccer skills for beginners.

ATHLETICS

Soccer	Chicagoland Men's Club team, 1997–Present—Captain, 2000–Present Oak Park High School, 1993–1997—Captain, 1995–1997—City Championship, 1997
Football	Oak Park High School, 1993–1997

Writing the Major Sections of a Chronological Resume

An Instant Resume Worksheet follows these tips on page 17. Use it to complete each section of your basic chronological resume. You might find it helpful to complete a section of the worksheet after reading the tips related to that section.

The Heading Section

Do not write the word "Resume" at the top of the page. This is redundant (it's perfectly clear that this is a resume), and for computer scanning purposes, it's essential to have your name appear on the first line of your resume.

The Identification Section

This section consists of your name, your address, your phone numbers, and your e-mail address.

Name

You want to present a professional image, so avoid using a nickname. But don't feel you must spell out your entire first, middle, and last names; in most cases, use just your first name, optional middle initial, and last name.

Address

Don't abbreviate things—such as Street to St.—and do include your ZIP code. If you might move during your job search, ask a relative, friend, or neighbor if you can temporarily use their address to handle your mail. As a last resort, arrange for a P.O. box at the post office. Forwarded mail will be delayed, which can cause you to miss an opportunity. If you plan to move to a new city during your job search, get a local address at the new location so that you appear to be settled there.

Phone Numbers

An employer is likely to phone you rather than write to you. For this reason, it is essential that your resume provide a phone number that is reliably answered during the day. There are several ways to accomplish this:

- **Use an answering machine or voice-mail service.** These are inexpensive and reliable ways to be sure you don't miss messages. Use a professional-sounding message for incoming callers to hear. Consider how a prospective employer would react to your message, and let that be your guide.

- **List an alternative phone number or two.** Many of the sample resumes that follow list a home number and an alternative phone number such as a work number, mobile phone number, or pager. You can list the number of a reliable relative or friend who will answer your calls if your home number is busy or unanswered. It is best to designate these numbers as "home" or "messages" or "answering service" so that an employer will know what to expect. Don't include a work number unless it gives direct access to your phone and is not picked up by others when you are not there. And be ethical and discreet about using your employer's time for your job search.

■ Make sure that anyone likely to answer your home phone is trained on how to handle messages from employers. And on your resume, always include your area code. You never know who will be calling—or from where.

E-mail Address

Even if you are sending a paper resume by regular mail, an e-mail address communicates that you are technologically up-to-date and gives an employer a reliable means to contact you at any time of day or night. If your search is being conducted online, an e-mail address—one that you check daily—is essential. You can obtain free e-mail accounts from providers such as Hotmail and Juno. With these accounts, you'll have access from any Internet-connected computer and can keep your job search correspondence separate from other e-mail.

You should now complete the Identification section of the Instant Resume Worksheet on page 17.

The Job Objective Statement for a Chronological Resume

You don't have to use a job objective statement on a chronological resume. Many (if not most) of the resumes in part 2 don't lead off that way. What they all do, however, is clearly answer the employer's questions: "Who are you and what can you do for me?" Many include a Summary or Profile or other introductory section instead of an objective. If you're writing a skills/functional resume, a job objective statement becomes more important because it is less obvious from looking at your resume what job you are interested in (see "The Job Objective Statement for a Skills Resume" under "Constructing a Skills Resume," later in this part).

Sample Job Objectives

■ A responsible general office position in a busy, medium-sized organization.

■ A management position in the warehousing industry. Position should require supervisory, problem-solving, and organizational skills.

■ Computer programming and/or systems analysis. Prefer an accounting-oriented emphasis and a solution-oriented organization.

■ Medical assistant or secretary in a physician's office, hospital, or other health services environment.

■ Responsible position requiring skills in public relations, writing, and reporting.

■ An aggressive and success-oriented professional, seeking a sales position offering both challenge and growth.

■ Desire position in the office management, secretarial, or clerical area. Position should require flexibility, good organizational skills, and an ability to handle people.

It's difficult to write a job objective that will not exclude you from jobs you would consider, without sounding as if you would be willing to do just anything. But a clear, focused objective is quite helpful to people reading your resume.

I see lots of objectives that emphasize what the person *wants* but don't provide information on what the person *can do.* For example, an objective that says "Interested in a position that allows me to be creative and offers adequate pay and advancement opportunities" is *not* a good objective at all. Who cares? This objective (a real one that someone actually wrote) displays a self-centered, "gimme" approach that will turn off most employers.

Look through the examples of simple but useful job objectives on the previous page. Most provide some information on the type of job the writer is seeking, as well as the skills he or she offers. The best ones avoid a narrow job title and keep options open to a wide variety of possibilities within a range of appropriate jobs.

I've included a Job Objective Worksheet on page 25. Go ahead and complete it now, along with the Job Objective section on the Instant Resume Worksheet on page 17. You should complete these worksheets even if you choose not to use an objective on your resume. You will find that writing an objective focuses your thoughts and will help you identify relevant skills and accomplishments when you are writing the rest of your resume.

Education and Training Section

Recent graduates should put their educational credentials toward the top of their resumes, because they represent the more important part of their experience. More experienced workers typically place their education toward the end of their resumes.

You can drop the Education section entirely if it doesn't support your job objective or if you don't have the educational credentials typically required for the position. This is particularly true if you have lots of work experience in your career area. Usually, though, you should emphasize the most recent and/or highest level of education or training that relates to the job.

Look at the sample resumes in this section and in part 2 for ideas. Then, on a separate piece of paper, rough out your Education and Training section. After you edit it to its final form, write it on the Instant Resume Worksheet on page 17.

Honors and Awards

If you have received any formal recognition or awards that support your job objective, you can mention them either in a separate resume section or in the Work Experience, Skills, Education, or Personal sections.

Work, Military, and Volunteer Experience Section

This section of the resume provides the details of your work history. If you have had significant work history, list each job along with details of what you accomplished and any special skills you used. Emphasize any skills that directly relate to the job objective you have stated on your resume.

List your most recent job first, followed by each previous job. Use additional sheets to cover *all* your significant jobs or unpaid experiences. You can treat any significant volunteer or military experience the same as a job.

Whenever possible, provide numbers to support what you did: the number of people served over one or more years, the number of transactions processed, the percentage of sales increase, the total inventory value you were responsible for, the payroll of the staff you supervised, the total budget you managed, and so on. As much as possible, demonstrate results using numbers. Specific results support your ability and lend credibility to your resume.

Emphasize your accomplishments! Think about the things you accomplished in jobs, school, the military, and other settings. Emphasize these things, even if it seems like bragging. Many of the sample resumes include statements about accomplishments to show you how this can be done. When writing about your work experience, be sure to use action words. Quantify what you did and provide evidence that you did it well. Take particular care to mention skills that directly relate to doing the job you want.

Use separate sheets of paper to write rough drafts of what you will use in your resume. Edit it so that every word contributes something. When you're done, transfer your statements to the Instant Resume Worksheet on pages 18–20.

Previous Job Titles

Remember that you can modify the title you had to more accurately reflect your responsibilities. For example, if your title was "sales clerk" but you frequently opened and closed the store and were often left in charge, you might use the more descriptive title "night sales manager." Check with your previous supervisor if you are worried about this, and ask if he or she would object. If you were promoted, you can handle the promotion as a separate job—and make sure that you mention the fact that you were promoted.

Previous Employers

Provide the organization's name, city, and the state or province in which it is located. A street address or supervisor's name is not necessary—you can provide those details on a separate sheet of references.

Use Action Words and Phrases

Use active rather than passive words and phrases throughout your resume. The following list includes many good examples. Look at the sample resumes in part 2 for additional ideas.

Administered	Implemented	Presented
Analyzed	Improved	Promoted
Controlled	Increased productivity	Reduced expenses
Coordinated	Increased profits	Reviewed
Created	Initiated	Researched
Designed	Innovated	Scheduled
Developed	Instructed	Set priorities
Diagnosed	Led	Solved
Directed	Managed	Supervised
Established policy	Modified	Trained
Expanded	Negotiated	Troubleshot
Guided	Organized	
Headed	Planned	

Employment Dates

If you have large gaps in your employment history that are not easily explained, use full years (rather than months and years) to avoid emphasizing the gaps. If you have a significant period of time during which you did not work, did you do anything else that could explain it in a positive way? School? Travel? Raising a family? Self-employment? Even if you mowed lawns and painted houses for money while you were unemployed, that counts as self-employment. It's much better than saying you were unemployed.

Professional Organizations

If you belong to job-related professional groups, it's worth mentioning, particularly if you are (or were) an officer or are active in some other way. Mention any accomplishments or awards.

Personal Information Section

Years ago, resumes traditionally included things such as your height, weight, marital status, hobbies, leisure activities, and other trivia. My advice is to not include this sort of information. Earlier I advised you to make every word count—if it does not support your job objective, delete it. The same goes here.

There are situations in which relevant extracurricular activities or hobbies can help you; if so, go ahead and use them. Look at the sample resumes and decide for yourself.

Although a personal section is optional, I sometimes like to end a resume on a personal note. Some of the sample resumes provide a touch of humor or playfulness as well as selected positives from outside school and work lives. This is also a good place to list significant community involvement, a willingness to relocate, or personal characteristics an employer might like. Keep it short.

Turn now to the Instant Resume Worksheet on page 20 and list any personal information you think is appropriate.

References Section

It is not necessary to include the names of your references on your resume. There are better things to do with the precious space. It's not even necessary to state "references available upon request" at the bottom because that is obvious. If employers want them, they know they can ask you for them.

It *is* helpful to line up your references in advance. Pick people who know your work as an employee, volunteer, or student. Your references do not have to be your supervisors or employers; they can be anyone who can speak about your work-related abilities. Make sure your references will say nice things about you by asking them just what they will say. Push for any negatives, and don't feel hurt if you get some. Nobody is perfect. Hearing about negatives up front gives you a chance to take someone off your list before he or she can do you any damage.

When you know who to include, type up a clean list on a separate sheet. Include names, addresses, phone numbers, and details of why these people are on your list.

Be aware that some employers are not allowed by company policy to give phone references. If this is the case, ask the employer to write a letter of reference that you can photocopy as needed. This is a good idea anyway, so you might want to ask for one even if it's not a problem to give phone references. I have refused to hire people who probably had good references but about whom I could not get information.

Keep copies of the list and any letters of recommendation and provide them when they are asked for. Do not attach them to your resume unless you are asked to do so.

The Instant Resume Worksheet

Directions: This worksheet will help you organize the information you need to complete a simple chronological resume. It also provides the basis for a skills resume. Write rough drafts for each of the more complicated sections that follow. Then complete the form with wording that's close to what you want to use in your resume.

Identification

Name: _____

Home address: _____

_____

Phone number and description (if any): _____

Alternative phone number and description: _____

Alternative phone number and description: _____

E-mail address: _____

Job Objective

_____

_____

_____

_____

_____

Education and Training

Begin with the highest level or most recent.

Graduate Degree

(Skip this section if you have not attended a master's or doctorate program.)

Institution name: _____

City and state/province (optional): _____

Degree or certificate earned: _____

Relevant courses, awards, achievements, and experiences: _____

_____

_____

_____

_____

College/Post–High School Training

Institution name: _____

City and state/province (optional): _____

Degree or certificate earned: _____

Relevant courses, awards, achievements, and experiences: _____

_____

_____

_____

(continues)

(continued)

High School

(This is usually not included unless it is the highest educational level you have attained.)

Institution name: _____

City and state/province (optional): _____

Degree or certificate earned: _____

Relevant courses, awards, achievements, and experiences: _____

_____

_____

_____

_____

Armed Services Training and Other Training or Certification

_____

_____

_____

_____

_____

Specific things you can do as a result: _____

_____

_____

_____

_____

Work, Military, and Volunteer Experience

(Begin with your most recent job.)

Name of organization: _____

Address: _____

Phone number: _____

Dates employed: _____

Job title(s): _____

Supervisor's name: _____

Details of any raises or promotions: _____

_____

_____

_____

Machinery or equipment you handled: _____

_____

_____

_____

Special skills this job required: _____

_____

_____

_____

List what you accomplished or did well: _____

_____

_____

_____

Next most recent job

Name of organization: _____

Address: _____

Phone number: _____

Dates employed: _____

Job title(s): _____

Supervisor's name: _____

Details of any raises or promotions: _____

_____

_____

_____

Machinery or equipment you handled: _____

_____

_____

_____

Special skills this job required: _____

_____

_____

_____

List what you accomplished or did well: _____

_____

_____

_____

Next most recent job

Name of organization: _____

Address: _____

Phone number: _____

Dates employed: _____

Job title(s): _____

Supervisor's name: _____

Details of any raises or promotions: _____

_____

_____

_____

Machinery or equipment you handled: _____

_____

_____

(continues)

(continued)

Special skills this job required: _____
_____
_____
_____

List what you accomplished or did well: _____
_____
_____
_____

Next most recent job

Name of organization: _____
Address: _____
Phone number: _____
Dates employed: _____
Job title(s): _____
Supervisor's name: _____
Details of any raises or promotions: _____
_____
_____
_____

Machinery or equipment you handled: _____
_____
_____
_____

Special skills this job required: _____
_____
_____
_____

List what you accomplished or did well: _____
_____
_____
_____

(If you need space for more jobs, attach additional sheets.)

Professional Organizations

_____
_____
_____
_____

Personal Information

_____
_____
_____

Write Your Basic Resume Now

At this point, you should have completed the Instant Resume Worksheet. Carefully review all dates, addresses, phone numbers, spelling, and other details. Now you can use the worksheet as a guide for preparing a better-than-average chronological resume.

Use the examples of simple chronological resumes later in this chapter for ideas when you create your own. Examples of skills resumes are included later in this section and in part 2. Look them over for ideas on writing and formatting your own.

Don't worry if your first attempt is not a wonderful, powerful, creative resume. That can come later. You need to have an acceptable resume first, one that you can use tomorrow to begin an active job search. So keep it simple and set yourself a tight deadline for having a simple resume finished so that the lack of one doesn't become a barrier to your job search.

If you have access to your own computer, go ahead and put the information you have collected into a resume format. Make sure you edit each section carefully and that the resume has *no errors at all*. If you do not have a computer or you are not a good typist, have someone else type your resume into a word-processing program for you. Whether you do it yourself or have it done, *carefully review it once more* for typographical or other errors that might have slipped in. Then, when you are certain that everything is correct, have the final version prepared.

Write a Skills/Functional Resume in Less Than a Day

Even though it takes a bit longer to write a skills (or functional) resume, the format has some advantages that might make it worth your time.

Why Consider Using a Skills Resume?

In its simplest form, a chronological resume is little more than a list of job titles and other details. Many employers look for people with successful histories in jobs similar to the open position. If you are a recent graduate or have little prior experience in the career you now want, you will find that a simple chronological resume emphasizes your lack of related experience rather than your ability to do the job.

A skills resume avoids these problems by highlighting what you have done—under the heading of Specific Skills—rather than jobs you have held.

If you hitchhiked across the country for two years, a skills resume won't necessarily display this time as a gap in your employment record. Instead, you could now say, "Traveled extensively throughout the country and am familiar with most major market areas." That could be a useful experience for certain positions.

Because it is a tool that can hide your problem areas, many employers do not like the skills resume. And a skills resume is probably not the best format for a wide-scale search that includes mass mailing (or e-mailing) your resume to potential employers and responding to want ads and online postings. But if you plan to pursue the active, targeted job search I recommend in this book, a skills resume will let you "put your best foot forward" for each opportunity you encounter. And if you have a problem that a traditional chronological resume highlights, a skills resume might help get you the opportunity to meet with a prospective employer rather than be screened out.

So if your work history is short or sporadic, you should consider doing a skills resume, even though it does take a bit more work to create a good one.

On the next page is an example of a basic skills resume for a recent high school graduate whose only experience has been in a fast-food restaurant. A skills resume is a good choice here because it allows the writer to emphasize her strengths without emphasizing that her work experience is limited.

Although the sample format is simple, it presents the writer in a positive way. Because her employment will be at the entry level in a nontechnical area, an employer will be more interested in her basic skills—those that can transfer from things she has done in the past—than in her job-specific experiences. The work experience she has is a plus. Also notice how she presents her gymnastics experience under Hardworking.

Constructing a Skills Resume

The skills resume uses a number of sections that are similar to those in a chronological resume. Here I will discuss only the sections that are substantially different: the Job Objective and Skills and Abilities sections. Refer to the discussion of chronological resumes for information on sections that are common to both types of resumes.

Don't be afraid to use a little creativity in writing your own skills resume. You are allowed to break some rules in this format if it makes sense to do so.

The Job Objective Statement for a Skills Resume

Although a simple chronological resume does not require a career objective, a skills resume does. Without a reasonably clear job objective, it is not possible to select and organize the key skills you have to support that objective. You should carefully construct your job objective statement. To see some example job objective statements, refer to "The Job Objective Statement for a Chronological Resume" earlier in this part.

Tips for Writing a Good Job Objective

The job objective you write should meet your specific needs. But here are some general things to consider when you write it:

1. **Avoid job titles.** Job titles such as "secretary" or "marketing analyst" can involve very different activities in different organizations. The same job can often have different titles in different organizations. Using such titles might limit you from being considered for such jobs as "office manager" or "marketing assistant." It is best to use broad categories of jobs rather than specific titles, so that you can be considered for a wide variety of positions related to the skills you have. For example, instead of "secretary," you could say "responsible office-management or clerical position," if that's what you would really consider and are qualified for.

2. **Define a "bracket of responsibility" to include the potential for upward mobility.** Although you might be willing to accept a variety of jobs related to your skills, you should definitely include jobs that require higher levels of responsibility and pay. The example in step 1 would allow the candidate to be considered for an office-management position as well as for clerical jobs. In effect, you should define a "bracket of responsibility" in your objective that includes the range of jobs you are willing to accept. This bracket should include

A sample skills resume

Lisa M. Rhodes
813 Evergreen Drive
Evansville, IN 47715
lisamrhodes@aol.com
Home: (812) 643-2173   Message: (812) 442-1659

Job Objective

Sales-oriented position in a retail or distribution business.

Skills and Abilities

Communications: Good written and verbal presentation skills. Use proper grammar and have a good speaking voice.

Interpersonal: Able to accept supervision and get along well with co-workers. Received positive evaluations from previous supervisors.

Flexible: Willing to try new things and am interested in improving efficiency on assigned tasks.

Attention to Detail: Like to see assigned areas of responsibility completed correctly. Am concerned with quality, and my work is typically orderly and attractive.

Hardworking: Have worked long hours in strenuous activities while attending school full-time. During this time, I maintained above-average grades. At times, I was working as many as 65 hours a week in school and other structured activities.

Customer Contacts: Have had as many as 500 customer contacts a day (10,000 per month) in a busy retail outlet. Averaged lower than a .001% rate of complaints and was given the "Employee of the Month" award in my second month of employment.

Cash Sales: Handled over $2,000 a day ($40,000 a month) in cash sales. Balanced register and prepared daily sales summary and deposits.

Education

Graduate of Harrison High School. Took advanced English and other classes. Member of award-winning band. Excellent attendance record. Superior communication skills. Graduated in top 30% of class.

Other

Active gymnastics competitor for four years. This experience taught me discipline, teamwork, and how to follow instructions. I am ambitious, outgoing, and willing to work.

the lower range of jobs you would consider as well as those that require higher levels of responsibility, up to and including the most responsible job you think you could handle. Even if you have not handled those higher levels of responsibility in the past, many employers will consider you for them if you have the skills to do them.

3. **Include your most important skills.** What are the most important skills needed for the job you want? Include one or more of these in your job objective statement. The implication is that if you are looking for a job that *requires* "organizational skills," then you have those skills. Of course, your interview (and resume) should show evidence that you have those skills, by giving specific examples.

4. **Include specifics only if they really matter to you.** If you have substantial experience in a particular industry (such as "computer-controlled machine tools") or you have a narrow, specific objective that you *really* want (such as "art therapist with the mentally handicapped"), it's okay to say so. But you should realize that narrowing your alternatives might keep you from being considered for other jobs for which you qualify. Still, if that's what you want, it's worth pursuing. (I would, however, encourage you to have a second, more general objective ready, just in case.)

5. **Research the job you want.** Read descriptions of your target job. Then emphasize in your resume the skills you have that are mentioned in these descriptions. The *Occupational Outlook Handbook (OOH),* created by the U.S. Department of Labor, provides brief descriptions of more than 250 major jobs, and I recommend it as a good source of information. You can find this book in library reference sections and bookstores, as well as on the Department of Labor's Web site at www.dol.gov. Another book, *America's Top 300 Jobs,* provides the same information as the *OOH,* but libraries are more likely to allow you to check it out. The *OOH*'s structure of organizing jobs into clusters (for example, "Service Occupations," "Sales and Related Occupations," and so on) is the one we used to organize the resumes in part 2 of this book.

Use the Job Objective Worksheet

Use the worksheet on page 25 to help you construct an effective and accurate job objective statement for your resume.

Finalize Your Job Objective Statement

Most employers are impressed by candidates who are very clear about the jobs they want and why they want them. Few interviews end well unless the interviewer is convinced that you really want the job and have the skills to do it. So it is essential to have a clear job objective.

Once you've settled that, you can go out and get interviews for jobs that closely approximate what you want. In interviews, support your interest in the job by presenting the skills and experiences you have and the advantages you present over other candidates. It sounds simple enough—and it can be, as long as you are clear about what you want to do and are well organized about finding it.

The Skills Section

This section can also be called Areas of Accomplishment, Summary of Qualifications, or Areas of Expertise and Ability. Look through the sample resumes in part 2 for other ideas.

The Job Objective Worksheet

Directions: Complete each of the following items. When you're done, you'll have a better idea of what to include in your job objective statement.

1. **What sort of position, title, and area of specialization do you want?** Write the type of job you want, just as you might explain it to someone you know.

   _____

   _____

   _____

2. **Define your bracket of responsibility.** Describe the range of jobs you would accept, from the minimum up to those you think you could handle if you were given the chance.

   _____

   _____

   _____

3. **Name the key skills you have that are important in this job.** Describe the two or three key skills that are particularly important for success in the job that you are seeking. Select one or more of these that you are strong in and that you enjoy using. Write it (or them) here.

   _____

   _____

   _____

4. **Name any specific areas of expertise or strong interest that you want to use in your next job.** If you have substantial interest, experience, or training in a specific area and want to include it in your job objective (remembering that it might limit your options), write it here.

   _____

   _____

   _____

5. **What else is important to you?** Is there anything else you want to include in your job objective? This could be a value that is particularly important to you (such as "a position that allows me to help families" or "employment in an aggressive and results-oriented organization"), a preference for the size or type of organization ("a small- to mid-size business"), or something else.

   _____

   _____

   _____

Whatever you call it, this section is what makes a skills resume different from a chronological resume. To construct it, you must carefully consider which skills you want to emphasize. You should feature skills that are essential to success on the job you want *and* skills that are your particular strengths. You probably have a good idea of which skills meet both criteria.

Note that many skills resumes emphasize skills that are not specific to a particular job. These types of skills are known as *transferable skills*. For example, the skill of being well organized is important in *many* jobs. In your resume, you should provide specific examples of situations or accomplishments that show you have that skill. This is where you bring in examples from previous work or other experiences.

Key Skills List

Here are the key skills for success in most jobs. If you have to emphasize some skills over others, these are ones to consider (if you have them, of course).

The Basics	**Key Transferable Skills**
Accept supervision	Instructing others
Get along with coworkers	Managing money and budgets
Get things done on time	Managing people
Good attendance	Meeting deadlines
Hard worker	Meeting the public
Honest	Negotiating
On time	Organizing/managing projects
Productive	Public speaking
Written communication skills	

In addition to these types of skills, most jobs require skills that are specific to that particular job. For example, an accountant needs to know how to set up a general ledger, use accounting software, and develop income and expense reports. These skills are called *job-specific* skills and are quite important in qualifying for a job.

Identify Your Key Skills

You resume should emphasize skills that are particularly important for the job you want. Include any other job-specific skills or other skills you have that you think are important to communicate to an employer regarding the job you want. Write at least three, but no more than six, of these most important skills on the following lines:

_____

_____

_____

_____

_____

Prove Your Key Skills

Now, write each of the preceding skills on a separate piece of paper. Then write any particularly good examples of when you used each skill. If possible, you should use work situations, but you can also use volunteer work, school activities, or any other life experience. Whenever possible, quantify the example by including numbers—such as money saved, increased sales, or other measures—to support those skills. Emphasize results you achieved and accomplishments.

The following is an example of what one person wrote for a key skill. It might give you ideas on how you can document your own skills.

Key Skill: Meeting Deadlines

I volunteered to help my social organization raise money. I found out about special government funds, but the proposal deadline was only 24 hours away. I stayed up all night and submitted the proposal on time. We were one of only three groups whose proposals were approved, and we were awarded over $100,000.

Edit Your Key Skills Proofs

Go over each "proof sheet" from the preceding exercise and select the proofs you think are particularly valuable in supporting your job objective. You should have at least two proofs for each skills area. After you have selected your proofs, rewrite them using action words and short sentences. Delete anything that is not essential. Edit each of your proofs until they are clear, short, and powerful. You can then use these statements in your resume, modifying them as needed to fit that format. Here is an edited version of the preceding skill statement in a form that's appropriate for a resume.

Key Skill: Meeting Deadlines

On 24-hour notice, submitted a complex proposal that successfully obtained over $100,000 in funding.

Sample Skills Resumes

Look over the sample resumes on the following pages to see how others have adapted the skills format to fit their own needs. These examples are based on real resumes (although the names and other details have been changed). I have included comments to help you understand details that might not be apparent.

The formats and designs of these samples are intentionally basic, and you can do them on any word processor. Many more sample resumes with more elaborate formats are included in part 2.

Sample Skills Resume 1:
A Career Changer with a New Degree

The next page presents the resume of a career changer. After working in a variety of jobs, Darrel went to school and learned computer programming. The skills format allows him to emphasize the business experiences in his past to support his current job objective. There is no chronological listing of jobs, and no dates are given for his education, so it is not obvious that he is a recent graduate with little formal work experience as a programmer.

Darrel does a good job of presenting his previous work experience and includes numbers to support his skills and accomplishments. Even so, the relationship between his previous work and current objective could be improved. For example, collecting bad debts requires discipline, persistence, and attention to detail—the same skills required in programming. And, although he is good at sales, how does this relate to programming?

To correct this, he might consider modifying his job objective to include the use of his sales skills (such as selling technological services) or emphasizing other skills from his previous work experience. Still, his resume is effective and does a decent job of relating past business experience to his ability to be an effective programmer in a business environment.

A Career Changer's JIST Card

The following sample JIST Card accompanies the first resume example. This nifty job search tool is covered in more detail in part 3.

Darrel Craig   (412) 437-6217
Message: (412) 464-1273
E-mail: DarrelCraig@aol.com

Position Desired: PROGRAMMER/SYSTEMS MANAGEMENT

Skills: Over 10 years of combined education and experience in data processing, business, and related fields. Programming ability in Linux, C++, Java, and VBA. Knowledge of various database and applications programs in networked PC, Mac, and mainframe environments. Substantial business experience, including accounting, management, sales, and public relations.

Dedicated, self-starter, creative, dependable, and willing to relocate.

A skills resume for a career changer with a new degree

Darrel Craig

Career Objective

Challenging position in programming or related areas that would best utilize expertise in the business environment. This position should have many opportunities for an aggressive, dedicated individual with leadership abilities to advance.

Programming Skills

Include functional program design relating to business issues, including payroll, inventory and database management, sales, marketing, accounting, and loan amortization reports. In conjunction with design, proficient in coding, implementation, debugging, and file maintenance. Familiar with distributed network systems, including PCs and Macs, and working knowledge of DOS, Linux, C++, Java, and VBA.

Areas of Expertise

Interpersonal communication strengths, public relations capabilities, innovative problem-solving and analytical talents.

Sales

A total of nine years of experience in sales and sales management. Sold security products to distributors and alarm dealers. Increased company's sales from $16,000 to over $70,000 per month. Creatively organized sales programs and marketing concepts. Trained sales personnel in prospecting techniques while also training service personnel in proper installation of security alarms. Result: 90% of all new business was generated through referrals from existing customers.

Management

Managed security alarm company for four years while increasing profits yearly. Supervised office, sales, and installation personnel. Supervised and delegated work to assistants in accounting functions and inventory control. Worked as assistant credit manager, responsible for over $2 million per month in sales. Handled semi-annual inventory of five branch stores totaling $10 million dollars and supervised 120 people.

Accounting

Balanced all books and prepared tax forms for alarm company. Eight years of experience in credit and collections, with emphasis on collections. Collection rates were over 98% each year, and was able to collect a bad debt in excess of $250,000 that the company deemed "noncollectable."

Education

School of Computer Technology, Pittsburgh, PA
Business Application Programming/TECH EXEC—3.97 GPA

Robert Morris College, Pittsburgh, PA
Associate degree in Accounting, Minor in Management

**2306 Cincinnati Street, Kingsford, PA 15171 (412) 437-6217
Message: (412) 464-1273   E-mail: DarrelCraig@aol.com**

Sample Skills Resume 2: A Resume That Incorporates Chronological Elements

Peter lost his factory job when the plant closed in the late 1990s. He picked up a survival job as a truck driver, and now he wants to make this his career. It allows him to earn good money, and he likes the work.

Notice how his resume emphasizes skills from previous experiences that are essential for success as a truck driver. This resume uses a combination format: It includes elements from both the skills and chronological resume formats. The skills approach allows him to emphasize specific skills that support his job objective, and the chronological listing of jobs allows him to display his stable work history.

The miscellaneous jobs Peter had before 1982 are simply clustered together under one grouping because they are not as important as more recent experience—and because doing this conceals his age. For the same reasons, he does not include dates for his military experience or high school graduation, nor does he separate them into different categories, such as Military Experience or Education. They just aren't as important in supporting his current job objective as they might be for a younger person.

An unusual element here is Peter's statement about his not smoking or drinking, although it works, as do his comments about a stable family life.

Peter also has a version of this resume in which the job objective includes supervision and management of trucking operations. He added a few details to the content to support this objective. When it made sense, he used the other version.

He got a job with a small long-distance trucking company driving a regular route, and now he supervises other drivers.

A skills resume that incorporates chronological elements

Peter Neely
203 Evergreen Road
Houston, Texas 39127
PNDriver@hotmail.com
Messages: (237) 649-1234   Beeper: (237) 765-9876

POSITION DESIRED: Truck Driver

Summary of Work Experience:	Over 20 years of stable work history, including substantial experience with diesel engines, electrical systems, and truck driving.

SKILLS

Driving Record/ Licenses:	Chauffeur's license, qualified and able to drive anything that rolls. No traffic citations or accidents for over 20 years.
Vehicle Maintenance:	I keep correct maintenance schedules and avoid most breakdowns as a result. Substantial mechanical and electrical systems training and experience permit many breakdowns to be repaired immediately and avoid towing.
Record Keeping:	Excellent attention to detail. Familiar with recording procedures and submit required records on a timely basis.
Routing:	Knowledge of many states. Good map-reading and route-planning skills.
Other:	Not afraid of hard work, flexible, get along well with others, meet deadlines, responsible.

WORK EXPERIENCE

1998–Present	CAPITAL TRUCK CENTER, Houston, Texas Pick up and deliver all types of commercial vehicles from across the United States. Am trusted with handling large sums of money and handling complex truck-purchasing transactions.
1988–1998	QUALITY PLATING CO., Houston, Texas Promoted from Production to Quality Control. Developed numerous production improvements resulting in substantial cost savings.
1986–1988	BLUE CROSS MANUFACTURING, Houston, Texas Received several increases in salary and responsibility before leaving for a more challenging position.
1982–1986	Truck delivery of food products to destinations throughout the South. Also responsible for up to 12 drivers and equipment-maintenance personnel.
Prior to 1982	Operated large diesel-powered electrical plants. Responsible for monitoring and maintenance on a rigid schedule.

OTHER

Four years of experience in the U.S. Air Force operating power plants. Stationed in Alaska, California, Wyoming, and other states. Honorable discharge. High school graduate, plus training in diesel engines and electrical systems. Excellent health, love the outdoors, stable family life, nonsmoker and nondrinker.

Sample Skills Resume 3: A Resume for Someone with Limited Work Experience

This resume uses few words and lots of white space. It looks better, I think, than more crowded resumes. I would like to see more numbers used to indicate performance or accomplishments. For example, what was the result of the more efficient record-keeping system she developed? And why did she receive the Employee-of-the-Month awards?

Andrea does not have substantial experience in her field, having held only one job. For this reason, the skills format allows her to present her strengths better than a chronological resume would. Because she has formal training in retail sales and is a recent graduate, she could have given more details about specific courses she took or other school-related activities that support her job objective. Even so, her resume does a good job of presenting her basic skills in an attractive format.

A resume for someone with limited work experience

ANDREA ATWOOD
3231 East Harbor Road
Grand Rapids, Michigan 41103
atwood@juno.com

Home: (303) 447-2111   Message: (303) 547-8201

Objective: A responsible position in retail sales.

Areas of Accomplishment:

Customer Service   Communicate well with all age groups.
Able to interpret customer concerns to help them
find the items they want.
Received six Employee-of-the-Month awards in
three years.

Merchandise   Developed display skills via in-house training and
Display   experience.
Received Outstanding Trainee award for Christmas
toy display.
Dress mannequins, arrange table displays, and organize
sale merchandise.

Stock Control   Maintained and marked stock during department
and Marking   manager's six-week illness. Developed more
efficient record-keeping procedures.

Additional Skills   Operate cash register and computerized accounting
systems.
Willing to work evenings and weekends.
Punctual, honest, reliable, and hardworking.

Experience: Harper's Department Store
Grand Rapids, Michigan
1995 to present

Education: Central High School
Grand Rapids, Michigan
3.6/4.0 grade-point average
Honor Graduate in Distributive Education

Two years of retail sales training in Distributive
Education. Also took courses in business writing,
computerized accounting, and word processing.

Sample Skills Resume 4: A Template-Based Format

Linda's resume is based on one included in David Swanson's *The Resume Solution*. It shows the resume style that he prefers, using lots of white space, short sentences, and brief but carefully edited narrative.

The format for this resume is based on a resume template that is provided with a popular word-processing program. That program offers several predetermined design options that include various typefaces and the use of other simple but effective format and design elements. Other resumes in this book have used similar templates, and this approach makes formatting a resume much easier, although sometimes it can be quite challenging to make your unique information fit into the constraints of a template.

Linda's resume is short but presents good information to support her job objective. It is based on the principle of "less is more."

A resume with a template-based format

6673 East Avenue   **(415) 555-1519** (leave message)
Lakeland, California, 94544   lindamwinston@aol.com

Linda Marsala-Winston

| **Objective** | Copywriter, Account Executive in Advertising or Public Relations Agency |

Experience

1999–Present   Great River Publishing   Southridge, WA
Copywriter
- Developed copy for direct-mail catalogs featuring collectible items, for real estate developments, and for agricultural machinery and equipment.

1996–1999   *Habitat* Magazine   Southridge, WA
Writer
- Specialized in architecture, contemporary lifestyles, and interior design.

1994–1996   Fullmer's Department Store   San Francisco, CA
Sales Promotion Manager
- Developed theme and copy for grand opening of new store in San Francisco Bay area.

1991–1994   Mehari, Inc.   Los Angeles, CA
Fabric Designer
- Award-winning textile designer and importer of African and South American textiles.

Education

1991   University of California   Berkeley, CA
- B.A., English.
- 30 hours of graduate study in Journalism.

1994   California State University   Fresno, CA
- M.A., Guidance and Counseling.

Professional Membership

San Francisco Women in Advertising

Sample Resume 5: A Combination Format

This is one of those resumes that is hard to put into a category—it is neither a skills nor a chronological resume, but combines elements of both. Remember that I have suggested you can break any rule you want to in putting together your own resume—if you do so for a good reason. Thomas's resume does break some rules, but he does so for good reasons, and the resume presents him well.

Thomas has kept his job objective quite broad and does not limit it to a particular industry or job title. Because he sees himself as a business manager, it does not matter much to him what kind of business he works in, although he prefers a larger organization, as his job objective indicates.

His education is toward the top of his resume because he considers it a strength. His military experience, although not recent, is also listed toward the top because he also felt that would help him. Note how he presented his military experience using civilian terms such as annual budgets and staff size, things that are easy to relate to a business environment.

Thomas has many years of experience with one employer, but he lists each job he held there as a separate one. This allows him to provide more details about his accomplishments within each job and also clearly points out that he was promoted. This nicely shows his progression to increasingly responsible jobs.

A resume that uses a combination format

THOMAS R. MARRIN
80 Harrison Avenue
Baldwin, New York 11563
Answering Service: (716) 223-4705
Email: tom_marrin@optonline.net

OBJECTIVE:

A middle/upper-level management position with responsibilities including
problem solving, planning, organizing, and budget management.

EDUCATION:

University of Notre Dame, B.S. in Business Administration. Course emphasis on
accounting, supervision, and marketing. Upper 25% of class. *Additional training:*
Advanced training in time management, organizational behavior, and cost control.

MILITARY:

U.S. Army–2nd Infantry Division, 1990 to 1993. 1st Lieutenant and platoon
leader–stationed in Korea and Fort Knox, Kentucky. Supervised an annual budget
of nearly $4 million and equipment valued at over $40 million. Responsible for
training, scheduling, and activities of as many as 40 people. Received several
commendations. Honorable discharge.

BUSINESS EXPERIENCE:

Wills Express Transit Co., Inc.—Mineola, New York

Promoted to Vice President, Corporate Equipment—1998 to Present

Control purchase, maintenance, and disposal of 1,100 trailers and 65 company
cars with $6.7M operating and $8.0M capital expense responsibilities.

- Scheduled trailer purchases, 6 divisions.

- Operated 2.3% under planned maintenance budget in company's
  second-best profit year while operating revenues declined 2.5%.

- Originated schedule to coordinate drivers' needs with available trailers.

- Developed systematic Purchase and Disposal Plan for company car
  fleet.

- Restructured Company Car Policy, saving 15% on per-car cost.

THOMAS R. MARRIN, Page 2

Promoted to Assistant Vice President, Corporate Operations—1997 to 1998

Coordinated activities of six sections of Corporate Operations with an operating budget over $10M.

- Directed implementation of zero-base budgeting.

- Developed and prepared Executive Officer Analyses detailing achievable cost-reduction measures. Resulted in cost reduction of over $600,000 in first two years.

- Designed policy and procedure for special equipment leasing program during peak seasons. Cut capital purchases by over $1 million.

Promoted to Manager of Communications—1995 to 1997

Directed and managed $1.4M communications network involving 650 phones, 150 WATS lines, 3 switchboards, 1 teletype machine, and 5 employees.

Installed computerized WATS Control System. Optimized utilization of WATS lines and pinpointed personal abuse. Achieved payback earlier than originally projected. Devised procedures that allowed simultaneous 20% increase in WATS calls and a $75,000/year savings.

Hayfield Publishing Company—Hempstead, New York.

Communications Administrator—1993 to 1995

Managed daily operations of a large communications center. Reduced costs and improved services.

Tips for Fine-Tuning Your Resume

Before you make a final draft of your skills resume, look over the sample resumes at the end of this section and in part II for ideas on content and format. Several of them use interesting techniques that might be useful for your particular situation. Also keep in mind the following tips:

- If you have a good work history, a brief chronological listing of jobs is a helpful addition to your skills resume. When you add this listing, your resume becomes a combination format resume, which combines the best of a chronological resume and a skills/functional resume.

- If you have substantial work history, begin the resume with a summary of your total experience, which provides the basis for details that follow.

- Remember that this is your resume, so do what you think is best.

- Trust your own judgment, and be willing to break a few rules if you think it will help you.

- Write the draft content for your resume on separate sheets of paper or on a computer.

- Rewrite and edit until the resume communicates what you really want to say about yourself.

- If you are doing your resume on a computer, print the "final" copy and ask someone else to review it for typographical and other errors.

- Even if you are having someone else prepare your resume, have someone else other than yourself review their "final" copy for any errors you might have overlooked.

- When you are sure that your resume contains no errors (and only then), have the final version prepared.

Adapt Your Resume for an Electronic Job Search

Thus far, I've talked about writing your resume and formatting it for printing on paper and viewing by human eyes. But job search is more complicated than it was ten or even five years ago. The Internet and e-mail have become important, widely used job-search tools. Even if you pursue a targeted job search as I've recommended—and therefore don't need to e-mail your resume to thousands of recruiters or companies—you can still use the Internet to make your job search easier and faster in the following ways:

- **Research.** The Internet is a vast resource where you can find information on companies, industries, job descriptions, salaries, and just about anything else you can think of. Use the Internet to compile and narrow down your target list of companies. Check these companies' Web sites for language you can use in your resume and cover letter or to see what relevant jobs they might have posted.

- **Speedy communication.** After you talk with a potential employer, you can quickly e-mail your resume and avoid mail delays. You can immediately apply online for a job at one of your target companies and, if your skills fit, could be interviewing the next day.

- **Follow-up.** Mass e-mailing to people you don't know is not a good way to conduct your search. But once you've established contact, e-mail is often the preferred method of communication with many businesspeople.

You'll need to create at least two different file formats for your electronic job search:

- **Word-processing file.** This is the original format you used to create your resume. If you used Microsoft Word, in many cases you can safely send your resume as an attachment to your e-mail message. Most employers and recruiting firms that receive your resume will be able to open, view, download, print, and file your MS Word resume.

  If you have used a different word-processing program, such as WordPerfect or Microsoft Works, you can try to convert your resume file to a Word-compatible format, if you know how to do so; or you can simply create a universal-format text resume, as described below.

  In some instances you will be required to "cut and paste" your resume into an online application, or you might be responding to a job posting that states "no attachments." In each of these cases, the text version will be required.

- **Text file.** ASCII Text is a plain-text file format that can be read by all computers. This kind of file cannot include formatting such as bold type, bullet points, or graphics. But the most important part of your resume—the content—will come through perfectly.

Converting Your Resume to E-mail Format

Here's how to create an ASCII text file from your word-processed resume:

1. Open your resume file.

2. Using the "Save As" function, give the file a new name, and choose the "Text Only" or "ASCII text" option.

3. Close the file.

4. Now open the new file and you'll see that a transformation has taken place. Your formatting has disappeared, bullets have turned into asterisks, and the font has been changed to Courier.

5. Review your resume to see if there are any obvious glitches or formatting problems. For example, sometimes apostrophes get turned into a funny assortment of characters, or square bullets change into question marks. With an ASCII resume, you can use only standard "typewriter" symbols (such as asterisks) as accents and graphics.

6. Add extra blank lines if necessary for readability. Don't worry about how long your resume is or whether it fits nicely onto a page.

7. If you have used a column format, you might have to reposition some text so that it makes sense.

8. Save the file (it will be saved with a ".txt" file extension rather than the standard ".doc" that is used for MS Word files).

Using Your Text File in Your Electronic Job Search

This new text file now becomes your e-mail and online application resume. Here's how to use it:

- **When applying for a job online.** If you are applying for a job listed on a company's Web site, you will usually be asked to "paste your resume here." To do this, open your ASCII text file resume, choose "Select All" and then "Copy." Switch back to the Web site, insert your cursor in the appropriate place, and type the "Paste" command (Ctrl + V). Your text resume will automatically flow into the box.

- **When responding to an ad that states "no attachments."** Paste your ASCII text resume into the body of your e-mail message, directly after a short cover letter. Use the subject line of your e-mail to say something relevant about yourself and/or the job you're applying for, for instance: "Re: CUSTOMER SERVICE JOB #459-A, 4 yrs. experience, customer ratings near 100%."

Following are two versions of the same resume—first in a traditional word-processed format, and then transformed into a text file.

A traditional resume

Meredith Gordon

617-243-5540
meredith@netcom.com
25 Edgeview Drive, Stoneham, MA 02180

GOAL

Pharmaceutical Sales

SUMMARY OF QUALIFICATIONS

- **SALES AND COMMUNICATION SKILLS:** Successful sales and customer service experience... proven communication abilities (listening, speaking, presenting)... strong problem-solving skills... ability to establish rapport with diverse individuals.
- **HEALTH/WELLNESS KNOWLEDGE:** Degree in Health Education and Promotion... internship experience communicating health issues to city employees and the public.
- **PERSONAL ATTRIBUTES:** Self-motivated and energetic... possess strong planning, organizational, and time management skills... professional in appearance and demeanor...enthusiastic, energetic, sincere, and hard working.

EDUCATION

Bachelor of Science in Health Education and Promotion, June 2002
Salem State University, Salem, Massachusetts

Internship: City of Salem Health Department, January–June 2002

- Assisted health educators in planning and carrying out various health education programs for more than 500 city employees as well as members of the community.
- Wrote, edited, designed, and coordinated printing and distribution of a monthly health newsletter distributed to all city employees.
- Prepared and delivered educational presentations on topics such as stress and safety.
- Attended and participated in professional meetings with health education staff.
- Provided staff support for tobacco and cardiovascular disease-prevention programs.
- Compiled a comprehensive list of smoke-free restaurants in Essex County.

EXPERIENCE

Front Desk/Customer Service Representative: Nauticus Fitness Center, Stoneham, MA, 2001–Present

- Provide customer-focused assistance to visitors and members; answer questions about programs, schedules, and referrals to health care providers located in the facility.
- Present program benefits and promote program registration.
- Recognized for problem-solving skills and ability to deliver customer satisfaction.

Sales Associate: Fitness Gear, Peabody, MA, 2000-Present

- Consistently earn commissions and incentives for sales performance as measured against monthly objectives.
- Personally set daily, weekly, and monthly goals and self-monitor performance.
- Completed sales training with emphasis on promoting product benefits.

ADDITIONAL QUALIFICATIONS

Computer Skills: MS Word, Excel, PowerPoint, Outlook, Internet applications.
Activities: Competitive tennis league.

A traditional resume converted to a text resume

```
Meredith Gordon
617-243-5540
meredith@netcom.com
25 Edgeview Drive, Stoneham, MA 02180

=====================================
GOAL:  Pharmaceutical Sales

=====================================
SUMMARY OF QUALIFICATIONS

* SALES AND COMMUNICATION SKILLS:  Successful sales and customer service
experience... proven communication abilities (listening, speaking, presenting)...
strong problem-solving skills... ability to establish rapport with diverse
individuals.
* HEALTH/WELLNESS KNOWLEDGE:  Degree in Health Education and Promotion... internship
experience communicating health issues to city employees and the public.
* PERSONAL ATTRIBUTES:  Self-motivated and energetic... possess strong planning,
organizational, and time management skills... professional in appearance and
demeanor...enthusiastic, energetic, sincere, and hard working.


=====================================
EDUCATION

Bachelor of Science in Health Education and Promotion, June 2002
Salem State University, Salem, Massachusetts

INTERNSHIP: City of Salem Health Department, January-June 2002
* Assisted health educators in planning and carrying out various health education
programs for more than 500 city employees as well as members of the community.
* Wrote, edited, designed, and coordinated printing and distribution of a monthly
health newsletter distributed to all city employees.
* Prepared and delivered educational presentations on topics such as stress and
safety.
* Attended and participated in professional meetings with health education staff.
Provided staff support for tobacco and cardiovascular disease-prevention programs.
* Compiled a comprehensive list of smoke-free restaurants in Essex County.


=====================================
EXPERIENCE

Front Desk/Customer Service Representative:  Nauticus Fitness Center, Stoneham, MA,
2001-Present
* Provide customer-focused assistance to visitors and members; answer questions
about programs, schedules, and referrals to health care providers located in the
facility.
* Present program benefits and promote program registration.
* Recognized for problem-solving skills and ability to deliver customer
satisfaction.

Sales Associate:  Fitness Gear, Peabody, MA, 2000-Present
* Consistently earn commissions and incentives for sales performance as measured
against monthly objectives.
* Personally set daily, weekly, and monthly goals and self-monitor performance.
* Completed sales training with emphasis on promoting product benefits.

ADDITIONAL QUALIFICATIONS
* Computer Skills:  MS Word, Excel, PowerPoint, Outlook, Internet applications.
* Activities: Competitive tennis league.
```

What Is a Scannable Resume?

You might have heard that many companies require "scannable" resumes. Using scanning technology, your resume is entered into the company database, which the company uses to search for candidates who match specific job qualifications. For the company to find a match, your resume must do the following:

1. **Contain the right words that match the employer's queries (known as "key words").** Key words are simply words that an employer or company uses to define the most important qualifications for a job they're trying to fill. Key words typically are nouns ("sales," "accounting," "customer satisfaction," "Bachelor's degree") rather than verbs ("increased," "achieved," "initiated") or adjectives ("successful," "excellent," "dynamic").

   If you have held jobs similar to the one you're seeking, your resume probably contains the right key words. You can learn more key words from job descriptions for similar jobs, and you might want to add some of these to your resume to increase your chances of being "found" in a key-word search.

   If you are looking for a position unlike anything you've ever done before, your resume might not be found by a key-word search. But if this is your circumstance, you're probably not looking for a job by these mass-application means, anyway.

2. **Be able to be read by scanning software.** What is considered "scannable" can vary dramatically from company to company. Advanced scanning software can read a variety of formats and font variations, but simple scanners will have trouble with anything out of the ordinary. For best results, use a simple, unadorned format, eliminate bold and italic type, remove bullets, and eliminate graphics. Place all text at the left margin, and use at least 11-point type.

   You can remove all potential scanning problems by sending your resume electronically, by e-mail or through a Web site application form. Your text or word-processed resume can enter the database directly, without having to pass through a physical scan.

   And if you prefer to send a hard-copy resume to be scanned, simply use the text version of your resume. It is 100-percent scannable.

2
P·A·R·T

Top Resumes Arranged in Groups of Related Jobs

Major Topics in This Part

Top Resumes Arranged in Groups of Related Jobs

The resumes in this section are arranged in groups of similar jobs. This section uses the same system developed by the U.S. Department of Labor. This system, which organizes about 250 major jobs into 11 major clusters, is the same system used in major career references such as the *Occupational Outlook Handbook* and all the books in the *America's Top Jobs* series. This arrangement allows you to quickly find resumes that are most closely related to jobs that you seek. You can also use the index to locate resumes for jobs like yours.

Tips on Using the Resumes

Browse through these resumes and take any ideas they give you to use in your own. Here are a few tips for reviewing them:

- **Review resumes for jobs similar to those you seek.** It makes sense to look at resumes for jobs similar to the ones you will seek. Doing so gives you ideas on how people present their backgrounds, the skills they emphasize, and other things that can make sense for you to use.

- **Look at resumes in other sections.** You will find interesting design, layout, and other techniques presented in resumes within other occupational groupings. If, for example, you are a new graduate, you might look at the resumes of other recent graduates. Doing so will give you ideas even if the resumes are for different fields. New graduates, for example, need to emphasize their school, extracurricular, and part-time work experiences more than do people with substantial work histories. Other new grads' resumes will show you how they handled similar issues.

- **Note ways to hide your weaknesses and emphasize your strengths.** Each resume in this section was written to present the person behind it in a positive way. Look for techniques you can use in your own resume to accomplish the same thing.

- **Don't copy.** Your resume should be YOUR resume and not a copy of someone else's. It's okay to borrow a good line here and there, but make certain that everything in your resume is true and that you can support it with examples.

About the Resumes in This Section

Most of the resumes in this section were submitted by members of the Career Masters Institute, the Professional Association of Résumé Writers and Career Coaches, and the

National Résumé Writers' Association. These professionals write resumes for a living, and most have years of full-time experience in doing so. They were asked to submit their best resumes, and, from the many that were sent, we selected those that were particularly good.

These are not just any resumes. Besides covering many occupations, they represent an enormous variety of writing styles, designs, formats, and content. Most resume books can't give you this kind of variety because their sample resumes are often all written by one person or selected to support one way of doing a resume.

Each sample is based on a real resume created for and used by a real person. Of course, the names and other details have been "fictionalized." We've included notes on them to point out features used in the resume or to give you information about the person's situation that is not obvious from reading the resume. Comments from the resume writer are also sometimes included. As you will see, each of these resumes is different, just as we are.

Note that the jobs listed here are major jobs that cover more than 87 percent of the labor market. But an enormous number of specialized jobs employing small numbers of people are not covered in this book. For example, you will not find resumes for optical scanning software developers or astronauts. There are also many specialized industries that are not covered. For instance, you will not find a resume for an electrical engineer employed in the petrochemical industry or a blasting specialist in the construction industry. Even so, most major jobs are represented, and this substantial collection of resumes provides enough examples to help you write your own.

Professional Assistance in Writing or Producing Your Resume

The resumes in this section were carefully crafted by experienced writers. They incorporate superior writing skill as well as skills in layout, design, editing, and self-promotion.

I trust that many of you can write and design a good resume if given the time. You are certainly capable of writing a basic resume like those presented in part 1, and I encourage you to write one. But you should consider getting some professional assistance if you need it. Writing a well-done resume requires a considerable amount of career self-knowledge. In most cases, the resumes in this book reflect the skills of the professional resume writers in providing career counseling. That is one of the reasons these resumes are so well done.

You can buy simple services such as word processing, basic layout, editing, and laser printouts from secretarial and typing services. These are often reasonably priced and can be found under the Yellow Pages headings of "Resume Services," "Secretarial Services," and "Word Processing Services." Many "quick" print shops provide similar services for reasonable fees.

Note that there is a big difference between basic word-processing services and the services provided by a professional resume writer. A print shop or secretarial service might charge you $50 to $100 to typeset your resume, but such a service will not fix your grammar errors, improve your use of words, ask for additional information, or spend much time formatting it. Secretarial or print-shop services will normally spend about 30 minutes on your one-page resume.

Services from experienced professional writers cost more, but you get more. Many will spend an hour or more with you going over your career goals, work experience, past accomplishments, education, and other life experience. Then they will spend one, two, or more hours writing your resume and creating a design and format to present you in the most attractive way. Often, you will get career counseling or career coaching as well as a professionally written resume.

Prices for these services vary based on how well prepared you are and how complex your background—the more time you need, the higher the cost. Resumes for new graduates, for example, will usually cost less than resumes for experienced professionals. Prices therefore vary, and are higher in some parts of the country than others.

Average prices for professional assistance in writing a resume fall in the range of $200 to $600, but could be higher for more complex situations. A review of a resume you did yourself and a few improvements might cost as little as $50 to $150. Some charge by the hour, and you should expect to pay as much as you would pay a good plumber: from $50 to $100 an hour or more.

This could be money very well spent for some people. The value is as much in what you learn about yourself as in the resume itself, because a professional writer will help you identify key skills and present them in a convincing way. A resume writer will also give you tips to overcome specific problems and job-search advice that is not easily obtained in any other way.

Be aware that almost anyone can and does sell resume, career coaching, and job-search services. There are no formal credentials required in most areas to sell these services, and some people have been cheated out of thousands of dollars. To avoid this, I suggest you work only with those who will tell you, over the phone, how much they charge for various services. If you feel pressured to buy something, you should get up and go elsewhere.

Resume writers who are members of a professional association often highlight their membership in their Yellow Pages ads. Members displaying the abbreviation CPRW (for Certified Professional Résumé Writer, awarded by the Professional Association of Résumé Writers and Career Coaches) or NCRW (for Nationally Certified Résumé Writer, awarded by the National Résumé Writers' Association) have to pass a rigorous resume-writing skills test and are required to adhere to a code of ethics that gives you protection from being cheated. Members of the Career Masters Institute are among the most experienced career professionals, and many have earned multiple industry credentials. Most members of these organizations have substantial experience and a sincere desire to help you succeed. If in doubt, I suggest you consider services from a CMI, PARW/CC, or NRWA member over those from nonmembers. A list of members of these organizations whose resumes are used in this book is provided in the appendix.

Management and Business and Financial Operations Occupations

Resumes at a Glance

Functional headings identify both specific skills and personal attributes that have led to significant success for this young accountant.

Jonathan Radeux

radeux@hotmail.com
1590 134th Avenue S.E. Apt 107
Vancouver, WA 99800

(425) 555-2222

ACCOUNTANT / TAX

Relationship Manager
Self motivated and resourceful, demonstrating effective communication skills, sound judgment, and ability to complete tasks in a highly professional manner.

Team Player
Repeatedly commended for "going the extra mile" to deliver superior results.

Knowledgeable
Internal & External Audits ● Internal Revenue Code ● R&D Studies ● FAS 109 ● Tax Research ● Tax Projections ● Deferred Taxes ● SEC Reporting

EDUCATION

CPA
CPA Candidate ● Test scheduled May 2002.

Formal
University of Washington, Seattle, WA
Master of Professional Accounting, 2000 ● Concentration: Tax ● GPA 3.4
B.A. Business Administration, 1999 ● Concentration: Accounting ● GPA 3.2

Professional
PricewaterhouseCoopers, LLP
Tax Consulting Foundation Training, 2000 ● 50 hours
Tax Update, 2001

Computers
Proficient in the use of Microsoft Office (Windows, Excel, PowerPoint, Word, Access) ● LexisNexis ● Westlaw ● CCH & RIA databases ● Oracle Financial ● Lotus Notes ● Microsoft Exchange ● Visio ● Windows NT

PROFESSIONAL EXPERIENCE

Staff Associate, Tax & Legal Services Group
PRICEWATERHOUSECOOPERS, LLP, Portland, OR ● 2000–2001

Surpassed normal reporting hierarchy, directly supporting Senior Manager and Partner on M&A and FAS 109 analysis, deferred tax studies, and R&D tax credit projects for major companies.

Worked at client sites 80% of time, interviewing and interfacing with a wide range of professionals: lawyers, senior technology engineers, tax directors, tax managers, vice presidents, and technology product managers.

Accomplishment statements detail this person's success.

- Established 80% utilization rate, 30% over average for local tax associates, by aggressively seeking new challenges and projects.
- Only Staff Associate in Portland tax office to earn performance bonus in 2000.
- Assigned increasingly challenging projects based on performance, initiative, teamwork, and professionalism.

Intern, Tax Compliance
ROTHCHILD WENSON & COMPANY, PLLC, Vancouver, WA ● 1999

Federal and State Compliance. 1120S, 1065, 1040, and 1041 forms.

AFFILIATIONS

Oregon Society of Certified Public Accountants

Bonded, Oregon and Washington States
Notary, Oregon and Washington States

1

Tax accountant (entry-level). *Alice Hanson, CPRW; Seattle, WA*

RAMANU JACHARI

20 Helen Street, Hanover Park, IL 60133
Residence: (630) 855 1071
Email: jachariramanu@hotmail.com

This resume was transformed by moving beyond task and duty statements to an achievements-based approach.

FOCUS: FINANCE MANAGER • DIVISIONAL ACCOUNTANT • ACCOUNTANT

Nearly 10 years' experience driving prudent revenue growth and offering expert financial counsel to key business decision-makers. Proven track record in exploiting fresh technologies, refocusing on continuous improvement, and reengineering existing business processes. Dedicated to translating company values into practical everyday operations and preserving strong business alliances with clients and vendors.

KEY CREDENTIALS   *Serves as a keyword summary.*

- **Strategic Financial Forecasting**
- **Business Plan Development**
- **Internal/External Audits**
- **Asset Management**
- **Profit & Loss Analysis**

- **Operating Budgets**
- **Financial Reporting**
- **Feasibility Analysis**
- **Variance Analysis**
- **Team Supervision & Training**

- **Yield Management**
- **Process Reengineering**
- **FOREX Compliance**
- **Debtor Negotiations & Mediation**

Software: Excel, Word, PowerPoint, Outlook, Access, BOSS 3 Airline Accounting (Visual Basic), C2000 Financial Accounting (Unix), Platinum (Financial & Management Information), Internet, email.

QUALIFICATIONS & TRAINING

Diploma in Oracle Programming, *Boston's Computer Institute,* India (1997)

Bachelor of Accounting (Commerce), *University of Bombay,* India (1989)

PROFESSIONAL EXPERIENCE

Finance Manager, *Boyd Smith & Partners,* Hanover Park, IL.. Mar 98–Present
Travel Division. *Staff: 2. Report to: Financial Controller. Revenue: US $6.4M.*
IATA-accredited travel agency servicing corporate management. Ranked 5th in top 10 agencies in Abu Dhabi.

Spearheaded a series of productivity and process improvements after thorough analysis of the travel division's operations, which contribute 20% of company's $US32M revenue. Identified top issues impeding workflows and staff productivity, and successfully achieved staff and management acceptance for change management initiatives. Managed complete monthly MIS, financial reports, budgets, forecasts and plans for the division.

- Established a highly productive and motivated team through responsible task delegation, ongoing encouragement, and active collaboration between staff and management during quarterly performance appraisals.
- Maximized interdepartmental relationships, restoring communication lines and forging solid partnerships between sales force, accounts staff and senior management.
- Successfully coordinated external and internal audits, completing all projects on time, in total compliance with government standards.
- Streamlined preparation, compilation and reporting procedures for fortnightly sales report to the Airlines, dramatically boosting turnaround times.
- Reduced payment terms for all doubtful debts. Mediated/negotiated payment deals, restored customer confidence, and preserved strong alliances. Manage all A/R and A/P functions.

Divisional Accountant, *Boyd Smith & Partners,* Hanover Park, IL ....Mar 97–Feb 98
Liquor Division. *Reported to: Finance Manager.*

Presided over entire accounts payable functions — invoices, reconciliations, payments, and vendor relations. Managed accounts receivable processes including payments, review, analysis, and follow-up. Supported the Finance Manager with end-of-month routines, stock reconciliations, commission calculations and payment, and MIS reports.

Accountant, *THWM Advanced Technologies* .... May 93–Oct 96

2

Finance manager/accountant (mid-level). *Gayle Howard, CPRW, CRW, CCM; Melbourne, Australia*

This one-page resume presents the key points of an experienced professional employed 15 years by the same organization

NESTER L. ARMISTON
30 E. Main Street
Belleville, Illinois 62221
(618) 555-7660

"Experienced"

PROFESSIONAL PROFILE

- More than 15 years experience as a Tax Auditor for the Internal Revenue Service, with additional duties involving quality control, staff training, audit selection and direct taxpayer assistance in person and via telephone.

- Experienced with Illinois and Missouri State Income Tax, Illinois State Retailer's Occupation & Use Tax, and Illinois Circuit Breaker returns.

- Proficient with database, spreadsheet, word processing, and automated tax preparation software applications. Recently completed the accredited National Tax Training School to maintain up-to-date knowledge of audit techniques, accounting methods, and IRS codes, rules and regulations.

- Able to distinguish between problems caused by computer errors as well as erroneous input. Can perform computations and other job tasks without being totally reliant on automated systems.

SELECTED TAX KNOWLEDGE AND SKILLS

This list style is a good way to pack lots of details into a small space

Federal Taxation	Exemptions and Filing Status
Tax Computations	Gross Income Inclusions/Exclusions
Gain/Loss on Sale/Exchange of Property	Capital Gains and Losses
Business Deductions	Depreciation
Accelerated Cost Recovery	Depletion
Amortization	Business/Casualty Losses
Self-Employment Tax	Estimated Tax
Income Tax Withholding	Payroll Tax
Tax Credits	Gain on Sale of Residence

EXPERIENCE

Note the lack of dates — helps "hide" age or recent unemployment

TAX AUDITOR, Internal Revenue Service
- Inspected books and records to determine and adjust taxpayer liability.
- Reviewed and corrected other tax auditor's work.
- Trained new staff members on all self-employed and non-self employed income, deductions, credits, and audit techniques; provided instruction on indirect methods of determining income including bank deposit analysis, net worth, source and application of funds, and cash analysis.
- Selected which returns would be audited.

Additional experience:
Successful small business owner responsible for all bookkeeping, accounting, sales, and financial management functions.

EDUCATION/SPECIALIZED TRAINING

- B.A. Degree, Business Education/Psychology, McKendree College, Lebanon, Illinois
- Accounting/Federal Taxation Courses, Southern Illinois University at Edwardsville
- Advanced Tax Auditor Training, Internal Revenue Service
- National Tax Training School, Monsey, New York

REFERENCES AVAILABLE UPON REQUEST

3

Auditor. *John A. Suarez, CPRW; O'Fallon, IL*

Julie Harrigan Willis

16 George Street, East Haven, CT 06512
julie-willis@aol.com   203-555-5594

EXPERTISE: Administrative Management — Corporate Meeting & Travel Planning

Experienced and accomplished administrative manager with a track record of contributions to productive, efficient business operations and positive professional relationships.

Areas of proven strength include:

- **Creating and implementing** operational systems and procedures.
- **Planning and executing** corporate travel and meeting arrangements.
- **Managing and monitoring** details of financial and operational activities.
- **Negotiating** contracts, leases, meeting amenities, billing arrangements.
- **Communicating and interacting** with colleagues, vendors, customers.
- **Directing and guiding** administrative staff and outside business services.
- **Responding rapidly and appropriately** to changing circumstances… troubleshooting problems and refocusing on new priorities.

> *"Julie has a way of working with people to get things accomplished with a minimum of contention… She has developed a smooth and flowing corporate administrative structure for the first time in our history."*
> John Eagle, President & CEO, Eagle's Legals

a ringing endorsement!

Professional Experience

ADMINISTRATIVE MANAGER — Eagle's Legals, Inc., New Haven, CT — 1998–Present — Manage all administrative functions for two-location, 12-employee company providing on-site trial assistance to attorneys nationwide. Charged with independent decision-making for day-to-day business activities and operational procedures. Primary goal is to provide a solid administrative foundation to enable top managers and trial specialists to perform effectively and achieve business goals.

The extensive nature of this manager's job duties required a rather long list, so "Contributions" were set apart as a separate heading to be sure they stand out.

- Supervise the company's travel activities including extensive air and ground travel, direct billing arrangements, and the logistics of shipping technology equipment for use in trial presentations.
- Manage HR functions: benefits administration, payroll, records, interviewing, employee orientation.
- Drive the process to gather staff billing data and create client invoices.
- Monitor cash balance and receivables; oversee collections; authorize payment for invoices; coordinate with bookkeeper.
- Maintain vendor relationships and negotiate prices and contracts. Manage office facilities for 2 locations.

Contributions:

- **Established operational policies and procedures** necessary for smooth business operations. Wrote corporate policy manuals and employee procedures manuals.
- **Developed corporate travel procedures** and established relationship with corporate travel agency — a business priority due to extensive travel and frequent last-minute changes.
- **Completely reorganized the company's administrative records.** Instituted new filing systems, procedures, and supervisory techniques to ensure the integrity of corporate records.
- **Established positive, productive vendor relationships.** Negotiated favorable billing policies and contracts; renegotiated existing contracts with in-place vendors. As a result, increased quality of business services received and improved cash flow.
- **Improved the efficiency of the company's billing procedures** through increased communication with staff members.

ADMINISTRATIVE MANAGER — Meeting Managers, Hamden, CT — 1996–1998 — Orchestrated meeting details and served as client liaison for successful meetings, symposiums, and sales training programs throughout the country for Fortune 500 clients including IBM, Echlin, and Pratt & Whitney.

Education

B.S. Psychology: University of Connecticut, Storrs, CT, 1990

Administrative manager. *Louise M. Kursmark, CPRW, JCTC, CEIP, CCM; Cincinnati, OH*

This resume helped Brian move from his long-time job managing residential properties to a higher-paid commercial property manager's position.

BRIAN MCLAUGHLIN

33 Fourth Street, Lindenhurst, NY 11736 • 631-729-4430 • b-mac@aol.com

— This building graphic is eye-catching and appropriate.

Facilities Manager / Electrical Engineer
Green Oaks Apartments, Lake Success, NY 1985 – present

Facilities Management

Construction Management

Project Management

HR/Staff Management

Tenant Relations

Budget Management

Inventory Control

Vendor Relations

Loss Control & Prevention

Contract Negotiations

Regulatory Compliance

Proposal Development

Information Systems

- Direct facilities-management operations of 266 housing units (five buildings) and common grounds for this organization's Congregate and Assisted Living for senior residents.
- Successfully restructured company practices, policies, and procedures resulting in dramatic improvements in areas of:
  - **General Management:** vendor selection, contract management, capital expenditures, inventory control, purchasing, staff development, and management/contractor relations.
  - **Technical:** HVAC, manual Building Management Systems (BMS), electrical, plumbing, blueprint preservation, and management of information systems.
- Coordinate emergency response procedures and act as primary point of contact for management, insurance agents, fire marshals, and town inspectors concerning Loss Control & Prevention issues.
- Oversee the hiring, training, scheduling, and supervision of 12 direct reports and define job responsibilities as dictated by the organization's ever-changing business needs. Instituted performance measurement tools that increased employee recognition and productivity.
- Gained greater flexibility in a $750,000 maintenance budget, achieving second-quarter savings of $16,000 through vendor changes, expense control, proposal development, and negotiations.
- Ensure the safety of residents and maintenance staff through continuous testing and maintenance of lighting, fire alarm, boiler and generator back-up systems; enforce mandatory use of protective gear during low/high-voltage work in accordance with local/national jurisdiction and OSHA regulatory compliance.

Chief Engineer / Facilities Manager
Briarcliff Gardens, Old Westbury, NY 1981 – 1985

- Directed a 6-year, $6.6 million grounds refurbishing project spanning 108,000 sq. ft. situated on 250 acres accommodating 3 golf courses, 15 tennis courts, Olympic pool, restaurants, 11-room dormitory, and 26 apartments/suites.
- Managed a $1M maintenance budget and staff in areas of HVAC, electrical, plumbing systems, computerized BMS, kitchen equipment/ appliances, and interior maintenance, repairs, and improvements.

Bachelor of Arts, Electrical Engineering
New York Institute of Technology

Certified Technician, EPA
Licensed Asbestos Handler

Preparing this resume helped Brian realize and value his skills and extensive knowledge, which he and his employer had been taking for granted.

Facilities manager. *Ann Baehr, CPRW; Long Island, NY*

5

PATRICIA M. PRICE

2304 Michael Street • Annandale, Virginia 22043
Home: 703-542-2983 • Cell: 703-451-3792
E-Mail: patmprice@yahoo.com

SUMMARY OF QUALIFICATIONS

FACILITIES MANAGER with experience in managing multi-site, mixed-use commercial properties and support services. Strong emphasis on client satisfaction, service delivery, and employee training. Noted as a dedicated and highly organized manager who is able to communicate at all levels. Available to travel and/or relocate.

Expertise Includes:

- Contract negotiations
- Staff supervision and training
- Capital and expense budgeting
- Cost control / reduction
- Regulatory and environmental compliance

- Vendor performance
- Project planning and coordination
- Lease administration
- Landlord / tenant relations
- Preventive maintenance planning

A strong team leader with the ability to develop partnerships that deliver results and meet objectives.

Only her most recent & relevant experience is described in detail.

PROFESSIONAL EXPERIENCE

HARMON & JONES REALTY SERVICES, Alexandria, VA   1990 – Present
An international commercial real estate and property management firm.

Facilities Manager (Fredericksburg, VA / July 1997 – Present)
Manage a 275,000-square-foot mixed-use commercial property on 32 acres. Facility has 2,000 employees on 3 shifts operating 7 days a week. Direct a staff of 10 to provide predictive/preventative maintenance as well as scheduled and emergency work-order services. Negotiate vendor contracts and monitor performance. Coordinate project scheduling to minimize impact on daily business and operations. Prepare detailed monthly financial reports for both HJRS and client.

Specific numbers and results give credibility to these accomplishment statements.

- Continuously evaluate operating expenses to maintain the most cost-effective methods of delivering services in line with client expectations. Achieved 11% savings over original budget of $2.5 million and under-ran FY 2000 adjusted goal by 5.44%.
- Challenged to resolve a possible indoor-air quality issue causing employee health problems. Arranged for environmental testing of possible sources of contamination, including soil samples and air handlers. Brought facility into compliance with OSHA guidelines as a result of audits.
- Supervised major upgrade of HVAC system to current regulations and ensured that engineers received training on new computerized monitoring system.

Area Manager (Richmond, VA / April 1995 – July 1997)
Managed 11 facilities throughout the Southeast for a health insurance client. Facilities totaled 315,000 square feet and included data centers, customer service and administrative offices, and call centers. Served as tenant representative and interfaced with landlord to resolve maintenance issues as well as address problems not covered under the lease agreement.

- Created and managed individual property budgets totaling $2.2 million.
- Partnered with Project Management and IT group to consolidate and close facilities.

6

Facilities manager. *Jean F. West, CPRW, JCTC; Indian Rocks Beach, FL*

PROFESSIONAL EXPERIENCE, continued

HARMON & JONES REALTY SERVICES
Assistant Area Manager (Baltimore, MD / July 1990 – April 1995)
Managed 2.3 million square feet of mixed-use commercial real estate owned by the regional telephone company. Handled contracts and vendor issues for 1,100 properties including data centers, switching equipment, administrative offices, and garages throughout Maryland. Partnered with teams from several companies to provide real estate solutions for the client. Set agendas and conducted ongoing monthly meetings with key team members to measure progress and revise strategies to achieve client goals.

▸ Reduced expenditures by 20% in 1995 and 2% in 1996, with some contracts reduced as much as 44%.

▸ Viewed as an outside vendor, overcame initial resistance from the close-knit telephone community. Traveled extensively to client offices throughout the state to meet with managers, assess their needs, discover their goals, and educate them on the benefits of the property management program. Translated client's corporate vision and goals into effective service delivery.

Previous experience includes 10 years of retail operations and sales management.

— Prior ten years summarized very briefly.

EDUCATION

University of Virginia, Charlottesville, VA
Bachelor of Science in Business Administration (1990)

LICENSES

Real Estate Sales License, State of Virginia (2000)
Real Estate Sales License, State of Maryland (1998)

PROFESSIONAL DEVELOPMENT

▸ Continuing education for licensure renewal
▸ Ongoing courses in real estate, personal development, and computer training
▸ Commercial Real Estate Training, Harmon & Jones Realty Services
▸ An Overview of Company and Real Estate Practices, Northern Virginia Community College
▸ Relocation Specialist Training

COMPUTER SKILLS

Strong technology skills, often serving as a resource and trainer to resolve computer and software problems for others. Proficient in MS Word, Excel, Publisher, PowerPoint, Access, Silent Flyer, Forms, intranet, e-mail and Internet communication.

Starts with a strong "value statement."

Andrea Gelman

7432 Oak Street, Burr Ridge, IL 60525   630-247-9742   a-gelman@msn.com

ADMINISTRATIVE MANAGEMENT EXECUTIVE

Delivering significant operational improvements that contribute to bottom-line profits.

Goes on to highlight the most important skills she brings to her job.

- Negotiating favorable contracts
- Developing effective standardized policies and systems to control and measure key functional areas
- Creatively attacking operational problems and devising winning solutions
- Justifying proposed changes through effective presentation of options and projected outcomes
- Maximizing the benefits of outsourcing non-core business functions

PROFESSIONAL EXPERIENCE

1987–Present   **MIDWEST BEEF,** Chicago, Illinois
              Manager, Transportation Services (1995–Present)
              Manager, Fleet Services (1992–1995)

The two most-recent positions are combined to avoid repetition.

Direct transportation and warehousing operations to support 4 producing plants and 7 distribution centers with national distribution of perishable products. Devise and implement strategies to maintain a tight operation and keep transportation costs to a minimum.

Manage $58 million annual budget. Negotiate warehousing and carrier contracts (truck and rail). Oversee company's regional truck fleets, selecting carriers and monitoring performance of both contract carriers and company trucks. Administer corporate automobile program for sales staff (275 autos). Oversee risk management for cargo, warehousing, fleet and carriers, working with attorneys and insurers to devise appropriate policies in conformance with legal and insurance recommendations.

- Initiated warehouse contract negotiation to capture annual savings of $110,000.
- Outsourced fleet transportation at one Midwest location, saving $60,000 and eliminating liability.
- Reduced auto fleet cost 2¢ per mile, resulting in $120,000 annual savings, by strengthening personal use policy and enforcing safety review procedures.
- Effectively controlled freight undercharge activities through strong contract and rate agreements, holding settlements to .02% of annual freight bill.
- Reduced leased rail fleet 12% by more closely tracking rail car locations through outsourced locator.
- Achieved 4% reduction in container fleet dead-head mileage through agreement with a major Gulf shipper.

        Manager, Carrier Claims (1987–1992)

Investigated, documented and filed freight loss and damage claims. Established cargo-inspection program and claim-filing procedure to allow for prompt claim creation and settlement. Implemented claim prevention programs to reduce company exposure to temperature and shortage losses.

- Reduced freight-claim receivables from $1.1 million to under $110,000. Achieved 80% collection ratio on claims settled.
- Captured annual fuel cost savings of $15,000 through redesign of employee reporting format.

1980–1987   **STANDARD TRUCKING,** Gary, Indiana
              Corporate Claims Manager

Administered customer service/adjustment policy for $2 billion company. Supervised department that investigated and negotiated $3 million in customer, warehouse and carrier claims annually.

- Compiled claim loss data by customer to determine account profitability.
- Initiated loss-prevention programs to attack early claim trends and encourage prompt corrective measures.
- Achieved .01% reduction in customer claim loss for annual savings of $400,000.

1977–1980   **MIDWEST NATIONAL BANK, Trust Officer,** Gary, Indiana

EDUCATION
Bachelor of Science, Business Administration — 1977 — Loyola University, Chicago, Illinois

MEMBERSHIP
Transportation Claims and Prevention Council — Council of Logistics Management

7

Administrative management executive. *Louise M. Kursmark, CPRW, JCTC, CEIP, CCM; Cincinnati, OH*

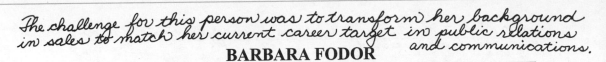

The challenge for this person was to transform her background in sales to match her current career target in public relations and communications.

BARBARA FODOR

666 Acton Avenue • Ridgewood, NJ 07450 • (201) 444-1111 • barbaraf@aol.com

PUBLIC RELATIONS / CORPORATE COMMUNICATIONS

Highly qualified professional with a diversified business background offers a solid academic foundation in journalism and public relations…. A published author who has won university journalism awards…. Computer-proficient with excellent knowledge of business software.

—— EDUCATION ——

Montclair University, Upper Montclair, NJ— BA Degree, May 2000 (GPA/3.8)
- Major: Communication with concentration in Journalism/Public Relations (GPA/3.9)
- Lambda Pi Eta, Beta Xi Chapter (National Communication Honor Society)
- Magna Cum Laude graduate / Dean's List
- *Print Journalism Award for 2000*
- Published writer with creative pieces appearing in both campus and national publications

Barbara's educational achievements are directly related to her current career goal, so they are placed near the top of her resume.

—— EXPERIENCE ——

Sales Representative: STAR PHARMA & CO., Newark, NJ   2000-2001

Promoted pharmaceutical products to over 140 private physicians for this Global Fortune 500 company. Part of dynamic sales team that effectively covered a large urban/suburban territory generating $4+ million annually.

- Brought sales ranking up by 66% in short time, achieving corporate sales objectives.
- Targeted specific practices to increase sales by reviewing monthly sales reports. Developed business through on-site visits, samples and promotional programs.
- Organized well-attended educational programs for physicians to promote company's products.

Account Manager: PHONE-TEL, Paterson, NJ   1998-1999

Serviced up to 300 corporate accounts, generating in excess of $1 million for this full-service telecommunications and Internet service provider. Addressed all clients' concerns, functioning in both proactive and reactive modes.

- Regularly followed up with accounts by phone and in person to build rapport and add new products and services.
- Served as consultant in evaluating needs of each client, taking into account system requirements and costs.
- Part of team that made presentations to clients. Secured four million new minutes and locked in $400,000 in term contracts over a six-week period.
- Maintained an account attrition rate of .0003, far below the industry standard of .02.

Customer Service Representative: SOS TECHNOLOGIES INC./Card Corporation, Newark, NJ   1995-1998

Responsible for customer service activity for imprinters, cards and consumable products. Handled approximately 50 calls daily, processing a high volume of orders (up to $20,000) using MRP system.

- Provided sales support for 25 sales reps and 40 dealers (domestic & international). Expedited orders to ensure fastest delivery possible. Authorized returns and credits.
- Conducted cross-departmental meetings using TQM approach. Improved communication, resulting in achieving priority goals on regular basis.

Promotions/Inside Sales: CORPORATE ENTERTAINMENT, Fort Lee, NJ   1990-1995

Responsible for marketing and sales support, serving as chief liaison with vendors and independent sales reps nationwide. Supervised an office staff of three.

- Marketed electronic equipment nationwide. Profits jumped 32% over previous year.

—— COMPUTER SKILLS ——

Windows 95/98	MS-Office 97	Lotus 1-2-3
Word / Excel / Access	PowerPoint	WordPerfect

8

Public relations (entry-level). *Vivian Belen, NCRW, CPRW, JCTC;*
Fair Lawn, NJ

The great amount of detail in this resume is appropriate for a senior-level executive.

GRIET L. DIERXSENS
GDierxsens@yahoo.com

970 Lakeside Boulevard
Grosse Pointe Woods, Michigan 48111
810.771.3773 cell

EXECUTIVE MARKETING/ADVERTISING MANAGEMENT PROFESSIONAL with demonstrated leadership abilities that include creating strategic vision, generating financial success and delivering positive operating results across multiple business functions, in international service and product markets. Recipient of numerous awards. *Areas of Expertise:*

- eBusiness, Interactive Marketing
- Global Operations
- Information Technology
- Global Sourcing
- International Sales & Marketing
- Mentoring & Team Building

- International Advertising Strategy
- Strategic Planning
- Public Relations
- Strategic Partnerships & CRM
- Profit Optimization
- Dutch & French Language Fluency

PROFESSIONAL EXPERIENCE

"Blue-chip" client names are identified throughout because these important relationships will carry over to the next job.

Vice President, Managing Director
CAMPBELL EWALD — WARREN, MICHIGAN (1997 to Present)
(One of the world's largest advertising agencies. Clients include DaimlerChrysler; British Telecommunications; Playstation.com (America), Inc.; Dayton's Departments Stores; General Electric; Bell Canada; Washington Mutual; and Target.)

Led daily production, operation, recruiting and HR activities with responsibility for $40 million revenue plan; included direction of 260-employee team for creative design and content, technical design and implementation, online media planning, business development, strategic planning, logistics, localization, public relations and corporate development for global clients.

Actions: Developed and managed $30 million convergence marketing budget as component of leasing automotive manufacturer's $1 billion marketing budget, ensuring seamless transition between direct mail, television, radio, catalog and print advertising campaigns and online campaigns. Also, developed and implemented international interactive strategy for leading automotive manufacturer spanning Asia, South America, Africa and Europe and successfully managed channel conflict by developing and implementing a dealer lead-generation solution.

Established stand-alone research group, world-class strategic consulting group and leading client services organization within company and solidified key client relationships. Implemented call-center cost-reduction strategy and increased office from 30 to 260 employees in 14 months along with complete knowledge transfer system and new employee mentoring program, a company first. Also, facilitated first global interoffice production for one client across 12 offices.

Accomplishments:
- Increased annual revenue 300% via client growth and new business development.
- Only senior manager to meet revenue targets in contracting business climate.
- Acquired first new client for local office and first client that crossed all service lines with estimated $7 million in revenues (first year).
- Expanded local client base to include eight additional Fortune 500 clients.
- Established research group, which generated $2 million+ revenue in first year; established consulting group, which generated $2.5 million+ in first year.
- Held operating expenses to 89% of budgeted projections.
- Realized remarkably low turnover (4% when industry average is 30%).
- Produced award-winning product: Best Use of Technology, Best eCommerce Site, GLIMA *(Great Lakes Interactive Marketing Association)*, 1999 and 2001.

9

Advertising/marketing (senior-level). *Jennifer Nell Ayres; Clarkston, MI*

PROFESSIONAL EXPERIENCE *(CONTINUED)*

General Manager
SAATCHI & SAATCHI ADVERTISING – NEW YORK, NEW YORK (1994 to 1997)
(Major worldwide commercial and communication solutions company. Clients included Kellogg's, Hasbro, Mayo Clinic, FedEx, MCI, Volkswagen, Marriott and U.S. Postal Service.)

Led worldwide daily production activities, overall P&L, and 50-employee team for localization, creative design and content, technical design and implementation, media planning, business development, strategic planning, marketing, public relations and global client development.

Actions: Launched international division; developed and implemented integrated print/direct-mail product introduction marketing campaign with CRM data collection component; negotiated strategic alliances; acquired new clients including Rousch Racing, NBC, Delta Airlines, Samsonite, Treetorn, Hasbro, FedEx, Zenith, Volkswagen, Marriott and U.S. Postal Service.

Accomplishments:
- Launched international division, earning $3.5 million revenue in first year.
- Transformed production model in seven months from regional boutique to international company with offices in Detroit, Los Angeles, New York, Houston, London, Berlin, Brussels and Dublin.
- Increased annual revenue 42% via client growth and new business development.
- Attained $1 million in first quarter global sales for start-up division, representing 88% of total sales.
- Newly acquired clients resulted in $5.7 million revenue in first year.

Director, Consulting
BOWER GLOBAL SOLUTIONS – BRUSSELS, BELGIUM (1988 to 1994)
(The world's largest software localization company. Clients included Microsoft, IBM-Lotus, 3Com, Oracle and Novell.)

Managed all office activities including overall P&L and proposal process. Launched consulting division with resources in six regions generating $2.5 million revenue in first six months and provided strategy on new product offerings, product diversification, brand positioning, marketing campaigns and sales management. Key clients were 3Com, Visio, The Associates and InterWorld. Key client strategist for Netscape, Adobe, Attachmate, Morgan Stanley, Johnson & Johnson and Amazon.com.

Previously: **Director, Advertising Business, and Manager, Business Development**

Manager, U.S. Import/Export – WORLD EXPORT ASSOCIATES – PARIS, FRANCE (1983 to 1985)
Secured export licenses for advanced computer hardware via COCOM and U.S. Defense Department, negotiated letters of credit payment and established financing for large contracts. Handled all aspects of client delivery from licensing, international delivery, payment and document translation. Turned around office from $900K deficit to $3 million profit in 15 months.

EDUCATION & AWARDS

M.A. in Advertising – NEW YORK UNIVERSITY – New York, New York (1995)
Nine Addy Awards *(detailed upon request)*

VOLUNTEER ASSOCIATIONS

Board of Directors & President of Volunteers – New York Symphony (1995 to 1997)
Board of Directors – Junior League of New York (1996 to 1997)
Member – Junior League (1994 to Present)
Board of Directors – ACROBAT (1997 to 1999)

GRIET L. DIERXSENS
GDierxsens@yahoo.com

970 Lakeside Boulevard
Grosse Pointe Woods, Michigan 48111
810.771.3773 cell

Robert wanted to advance from the regional to the national management level. He was looking for an executive position developing and implementing strategic communications/public relations campaigns.

ROBERT PATE

6092 Prospect Avenue
Hackey, WA 02975
H: (307) 359-1094 ◆ O: (307) 359-0139 ◆ Email: rpate@worldnet.att.net

---

EXECUTIVE PROFILE

PUBLIC RELATIONS / COMMUNICATIONS MANAGEMENT SPECIALIST

Talented communications professional offering 10+ years' proven ability to meet diverse and ever-changing external / internal communication needs within various business settings. Highly successful in designing and implementing creative and influential public, media, community, and employee relation strategies, using a wide range of tools and messaging vehicles. Strong leader and team player; excellent multitasking skills.

**Strategic Communications / Public & Media Relations / Government Relations
Issue Management / Grassroots Communications / Events Management**

PROFESSIONAL EXPERIENCE

1995 – Present **Paper International Corporation**
Advanced rapidly through positions of increasing complexity and responsibility with one of the largest forest-supply companies in the world.

REGIONAL PUBLIC AFFAIRS DIRECTOR, Hackey, WA (Jun 1997 — Present)

Promoted and transferred to provide internal strategic and tactical consultation on public affairs, issue management, and community relations for 5 major operations and a 1-million-acre forest within a 2-state southeastern region. Develop and manage budgets. Direct all media relations and serve as the registered lobbyist, coordinating government relations at the local and state levels.

- Favorably influenced state and local legislation, proposals, and regulations, including passage of 2 statewide sales tax exemption bills, a $1.8 million county tax exemption, and a 40% economic obsolescence credit.
- Directed crisis communications, effectively bolstering public support during a period of intense controversy and overachieving goals of maintaining positive public opinion at 50% or higher as measured in polls.
- Defused negative public perception and rebuilt community trust following crisis resolution through a series of judiciously executed external communications and public education campaigns.
- Strategized and deployed proactive campaigns utilizing appropriate, cost-effective mixes of print/broadcast media, outdoor advertising, earned media, sponsorships, charitable contributions, direct mail, and speaking engagements.
- Managed advertising and issue management firms in creation of several critically acclaimed and national award-winning television spots. Collaborated with agencies on location selection, talent, and message development.
- Enhanced public opinion through promotion and management of a highly successful educational mill-tour program that has hosted more than 15,000 visitors since inception.
- Gained positive media coverage and fostered strong relations with regional press members; responded to inquiries, conducted press tours, prepared staff prior to media interviews, and drafted op-eds for corporate executives.
- Initiated, built, and managed a grassroots network that has successfully lobbied at the local, state, and federal levels. Coordinated grassroots communications and educated staff with briefings and written materials.

10

Public relations executive. *Michelle Dumas, CPRW, NCRW, CCM, JCTC, CEIP; Somersworth, NH*

ROBERT PATE

COMMUNICATIONS MANAGER, Bethel, ME (Jan 1997 — May 1997)
COMMUNITY PROGRAMS MANAGER, Bethel, ME (May 1995 — Jan 1997)

Recruited to accelerate community involvement in a new program designed to increase name recognition and promote goodwill. Created and launched communication strategies involving public outreach, earned media, and direct mail for programs in 8 markets. Promoted and charged with additional and concurrent responsibility for leadership of 5 staff, all external communications, marketing, and customer service.

- ♦ Spearheaded high-impact communications strategy design and deployment, leading successful launch of new community-outreach programs in 6 diverse metropolitan areas in under 17 months.
- ♦ Identified and built relationships with supportive local non-profit and activist groups. Established partnerships with schools, achieving optimal program visibility and community involvement at the lowest possible cost.
- ♦ Built alliances with business partners, including Compaq and Sea World. Designed incentives for involvement, successfully increasing public awareness and driving participation levels that exceeded all expectations.
- ♦ Orchestrated and structured events to maximize press coverage and publicity by increasing the "human interest" story value. Introduced a popular program mascot, wrote speeches, involved key community leaders, and personally represented the company as an on-air spokesperson.
- ♦ Created and implemented a complete set of customer service protocols that were successful in improving both the timeliness and quality of communications with customers and increased satisfaction rates 45%.
- ♦ Wrote and produced newsletters for each market; planned and managed trade show booths, promotions, and business-to-business advertising campaigns.

1990 – 1995   **AAA Chemical Company**

LEGISLATIVE ASSOCIATE / ASSISTANT, Washington, DC (1993 – 1995)

Implemented strategies to meet federal legislative and regulatory objectives for this leading intermediate chemical manufacturer. Monitored legislative and regulatory activities, assessed and briefed management on importance of proposed actions, and prepared legislative position papers. Maintained grassroots communications.

Developed and cultivated relationships with members of Congress, federal agencies, and trade association representatives. Planned and implemented corporate activities during the 1992 Democratic and Republican conventions, managing a $300K budget.

1981 – 1990   Early career includes work as a research assistant and analyst with Research Associates International in Arlington, Virginia.

EDUCATION   **B.A., Government and Politics** — University of Maine, Orono, MC (1986)

Additional training in Executive Management/Leadership, Crisis Communications, Media Relations, Lobbying, Grassroots Communications, and Issue Management

COMPUTER SKILLS

Strong computer skills; proficient with word processing, desktop publishing, and multimedia applications, including MS Office (Word, Excel, Access, PowerPoint). Highly Internet savvy and comfortable with utilizing new media technologies for communications and advertising.

MING QUON DU

955 Breakwater Court — Ventura, CA 93004 — Tel: 805-647-1116 — E-Mail: mqdu@dock.net

PROFESSIONAL SUMMARY

Financial industry keywords are highlighted.

Comprehensive range of experience and formal training in *Budget Analysis and Accounting.*

Prepared to undertake higher level responsibilities in:
CORPORATE CREDIT–CARD MANAGEMENT — ONLINE BANKING SERVICES — COMPUTERIZED ACCOUNTING

ADDITIONAL QUALIFICATIONS

- Adept at managing multiple tasks and resolving or minimizing problems by identifying them in their early stages.
- Computer proficient in accounting software such as **MAS90**, **FAS**, **J.D. Edwards,** and **Excel**.

CAREER HISTORY

The chronological format makes the most of this person's progressively responsible and 100% relevant experience.

ADVANCED DIGITAL CORPORATION — Santa Barbara, CA (1998–Present)
[Advanced Digital provides nearly 500 financial institutions and over 10 million potential banking customers with global Internet banking services.]
Budget Analyst
Automated and standardized manual accounting procedures for server-based platforms; served as primary financial liaison to the programming group on this project. Analyzed and reconciled corporate Visa program accounts, representing 100 in-house cardholders with $1K to $500K limits, used primarily for IT capital acquisitions. Created a fixed asset and depreciation ledger, which supports capital computer acquisitions from $5K to $500K.

KINKO'S COPIES, CORPORATE OFFICES — Ventura, CA (1997–1998)
Senior Accounts Payable (A/P) Specialist
Directed full-cycle accounts payable and receivable processing, account reconciliation and cash drawer balancing for 20 regional stores. Supervised and trained 3 junior specialists in A/P tasks such as posting month-end closing and journal entries.

ACCOUNT TEMPS — Santa Barbara, CA (1996 - 1997)
Financial Consultant/Junior Accountant on temporary accounting projects, including the Cottage Hospital annual budget.

BIG FIVE SPORTING GOODS, INC. — Oxnard, CA (1994–1996)
Accounting Clerk
Transacted bank deposits and wire transfers. Reconciled expense accounts. Calculated and tracked commissions of sales staff. Computed sales tax. Input inventory data from manufacturer's production sheets.

TRI-COUNTY MANPOWER, INC. — Ventura, CA (1987–1994)
Accounts Payable Clerk
Automated A/P for human resources supplier. Controlled daily cash sheet. Disbursed checks.

EDUCATION

This important information appears late in the resume, so it is highlighted to be sure it is not overlooked.

Certificate in Business Management and Computerized Accounting — Sawyer College, Oxnard, CA (1990–1991)
Associate Degree in Liberal Arts and Sciences — Moorpark College, Moorpark, CA (1985–1987)

11

Budget analyst. *Roleta Fowler, CPRW, CEIP; Fillmore, CA*

FREDERICK R. PRENTICE
4060 Cleveland Avenue
St. Louis, MO 63110
(314) 771-8908
prentfr@compuserv.com

PROFESSIONAL SUMMARY

Budget Analyst with expertise in the analysis of financial operations, estimation of future revenues and expenditures and preparation of corporate budgets. Equally strong qualifications in management reporting, tax preparation and reporting and profit sharing plans. Recognized by senior management and promoted to positions of increasing responsibility based on outstanding performance, leadership, technical expertise and teamwork.

STRENGTHS

- Easily translate and present complex financial data into clear, concise management reports.
- Providing superior service with proven ability to work effectively with internal customers.
- Effective team leadership, project management and staff training experience.
- Key skills: Analytical, detail/follow-through, problem solving and computer systems.

PROFESSIONAL EXPERIENCE

<u>**MISSOURI MUTUAL**</u> • St. Louis, MO • 1991–Present

Budget Analyst, 1996–Present

- Promoted through increasingly responsible assignments in finance. Provide team leadership and training to junior members as well as manage key projects in department.
- Provide technical support and work closely with the chief financial officer in preparation of annual budgets at a regional financial services organization.
- Review budget estimates for accuracy and conformance with procedures, regulations and corporate objectives.
- Consolidate departmental budgets throughout the company into operating and financial budget summaries.
- Submit preliminary budgets to senior management, providing supporting statements to justify or deny funding requests.
- Monitor operating budget through ongoing review of reports and accounting records to ensure that allocated funds are spent as specified.
- Assess system limitations, recommending best method for minimizing future system development problems and improving efficiency.

Highlights:

- *Chosen to develop enhancement requirements for budget systems. Created and implemented training manual for users.*
- *Contributed to the development of new budget procedures and policies that improved accuracy and accountability. Conducted training sessions for company management on new budget procedures.*
- *Coordinated financial analysis project and developed capital improvement budget.*
- *Earned "Employee of the Month," "Team Player" and other employee recognition awards.*

Tax Reporting Analyst, 1993–1996

- Performed analysis and quality control functions; ensured accuracy of various Federal tax forms prepared for company's clients.
- Tested system and conducted audits of tax reports to ensure IRS compliance and integrity of all recorded transactions.

12

Budget analyst. *Louise Garver, MA, JCTC, CMP, CPRW; Enfield, CT*

FREDERICK R. PRENTICE – Page 2

Tax Reporting Analyst continued....

- Reviewed transactions to test accuracy of database edit and control features; effectively resolved problems on tax reporting information.
- Independently produced "exception" tax reporting forms for federal and state tax purposes; addressed inquiries from state agencies related to audits of "exception" reports.
- Prepared and electronically filed daily state tax returns to appropriate state agencies.
- Reconciled and balanced house ledger accounts; ensured adherence to payment schedule.

Highlights:

- *Achieved leadership and teamwork awards for initiating and implementing new tax reporting database.*
- *Named "Employee of the Month" in recognition of outstanding contributions and service.*

Prior: Accounting Specialist (1991–1993).

EDUCATION

B.S. in Accounting,1991
University of Connecticut, Storrs, CT

This resume — highlighting training, project, and staff leadership roles — successfully positioned this person for a higher-level role with another company.

Keeping insurance costs down through intelligent claims management.

The graphics and design make this resume stand out.

David Letterman
900 Cameron Way
Anderson, IN 46011
(317) 642-0000
dletterman@yahoo.com

Independent claims consultant specializing in industrial emissions violations claims settlements, with strong network of lab experts and legal and government contacts. Seeking a potential leadership role with physical damage unit of progressive insurance group. Excellent insurance claims record with solid damage expertise in industry, regulatory, technical, and auto.

Professional Experience:

Independent Claims Consultant for General Motors Divisions,
State of Indiana, doing business as Mid-State Appraisals, Anderson, Indiana.
1990–Present

❖ Eliminated costly and unnecessary expenses resulting in millions of dollars of savings for GM divisions with regard to industrial emissions and related technical matters.
❖ Set up and maintained claims database (15,000-plus claims) to eliminate duplication and produce reports, and developed solid relationships with division security to pursue fraudulent claims; recovered thousands of dollars for damage to company property.
❖ Referred to various GM divisions to help contain claim expenditures through implementation of settlement agreements, and developed mutual respect with UAW union representatives in helping to resolve problems.

Claims Adjuster, Underwriters Adjusting Co., Indianapolis, Indiana.
1984–90

❖ Responsible for physical damage claims; represented Continental Companies and numerous other insurers as well as self-insured entities.
❖ Joined National Catastrophic Team; held draft authority; set up and ran drive-in claims services at various agencies; trained new employees; responsible for 23 counties in north-central Indiana.

Extensive Auto Body Experience, Don's Auto Body, Lapel, Indiana. *1974–84*

Expert auto detailing with specialty focused on exotics, collector's items, and sports automobiles.

Special Information:

❖ Broad area of consulting helped develop large No. of contacts with technical expertise used in business.

❖ Expertise in client relations, technical issues in industrial emissions, damage claims investigation and settlement.

❖ Served on National Catastrophic Team for six years in an underwriting role serving large area with multi-task responsibilities.

❖ Solid networking skills.

❖ Extensive auto detailing, auto body experience.

Interesting two-column format.

13

Insurance claims adjuster. *Jon Shafer; Anderson, IN*

ROBERT P. MC MANN
555 Swartman Road
Ballston Center, New York 55555
(555) 555-5555

CAREER OBJECTIVE: Police / Insurance Investigator

QUALIFIED
by:

- 21+ years experience in law enforcement; 8 years in an investigative capacity.
- Extensive specialized training in all aspects of investigation including fire cause, homicide, robbery, traffic-related, and family issues.
- Persistent, thorough, and prompt in completing assigned projects.
- Excellent communication and interpersonal skills; reputation as an effective interviewer.
- Ability to work well independently or as part of a team.
- Qualified "Expert Witness" in Arson Investigation, U.S. Federal Court - 1995.
- Qualified "Expert Witness" in Arson Investigation, NYS - Schenectady County Court.

PROFESSIONAL EXPERIENCE:
Schenectady City Police Department, Schenectady, NY
INVESTIGATOR / DETECTIVE - 1988 - present

- Investigate all felonies assigned by supervisor and those that occur during shift.
- Manage investigative projects independently; analyze problem; exhaust all leads.
- Prepare detailed investigative reports, resulting in criminal prosecution and conviction.
- Successfully elicit confessions for such crimes as homicide, robbery, and arson, applying effective communication and interview skills.
- Appointed Deputy Federal Agent (DEA) for Capital District Drug Enforcement Task Force; served as undercover agent from 1991 - 1993.
- Work effectively with federal, state, and local enforcement agencies throughout the Capital District and surrounding areas.

TRAFFIC ACCIDENT INVESTIGATOR - 1986 - 1988

- Investigated condition and cause of accident. Issued tickets; wrote and filed detailed report on incident. Appeared in court as witness in traffic accident/violation cases.

PATROLMAN - 1975 - 1986

- Functioned as an undercover Vice Officer for one year in 1975; General Patrol from 1976 - 1986.
- Handled all types of cases including shoplifting, burglaries, robberies, traffic-related, domestic, and child abuse situations.

Awards/Recognition: Recipient of 18 Commendations for Outstanding Achievement in Police Work from the Schenectady City Police Department, City of Schenectady, and County of Schenectady.

CERTIFICATION:
Certified - Level I & Level II NYS Fire/Arson Investigator
CPR Certified - New York State

VOLUNTEER/COMMUNITY INVOLVEMENT:
Volunteer - Special Olympics, Albany, NY

14

Insurance investigator. *Barbara M. Beaulieu; Scotia, NY*

Robert P. Mc Mann   **Page 2**

MILITARY EXPERIENCE:
   U.S. Army - 1968 - 1971
   Republic of Korea - 1968 - 1969
   Republic of Viet Nam - 1970 - 1971
   Rank Achieved: Sergeant / Honorable Discharge

PROFESSIONAL AFFILIATIONS:
   Member - Schenectady Patrolmans P.B.A.
   Member - International Association of Arson Investigators - National
   Member - International Association of Arson Investigators - Local #23

EDUCATION:
   Schenectady County Community College, Schenectady, NY
   Concentration: Police Science

   Ricker College, Houlton, ME
   Concentration: Business Administration

PROFESSIONAL TRAINING:
   Attended numerous technical training, courses, and seminars throughout my career
   including:
   - Basic Course For Police - Bureau of Municipal Police - 1975
   - Doppler Radar Operator - Bureau of Municipal Police - 1979
   - Radar Operator - Bureau of Municipal Police - 1988
   - Basic Crash Management - Bureau of Municipal Police - 1988
   - Intermediate Crash Management - Bureau of Municipal Police - 1988
   - Technical Crash Management - Bureau of Municipal Police - 1989
   - Advanced Crash Management - Bureau of Municipal Police - 1989
   - Fire Behavior/Arson Awareness - State of New York Fire AC - 1989
   - Fire Cause & Origin - New York State Fire Academy - 1989
   - Practical Homicide Investigation - Investigative Consultants - 1989
   - Identi-Kit System - Identi-Kit Co. S&W - 1989
   - Fire/Arson Investigation - New York State Fire Academy - 1989
   - Fire Investigator Level II - New York State Fire Academy - 1990
   - Fire Investigator Level I - New York State Fire Academy - 1990
   - Juvenile Fire Setter - Capital District Fire Investigators - 1992
   - Fire/Arson Seminar - New York State Fire Prevention - 1992
   - 92 NYSP Sex Offense Seminar - New York State Police - 1992
   - 93 NYS Fire Investigation Training - New York State Arson Investigation - 1993
   - Arson Seminar - New York State Fire Academy - 1993
   - DPF & Search & Seizure - C-NET Schenectady County - 1993
   - Electrical Fire Cause Determination - New York State Fire Academy - 1995

REFERENCES ON REQUEST

This resume was designed to reflect Robert's law enforcement and investigative experience. It also highlights his career accomplishments, awards, special assignments, and special training (resume writer's comments).

Felix sent this resume out 7 times, got 3 interviews and 2 job offers. The job he took paid $8500 more a year than his previous job.

Felix Delgado, MCSE, MCP

33299 St. James Street ● Danville, VA 24540
Home: 434-555-5521 ● Cell: 434-555-1124 ● E-mail: felix@envision.com

---

COMPUTER SYSTEMS MANAGER

Project Management ● Strategic Planning & Analysis ● Staff Training

Focused, dedicated, and highly motivated professional offering solid contributions and a diverse systems background. Budget- and time-conscious individual. Exceptional dedication to growing with cutting-edge technologies and seeking to achieve beyond expectations in every endeavor. Motivational leader and communicator capable of building cohesion and project engagement across all levels of staff, management, vendors, and customers.

PROFESSIONAL EXPERIENCE

Millennium Computers, Inc.; Danville, VA   **05/1999 to Present**

ADVISORY I/T PROFESSIONAL
Train staff in new technologies. Write and edit REXX and PERL scripts. Develop and modify client/server applications using Visual Basic 6 in a lab environment. Develop academic VB.NET, C++, and SQL 7/2000 applications.

- Migrated 7000 laptops from Windows 98 to Windows 2000 and trained new users.
- Updated server tools and utilities on Windows NT, Windows 2000, Netware, and OS/2 platforms at offices all over the United States.

Just-In-Case, Inc.; Richmond, VA   **03/1998 to 05/1999**

SENIOR WEB PROGRAMMER
Programming Team Leader. Project Manager and Coder for both static and eCommerce Web sites. Designed and integrated Web site and database applications. Assisted the Data Center Manager with networking, NOS, and desktop issues.

- Developed a client training solution for the sales team after assessment of client and customer needs and extensive research of various technologies including Citrix ICA Server technology and third-party software.
- Completed 6 backlogged Web projects before the two-month deadline and received a promotion as a result.

Brilliant Designs, Inc.; Richmond, VA   **02/1997 to 03/1998**

NETWORK / SYSTEM / DESKTOP ADMINISTRATOR
Senior NT and application architect. Installed, configured, and deployed servers and end-user PCs. Maintained and monitored network servers in NT domain and all network-related connectivity devices. Monitored PBX- and telecommunications-related services and devices. Maintained all network print devices as well as copiers and fax machines. Assisted marketing department with Internet and intranet sites. Supported network and desktop administration teams. Supported end users.

- Solely led Y2K and Disaster Recovery Operation with a 100% success rate.

15

Computer systems manager. *Amy Whitmer, CPRW; Louisville, KY*

Felix Delgado; Résumé, page 2

Crystal Clear Solutions; Roanoke, VA   **06/1995 to 02/1997**

SENIOR HARDWARE TECHNICIAN
Built and repaired computer systems. Provided technical assistance and training to internal departments. Installed and configured testing software. Verified system operation. Tested, diagnosed, and repaired all hardware-related components returned by customer.

OTHER EXPERIENCE

Data Systems Corporation   **1992 to 1995**
Logistics Manager and IT Support

Great Alliance   **1986 to 1987**
A/V Technical Manager

University of Virginia   **1984 to 1986**
A/V Student Manager

TECHNICAL SKILLS

- Windows 95, 98, 2000, NT
- Win2000 Advanced Server/ServerPro
- Exchange 5.5
- Citrix MetaFrame/ WinFrame
- Access 97, 2000
- T-SQL & SQL 6.5/7 Server Administration
- IIS
- Visual Basic

- PERL
- REXX
- WinBatch & WinBatch Studio
- HTML, XHTML, IHTML, XML, DHTML
- JavaScript
- ASP
- Homesite
- Visual Studio
- Visual InterDev

- SMS
- FrontPage
- SMLSpy
- OptiPerl
- ScriptBuilder
- TextPad
- LiquidFX
- ColdFusion Studio
- Flash
- Swish
- PhotoImpact6
- Cool3D

CERTIFICATIONS & EDUCATION

Microsoft Certified Professional • Microsoft Certified Systems Engineer

Bachelor of Science in Computer Science
University of Virginia — 1986

Currently Pursuing:
Microsoft Certified Database Administrator • Microsoft Certified Solutions Developer
Cisco Certified Network Associate • Citrix Certified Administrator

PROFESSIONAL AFFILIATIONS

Software Contractors Guild (http://www.scguild.com/)
International Webmasters Association (http://www.iwanet.org/)
HTML Writers Guild (http://www.hwg.org/)

This introduction gives an almost instant profile of this individual's significant expertise.

Sandra T. Chan

122 Oleander Lane
Ridgewood, NJ 07464

fax: 201-555-1212

email: stchan@aol.com
residence: 201-555-1212

INFORMATION TECHNOLOGY EXECUTIVE

Acquisitions / Divestitures / Start-up / Turnaround / Fast-Track Growth / International

Astute comprehension of business and financial issues with an ability to rapidly develop and deploy IT solutions. Former ex-pat with in-depth understanding of international business. Excellent negotiator who understands both the IT and business sides of issues. Superb developer of operational plans with equally strong program execution abilities. Leader with extensive experience directing large, globally deployed, high-performing teams.

- WAN and LAN Technologies
- Security and Data Recovery
- Remote Systems Access
- Client/Server Architectures

- Network Engineering
- Infrastructure Design
- E-web hosting
- System & Multiuser Interface

PROFESSIONAL EMPLOYMENT

DIRECTOR — GLOBAL INFRASTRUCTURE ORGANIZATION

Total Telecomm Solutions, Waldwick, NJ   *1998 – present*

Promoted and given responsibility for budgets of $112 million for WAN and e-infrastructure and $89 million for operations as part of an overall CIO budget of $1.9 billion and an infrastructure budget of $1.1 billion. Support over 200 associates deployed globally in 25 countries. Responsible for US Western Region, Canada, Caribbean/Latin America, Asia/Pacific and e-Infrastructure. Support all e-web hosting, both internal and external, as well as network security. Manage all network connectivity from the desktop, including hosting of Total Telecomm Solutions' web applications and connection to external networks.

- Quadrupled bandwidth and reduced unit cost by 40% in 18 months in the US, Europe and Asia.

- Created a flexible IT infrastructure to allow for acquisitions and divestitures:
  - Divested $19 million (20%) of WAN, e-Infrastructure, LAN operations, network monitoring, voice communication and email in multiple countries simultaneously, along with 40 associates in the formation of Nedco to ensure viable infrastructure for both companies.
  - Spun off $5 million of a total $62 million budget for infrastructure operations and 10 associates for the creation of Systemex within a six-month time frame.
  - Disaggregated $1.6 million of a total $20 million infrastructure operations budget and 3 associates in the spin of New Systems to Dynamic in a nine-month time frame.

- Integrated CIO global Infrastructure operations of $100 million through negotiation with Europe and Saudi Arabia to agree to a merged network that incorporated corporate and business unit requirements.
  - Ensured that Company has one look to its customers — common look and feel — and still accommodated local cultures and business practices.

- Created a common PC security platform for the corporation: Replaced manually deployed software with a single online tool used by over 100,000 Total Telecomm Solutions associates worldwide that greatly reduced virus threats and hacking attempts.

- Achieved cost reduction of $6 million through negotiation of a global contract for data services.

- Planning IT infrastructure requirements for the sale of manufacturing plant with an anticipated sale price of $4 billion.

- Planning for reduction of IT infrastructure expense to 5% of revenue (currently 8%) through re-negotiation of contracts.

Every bullet item is quantified with some exceptional result.

16

IT executive. *Fran Kelley, MA, CPRW, SPHR, JCTC; Waldwick, NJ*

Sandra T. Chan

fax: 201-555-1212 | email: stchan@aol.com | residence: 201-555-1212

─────── **PROFESSIONAL EMPLOYMENT, cont'd.** ───────

SENIOR MANAGER — INTERNATIONAL BUSINESS MANAGEMENT
Global Infrastructure Systems and Operations, Total Telecomm Solutions, Waldwick, NJ   *1996 – 1998*
Participated in the start-up of Total Telecomm Solutions' CIO Infrastructure Operations.

- Within six months, created International Operations business model including WAN, supporting financials and funding for the newly created Total Telecomm Solutions, Inc.
- Developed Charge Back and International Operations models.
- Aggregated multiple engineering teams to build a single team to deploy a single WAN budget of $76 million for 130,000 associates in 60 countries.
- Deployed Total Telecomm Solutions Remote Access to 20 countries outside of the US.

SENIOR MANAGER — ASIA PACIFIC IT
CoTelco, Tokyo, Japan   *1989 – 1996*
Responsible for building Infrastructure for CoTelco expansion into the Asia/Pacific region. Supported a team of 90 people in 11 countries.

- Migrated 2,800 associates from mainframe to desktop environment in 12 countries.
- Built an international network and processing centers to support email, voice and access to common systems for 32 sites.
- First region in CoTelco to complete corporate mail networking/client server implementation and to upgrade processes and facilities.
- Migrated systems from dial-up/asynchronous networks to TCP/IP over six years.

SENIOR MANAGER
Engineering Laboratories, Tokyo, Japan   *1988 – 1989*
Responsible for software licensing. Presented at numerous technical conferences globally.

─────── **PRIOR PROFESSIONAL EMPLOYMENT** ───────
Several positions in Applications Development and Business Analysis for CoTelco supporting staffs of 25 – 40.

EDUCATION
MS — Computer Science, MIT, Cambridge, MA
BS — Political Science, MIT, Cambridge, MA

EXECUTIVE EDUCATION
Barnard College — two week *Strategic Thinking* Executive Education Program — 1999

PROFESSIONAL AFFILIATIONS
Member — Global Customer Advisory Council — 2000 – present
Major telecommunications companies participate.

Member — Customer Advisory Council — 2001
Major networking companies participate.

LANGUAGES
Basic Japanese — oral

This individual found a new, higher-paid position within two months!

a chronological format is used here to emphasize this individual's strong work history in the sometimes volatile high-tech industry.

Robert Lancaster

55 Tern Lane, Londonderry, NH 07946
(603) 647-5555 • (603) 647-5556 Fax • roblan@bsi.com

This check-marked list includes excellent keyword summaries.

EXECUTIVE – Technology Industry
IT Management / Project Management / E-Business / Business Development

☑ High-profile career spearheading the development, commercialization and launch of emerging e-commerce technologies from start-ups to Fortune 1000 companies.

☑ Business Model Expansion and Enhancement. E-Business Start-ups. Business Process Innovation and Creation. Strategic Partnering. Strategic Alliances.

☑ Competitive Analysis and Positioning. Technology Project Management.

Technical versatility in computer systems, hardware and software, web site design and development, database management, telecommunications, and accounting. Complex technology and internetwork integration expertise. Team-building exemplified in low turnover rate and internal promotions.

PROFESSIONAL EXPERIENCE

TECHNOLOGY IN MOTION, INC., Derry, NH   1998 – 2002
Vice President, Technology & Business Development
Given full responsibility for all technology aspects of e-commerce business development and resource management including computer systems, hardware and software, telecommunications, web site, financial systems, and secure e-commerce.

Accomplishments:
- Partnered with principals to launch start-up legal and medical seminar company. Developed integrated strategies leveraging new media for business development.

- Designed, developed and implemented 50-page web site with secure registration and book order forms, accommodating 680,000 potential registrants.

- Conceptualized and deployed data collection database, including registration records and reports, capable of utilizing real-time data and electronic data interchange.

- Researched and implemented credit-card program, including posting and reconciliation, electronic processing, shipment tracking and regulatory compliance.

TOPNOTCH TELECOM, INC., Somersworth, NH   1995 – 1998
Vice President – Operations
Driving force and founding team member for an innovative e-business model providing custom pre-paid calling cards. Developed advanced technology solutions. Full oversight for calling-card production (1 million cards within 2 years), security and shipment.

Accomplishments:
- Spearheaded start-up effort that captured Fortune 1000 client companies including Big Food Industries, Pharmaceuticals Plus, and Global Communications. Developed financial wire-transfer system within first 2 months.

- Designed, developed and maintained web site as well as phone card graphic design.

- Established special systems development and voice messaging of calling cards. Closely supervised PIN inventory and activation.

continued

17

IT executive. *Susan Guarneri, NCC, NCCC, LPC, CPRW, IJCTC, CCM, CEIP; Lawrenceville, NJ*

Robert Lancaster
(603) 647-5555 • (603) 647-5556 Fax • roblan@bsi.com   Page 2

PROFESSIONAL EXPERIENCE, continued

EVERY CITY INSURANCE AGENCY, INC., Blair's Landing, NH   1990 – 1995
Technology Advisor / Licensed Insurance Agent
Recruited to this financial services company to spearhead new technology-integration impetus and electronic systems deployment. Given full responsibility for information systems including computer systems design and maintenance, hardware/software, portability and purchase issues.

Accomplishments:

- Devised and rolled out successful electronic-payment systems for insurance agency and premium finance company, resolving operating discrepancies.

- Initiated and achieved incorporation status with federal, state and local authorities.

- Administered bank accounts, payroll, accounts payable and accounts receivable.

FINANCIAL SERVICES CORP., Blair's Landing, NH   1985 – 1990
Vice President (1986 – 1990), **Manager** (1985 – 1986)
Promoted to VP within one year based on successful and versatile track record for this financial services organization. Full latitude for technical operations and technology integration, including functional system requirements and network operating systems.

Accomplishments:

- Researched, developed and implemented integrated network and systems for custom premium finance software, in Novell-based PC-network and AS/400 terminal network.

- Hired and supervised 7 employees responsible for processing millions of dollars in financing. Initiated, developed and implemented employee training and policy notebook, resulting in increased staff motivation and productivity.

- As VP, assisted in securing additional institutional financing. Transitioned company in buyout phase to successor company.

EDUCATION
Bachelor of Arts, Political Science, University of New Hampshire, Durham, NH
New Hampshire Licensed Insurance Broker — Property/Casualty, Health/Life

COMPUTER SKILLS
Windows 2000 / 98...MS Office 2000...Access 2000...Excel 2000...Word 2000...
FrontPage 2000...QuarkXPress...Photoshop...HTML...Peachtree...Quicken...
MS Outlook...Internet Explorer...Netscape Navigator.

PROFESSIONAL ASSOCIATIONS
Computer Information Technology Systems — CITS
Society of Internet Consultants — SIC

Mr. Smith used this resume to showcase his business to contractors and to explore various business opportunities.

DANIEL SMITH

| 4223 Main Avenue | | (510) 643-1489 | Home |
| Berkeley, California 94702 | danielsmith@att.net | (510) 546-8965 | Mobile |

Construction Management ... Turnkey Operations ... Project Management ... Business Development

Diligent, results-oriented Superintendent experienced in asbestos abatement with proven success in winning contracts and managing construction of commercial, industrial, and residential buildings. Skilled in estimating equipment and manpower needed to complete projects on time without sacrificing quality. Highly developed organizational, planning, and time-management skills. Extensive supervision skills with contractors and employees on union and nonunion work sites. Self-motivated with initiative and attention to detail. Knowledge of California OSHA notification process, EPA, worker's compensation, bonding, and state, local, and federal regulations. Computer literate with experience in Windows 98 and Microsoft Word. Areas of skill include:

- Commercial Development
- Competitive Bidding
- Master Scheduling
- Contract Administration
- Building Code Compliance
- Field Construction Management

EXPERIENCE

all three jobs listed are concurrent. This shows that Mr. Smith is able and willing to tackle multiple projects at the same time.

1986 — Present   **Foreman**   Absestos Management, Vallejo, CA
Asbestos-abatement company with over 100 employees serving Northern California and Hawaii.
- Oversee asbestos abatement of refineries and manufacturing plants.
- Prepare proposals for competitive bidding.
- Manage construction crews of 2–15 contractors and employees.
- Prepare daily logs and field reports.
- Build required containments and double bag material.

1998 – Present   **Manager**   Industrial Services, Hayward, CA
Asbestos- and lead-abatement renovation company with 40 employees serving California, Ohio, and Pennsylvania.
- Plan and manage asbestos and reinsulation of wood mills, piping, boilers, and factories.
- Conduct project bidding and estimation.
- Complete projects on time without sacrificing quality.
- Manage employee recruitment, selection, and supervision.
- Reconcile $500,000 in accounts payables and receivables.
- Manually inventory stock and maintain supplies.

2000 – Present   **Foreman**   Environmental Services, Vallejo, CA
Asbestos- and lead-abatement demolition company with over 150 employees serving Northern California.
- Plan demolition of one-story buildings to high rises and interior demolition projects.
- Supervise and ensure worker safety of crews ranging in size from 2–20 employees.
- Schedule clearances and air samples.

CERTIFICATIONS

- Lead Abatement / Monitoring
- Asbestos Abatement
- BLS / CPR
- DHS Lead Monitoring

PROFESSIONAL MEMBERSHIPS

- Napa Solano Builders
- Shasta Builders Exchange

18

Construction manager. *Leatha Jones, CPRW, CEIP; Orinda, CA*

JOE WHEATLEY

3806 40TH Street
Lubbock, TX 79413

jwheat11@aol.com

Home: 806.788.1111
Mobile: 806.239.1555

CONSTRUCTION ENGINEER / PROJECT MANAGEMENT

Motivated, talented professional with the ability to plan, develop, and complete projects efficiently. Excellent time management and human relationship skills. Anticipate completion of BS in Construction Engineering spring 2002. Qualifications include:

- Problem Resolution
- Teambuilding & Leadership
- Hands-on Experience

- Customer Relationships
- Quality & Productivity Improvement
- Engineering & Project Management

EDUCATION

Since this person is looking for his first professional position, his education is highlighted right up front.

Bachelor of Science, **Construction Engineering,** Texas Tech University, Lubbock, TX, Spring 2002
- Worked throughout college career and earned a 3.1 GPA.
- Named to Dean's List, Spring 2001.
- Successfully completed Fundamentals of Engineering Exam, Fall 2001.

Presentations:
- Estimated, scheduled and presented group project to owner for a cafeteria addition.
- Developed and presented a business and marketing plan for a mobile car wash.
- Presented in PowerPoint format a project that demonstrated the successful resolution of a construction-specific problem.

Awards:
- West Texas Home Builders Scholarship, 1998 to Present
- National Associated General Contractors Scholarship, Spring 2001 to Present
- College of Engineering Scholarship, Spring 2001 to Present

Specialized Courses:
- Construction Management
- Contracts & Specifications
- Engineering Design
- Professional & Business Communications

- Computer Programming
- Statistical Methods
- Cost Estimating
- Cost & Profit Analysis

Powerful, positive comments such as this one are sprinkled throughout.

Honor Graduate, Coronado High School (CHS), Lubbock, Texas, May 1998
- Lettered two years Varsity Basketball; received All-Academic Athlete Award.
- Participant: National Honor Society and Bell Crew Spirit Squad.

"Joe is a winner in every aspect of the meaning of the word." ___Barry Voss, CHS Basketball Coach

RELEVANT EXPERIENCE

His two internships are listed as "Relevant Experience."

Assistant Project Engineer (Internship)
Huber, Hunt & Nichols, Dallas, TX, May to August 2001
National engineering company with six to eight billion under contract; ranked 24th in ENR Top 400 Contractors. Responsibilities included submitting products, reviewing projects and contract documents, scheduling, analyzing costs, writing technical materials, expediting field work/workers, processing photos, researching concrete mix design and customizing concrete-pour logs for computer.

- Analyzed and cut costs for project by at least 10%.
- Developed a computerized system for data retrieval; taught project engineers how to input and access files.
- Resolved complex technical problems and conducted business effectively via phone.
- Developed, maintained and expedited schedule for small phase of a large construction project.

"What an asset Joe turned out to be, exceeding all expectations for a summer intern...."
___Clint Brit, Project Engineer, Huber, Hunt & Nichols

19

Construction manager. *Lynn Hughes, MA, CPRW, CEIP; Lubbock, TX*

JOE WHEATLEY

jwheat11@aol.com

Page Two

Sales & Estimating Trainee (Internship)
RSM Builders Supply, Lubbock, TX, February to August 2000
Mid-sized door, frame and hardware supplier serving the Amarillo and Lubbock area. Estimated, prepared bids, worked in inventory control, assisted customers and contributed to good client relationships. Became proficient in material take-off from contract documents, plans and specifications. Taught staff how to utilize the computer effectively.

- Increased company's ability to take on more work through effective organization and relieving owner of many of his responsibilities.

ADDITIONAL WORK EXPERIENCE) *Other employment is listed here and takes second rating to the internships.*

Owner/Operator
Joe Wheatley Mobile Car Care, Lubbock, TX, 1999 to Present
Developed a mobile car-wash business with 25 regular clients and $5K profits annually.

- Selected equipment and assembled car-wash trailer.
- Maintained excellent client relationships with a 100% satisfaction rate.

Owner
Wheatley Lawn Care, Lubbock, TX, 1996 to 1999
Bought lawn care business. Services included fertilizing, chemical application, tree and brush trimming and mowing.

- Increased client base by over 60%; drove profits to over $15K yearly.

"Joe's work ethic and sense of responsibility is something rarely seen in today's society of youth... I think he will be very successful in whatever endeavor he pursues."
___Michael Salazar, Senior Systems Engineer, Mainline Information Systems

TECHNOLOGY

Expertise includes Primavera Project Planner (P3); TK Solver; Micro Station; MS Word, Excel, Access, and PowerPoint; and Internet research.

ASSOCIATIONS / COMMUNITY

Student Member, Association of General Contractors
Member, Society of Engineer Technologists
Participate in Big Brothers/Big Sisters of Lubbock, sponsoring the same child since December 1998

"I would highly recommend Joe Wheatley to any construction company with which he would seek employment."
___Clint Brit, Project Engineer, Huber, Hunt & Nichols

Victor L. Stephens
234 Lynwood Court ◆ Deltona, Florida 40100 ◆ (407) 555-1111

OBJECTIVE

Building / Construction Project Manager

Notice the many adaptive skills he mentions here

SUMMARY OF QUALIFICATIONS

- Over 18 years of comprehensive experience in management and supervision of residential and commercial construction.
- Extensive knowledge of building products and practices from ground to roof.
- Strong track record in managing complex projects, keeping them on schedule, and maintaining high quality standards.
- Self-motivated. Excellent record of dependability and reliability. Good decision-maker. Resourceful.
- Talent for picking the right people for the job.
- Ability to prioritize, delegate, and motivate.

Note the use of different bullets

HIGHLIGHTS OF TECHNICAL EXPERIENCE

Construction Management

He includes lots of accomplishments and numbers

- Hand-picked by USA Home Industries Corporation as *Construction Expert / Supervisor* for an emergency temporary housing project following a major earthquake in Japan; work had to be completed within 14 days.
- Provided expert supervision and training of personnel for the immediate construction of 100 houses at the Japan job site. Supervised the assembly and on-site painting of all homes by 500 subordinate Japanese and American employees.
- Completed the construction, assembly, and painting within budget and on schedule which resulted in USA Homes being awarded the contract for the construction of 900 more emergency homes.
- At Miles Construction, supervised the development and construction of total custom residential homes ranging in value from $300,000 to $500,000. At Morgan Construction, supervised the simultaneous construction of 33 semi-custom homes ranging in value from $100,000 to $135,000.
- Read blueprints, ordered lumber, windows, and all other materials needed to construct the houses.
- Supervised crews of up to 300 employees. Scheduled workers and subcontractors. Assigned tasks so that all houses were active every day.
- Trained workers on-the-job. Watched for safety hazards.
- Achieved consistent high quality control in compliance with codes and inspection standards. Assured strict adherence to projected scheduling and costs.
- Established and maintained reputation for high quality customer service. Quickly resolved problems that might have hindered progress or created disputes.

Painting Management

- Handled interior and exterior residential and commercial painting, primarily for new construction. Did all preparatory work, such as priming and sanding.
- Meet with customers. Did all bidding. Ordered necessary materials.

20

Construction project manager. *Connie S. Stevens; Radcliff, KY*

Victor L. Stephens
234 Lynwood Court ◆ Deltona, Florida 40100 ◆ (407) 555-1111

➤ Expert with airless paint sprayer, lacquer, brush and roll, spray enamel, mixing and matching colors. Repaired own equipment.
➤ Did taping and floating. Blew Monterey or orange peel texture, and blew acoustic on the ceilings.
➤ Stripped and refinished hardwood floors and antique furniture.
➤ Supervised crews of six workers. Prepared payroll, withheld taxes, handled accounts payable and receivable. Advertised and marketed the business.

WORK HISTORY

USA HOME INDUSTRIES CORPORATION ◆ Louisville, KY
➤ **Construction Expert / Supervisor** ◆ Apr 93 - Present

STEPHENS' HOUSE PAINTING ◆ Elizabethtown, KY
➤ **Owner / Painter** ◆ Feb 89 - Present

MORGAN CONSTRUCTION ◆ Elizabethtown, KY
➤ **Construction Foreman** ◆ Aug 84 - Apr 93

MILES CONSTRUCTION & CONTRACTING ◆ Louisville, KY
➤ **Construction Supervisor** ◆ May 78 - Aug 84

EDUCATION

GRADUATE ◆ Elizabethtown Vocational-Technical College ◆ Elizabethtown, KY ◆ 1975
➤ **Two-Year Carpentry Program**

GRADUATE ◆ North Hardin High School ◆ Radcliff, KY

After working his way up as a carpenter and painter, Victor then had years of experience in supervising construction projects.

Four bulleted statements highlight this individual's most-important qualifications.

John Carpenter

40 Watertown Street
Binghamton, New York 13747

(607) 666-9999
hammertime@aol.com

Chief Estimator/Project Manager

Qualifications

- **Five years of experience as Chief Estimator and Project Manager.**

- **Fifteen-plus years of local engineering, design and construction expertise** in the upstate New York building industry, preparing bid estimates and managing $300,000 to $3 million construction projects.

- **Senior construction generalist with a diverse skills.** Excel within small construction companies that require "wearing many hats." Proven expertise in business development; project management for both fieldwork and administrative projects; estimating via computer applications; drafting and architectural drawing; and management of shop, carpentry and millworking operations.

- **Innovative information manager.** Repeatedly automated bidding and construction processes for past employers, increasing production and decreasing overhead. Advanced user:

  AutoCAD version 10, Generic CAD version 6, Construction Management Systems estimating software, Super Project, Varco Pruden, VP Command building design and drafting program, Novell Networking, Access, Excel, Lotus 1-2-3, Microsoft Office, GTCO digitizer tablets and HP Draft Pro Plotter.

Education and Credentials

A.A.S. Degree, Construction Technology: State University of New York, Canton College, 1984
Certified Engineer Technician: A.S.C.E.T. Professional Engineering Society.

Estimating Experience

Estimator and Project Manager   1999 – present
JAMES SMITH AND SONS CONTRACTING COMPANY, Vestal, New York
Utilize in-depth knowledge of project costs, purchasing, construction techniques and technology, and local construction services market to estimate and manage large construction projects.

- Bid and supported 4 major contract wins in FY2001, cumulatively valued at $6 million.
- Manage estimating projects that generated over $10,000 per month in gross sales FY2001.
- As chief estimator, identify upcoming opportunities and generate 3–4 project estimates a month.
- Win 1 of every 3 estimates the company decides to submit.
- Manage a millwork shop generating $400,000 in annual gross sales with 30% net profits.

Accomplishment statements are brief yet powerful.

Chief Estimator and Project Manager   1994 – 1999
ARCHER AND SONS, Binghamton, New York
Prepared estimates, assisted proposal and business development team, and managed major construction projects throughout New York State.

- Projects included: The Marriott Hotel, Cornell University; The Law School Renovation Project, Cornell University; various Taco Time Restaurants; and school building upgrades in upstate New York.
- All projects came in on time, within 10% of originally prepared cost estimates.

Estimator/AutoCAD Drafter   1985 – 1993
WAY-LAN CONSTRUCTION COMPANY, INC., Binghamton, New York

21

Cost estimator. *Alice Hanson, CPRW; Seattle, WA*

Note the precise objective. This individual knows what she wants, and her resume fully supports her goal

COLLEEN E. MURPHY
5 Arbor Way
Peekskill, NY   10566
H (914) 739-1997
W (914) 761-3400

OBJECTIVE

A position in Educational Administration for a Technical/Occupational High School which will fully utilize strong leadership abilities, innovative organizational skills and a successful, diverse track record in education.

OVERVIEW

- Organized, take-charge education professional with exceptional follow-through abilities and excellent management skills; able to plan and oversee projects from concept to successful conclusion.
- Demonstrated ability to effectively prioritize a broad range of responsibilities in order to consistently meet deadlines.
- Proven budgetary and planning capabilities; weathered severe financial situations without eliminating instructional staff while simultaneously strengthening programs.
- Strong interpersonal skills; able to work effectively with individuals on all levels.
- People person, sensitive and perceptive; demonstrated ability to develop and maintain sound relationships with students and staff alike.
- Effective motivator of self and others.

CERTIFICATIONS

School District Administrator
School Administration and Supervision
School Guidance Counselor
Teacher N-6, 7-12, Social Studies

EXPERIENCE
1987 - Present

1989 - Present

BOCES SOUTHERN WESTCHESTER CENTER FOR TECHNICAL AND OCCUPATIONAL EDUCATION, Valhalla, NY

Supervisor: Basic Occupational Education
- Oversee and direct all aspects for twelve vocational training programs which service students with diverse specialized needs including those with sensory impairments.
- Provide supervision and evaluation of: Teachers; Teacher Aides; Counselors; Academic Teachers; Sigh Language Interpreters; Spanish Translators; Job Placement Staff; Clerical Support and Curriculum Development.
- Spearheaded establishment of VESL (Vocational English as a Second Language) program.
- Provide supervisory support for the Career Assessment Center; provide facilities for graduate students in Guidance/Counseling to experience Vocational Evaluation and Career Counseling, ensuring that future counselors are knowledgeable regarding BOCES.
- Oversaw operation of the Technical Alternative High School which substantially reduced the rate of student drop-outs.
- Developed programming for academic pull-outs thereby enabling students, needing further academic courses, to attend technical training who ordinarily could not come to BOCES.
- Coordinated program with the Special Education Division providing emotionally-fragile, and less capable students with the opportunity to experience Basic Occupational Education and discover areas for training and employment success.

1987 - 1989

Guidance Counselor
- Provided counseling to secondary and classified students.
- Served as Liaison with V.E.S.I.D. and the Westchester Private Industry Council.
- Oversaw Adult Placement/Counseling in Secondary Programs
- Planed and implemented G.E.D./Vocational programs at the Westchester County Correctional Facility

22

Vocational education administrator. *Mark D. Berkowitz, NCCC, CPRW; Yorktown Heights, NY*

COLLEEN E. MURPHY   Page Two

1976 - 1987   **HOLY NAME OF MARY SCHOOL**, Croton, NY
                 Principal
                 • Developed and implemented new programs into curriculum: Drug and Alcohol
                   Abuse Counseling; Foreign Language study; Computer Literacy; and various
                   volunteer experiences.

1974 - 1976   **Guidance Counselor**

1970 -1974   **Teacher:** First and Second Grade Self-contained; and Departmental Grades 5,6,7 and 8.

EDUCATION   **PACE UNIVERSITY**, White Plains, NY
                   Special Education Administration - 6 Credits   1991

                   LONG ISLAND UNIVERSITY, Dobbs Ferry, NY
                   Family Therapy: 24 Credits   1980

                   MANHATTAN COLLEGE, Riverdale, NY
                   School Administration and Supervision: 18 Credits 1978
                   Master of Arts: Counseling Psychology   1977

                   LADYCLIFF COLLEGE, Highland Falls, Ny
                   Bachelor of Arts: Psychology/Social Studies   1971

ADDITIONAL   **PUTNAM/NORTHERN WESTCHESTER BOCES**, Yorktown Heights, NY
SPECIALIZED   **Seminar: Introduction to Computers**   1985
TRAINING

                   YALE UNIVERSITY, MEDICAL SCHOOL, New Haven, CT
                   Seminar: Drug and Alcohol Abuse Counseling   1987

                   STATE EDUCATION DEPARTMENT, NY
                   Seminar: Adult Career Counseling   1988

REFERENCES   Available upon request.

Lucretia Washington ✑ 805 127th Street, New York, NY 00000 ✑ (000) 000-0000

URBAN ELEMENTARY SCHOOL PRINCIPAL

A nontraditional format that presents this job seeker as a results-oriented and creative administrator

Education and Certifications:

Fordham University, New York, NY
MASTER OF ARTS, Supervision and Administration — Urban Core Concentration, 1991
BACHELOR OF ARTS, Elementary Education, Minor in Social Science, 1978

NEW YORK STATE CERTIFICATES: Supervisor/Principal; Regular Elementary Teacher; Spanish Language Teacher; Trauma Counselor; Alcohol and Substance Abuse Counselor

Experience: CITY OF NEW YORK, BOARD OF EDUCATION   1984 to present

Principal, P.S. No. 18, South Bronx (1992 to present)
In first experience as a principal, recruited to take charge of this K-5 elementary school in an impoverished area following ouster of former principal. Encountered a situation of 30% declining enrollment due to the school's reputation for crime and drug activity. Was challenged with turning the school around without being given any real control over personnel or budget. During tenure:

Presents concrete outcomes of her efforts

- ✑ Rallied community and parental support by sharing with them a vision based on the belief that all children are gifted and talented in their own way. Inspired an increased effort by the PTA to raise funds, previously averaging $5,000 annually, to $50,000. Used funds to enrich the curriculum with classroom study aids, science and art materials and the services of part time instructors.
- ✑ Fostered cooperation and teamwork among teachers, overcoming their strained relationships and perceptions of malingering. Created common reading groups and planning periods, arranged for inservice workshops as budget allowed, and accompanied teachers on retreats.
- ✑ Wrote proposals for special programs, receiving several mini grants from the Board of Education.
- ✑ Raised percentage of students who were able to read at or above grade level from 38% at outset to 56% two years later. Awarded commendation by the Chancellor of Schools.

Grade Five Chairperson, Bronx Borough Schools (1990 to 1992)
Appointed liaison between teachers and administration of six schools and chaired cluster meetings.
- ✑ Observed and assisted teachers with implementing curriculum changes in math and health.
- ✑ Implemented the D.A.R.E. program and served as Substance Awareness Coordinator.
- ✑ Organized and handled details of class trips and elementary school graduations.
- ✑ Filled in for Vice Principal of Martin Luther King School during his frequent absences.

Classroom Teacher, Grades Four and Five, P.S. 87, Manhattan (1978 to 1990)
- ✑ Involved in a community based parallel program designed to offer students, parents and teachers a substantive choice among instructive learning styles.
- ✑ Planned and implemented a tutorial project to upgrade students' math and reading skills by working with exemplary high school students. This helped to increase overall CAT scores above national percentile and grade equivalents.
- ✑ Awarded Teacher of the Year recognition in 1989.

Memberships:

New York State Educational Association
New York County Educational Association
New York City Juvenile Conference Committee

National Association of Elementary School Principals
National Council for Multicultural Education
Harlem Pride Community Service Organization

23

Elementary principal. *Melanie Noonan, CPS; West Paterson, NJ*

Effective use of a
graphic and slogan.

Education is a journey – not a destination.

Elaine L. Baraga

275 Rivers Road ■ **Minneapolis, MN 55104** ■ **612.555.4242** ■ **School: 612.555.3679** ■ **baragausbell.com**

Although the word "objective" is not used, this introduction serves as a very clear objective statement.

Elementary Education Administrator ...

offering educational leadership skills in facilitating an inviting, positive and safe learning environment for students. My promise is to promote district operational and service goals.

PROFILE BACKGROUND

Educator with over 14 years of diverse teaching and leadership roles facilitating educational goals at the school and district levels. Successful working with teachers, administrators, boards, parents, students and the community to develop positive programs and dynamic community relationships focused on student-centered education. Demonstrated abilities with fiscal management, collective bargaining, long- and short-range planning, staff mentorship and guidance, program development, communications, and policy.

STRENGTHS:
Gift for empowering others ■ Staff mentoring ■ Student guidance and discipline
Project and program management ■ Concern for others ■ Articulate communicator
Belief that students come first ■ Motivational skills ■ Organizational skills

EDUCATION & CREDENTIALS

Endorsements used here and at the bottom of second page.

"I have found Elaine to be a dedicated, responsible, and student-centered educator. She will be an asset as a principal to any district."
– Jane Brown, Principal

- Minnesota Principal and Superintendent Licensure
- Minnesota Elementary Teaching (K-6) Licensure

UNIVERSITY OF MINNESOTA – Minneapolis, MN
- **Sixth Year Certification, Educational Administration**, 2001
- **Master of Science, Educational Administration**, 1994

ST. MARY'S UNIVERSITY – Winona, MN
- **Bachelor of Science, Elementary Education**, 1988

PROFESSIONAL DEVELOPMENT
- **Leadership Training**: Ongoing attendance at MEA Summer Leadership Conferences

PROFESSIONAL HIGHLIGHTS

CAREER PATH
ADMINISTRATION
PINEWOOD ELEMENTARY SCHOOL – Minneapolis, MN, 2000–present
Field Experience: Superintendency (2001–present)
- Helped pass a successful referendum, launched a 403-B TSA Plan for certified staff, and revised the elementary student handbook.

Field Experience: Elementary Administration (2000–2001)
- Produced a monthly "Principal's Calendar" for staff, providing information on events and issues.
- Attended the State of Minnesota Principals Convention and regional meetings for principals.

TEACHING
PINEWOOD ELEMENTARY SCHOOL – Minneapolis, MN, 1991–present
Teacher (K-6)
Classroom Teaching ■ Chapter One / Title One Lead Teaching ■ Reading Specialist
Enrichment Program ■ Physical Education

ST. JAMES ELEMENTARY SCHOOL – St. James, MN, 1988–1991
Teacher (Grade 1)

MONTOMERY DAY SCHOOL – Alberta Canada, 1987–1988
Teacher (K-6)
English as a Second Language ■ Physical Education ■ Coaching ■ Science ■ Social Studies

24

Elementary education administrator. *Barb Poole, CPRW, CRW;*
St. Cloud, MN

EDUCATOR LEADERSHIP & TEAM CONTRIBUTIONS

✓ **Student Store Co-Founder.** Partnered with teaching colleague in 2000-2001 to establish and facilitate Lion Paws, an on-site school store for students. Enterprise enabled students to earn "paws" for positive behaviors and apply them toward purchasing age- and school-appropriate merchandise. **Co-directed all activities:** Incorporation, policy/procedure development, purchasing, display case/store setup and merchandising, order form design, information and communications disbursement, community sponsorships, and an auction to maximize students' spending power and reduce inventory.

✓ **PER Committee Chairperson.** Developed agendas for and coordinated four annual meetings during pilot phase of the Minnesota Graduation Standards implementation. Led decision-making teams regarding the development of learner outcomes. Published the community-targeted PER Report.

✓ **Mentorship Project Mentor.** Applied peer observation techniques in observing and orienting teachers new to the district. Mentored inexperienced and seasoned teachers with varied experience. Provided input for administrators regarding evaluations.

✓ **Education Association President.** Collaborated with elementary and secondary administrators as well as school board members to address budget and communication issues. Achieved improved teacher/board communications by encouraging increased attendance at board meetings.

✓ **School Board Advisory Committee.** Reviewed school district audits, researched legislative statutes, and introduced information on a fund transfer that was successfully adopted — avoiding staff cutbacks.

✓ **Strategic Planning Committee.** Charter member of committee representing students, parents, administrators, teachers, and the community at large. Developed the Mission and Belief Statements. Appointed to Staff Development Subcommittee, 2001, to provide staff training commensurate with the Strategic Planning Committee's extensive curriculum development.

✓ **Communication Audit.** Conducted an audit (survey and data collection/analysis) for the school district to determine the method of communications (free "shopper"-type newspaper) most likely to reach the largest population. Subsequently passed a referendum helping to support this type of communication.

✓ **Elementary Specialist Scheduler.** Revamped and developed scheduling at the kindergarten through sixth grade levels that facilitated continued prep time for classroom teachers; accommodated Music, Art, and Physical Education specialists; and reduced class sizes.

✓ **Stop, Think, Resolve Program.** Teamed with colleagues to create and implement this program in 2000. The STR concept is to create disciplinary consequences for students with habitual disruptive behavior. Program allowed students an opportunity to stop, think, and resolve issues that interfere with personal or others' learning. Facilitated team meetings to develop goals and plans of action. Rewrote the "Discipline" section of the student handbook to incorporate age/behavior-appropriate policies, secured the physical space, and hired STR staff. Maintain behavior plans and other recordkeeping.

✓ **Chapter One Program Planning Workshop.** Helped develop and coordinate this evolving program.

PERSONAL SNAPSHOT

- Community Volunteerism: Community Education Advisory Council ▪ Church, Youth, School, & Community Groups
- Interests: Avid Reader ▪ Travel ▪ Sewing/Crafts ▪ Cross Country Skiing ▪ Golf ▪ Sports Spectator

REFERENCES / WORKING CREDENTIALS ENCLOSED

Endorsement

"… [Elaine Baraga] would make an excellent administrator… I frequently seek out her opinion when dealing with difficult problems… a valuable member of our district's educational team… respected by students, parents, peers and supervisors." – Greg Olin, Minneapolis Board of Education

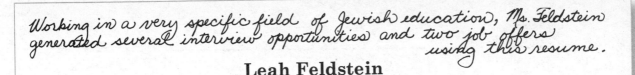

Working in a very specific field of Jewish education, Ms. Feldstein generated several interview opportunities and two job offers using this resume.

Leah Feldstein

165 Northwood Drive, Yardley, PA 19067 ▪ 215-270-3312 (h) ▪ 215-512-7756 (c) ▪ leahf@msn.com

OBJECTIVE

An administrative position in Jewish education that will utilize organizational, programming, and supervisory skills, in an environment that will benefit from an effective educator and promoter of Judaic principles and values.

SUMMARY

♦ **Administratively experienced** school board president and classroom manager
♦ **Enthusiastic educator** with excellent curriculum writing and programming skills
♦ **Judaically knowledgeable** with proven success in classroom
♦ **Creative** in educational settings and problem-solving situations
♦ **Continuing student** with love of learning new teaching methods and maintaining knowledge of classroom topics

EXPERIENCE

Mispallelim Synagogue, Erdenheim, PA (9/1999 to present)
Teacher of 4th Grade
♦ Effectively manage classroom of 32 students
♦ Write and implement lessons for curriculum
♦ Promote love of Judaism through classroom instruction and practical application
♦ Instill confidence in Hebrew reading and writing
♦ Plan special events and field trips relevant to educational experience
♦ Inject creativity into lessons: arts and crafts, poetry, journal writing
♦ Actively promote a Kehillah in classroom

Adath Jeshrun Synagogue, Churchville, PA (9/1999 to present)
School Board Member (9/1999 to 9/2000)
School Board President (9/2000 to present)
♦ Oversee duties and supervise progress of school board director and members
♦ Develop and nurture relationships with parents, executive board, and synagogue community
♦ Lead school board in textbook selection and acquisition
♦ Responsibly monitor and abide by budget
♦ In process of writing curriculum for entire school
♦ Expanded Family Education program from two grades to all, Gan through Hey
♦ Increased junior congregation attendance with innovative program
♦ Developed effective new discipline policy
♦ Assisted in grant-writing project resulting in award of Mishpacha seed grant from Auerbach Central Agency for Jewish Education

♦♦♦

25

Elementary education administrator. *Andrea Peak, CPRW; Louisville, KY*

Ohev Shalom Synagogue, Richboro, PA (9/1997 to 6/1999)
Teacher of 2nd Grade
- Successfully taught all 2nd grade students to read Hebrew by end of year
- Promoted love of Judaism and a Kehillah for the class
- Taught Mitzvot and Jewish values through special field trips and projects, including visit to emergency room and raising money for charity for disabled children
- Nominated for Disney Teacher of the Year

Jewish Community Hebrew School, Boston, MA (9/1994 to 6/1997)
Teacher of 4th Grade
- Fostered fluency in Hebrew reading and writing
- Wrote lessons for curriculum
- Developed creative teaching style, including poetry and journal writing
- Sought new, fun ways to engage students in active learning

Silver Mechanical, Philadelphia, PA (2/1992 to 8/1994)
Client Services/Sales Representative
- Acted as liaison between corporate clients and company
- Managed and administered accounts

EDUCATION

Syracuse University, Syracuse, NY
Master of Arts in Political Science (1997)

Smithson University, Chester, PA
Bachelor of Arts in Sociology (1993)
Graduated with Honors: Magna Cum Laude

Graham College, East Park, PA
As a high school student, participated in program offering Education courses leading to teaching certification (1988 to 1989)

CONTINUING EDUCATION

Temple University, Philadelphia, PA
Completed Philadelphia Literacy Network Course (PLN), 3 graduate credits: Tefillot with Meaning (2000)

Auerbach Central Agency for Jewish Education, Melrose Park, PA
Nominated as Mentor Teacher; currently enrolled in Mentor course
Various workshops and courses (1995 to present)

Graham College, East Park, PA
Level 1 and 2 Ulpan courses, refresher for teaching Hebrew (1999 to 2000)

COMMUNITY ACTIVITIES

Member of Hadassah and Ort
Internship, Anti-Defamation League, 1993

◆ ◆ ◆

This individual works in educational program administration.

OLIVIA R. DONOVAN

830 Raven Lane, Toledo, IA 50159
Home: (515) 296-5555 · Cell: (515) 795-3333
ordonovan@pionet.net

MANAGEMENT PROFESSIONAL

**Leadership · Financial Management · Human Resource Management
Marketing · Customer Service**

Over 10 years' management experience in the travel industry, including four years as Office Manager with Council Travel. Demonstrate professionalism, competence, and maturity while representing company values at all times. Successful track record in demanding, fast-paced environment requiring stamina, patience, and time management skills. Effectively develop quality teams and relationships that ensure high levels of customer satisfaction as proven by awards for management and sales. Excellent conflict resolution skills. MBA degree.

Eager to apply business management skills and leadership to ensure the achievement of sales, revenue and profit goals as Senior Manager.

PROFESSIONAL EXPERIENCE

OFFICE MANAGER, Council Travel, Toledo, IA 1996 – present
Parent company: Council on International Educational Exchange
Prepare and maintain forecasted budgets; analyze and prepare monthly financial statements; recruit, develop, and motivate full-time staff of three; provide highest level of service to internal and external customers; resolve customer complaints; maintain comprehensive knowledge of all products and services; and actively seek out, initiate, and participate in state-wide marketing opportunities.

Accomplishment statements are divided into three key areas. This increases their impact and ensures they are not lost in a sea of text.

Financial Management/Marketing Accomplishments:

- Participated in start-up venture of Iowa branch office.
- Generated retail sales from $0 to $2 million in three years using aggressive marketing campaigns at numerous university and college locations throughout Iowa.
- Established critical teacher, youth, and student markets to stabilize office in volatile industry.
- Streamlined marketing expense by 50% while doubling sales in 1999; stabilized personnel expense.
- Implemented successful service charge that became model for company-wide sliding scale.

Human Resource /Customer Service Accomplishments:

- Developed creative and rewarding incentives to motivate agent productivity and broaden product-selling base.
- Handled in-bound international callers at WYAW (With You All the Way) desk in Boston, MA to broaden diversification experience.
- Enhanced existing interview and hiring manual as part of Master of Business Leadership project.

Honors and Awards:

- National Manager of the Year (2nd Place) 1998 – 1999
- Office Team Silver Award for Sales 1998 – 1999
- Central Regional Manager of the Year for Council Travel 1996 – 1997
- Chosen as member of Air Products Task Force, 1996

Continued on Page Two

26

Educational program administrator. *Marcy Johnson, CPRW, CEIP; Story City, IA*

PROFESSIONAL EXPERIENCE *(continued)*

ALUMNI DIRECTOR, STA Catholic Student Center, Simpson College, Indianola, IA 1992 – 1996
- Established planned-giving program and marketing plan to raise $5.2 million.
- Raised $1 million for Simpson College Theology Chair.
- Manipulated MIS donor base to facilitate mass mailings to alumni base of 13,000.
- Coordinated alumni functions with volunteers for typical 500 person gatherings.

RETAIL MANAGER, International Travel Associates, Inc., Des Moines, IA 1988 – 1992

- Promoted from Contracting and Group Air Purchaser to Manager within one year.
- Supervised seven full-time agents in stand-alone retail store and five agents in satellite office.

OTHER TRAVEL EXPERIENCE

MANAGER, The Travel Connection, Inc., Clarion, IA 1986 – 1988
OFFICE MANAGER, Adventure Coaches, Inc., Des Moines, IA 1985 – 1986
INTERNATIONAL TRAVEL CONSULTANT, Worldwide Travel, Ames, IA 1983 – 1985

TECHNOLOGY SKILLS

Strong working knowledge of Sabre, Travcom, Microsoft Office (Word, Excel, Access) and Internet.
Thoroughly familiar with ticket printers, cash registers, and other shop machinery.

LICENSES AND CERTIFICATIONS

Certified Travel Consultant (CTC five-year program testing) 1989 – present
Iowa Insurance License for Life, Health and Accident 1988 – present
Pan Am International Tariff Certification, London, UK 1983

EDUCATION

MBA, Upper Iowa University, Des Moines, IA 2001
Major: Human Resources
Current GPA: 3.9/4.0

BS, Upper Iowa University, Des Moines, IA 1994
Emphasis: Marketing
Graduated Cum Laude

This resume uses lots of accomplishments with numbers to quantify them — an effective approach!

SAMUEL LEVIN

000 North West Ave.
Anywhere, USA

Telephone (000) 000-0000
Facsimile (000) 000-0000

EXPERIENCE SUMMARY

SENIOR ENGINEERING / PLANT OPERATIONS MANAGER with 20+ years experience in the garment industry. Skills in strategic planning and operation of multi-million dollar, multi-site manufacturing operations have resulted in productivity increases of as much as 35% and $1.5 million savings for a single site. Strengths include:

- New plant start-up, industrial engineering, and operations management
- Multi-national staffing, employee relations/participation management, and supervisory/operator training
- Quality assurance, material utilization, productivity/performance improvement

Global orientation; considerable experience with multi-national companies. Fluent in Italian and English; working knowledge of French and Russian; Spanish in progress.

PROFESSIONAL EXPERIENCE

MANAGEMENT CONSULTANT   1987-Present
United States, Russia, Pacific Rim

Management consultant specializing in industrial engineering and manufacturing operations.

- Hong Kong-Leningrad Joint Venture: Project Manager with P&L responsibility for new denim jeans factory in the USSR. Full accountability for turnkey production and finishing facility, including factory design, engineering, and operations. Designed training programs which brought 350 unskilled operators to levels of competence. Delivered ongoing business solutions to a complex project, overcoming considerable logistical, cultural, and socio-political barriers.

- Mademoiselle, New York, New York: Implemented cutting, sewing, and finishing room engineering program and quality improvement program for dress shirt manufacturer. Increased productivity by 35% without additional staffing, with resultant annual savings of $1.5 million. Reduced seconds and rejects from 2.8% to 0.8%, a savings of approximately $360,000 annually.

DIVISIONAL ENGINEERING MANAGER   1984-1986
ENGINEERING MANAGER   1981-1984
Liz Claiborne, Canada and Europe

As Divisional Engineering Manager, responsible for industrial engineering, material utilization, product development and specification, research and development for the Continental Europe Division comprised of six production facilities and one finishing center, employing some 2,500 individuals.

- Increased labor productivity 4.5%, a savings of $1.7 million.
- Improved material utilization 1.5%, a savings of $700,000.
- Improved planning/calendaring systems with rationalization to shorten product development cycle.
- Implemented engineering program for distribution centers in the U.K. and Germany.
- Set up centralized sourcing operation in Ireland, processing over 2 million units per year.

27

Engineering/plant operations manager. *Susan Britton Whitcomb, CPRW; Fresno, CA*

SAMUEL LEVIN
Page Two

PROFESSIONAL EXPERIENCE

Liz Claiborne (continued)

As Engineering Manager, directly supervised and trained staff of 12 industrial engineers, working closely with plant managers on engineering projects in five Japanese facilities employing some 1,500 individuals.

- ▸ Increased direct labor productivity 18% over three-year period, a savings of $1.5 million.

- ▸ Improved material utilization by .8%, a savings of $250,000 per year based on 8 million units.

- ▸ Directed set-up and engineering of centralized washing and finishing facility processing 30,000 units per day.

MANAGEMENT CONSULTANT   1976-1980
Italy

Projects for Italian manufacturers:

- ▸ Converted children's wear manufacturing facility to denim production with direct accountability for engineering, operations, and training. Project was completed on schedule with all operators producing near 100%. Served as interim Plant Manager.

- ▸ For manufacturer of men's and ladies outerwear, re-engineered facility from one plant employing 280 to six separate manufacturing units. Employed management and human relations skills to obtain buy-in from labor and accomplish reorganization without significant downtime.

MANAGEMENT CONSULTANT   1969-1976
Projects for U.S. and Italian companies included:

- ▸ Sewing room engineering for dress slacks manufacturer (The Dress Manufacturers, Chicago, IL).

- ▸ Cutting room engineering for outerwear manufacturer (The Outerwear Co., Chicago, IL).

- ▸ Design and implementation of Operator Training program for 1,500 operators and Statistical Quality Control program for 1,200 operators of a men's suit manufacturer (Bella Bella, Italy).

EDUCATION

Mechanical Engineering Degree
Apparel Industry Specialization Course
G.S.D. Certification
Computer Literacy: Windows, Excel, Microsoft Word, WordPerfect

AFFILIATIONS

Member, Institute of Industrial Engineers

References Upon Request

An attractive, sharp color photo of a harvesting machine at work makes for a striking presentation.

Farm Resume Presentation

Rees D. Tyler

11105 US Hwy 69 · Story City, IA 50248
Phone: (515) 733-4981 · Cell: (515) 233-0131
rdtyler@prairieinet.net

The farm resume is a fairly new concept for farmers competing for rental acres.

Farm manager. *Marcy Johnson, CPRW, CEIP; Story City, IA*

Nontraditional areas of interest are included with more-traditional information. This is especially helpful when a person is unable to include a cover page.

Rees D. Tyler

11105 US Hwy 69
Story City, IA 50248

rdtyler@prairieinet.net

Phone: (515) 733-4981
Cell: (515) 233-0131

SUMMARY OF QUALIFICATIONS

Progressive farmer with over 30 years of experience farming 2,000 acres (475 acres owned; 1,400 acres cash rented; 125 acres custom farmed). Business experienced 1,200% continued growth using up-to-date technology, modern and well-maintained equipment, and sound marketing practices. Converted entire operation to 20-inch rows in 1997.

MANAGEMENT OBJECTIVE

My philosophy is to enrich and maintain the land through yearly soil testing and appropriate fertilization practices with the goal of producing a top-quality product and lifestyle for my family. Efficiency is my strength, and intense management throughout our operation is the key to staying competitive.

I have committed myself to success by taking a proactive rather than a reactive approach to farming. Our enhanced profitability comes from maintaining our equipment, participating in teleconferences on farming topics, attending machinery shows, staying abreast of new seed genetics, developing excellent relationships with other farmers and professionals, and utilizing outside support and consultants to manage today as well as position ourselves for a future in farming. Several part-time employees, my wife, Mollie, and semi-retired father, David, assist me in achieving my management goals.

ENVIRONMENTAL STATEMENT

- Minimize erosion by building and maintaining grass waterways wherever necessary.
- Control wind erosion by minimum tillage of cornstalk ground and no-till soybean acreage.
- Encourage appropriate tiling necessary for good drainage.
- Maintain soil fertility by yearly testing and fertilizer application as advised by experts.
- Use premium diesel fuel for maximum care of equipment.
- Make use of environmentally friendly injection methods to apply manure to 240 acres.

TECHNOLOGY AND COMPUTER PROFICIENCY

- Farm Works Computer Software used to maintain current farm records.
- Global Positioning System (GPS) installed in combine with data read and analyzed using Farm Works computer software in home office.
- DTN market and weather tracking system monitored daily.
- Market fluctuations tracked using Internet and daily e-mail updates on commodity prices.
- Sophisticated computer systems used in planter and spraying equipment to ensure accurate applications.
- Soil sampling done on a four-year rotation basis utilizing the knowledge of CENTROL Scouting Services.

Rees D. Tyler

FINANCIAL AND RISK MANAGEMENT STRATEGIES

- Wayne E. Jones, Vice President, First American Bank, Perry, IA – Phone (515) 826-2432.
- Marshall Boggs, Agent, Boggs Realty & Insurance, Murray, IA – Federal Crop Insurance.
- Lisa Evans, Agent, Farm Bureau Mutual Insurance Company, Ames, IA – $3 million umbrella liability insurance.
- Contract one-half grain crop before harvest.

PARTIAL LIST OF EQUIPMENT

TRACTORS:	STX 375 Case IH (2001) 7410 John Deere (1999) 8100 John Deere (1997) 8400 John Deere (1995)	**HARVEST:**	9650 STS John Deere Combine 850 Bu. Grain Cart With Scale
PLANTER:	1780 John Deere 24-Row (20" rows)	**GRAIN STORAGE:**	Continuous Flow Grain Dryer With 15,000 Bu./day capacity 200,000 Bu. On-Farm Grain Storage
TILLAGE:	John Deere Field Cultivator John Deere Disc John Deere 40' Rotary Hoe Case IH Ecolo-Tiger Chisel Plow	**SPRAYER:**	80' Redball 1350-gallon tank

BIOGRAPHICAL BACKGROUND)

This and other nontraditional areas of interest help prove to potential landlords that this person will do a good job for them.

While still in high school, I started custom plowing for other farmers using my father's equipment. After graduation, I worked at the Department of Transportation for two years, continuing to help on the family farm after hours and weekends until I was able to cash-rent 50 acres in 1968. Shortly after my wife, Mollie, and I married in 1970, I was able to purchase our first tractor, a 1206 International. Since that time, our farming operation and family have continued to grow. We have three children: Tricia is married and lives in Phoenix, AZ; Brooke is married and lives in Creston, IA, with their two children; and Chris recently graduated from Simpson College and is currently enrolled at The University of Iowa in an Actuarial Science graduate program.

I am a basketball fan and enjoyed following my favorite player, son Chris, until his college graduation. We don't know who to cheer for now — the Hawks or the Clones! I served two years as treasurer of our local Athletic Booster Club, managing a yearly budget of more than $20,000. I also organized and supervised a yearly basketball tournament when our booster club was beginning a $150,000 fund-raising drive to build a new all-weather track and field. Numbers are my passion, and playing cribbage is my favorite way to unwind and relax. We enjoy traveling to visit our children and spend time with the grandkids. Olivia, 3 years old, can already spot a John Deere combine in the distance!

This person wanted to emphasize both his veterinarian qualifications and his management expertise.

Andrew T. Eckberg, DVM
2323 Old Hunting Trail, Lexington, KY 40508
(606) 791-7710
horsedoctor@juno.com

Farm Manager — Veterinarian

Effective business manager with more than 10 years' experience in farm management and veterinary care.

Proven ability to direct large-scale establishments, with complementary strengths in business operations, personnel management, and veterinary care.

Experience

1998-2002
BLUEGRASS STABLES, Lexington, Kentucky
General Manager

Full management responsibility for 200-acre, 15-employee equine-breeding and -training farm with absentee owner.

- Provided year-round care to 8 stallions and supervised more than 250 breedings annually. Significantly improved and maintained the quality of the breeding operation.
- Managed the training division for 60-70 thoroughbreds, overseeing their care and preparation for racing.
- Turned around a losing operation in the first year, increasing profit-to-loss ratio by over 300% and continuing to maintain a stable and profitable business.

1990-1998
EQUINE SPECIALISTS, Lexington, Kentucky
Managing Partner / Equine Veterinarian

Provided veterinary and consulting services to owners of thoroughbred race horses. Clients ranged from small operations to large, full-scale breeding and racing organizations.

- Started and built successful practice based on top-quality services and excellent client relationships.
- Served as on-site veterinarian at several racecourses over a 40-week annual racing season.

1988-1990
EMERGENCY PET CARE, Danville, Kentucky
Veterinarian

Gained diverse experience providing emergency veterinary care to small animals for clinic offering 24-hour service.

Education

Doctor of Veterinary Medicine, 1988
Bachelor of Science in Biology, 1985
OHIO STATE UNIVERSITY, Columbus, Ohio
Internship: CAROLINA BREEDERS FARM, Asheville, North Carolina, 1987-1988
- Foaled over 200 mares and provided care to 15 stallions.

Certification

- Licensed in Ohio, Kentucky, Virginia and Maryland.

Affiliations

- American Association of Equine Practitioners
- American Veterinary Medical Association
- Kentucky Veterinary Medical Association
- American Society of Farm Managers and Rural Appraisers

29

Farm manager. *Louise M. Kursmark, CPRW, JCTC, CEIP, CCM; Cincinnati, OH*

Summary provides essential keywords, including professional competencies, specific computer skills, and bilingualism.

DAVID LANCOME

410-927-5381

8127 Mountainspring Valley Road
Severna Park, Maryland 21125

email: dlancome@earthlink.net

FINANCIAL ANALYST with cost management, operating, and consulting experience. Combine strategic planning and finance qualifications with strong business-development, negotiation, and leadership skills. Research background includes assessment of international and multinational companies.

- Financial Planning and Analysis
- General Accounting and Reporting
- Budgeting and Forecasting
- Cost and Variance Analysis

- Data Collection/Research/Analysis
- Acquisition Sales and Margin Forecasting
- Project Planning/Management
- Cash Management and Optimization

Proficient in SAP, Windows 98 and NT, Office 2000, Excel, PowerPoint, Internet. Speak, read, and write German.

PROFESSIONAL EXPERIENCE

LEAD FINANCIAL ANALYST/SCHEDULER — SYSTEMS DEVELOPMENT & TECHNOLOGY
Trouvaille Corporation — Electronic Systems and Sensors Sector, Baltimore, MD   1999–Present

Financial Consultant to Strike and Combat Program area. Scope of responsibility is diverse: budgeting, cost management, cost following, scheduling, and forecasting; prepare monthly budget reviews, including variance analysis; interact daily with technical community and various levels of management. Participated in development of new **Earned Value Management** system, and in implementation of new SAP (corporate accounting system). Act as liaison between technical and business staff. **Security Clearance** — Secret. **Commendation:** Teaming and communication skills.

Numbers and results are set off in bullet-point statements and further enhanced with bold type.

Achievements:
- Instrumental in obtaining $10 million contract from 10K investment.
- Accomplished **#1 ranking** in division for Acquisitions, **#1** in Inventory Management, **#2** in Sales, **#3** in Margin in comparison to objectives for second half of 2000.
- Selected to develop new operating and desktop procedures for SAP Improvement Integrated Product Team and engineering personnel.
- Aided in designing and implementing schedules with a given set of cost objectives. Independently maintain these schedules.
- Improved cost visibility to upper management.

PRICING ASSOCIATE – CONTRACTS AND PRICING
Airsistance Corporation — Military Aircraft Systems Division, Pico Rivera, CA   1998–1999

Aided in developing new estimation system for corporate management. **Created**, compiled, and maintained databases. Assisted with collection, analysis, and preparation of cost related data for pricing, cost estimates, and economic analysis for proposals through mainframe accounting systems. Served as liaison between business and engineering groups to ensure profit goals were met. **Assigned focal point for network printer installations. Security Clearance** — SAR (Special Access Required). **Commendation:** Cross-Function Teaming Skills, proactive participation in proposal development.

INTERN, EXPORT ASSISTANCE
U.S. Commercial Service, U.S. Dept. of Commerce, Oceanside, CA   1997

Selected to advise clients on exporting financial services. Designed marketing information to promote upcoming international trade fairs. Aided in **extensive Internet-based** research and preparation of presentations for foreign markets.

EDUCATION

Currently working toward MBA in Finance, Johns Hopkins University, Baltimore, MD

Bachelor of Arts, International Business, specialization in Western Europe with an emphasis on German, San Diego State University (CIBER Program), California. December 1997.

Investment Opportunities in Europe—UCLA Extension course on assessing foreign companies and valuation techniques of foreign investment instruments. Fall 1998.

30

Financial analyst. *Myriam-Rose Kohn, CPRW, JCTC, CCM, CEIP; Valencia, CA*

Resume graphics are not for everyone, particularly for "formal" jobs, but this one works well

HERMAN WINTHROP, C. P. A.

He also used the resume without the graphic, as appropriate

24 Thistler Drive
Greer, South Carolina 29651
(864) 555-7433 (H)
(864) 555-8456 (O)

Financial Reporting...Strategic Planning...Analysis
Distribution and manufacturing environments

Financial Management Executive with more than 10 years of progressive experience in highly visible corporate positions. Expertise in strengthening internal controls to improve forecasting, investments, financial reporting, cost accounting, inventory reserves, and overall performance of multi-million dollar operating divisions. Effectively use an empowering, participatory management style that breeds accountability, teamwork, continuous improvement, and results.

PROFESSIONAL EXPERIENCE

RYOBI NORTH AMERICA INC., 1989-Present
Director of Finance/Controller, Ryobi Motor Products, Anderson, South Carolina (1995)
Controller, Ryobi America Corporation, Anderson, South Carolina (1995)
Senior Financial Analyst, Ryobi North America, Inc., Easley, South Carolina (1989)

Scope of responsibilities:
A/R, A/P, G/L, Payroll, Treasury, Budgeting, Forecasting, Income Statements, ROI/Expense Analysis, Inventory Turnover Analysis, Due Diligence on Equity Investments

Emphasizes results rather than "duties"

Accomplishments:
- Implemented an insurance consolidation program that increased coverage and saved $500,000 in annual premiums.
- Established standard product costs and departmental overhead rates, resulting in accountable spending and reporting procedures.
- Analyzed financial and marketing data; recommended the discontinuance of a joint venture that saved a $3 million company investment.
- Managed a successful $50 million commercial paper program that allowed company to borrow money on the open market and loan it back to subsidiaries at a lower interest rate.
- Balanced a $7 million division within $2,500.
- Prepared consolidated monthly sales and profit reports. Presented reports and any variance analysis directly to CFO's and corporate Boards of Directors in the U.S. and Tokyo.

THE RIVERSIDE PUBLISHING COMPANY, 1986-1989
Accounting Analyst, Chicago, Illinois
- Coordinated financial, accounting, and marketing data with an emphasis on budgeting, forecasting, and financial reporting.
- Enhanced computerized reporting systems for marketing, customer service, accounts payable, and inventory control departments.

EDUCATION

ILLINOIS STATE UNIVERSITY, Normal, Illinois
Bachelor of Science in Accounting

References Available Upon Request

31

Director of finance. *John A. Suarez, CPRW; O'Fallon, IL*

FRANK FINANCIAL SERVICES

119 Old Stable Road
Lynchburg, Virginia 24503
Home (804) 384-4600   Office (804) 384-4700

SENIOR BANKING & FINANCIAL SERVICES EXECUTIVE

Global Marketing & Business Development / Portfolio Development & Management
Transaction Banking Services / Strategic Planning & Organization Development
New Venture Start-Up / Risk & Asset Management / Product & Service Pricing

MBA in Finance. CPA Certification.

Employed for many years by the same employer, this resume presents this experience in creative and effective ways

PROFESSIONAL EXPERIENCE:

FIRST BANK, Lynchburg, Virginia   *1973 to Present*

Distinguished management career with one of the highest rated financial institutions in the U.S. (Standard & Poors, Moody's). Spearheaded high-profile and financially successful business development programs which successfully expanded First's presence throughout emerging business and international markets. Career highlights include:

Senior Vice President, Transportation & Leasing Group (1989 to Present)

Promoted from Senior Vice President of Maritime Division to develop and direct the entire Transportation and Leasing Group of First. Given complete responsibility for building a portfolio of four independent operating divisions (Marine, Air, Rail, General Leasing) targeted to distinct business markets worldwide.

Scope of responsibility includes a professional staff of 20 and a $600 million risk asset portfolio (loans, leases, lines of credit and letters of credit for secured transportation equipment financings). In addition, build and direct fee-generating banking relationships with customers worldwide (e.g., cash management, foreign exchange, depository, investment management, trust).

Emphasizes accomplishments

- **Delivered 6% of the bank's total earnings in 1994** ($7 million in net income with ROA of 1.6% and ROE of 15%. Achieved net interest margin of 2.4% and efficiency ratio of 37%. Continue to maintain portfolio with no non-performing assets.

- Further expanded the global market penetration and financial success of the Marine Transportation Division. Continued to build loan portfolio from $100 million to $225 million, DDA portfolio to $20 million and annual fee income to an average of $700,000.

- Built Rail Transportation Division from 1988 concept into a $120 million loan portfolio, $2 million deposit base and $200,000 in annual fee income. Established business infrastructure, sales/marketing organization, lending and credit administration policies and internal administration.

- Appointed President of First Maryland Leasecorp in 1992, responsible for the management of a general leasing division (e.g., FFE, computer technologies, medical and manufacturing equipment, robotics). Built portfolio to $170 million.

32

Finance executive. *Wendy S. Enelow, CPRW, JCTC, CCM; Lynchburg, VA*

FRANK FINANCIAL SERVICES - *Page Two*

Senior Vice President, Maritime Division (1981 to 1988)

Senior Manager with full responsibility for the strategic planning, development, staffing and management of a newly-created global banking division. Launched worldwide marketing programs targeted to shipping centers and vessel owners throughout the U.S., London, Latin America, Greece and Hong Kong. Built portfolio of transaction banking and relationship banking services to provide a single point of contact to key account base.

- Built loan portfolio from $15 million to $100 million, deposits to $10+ million and fee income to more than $300,000.

- Established long-term and profitable relationships with major shipping lines worldwide.

- Captured virtually the entire Port of Lynchburg's maritime community (e.g., stevedoring companies, steamship agencies, freight forwarders, customhouse brokers). Outplaced all previous competition.

- Led the design of a series of industry-specific banking, cash management and service programs for the U.S. maritime industry.

NOTE: Retain full operating control of the Maritime Division in current position.

Same employer, different jobs

Vice President & Manager, London Branch (1979 to 1980)

Accepted one-year reassignment to direct the business development effort of First's U.K. operation. Built relationships with corporate and industrial accounts for lending, depository and financial management services. Worked cooperatively with another vice president responsible for internal branch operations, staffing, transaction processing, accounting, lending, credit and headquarters reporting.

- Assisted in building loan portfolio from start-up to over $100 million within first year.

- Established key account relationships with major European corporations.

Vice President, Latin American Division (1973 to 1978)

Marketed First's relationship and transaction banking services to U.S. headquartered multinational corporations with operating divisions, subsidiaries, joint ventures and other business interests throughout Latin America.

- Established a critical business relationship to manage 50% of their U.S. documentary collection service. Processed tens of millions of dollars in annual transactions at a substantial profit return to the bank.

- Captured Latin American corporate accounts within a highly-competitive international banking market.

EDUCATION: **MBA / Finance Major**, University, 1973
BS in Economics / Finance Major, University, 1968
CPA, State of Virginia, 1980

PROFESSIONAL ACTIVITIES:

Affiliations   Member, Finance Committee & Board of Directors, Coco, Inc.
($1 billion gross revenue, 530-site retail convenience chain)

Publications   Published Author, <u>Euromoney</u> (1992, 1995)
(Articles on ship and rail equipment financing)

Leslie devoted much time and energy, working long hours and weekends, to her position in restaurant management.

LESLIE PETTY

8400 Industrial Parkway
Plain City, Ohio 00000
(000) 000-0000

When she learned of an opening in wine sales, she jumped at the chance and had her resume prepared.

FOOD AND BEVERAGE MANAGER with 18 years experience in the management of upscale, multi-million dollar, full-service restaurant, lounge and hospitality operations. Rapidly attained promotions of increasing responsibilities. Catalyst for change, transformation and performance improvement. Consistently successful in increasing service standards, quality and profitability. Responsibilities/skills include:

- Menu and wine list development
- Wine seminars
- Organizational development/leadership skills
- Superior communication/public relations skills
- Project management/marketing strategies
- Aggressively promote service/increase revenues

- P&L/budget accountability
- Inventory and cost control
- Staff supervision/development/motivation
- Cooperative teamwork at all levels
- Turnaround strategies/productivity improvements
- Forecasting revenues/covers

EDUCATION/TRAINING

UNIVERSITY OF PITTSBURGH
Bachelor of Science, Life Sciences (1982)

Harrision's M-TOP, in-house seminars. Topics include: Effective Leadership, Evaluating Performance, Communication Skills and Employee Motivation Techniques, Service That Sells (John Sullivan, Spring, 1996), Team Building Skills (Educational Marketing Services. May 1997)

Certificates
Six Week Introduction to Wine Seminar, Henry's Wines, Inc. (1998)
Serving Alcohol with Care, The Educational Institute, American Hotel & Motel Association (1994)

PROFESSIONAL EMPLOYMENT

HARRISON'S HOTELS & RESORTS   1991 - Present

Restaurant Manager (1996-Present)
Liberty, Ohio

Manage operation of 90-seat, full-service restaurant, lounge and 215-guest room service. Report to the General Manager. Supervise and conduct performance evaluations for 24 employees. Consistently receive ratings above regional average for guest service satisfaction in all three outlets.

- Reduced outlet turnover to below total hotel's average; improved guest satisfaction index to corporate average.
- Maintain labor and beverage cost below budgeted goals.
- Conducted three Alcohol Awareness seminars for management and staff of the Food and Beverage department; 99% of attendees passed and received their certification.

Restaurant Manager (1994-1996)
New Rochelle Plaza Hotel, New Rochelle, New York

Managed the operation of 170-seat, full-service restaurant, lounge, and 364-guest room service. Reported to the Food & Beverage Director. Supervised and evaluated 37 employees.

- Improved guest satisfaction index to above corporate average by intensely retraining service staff in all outlets, especially Room Service.
- Successfully organized, marketed and executed Wine Maker Dinner series with wineries from the NY Finger Lakes.
- Conducted four Alcohol Awareness seminars for all Food and Beverage employees.
- Conducted numerous wine seminars for employees and staff managers.

33

Restaurant manager.   *Susan D. Higgins, CPRW; Plain City, OH*

Leslie Petty

A cover letter and this resume were bound in a presentation folder. Leslie got the interview... and the job.
(Resume writer's comments)

Page Two

PROFESSIONAL EMPLOYMENT (continued)

HARRISON'S HOTELS & RESORTS

Banquet Services Manager (1992 - 1994)
New Rochelle Plaza Hotel, New Rochelle, New York

Rapidly promoted to Banquet Manager (after only two weeks on the job.) Managed the operation of an 18,000 sq. ft. area (grand ballroom and 12 meeting rooms.) Actively involved in the planning and successful execution of all catered events. Supervised 45 employees.

- Reduced turnover.
- Reduced and controlled costs necessary for repairs and maintenance of banquet facilities.

Restaurant Supervisor (1991 - 1992)
The Town Grill, Liberty, Ohio

Assistant to the Restaurant Manager. Primary responsibility for guest service, staff training and A.M. supervision of a 92-seat restaurant, lounge, and 215-guest room service. Supervised and evaluated 15 employees.

- Developed a new restaurant wine list and introduced it to staff.
- Conducted three wine-tasting seminars introducing new promotions to all service staff.

THE ORIGINAL DELI, Liberty, Ohio   1991

Sales Manager

Responsible for menu planning, purchasing, production and staffing of a wholesale sandwich and catering company. Catered mostly outside events such as cookouts and golf outings.

TOP TOWN RESTAURANT, Liberty, Ohio   1987 - 1991

Restaurant Manager

Managed day-to-day operations of a full-service restaurant and lounge. Supervised 60 employees. Compiled two wine lists and extensive description packets for all five Top Town restaurants. Recipient 1989 Employee of the Year.

R. FLOWERS CORPORATION   1981 - 1987

Assistant Manager (1986 - 1987)
Mary's Seafood and Tavern, Liberty, Ohio

Managed full-service, 165-seat restaurant and lounge. Supervised 40 employees. Developed effective restaurant reservation system.

Dining Room Supervisor (1981 - 1985)
Meg's Restaurant, Grove City, Pennsylvania
Full-service, 430-seat restaurant in historic P & LE Railroad Station

Coordinated scheduling of all front-of-house service staff. Rapidly promoted from server, to supervisor, to Maitre 'd in charge of restaurant seating. Developed and fine-tuned restaurant's reservation system. Participated in developing and writing company's training manual for host personnel. "Trainer," instrumental in opening two new R. Flower's restaurants in Ohio.

This resume is targeted to a particular organization.

CONFIDENTIAL

M. HOWARD CRANSTON, JR.

6109 Cook Drive, Apt. H   Montgomery, Alabama 36100   mhc11@yahoo.com   ✆ 334.555.5555

WHAT I CAN BRING TO THE **FAITH CHAPEL** AS A **FUNERAL EIRECTOR AND EMBALMER**

These three specific attributes correspond to the unique needs of the profession and this employer.

- **Compassion** to anticipate our families' needs
- **Skill** to preserve the living image of the deceased
- **Dedication** to make each burial a seamless integration of details

RECENT WORK HISTORY

- **Licensed Funeral Director** and **Embalmer**, Prattville Memorial Chapel and Memory Gardens, Prattville, Alabama, February 01 – Present

  I perform the full line of services for Prattville Memorial Chapel. The organization is a six-year-old, family-owned operation that services about 160 calls each year from the five counties it serves.

- **Forensic Technician**, Alabama Department of Forensic Science, Office of the Medical Examiner, Montgomery, Alabama, November 98 – January 01

  I helped perform autopsies on those who died of suspicious causes and gathered fingerprints and evidence in cases of homicide, suicide, and accidental deaths. I was bound by the stringent standards that bind all information submitted to courts of law.

- **Licensed Funeral Director** and **Embalmer** *and later also* **Merchandising Manager** *promoted to* **Assistant Manager** of White Chapel (a corporate division of Leak-Memory Chapel) *promoted to* **Manager** of White Chapel *promoted to* **Manager**, Leak-Memory Chapel Operations, Leak-Memory Chapel, Montgomery, Alabama , January 70 – October 98

  Leak-Memory is the capital city's most well-respected and oldest funeral home.

LICENSES

- Embalmer's license number 0000; Funeral Director's license number 11111. Both expire October 1, 2002. (Alabama enjoys full reciprocity with Florida.)

SERVICE TO MY COMMUNITY

- One of the first in the industry to volunteer to remove and transport eye tissue to eye banks up to 90 miles away.

EDUCATION

- Diploma, John A. Gupton College of Mortuary Science, Nashville, Tennessee

COMPUTER LITERACY

- Fully proficient in FALCON (SCI's proprietary program developed for the funeral industry to generate contracts, help with bookkeeping, and store personal data about the deceased).

- Working knowledge of Internet search protocols, Windows 98.

CONFIDENTIAL

34

Funeral director. *Don Orlando, MBA, CPRW, IJCTC, CCM; Montgomery, AL*

This chronological format works well for this entrepreneurial job seeker.

DIANE HILL
2000 East Drive
Savannah, Georgia 31412
(912) 920-5555
dhill@aol.com

It clearly shows her upward movement in each job and points her to a new job with even more responsibility.

Summary

HUMAN RESOURCES DEVELOPMENT MANAGER with proven and verifiable record of improving business results through training and developmental solutions. Directed activities of training staff while managing overall training program for 5,500 employees. Established consulting firm focused on performance technology applications to assist client companies.

Professional Experience

PERFORMANCE ACCELERATION, INC., Savannah, Georgia   1999 to Present
President

- Designed and developed an international management-training program and Total Quality Management workshop for client companies.

- Successfully facilitated customer-focused sales workshops for Chrysler sales and service employees.

- Facilitated world-class manufacturing workshops for start-up companies across the state of Georgia while consistently receiving excellent participant evaluations.

- Counseled and trained recently downsized individuals regarding career planning and job search strategies.

ABC COMPANY, Macon, Georgia   1991 to 1998
Manager, Training and Development, 1993 to 1998

- Implemented a sales-negotiations training program that resulted in $4.7M in sales revenue.

- Co-sponsored company-wide implementation of successful Continuous Process Improvement initiative.

- Influenced business units to effectively double training budget while operating in a mature market.

- Compiled individual development plans for managers and counseled them on job enrichment activities.

Training Specialist, 1991 to 1993

- Researched, designed, and developed training programs for sales, customer service, and supervisors.

- Introduced a modular training program for 450 customer service representatives.

- Compiled and conducted all sales orientation training.

35

HR/training manager. *Carol Lawrence, CPRW; Savannah, GA*

DIANE HILL

Professional Experience (continued)

ENERGY AND AUTOMATION CONCEPTS, Raleigh, North Carolina   1988 to 1991
Manager, Sales Training, 1990
- Conducted needs analysis of sales force and developed a three-tiered training program.

- Directed activities of six sales trainees with positive results while coordinating technical training for 135 sales engineers.

- Established program to assign point values to training activities and track points for each engineer.

Coordinator, Trade Shows and Meeting Planning, 1989
- Effectively created, planned, and supervised company participation in 22 major trade shows and 12 company events annually while traveling 70% of the time.

- Innovated and planned special events for executive management and key clients such as golf tournaments, dinner dances, etc.

- Successfully managed $1M budget

Communications and Public Relations Specialist, 1988
- Composed and edited all press releases, newsletters, and slide shows; managed media relations.

- Initiated a focus marketing communications program resulting in a 33% sales increase in the pulp and paper industry.

Certifications

Acclivus Sales Negotiations	Situational Leadership
D.D.I. Targeted Selection	Time Systems Inc. Organizer Workshop
S.P.I.N. Sales Training	Selling with Style
Benchmarks 360-Degree Tool,	Partners in Quality (Atlanta Consulting Group)
Center for Creative Leadership	Adventures in Attitudes

Affiliations

International Society of Performance Improvement   American Society for Training and Development

Education

M.S., Human Resources Development, 1996	Georgia State University, Atlanta, Georgia
A.B.J., Public Relations, 1988	University of Georgia, Athens, Georgia
Intensive French, 1986	University of Paris, Sorbonne

Noelle Washington

noellewashington@yahoo.com

78 Linden Street, Apt. 3-B
Reading, MA 01867
Home (781) 555-0993
Office (617) 555-2014

Training Specialist

HIGHLIGHTS

- Experience designing and delivering technical training and writing technical documentation; proven ability to explain complex technical products and processes to end users of all capability levels.
- Effective communications skills — writing, speaking, presenting, persuading, influencing.
- Demonstrated ability to work in collaborative teamwork relationships and to lead multi-faceted group activities.
- Goal-oriented, with solid planning and organizational abilities complemented by meticulous follow-through.

PROFESSIONAL SKILLS

- Documentation writing
- Team building and facilitation
- Curriculum development
- Program management
- Public relations
- Presentations

Education

BOSTON UNIVERSITY, Boston, MA: **M.Ed. in Human Resource Development**, 2001
SALEM STATE COLLEGE, Salem, MA: **B.S. in Education**, 1991

Professional Experience

This section shows that Noelle made her career transition in small steps rather than giant leaps.

EDUCATION CONSULTANT, SIEBEL END USER EDUCATION,
Siebel Systems, Inc., Boston, MA

2000–Present

Her transition to a well-paid training technical-writing role with a technical systems company followed five years of teaching elementary school and then three years in a training position with a non-profit social service agency.

Plan and deliver customized classroom training to support new and upgraded installations of Siebel systems at client sites. Work with project team to learn specific client business processes and system features, then design and deliver training programs to achieve high levels of comfort and proficiency among diverse technical and nontechnical end users. Adapt training style to meet specific client needs.

Prepare comprehensive documentation (training curriculum and exercises, instructor's manual, "train the trainer" materials, end user manual) to support training program and coordinate with specific client systems and processes.

- **Consistently earn high ratings (4 to 5, "Good" to "Outstanding") on client evaluation forms** distributed at the conclusion of each program.

TRAINING SPECIALIST, ABCD, Boston, MA

1997–2000

Directed the training function for 500-employee social service agency (a certified CEU provider), serving as both manager/coordinator for all details of the training program and as presenter/facilitator for selected courses and teams.

Prepared training schedules; managed budget; coordinated all meeting details; identified and engaged outside training professionals; encouraged in-house experts to deliver courses; publicized events both internally and externally; monitored and measured effectiveness of all programs.

...continued on page 2

36

Trainer. *Louise M. Kursmark, CPRW, JCTC, CEIP, CCM; Cincinnati, OH*

Noelle Washington

Professional Experience

TRAINING SPECIALIST, ABCD — continued

As the agency's training resource, interacted with all levels of management. Frequently requested to participate in meetings and on program planning teams. Served on the agency's Facilitation Committee and Diversity Committee.

- **Expanded marketing initiatives** to make training programs available to individuals outside the agency.
- Initiated planning for **ABCD Training Institute,** a revenue-generating educational arm.
- **Coordinated large-scale events**, including a community-wide program for 230 participants that featured a nationally known outside speaker and delivered $5K profit.
- Completed training in **group facilitation and teaming** and began the process of delivering this training to groups and committees within the agency.
- Reconvened and led the agency's **Training Advisory Board,** a collaboration with clinical managers designed to evaluate current training and develop new topics.
- Developed information packet and orientation program for inexperienced in-house speakers.

TEACHER, James M. Curley Elementary School, Boston, MA   1992–1997

Developed curriculum and implemented teaching programs for students of all ability levels. Assessed learning needs of individual students and developed effective teaching strategies for a variety of learning styles. Evaluated and selected training materials.

Regularly delivered group and one-on-one presentations. Contributed to team activities with other education professionals, administrators, and parents.

- **Boosted achievement test scores** by 2% in reading and 1% in math in one school year.
- **Teamed with teachers and administrators** to design and implement programs to ensure uniform development of students prior to advancement.
- **Chaired Student Aid program,** working closely with parent organization representatives to oversee implementation of a program that assisted needy students on an individual basis.
- As Membership Committee delegate, **attained 100% faculty membership and participation** in inner-city school PTA program.

Volunteer Experience

PROGRAM LEADER, Rosie's Place, Boston, MA

Implemented outreach initiative that provided information and generated funds for homeless-women's shelter.

- **Trained staff and volunteers** in communication skills and ways to relate to clients.
- **Prepared and delivered presentations** that reached over 7000 people and heightened public awareness of homeless-women's issues.

Lori has no "job objective" as such, but presents her Key Credentials and experience up front.

Lori Aman
771 Backwood Road
Middletown, New York 08749
(808) 771-8737

Profile

Fifteen years of professional experience in personnel and recruiting for both retainer firm and contingency agencies.....background includes applications in operations, business development, and human resources.....possess strong organizational and interpersonal skills.

Summary

Broad-based responsibilities in the following areas:

- Recruitment
- Research Analysis
- Screening and Interviewing
- Candidate Development
- Job Development
- Consultative Sales
- Employer Liaison Functions
- Search Plan Development

Experience

She uses experience statements from all jobs allowing her to emphasize those she thinks are most important

- Developed candidates for executive level positions.
- Worked on Director Level searches for Marketing and Sales, Business Development, Strategic Planning, Environmental Affairs, and Formulations.
- Wrote search plans for clients, detailing information.
- Extensive experience in recruiting of professionals.
- Create advertising campaigns and develop sources of qualified applicants through an extensive network of referrals.
- Perform pre-screening and collection of candidates, interviewing and reference checks, and employee orientation.
- Work closely with Presidents of companies, Hiring Managers, and Human Resources to assess technical personnel needs.
- Directly supervised staff of five recruiters. Performed extensive training and development of professionals in technical areas.
- Strong background in business development efforts including client needs assessments, acquiring new accounts, and cultivating existing relationships.
- Conduct client presentations and negotiate contract terms.
- Responsible for managing projects from start to completion. Staffed entire departments for newly formed corporations.

Employment

1995-Present	Farn/Kaerry International, Princeton, NY *Associate*
1991-1995	Toucher Associates, Inc., Iselin, NY *Recruiter/Manager*
1981-1991	Jonn Law Associates, Sayreville, NY *Recruiting Supervisor*

a short listing of jobs is enough here

Education

Kean College of New York
Degree program: Psychology

← a good way to present education but no degree

37

Recruiter. *Beverly Baskin, MA, NCC, CPRW; Marlboro, NJ*

While he has an extensive employment background and impressive accomplishments, Roger prefers a one-page resume.

Roger E. Milton

3245 Main Street	Office: (414) 722–7947
Appleton, Wisconsin 54914	Home: (414) 875–1874

Thus, I included only select accomplishments and listed fewer responsibilities for past positions.

Summary of Qualifications

Results–oriented, profit–driven executive with excellent qualifications in plant management and staff development gained through 20+ years experience. Demonstrated success in implementing processes and building operations which have consistently reduced operating costs, improved production yields, and increased profitability. Strong supervisory and leadership abilities, with a proven capacity to build effective, productive teams.

Strong opening summary succinctly describes his strengths.
(Resume Writer's Comments)

Experience

XYZ Corporation, Appleton, Wisconsin   June 1982–Present

Production Superintendent, Main Street Plant
- Full P&L responsibility for Manufacturing and Finishing Departments, warehouse and shipping operations.
- Directly supervise 8 salaried shift supervisors and an assistant superintendent. Indirectly supervise 200 union employees and 40 temporary employees working on three shifts.
- Instrumental in the transfer of Finishing operations to Main Street Plant which resulted in increased utilization of direct labor pool and reduced supervisory and staff costs.
- Improved profits through better communications with hourly employees, development of an effective Plant Maintenance Program, and supervisory shift control and reporting.

BYT Company, Inc., Neenah, Wisconsin   April 1979–June 1982

Production Superintendent
- Supervised 7 employees directly, and 200 indirectly in this unionized three–shift production facility with an annual inventory valued at $8MM.
- Reduced unfavorable labor and material usage variances through improved communications and reporting procedures, and installation of shop floor controls.

CSZ Corporation, Education Division   October 1973–April 1979

Operations Manager, Green Bay, WI (6/77–4/79)
- Full P&L responsibility for three facilities within division. Developed a profit improvement program which increased 1977 profits 22% through staff and administrative cost reductions.

Procurement and Plant Manager, Green Bay, WI/Fairfield, MD (1/76–6/77)
- Procured shipping and production supplies as well as items for resale.
- Decreased direct labor cost by 7% while increasing production by 21% at the Fairfield facility.

Plant Manager, Green Bay, WI (10/73–1/76)
- Decreased manufacturing expense by 11% while maintaining same rate of production.

Education

B.A. in Biology — University of Wisconsin–Madison	1972
Management Seminars and Courses — University of Wisconsin System	1975–1981

38

Production superintendent. *Kathy Keshemberg, NCRW; Appleton, WI*

This resume shows a successful transition from military leadership to manufacturing leadership.

THOMAS F. DAWSON

4578 SUNRISE DR
ORISKA, ND 58585
701-252-8111

OBJECTIVE

Seasoned manager with significant success delivering impressive contributions to productivity and profit seeking to provide that experience in the role of Production Manager or Plant Engineer.

PROFESSIONAL EXPERIENCE

WATSON MILLWORK, Oriska, ND — May 2000 – Present
MAINTENANCE SUPERVISOR – TWO PLANT LOCATIONS.
- Coordinate repairs with production staff.
- Identify and order repair parts.
- Reduced downtime by implementing a preventative maintenance program.

UNDERWOOD FINISHING SYSTEMS, Grand Forks, ND — Jan. 2000–May 2000
DRYEND SUPERINTENDENT (MANAGEMENT/SUPPORT/LEADERSHIP ROLES)
- Increased production throughput by 30%.
- Increased line utilization to 80–85% from 45–50%.
- Decreased product rejects by 6%.
- Implemented a JIT packaging-supply program.
- Utilized and taught TOC measures to improve and train employees to foster a continuous improvement process.
- Monitor and control labor spending.
- Supervise 22 subordinates, 1 supervisor, and 3 working supervisors.

GLENBURN, Minot, ND — 1997–1999
PLANT ENGINEER (MANAGEMENT/SUPPORT/LEADERSHIP ROLES)
- Completed 45 projects in 13 months on time and on budget.
- Designed new racks and racking method, resulting in a 100% increase in throughput per hour (3600 sq. ft. to 7100 sq. ft.).
- Developed a more efficient method for electrostatic spraying of plastic parts.
- Developed and implemented an energy-saving program that saved more than $100,000 while increasing use of cost-effective natural gas 15% in less than one year.
- Instrumental in the development of an improvement process that resulted in moving a plant's revenues from loss to profit.
- Collaborated with DNR on environmental issues.
- Assisted the Director of Safety on OSHA and other safety issues.
- Established and maintained accountability for maintenance budget.
- Mentored 2nd and 3rd shift production supervisors on managerial skills and that helped them develop positive functional relationships with subordinates.
- Mentored production superintendent and production supervisor of Atlanta facility on an improvement process that increased profit by $50,000 per month in just 3 months.

39

Production superintendent. *Julie Walraven; Wausau, WI*

THOMAS F. DAWSON   PAGE TWO

PROFESSIONAL EXPERIENCE – *Continued*

METLIFE/PHYSICIAN'S MUTUAL, Rugby, ND   1996–1997
ACCOUNT REPRESENTATIVE
- Leading national sales representative for Physician's Mutual medical supplemental insurance.
- Leading regional sales representative for MetLife property and casualty.

HOWESS OFFICE PRODUCTS, Grayville, ND   1995–1996
ACCOUNT REPRESENTATIVE
- Called on various accounts and took orders for office supplies.
- Assisted customers with office design and layout.

The abilities he developed in the military served him well in corporate life.

MILITARY EXPERIENCE)

US MARINE CORPS/US ARMY   1967–1995
RETIRED MAJOR, US ARMY
- Entered Marine Corps in 1967 as an E-1 Marine Corps private, to E-7 Gunnery Sgt.
- Entered US Army reserve 1976; Staff Sgt. to Platoon Sgt. 1980
- Commissioned 2nd Lt. 1980; retired Major 1995.
- Training Officer (experience at Battalion and Brigade) for 5000 people.
- Logistics Officer, asset management at Battalion and Brigade (responsible for $465 million in first year.
- Personnel Officer, responsible for administration, recruiting, and retention of both Battalion and Brigade.

EDUCATION

- University of San Francisco, Visalia, CA — Human Relations and Organizational Behavior, 2 years
- College of the Sequoias, Visalia, CA — Police Science, 2 years
- Command and General Staff College, Ft. Leavenworth, KS, 1 year
- Armor Officer Advance Course, Ft. Knox, KY, 6 months
- Armor Officer Basic Course, Ft. Knox, KY, 4 months
- Intelligence Officer Basic Course, Ft. Huachuca, AZ, 6 months
- Intelligence Officer Security Course, Ft. Huachuca, AZ, 3 months

SPECIAL SKILLS AND ABILITIES

- Interaction management techniques including TQM, TOC, JIT, and various team building courses and leadership training
- Computer literate, experienced in Excel, Outlook, Enable, WordStar, Dbase 3, and Harvard Graphics

Gerry Henderson
1500 Marlboro Place
Los Angeles, California 33353
(000) 111-2222

SUMMARY OF QUALIFICATIONS

With Gerry's strong track record, I highlighted accomplishments right away.

- Successful, proven leader with ability to direct operations of a multi-million dollar, high volume manufacturing facility.
- Strong human resource/personnel skills. Create successful team environments that foster employee satisfaction, lower costs, and higher productivity.
- Initiate and nurture profitable relationships with vendors and customers.
- Develop new ways to reduce costs and increase efficiency.
- Work closely with company controller to maintain knowledge of financial health of company, areas needing attention and areas to capitalize on.

ACCOMPLISHMENTS

The summary quickly conveys his strongest areas and lead to accomplishments without overwhelming the reader.

Because his scope of responsibility was unusual, we used the resume to show how he capitalized on these opportunities (resume writer's comments).

Big Boy's Bakery

✓ Created new products and directed their development from concept to implementation. Project Manager overseeing the development of new products for Hardee's that generate over $300,000 in sales.

✓ Increased scores on inspections from "low satisfactory" to "excellent" and "above average." These inspections conducted by FDA, military agencies, and outside agencies contracted by customers. Accomplished by implementing good manufacturing processes.

✓ Implemented training programs to make employees knowledgeable about OSHA and EPA regulations to increase compliance. Established a successful working relationship with these agencies.

✓ Initiated "Waste Watcher" program in all departments. Program encouraged each department to implement cost saving ideas wherever possible. In 1994 this program saved more than $200,000.

✓ Initiated contact with potential new customer. Followed through and secured customer that will generate $360,000 in sales (1995).

Tummy's Bakery

✓ Implemented "Daily Diary" program. All supervisors filled out diary each day. This proved very beneficial to the organization when responding to a sexual harassment case.

✓ Created a management style that demonstrated management concern to employees. When beginning position employees were in negotiations to unionize. Vote was taken six months later and was voted down.

✓ Wrote employee handbook which was reviewed and approved by company headquarters.

40

Director of operations. *Sandy Adcox Saburn, CPRW; Charlotte, NC*

Gerry Henderson   **Page 2**

EXPERIENCE

<u>AMERICAN BAKERIES</u>
BIG BOY'S BAKERY, San Francisco, California
Director of Operations   1992-Present
* Supervise a high volume manufacturing plant with over $15 million in sales and 70 - 100 employees on three shifts working 24 hours per day.
* Work closely with Production, Engineering Maintenance, Shipping, Sanitation, and Fleet Maintenance (120 vehicles) departments.
* Oversee military contracts ensuring stringent regulations are met. Contracts include Camp Lejuene, Fort Bragg, and Seymour Johnson AFB.
* Provide information to sales managers regarding pricing and product knowledge.

TUMMY'S BAKERY, Birmingham, Alabama
Director of Operations   1989-1992

PALM BEACH BAKING, Orlando, Florida
Assistant Plant Manager   1978-1989
* Implemented and monitored quality control programs.
* Responsible for all personnel relations including hiring and training.
Production Manager   1977-1978

NATIONAL BRANDS, INCORPORATED, Frankfurt, Kentucky
Production Supervisor   1976-1977
Group Leader   1976
Production and Shipping   1973-1976

EDUCATION

FLORIDA STATE UNIVERSITY, Tallahassee, Florida
B.S. Degree

PROFESSIONAL TRAINING

* *Southern Baking Institute*, Manhattan, New York
* *American Management Association* courses
* *Howard Evans Course* - Effective Speaking and Human Relations
* *Scientific Baking*, Manhattan, New York
* *Various Seminars* on topics that include: Americans with Disabilities Act, environmental concerns, and computer usage

AFFILIATIONS

American Society of Bakery Engineers (ASBE)
Southern Bakers Association (Program Chairman, 1994)
Optimist Club
Rotary Club of Orlando, FL

Facing the transition of his current employer's manufacturing operation to Taiwan, this individual was looking for a manufacturing management position with another company.

Stephen T. Caruthers
126 Old North Road, Elizabeth, NJ 07201
908-759-5566 Home ▪ 908-203-8899 Mobile ▪ stcar@worldnet.com

SENIOR MANUFACTURING & OPERATIONS MANAGEMENT
Specialty Consumer Products and Components Manufacturing

Manufacturing industry manager with 20+ years of experience in high-quality, high-rate operations, labor relations, quality control, safety and engineering. Proven track record of consistent contributions to increase productivity, quality, cost effectiveness and profitability. A persuasive leader and team builder skilled in cross-functional team collaborations with all operating departments. Key player in strategic planning. Expertise in:

✓ Manufacturing / Production Planning	✓ Performance Improvement	✓ IT / ERP Initiatives
✓ Inventory / Materials Management, MRP	✓ Cost Reductions / Controls	✓ Team Leadership
✓ Process Redesign / Reengineering	✓ Quality Management / TQM	✓ GMP / JIT
✓ Cell Manufacturing Operations	✓ Vendor Negotiations	✓ Safety / OSHA

Delivered performance improvements through cost reductions, production efficiency, statistical process controls (SPC) and company culture of continuous improvement. Proven problem-solving and decision-making skills. Promoted through increasingly responsible technical, production, quality and plant management positions.

This section of his resume emphasizes his achievements, **PROFESSIONAL EXPERIENCE**

scope of experience, and recent training to offset his lack of a college degree.

ACCURATE MEASURE INSTRUMENTS, Elizabeth, NJ   1979 – present
Market leader in design, manufacturing, sales and distribution of electronic measurement and temperature devices (Cal-Tec, Arrow and Beam) sold to the mass retail market (Fortune 100 companies). $24 million annual revenues.

Plant Manager (1998 – present)
Direct manufacturing, planning, inventory control, quality, maintenance and engineering for 380,000-square-foot manufacturing facility. Manage 7 direct reports, 23 indirect reports and 410 unionized employees.

- **Production Improvements.** Increased production efficiency from 85% to 98% within first 2 years through ongoing employee training, good manufacturing practices (GMP), and cell manufacturing. Develop and maintain performance measurements for key cost elements to ensure annual performance improvements.

- **Capital Expansion.** Key player in transition of manufacturing to offshore facility in Taiwan. Conducted on-site evaluation of overseas vendor capabilities, land selection, new facility design and budget development.

- **Technology Implementation.** Championed active use of ERP (Enterprise Resource Planning) software for manufacturing enterprises, integrating manufacturing into cross-departmental functions. Initiated computer-generated reporting for improved inventory control and customer service.

- **Operations Management.** Pioneered streamlined processes and standardized operating procedures. Reduced components and finished goods inventories by 22% in 2001 (cost reduction of $880K), including the reduction of electronic calibration category by 80%. On target to reduce inventories by 17% in 2002.

- **Relationship Management.** Maintain positive relations with union leaders, employees, outside vendors and suppliers, executive management, customers and industry colleagues. Revitalized customer service by upgrading customer return responsiveness from a low of 20 days to a consistent response time of 2 – 3 days.

- **Safety Management.** Lead all safety programs as Director of the Safety Committee. Won "Focus Award" from the State of New Jersey for the effectiveness of safety programs, which led to $250K insurance rebate.

- **Staff Development, Training & Recruiting.** Oversee training for production supervisors and 320 hourly employees, focusing on safety, GMP and quality. Lead meetings for supervisors and group leaders, as well as retail store checks and vendor visits. Saved $87K in labor costs in fiscal year 2001.

continued

41

Plant manager/operations executive. *Susan Guarneri, NCC, NCCC, LPC, CPRW, IJCTC, CCM, CEIP; Lawrenceville, NJ*

Stephen T. Caruthers
908-759-5566 ▪ stcar@worldnet.com

Page 2

PROFESSIONAL EXPERIENCE

Quality Control Manager (1993 – 1998)
- Directed competitive product testing and new design testing. Trained and developed production staff in best calibration procedures for accurate products. Monitored product accuracy and reliability by reviewing daily production audit records, SPC charts and warranty returns. Oversaw UL and CSA factory inspections.
- Chosen to lead project management of new sales catalog, in collaboration with new CEO, as well as cross-functional departments and outside vendors; produced a full-color, 24-page, top-quality sales collateral tool.
- Initiated systematic quality-inspection procedures, which led to a 30% reduction of quality department staff without any loss of quality level. Initiated close communications with suppliers and a corrective action system, which contributed to continuous improvement of quality issues.
- Utilized self-directed work teams to problem-solve highest cost scrap items, reducing cost of top 5 by 42%.
- Selected to begin corporate initiative for ISO 9002 certification. Achieved most advanced ranking (out of 6 divisions) — just months short of certification — before initiative was abandoned due to cost constraints.

Engineering Assistant (1992 – 1993)
- Conducted research and testing on new product design and development and prepared product-variation samples for sales and marketing departments. Supervised tooling inventory update, in-house and at vendor.
- Tracked cost reduction proposals and assisted in cost reduction implementation. Maintained accurate product bills of materials and database documentation. Maintained product sample archives.

Shipping Manager (1991 – 1992)
- Directed product shipments through cross-functional collaborations with manufacturing, sales and customer service departments. Consistent record of on-time deliveries at lowest possible cost.
- Saved $100K of annual costs for freight carrier services by researching all carriers' rate schedules and negotiating first-ever, low-cost corporate contract with major carrier.

General Production Foreman (1990 – 1991)
- Complete oversight for electronic caliper assembly lines and all subassembly operations including production, safety and quality, ensuring cost-effective delivery of high-quality products on schedule.

R & D Assistant (1980 – 1990), Production Line Repairs (1979 – 1980)
- Collaborated with Engineering in product-development phase of multimillion-dollar product line of mechanical calibrators. Chosen to head pilot run and production run on semiautomatic assembly line.
- Key player in start-up of electronic measurement devices department. Assisted Engineering in incorporating innovative new technology. Managed project for 9 months before transferring unit to production department.

EDUCATION & PROFESSIONAL DEVELOPMENT
Ongoing Professional Development through professional seminars and classes in:
- ✓ Introduction to Industrial Engineering (NJIT)
- ✓ Achieving Results Through Teams
- ✓ Best Practices for Process Improvement
- ✓ Problem Solving
- ✓ Inventory Management
- ✓ Systems and Technologies
- ✓ JIT / MRP II
- ✓ ISO 9000
- ✓ Master Planning

A.A.S. Program, Electrical & Mechanical Technology – 66 credits earned (GPA 3.96)   1992 – 1997
South Brunswick County Community College, Monmouth Junction, NJ

COMPUTER SKILLS
Windows 98, MS Office 2000 — Word, Excel, Access, MAPIC (ERP software), Internet Explorer.

PROFESSIONAL ASSOCIATION
American Production & Quality Control Society — APQCS (Member since 1992)

This person has been very successful in attaining interviews using this resume.

This resume, with its clear font (Verdana) and emphasis on solid accomplishments, was very effective for this individual in a highly competitive field.

MARY L. HOLLIS, CPCU

8600 Arbor Road • Lodi, California 95220 • (209) 367-3379 • mhollis@gateway.net

INSURANCE UNDERWRITER

Corporate Vision & Image / Transition Management / Best Practices / Start-up Venture Coaching / Consensus Building / Organizational Development / Matrix Management Human Resources / Team Leadership / Loss Trend Analysis / Workflow Optimization

Innovative 20-year career distinguished by promotion to challenging assignments. Expertise in operations management, subrogation, multi-lines representation, policy underwriting, administrative affairs, and technology systems integration. Effect loyalty, efficiency, and high quality standards among staff through personal example and leadership. Strong planning, organizational, and communication skills. Creative problem solver.

CREDENTIAL

Chartered Property Casualty Underwriter (CPCU)

PROFESSIONAL EXPERIENCE

ENCOMPASS INSURANCE, Sacramento, CA   1986–Present
A leader in personal insurance products sold through a countrywide network of independent agents; 9 locations in California, Massachusetts, New Jersey, Georgia, Pennsylvania, Illinois, Ohio, Texas. Subsidiary of Allstate Insurance.

Divisional Claims Manager/Subrogation — Western Subrogation Center (2000–Present)
Operations Manager/CNAPI (1995–2000) • **Operations Supervisor** (1990–1995)
Operations Supervisor (1986–1990)
Advanced through a series of increasingly responsible management positions to current promotion as Divisional Claims Manager/Subrogation in charge of 32 states. Provide strong and decisive leadership to gain cooperation and support of 20 subrogation representatives. Specialize in recovery services including subrogation, reinsurance recovery, premium audit and third-party administration. Focus efforts on problem solving to improve recovery and increase customer satisfaction and retention.

Create and develop organizational models and lead matrix management systems transcending all core business, operating, financial, and human resource functions. Direct full strategic P&L management to achieve/surpass annual goals and objectives of the division.

Key Accomplishments and Values Offered

➢ Presented with "Superior Performance for Excellence Award" for outstanding performance in building infrastructure, redesigning operating processes, and delivering profitability.

➢ Executed the successful transition of four branch offices into one centralized unit resulting in best-in-class underwriting services, workflow optimization, and yield improvement.

➢ Launched Joint Opportunity Analysis (JOA) and Cost Benefit Analysis (CBA) to support operations.

➢ Exceeded all corporate standards for productivity, efficiency, and operations management.

➢ Guided a series of complex reorganizations, new start-up ventures, and other corporate acquisitions/mergers involving Allstate, CNAPI, and Continental from 1994 to 2000.

➢ Led division to gross margin improvement; captured $23 million in subrogation recovery.

➢ Championed the design and implementation of performance-improvement and customer-service initiatives throughout national claims centers.

42

Insurance underwriter. *Anita Radosevich, CPRW, JCTC, CEIP; Lodi, CA*

MARY L. HOLLIS, CPCU Page 2

PREVIOUS PROFESSIONAL EXPERIENCE 5 Years
Underwriting Services Supervisor/Personal Line Underwriter/Case Coordinator

- ➢ Streamlined all aspects of underwriting, reporting, and compliance functions.
- ➢ Supervised Personal Lines Department, reporting to the President. Successfully negotiated and established a $100,000 account.
- ➢ Interfaced extensively with customers to ensure excellent customer service; quickly resolved problems and conflicts.
- ➢ As Case Coordinator, effectively trained and supervised 200 nursing staff to increase performance in a high-pressure healthcare/medical environment.

KEY SUCCESS FACTORS

Operations Management & Organizational Development

- ➢ Stimulate employee empowerment, participative leadership, and process reengineering.
- ➢ Direct regulatory affairs including insurance audits and reporting to ensure compliance/best practices with local, state, and federal requirements.
- ➢ Initiate and set standards to implement superior underwriting operations, customer management, and internal communications.
- ➢ Drive forward innovative customer-management initiatives to expand level, scope, and caliber of multi-branch service centers.
- ➢ Spearhead design and implementation of Total Quality Management (TQM) programs to support company-wide continuous quality improvement initiatives.

Team Building & Organizational Leadership

- ➢ Create techniques to keep team members focused and productive during major corporate mergers and change initiatives.
- ➢ Assemble and facilitate team to guide corporate planning and define corporate vision.
- ➢ Rechannel negative energy, differing opinions, and opposing viewpoints into a positive team.
- ➢ Build trust and teamwork in teams to ensure a successful, quality-oriented work unit.
- ➢ Serve as liaison for the United Way in support of annual fundraising campaign.

Technical & Nontechnical Communications

- ➢ Piloted technology integration, process automation, MIS functions, and an innovative company-wide adjuster's workstation design (PLUS), which increased efficiency and productivity to support company's high-growth initiatives.
- ➢ Introduce leadership training, technology training, and communication skills training for top-level association management for western branch offices.

EDUCATION AND PROFESSIONAL DEVELOPMENT

University of Louisville, Louisville, Kentucky
Indiana University, Bloomington, Indiana
Undergraduate Studies: Liberal Arts

Attained designation as **CPCU,** American Institute for Chartered Property Casualty Underwriters, Insurance Institute of America, Malvern, Pennsylvania

Courses in: Personal Risk Management and Insurance, Insurance Company Operations, Principles of Risk Management and Insurance, Elements of Supervisory Management, Legal Environment

Seminars: Management, Motivational Speaking, and How to Lead a Team

This resume points this person's background toward a sales position, using a well-developed objective and profile section.

PHIL W. SHEEN

The actual experience section is saved for last (resume writer's comments).

#15 Peak Court
St. Louis, Missouri 63026
(314) 555-0223

OBJECTIVE

Seeking to apply a successful corporate finance career toward a sales/marketing position. Looking for an opportunity to help a company improve market share and overall profitability using creative problem solving, self-motivated leadership, and professional business relations skills.

Note that Phil is seeking to transition away from corporate finance.

PROFESSIONAL PROFILE

- Six years of progressive experience in the banking industry with a solid track record of promotions for outstanding performance and ability to manage projects to completion with quality results.
- Accustomed to constantly having to "sell" my point of view to senior banking executives, with potential to impact the performance of millions of dollars in company assets.
- Consistently recognized for creativity in problem solving, training, and staff development. A proven team leader who combines high-tech analytical skills with interpersonal communication skills.

Key Strengths include:

Negotiating	Market Analysis
Time Management	Human Relations
Teamwork	Staff Development

EDUCATION/SPECIALIZED TRAINING

- Bachelor of Science Degree, Accounting, St. Louis University, 1989
- Bachelor of Science Degree, Business Administration, St. Louis University, 1988
- Loan Review Certificate Course: Bank Administration Institute
- Computer Skills: WordPerfect, Lotus, Quatro Pro

PROFESSIONAL EXPERIENCE

Commerce Bancshares, Inc., St. Louis, Missouri, 1992-Present
Senior Loan Review Analyst
Assess the repayment risk of loans ranging from $500K to $15M. Identify problems relating to cash flow, collateral, and credit history; negotiate loan grades accordingly. Obtain information in person and via telephone from other finance officials to evaluate and support credit decisions. Prepare reports and present analysis to top management including vice presidents, presidents and CEO's.
- Trained 4-5 staff members on procedural, technical, analytical and communication issues. Personally coached individuals to help them gain the confidence to act more independently.
- Studied fluctuation in interest rates, market trends, and other economic factors to further determine overall loan quality.
- Scheduled review activities to ensure a quick turnaround and maintain cost effectiveness.
- Promoted to a senior-level position within three months of employment.

Magna Group, Inc./Landmark Bancshares, Inc., St. Louis, Missouri, 1990-1992
Senior Assistant Credit Analyst
- Supervised and performed loan reviews; prepared reports for management.
- Promoted to Analyst-in Charge within six months and to a senior-level position within twelve months of employment.

Additional Experience: Grocery/Produce Clerk, Straub's, St. Louis, Missouri, 1984-1990

References Available Upon Request

43

Loan review analyst. *John A. Suarez, CPRW; O'Fallon, IL*

Note the many acronyms and banking terms in this resume. These are used to paint this person as an insider and as an expert in his field.

JAMES ROBERTS
10 Lake Street, Ramsey, New Jersey 07640
Pager: (212) 654-3278 ■ Home: (212) 324-9834 ■ E-mail: Jroberts@aol.com

RETAIL LOAN OFFICER

Proactive, results-oriented mortgage specialist with extensive experience in originating, processing and closing mortgage loans. Skilled in analyzing client needs and recommending appropriate mortgage products. Expertise with following types of loans: Conventional, ARMS, Jumbo, FHA, COFI, IndyMac, HELs, and HELOCs.

SUMMARY OF QUALIFICATIONS

- Over 6 years' experience in originating and closing mortgage loans.
- Outstanding record in converting referrals to closed loans. Effective in overcoming rate objections.
- Excellent interpersonal and communication skills; sensitive to customer needs.
- Honest, energetic, hardworking, and analytical; excellent decision-making capabilities.

RELEVANT EXPERIENCE & ACCOMPLISHMENTS

2000–Present **FINANCIAL SERVICES CONSULTANT**
ERA FINANCIAL SERVICES, Demarest, New Jersey
Wholly owned subsidiary of ERA Realtors. Report to Regional VP of Sales. Submit complete and accurate mortgage applications for underwriting. Cross-sell insurance and title services. *) job duties*

- Successfully closed over $15.2 million in loans in 10 months.
- Manage on average 20 loans with a $6 million pipeline.
- Developed close and loyal relationships with many in-house realtors.
- Achieved Ambassador Club designation for exceeding income goals.

Accomplishments (set apart with bullets) are clearly distinguished from job duties and contain lots of solid numbers that add credibility.

1997–2000 **MORTGAGE LOAN OFFICER**
NORTHWEST MORTGAGE CORPORATION, Totowa, New Jersey
Large New Jersey mortgage company. Submitted mortgage applications for underwriting. Handled mortgage needs of 4 bank branches. Involved in marketing and promotion of mortgage services. Received extensive sales training.

- Recipient of "Gold Circle" award for 1998 and 1999 for being a top 10% producer.
- Tripled income within 3 years.
- Initiated and closed $43 million in loans. Managed on average 30 loans with an $8 million pipeline.
- Maintained 94% customer satisfaction rating while exceeding profitability requirements.

1995–1997 **MORTGAGE LOAN OFFICER**
SMITH & KOLINSKY, New York, New York
Regional mortgage broker specializing in co-ops and condominiums in New York City. Initiated and processed mortgage loans. Selected banks for loan approvals. Developed key banking relationships.

- Expanded business by networking with various contacts and building relationships with New Jersey banks.

1986–1995 **SENIOR CORPORATE FOREIGN EXCHANGE ADVISOR**
HONG KONG AND SHANGHAI BANKING CORPORATION, New York, New York
Large, full-service bank. Bought and sold foreign exchange, executed customer orders as required, and developed relationships with banks and analysts. Trained and managed new traders.

- Grew business by significantly increasing number of Fortune 500 customers.
- Promoted twice for superior performance.

EDUCATION

MBA–Finance, Fordham University, New York, New York 1986
BBA–Finance, Magna Cum Laude, Manhattan College, New York, New York 1981

44

Loan officer. *Igor Shpudejko, CPRW, JCTC, MBA; Mahwah, NJ*

This individual secured a high-level internal consulting position with a major hotel group.

Michael J. Montgomery

11412 40th Avenue Court, NW
Gig Harbor, Washington 98832
Telephone (253) 822-9328   Mobile (253) 516-4900
micmontgomery@aol.com

HOSPITALITY INDUSTRY SENIOR EXECUTIVE / CONSULTANT

Strategic Planning / Business Solutions / Team Leadership & Training / Capital Planning / Budgeting / Contract Negotiations / Consultive & Solution Sales / Customer & Public Relations

Fast-track professional and mentor offering more than 25 years of experience in reversing negative sales trends, controlling costs, training, and proactively identifying and resolving operational problems. Expansive, entrepreneurial thinker with outstanding record of achievement implementing new business concepts, delivering innovative business solutions, and facilitating operations transitions with risk-management alternatives and a high level of ethics.

- Outstanding success developing and maximizing key strategic partnerships with community-based leaders and businesses to drive revenue gains.
- Exceptionally well organized, with a track record that demonstrates self-motivation, creativity, and initiative to achieve both personal and corporate objectives.
- Pioneering career reflecting cross-functional team leadership and decisive management style to consistently outperform market competition.

CAREER HIGHLIGHTS

This "Career Highlights" section is a good way to bring to the front his truly impressive career achievements without deviating from the traditional chronological format often preferred by employers.

Inventoried existing initiatives for major clients, reinventing business strategies, processes, and systems to achieve increased competitiveness, market share, and heightened market valuation. **Delivered revenue gains up to $4.5 million.**

Identified and cultivated opportunities to formulate an ever-expanding circle of reciprocal market development. **Built lucrative strategic partnerships for win-win co-marketing and revenue growth.**

Profiled in Tacoma's *Business Examiner* and *The News Tribune* as a "Key player...[whose departure] is viewed as the loss of a cooperative comrade-in-arms" and "a big loss for downtown."

Trained GM-level management on the principles of in-depth analysis of profit and loss statements, cost analysis, human resource reports, and regulation compliance protocols.

Instilled vision, attaining and surpassing company goals and sales expectations while maintaining quality, safety, and customer-service integrity through total quality management practices.

Experienced in operations restructuring to address business growth, cost reduction and avoidance, and service improvement.

PROFESSIONAL EXPERIENCE

Sheraton Tacoma Hotel / The Kimpton Group — Tacoma, Washington 1993 – 2000
Sales & Marketing Director, General Manager, and Director of Operations

Senior Operations Executive with full management responsibility for three Seattle properties and Tacoma's largest downtown hotel and convention center. Directed all related staffing, guest service, pricing, financial analysis / reporting, quality, and property management operations. Consulted with general management to coordinate integrated operations, services, and marketing programs.

45

Hotel manager/executive. *Debbie Ellis; CPRW; Danville, KY*

Michael J. Montgomery • Page 2

PROFESSIONAL EXPERIENCE (Continued)

- Initiated a series of operational improvements to deliver record revenues and market share gains, increasing rates by 48.7% and occupancy by 27.5%.
- Increased sales productivity 20% and gross operating profit by over 15% annually.
- Introduced new training and performance standards for all levels of management and staff, resulting in a 46% decrease in employee turnover and a full 63% reduction in employee accidents.
- Held position in top 10% for total customer satisfaction within Sheraton Hotels worldwide during 9 of 10 quarters during tenure.
- Captured leading market share, highest occupancy, and highest daily rate in area.

San Jose Hilton & Towers — San Jose, California   1992 – 1993
Director of Sales & Marketing

Sales and Marketing Manager with full responsibility for the design, development, and implementation of the property's promotional programs on behalf of one of the world's premier hospitality organizations.

- Recruited to plan and direct the start-up of sales and catering departments.
- Trained both permanent and contract staff in quality-based service.
- Compiled initial strategic business / marketing plans and budget forecasts, creating policies, procedures, standards and performance goals.
- Built initial client base to over 60 corporate accounts in the highly competitive San Jose market.

Red Lion Hotel — San Jose and Sonoma County, California   1985 – 1991
Director of Sales and Director of Marketing

Fast-track promotion through nine increasingly responsible assignments to final position as Director of Marketing for the four-star, 500-room, 500-employee San Jose hotel. Achieved a significant increase in banquet sales through aggressive personal management of key customer relationships and operating within the highest standards of quality and service.

- Secured two major film projects utilizing guest rooms and offices.
- Increased transient room nights by 12.5% and group room nights by 9.5% during first twelve months.
- Averaged highest per-room revenue of any airport property in the U.S. three of five years during tenure.
- Increased corporate accounts, generating more than 24,000 room nights annually.

PROFESSIONAL AFFILIATIONS

- Vice President Executive Board and Board Member, Tacoma / Pierce County Convention & Visitors Bureau 1995 – Present
- Executive Board Member, Tacoma Theatre District 1996 – Present
- Executive Board Member, Regional Urban Design Assistance Team 1997 – Present
- Executive Board Member, Network Help for the Homeless 1996 – Present
- Executive Board Member, Cultural Tourism Task Force 1995 – Present
- Member, Tacoma Rotary Club 1998 – Present
- Member, Asian Chamber of Commerce 1992 – 1993
- Executive Board Member, San Jose Conventions & Visitors Bureau 1992 – 1993
- Executive Board Member, Sonoma County Business Association 1991 – 1992
- Executive Board Member, Sonoma County Conventions & Visitors Bureau 1991 – 1992
- Advisory Committee, California State Tourism Office 1985 – 1991
- Executive Board Member, San Jose Chamber of Commerce 1985 – 1991

Joel I. Geller

323 West 47th Street
Elmira, New York 00000

Office: (000) 000-0000
Home: (000) 000-0000

Management Consultant

Management executive with 20 years experience in operations, strategic planning, and competitive market development who took a new venture from zero to $88 million in annual sales.
- Conducted feasibility analyses and total project planning for corporations and non-profits.
- Negotiated agreements for successful company acquisitions, buyouts and takeovers.
- Created and managed several business entities simultaneously with high percentage ROI.

Hands-on operations, product development and management resulting in increased profitability.
- Developed comprehensive business and strategic plans, corporate image programs, promotion and ad campaigns.
- Consistently increased annual profit margins and returns on investment while reducing debt.
- Designed proposals, wrote and administered grants for CAP agencies and PIC's.

Team motivator with ability to identify and solve problems. Supervised staff and consultants.
- Established efficiency, quality control standards, internal and external controls.
- Developed goals, measurement and feedback loop to Quality Action Teams for continuous improvement.

PROFESSIONAL HISTORY

Management Consultant
1973 to Present

Consultant to fortune 500 companies, non-profit agencies and private industry councils. Provide expertise in areas of business development, marketing, promotions and strategic planning.
- Successfully solved high tech problems related to telecommunications equipment.
- Instrumental in company turnarounds through aggressive and innovative promotions.

Executive Vice President
Division Consultants, Ltd., Inc., 1978 to 1995

Founded corporation specializing in the sales and service of state-of-the-art telecommunications equipment, both hardware and software. Analyzed communications traffic patterns and performed theoretical programming.
- Successfully opened new markets worldwide.
- Generated over $7 million in gross annual sales.
- Negotiated all major service contracts in excess of $10 million.

Regional Vice President
J.G. Communications Inc., 1977 to 1978

Developed corporation from solely service business to sales and marketing of telecommunications equipment. Created tax shelters for other corporate entities. Designed creative sales plans to penetrate the New England and national markets.
- Generated $10 million in sales within first year.
- Realized $800 thousand profit on first year sales.
- Successfully sheltered $1.3 million first year of operation.

46

Management consultant. *Betty Geller, CPRW; Elmira, NY*

JOEL I. GELLER   *Page Two*

Regional Manager
A&S COMMUNICATIONS, 1975 to 1977

Full P&L responsibility for sales region. Recruited/trained sales professionals which converted Terryphone and other A&S customers to Interconnect. Developed strategic marketing and account development plans, innovated solutions to meet customer needs, and personally managed key account presentations, negotiations and closings.
- Generated $1 million in sales in six months.
- Increased revenues by 300% through creative sales training.

Deputy Commissioner On Aging Region Two/Acting Region One
New York State Department, 1970 to 1975

Reported to the Commissioner on Aging. Reviewed and evaluated state and federal grants and programs, interpreted political trends, collected and analyzed information on gerontology.
- Implemented directives and new programs under the Older Americans Act.

EDUCATION

Harvard University, Cambridge, MA
MBA, MS Economics

University of New Hampshire, Durham, NH
MS Gerontology

University of Puget Sound, Tacoma, WA
BS Economics, BA Business

REFERENCES FURNISHED UPON REQUEST

Joel is a management consultant with a specialization in communications. He's very well educated – but also older, so I left off dates of education. He used this resume to find work as a consultant, not for a regular office job (resume writer's comments).

CATHY CANDIDATE

119 Old Stable Road
Lynchburg, Virginia 24503
(804) 384-4600

An overview of her key skills up front

CAREER PROFILE

Project Planning & Management / Organization Consulting / Process Design & Performance Improvement
Economic Impact Review / Technological & Data Analysis / Econometric & Statistical Methodologies
Client Relationship Management / Interpersonal Communications / Public Speaking & Presentations

PROFESSIONAL EXPERIENCE:

Consultant   1994 to Present
INC. Processes, Inc., Lynchburg, Virginia

Note her use of words that show she is an achiever who stands out

Recruited to join this exclusive management consulting group specializing in process improvement, internal reengineering and performance management projects for corporate clients nationwide. Consult with clients on broad organizational issues including process redesign, information technology, strategic planning, staffing, restructuring, cost/benefit analysis, quality management, benchmarking and productivity/efficiency improvement.

- Currently working with one of the largest telecommunications corporations in the U.S. to facilitate the redesign of the Work Management Centers, introduce quality-based initiatives and achieve reorganization objectives. Work cooperatively with team leader and 10 client company personnel.

- Launched project with extensive consultation regarding process improvement, travelled to 13 states to collect data regarding specific operations, and followed through with data compilation, analysis and reporting. Currently completing final recommendations for work flow redistribution, staff realignment and introduction of several technology interfaces.

Economist   1991 to 1994
U.S. Department of Labor, Occupational Safety & Health Administration, Washington, D.C.

Promoted to **Economist** in 1993 and assigned to a 6-member, high-profile project team developing OSHA's regulations for ergonomic protection throughout the U.S. workforce. Worked cooperatively with attorney, health standards specialist, RN and other project team members to conduct a nationwide study, analyze data, determine economic and technological feasibility, and author final regulations.

- Conducted an extensive review of statistical data from previous ergonomic studies, managed 35 on-site evaluations at corporate and industrial sites nationwide, and coordinated the data collection, analysis and reporting function. Consulted with the Centers for Disease Control to prepare final data interpretation.

- Assisted in preparation of briefing materials for the Secretary of Labor, National Economic Council and Council of Economic Advisors.

- Traveled nationwide to present OSHA ergonomic and regulatory information to professional associations and industry trade groups.

As **Regulatory Economist** (1991 to 1993), developed and wrote regulatory impact analyses to determine the impact of OSHA regulations on U.S. businesses, specific industries and the general labor market. Prepared and applied econometric and statistical methodologies.

47

Consultant. *Wendy S. Enelow, CPRW, JCTC, CCM; Lynchburg, VA*

CATHY CANDIDATE - Page Two

U.S. Department of Labor, Occupational Safety & Health Administration *(Continued)*:

- Appointed Project Manager for <u>Survey on Ergonomic Hazards and Hazard Prevention Programs</u>. Oversaw national survey of 9000 businesses from all major industries. Determined the survey sampling and statistical methodology to produce valid data, wrote survey instrument and led project implementation. Directed a staff of 30 contractors and a $1.5 million project budget.

- Appointed Project Manager for OSHA's <u>Electrical Power Generation, Transmission and Distribution</u> final rule. Prepared studies on changes in capital, operating costs, prices, economic growth and market concentration within the electric utility industry resulting from introduction of final rule. Directed project team of four contractors and two economists.

- Authored four industry-specific regulatory impact analyses.

Development & Fundraising Supervisor   1990 to 1992
Public Interest Group, Falls Church, Virginia

Promoted from staff position to Supervisor responsible for a team of 30 employees developing and expanding the membership base for contracted public interest organizations. Developed scripts to inform members of current legislative activity directly impacting each organization and the continued need for fundraising and outreach support.

- Planned and directed high donor fundraising campaigns three times a year. Consistently delivered contributions well over projections.

Marketing Associate   1989
Business Systems, Alexandria, Virginia

Worked cooperatively with the Vice President of Marketing to orchestrate the start-up of this company's first full-scale marketing department. Researched economic and demographic data to identify new target markets for the introduction of leading edge accounting software and applications. Designed, wrote and produced advertisements, brochures, sales collaterals and other promotional literature.

- Led software presentations to consulting groups, accounting firms and major computer hardware manufacturers (e.g., HP, IBM) to establish strategic selling partnerships and expand end-user market.

Equal Opportunity Intern   1988 to 1989
U.S. Department of Labor, Office of Federal Contract & Compliance Programs, Washington, D.C.

Selected from a competitive group of candidates for a one-year internship with OFCCP. Responsible for the extraction, compilation and reporting of economic and statistical data for various OFCCP studies, projects and analyses.

- Traveled to regional offices to conduct accountability reviews and audits pertaining to internal regulatory compliance and management efficiency. Wrote/edited findings and recommendations for enhanced organizational development.

EDUCATION:

MBA / Business Economics, 1990

BS / Business Economics & Public Policy, 1988
Concentration in Management & Organizations

Heather Flynn

2 Bronxville Road, Yonkers, NY 10708
HFlynn01@aol.com

This conservative-looking resume plays down the individual's youth and plays up her extensive achievements and transferable skills.

(914) 961-2588 Home
(914) 749-4733 Mobile

SUMMARY OF QUALIFICATIONS

- **Health Services Manager** with strong leadership and team building capabilities. Quickly advanced career in healthcare industry through professionalism, willingness to accept new challenges, and contributions to the development of innovative programs.

- Effective trainer of staff, interns, and volunteers in both formal and informal programs.

- Speaker at conferences, board meetings, schools, and community organizations.

- Strong technical knowledge—Microsoft Word/Excel/PowerPoint, e-mail, and Internet.

- Demonstrated competencies in:

Staff Management and Development	**Public Speaking**
Project/Event/Change Management	**Training**
Problem Solving and Decision Making	**Writing**
Performance Improvement	**Quality Assurance**

PROFESSIONAL EXPERIENCE

Jewish Home for the Aged, Bronx, NY   1995 to Present
800-bed long-term-care facility with national reputation and 1,200 employees.

—Program Coordinator, Quality of Life Programs (2001 – Present)
—Program Coordinator, Volunteer & Resident Transport Services Dept. (1998 – 2001)
—Assistant to the Director, Volunteer & Resident Transport Services Dept. (1995 – 1998)

Her job titles are not bolded.

As a **Department Head with Administration responsibilities**, accountable for developing and managing operations of resident quality-of-life programs and related staff; planning annual goals and objectives; directly supervising 25 wheelchair aides; and indirectly managing 34 employees in the Therapeutic Activities Department. Serve on facility-wide improvement and planning committees. Deliver educational and motivational training workshops. Volunteer for the organization's ongoing special events, fundraisers, holidays, and activities. Highlights:

Her functional, and more-senior, role as Department Head is highlighted in bold type.

- **Led the development of an innovative grant program to provide university-level courses to residents.**

- **Designed and delivered orientation for Mercy College faculty** specific to instructing this special population in a long-term-care environment.

- **Instituted a residents' computer center** to teach e-mail, Internet applications, and word processing. Hired instructors, sourced equipment, and tailored classes to meet needs.

- **Trained volunteers and employees—at all levels**—in healthcare mandatory courses, a facility-customized service-excellence program, and procedures for monitoring Special Care residents in large-group activities. Contributed to the design of many of these programs.

- **Transformed the Resident Transport Services Department resulting in 98% resident satisfaction ratings.** Conducted a needs assessment, increased communication, improved attendance, restructured policies/procedures/schedules, and provided staff training.

- **Spearheaded the expansion of intergenerational activities** from approximately five visits per year in 1996 to well over 300 per year presently.

48

Health services manager. *Kirsten Dixson, JCTC, CPRW, CEIP; Bronxville, NY*

Heather Flynn

Jewish Home for the Aged (continued)

- **Created an internship program to foster a mentoring environment for at-risk students** that expanded their employment opportunities.

- **Co-chaired 2000 "Rhythm on the River" Concerts resulting in largest attendance to date.**

- **Collaborated with a contract librarian to design the plan for an in-house library.** Supervised the librarian to implement this plan and developed his position description.

- **Wrote a Resident Transport Services Employee Handbook** to document self-developed policies, procedures, and training.

- **Established Joint Commission Accreditation for Healthcare Organizations standards** for Volunteer and Resident Transport Services Departments and Quality of Life Programs.

- **Improved staff acceptance of volunteers.** Converted negative prior experiences by educating volunteers on behavior and reporting measures, and staff on appropriate mentoring and /or utilization of volunteers.

- **Directed first participant (from Japan) in a year-long International Internships Program**.

- **Promoted from an initial temporary assignment** based on successful management of Volunteer Department operations in absence of the Director.

PrimeHealth, Baltimore, MD — 1994 to 1995
—Administrative Assistant

Assisted the Senior Vice President, Managed Care, of this Fortune 500 HMO with 2,000 employees. Accountable for office management and corporate communications. Highlights:

- Developed original office procedures.

- Selected, trained, supervised, and terminated permanent and temporary support staff.

- Increased cost controls by checking accuracy of accounts receivable and payable documents.

Previous experience as a Psychometrist at a Center for Counseling and Psychological Services and as an Assistant at the Baltimore Department of Education. Details available on request.

EDUCATION / TRAINING

Bachelor of Arts, Psychology, Johns Hopkins University, Baltimore, MD } *Her graduation date is omitted so her age is not apparent.*

Seminars in Management, Motivation, Quality Assurance, Performance Improvement, Resident Rights, Resident Abuse Policy, Privacy/Confidentiality, Body Mechanics, Infection Control, Special Care/Dementia, Safety and Security, and Volunteer Management.

MEMBERSHIPS

New York State Association of Directors of Volunteer Services — 1998 to Present
United Hospital Fund — 1998 to 2000

This individual was seeking a new challenge at the same level or slightly higher in the same industry.

Eduardo Fernandez, MBA, PT

Home: (718) 221-8843
Fax: (718) 221-5417

659 Simmons Street, Brooklyn, NY 11229

Mobile: (718) 669-2591
E-mail: Egf888@msn.com

PROGRESSIVE HEALTHCARE ADMINISTRATOR

Consistent track record of program development and revenue growth. Cross-functional experience in start-up, strategic planning, and administration of physical therapy and rehabilitation services. Solid clinical background as a Physical Therapist. Excellent communication, team building, and problem-solving skills.

Resume focuses on his healthcare management & consulting experience.

- Cost Containment & Revenue Growth
- Staff Development & Retention
- Patient Satisfaction Improvement
- Finance & Budget Administration
- Marketing
- Introduction of New Services

PROFESSIONAL EXPERIENCE

Facility Director   1998 to present

BONNER REHABILITATION CLINIC, Brooklyn, NY   *Comprehensive rehabilitation clinic providing therapy service and wellness programs*

Direct strategic planning, marketing, human resources, service delivery, program evaluation, and financial affairs. Serve as a consultant to business and industry on wellness, rehabilitation, and ergonomic issues. Monitor claims and reimbursement.

- Over a 3-year period, increased productivity 43% while maintaining high employee morale and increasing staffing by just 1.5 FTEs.
- Increased revenue 38% per year by leading the district to increase both physician and patient referrals.
- Controlled costs at a 5.9% increase per year.
- Developed an effective marketing strategy targeting office managers and nursing staff.
- Introduced new services: wellness program, back education program, and functional capacity evaluations.
- Implemented patient satisfaction surveys. Maintained patient satisfaction rates of 90-95%.
- Established a patient-education program that increased patient compliance with therapies.

Assistant Professor / Consultant   1994 to 1998

COLLEGE OF MOUNT SAINT VINCENT, Department of Physical Therapy, Riverdale, NY

Developed Physical Therapy bachelor's degree program. Planned and implemented objectives, curriculum, courses, and policies. Recruited faculty and students. Prepared and administered budget. Served on or chaired a variety of committees.

- Prepared the way for this program to be accredited by CAPTE at the end of the second academic year.

Director, Physical Therapy and Outpatient Rehabilitation Services   1987 to 1994

ALLIANCE MEDICAL CENTER, Rochester, NY *Physical therapy and rehabilitation network consisting of three hospitals and a medical park*

Oversaw strategic planning, marketing, staffing, service delivery, financial affairs, and program evaluation. Managed a budget of $1.7 million. Hired, trained, supervised, and evaluated 36 full-time employees.

- Fostered improved value and respectability of physical therapy services within network.
- Led department through two successful JCAHO reviews.
- Instituted employee back-safety training and workplace reviews to decrease injuries from ergonomics.
- Effectively recruited and retained staff. Demonstrated open communication and respect in dealing with employees. Established a cross-training program and a career ladder.

Prior Experience includes positions as Physical Therapist and Director of Physical Therapy Rehabilitation Services.

PROFESSIONAL PROFILE

Education   **MBA** (Executive Track), 1992: NEW YORK UNIVERSITY, New York, NY
BS in Physical Therapy, 1981: UNIVERSITY OF MIAMI, Miami, FL

His early career experience in direct patient care is mentioned only briefly.

Licensure   Physical Therapist License, New York

Affiliations   American Physical Therapy Association; American College of Health Executives (Associate)

49

Health services manager/administrator. *Rima Bogardus CPRW; Cary, NC*

With an advanced degree and years of related experience, this person manages laboratory operations and staff.

GAIL WILSON

1978 South Route 9W
Congers, NY 10920
(914) 268-1997
gailwilson@yahoo.com

OBJECTIVE

A position in clinical management which will utilize my technical expertise and strong organizational abilities, and benefit from my successful 20-year track record.

PROFILE

- Organized, take-charge technical/clinical management professional with exceptional follow-through abilities and detail orientation; able to plan and oversee projects from concept to successful conclusion.
- A resource person, problem solver, troubleshooter, and creative turnaround manager.
- Possess strong interpersonal skills; able to work effectively with individuals on all levels; effective motivator of self and others.
- Adept at developing procedures to maximize efficiency.
- Versatile; proven ability to manage multiple projects.
- Possess current knowledge of OSHA and CLIA regulations; able to disseminate to physicians.
- Experienced in the use of Technicon H-1, Coulter S Plus, Kodak Ektachem, Ortho ELT-8, Coulter STKS, NUA 900, Clinitek 200, Baxter Paramax, Abbott TDX, DuPont ACA; and the Cerner Laboratory and Medstar computer systems.

These important details for a technical job are placed appropriately toward the top.

**CERTIFICATIONS
AND PROFESSIONAL
MEMBERSHIPS**

Board of Registry of American Society of Clinical Pathologists
Certified Medical Technologist (MT #64131)
American Society of Medical Technologists
International Society for Clinical Laboratory Technology
Clinical Laboratory Management Association
American Association of Clinical Chemists

EXPERIENCE
June 1996–Present

SMITHKLINE BEECHAM CLINICAL LABORATORIES, White Plains, NY
Supervisor: Patient Service Center at the Kaiser Permanente facility.

- Serve as liaison between Smithkline Beecham management and Kaiser Permanente.
- Supervise staff of 12, overseeing three phlebotomy stations and one stat library.
- Maintain budget of $1.2M.
- Achieved unprecedented contract renewal from Kaiser Permanente, a first in the preceding 10-year period.
- Negotiated 18-month standing orders for specific lot numbers of controls, which eliminated the need for frequent recalibration and decreased waste of reagents.
- Order and evaluate new equipment, such as Beckman E4A, which accelerated procedures, cutting turnaround time by 40%. The E4A also yielded a higher level of reproducibility results, decreased costs per test, and cut maintenance time.
- Set up new inventory system for stock supplies, decreasing need for emergency orders.
- Present monthly in-service training programs for staff.
- Ensure maintenance of all records and material as required by OSHA, CLIA, and the New York State Department of Health.
- Produce and provide all QC and QA materials and quarterly reports to both SBCL and Kaiser Permanente.
- Schedule, evaluate, and discipline staff as necessary.
- Named as EXCEL WINNER (January 1998) on the basis of outstanding accomplishments in running the Kaiser Permanente lab.

Emphasis is on results, responsibilities, and accomplishments.

November 1994–
September 1996

NYACK HOSPITAL, Nyack, NY
Staff Medical Technologist• Night Shift
Provide emergency laboratory work in clinical laboratory handling trauma cases.

July 1994–December 1994

HELEN HAYES HOSPITAL, West Haverstraw, NY
Staff Medical Technologist• Evening Shift
Sole MT on hand for emergency lab work in a Rehab Hospital, using mostly manual techniques.

50

Clinical laboratory manager. *Mark D. Berkowitz, NCCC, CPRW; Yorktown Heights, NY*

A good example of how technicians can move into management, although it often requires more education.

GAIL WILSON *page 2*

August 1993–July 1994	**PIEDMONT HOSPITAL**, Atlanta, GA **Staff Medical Technologist, Night Shift**

- Provided emergency laboratory work in clinical laboratory handling trauma cases.

November 1987– December 1992	**INTERNATIONAL GENETIC ENGINEERING, INC.**, Santa Monica, CA **Process Manager/Research Associate** **Process Manager:** *Osteogenesis Project* 1990–1992

- Promoted into newly created position.
- Supervised scale-up of purification process.
- Oversaw and scheduled employees and experiments.
- Ordered all supplies.
- Maintained and verified records pursuant to FDA filing. Patent issued: 1993.
- Project currently in human clinical trials.

Research Associate 1987–1990
- Extensive participation in projects: Mammalian cell culture, small animal surgery (rats), monoclonal antibody production, antibody production in rabbits, protein purification by conventional purification.
- Organized project lab.
- Oversaw organization of vivarium.

March 1984–January 1987	**CANCER CENTER OF HAWAII: CLINICAL SCIENCE UNIT**, Honolulu, HI **Research Associate**

- Oversaw protocol preparation of laboratory phase of clinical research projects.
- Coordinated lab activities with participating hospital institutions.
- Supervised technical aspects and arrangements of new experiments and projects.
- Facilitated purchase of lab supplies and equipment.
- Compiled and analyzed research data.
- Abstracted clinical data from patient charts.
- Set up human tumor stem-cell assay in soft agar for chemotherapy drug-sensitivity assays.
- Performed immunological assays: e.g. quantitative immunoglobulins, T and B cell assays, lymphocyte stimulation tests, HLA typing, antibody production in rabbits, minimal monoclonal antibody work.

June 1980–July 1987	**STRAUB CLINIC AND HOSPITAL, INC.**, Honolulu, HI **Staff Medical Technologist**• **Night Shift**

August 1978–June 1980	**UNIVERSITY OF HAWAII: BEHAVIORAL BIOLOGY LABORATORY**, Honolulu, HI **Research Associate**

- Collected and processed blood and saliva specimens from healthy individuals participating in behavioral genetic study.

EDUCATION	**UNIVERSITY OF HAWAII**, Honolulu, HI **Master of Science: Biomedical Genetics** 1983

- *Graduate Courses:* Biometry, Genetics, Population Genetics, Immunology, Molecular Genetics, Immunogenetics.
- *Thesis Project:* Quantitation of alpha/beta globin ratios in alpha thalassemia patients using polyacrylamide gel electrophoresis.

LOYOLA UNIVERSITY, New Orleans, LA
Bachelor of Science: Medical Technology 1970

CHRISTOPHER JADEN

369 Harborside Drive • Lakeland, Florida 33810 • (941) 555-5555

SUMMARY OF QUALIFICATIONS

Lists many Key adaptive skills

➤ Significant experience and skill in negotiations, management, purchasing, leasing, staff supervision and construction/renovation.

➤ Strategic thinker and planner able to quickly grasp needs and concerns in vastly distinct areas of responsibility.

➤ Exceptional program development and implementation skills; team-focused management philosophy.

➤ Extremely organized and resourceful; strong, goal-oriented work ethic.

➤ Strong communication skills, including the ability to effectively interface with all levels of staff and clientele.

PROFESSIONAL EXPERIENCE

Emphasizes accomplishments and responsibilities within major clusters

Manager — Sand Key Development Company, Lakeland, Florida (1992-Present)

Property Development
- Travel to various property sites and assist in the preparation of financial analyses and market feasibility studies of potential property acquisitions.
- Meet with county officials to assist in obtaining rezoning ordinances and facilitate construction; work with construction companies to secure permits and establish construction schedule.
- Set up temporary rental facilities; work with advertisers in the print, radio, and television media to coordinate marketing campaigns and promotions.
- Inspect units during and after construction to ensure building code standards are met; provide progress reports to owners.

Property Management
- Negotiate lease and rental agreements; oversee capital improvements, maintenance and modifications for 900 residential units.
- Supervise accounts payable/receivable duties, including monthly rent collections in excess of $500,000 and expenditures for payroll, subcontractor fees, and supply purchases.
- Prepare yearly budgets; assist legal staff in the preparation and presentation of materials for legal proceedings.
- Ensure that contract guidelines and community regulations are followed.

Personnel Management
- Hire and supervise a staff of 35 people, including maintenance, security, and clerical personnel.
- Handle employee relations; direct and supervise employment and recruitment efforts.
- Solicit and assess bids from subcontractors; supervise completion of work.
- Oversee a community of 2500 residents and work to resolve issues and concerns which arise on a daily basis.

Assistant Manager (1990-1992)
Grounds Superintendent (1986-1990)

Use of numbers help strengthen his achievements

EDUCATION

Bachelor of Science - Business Administration (1994)
University of Central Florida, Orlando, Florida

51

Property manager. *E. René Hart, CPRW; Lakeland, FL*

Meredith Lee

98 Seaview Avenue, Revere, MA 02151 ● (617) 555-9821

PROFESSIONAL PROFILE

Emphasis on Key skills

Experienced **property manager** with a solid record of industry accomplishments.

- Proactive business manager who combines close attention to detail with planning and goal-setting to achieve long-range objectives.
- Creative problem solver and effective negotiator.
- Highly motivated and enthusiastic; able to manage multiple projects simultaneously.
- Strong leadership skills and the ability to manage and motivate staff.

EDUCATION

MBA   BOSTON UNIVERSITY, 1986 ● Concentration in Finance
BA   PACE UNIVERSITY, 1983 ● Majors in Economics and Finance

EXPERIENCE
1990-Present

Emphasis on profits and results — things an investor would want in a manager

Property Manager ● HUB PROPERTIES, Boston, Massachusetts

Provide total property management for 52 buildings comprising 260 residential and retail units. Responsible for building management and maintenance, marketing, leasing, tenant relations and retention, financial reporting, budgeting, collections, negotiating contracts with tenants and vendors. Supervise staff of 6.

- Maintain occupancy rate in mid-90% range through combination of proactive measures (effective marketing; thorough screening of prospective tenants; cultivating referrals through a bonus system) and a strong customer service focus that results in excellent tenant retention and low turnover.
- Consistently achieve a satisfactory return on the owner's investment.
- Instrumental in the purchase of 11 pieces of real estate, providing analysis of building, neighborhood, and leasing prospects as well as detailed cost estimates for remodeling/repairs.
- Achieved successful turnaround of newly purchased vacant or poorly run buildings, applying an intensive effort to make them marketable and income-producing within a short time frame.
- Analyzed company's computer needs and installed updated system that includes word processing, spreadsheet, and property management and construction software.

1986-1990

Project Manager ● BODY STOPS, INC., New York, New York

Managed the development and maintenance of all Body Stops retail stores in Northeast Division (15–25 new stores per year) from Letter of Understanding through opening.

- Ensured construction met quality standards and stores were completed within established time frames and budgets.
- Managed $12MM construction budget and additional maintenance budget.
- Directed all remodeling of existing and acquired stores,
- Established and maintained positive working relationships with general contractors, architects, vendors, property owners and company officials.
- Developed a computerized revitalization program for existing stores to produce long-term financial forecasts, monitor budgets and expenses, and ensure completion of annual maintenance programs.

1983-1986

Project Cost Accountant ● WASTE MATERIALS CO., Hauppage, New York

Coordinated field accounting on EPA-contracted hazardous-waste cleanup projects. Tracked financial data and generated financial and close-out reports on approximately 25 ongoing projects representing yearly contracts of $12 million.

52

Property manager. *Louise M. Kursmark, CPRW, JCTC, CEIP, CCM; Cincinnati, OH*

This resume showcases the candidate's knowledge of foreign markets as well as his experience with travel, particularly in the Far East.

JOSEPH DONALDSON

333 Maple Avenue, Suite 4A   nationalbuyer@aol.com   **Tel: (201) 444-8888**
Paramus, NJ 07652   **Fax: (201) 444-8880**

PURCHASING / EXPORT SALES

International Trade — Finance

Entrepreneurial senior manager offers extensive experience sourcing/procuring fine chemicals and industrial materials from international suppliers. Proven record of reducing material costs and increasing profit margins through savvy negotiations and cost-control methods.

—— *Areas of Expertise* ——

Contracts / Negotiations / Pricing / Cost Control / Letters of Credit
Foreign Exchange Rates / Market Trends / E-Commerce

A worldwide traveler, recognized for establishing profitable relationships with vendors throughout the Far East, India, North and South America.

CAREER EXPERIENCE

NATIONAL BUYER, INC., Paramus, NJ   1999–Present

Purchasing Agent/Consultant

Founded this importing company to provide consulting services to companies seeking more economical suppliers in the Far East.

Accomplishments

- Sourced new international suppliers for automotive parts distributor servicing the after-market. Established three new suppliers within four months, reducing company's material costs by over 25%.

- Provided marketing services to Indian fine-chemical companies seeking to distribute their products in US market.

- Created additional revenues for retailer through online sales. Developed new business in the Far East for this company.

AMERICAN CHEMICAL CO., New Brunswick, NJ   1995–1999

Foreign Purchasing — Vice President

Directed procurement of fine chemicals for this international importer/distributor with annual sales of $55 million, servicing the textile industry. Responsible for material purchases of $20 million. Supervised a staff of two.

- Instrumental in redirecting company's efforts from manufacturing to an importing/repackaging operation. Reduced operating expenses 75%, saving over $3 million per year.

- Developed new purchasing relationships in Asia that allowed company to reduce raw material costs by 60–75%. Added $2 million to annual revenues.

- Reduced costs of raw materials by 40% through extensive price negotiations with Chinese suppliers. Resulted in cost savings of $1.5 million, allowing company to compete in US marketplace.

- Negotiated financing and payment terms for all purchases.

Continued....

Accomplishments are quantified, particularly the amounts he saved his employers and the amount of revenue generated.

53

Purchasing agent. *Vivian Belen, NCRW, CPRW, JCTC; Fair Lawn, NJ*

JOSEPH DONALDSON   Page 2

(201) 444-8888

CAREER EXPERIENCE (continued)

RITE DYESTUFFS CORPORATION, Union City, NJ   1994–1995

Export Sales & Foreign Purchasing — Vice President

Took company from buyer of scrap chemicals with $10 million in revenues to importer of first-quality product. Created repeat-business marketing strategy.

- Penetrated new markets in Canada and Mexico, soliciting 10 new accounts in one year.
- Recruited new company president to lead transition from wholesale marketing approach to developing pulp/paper industry base. This strategy continued to increase company revenues by $5.5 million in subsequent years.

BEST INDUSTRIES, Paterson, NJ   1991–1994

Purchasing Manager/Export Sales

Purchased fine chemicals, commodity products and industrial supplies for this $100 million importer/wholesaler servicing the paper, leather, ink and textile industries.

- Generated $3.5 million in annual sales by marketing to Canadian and Mexican manufacturers as well as wholesale distributors in South America.
- Increased profit margin to 40–45% on export sales by recouping duty rebates.
- Coordinated the logistics of purchase and resale of imported products to foreign markets, including Canada, Mexico, South America and Far East.
- Managed field request from 10 foreign agents to ensure consistent approach to customers' needs for samples and commission disbursements.

PREVIOUS EXPERIENCE includes related work in purchasing and exporting.

EDUCATION

- Columbia University, New York, NY — MBA Degree/Finance
- Temple University, Philadelphia, PA — BA Degree/Political Science

References available on request.

This job-seeker faced several obstacles—not having a degree, being older, and having to compete with new college graduates.

JACK A. RUSSO
8129 Rothbury Way, Sacramento, CA 92677 • Tel: 916-249-1777 • Mobile: 916-804-9992 • Email: russo@lucky.net

SENIOR BUYER
PROCUREMENT / DISTRIBUTION / SALES & MARKETING MANAGEMENT

TOP-PRODUCING PROFESSIONAL WITH PROVEN ABILITY TO CAPITALIZE ON MERCHANDISE TRENDS TO ACHIEVE MARKET DOMINANCE

DYNAMIC PROCUREMENT EXPERT combines over 20 years' experience in procurement, merchandising, inventory control and management with a solid track record of progressive growth and sustainable revenue streams. Expertise in product development with extensive background in Grocery, Frozen, Dairy, Meat, Deli and Service Deli. Possess highly transferable marketing and sales concepts and skills to produce outstanding results regardless of industry or product. Highly motivated professional who is driven by a profit motive to achieve phenomenal results. Extremely effective in fast-paced and stressful situations. Willing to relocate.

VALUE PROPOSITION

MASTER of EXECUTING STRATEGIC PLANS TO EXCEED PROJECTIONS AND INCREASE REVENUE
- Demonstrated ability to approach business in both creative and analytical ways to increase all aspects of performance.
- Dynamic ability to generate profitable sales and profit growth by focusing on results. **Have met and exceeded every goal since becoming a buyer.**
- Combine strong leadership and management skills to maximize assets in both vendor relations and corporate growth.
- Deliver increased profitability through astute market projections, attention to customer needs and ability to capitalize on market niches.
- Offer powerful negotiation and presentation capacity combined with attention to detail and keen vendor-management skills.
- Proven ability to communicate with manufacturer representatives to identify and negotiate sales opportunities and successfully execute programs and promotions.

A TRUE LEADER BUILDING A SOLID REPUTATION FOR MAINTAINING COHESIVE RELATIONSHIPS

PROFESSIONAL CAREER PATH

LUCKY STORES, INC., Sacramento, CA   1977–present
Fast-track promotion through increasingly responsible positions in distribution and procurement. Recruited to each successive position based on consistent contributions of performance, category growth and gross profit. Career highlights:

Buyer – Frozen, Dairy and Private Label (1992–present)
Manage and direct all aspects of procurement for 120 stores encompassing three divisions within California, Washington, and Oregon. Scope of responsibility includes item selection, cost negotiation, vendor selection, service level, inventory turns as well as gross profit and category growth for Frozen Food, Dairy and Private Label products. Key areas include 2,000 SKUs from over 200 vendors nationwide. Control and allocate inventory value in excess of $5 million and volume of $75 million.

KEY CONTRIBUTIONS
- Increased grocery turnover 3 points by reducing safe stock and increasing weekly orders.
- Dramatically increased gross profit by increasing deal, incentive and diverter buys.
- Championed development of Frozen category into highest gross-profit category for Lucky Stores.
- Achieved unparalleled increase in service level to 99%.
- Consistently exceeded company standards for service level, inventory turnover and gross profit.
- Spearheaded frozen-dinner category review, which generated over $500,000 in new item profits in one month.
- Developed and implemented innovative corporate seasonal-turkey program for over 500 stores. Managed and directed all phases of procurement, storage and distribution.

Buyer — Grocery, Frozen and Dairy (1989–1992)
Buyer — Meat and Deli (1988–1989)
Buyer — Service Deli (1986–1988)
Warehouse Foreman (1978–1986)
Order Selector (1977–1978, 6 months)

The objective of this resume was to emphasize the individual's hands-on experience and his extensive, successful career as a buyer.

EDUCATION

University of California, 1974–1976, 1978
Coursework in Business Management

Highlights of Continuing Education:
- Various workshops and seminars relating to sales and management focused on motivation and leadership.

54

Buyer. *Diana C. LeGere; Salt Lake City, UT*

MICHAEL LEE

231 Main Way
Vallejo, California 94590

(707) 555-3261 Home
(707) 555-5564 Work

Profit-Driven **Purchaser** *qualified for corporate procurement opportunities with an industry leader that will benefit from my proven ability to secure quality vendors, streamline acquisition, and deliver cost savings.*

Although this person is a recent college graduate, his extensive and highly relevant military experience is showcased first, with his education placed at the end of the resume.

QUALIFICATIONS

- ◆ Budget Control
- ◆ Bid Review
- ◆ Strategic Sourcing
- ◆ Cost Containment

- ◆ JIT Purchasing
- ◆ Vendor Relations
- ◆ Contract Administration
- ◆ Buy vs. Lease Analysis

PROFESSIONAL EXPERIENCE

Contract Buyer Administrator — Edwards Air Force Base, California   1997 to Present

Certified Level II Contracting Acquisition Professional with full responsibility for directing procurement activities for all 12,000 personnel. Areas of responsibility include:

Procurement
Prepare, evaluate, and award bids and proposals for construction contracts. Counsel customers requesting purchases on matters such as purchasing substitute items, volume buying terms, delivery dates and expediting equipment acquisition. Investigate vendor quotes according to quality, cost, and delivery options for products and services. Perform cost and price analysis on necessary contract changes and write modifications to contracts and delivery orders. Organize purchase request data.

Vendor Relations
Establish pricing objectives and negotiate with contractor personnel. Monitor contractor progress, ensure compliance with federal and state labor laws and terms and conditions of contract. Follow up and expedite simplified acquisitions, ensuring purchases are delivered on time. Recover government property and correct shipment discrepancies.

Database Management
Operate base contracting automated system (BCAS) software, hardware, and peripherals for internal and external customers. Monitor efficiency of hardware system and load and troubleshoot new software and software updates on local area network. Maintain BCAS database and ensure standard data format is upheld by all personnel and remote users. Train BCAS users/customers on data-entry procedures and the preparation of manual purchase requests.

Accomplishments:
- ◆ Solicited written and verbal quotes and used aggressive purchasing techniques to procure over $700,000 in supplies.
- ◆ Recovered tools valued over $1,750 for the 60th Transportation Squadron.
- ◆ Loaded over 140 purchase requests valued in excess of $4.8 million into ordering system within 90 days.

CONTINUED

55

Buyer. *Leatha Jones, CPRW, CEIP; Orinda, CA*

MICHAEL LEE

231 Main Way
Vallejo, California 94590

Page 2

(707) 555-3261 Home
(707) 555-5564 Work

Professional Experience, continued:

- Awarded $480,000 in delivery orders at close of fiscal year.
- Awarded $22,000 to purchase emergency generator, which alleviated loss of power problems and ensured continuous mission support during power outrages.
- Without interruption to ROTC class schedule, arranged for immediate repair of furniture valued at over $7,000 that was shipped damaged.
- Processed modifications to change accounting and classification date for contract valued at over $22,000, saving the government $600 in prompt-payment discounts.
- Facilitated labor interviews to verify if contract employees received authorized wages.

Assumed additional responsibilities as Alternate Unit Deployment Manager, Alternate Unit Ancillary Training Manager, and Alternate Unit Hazardous Material Representative.

Structural Specialist — Edwards Air Force Base, California

1993 to 1997

Constructed and repaired metal, masonry, wood, and prefabricated structures and fixtures. Performed all phases of welding. Assisted the RH-3 Mobility Team and served as Assistant Vehicle Monitor.

Accomplishments:
- Regularly inspected all 24 Cantonments branch vehicles to ensure they met shop and squadron standards.
- Established an AFOSH- and OSHA-compliant respirator-maintenance operating instruction.
- Instructed training classes on proper layout and installation of suspended-ceiling construction.

EDUCATION AND TRAINING

Level II Contracting Certification, Edwards Air Force Base, California
— Contracting Fundamentals
— Contract Pricing
— Intermediate Contracting Fundamentals
— Intermediate Contract Pricing
— Government Contract Law
— Supervisor Safety
— Operational Risk Management Awareness

B.A. Law Enforcement Chaplaincy, Trinity Biblical University, Anticipated June 2002
A.A. Contracts Management, Community College of the Air Force, Anticipated June 2002
A.A. Construction Technology, Community College of the Air Force, June 2000
A.A. Liberal Arts, Solano Community College, June 1999

Because his degree appears at the end of his resume, it is seen as an additional credential rather than as a primary qualifier as it would be for someone without experience.

Self-employed for 20 years, he envisioned, built, and negotiated the sale and acquisition of several corporations. The functional format highlights three key areas — Marketing, Operations, Sales — in two sections. The Professional Summary diminishes the fact that he's only been with one company and his only experience is in retail (resume writer's comments).

CHARLES B. FELLOWS

234 West Anne Avenue
San Diego, California 90222

E-Mail: charles@msn.com

Business (202) 223-3333
Fax (202) 222-2222

PROFESSIONAL QUALIFICATIONS

QUALIFIED FOR SENIOR MANAGEMENT capacities requiring an excellent performance record in strategic planning, development, and leadership of high-growth business opportunities. Strengths in the areas of:

- **Marketing** -- Anticipated and capitalized on market trends, identified target markets, and positioned company to capture leading regional market share.

- **Operations** -- Established full range of internal operating systems for start-up business, enabling organization to experience 25% annual growth.

- **Sales** -- Recruited, coached, and developed intelligent, highly-skilled sales teams, generating sales of 300% above industry average.

EXPERIENCE & ACCOMPLISHMENTS

MARKETING -- Seasoned marketing manager with excellent sense for, and ability to capitalize on, economic and consumer trends. Held full responsibility for marketing cycle including market planning/timing, product selection, and presentation.

- Designed and executed marketing strategies which attracted top 5% of income-earners.

- Led re-engineering of profit centers in anticipation of increased discounter competition; concepts enabled company to thrive while 22 other businesses closed their doors.

- Developed progressive marketing schematic and negotiated exclusive contract with manufacturer to tap lucrative new niche market.

SALES -- Motivational sales manager with excellent record for attracting and retaining qualified sales professionals. Developed and implemented ongoing sales training. Hired and supervised sales and support staff for multi-unit operations.

- Delivered strong and sustained profit growth in highly competitive markets, growing annual sales from start-up to in excess of seven-figures.

- Coached sales associates in product knowledge, client knowledge, presentation, listening, closing, and follow-up skills to generate average sales per square foot of $500 (industry average is $150-175).

- Recruited and developed interns who went on to hold management responsibilities with national companies.

OPERATIONS -- Hands-on business manager with experience in full range of operations, including strategic business planning, finance/accounting, MIS, human resources administration, customer service, purchasing, and inventory management. Excellent financial skills for effective forecasting, budgeting, and negotiations. Wrote policy and operations manuals.

- Directed the acquisition, consolidation, and sale of businesses which generated a 20% ROI.

- Negotiated long-term leases at well below market ($1.25/sq.ft. full service vs. market rate of $6.50/sq.ft. triplet net).

- Secured credit terms for specialty stores normally afforded to only regional companies.

PROFESSIONAL SUMMARY

Chief Operating Officer -- Thielen Corporation, Fresno, California (1976-Present)
Bachelor of Science Degree in Marketing -- California State University, Fresno
Graduate Studies in Marketing -- Virginia Commonwealth University
Travel -- Extensive business travel to New York, Chicago, Dallas, San Francisco, London, Milan, Paris, and Hong Kong.
Language -- Conversational and business Spanish. Understand European and Oriental business culture.

◆ ◆ ◆

56

Senior manager. *Susan Britton Whitcomb, CPRW; Fresno, CA*

Introduction

Dana T. Singer

dtsinger@austin.rr.com

The slogan and list of five general career achievements will catch the interest of readers looking for a seasoned, successful business leader.

7551 Texas Trail
Austin, TX 78728
Home: 512-555-8345
Office: 512-555-0904

Senior Management Executive

Driving Strategic, Profitable Growth for Start-up to Fortune 500 Organizations *) Slogan*

Creative business strategist with a strong record of career achievements that include:
— Leading fast-growth start-ups
— Revitalizing flagging operations
— Delivering strong and sustained revenue growth
— Consolidating and cost-cutting to improve profit performance
— Repositioning sales strategies for long-term growth

Career achievements

Multimillion-dollar P&L responsibility for Fortune 500 and early-stage companies with US and international operations. Extensive M&A experience, from assessment through integration. History of identifying and capturing beneficial strategic partnerships.

Unquestionable integrity and total commitment to providing outstanding customer service and creating value for shareholders.

Experience and Accomplishments

Safety Software (Subsidiary of Software Central, Inc.), Austin, TX   **1999–Present**

World's largest provider of public-safety software and consulting services — $500MM revenue, 12 global locations

PRESIDENT

Brought on board to spearhead rapid, profitable growth — to create and execute growth strategies, develop a strong management team, acquire and integrate complementary businesses, negotiate strategic alliances, and drive sales/business development. Manage P&L, operations, and sales. Directly manage 4 VPs who oversee 400 employees in the US, Europe, and Asia.

- Grew revenues from $120MM to $500MM through acquisition and organic growth.

- Increased EBITDA from 10% to 17% through consolidation strategies.

- Spearheaded active acquisition drive and managed due diligence, negotiations, and integration for 5 acquisitions in 2 years.

- Retained experienced, entrepreneurial managers in each location, successfully renewing management contracts of more than 80% of original business owners into second year of Safety Software ownership.

- Vigorously pursued strategic partnerships to build visibility, support the development of complementary products and services, and firmly position Safety as the industry leader. Partners include:
  — Manufacturers of handheld and in-vehicle data terminals
  — Professional associations within the law-enforcement and fire-prevention fields
  — Leading online training companies specializing in public-safety training
  — Major web portals with high visibility and credibility in the public-safety industry

CORPORATE VICE PRESIDENT, SOFTWARE CENTRAL, INC. (concurrent role)

Participate in strategy and business planning as a member of the executive team of Software Central, a fast-growing $200MM conglomerate of niche software providers.

- Instrumental in acquisition of P-Plus, the market-share leader in PDA peripherals.

- Leveraged Safety Software's law enforcement expertise to position Software Central for growth opportunity in public-safety database enhancement.

57

Senior executive. *Louise M. Kursmark, CPRW, JCTC, CEIP, CCM; Cincinnati, OH*

Dana T. Singer

dtsinger@austin.rr.com

Bulleted items throughout the resume include numbers and percentages that support the career achievements listed in the introduction.

Page 2
Home: 512-555-8345
Office: 512-555-0904

Tempco, Inc., Austin, TX   **1997–1999**

Regional staffing organization with $360MM revenue and 24 branches throughout South / Southwestern U.S.

VICE PRESIDENT / GENERAL MANAGER

Invigorated and refocused a stagnant organization, providing turnaround leadership to build revenues, cut expenses, and dramatically boost profitability.

Held total P&L responsibility for $360MM organization with $140MM operating budget and 2800 employees. Directed all facets of strategy, operations, and sales.

- Grew pre-tax profits by 30%.

- Spurred revenue growth of 22% after several years averaging 3%.

- Built high-performance sales staff by transitioning order-takers to partnership managers; improved commission compensation and provided opportunities for advancement.

- Slashed employee turnover 40%.

- Transformed the sales strategy, focusing on major corporate partnerships and national accounts. Identified and capitalized on strategic opportunities to create win-win solutions for client / partner organizations. E.g., teamed with small, growing companies and delivered cost-effective hiring solutions that led to major national contracts as companies grew.

United Telecom, Houston, TX   **1983–1997**

A global leader in integrated telecommunications solutions

VICE PRESIDENT SALES: SPECIAL MARKETS DIVISION, 1994–1997

Led sales, marketing, distribution, and project management for Fortune 100 accounts with domestic and international installations. Directed the activities of 5 senior managers overseeing 320 sales employees. Product technology included two-way radio, paging, mobile data, and fixed data.

- Grew area operations from $40MM to $100+MM in revenue with a 21% pretax profit.

- Redirected sales teams toward key account management. Created telemarketing program to support lower-tier accounts and challenged direct-sales staff to deliver revenue growth through account penetration and consultative sales. Individual sales production increased from $900K to $1.7MM annually.

REGIONAL MANAGER / DISTRICT SALES MANAGER / ACCOUNT EXECUTIVE, 1983–1994

- Consistent top performer with an unbroken record of meeting goals — every quarter — in progressively responsible sales and sales management roles.

Education

Graduate School of the University of Texas   **Austin, TX**

Graduate-level certification programs in Marketing, Management, and Acquisitions

Rice University   **Houston, TX**

BS Business Administration, 1983

Alan B. Snyder

One Sylvan Way
Bedminster, NJ 07470

email: absnyder@hotmail.com

Office: 973-555-0904
Residence: 973-555-1212

With a track record of significant results, this financial executive is poised to advance to a CEO position.

────────────── **CAREER PROFILE** ──────────────

CEO / CFO / COO

**Pharmaceutical, Biotechnology, Manufacturing, Banking, Marketing, Real Estate, Advertising
IPO, Outsourcing, Turnaround, Acquisitions, Divestitures, Fast Growth**

Highly experienced Executive with expertise in all aspects of Business Management and Development. Decisive leader, with an ability to energize teams for high performance. Diversified problem-solver, able to move seamlessly from strategy to operations.

Areas of Expertise

- Information Technology
- Relationship Management
- Sales / Marketing

- Finance / Auditing
- Human Resources
- Venture Capital

PROFESSIONAL EMPLOYMENT

Alan's resume emphasizes his broad experience in both the financial and general business areas.

CHIEF FINANCIAL & ADMINISTRATIVE OFFICER

Dearborn, Inc., Chatam, NJ   1999–present
Direct report to the Chairman of the Board of this company with annual revenues of over $10 million specializing in healthcare, technology, and drug discovery. Oversee a budget of $12 million and direct activities of a staff of 50 management professionals. Manage the design and implementation of financial systems as well as the general management of the Accounting, Information Technolog,y and Human Resources Departments.

- Reduced property, casualty and health insurance costs by 20% through analysis and revision of risk-management programs.

- Led the team that prepared financials for negotiations with venture capitalists in initiatives valued at $10 million, $20 million, and $40 million.

- Participated in structuring a $12.5 million operating agreement with strategic, publicly held European business partner.

- Reduced operating costs by 50% and increased efficiency tenfold through restructuring of voice and data infrastructure.

- Reduced monthly book close time by 67% and produced enhanced data through initiation of new ERP system and leadership of implementation team.

- Negotiated with Chief Technology Officer and development team in the acquisition of a technology company with a $5 million convertible-debt instrument.

- Raised $20 million of venture capital for software and drug development subsidiaries valued at $15 million–$18 million each.

- Established 401K Plan for over 200 employees.

- Reorganized company's capital structure by conversion of two LLCs to a more profitable structure.

58

Senior executive. *Fran Kelley, MA, CPRW, SPHR, JCTC; Waldwick, NJ*

Alan B. Snyder

email: absnyder@hotmail.com   Office: 973-555-0904   Residence: 973-555-1212

page two

PARTNER

Accounting Advantage, Inc., Wayne, NJ   1981–1999

Managed all aspects of firm providing financial services to start-up and small businesses in technology, manufacturing, and marketing. Produced annual revenues of over $1 million. Provided professional services for the implementation of financial controls, debt structuring and banking relationships, plan and deployment of exit strategies, and structuring of transactions with tax considerations. Served as the Internal Auditor responsible for relationships with external auditors and regulatory agencies, operational audits, and review of credit files for New Jersey Bank and the Bank of Northern New Jersey.

- Negotiated a six-fold increase in credit facilities, from $600,000 to $3.6 million, that accelerated manufacturing company's growth from $5 million to $16 million in four years.

- Increased a manufacturing company's margins by 10% through revision of the reporting structure and institution of cost controls.

- Structured and managed the sale of an insolvent $44 million distributorship that produced a 47% distribution of $5 million to unsecured creditors.

- Enabled a cash-poor media company to increase its sales from $500,000 to $5 million in one year by implementing cash-flow strategies needed to expand, negotiating a partner buyout, and securing working capital lines of credit, equipment leases and $2.5 million of venture capital.

- Assisted in the Initial Public Offering of two $10 million banks that grew to $60 million and $100 million: Coordinated internal audit and compliance efforts, acted as liaison with State and Federal Reserve auditors, and reduced external auditing costs by 25%.

- Reduced accounting staff of $20 million publishing firm by 75% through design and implementation of an outsourcing program.

- Negotiated $2 million credit line and cash-management facility that spurred the growth of a company from $3 million to $12 million in two years and reduced the cost of funds by 40%.

- Reviewed credit files for loans of $100,000 to $1.5 million for technical compliance and credit quality.

PRIOR PROFESSIONAL EXPERIENCE

Developmental positions as Assistant Controller and Senior Accountant.

EDUCATION

MS — Taxation   Rutgers University, New Brunswick, NJ
BA — Economics   Princeton University, Princeton, NJ

EXECUTIVE EDUCATION

Creating Value Through Financial Management — New York University   November 2000

PROFESSIONAL AFFILIATIONS

NJ State Society of Certified Public Accountants   NY State Society of Certified Public Accountants
American Institute of Certified Public Accountants

CPA Certification — NJ & NY

This resume clearly demonstrates Ms. Sanderson's role as an achiever within "the system."

ELAINE SANDERSON

She defines her audience here and uses the rest of the resume to reflect her value to these organizations.

1935 Saw Grass Drive
Chapel Hill, South Carolina 27514
H: (919) 599-1834/W: (919) 214-3270
serverplan@nc.ll.com

OBJECTIVE

Human services, education or related nonprofit leadership opportunity where proven federal, state, and local executive experience and achievements will be valued.

SELECTED RECENT AWARDS

- **"Class Award"** presented by Vice President Dick Cheney for excellence in reinventing government. Reduced 464 pages of federal eligibility forms for 6 programs in 5 federal agencies to an 8-page common form.
- **Leadership Awards:** Federal/National Head Start Association; Southeastern Regional Head Start Association; North Carolina Head Start Association; Kentucky Head Start Association; Alabama Head Start Association; Florida Head Start Association; Georgia Head Start Association; also received multiple local awards for leadership and commitment to at-risk children and families.
- **Assistant Secretary's Award for Outstanding Federal/State Relations** (1996).
- **1999 Leadership Award** from Alabama College; this award was presented at commencement in May 1999 to recognize commitment to diversity/inclusion.
- **Family Advocacy Award** presented by Tau Phi Alpha Fraternity for initiating the first project in the nation where members of the Tau Phi Alpha Fraternity mentor Head Start children and families.
- **President's Award** of the Alabama Association for Community Action: presented to one person who has demonstrated outstanding leadership and caring for at-risk families and communities.

SKILLS SUMMARY

- Program Supervision/Development
- Policy Development/Management
- Multi-Ethnic/Multi-Cultural Inclusion
- Grant Writing/Resource Development
- Complex Issues Development
- Team Building/Staff Recruiting
- Legislative Testimony (all levels)
- Group Facilitation
- Budget Management/Analysis
- Media Affairs/Public Affairs
- Spanish Language Proficiency

- Strategic Planning/Implementations
- Major Partnerships/Collaborations
- Political Skill/Process Expertise
- Visioning Expertise
- Coaching/Mentoring
- Community Collaborations
- Facilitation/Volunteer Project Management
- Nonprofit Community Network
- Venture Development Processes
- Huge Volunteer Network
- Public Speaking (300+ speeches)

PROFESSIONAL EXPERIENCE

GOVERNOR'S OFFICE, Office of Community Involvement (loaned federal executive), Raleigh, NC
Director/Consultant to the Governor (1992 – Present)

- Plan and perform policy development for children, youth, families and communities. Provide comprehensive support and implementation work for the Governor's post-Summit Volunteer priorities and Communities of Promise in all 100 North Carolina counties. Represent Governor at volunteer summits and ceremonies.
- Identify and pursue partnership development work across the state with churches, schools, foundations, corporations, nonprofits, and volunteer agencies. Work closely with local elected officials and NCACC.
- Expand and strengthen volunteer services throughout North Carolina. Write grants and perform resource development for North Carolina's volunteer sectors through partnerships and collaborations with large corporations, small businesses, advocacy organizations, Chambers of Commerce, NC Committee for Citizens in Business and Industry, United Way, NC Association of County Commissioners, National Association of County Commissioners, Points of Light Foundation, Inc., Volunteer Administration Association, and AARP.
- Promote Learn & Serve America, Corporation for National & Community Service, and AmeriCorps programs.

59

Government executive. *John M. O'Connor; Raleigh, NC*

ELAINE SANDERSON, page 2

US DEPARTMENT OF HEALTH & HUMAN SERVICES, ADMINISTRATION FOR CHILDREN AND FAMILIES (ACF), Mobile, AL
Regional Administrator (1988 – 1992)

- Responsible for a $4 billion federal agency spanning eight Southeastern states. Internal operating budget exceeded $8 million. Won recognition and multiple awards throughout this time.
- Supervised and directed 225 ACF staff professionals. Provided leadership, direction, financial, and policy oversight to 19 separate programs serving children and families, including: Child Care, AFDC, Child Support Enforcement, Child Welfare Services, Employment/Training Programs, Head Start, Runaway Youth, foster care, adoption programs, and many other family-focused, community-based programs.
- Established, developed, and created public relations and media communications programs to ensure the finest coverage of organizational/program public affairs. Handled difficult problems with media.
- Recognized for intergovernmental strategies and achievements.
- Refined the organizational human resource structure to create a more efficient system of communication and management within programs. This work required extensive intergovernmental communications, program analysis, and leadership role in all human resource activities.
- Implemented human resource strategies in all aspects of human resources, including EEO, Mentoring/Coaching, Total Quality Management, and Counseling.
- Developed team concept in the organization and established quantitative budget and operational reviews to improve management and program quality especially in 336 Head Start grantees.

US DEPARTMENT OF HEALTH & HUMAN SERVICES, FAMILY SUPPORT ADMINISTRATION, REGION II, Tuscaloosa, AL
Regional Administrator (1984 – 1988)

- Supervised a staff of 62 people and a $2 billion agency.
- Achievements included ensuring Region II led the entire nation in Child Support Collections with a 350% increase in four years. Ongoing results from these initiatives include over $1.6 billion collected in 1995.
- Analyzed all programs and operational processes for the Family Support Administration that preceded ACF.
- Responsible for the AFDC, Child Support Enforcement, JOBS, and selected child-care programs.
- Identified improved ways to help the agency administer the AFDC, child care, Work Incentive and Repatriation programs. Recognized for expert handling of sensitive, volatile issues.
- Achievements during my tenure included assisting the eight Southeastern states to significantly improve AFDC error rates; also assisted in critical improvements and changes in the organizational effectiveness of OFA.

OFFICE OF REFUGEE RESETTLEMENT, Washington, DC
Regional Administrator (1977 – 1984)

- Managed a high-profile, volatile, and controversial federal agency in the eight Southeastern states.
- Responsible for assisting in the federal response to the Haitian and Cuban crises of 1980.
- Testified before Congress on the Refugee and Cuban-Haitian Entrant programs.
- Handled crisis situations and worked closely with the media, state and local elected officials in Florida, including the Governor. Served as liaison to the Federal Task force on Refugee issues.
- Additionally, dealt with concomitant influx of Southeast Asian refugees. Achievements included low welfare dependency among refugees in Region II and strong state relations.

EDUCATION

GEORGETOWN UNIVERSITY, Washington, DC
Master of Public Administration with Distinction, 1978

PORTLAND UNIVERSITY, Portland, OR
Bachelor of Arts in Modern Languages, 1976

Using this resume, Ms. Sanderson landed a senior-level role coordinating program services at a major university.

Further Executive Reference Letters and Contact Information Available

This individual is currently employed, but she wanted to have her resume ready since she works in the volatile telecom industry.

Michelle A. Sanchez

172 Ivy Trail
Cupertino, CA 92867

email: sanchez.ma@silicon.rr.com
cellular: 714-505-0705

office: 714-555-8409
residence: 714-492-1212

Business Development Executive
International, Start-up, Fast-Track Growth

Leader with progressive experience in all aspects of strategic partnership relationships. High-level negotiations with senior decision-makers to launch breakthrough multimillion-dollar global initiatives.

AREAS OF EXPERTISE

- Senior-Level Negotiation
- International
- New Business Development

- Executive Relationship Management
- Matrix-Management of Global Virtual Teams
- Strategic Partnership Sales

Entire resume emphasizes Michelle's strong, progressive career development.

Professional Employment

DIRECTOR — GLOBAL ACCOUNTS
Advanced Telecommunications, Inc. — Multinational Accounts Division, Cupertino, CA   2000–present

Responsible for meeting an annual revenue quota of $3 million in first year of this highly visible investment program forecasted to grow exponentially within the next 12–18 months. Manage critical relationships with five strategic partner companies—DSE, Tya, Kenta, Protel and BTB—with whom Advanced currently does $250 million–$300 million in annual business. Interface with Senior VPs, Directors and National Account Managers. Assemble and oversee global resources from sales and technical teams in Europe, South America and Asia to design and deliver customer solutions. Update President quarterly and as needed regarding results. Internally interface with CTO and CIO as well as Senior VPs of Procurement, Engineering, Sales, Systems and Product Development.

RESULTS:
- Uncovered opportunities valued at over $20 million in five companies.
- Negotiated a $1 million contract with Tya for network services.
- Received executive-level recognition for successful development of executive-level relationships.
- Currently negotiating global contracts of $7 million in Europe and $1 million in Latin America and Mexico.
- Positioned company to successfully convert existing service contracts with competitors to Advanced Telecommunications.

Information here shows that she advanced to this position in a consistent, deliberate way.

DIRECTOR — STRATEGIC PARTNERSHIP SALES
Alphaserve Wireless, Santa Barbara, CA   1997–2000

Promoted to this position and given DSE and Protel accounts for this start-up program. Responsible for a $3 million annual revenue target for sales of digital broadband radio services to wholesale and commercial accounts.

RESULTS:
- Sold $5 million digital broadband radio private-campus network to Protel ICN division.

SENIOR MANAGER — NATIONAL ACCOUNT SALES
Managed the establishment of Alphaserve as a key provider of alternative access services in the West.

RESULTS:
- Strategically positioned Alphaserve in new market of ISPs.
- Closed $10 million Master Services Agreement with Internetworking, Inc.—the first of its kind.
- Increased revenues 150% in the first five months in the position.
- Negotiated Carrier Interconnect Agreements to increase market availability.
- Participated in the development of a strategic national accounts program for wireless access.
- Successfully negotiated real estate deals that supported Santa Barbara network development.

60

Business development executive. *Fran Kelley, MA, CPRW, SPHR, JCTC; Waldwick, NJ*

Michelle A. Sanchez
Page 2

email: sanchez.ma@silicon.rr.com
cellular: 714-505-0705

office: 714-555-8409
residence: 714-492-1212

page two

Professional Employment, cont'd.

NDJ Telecommunications Company, San Francisco, CA   1988–1997
Progressive development to positions of increasing responsibility during this nine-year period.

CURRICULUM MANAGER — NATIONAL TRAINING ORGANIZATION — 1995–1997
Managed the development and delivery of strategic and tactical training programs for several hundred National Account Executives and Sales Managers. Responsible for a multimillion-dollar training budget. Selected and negotiated with key consulting firms to design and deliver courses. Participated with consultants in the design of Sales Management programs for national sales conferences.
RESULTS:
- Launched the first strategic leadership course for Executive Sales Directors in Corporate National Accounts.
- Designed the first full course curriculum for Mid-Market Sales Managers.

SENIOR MANAGER — NATIONAL ACCOUNT SALES — 1990–1995
Promoted to this position to manage four national accounts: Western Telecomm, MDDT, Western Net and West Bank. Managed five National Account Managers with a $30 million annual revenue target.
RESULTS:
- Consistently exceeded annual revenue goals by 120%.
- Negotiated with team for long-term contracts for over $65 million in revenue.
- Generated over $10 million in new revenue in 12 months through establishment of new Local Exchange Carrier market for NDJ in the West.

NATIONAL ACCOUNTS MANAGER — 1988–1990
Managed the Western Telecomm account with an annual revenue target of $4 million. Identified key revenue opportunities, negotiated long-term contracts and managed account-support functions.
RESULTS:
- Doubled existing base revenue in two years from $4 million to $8 million.

Prior Professional Employment

Position as National Accounts Manager for General Telco as well as various sales and sales management positions at Western Telecommunications.

Education

BA — State University of New York — Albany, NY

Awards

- Alphaserve Spirit Award for outstanding corporate achievement: sole recipient from National Account Sales — awarded 1,000 stock options — 1999.
- Alphaserve President's Club Award — 1998 and 1999.
- NDJ Chairman's Inner Circle National Award for 1988, 1991 and 1992.
- NDJ Director's Cup Award for seven consecutive years for outstanding achievement.

Professional and Related Occupations

Resumes at a Glance

This architect is a senior manager. The majority of the first page of his resume is devoted to project highlights because Adam prefers the hands-on project development to running the company.

ADAM STEPHENS, AIA

6530 High Street
Worthington, OH 43085

Home: (614) 436-1212
E-mail: adam@architectstar.com

SENIOR-LEVEL MANAGEMENT PROFESSIONAL
Expertise in Large-Scale Project Development

Providing Professional Planning, Architectural Design, and Engineering Excellence...

Accomplished executive with almost 25 years' comprehensive experience in fast-paced, growth-driven environments and demonstrated skills in relationship building, community interaction, and driving sales and developing markets within competitive venues. Talented leader with highly effective interpersonal skills and rare blend of business acumen, creativity, and program-development abilities. Outstanding history of successfully managing projects from conception, through development, to implementation. Self-motivated, inclusive, decisive, and thoroughly committed to professional excellence.

AREAS OF EXPERTISE

- National / International Markets
- Business / Strategic Planning
- Sales / Contract Negotiations
- P&L Management / Budgeting
- Client Needs Analysis / Relations

- Hiring / Training / Supervision
- Public Speaking / Presentations
- Major Account Development
- Marketing Research / Expansion
- Team Building / Group Leadership

REPRESENTATIVE PROJECTS

- Vern Riffe Center for Government and Performing Arts, Columbus, OH — State's largest building.
- Franklin County Government Center — The largest Franklin County building, 650,000 ft^2.
- Project '88 Wastewater Treatment Plant — City of Columbus's largest engineering assignment.
- NASA Lewis Research Center, Cleveland, OH — $10M fee.
- Ft. Benjamin Harrison Finance Accounting Center renovation, Indianapolis, IN — 1.2M ft^2, $7M fee.
- Ohio Department of Transportation/Public Safety Headquarters, Columbus, OH — 750,000 ft^2, $90M construction cost.
- Ohio Department of Youth Services, Columbus, OH — Three separate juvenile detention campuses.
- U.S. Pentagon, Arlington, VA — 1.6M ft^2 basement renovation, $365M construction cost.
- United Parcel Service Air Cargo Distribution Hub, Louisville, KY — $2.8M remodel.
- The Ohio State University main library renovation feasibility study, Columbus, OH — $60M-$80M project.
- Guangzhou Airport design competition, Guangzhou, China — $1.5B airport.
- The Ohio State University, Farmington dormitory, Columbus, OH — $1M.
- Schottenstein Arena, Columbus, OH — $2.5M addition.
- University of Cincinnati Recreation Center, Cincinnati, OH — $1.6M.
- Mall of Atlanta, Dalton, GA — $2M renovation.
- Louis Weinberg Synagogue, Cincinnati, OH — $1M remodel.
- St. Paul's Cathedral, Columbus, OH — $2.8M renovation.

61

Architect (senior-level). *Janice Worthington, MA, CPRW, JCTC, CEIP; Columbus, OH*

CAREER PROGRESSION

International Architectural Design Place (www.iadp.com) — Columbus, OH
[Professional planning, architectural design, and engineering firm producing high-quality building and facility designs and providing environmental solutions to restore ecosystems and protect the earth's resources. Employs 18,000 in 920+ offices worldwide.]

Senior Vice President/Regional Manager (1993–Present) — Columbus, OH
Manage ten regional offices (employing 1,200), including accounting, HR, legal, recruiting, and IMS. Liaise with management and staff to generate/implement plans to attain overall growth/development, attain profit goals, and meet customer needs while achieving short- and long-term business priorities. Oversee proposal development/presentation, negotiations, and contract closing of major architectural/engineering project sales to high-profile and high-dollar regional and international clients. Recruit, hire, and mentor senior staff.

Team with office managers to develop and revise multidiscipline business plans reflecting each office's sales, cash collection, growth strategies, and overall P&L. Participate in development of new markets and direct ongoing projects. Co-manage business line concentrating on strategic planning, coordination of resources, revenue growth, and IRS name recognition within the A/E "facilities" segment. As member of senior management committee, report directly to senior-level management on strategies impacting operational efficiency.

Contributions:

♦ **Accelerated regional revenues 200%** ($35M to $105M) **and profits 280%** ($5M to $19M) between 1995 and 2000 through industry and competitor analysis combined with aggressive business plan that maximized potential of existing accounts. Revenues for 2001 anticipated to **increase an additional 13%.**

♦ **Established and opened three new office locations** (Columbus, Cincinnati, Washington, DC) employing 530 professional and technical staff.

♦ **Teamed with senior management to found IRS/Telecommunications** ($38M/annually). Originally based in Washington, DC, it now operates in approximately 10 IRS office locations through the U.S.

♦ **Entrusted to lead sales and client management for one of IRS' largest project assignments** ($42M fee), the U.S. Pentagon basement renovation.

Office Manager (1987–1993) — Columbus, OH
Accepted challenge to direct sales growth strategy, penetrate new accounts, define tactics for marketing initiatives, develop metrics to improve performance, preside over all new business development, and provide overall P&L management. Supervised and ran office efficiently and seamlessly, resolving all day-to-day and recurring problems. Oversaw recruitment of new hires and planned/implemented sales training.

Contributions:

♦ **Facilitated market diversification** into design/engineering, civil water/wastewater engineering, transportation engineering, and environmental engineering by making key hires based upon credentials and compatibility with company philosophy and goals.

♦ **Nurtured geographic growth with establishment of IRS offices** in Washington, DC, and Cincinnati, OH.

PROFESSIONAL PROFILE

EDUCATION: THE OHIO STATE UNIVERSITY — Columbus, OH
                     B.S. in Architecture; minor in Business Administration (1978)
                     OXFORD UNIVERSITY — Oxford, England
                     Graduate courses in British Economics and Urban Design (1977)

AFFILIATION: Registered Professional Architect, Ohio — Registration #8384
                     American Institute of Architects
                     Architect's Society of Ohio
                     Department of Defense — Top Secret Security Clearance

COMMUNITY SERVICE: United Way Cabinet 2001
                     Columbus Zoo, Board Secretary 2001 (Board member since 1982)

Keywords are divided into three areas: project management, business management, and sales. They are used to show that his knowledge extends beyond landscape architecture.

Clayton Garner

7245 N. Longmoor, St. Joseph, MO 6450 ● Phone: (816) 432-9095 ● Email: Clay9865@yahoo.com

LANDSCAPE ARCHITECT / PROJECT MANAGER

**Landscape Design / Multi-Project Management / Business Development
Market Development / Profit & Loss / Quality Control / Client Presentations
Human Resources / Cost Reduction / Multifunction Experience / Customer Retention**

SUMMARY OF EXPERIENCE

Landscape Architect, 1997–Present   **Braeden's Landscape Service, Inc., North Kansas City, MO**

Includes quantitative statements that support the skills he has in the three areas included in his keyword list.

- 2001 Designers Award, Kansas City Flower, Lawn & Garden Show, for best overall Landscape Design.
- 2000 Kansas Streetscaping Award, Kansas Department of Transportation, for Sprint Campus facility.
- Collaborated with business associate in development of commercial landscaping department launched in 1998. Landscape Department has been profitable from startup.
- Increased combined landscape department sales 650% from $700,000 to nearly $5,250,000 and maintained gross sales volume while reducing labor costs by 30%.
- Clients include Global Construction, Zimmer, J. M. Fahey, Holland Corporation, North Kansas City School District, Cities of Gladstone, Liberty, Platte City and Parkville.
- Manage 75–125 projects per year, while bidding over 500 projects yearly.
- Oversight of on-site construction managers, job foremen, nursery, equipment, subcontractors and purchasing.
- Administration of human resources development, evaluating department policies and guidelines, hiring and firing, performance appraisals, employee retention, pay scales, trade-show scheduling and staff training.

Senior Project Manager/Senior Commercial Estimator, 1995–1997   **Fulton's Lawn & Garden, St. Joseph, MO**

- Coordinated with multiple departments, including operations, nursery, maintenance and administration, for bidding, design and sales of commercial landscape projects.
- Clients included J. E. Dunn, Walton, DiCarlo and Turner.
- Exceeded all sales goals during tenure, with 1997 sales surpassing $2,200,000.
- Trained commercial estimators/project managers.
- Bid more than 400 jobs per year, including multimillion-dollar projects.

Landscape Designer, Merchandising/Retail Sales Manager, 1993–1995   **Stanton's Landscaping, Inc., Parkville, MO**

- Coordinated with multiple departments, including administration, irrigation, maintenance, and nursery for design and sales of residential landscaping projects.
- Computerized nursery and updated computers for bar-code integration.
- Supervised landscaping crews. Trained nursery personnel.

COMPUTER PROFICIENCY

- Proficient in IBM Systems and Macintosh systems, and Window 98 Operating Systems.
- Experienced with AutoCAD, RainCAD and LandCAD, and Microsoft Excel, Word and Access.

MEMBERSHIPS

- Greater Kansas City Area Chamber of Commerce, 1999–Present
- St. Joseph Chamber of Commerce, 1997–Present

EDUCATION, CERTIFICATIONS & PROFESSIONAL DEVELOPMENT

- BLA, Bachelor of Landscape Architecture, 1992: Iowa State University, Ames, Iowa
- Registered Landscape Architect, Iowa and Kansas, 1998
- Certification in Water Management, 1998
- Member of CLARB, Council for Landscape Architecture Registration, 2000
- Fulton's Sales Training, January 1995, 1996 & 1997
- RainBird Seminars: Interviewing Techniques — January 2000; Retaining Employees — January 2001
- Industrial Sales Professional Training, Employee Benefits and Resources Seminar — February 2000

62

Landscape architect. *Karen M. Silins, CRW, CCA; Kansas City, MO*

The unusual format of this resume was intended to position Mr. Smith for advancement into more-challenging, design-focused landscape architecture positions.

Bruce T. Smith

307 Colonial Road
Portland, ME 08672
(207) 954-1035 – bsmith@email.com

REGISTERED LANDSCAPE ARCHITECT
Creative, design-oriented landscape architect with 10+ years' experience

Talented landscape architect offering complementary blend of artistic/graphic and technical qualifications, and experience spanning residential, commercial, institutional, and mixed-use development projects. Detail-focused project manager, well-versed in all landscape design project phases, conceptual design through final construction. Tenacious and thorough in following through with projects. Strong communication and interpersonal skills.

Qualifications Summary

— Landscape Architecture & Design
— Site / Land Use Analysis & Planning
— Project Planning & Management
— AutoCAD r14/r13 / SoftDesk Civil 8.0

— Environmental Regulations & Permitting
— Development Regulations & Processes
— Contract Documents Production
— Construction Methods & Materials

Professional Highlights

Used this format to eliminate redundancy in job descriptions!

LANDSCAPE ARCHITECT & PROJECT MANAGER
Landscape Associates, Inc. – Portland, ME (1998 – Present)
Fowles Associates, Inc. – Gilmanton, NH (1996 – 1998)
Ziemba Associates – North Berwick, ME (1995 – 1996)
Johnson & Sons Associates, P.C. – Portland, ME (1987 – 1991)

Contributed technical and design expertise, performed landscape design, managed projects, and headed production of design drawings/contract documents for landscape architectural and multi-disciplinary engineering firms. Worked on diverse commercial, industrial, residential, institutional, and mixed-use development projects. Earned professional reputation for rare blend of artistic design, technical, and managerial qualifications — consistent ability to produce time sensitive, high-pressure projects on time and within budget. Recent highlights include:

➤ **Berwick Public Schools — public school design/construction projects:** Current project manager working closely with architectural firm; developed design schemes and earned approval for design development phases for four middle and elementary school facilities accommodating 400 – 1300 students each.

➤ **Lucent Technologies R&D facilities expansion — 500,000 sq. ft.:** Headed production of contract design documents, inception through final bid documents, developing the largest set of drawings issued on a single project in history of the company. Earned praise from reviewing agencies for design drawings produced to secure local and state environmental permits. Executed grading studies and recommended/coordinated design modifications to meet challenges of construction on steep topography.

➤ **Athletic facilities and fields:** Designed and produced landscape architecture drawings for new sports facility, new soccer field, renovation of three existing baseball and soccer fields, and associated parking and bus loop. Overcame challenges associated with construction in a floodplain and in close proximity to wetland resource areas, earning approval for project by local Conservation Commission.

➤ **Bell Atlantic Mobile, mobile telephone switching office — 25,000 sq. ft.:** Performed site planning and produced complete site plan package, managing all site grading, layout, utilities planning, and planting.

➤ **Residential subdivision — 200-acre parcel:** Utilized digitizer and AutoCAD to transpose engineering plans and topographic surveys; produced development scheme for residential subdivision.

➤ **Various commercial and institutional projects:** Completed earthwork computations and grading, developed construction documents, played key site-design role, and secured permits for construction of a post office, office/warehouse facility, hospital parking expansion, and two Marriott-owned executive-stay hotels.

Education & Credentials

BACHELOR OF LANDSCAPE ARCHITECTURE (1987)
SUNY College of Environmental Science and Forestry — Syracuse, NY

Landscape Architect — Maine State License

63

Landscape architect. *Michelle Dumas, CPRW, NCRW, CCM, JCTC, CEIP; Somersworth, NH*

This self-employed land surveyor wanted public employment. The resume addresses employers' concerns about hiring someone who has owned and managed his own business...

JASON E. LAWRENCE, PLS

5555 N.W. 56th Avenue
Portland, OR 55555
(555) 555-5555

PROFESSION: LICENSED PROFESSIONAL LAND SURVEYOR

QUALIFICATIONS *the qualifications here show experience up front...*

- Over 15 years' experience as licensed surveyor. Extensive CAD office and field experience for large-scale public works, DOT roadway projects, commercial projects, and private land surveying as Senior Land Surveyor with public utility company and Manager of private land survey firm.
- Supervised survey staff of up to eight using total stations and electronic data collectors for route, construction layout, mapmaking, land division, ALTA, boundary, and topographic surveys.
- Excellent administrative skills for business planning, budget forecasts, fiscal administration, personnel supervision, and general administrative operations.
- Qualified for high-profile positions requiring presentations before, and interaction with, elected officials, development services representatives, the real estate community, and the general public.
- Technical skills: AutoCAD (version 12), GPS, GIS, and other industry-specific software.

PROFESSIONAL EXPERIENCE *and the company name is de-emphasized...*

MANAGER / PROFESSIONAL LAND SURVEYOR   6/79-Present
Jason E. Lawrence Land Surveying, Portland, Oregon

Manage full scope of technical functions and administrative operations for leading land survey firm servicing government agencies, the telecommunications industry, developers, and private sector clients. Directly manage all phases of the survey process including estimating, proposals, project budgeting, office mapping, scheduling, field operations, and quality assurance. Interact regularly with engineers, County/City planners, contractors, and clients. Supervise computer draftsmen, land surveyors, instrumentmen, rodmen/chainmen, and internal support staff.

Representative project list includes:

- Right-of-way engineering -- 20-mile extension of Interstate 5 for the Department of Transportation.
- Topographic surveys -- over a dozen cellular tower sites for Pacific Cellular and PacTel Communications.
- Subdivision surveys -- mountain recreational subdivision developments (300-lot project; 80-acre project).
- Pole line staking and substation surveys -- Northwest Gas & Electric.
- A.L.T.A. surveys -- statewide lenders and title companies.

Accomplishments / Contributions:

- Successfully presented dozens of projects before the County Board of Supervisors and Planning Commission, winning approval for variances and parcel maps previously opposed in public hearings.
- Achieved consistent annual growth in revenue and profits, expanding staff from one part-time to eight full-time employees and doubling office space to accommodate increase in business.
- Earned reputation for quality, timely completion of projects, and total customer satisfaction.

SENIOR LAND SURVEYOR   6/73-6/79
Northwest Gas and Electric, Portland, Oregon

Directed survey crew of 4-6 on the $230 million Hood hydroelectric plant and other public works projects. Supervised layout of horizontal and vertical control, obtained data for microwave communication system and transmission tower lines, supervised construction staking of towers and switchyards, and performed Field Engineer responsibilities for route selection of over 50 miles of new power lines.

EDUCATION, LICENSURE, AFFILIATIONS

Bachelor of Science Degree, Land Surveying -- Oregon State University, Portland
Associate of Science Degree, Engineering -- Portland City College
Professional Land Surveyor (License #PLS 4998) -- State of Oregon
Member -- Oregon Land Surveyors Association and Surveyors Historical Society

•••

He was selected for an interview from a very competitive candidate list (resume writer's comments).

64

Surveyor. *Susan Britton Whitcomb, CPRW; Fresno, CA*

John T. Someone

1234 Country Road, Somewhere, Louisiana 00000 (318) 555-5555

OBJECTIVE

A challenging and rewarding **engineering/drafting position** with an innovative organization that offers opportunities for educational growth and advancement to upper management through the demonstration of my full potential.

HIGHLIGHTS OF QUALIFICATIONS

- Over eight years experience in engineering and drafting with knowledge in both structural and architectural buildings.
- Proficient in Intergraph Microstation and Autocad computer programs.
- Only draftsman for $6.8 million sawmill construction project; handled most of the design work.
- First draftsman on papermill project for Federal Paper Board Company with a budget of $110 million.

PROFESSIONAL EXPERIENCE

ARCHITECTURE FIRM, Somewhere, Louisiana
CADD Operator (December 1993 - November 1995)
Served as a member of a production team, utilizing Bentley System's Intergraph Microstation and MS Dos 6.0 to create architectural design drawings and plans for the construction of shopping malls and commercial/department stores.
- Launched layouts and followed through until construction on an extensive shopping mall project for Oak Hollow Mall in High Point, NC.
- Worked on numerous department store layouts and details for customers such as Dillards, JC Penney, Goodies, and Books-a-Million.
- Set up and organized an Archive Library of finished projects for future use and reference.

FISKE, HEARD & DANIEL, Anytown, Louisiana
Drafter II (February 1992 - December 1993)
Collaborated with engineers, architects, designers, and drafters of various disciplines to produce civil, structural & architectural design drawings on Pulp & Paper and Gas Compressor Station projects. Utilized Autocad, with a Structural Steel Template, Quick Dos, and Flexicon capabilities to design these drawings. Recent jobs include:
Federal Paper Board Company, Inc. , Paper Mill Modernization Project ($110 Million budget)
- Launched layouts for the addition of a refiner building & control center to Federal Paper Board Company's papermill in Riegelwood, NC. Implemented the structural steel and concrete designs for these buildings as conceived by engineers' calculation.
Michcon Gas Company, Engineering Services, Compressor Station Construction Project
- Instituted the design layouts of a compressor building and yard foundations at their Kalkaska County, MI compressor station, while updating the overall quality of other project drawings.
James River Corporation, Lime Kiln Installation Project
- Revised structural steel, concrete, and architectural drawings pertaining to the refiner and filter building areas of their mill in Naheola, AL. Strived to improve the consistency and accuracy of Design Layouts and formatted a floppy disk library of all project drawings at the customer's request.

This resume breaks down various project experience. Originally three pages, it included other work experience which I shortened to reflect only relevant work experience (resume writer's comments).

Resume Continued...

Drafter. *Melanie Douthit; West Monroe, LA*

John T. Someone   **Page 2**

HOWARD INDUSTRIES, INC., Laurel, MS
Design Drafter (August 1990 - February 1992)
Operated a network computer-aided design program to generate a complete bill of materials & detailed drawings for the construction of Three-Phase Padmount Electrical Transformers. Employed Autocad to revise drawings produced by the Network Logic Processor.
- Processed an average of 7 orders per week for utility and power company customers. Each order consisted of entering the initial design data into the Network system, updating the computer - data printouts and bills of materials, as well as ordering and revising the drawings, then releasing the order to a checker. Upon recieving the order back from checking, responsible for correcting errors, getting copies of all drawings, and issuing the order to the plant.
- Trained new personnel in the procudures of processing an order.

POWELL CONSTRUCTION & MAINTENANCE COMPANY, Howard, MS
Design Drafter (December 1987 - August 1990)
Engineered and designed layouts for the construction of sawmills, pole mills, paper mills, and their related equipment. conducted varioius board-drafting work involved to produce structual steel & concrete layouts and details, as well as shop fabrication drawings required on these projects. Some of these projects include:
Biewer-Wisconsin, Inc., Sawmill construction Project ($6.8 Million Budget)
- Pioneered the design layout of a Lumber and Waste Handling System for their new Prentice, WI location. Participated solo on this endeavor for approximately 8 months, then filled the position of Lead Drafter for the completion.
Barge Forest Products, Waste Handling System Design
- Designed a Chip-Loading System, consisting of a chip screen, a chip conveyor, and a railcar chip spreader for their Macon, MS sawmill. Laid out and detailed all related support steel and concrete foundation work.
Martin & Sons Lumber Company (Martco), Sawmill Turn-A-Round
- Designed a board "unscrambler" unit for the lumber handling system at their Lemoyen, LA mill. Created detailed drawings of this unit for shop fabrication purposes.

BYERS ENGINEERING, INC./AT & T Field Office, Hattiesburg, MS
Civil Drafter (December 1986 - November 1987)
Produced street, road, and highway layouts on an AT&T project to replace their existing buried telephone coaxial cable with another more technologically advanced version.
- Pinpointed the location of exisitng and new telephone cable along a route from Jackson, MS to New Orleans, LA through the use of inked civil and topographic drawings.

TENNESSEE GAS PIPELINE COMPANY, Houma, LA
Engineering Technician (Pipeline Inspector) (May 1981 - June 1986)
Supervised and inspected the construction of natural gas pipelines and their related facilities in the Gulf of Mexico and the southern portion of the United States.

EDUCATION

PEARL RIVER JUNIOR COLLEGE, Somewhere, MS
Associate of Applied Science- Architectural & Drafting Technology

UNIVERSITY OF SOUTHERN MISSISSIPPI, Hattiesburg, MS
Graphics and Commercial Art

Excellent References Available Upon Request.

RONNIE DRAKE

Graphic serves as an immediate eye-catcher.

12 Bronson Avenue, Brentwood, NY 11717 • (631) 988-3243 • cadlady@hotmail.com

Resume begins with a straightforward title rather than a wordy objective. ——(**CAD OPERATOR/DRAFTSPERSON**

QUALIFICATIONS

Summary of her technical and administrative skills.

- Offer eight years of field and office experience with New York/New Jersey-based engineering firms
- Maintain excellent technical skills in areas of cartography and industry-specific software
- Manage all phases of projects from field to finish, encompassing:
  Field: Subdivision, Construction, and Steel (precision) layout; boundary, ALTA, topographical, and environmental surveys; appropriation maps and wetland delineation
  Office: Manual and computerized drafting; title searches; legal descriptions; client relations, contractor negotiation and inventory control; and staff management

PROJECT HIGHLIGHTS

- *New Jersey Department of Transportation* — Pedestrian Bridge (Construction)
- *New Jersey Dormitory Authority* — The Five Boroughs (Appropriation Maps)
- *New Jersey Parks Department* — Wild Pond Park (Topographical/Layout)
- *Town of South Hamptons* — Bar Beach (ALTA/Topographical)
- *Westport Corp.* — Manny's, Spiegel, and Pennywhistle's at Southern State Mall (Construction/Steel)
- *Tri-way Building Co.* — Kiddy Time, Tutor Academy and East Kindergarten (Layout)
- *Structural Technical Co.* — County Grounds at Corvin West (Subdivision)
- *FJC Brothers* — Lawrence Captree, East Islip (Environmental)

TECHNICAL SKILLS

Equipment:		**Software:**	
	Nikon DTM820		AutoCAD 2000 release 14
	Nikon 750		SurvCADD 2000 release 14
	Sokkia SDR33		COGO
	Sokkia Set3		DTM
	Topcon		Contours
	Wild TC500		Windows 98
	Data Collector HP48/TDS Software		WordPerfect
	Levels (Leica, Wild and Nikon)		Quickbooks

PROFESSIONAL WORK HISTORY

Party Chief/Draftsperson, Suburban Technical Engineering, Oakdale, NY	1997 – present
Party Chief, Van Wyle, Turner & Harrison, East Islip, NY/Wayne, NJ	1995 – 1997
Party Chief, Henry, Powers & Leekman, Port Anderson, NY	1993 – 1995
Draftsperson/Rodperson, Coleman Bleekman, East Orange, NJ	1987 – 1993

EDUCATION

Associate in Applied Science, Drafting, Suffolk County Community College, NY 1992
Certificate of Completion, Blueprint Reading, Drafting and AutoCAD, BOCES, Deer Park, NY, 1987

Ronnie faxed her resume three times and was offered all three positions!

66

Drafter/CAD operator. *Ann Baehr, CPRW; Long Island, NY*

This person wanted to keep his options open for work in service, test, or manufacturing departments. The work is similar, so he needed only one resume.

WALTER G. MILTON

146 Jackson Drive, Palmyra, New York 14120 ● (716) 839-3635 ● wgm232@prestige.com

ENGINEERING, SERVICE, OR TEST TECHNICIAN

- Troubleshoot equipment usage, parts assembly, and production activities to identify problems and complete cost-effective repairs.
- Calibrate and use a wide variety of standard and specialized precision-measuring instruments and testing devices, including calipers, oscilloscopes, voltmeters, ohmmeters, and viscometers.
- Work from complex and involved drawings and specifications, such as schematics, wiring diagrams, engineering rework and change orders, parts layouts, and engineering/military standards.
- Set up machines to ensure efficient operation and high-quality production.
- Maintain accurate and detailed records and write procedures in ISO 9000 format.
- Utilize computers to prepare reports, develop spreadsheets, document corrective actions, track materials and returns, and run tests.
- Assist technical staff and provide instruction to co-workers and new employees.
- Demonstrate excellent communication and interpersonal skills and interact efficiently with production and engineering personnel.

This summary covers all the bases, and the list of accomplishments makes a strong case for his being very productive and highly regarded.

EXPERIENCE

1995–Present   HELFER ELECTRONICS, Rochester, NY
Engineering Technician
Operate over 20 different machines, including color and bar-code printers. Check for transmission and reflection densities. Analyze moisture content and correct irregularities. Verify machined parts against certification specifications. Conduct random audits to achieve smooth and uninterrupted operation.

Accomplishments:
- Reduced downtime by performing preventive maintenance and ensuring efficient machine operation.
- Improved steam cleaning of ink pans, resulting in 80% reduction of man-hours.
- Received Certificate of Excellence for assisting and training co-workers and exhibiting teamwork philosophy from both peer and supervisor standpoints.

1991–1995   LABEL-IT PRODUCTS, INC., West Henrietta, NY
Senior Technical Service Technician
Performed field service and bench repair of marking, labeling, ink-jet printing, and bar-code products. Trained customers, service-department technicians, and sales personnel in equipment operations. Serviced major accounts, such as Xerox, IBM, Kodak, and General Motors. Diagnosed and solved problems with computer hardware and software required to run products. Utilized a variety of instruments, including calipers, oscilloscopes, voltmeters, ohmmeters, gauges, and multimeters.

Accomplishments:
- Earned Gold Star Award for Outstanding Performance as Employee of the Year.
- Promoted to Senior Technician within first five months of employment.

1988–1991   NASHTRONICS, INC., Macedon, NY
Manufacturing Test Technician
Tested manufacturing processes and prototypes for airplane engines used in military and civilian applications. Developed motors from initial stage to final testing and shipment. Performed troubleshooting, identifying and resolving problems related to production, assembly, inventory, and repairs. Worked within government specifications and regulations.

EDUCATION AND AFFILIATION

Monroe Community College, Rochester, NY: <u>**A.A.S., Electrical Engineering Technology**</u>, 1988
SUNY College of Technology, Purchase, NY: <u>**Additional courses in**</u> ISO 9000, Total Quality Management, Soldering, Forklift Operations, AutoCAD 14, JIT Procedures, Introduction to Excel, Introduction to Word
Society of Manufacturing Engineers (SME): <u>**Member**</u>

Shows that his twelve-year-old degree has been updated.

67

Engineering technician. *Freddie Cheek, CPRW, CWDP; Amherst, NY*

RICHARD MEZARD

56 Forest Dr. ◆ Jacksonville, FL 32223
Ph: (734) 555-9996 ◆ e-mail: richmezard@hotmail.com

EXPERIENCE SUMMARY

Over 13 years of progressively responsible experience and measurable achievements in the electrical / engineering industry. Combine leadership strength with proven technical acumen and electrical knowledge to consistently drive results in productivity, cost management, quality and process.

PROFESSIONAL QUALIFICATIONS

- Software Engineering for Programmable Logic Controllers / Material Handling Conveyors and Automation Systems / Robots
- Electrical Controls for Industrial Automation Cells and Systems / Technical Writing / Technical Training
- Technical Needs Assessment / Systems Implementation / Applications Development / Project Engineering On-Site Management
- Technical Troubleshooting / Hardware Development and Engineering / Program Implementation
- Ability to read electrical, mechanical, hydraulic, pneumatic and instrumentation drawings

CAREER PROGRESSION

WEBB BROTHERS, INC. – Farmington, MI   1996 to Present
FIELD ENGINEER TECHNICIAN

Manage wide variety of field engineering technician activities including start-up and debugging for this worldwide $250M material-handling company. Manage efforts of five electricians, direct daily crew assignments and oversee scope of project from initial startup phase to successful completion. Provide troubleshooting and training of customer technicians, resolve customer issues and offer production support relating to customer and/or vendor issues. Perform technical writing of programs and project documentation and complete punch/deficiency list and standby requirements per customer contract specifications.

Key Contributions

- Boosted cycle time and trimmed downtime ($10K/minute) by developing alert system for conveyor system faultage.
- Corrected critical material design flaw by implementing control/logic fix and a system misalignment by changing parameters in VFD (Variable Frequency Drive).
- Developed standard block of code that was eventually integrated by other engineers in their programs.
- Interceded on stalled job and managed completion of necessary actions to deliver project on time.

These are emphasized to indicate the value he brought to each position.

JEFFERSON SYSTEMS – Troy, MI   1993 to 1996
ELECTRICAL ENGINEER

Promoted to electrical engineer position after just six months as lead technician, with responsibility for performing extensive design of software, panels, conveyor-device layouts and various models of conveyor systems. Supervised efforts of electrical staff of 3 and managed troubleshooting and tuning of systems.

Key Contributions

- Developed an Elpo delivery system and hook conveyor to replace obsolete procedure.
- Proactively studied software, hardware, national electric codes and literature to successfully transition into role of electrical engineer.

ELECTRIC CONTROLS, INC. – Dearborn, MI   1988 to 1993
FOREMAN/ELECTRICIAN

Initially hired as apprentice electrician before assuming role of job foreman. Supervised 9 direct reports; scheduled assignments, hours and manpower. Trained electricians in various jobs and resolved internal conflicts.

TECHNICAL SKILLS ⟩ *This provides a concise listing of his important qualifications.*

Ladder logic on Allen-Bradley PLC 2, 3 and 5 using AB 6200,-AI, Modicon and Taylor; RSLogix 5000, RSLinx, RSNetWorx, ControlLogix, SLC-5, 500, HMI using PanelBuilder, Mitsubishi programmable controllers, PC-based controls using FloPro, Wonderware, Visual Basic version 4.0 & 6.0, Devicenet and ControlNet.

68

Engineering technician. *Kim Little, JCTC; Victor, NY*

This resume was specifically targeted to the automotive industry, which uses engineers with aerospace backgrounds.

JACK WILLIAMS

5469 Squirrel Lake Road – Trenton, MI 48180

(555) 231-2110 (Home) – (556) 456-9878 (Cell) – williams@mediaone.com

AERONAUTICAL ENGINEER

Award-winning Project Manager and Product Engineer with expertise in identification of the root cause of hardware and software problems. 10+ years of experience in technology including combustion, structural, mechanical, electrical, and computer control. Expertise in process control, problem solving, and quality-improvement techniques. Background with state-of-the-art computer simulators. Excellent communication and team-building skills. Degree in Aeronautical Engineering.

- Project Management
- Systems Maintenance
- Research and Development

- Technical Problem Solving
- Engineering Design
- Cost Reduction

PROFESSIONAL EXPERIENCE

NASA–Johnson Space Center, Houston, TX
Held assignments in areas with the most problems, due to ability to substantially reduce the number and frequency of those problems.

Experiment Designer/Shuttle Upgrade Team Member, 1995–Present

Challenged to integrate controls and power requirements with new computer and electrical systems while maintaining operational capabilities of the current hydraulic system. Briefed management and tested hardware with simulators.

- Produced qualifications for actuators, gears, and power supplies that met the operational requirements of the space shuttle.
- Defined specifications for electromechanical actuator system to replace the hydraulic system.
- Devised long-term contamination control plan for propellant-production plant on Mars. Defined testing needed to classify Martian environment and to ascertain the effects of Martian dust on filtration devices.
- Designed filtration experiment for Martian Lander as part of the long-term contamination control plan. Provided detailed schedule for experiment design, test, evaluation, and manufacture.

Space-Station Propulsion Component Designer, 1992–1995

Developed requirements for the components of the space-station propulsion module and ground-support equipment. Managed R&D and testing of components (thrusters, valves, propellant storage tanks, filters, heaters, and instrumentation) to ensure compliance with requirements. Resolved thruster chamber pressure-spiking problem. Recommended and scheduled biweekly status meetings with upper management to keep management up to date on technical and schedule issues. (Recommendation implemented.) Utilized rigid body dynamics to determine component-loading and vibration requirements.

- Designated co-leader of team that planned servicing systems for propulsion modules.
  - Resolved technical and schedule problems associated with hardware development.
  - Reduced maintenance time 10% for propulsion modules by initiating design changes.
  - Resolved thruster-valve design problems by initiating a new design that reduced cost by 25% and improved schedule by 6 months.

69

Aeronautical engineer. *Sally McIntosh, NCRW, CPRW, JCTC; Jacksonville, IL*

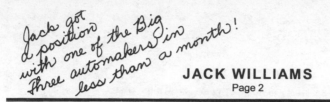

Jack got a position with one of the Big Three automakers in less than a month!

JACK WILLIAMS
Page 2

Assistant System Manager, Orbital Maneuvering System, 1989–1992

Provided technical management of the Orbital Maneuvering System (OMS) on the space shuttle fleet. Developed structural-load simulations for use in creation of hardware design elements. Trained astronauts on the capabilities and design of the OMS system.

❖ Served as team leader for the OMS and Reaction Control Systems (RCS) Fleet Leader Test Program. Defined scope of the OMS/RCS test program. Utilized test program to identify and resolve hardware problems before the shuttle fleet was affected. Measured vibration and analyzed frequency for detecting and analyzing combustion instabilities; rigid body dynamics used to determine component-loading and vibration requirements. Designed requirements for developing, testing, and using simulators for systems testing OMS and RCS.

♦ Shortened flight turnaround time by four weeks.

♦ Reduced costs 99% ($1M to $10K) and turnaround time to 2 weeks (from 6–12 months) by initiating reaction-control thruster-repair program. Resolved in-flight and ground turnaround and explosive residue problems without affecting schedule.

♦ Eliminated one week of ground testing between missions by developing new on-orbit checkout procedures to test Shuttle OMS/RCS systems on-orbit instead of on the ground.

❖ Developed procedures and ground support equipment for testing the zero-gravity propellant-acquisition devices. Trained engineers and technicians on the use of equipment.

❖ Reduced component removal and replacement. Lowered contamination of system and associated contamination-related problems with systems while maintaining overall performance requirements.

❖ Presented Silver Snoopy Award for significant contributions to shuttle safety by Eileen Collins, the first female Shuttle Commander. (Award given to less than 1% of NASA and contractor workforce.)

Liquid Propulsion Systems Engineer, 1986–1989

Engineered post-Challenger checkout procedures for the Shuttle Orbital Maneuvering System and the Shuttle Reaction Control System. Redesigned Reaction Control System thrusters to include added safety features. Monitored testing of Orbital Maneuvering and Reaction Control Systems. Reviewed shuttle payloads to ensure propulsion systems met the requirements to fly on the shuttles. Certified maintenance depots for performing routine maintenance on shuttle components. Oversaw testing of the Orbital Maneuvering and Reaction Control Systems for the shuttle.

❖ Pioneered and certified procedures and hardware for testing the Shuttle Orbital Maneuvering and Reaction Control Systems.

❖ Managed the redesign of shuttle thrusters.

EDUCATION

B.S. in Aeronautical Engineering, Purdue University, West Lafayette, IN, 1986

Computer Experience — IBM, Mac, HP, VAX, Cray, MS Office, Artimus, MS Project, Pro-Engineer, Ada, VMS, DOS, MacOS, Windows, X-Windows, Unigraphics, Unix

Seminars and Additional Training — ISO-9000, Automotive Mechanics, Design of Experiments, Orbital Mechanics, Cryogenic Engineering, Dynamic Systems Engineering, Creative Team Problem Solving, Pro-Engineer, Statistical Process Control, Productive Meeting Management, Project Management, Situational Leadership, Influence and Leadership, Contract Management, Time Management, Effective Briefings, Effective Oral Presentations

Although most chemical engineers work in the production of chemicals, Darwin applied his technical knowledge to several industries.

Darwin Glassman

12566 Nancylynn Lane   Tempe, AZ 55555   (555) 000-0000

SUMMARY OF QUALIFICATIONS:

- Experienced Journeyman Pipe Fitter/Plumber Foreman/Chemical Engineer/Facilities Manager....

- Trained/supervised crew of 6 for installation of hazardous piping....

- Skilled at Clean Room protocol/piping installations....

- Provided QC inspections of all materials/work to assure use of proper pipe/fittings....

- Expertise in DI water systems/industrial waste lines/supply side/ potable/non-potable/deionized water systems/hazardous waste....

- Detailed/designed Alpha/Beta installations without aid of blueprints... trained detailers to design areas....

- Utilized transitional piping concept for all line connects....concept became state-of-the-art concept for piping procedures....

- Built new Hazardous Waste Room....pre-fabbed gas/liquid systems/ supplies/returns....

- Recommended installation/hook-up/pressure testing of systems be handled by one group....created significant savings of time/money....

- Constructed prototype of Enfield piping....brought project in under bid/ no leaks....brought project in at 25% of labor time allowed....

- Formulated concrete ....added mixes to test for strength/durability....

- Designed vessels/chemical processes for manufacture of soaps....

- Conceived plans for new processing tanks....

- Excellent communication skills....creative....innovative....adaptable.... problem solver....seek challenges....team player....strong leader....

EDUCATION/TRAINING:

CALIFORNIA POLYTECHNICAL INSTITUTE - Pomona, CA
Bachelor of Science: Chemical Engineering

CERTIFICATIONS:
Journeyman Pipefitter/Plumber - Orbital Welding - Silver Soldering Soldering Med Gas - DI/PVDF Installs - Enfield/ASAHI/Fuseal/ Ryan-Herco - Plastics: PVC/ABS/CPVC - Hazardous Waste Piping

70

Chemical engineer/pipefitter/hazardous plumber. *Fran Holsinger; Tempe, AZ*

His many certifications and qualifications should open greater opportunities.

PROFESSIONAL HIGHLIGHTS:

JOURNEYMAN PIPE FITTER/PLUMBER/FOREMAN

- ◇ Installed hazardous piping lines for new FAB-C wing at Micron....
- ◇ Built piping/ racks to handle acids/slurry/waste lines....utilized double containment pipes....
- ◇ Designated as *Key Person* during raw/finish construction....authorized to make emergency modifications....
- ◇ Handled live tie-in/tie-ins....
- ◇ Designed/constructed pipe layout for DI water system 10,000 gallon storage tank....
- ◇ Recorded As-Built deviations....
- ◇ Directed complete installation of numerous piping projects....
- ◇ Fabricated solvent waste systems/pickling/hydraulic/hazardous exhaust lines....
- ◇ Assembled complete RAS/WAS Pump Station single-handedly....

FACILITIES MANAGER

- ◇ Performed Scale Master duties for concrete company....
- ◇ Loaded/unloaded rail cars....transferred loads....
- ◇ Dispatched/routed materials....
- ◇ Ordered materials: cement/fly ash/silica sand....

CHEMICAL ENGINEER

- ◇ Oversaw chemical processes to manufacture soaps....
- ◇ Directed feasibility studies....implemented design program....
- ◇ Designed processing tanks/vessels....
- ◇ **Promoted** to included Production Engineering....

RACE MASTER

- ◇ Supervised complete "day of" race activities....
- ◇ Instrumental in raising $20 million for charities over 5 year period...

EMPLOYERS:

MICRON TECHNOLOGIES - Boise, ID
   Pipe Fitter Foreman: 1996
MOTOROLA/MOS-21/MOS-12/CS-1 - Mesa/Tempe, AZ
   Plumber/Hazardous Plumber: 1993 - 1996
KAISER STEEL/CSI - Fontana, CA
   Pipe Fitter/Welder: 1993
JATC/Riverside Local #364 - Colton, CA
   Apprentice Pipe Fitter/Plumber: 1987 - 1992
4TH ST. ROCK CRUSHER - San Bernadino, CA
   Facilities Manager: 1983 - 1987
RACE CENTRAL - San Bernadino, CA
   Race Master: 1981 - 1986
PILOT CHEMICAL CO. - Santa Fe Springs, CA
   Chemical/Design/Production Engineer: 1980 - 1982

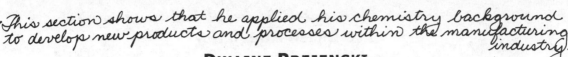

This section shows that he applied his chemistry background to develop new products and processes within the manufacturing industry.

DWAINE PREJENSKI

912 Dinlock Parkway
San Jose, CA 57522

408-277-8620
dprejenski@cs.com

Product Development Leader / Manufacturing Manager / Applied Chemist

Professional career reflects over 20 years of creative leadership and visionary capacities in complex, competitive, and highly regulated manufacturing environments. Established strategic plans, introduced systems, and developed operational overhauls that transformed corporate credibility and generated significant profit. Experience includes custom-design products and patent development in existing and start-up operations. Multiple product backgrounds include medical equipment, laboratory devices, and high-tech informational-storage systems.

Oversee all aspects of product development, manufacturing, finance, marketing, sales, risk management, raw materials utilization, and cost containment with a keen eye to detail. Intuitive understanding for customer expectation has led to a commitment to quality and the development of long-term consumer relations.

Selected Accomplishments

This section high-lights his strong record of accomplishments and notable contributions to productivity and cost reduction.

- Engineering experience extend to operation of 500 personnel, in a $300M division of a global manufacturing/distribution company with annual revenues in excess of $2B
- Key liaison between senior management and workforce to implement ISO 9000 & ISO 9001
- Led the charge to produce and commercially market floppy-disk data-storage systems for 3M, with annual sales over $300M for 15 consecutive years.
- Coordinated process and equipment overhaul to increase production yield from 14% to 97%.
- Reduced expenses $8M in 12 months, while sales grew $50M.
- Designed custom products now in consideration for patent; awarded "Most Innovative Process" and "Golden Step" awards for new product and team efforts.
- Researched operational processes of competitors to determine viability to utilize In-Line Activation; introduced control-system modifications that cut production down-time from more than 10% to less than 3%, while reducing defective-part output from 20% to less than 1%.
- Established production overhaul to reduce material and hazardous waste by 34%.

Career History

Product Development Strategist
Independent Contracts
Designed custom medical equipment for cardiovascular and diverse surgical applications.

1996—present
San Jose, California

Senior Process Engineer
Imagi-Corp
Responsible for laboratory technique and processes, equipment utilization, instrumentation, and quality control in data-cartridge and computer-tape manufacture

1993–1995
San Marillo, California

Manufacturing Process Engineer
GDM Production Company
Replaced antiquated magnetic slurry technology with industry-leading process technology. Responsible for equipment, process, product, materials and personnel to convert "tired system" to a world-class operation.

1985–1993
Catalina, California

Education and Affiliation

Bachelor of Science in Chemistry, Purdue University, West Lafayette, Indiana

Additional training in Lotus Notes, Excel, Word, PowerPoint, Sigma Plot, PLC Ladder Logic, Measurex Vision 2002, Wonderware systems, Maintenance Management System, and microprocessor machine language programming.

Active member of the American Society of Mechanical Engineers.

References Available Upon Establishment of Mutual Interest

71

Applied chemist. *Richard Lanham, MDiv, MA, MRE, CCM; Indianapolis, IN*

Mr. Rodriguez's resume emphasizes the breadth of his experience.

Frederico Rodriguez

P.O. Box 431
Ahmadi 62000
Kuwait

Tel: 965-366-1629
E-mail: rodriguezf@yahoo.com

270 NW 8196 Street
Miami, FL 33170
USA

SUMMARY

Civil Engineer with more than 5 years of project management, project engineering, and supervisory experience on projects ranging from $50K up to $150MM. Worked in multinational, multidisciplinary team settings. Communicate effectively with people at all levels. Dedicated, meticulous, capable of managing numerous projects at the same time. Excellent planning, analytical, and problem-solving skills.

EXPERIENCE

His resume highlights his multi-national and linguistic skills, which are important for a person wanting to travel worldwide while working for an American company.

Civil/Construction Engineer (1997–Present)
STEVENS ENGINEERING, LTD., Kuwait
- Serve as first Civil/Structural Engineer of a $150MM project for Kuwait Construction Company, the largest project in northern Kuwait. New center replaces old one destroyed during Gulf War.
- Supervise contractors and subcontractors on the project — 1,200 workers on site daily.
- Plan, schedule, and manage each phase of construction, including site preparation, earthwork, structural, buildings, drainage systems, shelters, and road work. Knowledgeable about piping, mechanical, electrical, and instrumentation.
- Ensure compliance with all governmental regulations as well as company specifications and standards for both quality and safety.
- Participate in, and sometimes lead, weekly construction meetings.
- Write site instructions, field memos, progress reports, and other correspondence.

Project Engineer (1997)
DIMENSIONS CONSTRUCTION, Miami, FL
- Engineered several phases of a $20MM construction contract for the Miami Medical Center main campus and 8 affiliates.
- Oversaw project planning, budgeting, scheduling, material take-offs, and construction of 9 ongoing projects ranging from $50K to $200K. Upgraded several facilities including multi-complex structures, utility buildings, training towers, and scientific laboratories.

Civil Engineer (1993–1997)
U.S. FEDERAL EMERGENCY MANAGEMENT AGENCY, Wilson, NC
- Managed a variety of civil and infrastructure construction projects following Hurricane Floyd's devastation of North Carolina. Projects included government, commercial, industrial, and residential structures; wastewater treatment facilities; and bridges.
- Directed project planning and development, budgeting, funding analysis, design approval and inspection, code compliance, project overview, status assessment, and close-out.
- Supervised a team of engineers, attorneys, and accountants.
- Served as the liaison among contractors, owners, and governmental agencies.

Consultant (1990–1993)
LEARNING RESOURCES, Fort Lauderdale, FL
- Developed and led seminars, workshops, and professional development courses to prepare students for board exams, professional registrations, and college/grad school entrance exams.
- Taught courses in mathematics, engineering, and natural sciences.

Professor Assistant (1989–1992)
CLEMSON UNIVERSITY, DEPARTMENT OF CIVIL ENGINEERING, Clemson, SC
- Developed and taught upper-level university engineering courses in Statistics, Strength of Materials, and Structural Analysis.

EDUCATION

M.S., Construction Management, University of Miami (1996)
B.S., Architectural/Civil Engineering, Clemson University, Clemson, SC (1992)

AFFILIATION

PE Intern: American Society of Civil Engineers

COMPUTERS

AutoCAD, Word, Excel, PowerPoint, Lotus 1-2-3

LANGUAGES

Fluent in Spanish and English; some knowledge of Arabic

Within three months, Mr. Rodriguez secured a new job with an American firm doing business in Europe & the Middle East.

72

Civil engineer. *Karen McMahan, JCTC; Durham, NC*

FRED SMITH

2764 Lark Street • Cupertino, CA 95245 • (408) 567-6789
fred@cs.com

OBJECTIVE: Electrical Engineer

PROFESSIONAL SUMMARY:
Innovative and self-motivated Electrical Engineer with extensive experience in high-end DASD disk drive control unit architecture and design. Skilled at building and working with different technical teams to successfully design, implement, simulate, and test complex logic designs.

WORK EXPERIENCE:

1985–Present   **IBM,** San Jose, California

Advisory Electrical Engineer / Technical Team Leader   1995–present
Architected and designed ESCON Channel Attachment logic for advanced RAID-5 CU Subsystem.
- Created two sub-teams tackling two main architectures, resolving major design issues in a more timely manner.
- Saved $2.4 million in development costs through creative chip redesign, keeping chip in original package size without loss of function.
- Integrated late architecture changes while still delivering chip on schedule.
- Developed and implemented plan for 10-person design-verification team when simulation area was determined to be understaffed.

Advisory Electrical Engineer / Logic Designer   1995–1996
Modified existing design of ESCON Channel Adapter Hardware for the 3990 Control Unit.
- Led sufficient simulation effort resulting in the on-time delivery of a defect-free design that powered up successfully.

Advisory Electrical Engineer / Technical Team Leader   1994–1995
Supervised and assisted logic design team responsible for DASD device attachment logic module for high-end supercomputer storage subsystem.
- Architected, designed, and simulated processor-based controller module for three independent disk read-write heads.

Staff Electrical Engineer / Logic Designer   1991–1994
Designed, implemented, and simulated receiver functional island for 9340 ESCON Channel Adapter Module.
- Implemented successful design-verification plan, eliminating the need for one design pass and resulting in $100K savings.

Senior Associate Electrical Engineer / Logic Designer   1987–1990
Resolved design and architecture issues arising from unique requirements of various product groups implementing new ESCON architecture.
- Represented Storage Division when negotiating the common ESCON architecture protocols.
- Developed ESCON standard CRC algorithm and benchmark tests.
- Defined the optical power control interface.
- Reduced by 30% the chip physical design and manufacturing cycle time for logic changes through new EC methodology still in use today.

EDUCATION: B.S., Electrical Engineering—San Jose State University

COMPUTER SKULLS: UNIX, IBM MVS/TSO, IBM VM/CMS, MS-DOS, and Windows

Note his use of numbers and emphasis on results.

73

Electrical engineer. *Gary E. Watkins; San Jose, CA*

John Edward Rameriz

eddierameriz@ieee.org

1004 Florida Ave.
Ellwsorth, IA 50014
(515) 382-8888

ELECTRICAL ENGINEER

Over five years of experience in analog circuit design with special expertise in LDO (Linear Regulator), including three years at Texas Instruments, Inc. Combine technical, analytical, and engineering qualifications for new product development, testing, and design verification to benefit the manufacture of integrated circuits meeting time-to-market demands. Unique combination of electrical and mechanical engineering background. Currently pursuing Master of Science degree in Electrical Engineering.

EDUCATION

This section allows an employer to see immediately John's unique combination of mechanical and electrical degrees.

IOWA STATE UNIVERSITY, AMES, IA
Electrical Engineering, Master of Science (currently attending)

WASHINGTON STATE UNIVERSITY, PULLMAN, WA
Electrical Engineering, Bachelor of Science 1995
Mechanical Engineering, Bachelor of Science 1994

Engineer-in-Training (June 1994)

Engineering Design Projects:
Development of an Anti-Lock Braking System for HEV
Design of A/D converter for PCM CODEC
Design of Voice SAR for ATM Network

Strategy was the name of the game for John. He was applying for an engineering position at the college he was attending, so his resume lists his educational information right after his profile.

AREAS OF EMPHASIS

A combination format was used here so his areas of expertise could appear on the front page, highlighting his crucial experience at well known Texas Instruments.

DESIGN –

- Conducted simulation, layout, and design verification at system and subsystem levels for Texas Instruments, Inc., cornerstone project; performed post-design verification, top-level simulations, laboratory analysis and characterization for second major project.
    - → Acted as liaison for Marketing, Manufacturing, Product Engineering, and Process Development departments.
- Designed support for Switch Mode Power Supply (SMPS) controllers.
- Designed analysis of Pulse Width Modulated (PWM) and Pulse Frequency Modulation (PFM) control schemes for SMPS controllers.

DESIGN VERIFICATION –

- Evaluated applicable use and ensured specifications for laboratory analysis and characterization of SMPS controller and Electro Luminescent (EL) Lamp Drivers.
    - → Provided marketing support and successfully launched new product into marketplace.
- Provided laboratory analysis and characterization of prototype ICs.

PROCESSING AND MANUFACTURING –

- Communicated with suppliers for tool capabilities and facilities requirements.
- Developed specifications for operations and maintenance of machine tools; developed fab-wide support tools requirements list.

Continued on Page Two

74

Electrical engineer. *Marcy Johnson, CPRW, CEIP; Story City, IA*

John Edward Rameriz
Page Two

WORK HISTORY

<u>**MICREL SEMICONDUCTOR / ELECTRONIC TECHNOLOGY CORPORATION**</u>, HUXLEY, IA   **1999 – PRESENT**
Design Engineer

Developed cornerstone design as member of 5-person engineering team working to achieve goal of establishing basic standard set of products and power management solutions to transition company focus from ASIC (Application Specific Integrated Circuits).

<u>**TEXAS INSTRUMENTS INC.,**</u> **DALLAS, TX 1996 – 1999**
Mixed Signal IC Designer — Power Management Products   1997 – 1999

Provided transistor-level design of analog Integrated Circuits (IC) to meet customer-specific goals and requirements for Fortune 500 Texas Instruments Inc.

Equipment Engineer — DMOS6 Wafer Fabrication Facility   1996 – 1997

Pursued company mission to establish flagship wafer-fabrication facility as part of elite 50-member start-up team.

ADDITIONAL EXPERIENCE

<u>**WASHINGTON STATE UNIVERSITY**</u>, PULLMAN, WA   **1991 – 1996**
Energy Conservation Engineer — Housing Services Maintenance   1994 – 1996

- Evaluated and analyzed energy usage in residence halls, developed energy conservation programs, and coordinated student conservation efforts.

Engineering Research Aide — Department of Mechanical Engineering   1991 – 1993

- Assembled experimental force dynamometer for grant from Boeing, Inc.
- Installed numerical control system on a production-milling machine.

<u>**USDA-ARS, SOUTHERN REGIONAL RESEARCH CENTER**</u>, NEW ORLEANS, LA   **1987 – 1990**
Mechanical Engineering Aide

- Produced and analyzed experimental composite yarns.
- Received recognition and cash award for service, USDA-ARS 1990.

TECHNICAL SKILLS

Cadence EDA tools, PSPICE, AutoCAD, Mathematical Analysis Software.
Programming in C and FORTRAN.

AFFILIATIONS

American Society of Mechanical Engineers
Institute for Electrical and Electronic Engineers

This two-page resume emphasizes results and rapid increase in responsibilities

EDWARD ENGINEER

119 Old Stable Road
Lynchburg, Virginia 24503
Home (804) 384-4600 Work (804) 384-4600

MANAGEMENT PROFESSIONAL
Engineer / Management / Consultant

Six years experience in the design, development and leadership of large-scale corporate actions to improve productivity, quality and efficiency. Facilitated significant cost savings through expertise in:

- Reengineering
- Continuous Improvement
- Statistical Design/Analysis
- Quality/Productivity Training

- Process Control & Improvement
- Manufacturing Methods
- Team Building/Team Leadership
- Project Management

PROFESSIONAL EXPERIENCE

Advanced Manufacturing & Process Engineer   1991 to Present
THE CORPORATION, Lynchburg, Virginia

Recruited into the corporation's Management Development Program and placed on a fast-track career path. Rotated through a series of increasingly responsible assignments in Engineering, Operations, Corporate Quality, Distribution and Manufacturing at The Corporation facilities in the U.S., Latin America and Europe.

Manufacturing Division, Lynchburg, Virginia (1993 to Present)

Promoted from Management Development Program to permanent professional position in Corporation's largest operating division (four business units with 5000+ employees and 15 manufacturing facilities throughout the U.S.). Given full responsibility and decision-making authority for design, development, implementation and leadership of an aggressive waste reduction program for raw materials, WIP and finished product.

Challenged to advocate program implementation and win the support of manufacturing management and staff throughout this nationwide division. Established cross-functional management teams (e.g., Quality, Manufacturing, R&D, Engineering) at each facility to research and identify specific areas for cost reduction within their organizations. Scope of responsibility includes process redesign, new product introduction, materials handling and resource management.

- Generated over $10 million in savings within first year with an additional $15+ million projected for 1995.

Results

Manufacturing Division, Caracas, Venezuela (1992 to 1993)

Planned and directed an aggressive program to optimize plant layout and methods for this multi-million dollar converting operation. Established, trained and managed a continuous improvement team of four professionals to facilitate project implementation and ongoing productivity improvements.

- Decreased material handling by 50% and reduced space requirements by 650 sqm.

- Designed and implemented Kanban system resulting in a 33% increase in productivity and 50% reduction in inventory.

- Decreased CCT by 50% to meet the corporation's performance objectives and reduced production costs by 15%.

75

Industrial engineer. *Wendy S. Enelow, CPRW, JCTC, CCM; Lynchburg, VA*

EDWARD ENGINEER   **Page Two**

Electronic Products Division, Silicon Valley, California (1991)

Introduced improved process control methodologies into an electronic cable assembly operation. Complemented changes to the manufacturing process with on-site training, feedback loops and designer/trainer involvement.

- Increased yield to 95% to meet IBM's quality supplier status requirements.

Industrial Engineering Consultant   1990
CONSUMER PRODUCTS MANUFACTURER, Bogota, Columbia

Completed two-month consulting assignment to troubleshoot and upgrade specific manufacturing areas for this large consumer products manufacturer.

- Designed sampling plan as the foundation for a plant-wide preventive maintenance program.

- Wrote software program to maximize plant capacity with minimal equipment, personnel and materials.

Assistant Industrial Engineer   1988 to 1990
INDUSTRIAL MANUFACTURER, Bronson, Michigan

Recruited for four internships while completing studies at the University of Michigan. Earned an excellent reputation for expertise in statistical theory and application.

- Invented a new measuring tool for shop materials that was subsequently utilized throughout the manufacturing facility.

- Planned and led 17 capability studies of specific product characteristics to determine their compliance with customer specifications. Utilized SPC techniques to measure product tolerances and performance.

- Conducted a large in-plant industrial experiment to identify improved process control methods to upgrade manufacturing and product capabilities.

Assistant Industrial Engineer   1988 to 1989
HOSPITAL, Detroit, Michigan

- Conducted a series of productivity monitoring and analysis projects throughout the manufacturing facility to validate worksheet model and variance analysis methodologies.

- Redesigned the corporation's central computer area to improve workflow, productivity and efficiency of operations. Orchestrated complete reconfiguration of equipment, personnel and infrastructure.

- Evaluated software prior to acquisition to determine its validity for specific flowcharting and reporting functions.

EDUCATION

B.S., Triple Major in Industrial Engineering, Mathematics & Statistics, 1991
UNIVERSITY OF MICHIGAN, Ann Arbor, Michigan

- Completed short-term projects with professors in the Engineering and Mathematics Departments. Conducted research experimentation, collected/analyzed data and reported results. Wrote code for random number generator algorithms.

PERSONAL PROFILE

Born in U.S. Lived in Portugal, Spain, Brazil and Denmark. Enjoy windsurfing, skiing and travel.

This resume was written to show Keith's qualifications for a position that did not exist at the company he was targeting! He was successful in influencing the company to create the position for him.

KEITH M. HICKSEY

47 North Bay Drive — West Chester, PA 19103 — 610-442-5116 — engineer@msn.com

TECHNICAL ANALYST

Senior-level electron microscopy specialist with more than 15 years' experience in industrial service laboratories. Utilized SEM, TEM, STEM, and EMPA to perform materials and product characterization in support of research, process development, and manufacturing. Competent and effective in managing an SEM / TEM materials characterization / FMA lab.

Repeated recognition for talent and expertise in a wide range of sample preparation techniques. Proven capability to use optical and electron microscopes for problem solving. Excellent hand-eye coordination, visual communication abilities, and spatial relationship skills. Unparalleled operating precision.

Skill set readily applicable to microelectronic materials and device characterization and failure mode analysis (FMA). Prepared and analyzed samples of devices based on InP, GaAS, and Si substrates for SEM and TEM. Analyzed optoelectronic (laser, modulator, detector, InP HBT) and semiconductor (CMOS, BiCMOS, RAM, RF) devices and materials.

TECHNICAL SKILL SET

- Electron / Optical Microscopy
- TEM / SEM Materials Characterization
- TEM / SEM Sample Preparation
- EDS / WDS Microanalysis

- Metallography
- Defect Analysis / Detection
- Macrophotography
- Laboratory Testing

EXPERIENCE

NATIONAL ENGINEERING SYSTEMS, Northampton, PA

Process Engineer — Optoelectronics Division, 10/00 to Present

Characterize structure of devices and materials through Scanning Electron Microscopy (SEM). Support design, process, and manufacturing engineering teams, as well as Failure Mode Analysis (FMA) and Metrology Lab. Immediately contribute to high-priority product-development projects. Consistently reduce entire process cycle time by routinely resolving process-development and manufacturing SEM characterization issues.

Accomplishments:

- Assigned ownership of Hitachi S-4700 FE-SEM; assumed full management and maintenance responsibilities for this equipment just two months after being hired. Train and certify users.
- Introduced and established Unified Technology Corp.'s Multiprep Polishing System, thus solving sample preparation problems and providing answers to critical characterization questions. Initiated contact with the Unified vendor, consulted with the lead applications engineer and sales representatives, then purchased supplies and outlined protocol for use.

SEMINCONDUCTOR NATIONAL, INC., Mesa, AZ

Senior Technician — Process & Materials Characterization Lab, 6/00 to 10/00

Conducted Transmission Electron Microscopy (TEM) sample preparation and materials characterization of semiconductor products, supporting research and development engineering teams and six wafer-fabrication facilities. Also analyzed samples on Hitachi FE-SEM.

Maintained and upgraded electron microscopes and supporting instrumentation. Provided training to junior technicians.

(continued)

76

Materials engineer/technical analyst. *Jewel Bracy DeMaio, CPRW, CEIP; Royersford, PA*

KEITH M. HICKSEY
610-442-5116 — engineer@msn.com

Senior Technician — Process & Materials Characterization Lab, continued

Accomplishments:

- Mastered application of the Union West Technology Tripod Polishing System for preparing Cross-section and Planar TEM Samples in just one month, then maximized its use, thus dramatically increasing overall lab production and yielding significant fab cost savings.

- Assumed responsibility for the high-priority development project, MRAM (magnetic tunnel junction) in the TEM lab. Collaborated with the engineering team to identify TEM requirements and priorities. Refined techniques to prepare high-difficulty samples. Observed, analyzed, and recorded structures in TEM.

- Demonstrated extremely sharp technical skills, including the ability to cross-section a 0.25 micron via and freestanding 1 micron feature. Received repeated recognition for superior sample preparation techniques, particularly noting sample thinness and preparation of samples for HR-TEM.

PENNSYLVANIA STEEL CORPORATION, Harrisburg, PA

Analyst — Research Department Electron Optics & Metallography Lab, 10/87 to 6/00

Performed materials characterization and defect analysis supporting research, development, processing, and quality control for the manufacture and application of steel products in three major production facilities. Conducted technical analysis utilizing TEM, SEM, EMPA and STEM. Produced TEM, SEM, and optical metallography samples.

Accomplishments:

- Supported operations of both the Electron and Metallography Laboratories by preparing and analyzing a wide range of research and production samples and by functioning as a liaison for up to 40 engineers.

- Developed and perfected difficult and novel sample preparation techniques for TEM to solve previously indeterminable technical issues. Specifically, introduced and perfected a technique for TEM cross-sections of zinc-coated sheet steel using ultramicrotomy to analyze interface.

- Supervised instrumentation service and maintenance; ordered, monitored, and tested all supplies. Sourced new equipment and vendors to facilitate the laboratory's characterization goals.

PROFESSIONAL TRAINING

HARRISBURG TECHNICAL UNIVERSITY, Harrisburg, PA

- Analytical Electron Microscopy
- Postgraduate Electron Microscopy
- TEM & SEM Sample Preparation
- Metallography

EDUCATION

PHILADELPHIA TECHNICAL INSTITUTE, West Chester, PA
Bachelor of Science Degree — Earth Science, Minor — Geology, 1987

Graphic adds a nice touch.

Raymond J. Smithson

1432 Bellvue Street • Chicago, Illinois 60042
Phone: 847-231-4533 • E-mail: rjsmith@yahoo.com

Summary of Qualifications

Mechanical Engineer and Production Supervisor with extensive plastics molding, die-casting, wave solder and SMT experience. Skilled at resolving complex manufacturing problems, refining production capabilities, and reducing work in progress. Demonstrated ability to increase productivity and decrease costs without compromising product quality. Interact effectively with Design, Process, and Quality Departments to ensure product quality and producibility. Open for relocation.

Areas of expertise include:

strong keyword summary.

Project management	Productivity improvements
Cost reduction strategies	JIT & lean manufacturing
Statistical process control (SPC)	Labor relations
Quality control	ISO 9000
Process documentation	Vendor relations
Team leadership & training	OSHA & environmental compliance

Professional Experience

MARTIN MARIETTA, Des Plaines, IL   1988 – Present
Senior Production / Quality Assembly Engineer (1998 – Present)
Manage final assembly of electromechanical switches and printed circuit assemblies for residential HVAC controls. Supervise a 3-shift crew of 35 union, toolmakers, and automation technicians.

Bullet lists throughout the resume emphasize his achievements.

- Achieved significant cost reductions on numerous projects through process redesign and material selection. Examples include:
  - ✓ Managed a large terminal insertion project, replacing equipment with newer, faster equipment that significantly decreased process time and resulted in savings of $248,840.
  - ✓ Reduced costs for a spray fluxer project by $72,335 by reducing foam fluxer for PCBs.
  - ✓ Developed an automatic trimmer to reduce hand operations, improving quality performance and on-time delivery and saving $57,289 on a single project.
- Conduct source selection and manage subcontracts for complex plastic and metal part assemblies and packaging. Work with material suppliers to accurately convey specification requirements and solve technical difficulties. Negotiate with supply and equipment vendors to consistently reduce costs below budget.
- Coordinate capability assessments, technical analyses and failure analyses to monitor quality control.
- Developed and implemented successful employee training and motivation programs that contributed to department quality improvements of 25–35%.

Senior Production / Manufacturing Engineer (1995 – 1998)
Supervised 39 production employees and technicians and resolved production problems with the operation of 32 plastic-molding machines. Improved production quality, cut costs, and reduced waste.

- Investigated product cost savings including labor set-up, scrap salvage, tool repairs and burden expenses to achieve annual cost-reduction goals.
- Improved production and decreased tooling changeover time by switching from a two-cavity to a four-cavity mold.
- Coordinated improved assembly floor plan to increase automation, improve efficiency, and eliminate down time.

77

Mechanical engineer. *Jean F. West, CPRW, JCTC; Indian Rocks Beach, FL*

Raymond J. Smithson - Page Two   **847-231-4533**

Senior Production / Manufacturing Engineer, continued
- Analyzed product designs and recommended improvements to design specifications relating to manufacturing procedures, machinery, tooling devices and piece-part designs to increase productivity, improve quality, and reduce costs.
- Monitored production line compliance with OSHA and environmental regulations.
- Negotiated with automation engineering to re-implement manufacturing processes that had been outsourced, resulting in improved quality control and subsequent cost reduction.

Production Engineer (1990 – 1995)
Attended trade shows and investigated alternate processes and equipment to boost production. Analyzed equipment failures and modified design of parts as necessary to correct problems.
- Altered line layouts to optimize product flow and minimize cycle times, reducing product-material costs by up to 50% on various projects.
- Identified high-cost piece parts and implemented changes to substitute equal quality but lower-cost parts to reduce product material costs.
- Developed work processes and procedures for each project and trained assembly operators.
- Improved JIT process to increase inventory turns by up to 80%.

Associate Production Engineer (1988 – 1990)
Established preventive maintenance procedures for new equipment. Designed workstations to minimize ergonomic injuries and meet safety standards.

Education

Bachelor of Science in Mechanical Engineering
University of Florida, Gainesville, Florida

Affiliations

Marietta Engineering Club, Former Chairman of Education Committee

Society of Plastic Engineers (SPE)

American Society of Mechanical Engineers (ASME)

Computer Skills

Microsoft Word, Excel, and PowerPoint

Technical Skills

Expertise in the operation of 32 machines including:

Thermoset 300-ton Stokes Machines	Thermoplastic Injection 40-ton Engel
Thermoset Compression/Transfer 150-ton Lawton	Thermoset 30–50-ton Newbury
Thermoplastic Injection 30–50-ton Newbury	Thermoplastic Injection 175-ton Vandorn

Additional Training

- *Wave Solder Training* — Six-month training at Schuller's, Phoenix, AZ
- *SMT Training* — Six-month training in Atlanta, GA
- *862 Data Collector Training* — One-month course
- *Geometric Dimension & Tolerance* — Included all engineering measurement tools
- *Statistical Training* — Honeywell
- *Ozone Depletion Training* — Martin Marietta
- *Supplier Productivity Initiative & Exhibiting Productivity Leadership* — Global Commodity Management

ample space allowed for highlighting this very important "Additional Training" information.

This person's goal was to demonstrate that he had abilities above and beyond his technical skills, which themselves are very strong. His resume shows that he also has significant background in sales and product development.

WESTON M. UBALLE

41 North 1st Avenue
Los Angeles, CA 90266

310-549-7162
westengineer@aol.com

PROFILE	Innovative technical expert offering extensive experience in product design, development, launch, and sale. Unique understanding of market demands, with proven ability to invent products that suit those requirements, thus driving and sustaining long-term revenue and profits. Knowledgeable regarding effective market research. Skilled at calling on customers directly and partnering with them.
EDUCATION	B.S., MECHANICAL ENGINEERING, <u>California Institute of Technology</u>, 1996
SOFTWARE	Unigraphics (UGS), Ansys, Adobe PhotoShop, Microsoft Word/Excel/PowerPoint, Internet, Email
EXPERIENCE	PACIFIC INTERNATIONAL CO., LOS ANGELES, CA *Major international manufacturer of industrial injection-molded products.*

5/00 to Present — **Design Manager** (Los Angeles, CA)

- ☑ Lead project development from cycle inception, to completion, to initial sale. Specialize in products for the food and beverage industries, as well as environmental, material handling, and medical fields. Direct project managers and design engineers.

12/99 to 5/00 — **Project Manager, Design Department** (Los Angeles, CA)

- ☑ Directed the company's first product launch into Asia (The Philippines), the largest project internationally. Designed a collapsible RPC (reusable produce container) that reduced produce-packaging costs while simultaneously positioning national produce suppliers to receive special environmental tax considerations. Projections: $10 million-$12 million revenue; $4.5 million profit.
- ☑ Launched a packaging product custom-tailored for an international produce leader that features cube efficiency, wash capability, and complete compatibility with European wash systems. This project is currently performing well in trials in Costa Rica, and projections are $30 million in the initial year.

12/98 to 12/99 — **Sales Engineer** (Orlando, FL)

- ☑ Fueled sales growth of a self-designed and patented collapsible agriculture container from $0 to $13 million first year, then $30 million sales in year two, with projections for $45 million in year three.
- ☑ Identified and called upon key, high-volume produce growers for whom this product would yield lower packaging costs, thus positioning them to not only purchase this product, but, in turn, package and market their goods for the first time to major national retailers.

3/98 to 12/98 — **Senior Design Engineer** (Atlanta, GA)

- ☑ Designed a point-of-purchase merchandising display for 2-liter soft drink bottles to be placed on the top shelf and automatically advance bottles forward to maintain facings. *Patent No. US D5514406: "Facing Maintainer for Beverage Containers," filed 2/99.*
- ☑ Developed an interface for soft drink manufacturers that increased warehousing space 50% by allowing pallet stacking three pallets high instead of two, still with sufficient stability. *Patent pending: "Three-Tier Pallet Stacking Mechanism."*

7/97 to 3/98 — **Design Engineer** (Los Angeles, CA)

- ☑ Created a collapsible agriculture container for the produce industry that simultaneously met the requirements and specifications of produce growers and retailers and smoothly flowed through a closed loop supply chain network. *Patent No. US 6945567: "Collapsible Carrier," filed 12/97.*
- ☑ Managed the six-month tooling development and implementation process for the 12 initial molds for the collapsible container. Subsequent to extensive sales and product use by customers in the field, re-designed tooling for a second-generation version that was lighter, stronger, and more cube efficient, thus better suited to serve the market.

78

Mechanical engineer. *Jewel Bracy DeMaio, CPRW, CEIP; Royersford, PA*

The challenge in creating this resume was to condense Robert's original four-page resume plus four-page addendum into a two-page resume that adequately reflected his expertise and experience. He had a long, impressive history as a mining engineer in both open-pit and under-ground mining.

Robert E. Arnold, M.Sc., P.Eng., P.Geol.

402 McAllen Drive
Lebanon, TN 37075

E-mail: rearnold@bellsouth.net

Home: (615) 826-4390
Office: (615) 683-9402

Professional Manager / Engineer • Open Pit and Underground Mining

Extensive experience in project management resulting in a strong combination of management and engineering skills. Manage and evaluate projects and properties from a technical, operational, logistical and financial perspective. M.S. in Geology; B.S. in Geology/Engineering. Proficient with leading PC applications (Microsoft Excel, Word) and industry applications such as Gemcom. Key strengths include:

- Project and Engineering Management
- Operations and Field Management
- Due Diligence Analysis

- Technical Writing and Documentation
- Budget and Cost Controls
- Government and Public Liaison

Professional Experience

PAZMINE, LIMITED • Crossville, Tennessee .... 1997 – Present
The US mine office of an Australian mining and refining company.

Consultant/Senior Mining Engineer – Provide technical and economic analysis and evaluation of mining projects at facilities throughout the US and Canada. Perform and direct feasibility studies and due-diligence analysis of new and existing properties and potential acquisitions. Work closely with senior management at various mine sites and make recommendations to improve production processes and control costs.
- Serve as technical liaison between mining projects, government agencies, joint venture partners, and corporate office.
- Organize public forums regarding impact of mining development on local environment.
- Assist company president with issues relating to long-term union situations and collaborate with consultants to reduce overhead and develop a more effective and efficient operation.

CROSSBAR RANGE MINING CORPORATION • Faro, Yukon .... 1995 – 1997
A large lead/zinc complex with two operating open pit mines and an underground deposit in the feasibility stage.

Superintendent of Exploration Projects – Oversaw budgeting, planning, implementation, and direction of multimillion-dollar exploration program, including supervision of office staff, field consultants, and contractors. Reported directly to President/CEO.
- Provided technical and management direction to drilling, geological, and geophysical programs.
- As member of senior management team, developed and presented technical solutions to meet company's short- and long-term objectives.

Chief Mine Engineer – Directed and coordinated computerized mine planning, pit engineering, surveying, grade control, and geological functions for 13,000-tonne-per-day lead-zinc mine. Supervised 14 technical staff members and monitored their performance to ensure compliance with proper engineering practices.
- Organized, launched, and managed company's first engineering department. Co-managed operation's field crews during early stages of production.
- Initiated and supervised major mine design change that added mine life and ore reserves to company's largest-producing mine.
- Facilitated more harmonious work environment in mining department by setting up lines of communication between technical and operations staff and between management and hourly workers.

Robert wanted to use this resume to obtain consulting projects in the U.S. or Canada.

79

Mining engineer. *Carolyn Braden, CPRW; Hendersonville, TN*

Professional Experience (continued)

ENVIRONMENTAL ENGINEERING, INC. • Jasper, Alberta..1993 – 1994
An environmental engineering company involved in contaminated real property evaluation appraisal, environmental audits, risk assessments, and project management of contaminated commercial and industrial sites.

Environmental Engineering Consultant – Conducted independent environmental audits, remediations, risk assessments, and cost analyses of commercial and industrial sites for appraisal firm. Compiled detailed histories of contaminated sites and prepared comprehensive programs and budgets for site remediation and reclamation.
- Established new technical arm of the company to develop policies and procedures to operate department more efficiently and effectively.
- Created business unit for established company that grew from small, break-even enterprise into profitable venture by developing practical, cost-effective procedures.

PIT RESOURCES CANADA LTD. • Cobblestone Gold Project • Newfoundland ....1989 – 1992
A multinational energy company with several ventures across Canada. Project was a 3,500-tonne-per-day, blast-hole, open-stope mine utilizing large rubber-tired equipment, including 50-tonne state-of-the-art electric haulage trucks. Mine and mill project employed 360 people at peak operations.

Project Superintendent – Directed crew in treating mine and mill effluent and in keeping complex functioning while mine was temporarily closed and during subsequent sale of property. Assisted potential buyers in evaluating mine facilities.

Mine Superintendent – Planned, budgeted, and supervised the engineering, geology, and mine operations departments. Member of senior management team responsible for mine operations.

Chief Mine Engineer – Supervised short- and long-range computerized mine planning, scheduling, forecasting, and production engineering.
- Prepared feasibility report on increasing daily mine production from 3,000 to 3,500 tonnes; subsequently supervised mining department in achieving this goal.
- Fostered better communications between mine and mill through initiation of weekly information-sharing sessions.
- Improved employee relations in the mine by opening lines of communication between staff and union, resulting in fewer grievances from the union.

Additional Professional Experience
Mining Consultant • Reliance Consultants Ltd. • Vancouver, British Columbia • 1987 – 1989
General Manager • Red Silver Mines Ltd. • Calgary, Alberta • 1985 – 1986
Chief Engineer • B & P Explorations Ltd. • Calgary, Alberta • 1980 – 1985

Academic Background

MASTER OF SCIENCE – Geology • University of Wisconsin
BACHELOR OF SCIENCE – Geology/Engineering • University of Vermont

Professional Affiliations

Association of Professional Engineers of Nova Scotia • 1997 – Present
Association of Professional Engineers of Yukon Territory • 1995 – Present
Association of Professional Engineers, Geologists and Geophysicists of Alberta • 1982 – Present

Edward was downsized and plans to be a self-employed consultant. To market himself, his resume functions as a brochure. This was a challenge because marketing typically is not consistent with scientific engineering personalities (resume writer's comments).

Professional Summary:

Health Physicist and Nuclear Engineer
with over 15 years supporting radiation protection activities
for Duke Power Company's three nuclear power stations.

A hands-on *problem solver* and scientist with the ability
to make connections and see possibilities outside the box,
and who takes pride in developing practical solutions.

Contact:
1010 Washington Drive
Charlotte, NC 28211
(704) 365-1234

Edward R. Schmidt, CHP, PE
Scientific/Engineering Consultant in Radiation Protection

Offering Expertise in:

Defining the Problem

A reputation for *listening* and
quickly linking theory and
common sense to client needs.

Constructive communication -
facilitated between scientists,
technicians, managers and teams.

Solving the Problem

Evaluation of radiation fields, instrument
selection and performance.

Investigation of unusual radioanalysis
and external and internal dosimetry
results.

Evaluation of plant emissions and
environmental results.

Auditing for compliance with standards
--with an open eye for what is better,
easier or more workable.

Delivering Solutions

Sensitive to urgent and time dependent
issues.

Reports that are to the point.

Recommendations for corrective
actions, simplifications or program
enhancements.

Training sessions.

Professional Experience:

Duke Power Company,
Charlotte, NC   1980-present
Health Physicist
Supervising Scientist
Senior Engineer
    Developed a practical beta radiation
    protection program in use over 14
    years without major revision.

Keane Monroe Corporation,
Monroe, NC   1977-80
Engineer
    Designed a solid state control to
    meet demanding schedule, cost and
    performance constraints. Set up
    facility to produce it.

**Fermi National Accelerator
Laboratory,** Batavia, IL   1973-77
Radiation Safety Officer

Credentials:

Health Physics Society, since 1977
Certified Health Physicist,
    comprehensive, since 1981
    power reactor, since 1983
Registered Professional
    Engineer (NC), since 1983
ABHP Part II Panel of
    Examiners, 1992-95
Author of 3 patents

Technical Publications Include:

"Improved Gamma source Calibration through Computerized Correlation of Data",
    Health Physics Society Annual Meeting, 1993
"Rapid Alpha Spectroscopy of Air Samples Without Chemical Preparation",
    Radiation Protection Management, October 1992
"A Practical Beta Radiation Protection Program",
    Radiation Protection Management, May 1986

Education:

**MS, Environmental Health
Engineering,**
Northwestern University, 1977

BS, Chemistry,
Illinois Institute of Technology, 1972

80

Nuclear engineer. *Debbie Sherrie, CPRW; Charlotte, NC*

Marc was a geological engineer with lots of project leadership experience but no promotion to management. He wanted to move up to manage a team of geologists.

Marc R. Brown

3003 Westheimer Road #506 • Houston, Texas 77082 • (281) 596-9206

His resume highlights his expertise in both technology and management.

GEOLOGICAL ENGINEERING SPECIALIST
Excellent Project Management and Business Development Qualifications

---

Multi-faceted geological engineering professional with twenty years' experience in business development, reservoir, geological and reserves engineering within Conoco Inc. Expert in cross-functional team leadership, resource management, project planning, technical analysis, proved-reserves documentation and reporting. Well-respected advisor on geologic modeling and probability methodology—authored and published article in the *Oil and Gas Journal*. Core competencies include:

- ➢ Reservoir Mapping & Petrophysics
- ➢ Gas Reserves & Deliverability Studies
- ➢ Strategic Business & Economic Analysis
- ➢ Risk Analysis & Risk Management

- ➢ SEC Reserves Compliance Reporting
- ➢ Internal & External Reserves Audits
- ➢ Acquisition & Disposition Analysis
- ➢ Drilling Project Management

PROFESSIONAL EXPERIENCE

CONOCO INC., Houston, Texas   1981 – Present
International Fortune 500 Company…Year 2000 Revenues of $39 Billion
Twenty-year career highlighted by a series of increasingly responsible project leadership assignments. Career highlights include:

Geological & Reservoir Advisor   (1997 – Present)
Assigned as integral member of asset management team to provide geological and reservoir expertise on a joint venture project between Conoco Inc. and Consolidation Coal Company. Assisted in the development and launch of an aggressive coalbed methane expansion drilling operation. Developed an integrated geologic and reservoir model to predict well performance, provide gas and water production forecasts, and support future development drilling programs. Built Monte Carlo model to determine probabilistic range of production flowstreams and reserves from current coalbed methane production and future development scenarios. Calculated SEC proved reserves and advised on internal / external proved reserves audits. Appointed as joint technical committee leader to assess drilling program performance, recommend future drilling projects, facilitate budget processes, and evaluate effects of reduced coalbed methane well spacing. Led team in well telemetry data capture / reporting to optimize field operations. Assisted with analysis and determination of the project's market value for potential sale. Coalbed methane expansion drilling has almost doubled gas volume — from 30 to 53 million cubic feet per day.

Geological Advisor   (1993 – 1997)
Assumed cross-functional reservoir engineering assignment with responsibility for Midland Operating Center proved reserves. Prepared gas reserves studies for domestic acquisition and disposition activities. Developed reporting process for SEC proved reserves, and advised on internal and external reserves audits. Led facilitation of paperless technology to expedite reserves data reporting and more efficiently manage auditing and recording functions. Authored article, "Probabilistic Model Better Defines Development Well Risks," that was published in the *Oil and Gas Journal*.

Marc received a job offer within 30 days!

81

Petroleum engineer. *Cheryl Ann Harland, CPRW, JCTC; The Woodlands, TX*

Marc R. Brown   **Page Two**

PROFESSIONAL EXPERIENCE
(Continued)

Senior Geologist   (1990 – 1993)
Accepted corporate headquarters assignment into worldwide exploration group to perform play analysis and track planning reserves projects for North American onshore operating areas. Assisted in the design/build of Conoco's initial probability methodology.

Geologist   (1981 – 1990)
Nine-year career in field development and exploration within the Permian and San Juan basins. Identified drilling and recompletion opportunities in both mature and undeveloped areas. Permian Basin projects included Wolfcamp carbonate debris flow infield exploration north of Howard-Glasscock Field (Chalk lease area), Siluro-Devonian (Fusselman) exploration, Central Basin Platform (southeast New Mexico) involving Langley Strawn infield exploration, and Permian carbonate reservoir characterization for waterfloods in the East Blinebry area. Identified San Juan Basin recompletion and drilling opportunities in Cretaceous gas sands on Jicarilla Apache leases, and evaluated Pictured Cliffs recompletion potential in the 29-4 Block area.

EDUCATION

University of Montana
MS, Geology 1981
(Structural Thesis)

University of Wisconsin
BS, Geology 1979

CONTINUING PROFESSIONAL DEVELOPMENT

Evaluating & Managing Petroleum Risk • Monte Carlo Simulation for the Oil and Gas Industry
Economic Evaluation & Investment Decision Analysis • Practical Exploration Techniques
Basic Reservoir Engineering • Reservoir Simulation for Practical Decision Making
Basic Wireline Well Logging • Well Completion Practices

PROFESSIONAL ASSOCIATIONS

American Association of Petroleum Geologists
Society of Petroleum Engineers
Geological Society of America

PUBLICATIONS

"Probabilistic Model Better Defines Development Well Risks"
Oil & Gas Journal (October 14, 1996, issue)

S A N D R A
H U G H E S

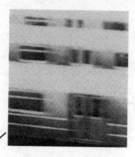

(212) 545 2323

(a sample of Sandra's work

E X P E R T I S E

- QuarkXPress

- Adobe Photoshop

- Adobe ImageReady

- Adobe Illustrator

- Macromedia Fireworks

- Macromedia Flash

- Macromedia Dreamweaver

- Mac and PC platforms

- Scanning and printmaking techniques

1505 West 58th Street — New York, NY 10123 — shughes@isp.com

AWARD-WINNING GRAPHIC AND VISUAL ARTIST

HIGHLIGHT OF SKILLS AND STRENGTHS

Combine solid background in fine arts with graphic skills, resulting in distinctive proficiency in both online and offline design techniques. Able to effectively analyze and communicate creative ideas with clients. Known for talent in applying wide range of styles to meet clients' needs. Specialize in corporate identity design, web design, and photo retouching. Recipient of international Amsted Award 1998, category graphic design.

GRAPHIC DESIGN *) creative area*

OBYR PHARMACEUTICALS, INC., New York, New York — Sep 1999 — Present
Web Design *for international pharmaceutical distributor.*

- Use Flash and Dreamweaver in developing high-quality and creative web pages.
- Take download speed for 56K- modem users into consideration during design.
- Enjoy working in team, but able to work independently.

TEENTRONICS.COM, New York, New York — May 1998 — Aug 1999
Web Design *for lifestyle Internet company geared toward teenagers.*

- Worked directly with Design Director on daily website updates and web graphics.
- Optimized photographs for web publication using Photoshop and ImageReady.
- Created web backgrounds and animated web banners.

Frequent interdepartmental communications led to overall success in maintaining identity consistency. Able to remain detail-oriented under tight deadlines and in fast-paced environment.

CORPORATE IDENTITY DESIGN *) creative area*

UP-N-GO, New York, New York — Finished project Oct 2001
Graphic Design for high-end fitness apparel firm.

- Given 100% creative control over design process of firm's marketing package.
- Handled logo design, brochure design and layout, photo scanning and optimization, color separation and prepress preparation.
- Applied traditional printmaking skills to produce unique posters for trade show.

PHOTO RETOUCHING *) creative area*

Use advanced Photoshop features on ongoing basis for variety of clients — Since 1996
and industries. Clients include multimedia artist, fashion magazine, jewelry designer. Projects include touch-up, color separation, web and print preparation, and high-resolution imaging.

EDUCATION

PARSONS SCHOOL OF DESIGN, New York, New York
Bachelor of Fine Arts — 1992
Emphasis on printmaking — wood and metal engraving

EXHIBITIONS

Exhibit print and graphic art in New York galleries on a regular basis since 1994.

She works – and likes to work – with different media and for various clients & industries, so her resume includes a representative example from three creative areas.

82

Graphic/visual artist. *Ilona Vanderwoude; Riverdale, NY*

Amy Lou Smithers

1234 Main Street, Aloha, Oregon 97007
Telephone: (503) 543-5555

Professional Profile

Appropriate emphasis on the business skills needed

Over 14 years of experience in developing, maintaining and maximizing sales production in the highly competitive home furnishings market. Proficient in all aspects of merchandising, training and customer service.

- Experienced in planning and conducting training seminars; able to develop effective presentations and tailor training programs to meet individual needs.
- Proven ability to develop a high level of referral and repeat business.
- Excellent follow-up and time management skills.

Experience

Design Consultant – 1992 to Present
Innovation Interiors, Tigard, Oregon
Call on local contractors and develop positive relationships to encourage referrals. Meet with customers, define needs, prepare estimates, make presentations and close sales. Plan and coordinate the installation process.
Accomplishments: Rated as #1 producer; consistently exceeded all sales goals.

Account Representative – 1984 to 1992
Advent Fabrics, New York, New York
Represented the fabric division to retail establishments and manufacturers in Washington, Oregon and Idaho. Managed over 550 existing accounts. Provided training at sales meetings and conducted customer training seminars.
Accomplishments: Successfully expanded the company's least productive territory; increased sales from $400,000 to $2,432,000 by demonstrating a thorough understanding of customer needs and providing relevant product education.

Sales Representative – 1978 to 1984
Design Group & Associates, Bellevue, Washington
Coordinated sales and customer service functions for accounts in Washington and Oregon. Also managed a 3,000 square foot designer showroom.
Accomplishments: Named "Rookie of the Year" in 1979.

Education

Bachelor of Arts – Interior Design, Portland State University, 1980
Sales Training – Dale Carnegie Sales Course, 1991

References

Provided upon request.

83

Designer. *Pat Kendall, JCTC, NCRW; Aloha, OR*

Samuel wanted to combine his broad expertise in the technology interface with his artistic and project-management skills and his more-traditional graphic arts background and training.

SAMUEL DeCONTE

Art Director ▪ Creative Director ▪ Senior Designer

10 Treadwell Avenue
New York, NY 10013
212-219-5555
sdec@xcom.net

EXPERTISE

✓ Industrial design art direction and product management

✓ Graphics design including digital graphics design

✓ Web design / interactive design

✓ Market research and competitive market intelligence

✓ Sourcing and contract negotiations

EDUCATION

1990 M.F.A.
Stonybrook University
New York, NY

1988 B.F.A.
Philadelphia
School of Design
Philadelphia, PA

SUMMARY

Experienced Creative professional and project manager. Innovative and resourceful, with demonstrated expertise in devising original solutions to complex problems. Natural analytical and research skills—creative problem solver. Proven abilities in communications, marketing research and customer service. Deadline-driven and reliable with a strong work ethic.

PROFESSIONAL EXPERIENCE

Art Director   1998 to present
SafeMode Commerce, New York, NY

Start-up company developing an Internet e-commerce authentication system (SafeMode System), which utilizes a cutting-edge electronic authentication device. Initial targeted clients include corporations, brokerage houses, and banking institutions with pilot deployment due in March 2002.

PROJECT MANAGEMENT

▪ Served in dual capacity of Art Director and Project Manager for the SafeMode prototype, saving $60K in personnel costs upfront. Established design direction, and managed design and development of SafeMode security device. Supervised 30 cross-functional team members and oversaw $150K project budget closely.

RESULT: Completed project, including tooling, within 4 months. Utilized quick thinking and decision-making skills to realize this project in record time.

▪ Sourced and supervised industrial design firm on-site for the plastic casing of the SafeMode. Co-negotiated contract, timeline, and deliverables.

▪ Served as liaison between vendors, the principal, and the chief engineer. Assisted in sourcing and provided ongoing oversight for electrical engineers, circuit-board designers, and molders. Supervised tooling production on-site.

▪ Saved $20K in SafeMode project by organizing the human factors focus groups, rather than hiring an outside marketing agency. Also wrote focus-group scripts to evaluate 7 preliminary models and moderated 12 focus-group sessions.

▪ Sourced and currently manage Canadian web design firm. Created information architecture and guide web design concept development. Collaborated with in-house counsel and principal to negotiate the contract, timeline, and deliverables.

▪ Provide in-house graphic design, HTML, and interactive design for brochures, advertisements, sales collateral, and other promotional materials.

MARKETING

▪ Developed a competitor report template and a competitor matrix and spear-headed strategy meetings on competitor analysis and strategic partnerships.

▪ Lead weekly presentations to executive management on SafeMode marketing and competitor issues, enabling them to make timely strategic decisions.

Continued

84

Designer/art director. *Susan Guarneri, NCC, NCCC, LPC, CPRW, IJCTC, CCM, CEIP; Lawrenceville, NJ*

SAMUEL DeCONTE

10 Treadwell Avenue
New York, NY 10013
212-219-5555
sdec@xcom.net

Design & Publishing Clients

America Online
Addison Wesley
Bantam Doubleday Dell
Booz Allen & Hamilton
Casilio
Chase
Channel Thirteen
Citibank
Colahan Saunders
Dentatus
Federal Express
General Binding
Hilton
HarperCollinsPublishers
Insignia
Island Graphics
Johnson & Johnson
Jungle Red Studios
Pfizer
Pharma
Random House
Showtime
Simon & Schuster
SUNY
UNDP
Vandenberg
Viacom

Page 2

Samuel's high-level technical competence makes him a unique candidate in the visual-arts field.

PROFESSIONAL EXPERIENCE, continued

Art Director   1996 to 1998
ImageArt, New York, NY
Fortune 500 company specializing in on-demand printing and outsourcing solutions for corporate clients, including Fortune 100 companies.

- Produced graphic design work (print) and trained in-house designers. Gained invaluable skills serving as liaison between ImageArt and clients.
- Instrumental in winning Johnson & Johnson national account ($60K quarterly). Wrote key proposal for color proofing and printing, and led proposal presentation on digital color issues to J&J executives.
- Originated system enabling Norbank to expedite national newsletter fulfillment by facilitating printing capability at any ImageArt location.

Designer   1994 to 1996
Hill Street Press, New York, NY

- Gained expertise in digital color-separation technology, which proved to be a key element in improving clients' color-printing projects.
- Interacted with clients to devise optimal design solutions. Ensured projects were completed on budget and on schedule.
- Clients included Balet and Albert Advertising, Giga Communications, Museum of Modern Art, Whitney Museum, Soho Press.

Fulbright Scholar & Professor of Fine Art   1991 to 1994
Stonybrook University in Rome, Italy

PROFESSIONAL ACTIVITIES

Associate Editor / Contributing Writer   1998 to present
Artist Magazine—65,000 readers in the US, Canada, Europe, and Japan.

Solo and Group Exhibitions, Public Works   1991 to present
Public and Private Collections—New York, Europe, and Asia.

Internationally Published Author   1991 to present
Articles, Books—Book Presentations, Catalogs, Interviews, Reviews, Video.

Guest Artist Lecturer and Instructor   1991 to 1995
Parsons School of Design, Philadelphia School of Design, Stonybrook University in Rome, U.S. Information Service in Paris, and Accademia di belle arti in Italy.

AWARDS & HONORS

- ✓ SafeMode prototype featured in prominent competitions including Industrial Design Association, NEW ARTS Awards (Business 2.0 Magazine), and Computer Products Magazine Awards (2001)
- ✓ U.S. Information Service Project Grant, Milan, Italy (1992 to 1993)
- ✓ Fulbright-Hays Fellowship Grant in Italy (1990 to 1991)

COMPUTER SKILLS

HTML, Lingo, GifBuilder, PageMaker, Illustrator, Photoshop, MS Office, Fetch, Quark, Premier, Director, Shockwave, Dreamweaver, SoundEdit 16.

Gene is a very experienced producer with many credits. But his essential information fits on one page.

Gene Gideon

128 Atlanta Avenue
Van Nuys, California 91400
818 • 475 • 9192

These are his top credentials and accomplishments

Guest Musical Comedy Director & Teacher - National Academy of Dramatic Arts
Founder, Artistic Director & President - Disneyland Youth Theatre, Inc.
Elected to membership of Distinguished Men of the Southwest - 1996
Managing & Artistic Director - Van Nuys Middle Theatre - 20 years
Resident Director - San Jose Music Circus
Graduate of Yale University

FILMS - Director

Young Hearts, Broken Dreams	Video Feature - Wrote, Directed & Produced
So Long Blue Boy	Starring Nelly King, Abe Frank, Enna Sykes
Inside a Kid's Head	Starring John Camparie
Numerous Documentaries	

THEATRE - Director

I Think I Killed My Wife	World Premiere Starring Dennis Manley	Hollywood
Demons: The Last Day of Edgar Allan Poe	World Premiere	New York City
Ferguson the Tailor	Pre-Broadway Musical Tryout	Santa Monica
Fiddler on the Roof	Starring John Price	San Jose
Dames at Sea	Starring John Baker	Santa Barbara
Finian's Rainbow	Revival	New Haven
United Crusade Show	Starring Robert Spoke, Jean Plain, Dan Dewy	State Music Center

THEATRE - Producer/Director

The Secret Life of Walter Mitty	East Coast Premiere starring Reva Williams
The Fantasticks	Five Year Run - Longest Musical Run in West Theatre History
The Wind in the Willows	World Premiere
Maxel (Multi-media musical)	World Premiere - Center Theatre
Stop the World I Want to Get Off	Isaacs Theatre & Opera House
Finian's Rainbow	LaPointe Auditorium
West Side Story	Choreographer - James Cohen
The Music Man	Mixed Arts Theatre
Oklahoma	Mixed Arts Theatre
Amahl and the Night Visitors	Variety Arts Center
The Boyfriend	Gordon Auditorium
Blithe Spirit	Disney Center Theatre
Rumpelstiltskin	Disney Center Theatre
Dark of the Moon	Disney Center Theatre
The Little Foxes	Disney Center Theatre
Come Back Little Sheba	Disney Center Theatre
The Devil and Daniel Webster	Disney Center Theatre
Awake and Sing	Disney Center Theatre

THEATRE - Producer

The Nutcracker Suite Ballet • Come Blow Your Horn • Wait Until Dark • What Do You Say To A Naked Waiter? • The Man Who Came To Dinner • Diary Of Anne Frank, etc.

THEATRE - Director

Anything Goes • Bloomer Girl • Brigadoon • Camelot • Carousel • Celebration • Damn Yankees • Guys and Dolls • 110 In The Shade • The King and I • Kiss me Kate • My Fair Lady • Pal Joey • The Student Prince • Hello Dolly • Pippin • Peter Pan • Little Mary Sunshine • You're A Good Man Charlie Brown • Oliver, etc., etc.

85

Director and producer. *Anne G. Kramer; Virginia Beach, VA*

BRENDAN PEEBLES
AEA, AFTRA, SAG
(212) 555-2546

Height: 6' 0"
Weight: 155

Hair: Brown
Eyes: Blue
Voice: Baritone

NEW YORK THEATRE

ANTHONY AND CLEOPATRA	Enobarbus (dir. Victor Hope)	New York Shakespeare Festival
BLUE WINDOW	Norbert (dir. Janet Wilkens)	Manhattan Theatre Club
KING JOHN	Chatillion/Melune	Riverside Shakespeare
OUR COUNTRY'S GOOD	Philip/Wisehammer	Wing and a Prayer Theatre Co.
THE CAINE MUTINY COURT-MARTIAL	Captain Queeg	MJT Productions
MUCH ADO ABOUT NOTHING	Antonio	Cressid Productions
MY DINNER WITH GOETHE	Wilhelm	Target Margin Theater
A NEW YORK HAMLET	Hamlet (dir. Elisa Burke)	Turnip Theatre Festival
THE LOVE OF THE NIGHTINGALE	Theseus/Chorus	Women's Workshop
THE TAMING OF THE SHREW	Curtis/Pedant	Survivor Productions
THE DIVINERS	Basil	Wing and a Prayer Theatre Co.
VIRGINIA	Leonard Woolf	Aphra Behn Theatre Co.
A WARSAW MELODY	Victor (dir. Mark Frehn)	Players Forum

REGIONAL THEATRE

OUTSIDE THE DOOR	Beckman (dir. Franco Paris)	Berkshire Theatre Festival
DEATH OF A SALESMAN	Ben	La Jolla Playhouse
A DOLLS HOUSE	Torvald (dir. Roberta Hogan)	Center Stage
SARITA	Fernando	Mark Taper Forum
A MATTER OF WIFE AND DEATH	Van Lust (dir. Tom O'Henry)	Pittsburgh Playhouse

FILM / TELEVISION

SHINE	Harvey	Fine Line Features
HITTING THE GROUND	Dr. Frances	Living Pictures Inc.
ONE LIFE TO LIVE	Sgt. Ferguson (Day Player)	ABC Television
SID AND MEL	Willie	NYU Student Film
AS THE WORLD TURNS	Conrad Hill (Recurring Under 5)	CBS Television

COMMERCIALS   Conflicts available upon request.

TRAINING   MFA: Rutgers University Professional Actor Training Program

SKILLS   Dialects: British, Cockney, Irish, New England, American Southern
Guitar, Fencing, Karate (brown belt), Motorcycle License.

*Another actor using a traditional resume format.
Usually attached is the actor's photo. This is
for a New York actor — an L.A. actor
might list film and T.V. credits first.*

86

Actor. *Dede Penick; Indianapolis, IN*

Work experience is grouped into related activities

REVA ANDREAS
SAG/AFTRA

Personal Management
GENE GIDEON ENTERPRISES
128 Atlanta Avenue
Van Nuys, California 91400
818 • 475 • 9192

Height: 5' 5"
Weight: 120
Hair: Blonde
Eyes: Blue

FILMS

The Wizard of Speed and Time		The Wizard Lt.
Private Popsicle (Voice Over)	Lead	Cannon Films
Satan's Blade	Featured	MC Productions, San Diega
Letting Go	Co-Star	USC Grad Film

TELEVISION

...Just A little More Love	Somi Productions

THEATRE

Play →   *Part →*   *"Employer" →*

Much Ado About Nothing	Margaret	Gordon Repertory Theatre
Sly Fox	Becky	Gordon Repertory Theatre
The Tavern	Virginia	Gordon Repertory Theatre
God of Vengeance	Basha	Gordon Repertory Theatre
King John	Blanche	Globe Playhouse
Cinders	Queen	Remarque Theatre, San Diego
Habeus Corpus	Felicity	Remarque Theatre, San Diego

SPECIAL SKILLS

Dance (Ballroom, Contemporary, Jazz) • Singing (Soprano, Alto) • Horseback Riding • Sewing, •
Swimming • Secretarial Skills (legal) • Bicycle Riding • Computers • Weapons • Drive a Car and Motor
Skooter.

TRAINING

Currently study with Gene Gideon • Commercial Workshop at Commercial Actor's Studio •
Various Workshops with SAF Conservatory • Comedy Improvisation with The Groundlings •
Shakespeare and Voice with Kate Fitzmaurice • Singing with Bob Garrett • Stage Combat with
Anthony DeLongis • Theatre Improvisation with Stephen Book and Philip Littel • Scene Study
Workshop with Mickey Rich • One year at Los Angeles Community College - Drama Major •
One year at San Diego Mesa College - Drama Major • U.S. Army - three years...

Actors' resumes include height, weight, and hair and eye color since many producers need to know this. Agents' phone numbers are listed so home address is not necessary (resume writer's comments).

87

Actor. *Anne G. Kramer; Virginia Beach, VA*

Katerina Boginskaya

P.O. Box 977 • New York, New York 11789 • (212) 443-5131
ballettteacher@optonline.net

PROFILE

Her notable experience with world-renowned ballet companies is highlighted in bold.

Classical Ballet Teacher with professional experience in classical and modern ballet, point, choreography, and teaching. Compose dance designed to suggest story, interpret emotion, or enliven show, coordinating dance with music. Instruct performers at rehearsals to achieve desired effects. Direct and stage presentation. Traveled extensively worldwide with the **Bolshoi Ballet Company** and **Russian State Ballet Company.**

TEACHING EXPERIENCE 2000 to Present

DANCE ELEK-TKA • New York, NY
JUNE CLAIRE DANCE CENTER • New York, NY
Classical Ballet Teacher
- Teach advanced classical ballet to modern dance.

1997 to Present

LONG ISLAND ACADEMY OF DANCE • Great Neck, NY
Classical Ballet Teacher
- Teach advanced classical ballet to students fifteen years old to adults.

Summers 1997 to Present

PHILADELPHIA DANCE CONSERVATORY • Philadelphia, PA
Classical Ballet Teacher/Choreographer/Dancer
- Choreograph, direct, teach, and perform in the Vaganova Festival.
- Staged Shopeniana (Les Sylphides), Piguita, and Swan Lake.
- Featured in various news articles specifying my directorship skills, dance style, and performances.

1997 to Present

TREND SETTERS • New York, NY
Classical Ballet Teacher
- Choreograph and teach ballet for students ranging from two years to adults; direct recitals.
- Created the first competition with solos and point dances. Through creative and innovative choreography, teaching, and coaching, students went on to place *First* and *Second Place* in competition, thereby increasing studio awareness and profitability.

1997 to Present

PRIVATE ACCOUNTS • Long Island, NY
Classical Ballet Teacher — Private Instructor

Summer 1998

"BACKSTREETS" • Manhasset, NY
Classical Ballet Teacher

1996 to 1997

NEW YORK BALLET INSTITUTE • New York, NY
Classical Ballet Teacher

1996 to 1997
1996 to 1997

GENEVIEVE'S SCHOOL OF DANCE • Bayside, NY
MARCHAND'S SCHOOL OF DANCE • Elmhurst, NY
Classical Ballet Teacher

Her experience is divided into two sections — teaching and professional (performing) — to highlight her two areas of expertise. If she were looking for performance roles, she could simply switch the order of these two categories and rewrite the "Profile" section.

PROFESSIONAL EXPERIENCE 1994 to 1997

BOLSHOI BALLET COMPANY • New York, NY
- Performances included Sleeping Beauty, Swan Lake, Raymonda, Don Quixote, La Bayadere, Giselle (pas-de-deux Act I), Faust, Spartacus, Romeo and Juliet.

88

Dancer and choreographer. *Donna Farrise; Hauppauge, NY*

Katerina Boginskaya
— Page Two —

PROFESSIONAL EXPERIENCE, cont. 1991 to 1997	<u>RUSSIAN STATE BALLET COMPANY (GORDEEV)</u> • Performances included Paquita, Classical (pas-de-deux), Ober, Shopeniana, Esmeralda (Diana and Acteon), La Fille Mal Gard (pas-de-deux).
GUEST PERFORMANCES 1997	Ilya Gaft Ballet Theater, NY ~ *Swan Lake* ~ *Dying Swan* Huntington Ballet Theater, NY ~ *Swan Lake* ~ *Nutcracker* Philadelphia Ballet Theater, PA ~ *Don Quixote* ~ *Paquita* ~ *Shopeniana* Haddad Youth Ballet, VA ~ *Nutcracker*
EDUCATION	<u>MOSCOW CHOREOGRAPHY INSTITUTE</u>, Moscow, Russia **Red Teaching Diploma (Honors)**, 1991 to 1995 ~ *One of two students who received the highest teaching diploma* ~ *Studied under Professor Golovkina* <u>VAGANOVA BALLET ACADEMY</u>, St. Peterburg, Russia **Diploma,** 1991 ~ *Studied under Dudinskaya*
SKILLS	~ *Speak Russian, English, and French* ~ *Teach Yoga, Malvaguo, School of Self-Defense*

While Derrick's primary position is as an elementary music teacher, his resume spotlights his part-time work as music director of several children's choirs, since that is his current job target.

DERRICK B. SAMPSON

26 East Barrington Street
Philadelphia, PA 19144
215-276-1872
musicman@yahoo.com

PROFESSIONAL PROFILE

current job target

Youth choir director with experience conducting church, mass, and school choirs.
Unique talent for revitalizing music programs, increasing participation, building a strong reputation,
and delivering improved performances.

EXPERIENCE

part-time work

PRAISE HOLY NAME YOUTH MASS CHOIR   Philadelphia, PA

<u>Music Director</u> - **1992 to Present:** Founded this community-based, youth and young adult, 100-voice, SATB gospel choir comprising vocalists and accompanying musicians from many churches and schools throughout greater Philadelphia. What originated as a summer program rapidly expanded to a year-round performance schedule at venues all over the tristate area. The choir performs on occasion for the City of Philadelphia's "Make It A Night" celebrations, yearly for the city's "Tree Lighting Ceremony," and has been invited to special events such as the New York Lincoln Center Festival.

- ♫ Recorded the album, "Worshipping Thy Name" in 1997; became the #4 request on 1110-AM (Gospel Highway 11).
- ♫ Preparing to record a second album in August 2002.
- ♫ Currently celebrating the choir's 10th anniversary.

MERION VALLEY PRESBYTERIAN CHURCH   Bryn Mawr, PA

<u>Children's Choir Director</u> - **1998 to Present:** Lead approximately 24 vocalists in 1st and 2nd grades in regular church performances as well as in annual Mother's Day productions, such as "Noah" and "Joseph & The Amazing Technicolor Dreamcoat."

HOLY HOPE CHURCH   Philadelphia, PA

<u>Music Director, Youth Enrichment Program</u> - **1998 to Present:** Teach general music classes in this Saturday morning program. Direct students at four distinct age levels in monthly choir performances.

PETER & PAUL'S LUTHERAN CHURCH   Philadelphia, PA

<u>Youth Choir Director</u> - **1993 to Present:** Expanded the choir from three voices to 20. This group participated in the African-American Lutheran Association Conference in 1999.

primary position

THE SCHOOL DISTRICT OF PHILADELPHIA   Philadelphia, PA

<u>General Music Teacher, Chase Valley Elementary</u> - **1996 to Present:** Teach six general music classes grades K-5, covering subjects such as music theory, rhythm and movement, and percussion instruments. Direct 120 3rd, 4th, and 5th grade students in unison elementary singing. Perform four concerts annually. Participate in the annual Northeast Cluster Music Program with choirs from eight area schools.

- ♫ Coordinated combined choir music at The American Federation of Teachers Convention in Philadelphia.
- ♫ Directed the Chase Valley choir, along with 800 voices in combined choirs, in the finale performance at the City of Philadelphia Public School Music Festival in 1998.
- ♫ Performed at Knowlton Mansion, broadcast live on TV Channel 29's "Good Day Philadelphia," in 1997.
- ♫ Participated in a feature presentation for WCAU-TV, Channel 10, in 1996.

| 1995 to 1996 | Long-Term Substitute | Weston Brook Elementary School | Philadelphia, PA |
| 1994 to 1995 | Long-Term Substitute | Brown Grove Elementary School | Philadelphia, PA |

89

Singer/music director. *Jewel Bracy DeMaio, CPRW, CEIP; Royersford, PA*

♪ **ANTHONY ("TONY") ZIMMERMANN** ♪
Three Blue Key
Birch, New York 00000-0000
Tel: (555) 555-5555 • Email: xxxxxxxx@aol.com

TOP PRODUCING MUSIC EXECUTIVE

RESULTS ORIENTED professional with a 20-year proven track record in strategic planning, development and business expansion • Ability to foster relationships with recording corporations, labels and artists • Unique talent in discovering new label interests and business ventures • Easily identifies up and coming trends with a talent for recognizing cutting-edge styles • Creating and recognizing hit singles • Dynamic, aggressive, persistent and consistent • Extensively versed in studio production • Experienced in both European and U.S. tour management • Confident decision maker and successful risk taker • Knowledge of music spans pop, rock, metal, R&B, alternative, rap, new age and country • Totally versed in state-of-the-art computerized environments • Areas of expertise include:

- ♪ ARTIST/LABEL PROJECT MANAGEMENT AND DEVELOPMENT
- ♪ NEGOTIATING/SIGNING NEW ARTISTS
- ♪ GENERATING, DEVELOPING AND IMPLEMENTING NEW LABEL BUSINESS
- ♪ TARGET AND CREATE INNOVATIVE LABEL INVESTMENT OPPORTUNITIES
- ♪ PRODUCTION MANAGEMENT AND DISTRIBUTION

an excellent overview of skills and abilities

PROFESSIONAL EXPERIENCE:

SPHERE PRODUCTIONS   New York, New York

PRESIDENT • 1986 - Present

Challenged to lead a successful music production company from inception through full operations. Discover and develop extreme talent into cross-over markets. Forecast future trends into mainstream music marketplace.

- Currently managing **Lynn Richardson**, an up and coming female performer.
- Produced MACHINE for **Paul Simon's** production company, *"Night After Night, LTD."*
- Discovered and launched career of **Jewel through** GRP *"Rap to Rock"* CD compilation of new artists.
- Participant in 20th anniversary **KISS** project and current **KISS** conventions (interviews and personal appearances).
- Maintain high-profile engagement with R&B artists **Elexus Quinn and Ziggy True** and pop/rock artist **Oona Falcon** (major attraction throughout Europe).
- Diverse areas of expertise encompass **Harper-Josef**, a New Age project.
- Contributed to the success of numerous music videos and films.
- Accountable for daily operations, including P&L, budgeting, marketing, strategic planning, staff development and contract negotiations.

(continued...)

90

Music executive. *Alesia Benedict, CPRW, JCTC; Rochelle Park, NJ*

ANTHONY ("TONY") ZIMMERMANN Tel: (555) 555-5555   - Page Two -

PROFESSIONAL EXPERIENCE: continued...

TOGA PRODUCTIONS   New York, New York

FOUNDER, CO-OWNER • 1982 - 1986

High-profile position in full service music and video production company. Managed projects for artists and groups. Provided live and video coverage for special events. Launched and produced video-magazine concept in association with The Industry Network System (TINS).

PROJECT/ARTIST HIGHLIGHTS:

♪   *Machine* (Paul Simon's Night After Night productions)
♪   *Rod Stewart* (1988 World Tour)
♪   *KISS* (20th anniversary project)
♪   *Oona Falcon* (European Starlight Express and tour)
♪   *Myth* (Beatles' attorney, Walter Hofer project)
♪   *Lynn Richardson* (up and coming female artist)
♪   *Jewel* (Rap to Rock GRP project)
♪   *Elexus Quinn and Ziggy True* ("Nothing is Meaningless" project)
♪   *Breakfast Special* (national tour)
♪   *Hunter* (former members with Billy Squire)
♪   *Hawkeye* ("Great Seal" film documentary, Mill Valley Productions)
♪   *Dreams* in Color (in association with Joe Serling)
♪   *Alexia* (managed by Rolling Stones partner, Pete Rudge)

PROFESSIONAL ATTRIBUTES:

◆ Founding member (drummer) of rock group KISS with Gene Simmons, Paul Stanley and Brooke Ostrander.
◆ Recipient of numerous awards and tributes in recognition of writing popular songs and lyrics.
◆ Featured in trade publications including *Modern Drummer*.
◆ Co-wrote and produced material for successful bands and major production companies.
◆ Instrumental in production of video projects and film clips.

EDUCATION:

Bachelor of Arts degree
University of Miami • Coral Gables, Florida

The design elements include the border, musical note graphics, different fonts, and spacing. They form a creative resume that is not "too much" for this experienced professional.

Martin had spent his entire career in hockey — first as a goaltender and then in hockey equipment sales — but wanted to transition into coaching.

MARTIN LaPIERRE

25 Osprey Road
Augusta, Ontario
A2B 3C3

Phone: (905) 888-7766
Fax: (905) 789-4455
Email: mlapierre@webcast.com

PROFESSIONAL GOALTENDING COACH

"Of all the goalies I have coached, Martin was the best at handling the puck and neutralizing the dump-in and opposing forecheck. His unique ability as a 'third defenseman' created a very quick transition to offense and spared many a defenseman from pressure and possible injury. I highly recommend Martin LaPierre as a goalie consultant, and I believe he would be an important asset to any hockey team."

- Jim MacLean, Commissioner I.H.L.
Former Coach of Philadelphia Flyers, Edmonton Oilers, and Vancouver Canucks

Martin faxed this resume to all NHL and minor-league hockey teams in North America! He landed an interview and an offer within ten days!

GOALTENDING / HOCKEY EXPERTISE

➤ Very sharp analytical eye, with the ability to identify and improve areas of weakness and habit while working within the goalie's own unique style.

➤ Outstanding player-development, team-building and leadership abilities — proven success motivating and inspiring athletes to play to their potential.

➤ Intimate understanding of goalies and the psychological/emotional requirements to playing at peak level.

➤ Equally skilled consulting and developing both young goalies and seasoned professionals.

➤ Keen eye for spotting less-obvious talent with the ability to then turn potential into skill.

➤ Personable nature, strong work ethic, and dedicated to team success.

➤ 35 years' hockey expertise as both a player and businessman.

➤ Specific goaltending coaching strengths include:

✓ **Advanced Puck Handling**	✓ **Advanced Use of Stick**
✓ **Goalie Mobility**	✓ **Angle Coverage**
✓ **Reading the Play**	✓ **Neutralizing the Forecheck**

PROFESSIONAL GOALTENDING CAREER

Port Huron Flags, International Hockey League (I.H.L.)   1974–1976
Coach: Jim MacLean
➤ Called up to New York Rangers to replace injured John Davidson (January 1976).
➤ Reached Finals (1976); Selected to All-Star Game (1975).

Greensboro Generals   1972–1974
Coaches: Don Carson, Ted Lansberg

St. Catharines Blackhawks   1971–1972
Coach: Frank Milner

Toronto Marlies   1969–1971
Coaches: Gus Bonham, Stuart Mazurski
➤ Reached Finals both years, playing with and against Gilbert Perrault, Marcel Dionne, and Steve Shutt.

91

Professional athlete/coach. *Ross Macpherson, MA, CPRW, JCTC, CEIP, CJST; Pickering, Ontario*

BUSINESS CAREER

BONELLO MARKETING CONSULTANTS   1999–2000
Owner/President   Markham, Ontario
➤ Focused on the invention, development, and marketing of three original products — gardening caddy, exercise machine, and fast-food packaging product.
➤ Directed all product design/development, market research, administration, and financial operations.

CCL (formerly Nardu 1989–94 and Tensports 1994–98)   1989–1999
Senior Sales / Marketing Representative   Markham, Ontario
➤ Contracted to sell, market, and promote Heaton, Jofa, Koho, Titan, and Canadien product lines throughout Greater Toronto and Southern Ontario, recognized as the largest hockey market in the world.
➤ Successfully brought Heaton goalie equipment from #3 position to #1 in only 2 years.
➤ Recipient of a variety of sales and business awards for excellence and achievement.

PEUGEOT SALES   1979–1989
Sales Representative   Head Office — New York, New York
➤ Hired to sell Micron, Canadien, I-Tech, and McLean equipment lines throughout Toronto market.
➤ Personally designed Canadien 6001 Mick hockey stick, the best selling hockey stick in Ontario 1985–92 (currently sold by VIC).
➤ Successfully recommended color-coordinating goalie pads to team colors, establishing a unique product distinction for Canadien equipment and introducing a standard still used today.

MAKIMOTO CORPORATION   1977–1979
Sales Representative   Head Office — Montreal, Quebec
➤ Introduced new hockey skate and athletic footwear line in Ontario market.
➤ Successfully increased Ontario sales from $0 to $2 million annually.
➤ Consulted with R&D team on product development.

PROFESSIONAL REFERENCES

Jim MacLean
Commissioner I.H.L.
Former Coach of Philadelphia Flyers, Edmonton Oilers, and Vancouver Canucks
Phone: (248) 866-7788

Mike Nardollilo
VP, Hockey Operations, N.H.L.
Former Coach of Toronto Maple Leafs, New York Rangers, and Ottawa Senators
Phone: (416) 987-7777

Stuart Mazurski
Director, Central Scouting, N.H.L.
Phone: (416) 444-5555

As a general rule, references are not included in resumes. In this case, it made sense to break the rule in order to leverage Martin's amazing references.

DON ANDREWS
BROADCAST JOURNALIST

**258 WEST 2ND STREET
MESA, ARIZONA 85201
602/844-1300**

PROFESSIONAL PROFILE	

- Quintessential news professional and winner of 20 awards for excellence in broadcast journalism, announcing and writing.
- More than 25 years of experience in radio and television, management and public relations, combined with Baccalaureate degree. Expertise includes:

Radio & Television Journalism	**Team-Building**
Public & Community Relations	**Management & Supervision**
On-Air Personality	**Motivation & Training**

- An accomplished, dedicated and self-confident veteran journalist; firmly committed; personable, credible and talented.
- Adept at resolving difficult situations with diplomacy and tact. Maintains productive rapport with news-makers, news sources, colleagues and the public; understands and honors deadline commitments.
- Creative and imaginative, with the drive and initiative to develop captivating news programming. Thoroughly professional in appearance and demeanor.
- Distinguished basso-baritone; speaking, writing and computer proficiencies.
- Reported on ABC, NBC, CBS, MBS, BBC and Armed Forces networks.
- Demonstrates pro-active, visible and motivated teamwork and leadership by example; guides and mentors associates.

BROADCAST JOURNALISM

1996 - Present

KFYI 910 Radio
News Anchor & Reporter
Phoenix, Arizona

Respected, recognized and credible morning-drive and mid-day news anchor and reporter for major-market news-talk station.

1994 - 1996

KTAR 620
News Anchor & Reporter
Phoenix, Arizona

News anchor and reporter for Pulitzer Broadcasting Company news-talk station.

- Recipient of two Team Journalism Awards for anchoring and reporting in 1994 and 1995.

1982 - 1986

KOY Radio & Edens Broadcasting Inc.
News Reporter & Anchor
Phoenix, Arizona

Electronic news gathering throughout the state on Arizona's first radio station.

- Winner of 14 awards for journalistic excellence from the *Arizona Press Club* and the *Arizona Associated Press Broadcasters Association*.
- Recognized for in-depth coverage of pertinent issues; provided network coverage of Arizona news of national interest on the *NBC Radio Network*.
- Recipient of numerous corporate *Incentives for Excellence Awards* for outstanding reportorial performance and achievement of goals.
- Successfully cultivated rapport with news sources including law enforcement, government, political and business leaders as well as public-issue groups.

Continued > > >

92

Announcer. *Brooke Andrews, CPRW; Chandler, AZ*

DON ANDREWS
BROADCAST JOURNALIST

1972 - 1980	*KOOL Radio - Television, Inc.*	Phoenix, Arizona

News Director - KOOL-FM

Provided insightful leadership to award-winning news team, set standards for journalistic professionalism, developed formats, recruited and mentored reporters.

- Winner of four awards for journalistic excellence from the *Arizona Press Club,* the *Associated Press Broadcasters Association* and the *United Press International Broadcasters Association.*
- Selected for coveted guest host position on *Dateline America,* covering for Charles Kuralt on the *CBS Radio Network.*

MILITARY

United States Air Force — Vietnam-era Veteran
American Forces Korea Network — Seoul, South Korea
RADIO & TELEVISION NEWS ANCHOR & REPORTER

Prepared and anchored TV and radio newscasts on nationwide networks.

- Anchored in-depth radio and television coverage of the American aerospace program, notably the Apollo moon missions including *Apollo XIII.*
- Covered United Nations peace negotiations between North and South Korea at Pamunjom and provided reports to ABC, CBS, NBC, MBS and the BBC.

PUBLIC INFORMATION OFFICEr — Williams Air Force Base, Arizona

- Directed public relations for *Apollo XVII* Astronaut Harrison "Jack" Schmitt during his flight training at Williams Air Force Base.;Coordinated media liaison activities for *USAF Thunderbirds* air show.

ACADEMIC CREDENTIALS

Edinboro State University — Edinboro, Pennsylvania
Bachelor of Arts: Humanities — **Major: Journalism**

Continuing Education

- Employee Relations - EEO/AA
- Fiscal Management
- Energy & Governmental Affairs
- Radio & Television Production
- Journalistic Ethics
- Desktop Publishing

AWARDS & HONORS

Winner of 20 awards for excellence in broadcasting, including:

Arizona Press Club
- **First-place Awards for News Reporting** in 1986, 1985, 1975, 1974, 1973.

Associated Press Broadcasters Association &
United Press International Broadcasters Association
- **Various awards for News Reporting** from 1973 through 1996.

PROFESSIONAL AFFILIATIONS

Past & Present

- Sigma Delta Chi - Honorary Fraternity for Journalism, Charter Member, ESU
- Pi Delta Epsilon - Honorary Fraternity for Journalism
- Phoenix Press Club - Former member, Board of Directors
- Arizona Associated Press Broadcasters Association
- Arizona Press Club

Continued > > >

One of the few three-page resumes in this book, it presents his substantial experience in an interesting and thorough way

DON ANDREWS
BROADCAST JOURNALIST

COMMUNITY INVOLVEMENT *Past & Present*	• Project Prevention - Board of Directors • Phoenix Little Theatre - Patron & Donor • Herberger Theatre Associates - Patron & Donor • Musical Theatre of Arizona - Patron & Donor • COMPAS Telethons & Auctions - Volunteer Fund-Raiser for the Arts

CORPORATE JOURNALISM

Arizona Public Service Company   Phoenix, Arizona
MANAGER & INFORMATION OFFICER   Palo Verde Communications

Positive impact on corporate image resulted in rapid advancement to Manager & Information Officer for the Palo Verde Nuclear Generating Station, the largest facility for the peaceful use of nuclear energy in the United States.

• Credited with successful transition of information and communication programs and staff from reactive to pro-active.
• Created and directed design and construction of the new *Energy Information & Visitors Center,* a 10,000 square-foot multi-media facility encompassing interactive exhibits, learning center, auditorium and offices.
• Produced magazines, newsletters, news releases, billboards and other communications targeting the media, the public and investors.
• Improved external and internal communications by modernizing communication products and methodologies via technology transfer to computers.

1980 - 1982

Phoenix Symphony Association   Phoenix, Arizona
COMMUNICATIONS & PUBLIC RELATIONS DIRECTOR

Total accountability for all communications regarding orchestral performances and activities, including publicity, media liaison and advertising.

• Coordinated fund-raising events and interacted with the community to increase concert attendance and ensure satisfaction of patrons.
• Recognized for extraordinary diplomacy during 1980 musicians' strike, disseminating concise, perceptive accounts of management position to media.
• Commended by the journalistic community for providing comprehensive information in a timely and factual manner.

REFERENCES

"You provide excellent news coverage on KTAR — you do a great job."
— Lynn Russell, *News Anchor, CNN Television*

"We're impressed by your knowledge and interest in the Space Shuttle System." — Shannon Lucid & Jon McBride, *NASA Shuttle Astronauts*

"His professionalism, dedication and loyalty were always beyond question. He demonstrated a spirit of innovation and creativity uncommon among his peers." — Gary Edens, *President, Edens Broadcasting Inc.*

"Thanks to your efforts, thousands of Arizonans now understand how important it is to give, [so] that those who are less fortunate can enjoy the [holiday] season." — John McCain, *U.S. Senator*

"I perceive Don to be a capable, honest journalist who is loyal to the facts and dedicated to fairness." — Dennis DeConcini, *former U.S. Senator*

PERSONAL

Additional information, photo and audio tape on request.

A spotty work history, an incomplete education, and a street address far from the centers of the recording industry were problems that had to be overcome in preparing this resume.

Lena Selden

1409 Northwest 186th Street ◉ Apartment 10a ◉ Miami, Florida 33000
[305] 555-5555 ◉ seldensound@juno.com

To position Lena well, her resume focuses on the names of the artists she has recorded and her work style.

S O U N D   E N G I N E E R

ARTISTS RECORDED:

- ◉ Michael Jackson
- ◉ The Commodores
- ◉ Atlantic Starr
- ◉ Lionel Richie
- ◉ Herb Alpert
- ◉ Vesta
- ◉ The Jacksons
- ◉ The Temptations

PROFILE:

- ◉ Gifted in patiently helping the artist make his or her music come alive
- ◉ Dedicated to meeting deadlines with only the best in technical production
- ◉ Always up to date in the art of finding the best value in recording equipment

WORK EXPERIENCE:

Music Director, Announcer (1999 – 2001)	WTTR-FM, Center State University, Montgomery, Alabama
Computer Operator (1997 – 1999)	Pacific Bell Telephone Company, Pasadena, California
Studio Engineer (1993 – 1997)	Commodores Entertainment Corporation, Los Angeles, California
Announcer, Traffic Manager (1990 – 1993)	WVVT AM & FM, Tuskegee, Alabama

EDUCATION:

- ◉ Pursuing B.S. (Management of Human Resources), Faulkner University, Montgomery, Alabama

AFFILIATIONS

- ◉ Board Member, National Black Programmers' Coalition.

   National president of this 8,000-member group asked me to set up my program that helps students prepare for broadcasting and recording careers. Students now benefiting at seven colleges.

93

Sound engineer. *Don Orlando, MBA, CPRW, IJCTC, CCM; Montgomery, AL*

Roberta was hired at her first interview the day after her resume was completed (resume writer's comments).

ROBERTA REPORTER

85 Alameda Avenue • Winston, California 95498
(707) 555-1212

OBJECTIVE   A position as City Reporter.

PROFILE

- Over 10 years experience in newspaper reporting, writing and editing.
- BA in Communication/Print Media including newswriting and publication.
- Excellent public and written communicator, skilled in expository style.
- Held different progressive positions to increase professional experience.
- Proficient in Microsoft Word, WordPerfect, PCWrite for IBM, and QuarkXPress.

EDUCATION

BA - Communication/Print Media, University of the West, Stanton, CA, 1994

RELEVANT EXPERIENCE AND ACCOMPLISHMENTS

REPORTER
- Gathered and wrote news and feature stories for The Winston News front page.
  - Interviewed public officials and reported events at weekly City Council meeting.
- Assembled and composed news stories for two-page business section.
- Produced black and white photographs to accompany stories.
- Organized, created and designed layout and paste-up copy for printing.

EDITOR AND WRITER
- Assigned stories, wrote and edited articles, reviews and copy for weekly campus newspaper at The Pacifican.
  - Created tabloid style magazine insert published once per semester.
- Supervised up to 10 staff members and students, scheduled assignments, and coordinated production of campus-wide circulation.

BROADCAST JOURNALISM
- Performed as radio host at campus AM station, KPAC, Stanton.
  - Read news hourly and played selected music.

EMPLOYMENT HISTORY

1994-present   **General Assignment Reporter and Business Editor** • The Winston News, Winston, CA
Gather and write news and feature stories with accompanying black and white photographs, when applicable, for twice-weekly city newspaper.

WORK HISTORY

1993-1994   **Managing Editor and Writer** • The Pacifican, Stanton, CA
Served as managing editor for weekly university newspaper. Created headlines, designed and laid out news pages.

1992-1993   **Page Editor and Senior Staff Writer** • Pacific Tide Magazine, Stanton, CA
Wrote articles and reviews, and edited copy for campus newspaper magazine insert. Edited health page, reported general features, and reviewed restaurants.

1989-1991   **Page Editor and Senior Staff Writer** • La Madrone Community College, Pittstown, CA
Edited and designed sports page, reported and edited general news for newspaper.

1985-1987   **Staff Writer** • The Liberty, San Juan, CA
Wrote and edited feature and news articles for monthly high school paper. Gained first experience as reporter.

PROFESSIONAL AWARD

Best Media Coverage and Fair Photo, Redway Empire Fair Board of Directors, 1995

94

News reporter. *Nancy Karvonen, CPRW, CCM, IJCTC, CEIP; Orland, CA*

Robert uses photos to demonstrate his skills

©1995 Photos by Robert Thomason

Robert C. Thomason
208 Griffin Street
Raleigh, North Carolina 27529
919-779-1132 or 919-662-9334

Objective
Seek position in corporate photography for the production of images
for news releases and promotional publications.

Experience

1992 to Present, Freelance Photography/Desktop Publishing, Garner, North Carolina
Developed an independent "zine" publication tabloid hobby model newspaper for subscription and newsstand distribution. Directly involved in the design, page layout, reporting, photography, marketing, and distribution. Promoted periodical through direct mail and trade shows. Produced promotional literature and authored readership survey forms.

1987 to 1995, News and Observer Publishing Company, Raleigh, North Carolina
Staff Photographer
Photographed news, features, and sports subjects as a general assignment photographer. Coverage area emphasized photojournalism in Raleigh - the state capital, surrounding counties and often throughout the state. Produced work under deadline and participated in a photo staff environment.

1986 - 1987, Killeen Daily Herald, Killeen, Texas
Staff Photographer
Photojournalist for this medium sized central Texas daily. Coverage emphasized military operations of the 1st Cavalry and 2nd Armored Division at the adjacent military post, Fort Hood.

1986, Cary News, Cary, North Carolina.
Staff Photographer
Provided photography for a "bedroom community" bi-weekly newspaper. Also produced self-generated articles and photography for features.

1983 to 1986, Conroe Morning News, Conroe, Texas
Photographer
Managed operations of a small town daily newspaper photo-lab. Photo coverage emphasized local city and county stories, high school football, and stand-alone features. Produced several special photography tabs as advertising sections.

1981 to 1983, Freelance Photography, Midland, Texas.
Provided freelance photography services to local advertising agencies for publications and news releases. Photographed localing sporting events for weekly sports newspaper distributed in the Midland-Odessa area.

1979 to 1980, Campbell University, Buies Creek, North Carolina
Photographer
Produced images for use by public relations and public information for news releases and in-house publications from brochures to the university newspaper and annual. Supervised student photographers in photo-lab skills and field photography techniques. Worked in department while as an undergraduate for the production of still images. Employed a summer to provide video services to basketball camp participants.

Professional Affiliation
National Press Photographers Association (NPPA)
North Carolina Press Photographers Association (NCPPA)

Professional Recognition
Participation in regional and local clip contests have provided recognition of photography
from the NPPA, NCPPA, and the Texas Community Newspaper Association.

Education
Bachelor of Science, Campbell University, Buies Creek, North Carolina, 1979.

Personal
Birthdate -September 9, 1957

Technical Experience
Mac and PC computers
Film and flatbed scanners
Leaf 3D portable scanner
Photoshop (image processing), Quark Express (desktop publishing)
Coreldraw (image & art processing), Ventura Publisher 5.0(desktop publishing)
WordPerfect 6.1(word processing) & Microsoft Word (word processing)
HotMetal Pro (HTML for Internet Home Page development)

Supplementary Information
Letters of reference, general references, writing samples, and portfolio available upon request.

Note the wide range of subjects and styles in the photographs

95

Photographer. *Robert Thomason; Garner, NC*

JONATHAN COHON - PROFESSIONAL PHOTOGRAPHER
"Creator of Images That Can Neither Be Ignored Nor Dismissed"

PROFESSIONAL SUMMARY:

Creative, adaptable and people-oriented individual with ten *plus* years of diversified experience...Familiar with every aspect of design and planning of all assignments...Remarkable sense of humor...Especially skilled at the most challenging of locations...Dedicated to excellence in customer service.

PROFESSIONAL EXPERIENCE:

PRISM STUDIO *Since 1986*
Specializing in Small Product, Commercial, Industrial, Automotive, Fashion/Glamour, Magazine Illustration, Architectural, Product Illustration, Special Events, and Annual Report Photography...Originally started this business in Hollywood, California...Relocated studio to Illinois in 1989.

J.C. ENTERPRISES, Palm Springs, CA *1984 - 1986*
Specialized in assignments with in-house public relations agencies, as well as General Public Relations and Social Events Photography.

FREELANCE PHOTOJOURNALIST, Palm Desert, CA *1983 - 1984*
Worked primarily for Copley News publications, including *Palm Desert Post, Cathedral City Citizen* and *Rancho-Mirage Chronicle*...Assignments included catastrophic, hard news and society page stories.

EDUCATIONAL BACKGROUND:

DAVID BLATTELL PHOTOGRAPHY, Studio City, CA *1986*
Apprenticeship Program (3 Months)

JULES PORTER PHOTOGRAPHY, Beverly Hills, CA *1986*
Apprenticeship Program (3 Months)

CLIENT LIST AND PORTFOLIO WILL BE FURNISHED UPON REQUEST.

The simple format of Jonathan's "company resume" provides just enough information to create general interest (resume writer's comments).

96

Photographer. *Joellyn Wittenstein, CPRW; Buffalo Grove, IL*

DAVID HULSE-STEPHENS
915 East Hill Road
Willits, California 95490
(707) 459-3661

Based on this resume, David was selected for an interview from among 60 highly qualified applicants (resume writer's comments).

OBJECTIVE

A position as Public Relations/Foundation Officer.

SUMMARY OF QUALIFICATIONS

- More than 9 years experience in graphic design, marketing, and foundation fund raising.
- Extensive graphic layout, design, production, marketing, and budgetary experience.
- Cutting-edge technical knowledge of computer, printing process and requirements.
- Accomplished in promotional processes—advertising and media campaigns.
- Knowledgeable of Lake and Mendocino counties through community and work activities.
- Excellent oral and written communications abilities—accomplished public speaker.

RELEVANT SKILLS AND ACCOMPLISHMENTS

PUBLICATIONS/MARKETING
- Scheduled, designed and produced internationally distributed 20,000-circulation journal.
- Published quarterly Mendocino County health-network newsletter with circulation of 3,000.
- Created, edited, and **produced quarterly newsletters** for several non-profit organizations.
- Designed and produced issue sensitive publication for U.S. Representative Dan Hamburg.
- Actualized numerous marketing catalogs, brochures, audio tapes and books for New Dimensions.
  - Developed, coordinated, and administered advertising campaigns in national magazines.
- Produced Waldorf School educational handbook, and State of California educational flyers.
- Developed **marketing research** and demographic survey for Mendocino College.

EVENTS PLANNING/FUND RAISING
- Spearheaded and promoted 24 public speaking series events over 4 years.
  - Attended by more than 1,500 registrants in one season, surpassing 90 percent capacity.
- Prepared and **monitored annual budgets** of more than $23,000 for speaker series.
- Presented welcoming talk and introduced world-class speakers at Star in the Well.
- Developed numerous fund-raising mailings, informational brochures, and marketing pieces.

Covers 10 years of work history

WRITING/EDITING
- Formulated copy for promotional catalogs, brochures, speaker series, and schedules.
- As managing editor, oversaw production for bi-monthly Mendocino Country Newspaper.
- Authored numerous personal profile feature articles in regional and national publications.
- Researched and **wrote news articles** on Mendocino County politics and entertainment.
- Composed **press releases** and radio public-service announcements, cultivated media contacts.

EMPLOYMENT HISTORY

Concurrent "jobs" some volunteer

1996-present	*Consultant/Events Coordinator*	MENDOCINO COLLEGE, Ukiah
1993-present	*Co-organizer/Producer*	STAR IN THE WELL SPEAKER SERIES, Ukiah
1988-present	*Director of Publications*	NEW DIMENSIONS FOUNDATION, Ukiah
1987-present	*Publications Designer*	HULSE-STEPHENS SERVICES, Willits

EDUCATION & TRAINING

University of California, Davis, Applied Behavioral Sciences

This is a good way to handle not having a degree

97

Public relations specialist. *Nancy Karvonen, CPRW, CCM, IJCTC, CEIP; Orland, CA*

Targeting a specific organization and opportunity, this resume is able to highlight the exact capabilities that will be of most value.

Alex Duart

P. O. Box 125 ❖ Prattville, Alabama 36000 ❖ duarta@hotmail.com ❖ 334.555.5555

Value to Variety Press International

As a **writer and editor**, I can translate your vision into written words that are read, remembered, and acted upon.

Capabilities you can use now:

❖ **Seasoned writer** who gets the best stories

❖ **Organized editor** who meets tight deadlines

❖ **"Turnaround" specialist** with solid track record

Work history with selected examples of success:

Business Owner, Champion Products, Montgomery, Alabama (99–Present)

❖ Found and served specialty markets, met customer needs, developed promotion plans, and controlled costs.

Editorial Director, Norpress Publishers, Montgomery, Alabama (89–91, 92–98)
One of the first employees of industry leader in natural resource magazines. Helped this aggressive company build a national circulation of 200,000.

❖ Transformed unfocused collection of promotional literature into major resource book. Found and wrote the stories, did most of the editing. Handled promotion. *Results:* Sold nearly 30,000 copies of this $25 technical manual. **Won $50,000 advertising packages.**

❖ Helped build five magazines. Did it all, from hiring writers to setting details of layout. Spun off full-color, slick magazine from tabloid. *Results:* Advertising up. **Successfully converted free publication to paid publication.**

❖ Convinced nation's expert to let me do in-depth story on his one-of-a-kind system. *Results:* Although other competitors had tried and failed, I got *all* the information. Expert impressed. Our **25,000 audited readers very happy.**

Editorial Director, The Colophon Press, Atlanta Branch, San Francisco, California (86–89)
Key contributor to two magazines this 100-year old house publishes.

❖ Major contributor and key researcher for flagship publications. *Results:* **Exceeded** corporate goals by **at least 15% every year for six years.**

❖ Developed and followed up on list of key decision makers in readers' markets. *Results:* **Always got the story. Manufacturers asked my opinion of their newest products.**

Results are included for each achievement.

Computer literacy:

❖ Expert in Word for Windows 2000 and WordPerfect
❖ Working knowledge of Excel, Lotus 1-2-3, Quicken, Peachtree Accounting, Windows

Skills that help build your productivity:

❖ Accomplished photographer comfortable with 35 mm and 2¼ x 2¼ formats
❖ Complete knowledge of paste-up procedures

Education:

❖ Attended Waller State University, Waller, Alabama: 30 semester hours in English

98

Writer and editor. *Don Orlando, MBA, CPRW, IJCTC, CCM; Montgomery, AL*

KYO TANAKA

75 Hillcrest Drive ❑ *East Haven, CT 06512* ❑ *(203) 469-2320* ❑ *kyotanaka@netzero.net*

PROFILE

Experienced technical writer / trainer with demonstrated skill in documenting software used for both non-technical users and technical support staff. Recognized for producing consistently clear, coherent documentation within deadline and with minimal supervision. Accustomed to collaborating closely with programmers during development and testing as an integral part of the software development team.

- ❑ Strengths include communication skills (both oral and written), organization and planning, meticulous proofreading, and project / schedule management.
- ❑ Experienced with computers and, in particular, with word processing programs and authoring systems (Corel WordPerfect, Microsoft Word, RoboHelp).

To avoid the appearance of "job hopping" each time the ownership of the company changed, company names are grouped and functions are combined.

EXPERIENCE

company names

MAAX INDUSTRIAL AUTOMATION AND CONTROLS, New Haven, Connecticut
AUTO-CONTROLS CORPORATION (purchased by Maax IAC 4/99)
HIGH RIDGE CORPORATION (purchased by Auto-Controls 6/97)

Technical Writer / Trainer, 1996–May 2001

function

Wrote detailed on-line and print instruction manuals for Windows NT-based and OS/2-based industrial gauging equipment.

- ❑ Manuals included a technical reference for setting up and maintaining the hardware as well as in-depth software documentation for daily use and system setup.

- ❑ Involved in each product during the development cycle and contributed significantly to software testing.

- ❑ Provided software training classes, for both an historical product and newer products, to customers and technical support personnel.

Technical Writer, 1994–1996

function

Researched, wrote, and often illustrated industrial-gauge manuals.

- ❑ Manuals include theory, safety requirements, installation and setup procedures, operator guides, and maintenance requirements.

- ❑ Also wrote detailed instructions for the computerized electronics or personal computers used to operate the gauges.

99

Technical writer. *Louise M. Kursmark, CPRW, JCTC, CEIP, CCM; Cincinnati, OH*

KYO TANAKA

Page 2

EAST HAVEN PUBLIC LIBRARY, East Haven, Connecticut

Indexer, 1993–1994

Assisted with the development of a local history index generated from newspapers dating back to the early 1700s. Focused primarily on individuals and their connections to events.

NORTHEAST HOME BUILDERS ASSOCIATION, Orange, Connecticut

Managing Editor, 1991–1993

Wrote and assigned feature articles, "spotlights" on local home-builder associations, and news items, as well as promotional material for the company. Proofread both the Xerox and blueline of the 20-plus magazines and all printing assignments. Established the editorial, feature, and production schedules for all the magazines.

EDUCATION

WESLEYAN UNIVERSITY, Middletown, Connecticut

Bachelor of Arts, English, 1991; Minor in Communications

Worked Sophomore, Junior and Senior years as a Resident Assistant for the University Housing Department. Served one year as a Peer Assistant. Active in intramural sports.

ACTIVITIES

- ☐ Senior Member of the Society for Technical Communication.
- ☐ Competitive soccer player (New Haven Adult League); avid rock-climber.

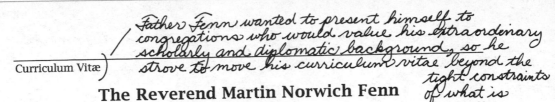

Father Fenn wanted to present himself to congregations who would value his extraordinary scholarly and diplomatic background, so he strove to move his curriculum vitae beyond the tight constraints of what is typically included.

Curriculum Vitæ

The Reverend Martin Norwich Fenn

3033 Colonial Drive
Montgomery, Alabama 36100
☏ [334] 555-5555 — mnfenn@knology.net

EDUCATION AND PROFESSIONAL DEVELOPMENT

○ M. Div, The St. Luke's School of Theology, University of the South, Sewanee, Tennessee, 1973. Top student in a class of thirty.

○ Unit in Clinical Pastoral Education, Yale University Hospital, New Haven, Connecticut, 1971. Selected for this competitive program that prepares pastors to deal with the entire range of personal crises in the lives of everyday people.

○ M.A. (History), University of Virginia, Charlottesville, Virginia, 1968. One of some 20 scholars nationwide to win a full Danforth Fellowship (full scholarship). Completed this program in a fraction of the time normally required.

○ B.A. (History), University of the South, Sewannee, Tennessee, 1967. Magna Cum Laude.

○ "Cross-Cultural Training," Episcopal Church, 1978. This intensive, two-month course prepares students to deal with vital, cross-cultural issues at every level.

○ "Motivating Communities to Reach Goals," Episcopal Church Training Movement, 1973–1976.

EMPLOYMENT HISTORY

○ Interim Rector, The Church of the Ascension, Martindale, Alabama, Jun 2001–Present.

○ Interim Rector, Trinity Church, Coller, Alabama, Feb 2001–Jun 2001.

○ Senior Counselor, Self-Discovery, Ft. Walton, Alabama, Jan 2000–Feb 2001.

○ Served Episcopal congregations for more than 27 years as senior executive and pastor at churches with up to 400 members. Beyond providing pastoral guidance, administered operational and mission budgets up to $200K.

- Episcopal Chaplain, St. George's, Alabama State University, Montgomery, Alabama, 1995–1999.

- Rector, Church of the Holy Comforter, Milliken, Alabama, 1986–1995.

- Rector, St. Alban's, Northboro, Alabama, 1983–1986.

- Rector, Grace Church, Selma, Alabama, 1981–1983.

- Interim Rector, St. Paul's, Union Ford, Alabama, 1980–1981.

- Chaplain to the Anglican Bishop in Jerusalem, Israel, 1978–1980. Served as the diplomatic interface between cultures in conflict for centuries.

- Curate, The Church of the Redeemer, Walton, Alabama, 1973 –1978.

Page 1 of 2

100

Protestant minister. *Don Orlando, MBA, CPRW, IJCTC, CCM; Montgomery, AL*

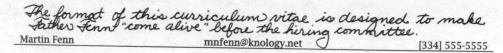

The format of this curriculum vitae is designed to make Father Fenn "come alive" before the hiring committee.

| Martin Fenn | mnfenn@knology.net | [334] 555-5555 |

HONORS

○ The Greek Award, 1973. Only one of 60 eligibles to win this award for excellence in the study of the Greek language.

○ Omicron Delta Kappa and Blue Key, 1966. This honorary organization draws its members from faculty recommendations for academic excellence and community service.

○ Phi Beta Kappa, 1965.

PUBLICATIONS

○ Regular columns on spiritual matters written at the request of the editor, *The Apostle*, 1986–1989.

○ Maius Imperium Proconsulare of the Emperor Caesar Augustus, unpublished master's thesis, 1968.

COLLEGE-LEVEL COURSES TAUGHT

○ Adjunct Professor of History, Conner College, Montgomery, Alabama, 1981–1983

- World Civilization, a comprehensive survey course that covered the period from prehistory to modern time.

- American History, a course devoted to the entire course of American history.

SERVICE TO MY COMMUNITY

○ Member, Board of Directors, AIDS Outreach, 1996–1999.

○ Director, Teenage Episcopal Camp Program, Camp Martin, 1973–1997.

○ Member, All American City Committee, Gadsden, Alabama, 1991–1993.

○ Board Member, Montgomery Area United Way, 1975–1978.

○ Member, Charter Board of Directors, Central Counseling Center, 1974–1978.

COMPUTER SKILLS

○ Proficient in word processors, database managers, Microsoft Windows, presentation software, Quicken, and Internet search protocols.

LANGUAGE SKILLS

○ Fluently able to read and write in Spanish, Hebrew, Arabic, Greek, and Latin.

This section paints a picture of who Rabbi Cohn is and what he has done. It emphasizes his philosophy and leadership style, which are of great interest to hiring committees.

Rabbi Ethan M. Cohn

45 Fellsbrook Drive, Melrose, MA 02176
(781) 555-3445   rabbicohn@juno.com

Profile

Philosophy

Dedicated to leading a vibrant Jewish community, promoting Jewish values and the essence of our tradition through leadership of both innovative and traditional programs that encourage participation in the full spectrum of Jewish expression through all of life's stages.

Key Strengths

Vision	Able to identify needs, envision programs, lead a community, and be an agent for change.
Execution	Skillful manager with strong organization and coordination skills; able to bring programs from idea to action.
People Skills	Empathetic and attuned to the diverse needs of the human soul. Able to build relationships in the community and work well with committees and staff.
Focus	Dedicated to developing activities that promote the fundamental purpose of the Synagogue as a center for Jewish religion, education, social action, and community.

Qualifications Summary

- Five years' experience as Associate Rabbi for large Temple with active and involved congregation.
- Track record of innovative program development and effective leadership of committees and initiatives encompassing all aspects of Temple life.

Rabbinical Experience

In this section, specific achievements are categorized under specific program areas.

1997–Present   **Associate Rabbi,** Both Shalom Temple, Melrose, Massachusetts
600-household Reform Temple

Perform all rabbinical functions: teaching, preaching, counseling, officiating at religious services and life-cycle events. Play a key leadership and coordinating role in Temple and community-wide activities and programs.

Key Contributions and Activities

Religious Services: Collaborate with senior rabbi on service improvements to ensure meaningful experiences and strong congregant participation.

- Co-edited and produced new prayer book for Friday night Shabbat worship. Instrumental in prayer selection, design and layout, and incorporation of transliteration. Participation in worship service has increased, particularly among congregants who don't read Hebrew fluently.
- Inaugurated and co-wrote new monthly service, *Refuat HaNefesh, Service of Healing and Strength of the Soul.* Attracted congregants to the service through outreach and publicity.

Social Action Program: Oversee committee and coordinate program in which more than 350 congregants participate in 50+ community service projects throughout the year.

- Reinvigorated social action pogram by developing new image, brochure, and kickoff program.

Youth Programs: Supervise religious education for students from 5th grade through Confirmation. Develop curriculum; oversee staff; develop and lead retreats.

College-Age Program: Inaugurate new outreach and communication programs.

- Created online newsletter distributed to more than 100 college-age students via e-mail.
- Conceived program of rabbinic visitations to college campuses throughout New England.

101

Rabbi. *Louise M. Kursmark, CPRW, JCTC, CEIP, CCM; Cincinnati, OH*

Rabbinical Experience, continued

Young Adult Congregation: Lead programs and activities for congregants 22-35 years of age with a strong focus on core values of worship, fellowship, and social action.

Outreach: Focus Temple outreach programs on integrating interfaith families and Jews by Choice into the congregation.

- Developed 2-year outreach plan/program that creates a structure for integrating new members into all aspects of Temple life. Established a mentoring program for those in the process of converting.
- Created educational programs on Jewish traditions and opened participation to the entire congregation, helping to reduce isolation of new members.
- Broadened program offerings for families of interfaith couples.

Senior Adult Program: Launch new program to address the needs of the Temple's most underserved population.

- Surveyed congregation and established well-attended programs ranging from entertainment to thought-provoking and challenging speakers.

Jewish Dating Service: Manage confidential Jewish dating service and supervise program director.

- Since 1997, program has served more than 800 single Jewish adults and led to 30 marriages and 9 Jewish children born of those marriages.

Web Site: Spearheaded development of the Temple's Internet presence, playing a key role in web site focus, content, and design.

Professional Activities and Associations

2000–Present	**President, Greater Boston Board of Rabbis (Member** since 1997)
1998–Present	**Board Member, Peaceful Village Retirement Home**
1998–Present	**Adjunct Faculty,** Boston University (teach undergraduate course on Jewish beliefs)
1998	**Co-Chair, Jewish Federation of Boston Annual Retreat** (involving 1200 people)

Prior Experience

1995–1997	**Student Rabbi,** Beth El Temple, Belmont, Massachusetts
1993–1994	**Chaplain Intern,** Mayo Clinic, Rochester, Minnesota
1992–1993	**Student Rabbi,** Temple Sinai, Jacksonville, Florida
1992–1993	**Rabbinic Intern,** University of Florida Student Union, Gainesville, Florida

Education

Hebrew Union College–Jewish Institute of Religion, Cincinnati, Ohio

1997	**Ordination as a Rabbi**
1995	**Master of Arts in Hebrew Letters**

Simmons College, Boston, Massachusetts

1993	**Bachelor of Science in Sociology**

Personal

- Married to Wendy Goldberg (marriage and family therapist) — one child, Sarah, born 11/15/01.

Not all priests lead parishes. Father Richards is a hospital chaplain and pastoral counselor.

REV. JOSEPH RICHARDS
9899 Hannum Avenue • Columbus, Ohio
614-899-9999 • Email: FrJoeRichards99@worldnet.att.net

DIRECTOR / MANAGER ~ PASTORAL / SPIRITUAL CARE

Creative, energetic and visionary leader called upon by God seeking opportunity to oversee and promote the spiritual and team-excellence of a dedicated staff. Promote a holistic approach to healing, combined with spiritual, religious, and emotional support and counsel to patients, families, and staff. Expertise in spiritual care and innovative approaches to spiritual ministry within the healthcare environment. Possess strong interpersonal skills and demonstrated strengths in written communication, organizational management, administration and facilitation. Excellent understanding and ability to foster relations with individuals from diverse faiths and multicultural milieus. Strengths include:

Community Relations • Interdisciplinary Relationship Management • Staff Relations
International Experiences • Spiritual Counseling • Corporate Parish Ministry • Mission Leadership
Program Planning / Development • Grief Counseling • All Faiths Ministry • Spiritual Outreach
Volunteer Programming • Committee Leadership • Computer Proficiency

CERTIFICATIONS / EDUCATION / TRAINING

Board Certified Chaplain — National Association of Catholic Chaplains

Clinical Pastoral Education • 1990–2000
Advanced & Extended Unit — Children's Hospital, Cleveland, Ohio — Emphasis in child spirituality
Emergency Department Chaplain Intern — Mercy Medical Center, Akron, Ohio
Chaplain Intern — Mental Health Rescue Crisis Center, Akron, Ohio
1600 hours of supervised training in hospital settings

Master of Divinity • Katholieke Universiteit Te Leuven, Louvain, Belgium • 1986–1989

Spiritual, Field and Pastoral Education with Theological Reflection
The American College, Louvain, Belgium • 1986–1989 and 1990–1991

Intense study in Canon Law
Katholieke Universiteit Te Leuven, Louvain, Belgium • 1990–1991

Bachelor of Arts in English Literature • Saint Meinrad College, Saint Meinrad, Indiana • 1986
Concentration in Philosophy • Minor in Psychology
100 hours of supervised training in a mental health facility

PROFESSIONAL EXPERIENCE

ST. JOAN OF ARC MEDICAL CENTER and CHILDREN'S HOSPITAL, Columbus, Ohio • 1994–Present
FULL-TIME PRIEST / CHAPLAIN

Recruited to serve as key resource in Roman Catholic tradition, providing spiritual needs within a 500+ bed tertiary-care, Level I Trauma Center and Level II Children's Hospital. Preside over daily community worship in a 250-person capacity chapel. Provide for more than 100 hours of weekly on-call coverage at four hospitals. Collaborate with Columbus area clergy and faith communities as a member of the Ecumenical Pastoral Care Team. Serve as primary consultant to the nascent Mercy Prayer Partners. Supervise the ministerial and educational development of more than 50 Lay Eucharist Ministers. Organize and facilitate annual workshops for area clergy.

- Established a dually accredited hospital CPE program, first ever in Ohio and in the CHP (Catholic Healthcare Partners) healthcare system.
- Guided numerous projects: chapel upgrades; maintenance and construction of the All Faiths Meditation Room.
- Spearheaded development of Community Clergy Advisory Board and established the initial groundwork to form the Cultural Diversity Group.
- Conducted very popular and widely attended in-service programs throughout Ohio introducing new approaches toward Mass Stipends and the Pastoral Theology of Sacrament of Anointing of the Sick.
- Championed the CHP (Catholic Health Partners)–Ohio Strategic Planning Pastoral Care Services Retreat in 1999, now a yearly event.
- Revised content and terminology for patient consent forms regarding family planning / fertility options as approved by the hospital IRB (Institutional Review Board).

102

Roman Catholic priest. *Deborah S. James, CPRW; Rossford, OH*

REV. JOSEPH RICHARDS
614-899-9999 • Email: FrJoeRichards99@worldnet.att.net

ST. JOAN OF ARC MEDICAL CENTER and CHILDREN'S HOSPITAL...*continued*

- Implemented Worship Needs Survey now being used in numerous hospitals throughout the Columbus and Cleveland areas.
- Authored MHP Northern Region Pastoral Care Services Vision Statement.

SAINT JOHN THE EVANGELIST CHURCH, Cleveland, Ohio • 1991–1994
ASSOCIATE PASTOR

Provided for spiritual needs and worship leadership for a 5,400-member congregation. Participated in a one-hour live weekly radio segment each Sunday.

- Offered pastoral care for the sick and family members at area hospitals and nursing homes, taking part in ethical consultations.
- Managed High School Chaplaincy Department and taught freshman and sophomore religion classes.
- Coordinated the high-school student and staff spiritual enrichment program.
- Designed and developed Adult Bible Study series.
- Guided the curriculum development of RCIA – Rite of Christian Initiation of Adults.

SAINT MICHAEL CHURCH, Toledo Ohio • 1989–1990
ASSISTANT TO PASTORS

Networked with deacons and lay ministers to develop a spiritually effective pastoral-care program for an 8,500-member congregation that served a countywide Catholic population. Provided biweekly pastoral care for hospitalized individuals.

ALL SAINTS ANGLICAN AND EPISCOPAL CHURCH, Waterloo, Belgium
Fall 1987–Spring 1989 • Fall 1990–Spring 1991

Trained as a pastoral minister in a 500-member congregation with a very diverse multicultural and ecumenical population. Fostered relations with Episcopalian ministers, a husband-wife team, and other lay leaders to develop and introduce individual spiritual care and successful public worship.

PROFESSIONAL WORKSHOPS AND CONFERENCES

Catholic Social Teaching & Church-State Relationships, Charles Curran, Cleveland, Ohio • 2001
Priest Prayer Days, Reverend George Aschenbrenner, S.J., Columbus, Ohio • 2001
Spirituality Symposium with John Shea, CHP, Cincinnati, Ohio • 2001
MHP Ohio Pastoral Care Services Strategic Planning Retreat • 2001
International Symposium, NACC, Baltimore, Maryland • 2001
Life is Precious to the Very End, MHP Palliative Care Forum, Columbus, Ohio • 2000

PROFESSIONAL MEMBERSHIPS AND INVOLVEMENT

Diocesan Priest, Roman Catholic Diocese of Columbus
Columbus Area Chaplain Association, CACA
Honorary Lifetime Member of the Catholic Knights of Columbus
Chairman: Hospital-wide Worship Committee • St. Joan of Arc Medical Center and Children's Hospital
Past Member: Institutional Review Board • St. Joan of Arc Medical Center and Children's Hospital
Founding Member: Hospital-wide CPE Professional Advisory Board

Amanda Paterson

19 Green Meadow Street ♦ Corning, New York 16773 ♦ (716) 655-8732

PROFILE:	Dedicated and self-directed professional with 20 years experience as an Educator, Child Services Advocate, Counselor and Public Relations Liaison. Outstanding leadership and motivational qualifications. Career highlights include:

These are all volunteer activities presented here {

- ◆ Developed and implemented tutorial program for at risk children at Woodlands Elementary School in collaboration with Conroe ISD and the YWCA. Expanded program to include parents in need (1992 - 1995).
- ◆ Coordinated summer enrichment program for disadvantaged youth of South Montgomery County (1992).
- ◆ Served as Program Director of The Woodlands Chapter of Jack and Jill, Inc.
- ◆ Recognized as "YWCA Outstanding Woman Honoree" for community service efforts.
- ◆ Served on Board of Review of The Boy Scouts of America.
- ◆ Committee member of Child Advocates of Houston (1996).

EDUCATION:

Prairie View A&M University
Prairie View, Texas
School Counselor Certification 1996
- Member of Honorary Counseling Society
- LPC Certification targeted for Fall 1996

This stay-at-home mom was re-entering the workforce after 12 years of working at home. She got a related job within 30 days.

Texas Southern University
Houston, Texas
M. Ed *Elementary Education* 1974

Texas Teacher's Certification in Grades K-6

Texas Woman's University
Denton, Texas
B.S., *Child Development* 1968

Practicum
LYNDBOROUGH HIGH SCHOOL, Lyndborough, NY
Served as Career and Financial Aid Counselor to Junior and Senior High School students

MONROE COUNTY COLLEGE, Nashua, NY
Counseled student on course selections and requirements. Ensured enrollees met requirements for TASP.

PROFESSIONAL EXPERIENCE:

WILTON DEVELOPMENT CORPORATION
Public Relations Liaison   1992 - Present

SERAFIN ANDERSON, M.D.
Office Administrator   1986 - 1989

MILFORD INDEPENDENT SCHOOL DISTRICT
Second Grade and Kindergarten Teacher   1977 - 1984

DURHAM INDEPENDENT SCHOOL DISTRICT
Third Grade Teacher   1975 - 1976

SOUTH FORK INDEPENDENT SCHOOL DISTRICT
Second and Sixth Grade Teacher   1969 - 1975

103

Counselor. *Cheryl Ann Harland, CPRW, JCTC; The Woodlands, TX*

Sarah L. Baker, RN, COHN-S, CEAP, LPC

723 St. Mary's Road • Goodlettsville, Tennessee 37072

Home (615) 851-3545 • Email: SBakerLPC@aol.com

Profile) *This section clearly outlines Sarah's areas of expertise and her numerous qualifications.*

LICENSED PROFESSIONAL COUNSELOR and REGISTERED NURSE with significant experience in **Occupational Health** and the development of **Employee Assistance** programs, combined with extensive professional training and education. Provide early identification and assessment of employee needs and problems that affect health and job performance.

- Well versed and proficient in the design and development of instructional health programs to meet employee needs and company goals.

- Identify and explore relevant employee issues and develop appropriate programs in multiple areas, such as alcohol and drug dependency, stress reduction, anti-smoking, weight management, hypertension, and other health and job concerns.

- Highly regarded for knowledge of available professional and community resources. Collaborate with Central Diagnostic and Referral (CDR) agencies for appropriate referrals and services.

- An accomplished change agent with an established track record in getting positive results working with employees, management, and healthcare professionals. Interact with all levels in a professional and diplomatic manner.

Education

MASTER OF ARTS IN COUNSELING — 2000
Trevecca Nazarene University — Nashville, Tennessee

BACHELOR OF SCIENCE IN NURSING — 1984
University of Tennessee, Knoxville — School of Nursing

Professional Experience

OCCUPATIONAL HEALTH NURSE SPECIALIST..1993 – Present
Textron Aerostructures International — Nashville, Tennessee

- Develop and maintain employee assistance and occupational health programs for manufacturing company with 1,400 employees (400 on first shift).
- Provide emergency care, pre-employment and monthly physicals, audiometric and eye testing, drug and pulmonary screening, asbestos and EKG testing.
- Counsel and support employees regarding personal health and family problems, referring them to appropriate CDR agencies as needed.
- Monitor OSHA compliance and recordkeeping and manage computer entry of records and reports for OSHA Log 200.
- Maintain inventory and quality control of all clinical equipment and supplies. Calibrate equipment nightly.

Continued . . .

104

Counselor. *Carolyn Braden, CPRW; Hendersonville, TN*

Sarah L. Baker

Professional Experience (continued)

SUPERVISOR / STAFF NURSE..1988 – 1993
Veteran's Administration Medical Center • Knoxville, Tennessee

- Worked as Relief Supervisor for four years, supervising nursing staff and overseeing patient care and treatment.
- Provided primary nursing care for Pulmonary Service in Diagnostic Medicine, Surgery Floor, for five years.

PULMONARY NURSE..1986 – 1988
Knox Home Health Care • Knoxville, Tennessee

- Managed caseload and provided direct home nursing care to pulmonary patients of area doctors.

EMERGENCY ROOM NURSE..1984 – 1986
Sevier County Hospital • Sevierville, Tennessee

Licensure & Certification)—

as seen in the previous "Education" section of her resume, Sarah had recently completed her master's degree in counseling. Here she highlights her licenses to help her secure consulting assignments in occupational health and employee assistance.

2000	**Licensed Professional Counselor** (LPC)
2000	Disability Management
1999	Certified Instructor — Crisis Intervention
1997	Physical Assessment
1995	**Certified Employee Assistance Professional** (CEAP)
1994	Certified Case Manager (CCM)
1993	Certified OSHA Recordkeeper
1991	**Certified Occupational Health Nurse Specialist** (COHN-S)
1990	Certified Emergency Medical Technician (EMT) – 21 CEUs
1988	Pulmonary Screenings
1983	Certified CPR Instructor

Professional Affiliations

American Association of Occupational Health Nurses — National   1993 – Present
- Chair, Election Advisory Committee; National Bylaws Committee

Tennessee Association of Occupational Health Nurses — State   1993 – Present

Middle Tennessee Association of Occupational Health Nurses   1993 – Present
- President; Vice President; Board of Directors
- Public Relations Committee; Nominating Committee

Employee Assistance Association — National, State, and Local   1992 – Present
- Secretary, Middle Tennessee Chapter

Lee Stephens

1111 North Hill Street ◆ Radcliff, Kentucky 40100 ◆ (502) 351-0000

Objective

Corrections Rehabilitation Counselor

Summary of Qualifications

- Master's degree in Counseling. Bachelor of Science degrees in Criminal Justice and Psychology.
- Over 20 years of experience in corrections.
- Excellent interpersonal skills with staff and inmate population and sensitive to their problems and counseling needs. A proven team-player who works well with people and can be counted on in any type of situation.

Professional Experience

FEDERAL CORRECTION FACILITY ◆ Any City, USA
Deputy Education Director & Operations Officer ◆ Mar 92 - Present

- ➡ Counseled inmates and correlated day-to-day administrative operations for this facility which provided vocational training and educational classes to prisoners. As Custody Control Administrator, handled all disciplinary problems; maintained a roster of all day and evening students/inmates and instituted a system to monitor student's progress and course completion. Developed and established a program to provide evening college classes. Coordinated with local universities to contract instructors.
- ➡ As Assistant Test Control Officer, administered and graded GED, DANTE, and ASIP tests. Awarded high school diploma, college semester hours, or certified students in vocational areas such as auto mechanics. Occasionally escorted prisoners into the city to take tests that could not be provided by any other means.
- ➡ Supervised six subordinate administrative employees. Acted as liaison to ten contracted teachers and resolved problems.
- ➡ Coordinated and established an inmate barber shop which resulted in an annual savings of $10,000.
- ➡ Consistently received commendable / outstanding ratings during security and safety inspections.
- ➡ Selected to attend Correctional Management Training which was usually reserved for prison wardens and correctional administrators.
- ➡ Coordinated and implemented educational programs for inmates to return them to civilian life with better employment skills.

FEDERAL CORRECTION FACILITY ◆ Any City, USA
Correctional Counselor ◆ Jul 86 - Mar 92

- ➡ As Counselor, had a case-load of approximately 150 inmates; counseled each inmate at least twice a month and provided advice concerning their personal problems. Counseled and advised families, arranged visits, and occasionally assisted spouses find lodging near the facility.
- ➡ Escorted and closely supervised inmates who were allowed to return home during times of family emergencies or death. Sat on Disciplinary Board and Parole Board and made recommendations for clemency, parole, etc., based upon thorough knowledge of each case. Issued medications and maintained an accurate, detailed record of medications which were dispensed. Served on the Classification Board; after careful review of records, made recommendations for custody-level of new arrivals and determined appropriate work assignments.

105

Counselor. *Connie S. Stevens; Radcliff, KY*

Lee Stephens

STATE CORRECTION FACILITY ◆ Any City, USA
Chief of Employment Branch ◆ Dec 80 - Jul 86
➥ Supervised 11 staff personnel and evaluated their performance. Provided employee training, guidance, and counseling.
➥ Managed the office responsible for providing work details to the community. Inmate details included such tasks as mowing grass, providing office-building maintenance, shop work, and routine repairs.
➥ Counseled and evaluated approximately 130 inmates. Ensured that prisoners' surroundings were secure at all times. Monitored their activities and assigned employment details based on the inmate's background and custody level. Assigned guards to escort prisoners.
➥ Attended weekly staff meetings with superiors and made recommendations. Attended semi-monthly in-service training sessions on various topics including riot control, apprehension planning and practice exercises, use of gas masks, and survival training.

REGIONAL CORRECTION FACILITY ◆ Any City, USA
Chief of Prisoners' Service & Supervision Branch ◆ May 76 - Dec 80
➥ As Chief of Prisoners Service Branch, supervised 25 employees. Assigned duties and evaluated job performance. Provided employee training and counseling. Managed the administration office, prisoner property and funds section, supply room, mail room, and probation and parole sections. Supervised all aspects of prisoner's processing into and out of the Regional Correction Facility.
➥ As Chief of Supervision Branch, supervised and managed the guard force consisting of 110 personnel. Awarded *Best Safety Program* twice in one year.
➥ Devised, developed, and implemented the Vocational Employment Training Program for minimum custody inmates. Work site supervisors provided inmates with on-the-job training in such areas as carpentry and plumbing. At the end of the program, inmates were given certificates to be used for future employment stating they had received vocational training in particular areas.
➥ Developed, staffed, and implemented an Escort Section which increased security and provided excellent inmate accountability. Supervised three guards whose responsibilities included scheduling appointments and escorting prisoners to medical and legal appointments.

Education

UNIVERSITY OF KENTUCKY ◆ Lexington, KY
Master of Arts in **Counseling** ◆ May 83

EASTERN KENTUCKY UNIVERSITY ◆ Richmond, KY
Bachelor of Science in **Criminal Justice** ◆ May 74
Bachelor of Science in **Psychology** ◆ May 74

Addendum containing information on additional training courses is available upon request

A very strong resume, it shows many examples of his accomplishments in his work with inmates. The resume also displays how his iniative has had a positive impact.

With a well-designed introductory page and an emphasis on key skills throughout, this resume presents an image of a creative and committed person who can do all sorts of useful things

━━━ **MELODIE KIMBER** ━━━

HUMAN SERVICE POSITION

Many key adaptive and transferable skills

Directly involved in human service work since 1991 in positions of increasing responsibility and authority ... experience in grant writing and government contracts ... diligent, compassionate and thorough professional who is committed to excellence ... effective communicator and motivator ... work well under pressure ... thrive in atmosphere of challenge, creativity and variety ... flexible work style—can adapt quickly to changing work and client needs ... assertive, hands-on leader with strong program implementation skills ... team player ... professional appearance and manner ... 2 yrs. college-level Spanish.

Strengths

- planning, implementation and coordination
- decisionmaking and goal setting
- supervisory and leadership
- fundraising and grant writing
- client and victim contact
- training and inservices
- writing and editorial
- document and form design
- budgeting and forecasting

Many work-related skills

106

Human service worker. *Beverly Drake, CPRW; Muskegon, MI*

MELODIE KIMBER

17 Spring Road
Milwaukee, Wisconsin 50000

(414) 555-0000

- ▶ language proficiency
- ▶ program planning and implementation
- ▶ writing and public speaking skills
- ▶ organizational and time management
- ▶ extensive computer background
- ▶ high work ethic and attention to detail
- ▶ strong problem resolution skills

HUMAN SERVICE POSITION

This is not so much a job "title" as a statement of what work she wants to do — a values-driven job objective

Emphasis is on key skills that could be used in a variety of positions

ACCOMPLISHMENTS AND EXPERIENCE

Human Service and Administrative Skills

- ▶ supervision and training of volunteer staff of 10+ for human service agency
- ▶ training and certification as victim advocate to provide counseling / assistance in court, hospitals, police stations
- ▶ successful initiation and implementation of emergency fundraiser for human service group
- ▶ speaker for community groups and agencies regarding human service topics
- ▶ assistance in organization of Sudden Infant Death Syndrome statewide conferences
- ▶ coordination and verification of data in government contracts; research and assimilation of business information
- ▶ responsibility for operational functions and development of policies and procedures for career consulting firm
- ▶ performance of needs analyses and implementation of business strategies
- ▶ human resource issues, including hiring and development of training programs

Writing, Editorial, and Media-Related

- ▶ media liaison with radio stations for human service group
- ▶ development of corporate marketing portfolio and procedure manual
- ▶ writing and setup of brochures, press releases and training manual
- ▶ production of prevention skills booklet for Wisconsin State workshops
- ▶ re-design, writing and editing of quarterly newsletters with countywide distribution
- ▶ co-author of workbook on Child Sexual Abuse

Technology Expertise

- ▶ self-taught Windows, PageMaker, Lotus, Excel, Quicken, Peachtree, AmiPro, Word, PowerPoint, WordPerfect
- ▶ conversion of manual accounting system to computerized system; data base and mailing list setup
- ▶ technical support and training to staff

WORK HISTORY

Business Development Coordinator, Startup Executive Training Corporation, Anytown, Wisconsin	1996 to present
Contract Administrator, Visionary Corporation, Anytown, Illinois	1992 to 1996
Editor and Victim Advocate, Important Human Service Group, Anytown, Wisconsin	1993 to 94
Office Administrator, Child Illness Group, Anytown, Illinois	1991 to 92

EDUCATION, RECOGNITION, AND MEMBERSHIPS

Bachelor of Arts in Communication—University of Wisconsin—1994
Associate of Arts in Accounting—Oakton Community College—1991
Member: Women in Communication; National Association of Female Executives (NAFE)
Thesis paper on gender bias recognized by Dr. Myra and David Sadker, Washington DC researchers

REFERENCES AND PORTFOLIO OF WRITING AND DESIGN WORK AVAILABLE

JOSEPH S. CATUCCI, C.S.W.

216-03 97th Road
Queens Village, NY 11428
(718) 479-1997
jsccsw@aol.com

OBJECTIVE

A position as Program Director of the Methadone Clinic that will utilize my expertise in treating substance abusers as well as my organizational skill and strong managerial track record, in order to maximize service, productivity, and profitability.

PROFILE

- Detail-oriented mental health-care management professional with exceptional follow-through abilities; able to oversee projects from concept to successful implementation.

- Demonstrated ability to coordinate multiple projects; can shift to cover a multitude of positions as needed.

- Effective program administrator with proven ability to positively affect the bottom line while improving quality of service delivered.

- Broad based general management qualifications with particular expertise in improving cost containment and staff retention.

- More than 13 years of experience working successfully with MICA (Mentally Ill Chemical Abusers) patients.

- Possess extensive expertise working with substance abusers.

- Demonstrated ability to resolve resistance to appropriate and productive behavior.

- Skillful in coordinating programs and interfacing with professional medical and administrative staff. Able to develop excellent rapport and work effectively with individuals on all levels, maintaining highest levels of professionalism.

ADDITIONAL QUALIFICATIONS

New York State **"R"** Certified
C.S.W. 1987
MICA Cross Training—Westchester County
15 years of experience as a psychotherapist

EXPERIENCE
1996–Present

MOUNT VERNON HOSPITAL, Mount Vernon, NY
Psychiatric Social Worker—Mental Health Services

- Function as Interdisciplinary Team Leader in an acute care psychiatric unit providing crisis treatment for individuals in need of emergency hospitalization by reason of being a danger to themselves or others.

- Manage staff of 10; oversee organization and administration of multi-disciplinary personnel: Psychiatrists, Social Workers, RNs, LPNs, and Nurse Assistants.

- Promoted to team leader based on consistent ability to address issues.

- Coordinate assessment evaluation and development of treatment and discharge plans for psychiatric population.

- Current treatment review statistics reflect that **the unit holds the second best statistics in Westchester,** a dramatic accomplishment for a program only four years young.

Group Therapist in Milieu Therapy (1997–Present)

- Serve as primary therapist in individual therapy.

- Member of committees: Policy and Psychoeducational Development.

107

Social worker. *Mark D. Berkowitz, NCCC, CPRW; Yorktown Heights, NY*

JOSEPH CATUCCI, C.S.W.

1986–1991   **CENTRAL NASSAU GUIDANCE & COUNSELING, INC.,** Hicksville, NY
Clinical Social Worker/Staff Development Chairperson

- Oversaw program development, staff development, in-service training, and administrative management.

- Assessed and evaluated staff educational needs; procured expertise to meet those needs.

- Directed crisis-intervention efforts.

- Supervised intake interview and diagnostic evaluation process.

- Developed initial treatment planning.

- Oversaw utilization review and supervised post-graduate social work students.

- Provided short-term individual psychotherapy, group work, and family and marital therapy.

- Achieved consistent high-quality evaluations in therapy delivered to alcohol and substance abusers, M.I.C.A., and S.P.M.I. patients.

1983–Present   **PRIVATE PRACTICE**
Psychotherapist

EDUCATION   **ADELPHI UNIVERSITY,** Garden City, NY   1983
Master of Social Work

         QUEENS COLLEGE, Queens, NY   1978
Bachelor of Arts
Graduated *Cum Laude*

REFERENCES   Available upon request.

This resume highlights this social worker's management and leadership potential, which enabled him to be appointed director of a Methadone Clinic. (Resume writer's comments)

JENNIFER C. MAYES
888 Layton Street
Tyler, Texas 75700
(903) 666-8888

many good skill statements are included

HIGHLIGHTS OF QUALIFICATIONS

- **Astute, professional Case Manager** with successful experience in managing large caseload of Medicaid-eligible, mentally-ill clients.
- Cognizant of **probation** system; experience in interviewing/observing offenders.
- Thorough knowledge of Medicaid guidelines and billing procedures.
- Highly **resourceful** and **organized**; proficiency in obtaining pertinent information to facilitate assistance for the client; schedule and organize tasks to achieve optimum productivity and timely completion of assignments.
- Ability to **understand, relate to,** and **communicate** with people of diverse cultures.
- Detailed and accurate in **report** writing/documentation; computer literacy in Windows, Microsoft Word, WordPerfect.
- Dedicated, responsible, goal-oriented.

For a recent grad, putting relevant education early makes sense

EDUCATION

NORTHEAST LOUISIANA UNIVERSITY – Monroe, Louisiana
Master of Arts Degree in Criminal Justice (1994)
Bachelor of Arts Degree in Criminal Justice; Emphasis: **Sociology** (1992)

DEPARTMENT OF HEALTH AND HOSPITALS – CASE MANAGEMENT SERVICES DIVISION
Certificate of Training – Case Management

PROFESSIONAL EXPERIENCE

HEALTHCARE PLUS   Monroe, Louisiana
Case Manager   1995

- Managed caseload of 12-15 Medicaid-eligible, mentally-ill clients diagnosed by psychiatrist and approved for case management services by the Office of Mental Health.
- Made home visits to complete Prior Authorization for target population; verified authorization.
- Prepared Intake and Service Agreement for each client.
- Analyzed clients' needs. Developed assessments and client service plans.
- Interacted extensively via telephone and in person with various agencies throughout community to link clients with providers to meet basic living, medical, financial, and employment needs.
- Located medical provider; coordinated transportation for client to receive medical care.
- Prepared extensive, detailed documentation; submitted to appropriate authorities.

U.S. PROBATION OFFICE   Monroe, Louisiana
Intern   1994

- Performed pre-trial services.
- Answered collateral requests.
- Observed Probation Officer's contact with offenders.

108

Social worker/case manager. *Ann Klint, CPRW, NCRW; Tyler, TX*

JENNIFER C. MAYES **Page Two**

NORTHEAST LOUISIANA UNIVERSITY
Graduate Assistant – Criminal Justice Department

Monroe, Louisiana
1993 – 1994

- Worked 25-30 hours per week while pursuing master's degree.
- **Published article** about the Johnny Gray Jones Youth Shelter in *Louisiana Youth Care* magazine.
- Researched and compiled study of detention in Ouachita Parish for presentation to Ouachita Parish Police Jury.
- Communicated with various agencies throughout Louisiana and coordinated preparation and organization of seminars sponsored by the Institute of Corrections and Juvenile Justice.
- Produced mailing lists and exams.

CADDO PARISH CLERK OF COURT
Office Assistant – Criminal Section

Shreveport, Louisiana
Summers, 1990 and 1992

- Entered data in computer for permanent records.
- Confirmed initial court appearances.

ADDITIONAL EMPLOYMENT EXPERIENCE

SNELLING TEMPORARY SERVICES

1994 – 1996

Held temporary assignments as secretary, clerk, and receptionist at various companies, including State Farm Insurance, Knowles Pharmaceutical, Superior Ford; served extended assignment with The W. P. Taylor Corporation.

THE W. P. TAYLOR CORPORATION
Receptionist

Shreveport, Louisiana
1994 – 1995

- Efficiently managed 8-line phone system for busy industrial manufacturing corporation.
- Produced correspondence and price quotes.
- Prepared all invoices for payment and costing purposes.
- Generated sales orders on SBT Accounting System.
- Maintained accurate records of all sales orders.

VOLUNTEER / COMMUNITY SERVICE

Volunteer, LOUISIANA COMMITTEE FOR THE PREVENTION OF CHILD ABUSE

Volunteer, – OUACHITA COTTAGE ABUSED CHILDREN'S CENTER

Volunteer, MONROE RONALD MCDONALD HOUSE

Volunteer, ST. JOSEPH'S NURSING HOME

Volunteer, NATIONAL KIDNEY FOUNDATION

Volunteer, MONROE POLICE DEPARTMENT

This resume does a good job of emphasizing key skills and making the most of her work and education-related experience to support her job objective.

~ ~ References Furnished On Request ~ ~

Though seeking a "formal" job, Britain highlights creative elements in this informal approach.

Britain J. Walker

Note the short statements and informal pencil bullets

1108 Fox Run Drive • Chicago, Illinois 60606 • 555-757-0422

Highlights of Qualifications

- Master's degree in mathematics with major in statistics
- Specialties in statistics and actuarial science
- Subspecialties in calculus, algebra, and trigonometry
- Ten successful years of applied mathematics in actuarial applications
- Five years' experience as an effective corporate actuarial trainer
- Proven ability to communicate technical data and theory to non-technical people
- Outstanding management, analysis, and interpersonal skills; highly creative

Experience

His personality shines through

Actuarial Supervisor • 1991-present
Polysystems of Chicago, Chicago, Illinois
- Trained coworkers and outside clients in CMO modeling techniques
- Headed team of six on CMO Project, reporting directly to vice president
- Supervised writing, editing, and production of CMO software instruction manual

Actuarial Assistant • 1986-1991
Capital Investments, Inc., St. Louis, Missouri
- Trained actuarial students, utilizing Tillinghast software

Graduate Math Teaching Assistant & Tutor for Athletic Department • 1983-1986
University of Nebraska, Lincoln, Nebraska

Education

- Master of Arts and Teaching in Mathematics
  University of Nebraska at Lincoln • GPA 3.27
  Major: Statistics • Minor: Educational Psychology

- Bachelor of Fine Art
  University of Nebraska at Lincoln • GPA 3.25
  Teaching Certification in Math an Art

- Actuarial Exams Passed: 100, 110, 120, 130, 135, 140 (110 hours)

Affiliations and Memberships

- Pi Mu Alpha, Math Honorary Fraternity
- Chicago Actuarial Association
- Business Professional Association
- Art Institute
- Goodman Theatre

109

Actuary. *Barbie Dallmann, CPRW; Charleston, WV*

This person had done a lot of job hopping, so she chose a functional format as the best fit for her situation.

GRACIELA M. RODRIGUEZ
3957 East 9th Street • Brooklyn, New York 11235
Cellular: (917) 887-6382 • Email: gmrodriguez@aol.com

These quotes add credibility.

PROFESSIONAL PROFILE

Innovative and talented **PROGRAMMING ANALYST** with proven ability to develop procedures to streamline and improve operations while enhancing system applications. Quickly identify problem areas and implement effective solutions to meet corporate goals.

"Gracie's primary strengths are her attention to detail, professional maturity, and personal commitment to developing thorough, quality work products." — Tom Brinks, Manager, Lead Solutions

"Gracie is an asset to any project she joins. She takes her responsibilities seriously. She also takes the initiative to go the 'extra mile' in ensuring the deliverables are accurate, timely, and quality-laden." — Sandra Styles, Manager, Lead Solutions

CAREER HIGHLIGHTS

The functional format allowed her to elaborate on her accomplishments instead of merely listing her duties.

Developed MS Access application system to generate "sign tags" displayed on merchandise shelves for a retail electronic chain of 41 stores to provide product information and pricing. *(Lead Solutions)*
- Conducted meetings to determine production of tag type and information to be displayed.
- Created a Graphical User Interface (GUI) to allow end users to request all store tag types.

Created an application that eliminated manual processing of over 10,000 credit-card transactions per day and assisted Sales Audit Department in reconciliation of funds. *(Lead Solutions)*
- Designed and implemented MS Access application using Visual Basic Applications (VBA) to generate various reports summarizing credit-card data and discrepancies including credit-card and cash-reconciliation reports.
- Provided Sales Audit Department the ability to determine discrepancies in funds received for credit-card purchases.

Streamlined process of pricing life-insurance products during the product-development stage. *(First Variable, Inc.)*
- Redesigned standard spreadsheet to allow changes of insurance and policy fees and added a table that contained values to be applied to standard cost of insurance rates.
- Redesigned spreadsheet to calculate rates based on data entered in the table to the standard cost of insurance rates.

Streamlined process of testing new life-insurance administration system by implementing spreadsheet information. *(Mutual Life)*
- Developed original spreadsheets based on actuarial specifications of policies used to determine policy values.
- New system provided accurate subaccount value used for variable life insurance policies and advised on fund additions or withdrawals from policies.

EMPLOYMENT HISTORY

LEAD SOLUTIONS, LLC (Consulting Firm) — New York, New York *1/1998 – Present*
Consultant — Provided solutions to fast-growing businesses and middle-market organizations delivering solutions designed to accelerate business performance for growth-oriented organizations.

110

Computer programming analyst. *Maria E. Hebda, CPRW; Trenton, MI*

Graciela M. Rodriguez
Cellular: (917) 887-6382 • Email: gmrodriguez@aol.com • Page 2

EMPLOYMENT HISTORY (Continued)
PACE UNIVERSITY — New York, New York *1/1996 – 12/1997*
Instructor/CIS Assistant — Maintained online tutorials in HTML, Excel and Introduction to Visual Basic.

FIRST VARIABLE, INC. (Life Insurance Company) — New York, New York *1/1993 – 12/1995*
Independent Contractor — Analyzed policy administration systems for compliance with product design, developed price product spreadsheets and tested reinsurance system.

INSURED LIFE RESOURCES (Life Insurance Disability Agency) — New York, New York *10/1991 – 12/1992*
Marketing Coordinator — Conducted market searches, produced marketing materials and tracked associated marketing campaigns.

MUTUAL LIFE (Life Insurance Company) — New York, New York *7/1988 – 10/1991*
Actuarial Analyst — Liaison between customer service and systems areas, calculated life insurance policy values and created spreadsheets that projected future staffing and expenses based on the number of life insurance/annuity policies sold.

PROFESSIONAL DEVELOPMENT
- Object Oriented Application Development with UML — Rational Software, 2000
- Object Oriented Application Development — The Learning Tree, 2000

COMPUTER PROFICIENCIES
Visual Basic • Visual Basic for Applications • HTML • Oracle 7 • Access • Excel • Monarch • Winbatch • Visio • Word • Internet • Email

EDUCATION
PACE UNIVERSITY, New York, New York
Master of Science — Computer Science

FORDHAM UNIVERSITY, New York, New York
Bachelor of Arts — Mathematics / Economics

This list allows an employer to readily see the individual's transferable skills without having to wade through job descriptions to find them.

NITALYIA

ALIMOVA

706 Paramont Way
Indianapolis, IN 46220
(317) 253-1258
nalimova@alimova.com

SUMMARY *of* QUALIFICATIONS

Project Management
Planning
    Key Result Areas
    Governance Strategies
    Risk Value Analysis
    Cost Analysis
    Timelines
Control
    Scope Management
    Status Reports
    Developer/Customer
      Feedback
Execution
    Presentations
    Team Leadership
    Quality Control
    Shared Learning

Customer Relationship Management

Motivator "We Can Do It Attitude"

Time Management

Problem-Solving

Professional Development Management

"Nitalyia juggles many tasks at once, asks for help when needed, and completes tasks with efficiency and integrity."
— Toni Williams
Supervisor

Professional & Personal References

Detail-oriented, high-energy **SYSTEMS ANALYST** with well-developed project management experience. Strong leadership skills demonstrated by an instinctive ability to guide and to motivate a diverse team to work at optimum levels in a high-risk/slow-feedback environment.

EMPLOYMENT HISTORY

ELI LILLY AND COMPANY, Indianapolis, IN
    Systems Analyst   1999 – PRESENT
- Identify and implement computer-based solutions to customers' business needs with integrity, energy and speed.
- Saved $10,000 by suggesting that Lilly perform a percentage of the software development cycle for the Online Report Submission Project, thereby minimizing costs, maximizing quality, and delivering multiple projects on time.
- Researched and developed the Medical Online Support System website. Presented and negotiated customer contracts to manage information more effectively; 200 people have noticed positive results in the medical community.
- Recruit Miami University Systems Analysis students; established Lilly scholarship.

HERCULES TIRE & RUBBER COMPANY, Findlay, OH
    Financial Programming Summer Intern   1998 – 1999
    Client Services Summer Intern   1996 – 1997
- Analyzed and implemented a program for integrating a receiving system with the factory maintenance system to determine whether the new inventory system was synchronized with the old; updated and created report of results.
- Performed analysis on purchasing reports to correct inaccurate totals, reviewed programs to determine "Year 2000" compliance and changed code in programs.

MIAMI UNIVERSITY, Oxford, OH
    Lab Consultant/Student Support Staff   1995 – 1999
- Provided technical support to end users with software and hardware questions, assisted in troubleshooting network problems, installed Windows NT and SmartCam.
- Monitored usage of computer lab and maintained facilities.

COMPUTER SKILLS

Environments: MS-DOS, Microsoft Windows 98, 2000 and NT, CANDE, VAX
Languages: BASIC, Visual C++, PASCAL, COBOL, ASSEMBLER, Java
PC Software: Microsoft Word, Works, Excel, Access, PowerPoint, WordPerfect for Windows, Lotus 1-2-3, Quicken, Quattro Pro, Oracle, Microsoft Project

EDUCATION

MIAMI UNIVERSITY, Oxford, OH
    Bachelor of Science in Applied Science Degree   1999
    Major: Systems Analysis   GPA: 3.8   *Magna Cum Laude*

    Formal Methods Program (1 of 8 graduates)   1996 –1999
    An experimental curriculum funded by the National Science Foundation designed to teach students how to create software specifications using first-order logic and to use these specifications in the development of software systems. See www.sas.muohio.edu/san/formal/.

This format also provides a great way to prepare for the interview process, as employers are sure to ask about the items in this column.

111

Computer systems analyst. *Sharon Pierce-Williams, MEd, CPRW;*
Findlay, OH

After an early career in social services, this person switched to an information-systems role with the same state agency.

Victoria Vartanian

vartanian@mediaone.net

PO Box 16603
Boston, MA 02112
617-381-2027

Her problem-solving abilities and aptitude for complex technical material are highlighted here.

> *Systems Analyst with the proven ability to analyze, document, troubleshoot and resolve complex technical problems in time-sensitive, mission-critical functions*

Expertise

- *Systems analysis*
- *Requirements definition*
- *Testing/debugging*
- *Problem resolution*
- *Product support and development*
- *Program documentation*
- *End-user training*
- *System conversion support*

Technical

- *SilkRadar*
- *Unicenter TNG Advanced Help Desk*
- *Trained in Oracle Discoverer*

Education Certification Licensure

- *M.A., Sociology, Tufts University*
- *B.A., Latin, Wheaton College*
- *Mass. Licensed Social Worker*

PROFILE

- Experienced in the analysis of complex information systems involving software system design, maintenance, testing/debugging, modification, end-user support and training

- Well-developed research and analytical skills with the demonstrated ability to diagnose and resolve defects

- A highly logical thinker with excellent oral/written communication and interpersonal skills and an aptitude for rapidly assimilating highly technical knowledge

- Effective collaborator and team leader with supervisory, training and planning experience

PROFESSIONAL EXPERIENCE

Systems Analyst
Massachusetts Department of Transitional Assistance   1998 – Present

Key member of the project team developing, testing and implementing Massachusetts' version of the federally mandated Family Assistance Management Information System (FAMIS). Known as BEACON (Benefit Eligibility and Control Online Network), this online NT-based system is used to control and process benefits programs statewide. Closely involved with analysis, testing, implementation and problem resolution. Work directly with development team members, including vendor representatives from Albion International, MAXIMUS and others.

Research, analyze and define requirements for all related eligibility programs. Develop and write detailed requirements-specification documents (including interface flow, root questions, procedures, edits, queries, verifications and reports). Review requirements documents from other team members. Resolve requirements issues with development team members.

Authored support tools including a non-citizen desk guide as well as more than 100 customer-service messages to assist end-users.

Review changes in state and federal regulations to determine impact on existing systems and recommend modifications. Document all regulatory and procedural changes and missing functionality across all programs that have an impact on system implementation.

Train users from central office units on the system and enhancements in preparation for deployment. Support technical staff in understanding the system application from a business perspective.

112

Computer systems analyst. *Bernice Antifonario, MA; Tewksbury, MA*

Victoria Vartanian

Comments

"Victoria's work is …

superior. She accepts

challenging

assignments and has

a knowledge base

which is an invaluable

asset. She is

resourceful, creative

and hard working.

Victoria is an excellent

team member."

Current Manager

This quote from her supervisor emphasizes her value to the organization.

(Professional Experience, continued)

Primary analyst for testing the interface between BEACON and the department's legacy benefit issuance system (FMCS), a critical and time-sensitive function in preparing the system for implementation. Create flow charts, orthogonal arrays and program narratives for developing test plans. Develop and execute test scenarios to identify pre-implementation problems. Create/respond to defect reports and suggest solutions. Retest and verify solutions and then track progress through extensive documentation during the entire process.

Selected for the triage team established to handle post-implementation problems. Receive and analyze reports and provide solutions or assign solution development to technical teams and policy groups. Pursue timely resolution to these mission-critical problems.

Supervisor
Massachusetts Department of Transitional Assistance   **1986 – 1998**

Supervised various groups of five or more social workers providing intake and case-management services for multiple eligibility programs administered by the department.

Trained staff in efficient and productive procedures and department protocols, emphasizing client services. Maintained current knowledge of regulations and procedures and implemented changes.

Motivated employees to achieve their best performance and maintain a high level of accuracy. Conducted performance reviews. Worked closely with individual employees experiencing challenges affecting their performance. Supported their efforts to overcome obstacles while continuing to emphasize the professional requirements of the position. Successfully transitioned these individuals into productive and effective employees.

Upon the consolidation of the intake and case-management functions, designed, documented and implemented a new screening system. Created the necessary documentation (forms, logs, tracking systems, etc.) to facilitate the implementation.

Social Worker / Systems Support
Massachusetts Department of Transitional Assistance   **1978 – 1986**

Interviewed and screened applicants and recipients through office and field assessments to determine program eligibility. Maintained a high level of knowledge of policies and procedures. Developed in-depth case management reports.

Selected for a special central-office support group to troubleshoot the implementation of the new Medicaid Management Information System (MMIS). Developed procedures and interpreted policy for management and field personnel. Provided daily systems support to department staff. Evaluated reports to identify, analyze and resolve system-wide problems and eligibility issues. Documented and escalated unresolved problems for correction.

References

available

upon request

Armed with this resume, Victoria set out to find a private-sector position.

This resume helped Barry receive many interviews for programming positions!

BARRY BARTHOLOMEW

77 Apple Valley Road
Princeton, NJ 08540
609-924-5555
barrybart@penn.rr.com

OBJECTIVE: Senior Systems Programmer

SUMMARY OF QUALIFICATIONS

⇒ Over 6 years' experience in computer operations, promoted twice in that time.
⇒ Computer Programming degree from The Computer Institute.
⇒ Dedicated, resourceful and reliable worker; can be counted on to get the job done.
⇒ Work well independently as well as cooperatively in a team environment.
⇒ Expert troubleshooter; strengths in analysis, logic and accuracy.

Hardware	Digital GEMS	IBM PC	AS/400	LAN/WAN Networks
Software	DEC/VAX VMS	UNIX	OS/VS JCL	COBOL Language
	CMS/XEDIT	Dos 7.0	Windows 95	IBM Assembler Language
	MS Office	OS/2	Sybase	

EXPERIENCE & ACCOMPLISHMENTS

1994–2002 Computer Operator III/Shift Leader   BLAKE CORPORATION, Newtown, PA

Provided computer systems operations to maintain the central computer system for daily operation of the state lottery.

- Oversaw the shift's triplex systems and activities-resolving problems (such as power shortages, tight deadlines and increasing capabilities) creatively and efficiently.
- Operated, monitored and controlled computers and associated equipment required to do batch processing of business applications in a real-time, on-line environment:
  — accurately performed the daily and weekly batch processing of reports and tapes.
  — ensured the central system maintained the daily time schedule of operations.
- Performed hardware and software testing and monitored systems progress via Digital Alpha Server 2100, digital tape drives, VAX VMS and UNIX software.
- Experienced with software packages, including installing, testing, debugging, maintenance, system enhancements, and new program applications such as installing new lottery games.
- Trained, supervised and evaluated technical staff of 3 computer operators, increasing employee retention by 60% through delegation and collaboration.
- Prepared daily report distributions (liability, system totals) for the state, weekly invoices and monthly cumulative reports as the Shift Supervisor.

1992–1994 Accounts Payable Data Entry   THE CORNING ORGANIZATION, Trenton, NJ

- Keyed/edited high volume of accounts payable invoices; entered cash receipts and disbursements, general ledger, and job cost adjustments.
- Trained 7 data entry operators to ensure accurate documentation of company files.

EDUCATION

Diploma, Computer Programming, The Computer Institute, Newark, NJ

BS, Public Administration/Business (Cum Laude), University of Tarrytown, Tarrytown, NY

113

Computer systems programmer. *Susan Guarneri, NCC, NCCC, LPC, CPRW, IJCTC, CCM, CEIP; Lawrenceville, NJ*

Gerald P. Mandel

1-2107 Creekside Drive
Plainfield, New Mexico 25536
(966) 778-6785
gpmandel@msn.com

Objective

Position as *a Mathematics / Statistics Textbook Editor*

Highlights

- Diversified background in mathematics/statistics in education and industry, including almost 10 years of experience in textbook reviewing.
- Goal-oriented decision maker with a keen eye for editorial detail.
- Proven administrative and organizational skills.
- Exceptional communication and interpersonal skills; easily develop rapport with peers.
- Skilled in using a PC with Lotus 1-2-3 for analysis and reporting.

Professional Skills

Textbook Editing

Notice how he organizes skills into subsections that have clear job assignment implications.

- Reviewed math and statistics manuscripts for several publishers.
- Ensured the soundness and clarity of mathematical principles.
- Validated the accuracy and relevance of all problems and solutions.
- Suggested improvements and corrections to presentation.
- Wrote supplemental exercises.
- Edited materials on a wide variety of subjects:

• Arithmetic	• Business Math
• Probability	• Trigonometry
• Algebra	• Postal Math
• Statistics	• SAT Preparation (Math and Verbal)
• Geometry	• GRE Preparation (Math)

Curriculum Planning and Test Development

- Wrote mathematics questions for the nationally administered National College Testing program.
- Designed mathematics tests in algebra, actuarial science, logic, calculus, probability, and statistics for the Learning Corporation.
- Developed SAT mathematics and verbal programs for the Radkin Educational Group.

Mathematician. *Beverly Baskin, MA, NCC, CPRW; Marlboro, NJ*

(*Teaching and Counseling*

- Taught full spectrum of college mathematics courses from developmental and survey math to advanced levels of calculus and statistics.
- Instructed Navy apprentices in applied mathematics at the Community College of Philadelphia.
- Taught high school mathematics courses from algebra through pre-calculus.

Experience)　　— *Jobs are arranged by category — an effective way to present his background clearly.*

1984–Present　　*Publishing Industry*

Specific dates are not mentioned.

Textbook Reviewer—four publishing companies:
Harriett Brace, Inc., San Diego, CA
E. C., Lexington, MA
Wordsworth Publishers, Belmont, CA
Prentier-Hall Publishing Co., Englewood Cliffs, NM
Test Developer—National College Testing Program, Iowa City, IA
Test Developer—Learning Corporation, Syosset, NY

Statistics

1986–1989　　*Statistical Analyst,* Coners Insurance Co., Cranbury, NM
1980–1985　　*Management and Cost Analyst,* US Government, Fort Monmouth, NM

Teaching

1983–Present　　**Instructor,** Kelly College, Madison, NM
Director of Placement and Testing, Jerrald County College, Cranford, NM

Education

MS in Mathematics (Cum Laude), Fairlaw Dickinson University, Teaneck, NM
BA in Mathematics, Rodriguez College, New Brunswick, NM
Post Graduate studies in Mathematics, Rodriguez College, New Brunswick, NM

This is a good example of a "modified" chronological resume. The chronological list of jobs is included, but the arrangement of skills is far more effective as presented here.

This individual's original resume was overwhelming, filled with statistics and information about his African banking background.

RENNY K. PARTUCO, Ph.D.

The challenge in preparing his resume was to distinguish between what was needed to capture attention and what could be added during interviews.

College of Management, Department of Economics
Central State University
Charlotte, North Carolina 29512
(704) 551-1994
rkpartuco@csu.edu

CAREER SUMMARY

Outstanding economics, econometrics, operations research, monetary policy, and statistics skills; expertise in designing and analyzing data. Seeking international consulting opportunity for a consulting firm or company that has business in and needs a consultant in Africa and Europe. Position should be based in the United States.

CONSULTING ROLES
Statistics Consultant
M.S. Statistician
Lecturer/Presenter
Monetary Policy Expert
Team Leader/Industry Issues

EXPERTISE
Business Forecasting
Business Analysis
IT for Banking/Business
Research (Published Professional)
Economics (Ph.D.)

SUMMARY OF QUALIFICATIONS

- Visiting Research Fellow at Central State University; previous senior-level work includes multiple projects in Lagos at the Central Bank of Lagos as Deputy Director of Research/Statistics.
  - Role as project leader has included heading projects in statistics, compliance, program design and implementation.
  - During this time, have been invited to participate in high-profile projects and have published over 44 papers on variety of related subjects.

- Expertise in designing and analyzing programs and projects for the banking industry regarding compliance, monetary policy, fiscal policy, statistics, econometrics and related projects.

- Excellent experience and knowledge of African business, banking and politics. Equivalently strong knowledge of Europe and related monetary, fiscal and banking issues.

- Outstanding training, teaching and public speaking skills. Multiple teaching engagements and assignments, including lecturer and fellow in the university system, management seminars, banking seminars, statistical management and modeling conferences in Europe, Africa and the United States.

- Additional business skills include business forecasting, modeling and analysis.

- Excellent applied knowledge and practical professional experience in solving problems in currency structure, inventory management, and distribution review and modeling.

- Experienced presenter, speaker and teacher in large and small group settings.

- Proven ability to lead teams, build positive team dynamics and communicate with multiple governmental or industry personnel. Solid personnel motivational skills to encourage cooperation and productivity.

TECHNICAL SUMMARY

Proficient in various operating systems, software, and languages, including *Microsoft Word, WordPerfect, Lotus 1-2-3, SPSS, TSP, EVIEWS, SX1, STATGRAPHICS. Past duties include Computer Operations Coordinator, Chairman of Research Computerization Committee and Chairman of Y2K Conversion/Compliance.*

115

Statistician. *John M. O'Connor; Raleigh, NC*

RENNY K. PARTUCO, page 2

EDUCATION

Ph.D. Economics, 1995, Statistics Econometrics, UNIVERSITY OF CALIFORNIA AT SANTA CRUZ
- Chosen as Fellow for Statistics International to perform statistics and analyses.
- Served as Co-Director of Statistics Consulting Lab to determine research needs, time lines and costs to physicians, physiologists and medical students.

M.S. Statistics, 1983, Central State University.
M.I.S., 1982, Major in Economic and Social Statistics, Elected F.I.S., London, U.K.
OND and HND, Agriculture, Major in Applied Statistics and Biometrics.

PROFESSIONAL EXPERIENCE

CENTRAL STATE UNIVERSITY, Charlotte, NC
Visiting Research Fellow — Current, 1998–Present

CENTRAL BANK OF LAGOS, Lagos, Nigeria
Deputy Director of Research — Statistics, 1991–Present
- Produced Economic and Econometric Modeling and Monetary Policy work for the bank. Design, coordinate and produce special project work including extensive research and review of policy in Lagos, Africa and Europe to determine policy and plan future research.
- Present critical information at board meetings regarding economic and econometric modeling and monetary policy that impacts the bank as a whole.
- Key projects included coordinating the Research Department Computer Training Programme since 1990.
- Additionally, coordinated CBN/FOS Collaboration in Statistics Production (External Trade, Producer Price Index, and National Accounts).
- Chosen as and completed work as Chairman of the bank's Y2K Computer Date Change Committee/Y2K Compliance program. Position included extensive research and writing of internal and external papers to carry out critical compliance activities.
- As an ongoing member of the Research Department Programs Committee, involved in program design, implementation and evaluation.

Assistant Director and Head Econometrics Office, 1986–1990
Principal Statistician and Head, Econometrics Office, 1980–1985
Senior Statistician/Economist, 1976–1979
- Researched, developed and produced multiple papers in the area of statistics, econometrics and monetary policy.
- Supervised research staff on all written projects and priorities.
- Developed and established complete computerized database for economic and financial statistics.
- Developed and implemented a Methodology of External Trade Indices during a work attachment at IMF.
- Designed, conducted and analyzed statistical surveys. Established CBN retail price indices and stock market indices.

NATIONAL ROOTCROPS RESEARCH INSTITUTE, Ministry of Agriculture, Lagos, Nigeria
Assistant Agricultural Superintendent, 1962–1971
- Collected, compiled and analyzed agricultural statistics/biometrics..

PROFESSIONAL AFFILIATIONS

Member, American Statistical Association
Member, International Association of Official Statisticians Section, International Statistical Institute
Fellow, Institute of Statisticians
Member, Nigerian Economic Society
Member, Vice President, and other roles, Lagos Statistical Association, since 1976

References Available Upon Request

Jacqueline had been trying to break into the field of museum management for some time, but found her unrelated work experience an insurmountable barrier.

Jacqueline San Miguel

9100 Wilshire Blvd.
Beverly Hills, California 90212
Mobile Voice (310) 215-6471
jsmiguel@aol.com

MUSEUM CURATOR / EXHIBITION & EVENT MANAGEMENT
Delivering Significant Contributions to Collection, Research, Archiving, and Education

Talented, resourceful, and dedicated professional offering a unique combination of cross-functional skills including 10 years of archiving experience handling public and private collections. Creative and enthusiastic with proven success in building and managing relationships with peers, artists, patrons, and the general public. Aggressive, decisive, and committed to personal and professional growth and opportunity. **MA Museum Studies.** Qualifications include:

This resume was designed to highlight the skills & credentials she had developed through her involvement in volunteer activities. These skills and credentials were more important to her career goal than her work experience as an actress and TV / film production assistant.

- Archiving / Research / Documentation
- Team Building & Leadership
- Oral & Written Communications
- Office Administration & Reporting
- Program Planning & Development

- Public Relations & Promotions
- Conservation & Interpretation
- Community Outreach
- Interactive Public Speaking
- Script Writing / Editing

CAREER PROGRESSION

MILLS COLLEGE ART GALLERY Oakland, California   1999 – 2001
Established in 1968, California's first public collection of modern art with over 6000 objects and drawings.

STUDENT ASSISTANT TO CURATOR

While a USC graduate student, hired to direct the administrative staff but was quickly recruited by the senior Curator / Director to address special projects including: marketing, community education, archiving and research projects, and assistance with new acquisitions, openings, and exhibitions.

Highlights: Developed and implemented a more user-friendly research / materials archive and implemented an innovative, highly visible promotional campaign to stimulate gallery attendance and improve community awareness and education. Recognized for outstanding contributions to several exhibitions providing site selection assistance, creative set-up solutions, and careful, reverent handling of artwork.

SAN SERVICES, LLC Los Angeles, California   1992 – 1999
Successful independent writer and consultant serving publishers and production companies worldwide.

FREELANCE WRITER / EDITOR

Independent provider of articles, academic essays, screenplays, editing, and consulting services to major publications and production companies throughout the U.S. and abroad.

Highlights: Columnist for *The Buzz*, a London-based arts magazine, reviewer for *The Daily Californian's* arts section, research consultant on *Easy Money* for screenwriter Paul Gray (*Liar Liar*, *Little Rascals*), and contributing editor for *Student Journal of American Studies*, a quarterly academic publication for the interdisciplinary community.

EDUCATION

University of Southern California – Los Angeles, California
Master of Arts, Museum Studies
Degree Awarded 2001

Mills College – Oakland, California
Bachelor of Arts, American Studies / Art History
Degree Awarded 1995

116

Museum curator. *Debbie Ellis, CPRW; Danville, KY*

Catherine A. Nottingham

934 Charles Drive   Rochester, Minnesota 55555-5555   (555) 555-5555

OBJECTIVE: Directorship of a medium to large urban or suburban library system that will utilize existing skills and experience while offering opportunity for professional advancement.

PROFESSIONAL EXPERIENCE:

HIAWATHA PUBLIC LIBRARY; HIAWATHA, MINNESOTA   **1992 - Present**
Library Director
Executive responsibility for management and operation of suburban library with two branches, 60 employees, annual budget over $1.1 million, and circulation of over 500,000 volumes per year.

A brief summary of her job-related skills

Answer to Library Board and Town Board of Hiawatha.
- Report to Library Board on budgetary and managerial issues.
- Work with Library Board to develop annual budget based on long-range goals.
- Present budget to Town of Hiawatha Board for approval.

Supervise professional staff:
- Implement employee evaluations.
- Establish goals and objectives for professional staff.
- Empower employees by moving responsibility down organizational chain.
- Institute training/development program for library staff.

Serve on committees of Twin Cities Library System:
- Co-Chair Town Library Directors' Council.
- Co-Chair Directors' Advisory Council.
- Automation Policy Committee.

Act as liaison between library and community:
- Serve on local Chamber of Commerce Board.
- Co-chair Town of Hiawatha Internet Committee,
  - Currently developing "Home Page".
  - Launched public access to Internet, September 1995.
- Collaborate with school district on Summer Reading Program with over 1300 children participating.

MAJOR ACHIEVEMENTS

Separating her key accomplishments reinforces a results orientation

Instituted five-year capital improvement campaign (1993-1997) and obtained grants to fund projects. **Campaign objectives realized in <u>four years</u>, one year ahead of schedule.** Campaign includes:
- Installation of new roofs and new carpeting in both branches.
- Installation of new HVAC systems in both branches.
- Construction of new entrances at one branch to comply with Americans with Disabilities Act (ADA) access requirements.

As part of Capital Campaign, developed three-year technology plan to upgrade library automation systems. Secured cooperation with Town of Hiawatha to participate in their equipment leasing plan and connect with their LAN. This innovation resulted in achieving goals **ahead of schedule** and at a **substantial cost savings.** Improvements implemented include:
- Migration from terminals to LAN's and WAN's.
- Migration from GEAC to CARL (Automated library systems handling circulation and O.P.A.C. catalog).
- Implementation of on-line catalog (CARL).
- Automation of office functions.

Increased annual budget by over 33% in three years:
- Justified increases to Town Board at time when budget cuts were proposed.
- Increased materials budget by 42% in three-year span.
- Increased personnel budget by 30% in three-year span.

117

Librarian.   *Arnold G. Boldt, CPRW, JCTC; Rochester, NY*

With substantial experience and credentials as a librarian, this resume emphasizes her high level of responsibilities, concrete accomplishments, and her many skills

Catherine A. Nottingham   Resume - Page 2

ADDITIONAL PROFESSIONAL EXPERIENCE:

ST. PAUL PUBLIC LIBRARY; ST. PAUL, MINNESOTA   1981 - 1992

Department Head, Interlibrary Loan & Centralized Reserves   1986 - 1992
Planned, coordinated, and managed all interlibrary loan and centralized reserves services for the Pioneer Library System, which encompassed over 100 individual branches in a five county region of southern Minnesota. Provided ILL services to Twin Cities Regional Library Council, school library systems, and MSILL on contract basis.

- Supervised staff of 18 employees.
- Recommended and implemented policy and procedural changes.
- Prepared and monitored departmental budget.
- Represented ILL services at Central Division Heads' meetings.
- Served on regional and state-wide committees relating to interlibrary loan.
- Provided training to member libraries on ILL services.
- Assisted in planning/implementation of automated circulation system.
- Chaired Office Automation Committee for Central Library.

Special Librarian, Central Library   1986
Established and coordinated usage of automated circulation system (GEAC) for Central divisions. Trained staff on use of GEAC and responded to user problems.

Science and Technology Reference Librarian   1981 - 1985
Selected titles and developed Science and Technology collection. Assisted member libraries with reference and collection development. Supervised pages, library assistants, and interns.

HARRIETVILLE PUBLIC LIBRARY; HARRIETVILLE, MINNESOTA   1978 - 1980

Acting Director   1979
Assumed Director's duties for seven month period shortly after move into new facility with doubled circulation.

Adult Services Librarian   1978 - 1980
Developed adult, reference, and Audio/Visual collections for large suburban library. Assisted Library Director in planning and management.

PROFESSIONAL AFFILIATIONS:

Minnesota Library Association:
    Continuing Education Committee
    Interlibrary Loan Committee

American Library Association

EDUCATION:

Master of Library Science
School of Library and Information Science
State University College at Cuylerville
Cuylerville, New York

Bachelor of Science, Biology
Holy Cross College
Worcester, Massachusetts

Cindi was seeking her first "real" job since completing her master's degree, so she had little to talk about in the areas of highlights, successes, or achievements. Instead her resume focuses on her variety of experience — including handling rare documents and converting systems from manual to computerized.

CINDI J. SMALLEY

204-667-4559
cjs3936@hotmail.com
5712 Roosevelt Way, Seattle, Washington 99243

LIBRARIAN

A vertical line is used to create a "navigational bar" along this left side of the page.

➤ Six years' library experience that includes software conversions, copy catalog for rare manuscripts, and circulation desk.
➤ Expertise in Library of Congress systems.
➤ Excellent computer skills with abilities in web page design. Experienced Internet navigator, providing first-level support for library patrons.

EDUCATION

University

Master of Library Science — June 2002
UNIVERSITY OF WASHINGTON — Seattle, Washington
Grade Point 3.90; Major areas of coursework:

Rare Books and Preservation	Collection Management / Retrieval
Information Resources	Government Documents
Electronic Databases	Internet Services

Bachelor of Science — Music / Bible Theology
WESTERN WASHINGTON STATE UNIVERSITY — Bellingham, Washington

Technical

MS Office, Front Page, Publisher, HTML, Galaxy, Dynix, Sirsi, Windows 95/98/00

Practicum

BOTHELL PUBLIC LIBRARY — Bothell, Washington
Provided direction to the public concerning Reference Materials and Reader's Advisories. As directed: Conducted demographic research for literacy grants; designed Reader's Advisory bookmarkers themed on UFOs and conspiracy theories; selected and culled volumes from donations; helped write first draft of Collection policy.

EXPERIENCE

Municipal

Types of jobs

1999–Present — RENTON PUBLIC LIBRARY SYSTEM — Renton, Washington
Circulation Clerk
Manage the flow of information concerning books, periodicals, research materials, government documents, and media recordings to the general public. Daily traffic: 200 patrons.
➤ Provided resolution for numerous issues including late returns or damaged goods; enforced library policy.
➤ Provided first-level Help Desk expertise for Internet and internal automation systems issues.
➤ Managed check-in and check-out requests.

Specialty

1998–1999 — SEATTLE THEOLOGICAL SEMINARY — Seattle, Washington
Copy Catalog
Researched and implemented cataloging procedures for rare books and manuscripts concerning early Protestant theology using the Library of Congress system as benchmark. Gained additional expertise in:
➤ Foreign language materials including subject matter in Greek, Hebrew, and German.
➤ Library of Congress systems concerning Microforms, Maps (Holy Land), musical scores, and film strips.

Conversions

1996–1998 — SHARON COUNTY LIBRARY — Sharon, Pennsylvania
Copy Catalog
Provided tactical support in the conversion from a manual system to Gaylord Galaxy enterprise software.
➤ Searched MARC and downloaded established catalog listings.
➤ Performed original cataloging for local and rare volumes, uploading and establishing new entries into the OCLC.
Notable
➤ One of two employees (out of 70) to receive perfect evaluations (5 of 5) in all twelve reviewable categories.

118

Library technician/librarian. *William G. Murdock, CPRW; Dallas, TX*

This resume was created for a full-time school tutor to help her obtain work after regular hours.

TUTORING FOR GRADES K THROUGH 4

Mrs. Sandra Farkel
(756) 299-3463
mrsfarkel0401@aol.com

Summary

Special emphasis on helping younger children in Kindergarten through grade four improve their basic academic skills. I enjoy working with children at this age and have considerable success in helping them learn—and to find joy in their accomplishments.

Experience and Skills

- Over 17 years of experience providing individual tutoring to children in school and private settings.

- Special emphasis on increasing basic reading and math skills.

- Extensive training in one-on-one learning techniques.

- Many years of success in helping children to make learning fun.

- Familiar with most school curriculum and can integrate remediation to specific weaknesses.

- Substantial experience in coordinating tutoring with teachers, psychometrists, counselors, and other professional school staff.

- Skills in individualizing tutoring to the specific needs of each child.

Training and Education

- Attended special one-year program at Ohio State University that taught skills for early childhood learning and development.

- Additional courses in elementary education at North Dakota State University.

- Intensive training in Early Prevention of School Failure program including diagnostic tests and techniques to assist children in basic academic skills.

- Many years of workshops in subjects such as teaching improved reading skills, learning styles, increasing comprehension, phonics, oral reading, individual teaching techniques, encouraging self-esteem in children, teaching to improve test-taking skills, and related topics.

119

Teacher assistant/tutor. *Michael Farr; Indianapolis, IN*

Mrs. Sandra Farkel

(756) 299-3463
mrsfarkel0401@aol.com

Experienced tutor available for children in grades K through 4.

Over 17 years experience tutoring children in school and private settings. College-level coursework on early childhood education and extensive experience and training in improving basic reading, math, and social skills. Excellent one-on-one skills and relate well to children. Successful in encouraging children to enjoy learning, gain confidence, and progress in their ability to read, comprehend instructions, understand basic math concepts and related academic skills. I also believe that self-esteem can be improved through individual attention and through mastery of basic skills. I have years of experience in helping children work up to grade level.

Hard-working, creative, caring, effective.

An example of a JIST Card to accompany Sandra's resume.

While her education and early work experience are in elementary education, this resume shows how that experience can relate to adults as well.

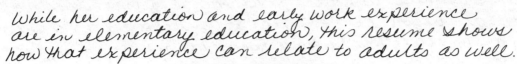

JON ELAINE ERICKSON
1132 Fuller Road • Hinsbrook, IL 00000
(555) 555-5555

PROFILE
- Dedicated **Literacy Coordinator / Teacher** with a track record of organizing programs and procedures to enhance operations and effectiveness of instruction.
- Professional, team-oriented approach: Work cooperatively with all levels of staff and treat each student with dignity and respect.
- Polished, persuasive presentation skills. Successful experience with fund-raising.

EXPERIENCE

PIPER LITERACY CENTER, Piper, IL
Literacy Coordinator / Adult Basic Education Instructor, 1990 to Present

- Report to the Director - Literacy Programs. Plan and implement workshops for students and tutors; conduct tutor training five times per year. Assist tutors in lesson planning, choosing appropriate resources, and handling special problems. Recruit volunteers and coordinate activities for special events.

- Manage record-keeping using Excel for 320 students and 220 tutors. Compile data and conduct quarterly and year-end analysis to submit to state grant-funding agency.

- Make presentations to promote programs at area organizations and clubs. Commended for success in increasing student and tutor bases each year.

- Actively involved in fund-raising for the Center. Originated and organized several successful promotions with area retailers and businesses.

- Initiated a joint venture with Tower Temporary Services to provide computer training for GED students.

- Teach two adult basic education classes for students with grade levels of 0-4.0. Plan lessons that spark and hold students' interest, maintaining high attendance rates.

- Earlier experience at the Center: Volunteer - Office Support and Special Projects (Summers 1986 to 1990).

WASHINGTON ELEMENTARY SCHOOL, Troy, IL
Teacher, 1985 to 1990

Includes skills that also apply to adult education

- Planned and presented individual and group instruction at the 2-4 grade levels.. Created a positive, nurturing environment conducive to learning.

- Improved students' reading comprehension and writing skills by utilizing a whole language approach with semantic mapping and journal writings.

- Tutored students who needed extra assistance after school; recommended diagnostic testing when appropriate.

- Enriched students' experiences with hands-on materials. Instructed students in mathematics using the Math Their Way method. Conducted weekly computer sessions, which reinforced skills in math, reading, and language arts.

EDUCATION

CENTRAL ILLINOIS UNIVERSITY, Troy, IL
B.S. in Elementary Education, 1985 • Endorsement in Special Education

She made a successful transition!

120

Adult and vocational education teacher. *Jennie Dowden; Flossmore, IL*

It takes awhile to notice that this resume does not list education or specific jobs held. This approach can be useful in hiding weaknesses or featuring strengths.

Peter J. Freeman

3456 E. Paterson Drive, Apt. 11
Portello, CA 94345

(451) 231-4656

OBJECTIVE

Leaves open a variety of options

Personal Development Specialist , with particular emphasis on *Teaching, Motivating, Empowering and Supporting people who want to live more meaningful lives. This line of work will probably include one or more of the following functions:*

- Adult Education
- Special Education
- Vocational Guidance
- Group Facilitating
- Keynote Speaking
- Crisis Counseling

QUALIFIED BY

- 11 years experience in personal development work.
- Demonstrated strengths in occupational and motivational counseling.
- Excellent background in developing highly motivated individuals and groups.
- Superior communication and interpersonal skills.
- Proven record of counseling individuals in becoming more effective people.

KEY SKILLS

- Speaking
- Presentation
- Supporting
- Leading
- Counseling
- Coordinating
- Training
- Mediation
- Facilitating

PROFESSIONAL CAREER

11 years of personnel development experience with the *Western National Bank,* specializing in:

- Motivational Counseling
- Human Resources
- Personal Development
- Career Counseling
- Team Building
- Staff Training

ACCOMPLISHMENTS

- Provided regular personal and career counseling to many levels of employees, in particular to those affected by employment transition and other crises, and assisted them in developing practical action plans for career recovery and growth.

- Worked with groups of employees to develop commitment to excellence and dedication to the highest performance standards, resulting in significant improvements in staff morale, customer service, and accomplishment of objectives.

- Personally conducted interviews with over 600 job applicants, and actively evaluated and screened applicants for over 150 positions, developing a high-level sense of the important elements that lead to success in the job market.

- Conducted over 200 effective presentations to management, staff, industry associations, schools and community groups on a wide range of topics, convincingly promoting issues, and winning audience support for new programs and changes.

- Conducted over 100 staff training sessions, covering issues ranging from new procedures, to interpersonal relations, to developing life goals and career objectives, resulting in a high degree of employee motivation and effectiveness.

121

Personal development specialist. *David M. Newbold; La Jolla, CA*

This page is written as if by someone else about Peter and allows him to speak about his experience in a different way.

PROFESSIONAL PROFILE

Peter J. Freeman

3456 E. Paterson Drive, Apt. 11
Portello, CA 94345

(451) 231-4656

SUMMARY

Peter is seeking to make a career change into a field which has one or more of the following characteristics::

- Supporting people in taking responsibility for their lives and reaching their true potential.

- Teaching or training people - in a classroom, tutorial or seminar environment - to develop vocational or life-enhancing skills, such as learning to use a computer, transitioning into the workforce, or adapting to major life changes.

- Planning, organizing and participating in programs designed to support or promote humanitarian goals, such as feeding the hungry, educating the poor, being a "big brother" to gang members, or counseling children from broken homes.

- Working in the field of career/vocational guidance, helping those seeking employment in organizing their job search, providing advice, assistance and resources in support of career development, and helping those recently graduated to choose the right career.

STATEMENT OF VISION AND VALUES

- Peter believes that all people have the innate need to develop their true potential and to excel in areas where they can play a vital and meaningful role in the forward progress of humanity.

- He seeks to enter a field in which he can teach, motivate, empower and support such people and help them realize more satisfying and enjoyable lives resulting from making meaningful contributions in the field(s) of their choice.

- His value system recognizes that it is his function to contribute from the depth of his extensive knowledge and experience to the continued growth of humanitarian causes, and to play his part in relieving the suffering and waste in human life that continues to anchor our progress as a planet to the past.

PERFORMANCE PROFILE

As a businessman, Peter has had an excellent record of achievement, which has been primarily attributable to the following characteristics:

- **Problem Solver** \ · investigative, logical, clear-thinking and organized
- **Accountable** \ · takes responsibility · finishes projects on time · fair and honest
- **Skilled With People** \ · enthusiastic · sense of humor · motivational · tactfully direct
- **Action-Oriented** \ · makes things happen · fresh new approaches · gets people excited
- **Communicator** \ · a natural catalyst for information flow · a polished presenter/facilitator
- **Visionary** \ · entrepreneurial · assumes ownership · goal-oriented · responsive to change
- **Strong Leadership** qualities with a winning attitude that positively affects others.
- **Organized & efficient** · resourceful · methodical · strong drive to excel

AREAS OF EFFECTIVENESS

- Communicating verbally & in writing
- Supporting personal development
- Teaching, training and seminar leading
- Planning and directing

- Creating with innovative ideas
- Using intuition to make the right decisions
- Fostering solid inter-personal relationships
- Transition counseling and career guidance

"Life is action and passion; therefore, it is required of a man that he should share the passion and action of the time..."
— Oliver Wendell Holmes, Jr.

Anne Marie Dessimoz

1000 South Michigan Avenue
Elmira, NY 00000
Home: (212) 555-5555
Business: (212) 222-2222
artsfan@prodigy.net

I used a functional format which includes a Summary to highlight artistic and creative abilities as well as accomplishments. Key points are in bold type. (resume writer's comments)

Professional Objective   Director of Arts Education

Summary of Qualifications

- Ability to apply creative thinking skills toward short- and long-range goals and problem-solving.

- Experience in program presentation and group facilitation.

- Ability to interact with the public in a professional and concerned manner.

- Facility to work independently and with a multidisciplinary team.

Professional Experience and Skills

- Implemented comprehensive **Summer Creative Arts Program** for youth ages 7 to 15. Benchmarked model program in Dover, Massachusetts. Sought and received donations, grants, and in-kind services from local organizations and individuals.

- Identified need for unique, self-guided **family program** and created the **At Matts Club** for students from preschool to high school. Designed evaluative material.

- Initiated collaboration with two schools and two cultural institutions for development of **in-school, interdisciplinary program based on art and nature/environment** for 1998–9 school year.

- Planned and coordinated **biannual art festivals** that attracted people who previously did not visit the museum.

- Successfully marketed summer camp, doubling enrollment by the second year.

Administration and Management

- Supervise and monitor Education Center facility.

- Annually **interview and contract over 30 local artists** and professionals for short- and long-term programs.

- Plan and monitor Education Department budget in excess of $70,000.

- Supervise and evaluate all Education Center and program staff.

- Administer ongoing docent program.

- Responsible for **development of short and long range plans** for the Education Department.

122

Director of arts education. *Betty Geller, CPRW; Elmira, NY*

Anne Marie Dessimoz, page 2

Community Relations and Marketing	• Serve as liaison between museum, schools, social service agencies and general public. • Research and evaluate art education needs of surrounding school districts and develop **thematic tours to enhance curricula.** • In conjunction with local organizations/programs, develop museum based hands-on experiences and **outreach programs** to meet their educational goals. • Co-facilitated unique, **interdisciplinary Teacher Training** course with two area museums. • Develop and implement Intensive **Docent Training course involving local professionals.** Recruit volunteers from general public. • Solicited public relations and design work from local agencies/media for promotion of educational programs and events.
Employment History	*1994 to Present:* **Curator of Education** Valley City Art Museum Valley City, New York *1993 to 1994:* **Account Manager** Harrison Temporaries Valley City, New York Filled the temporary needs of corporate and small businesses. Off-site marketing of first-rate temporary agency.
Education	**Palazzo Spinelli** **Instituto dell'Arte e Restauro** Florence, Italy Graduate Fine and Decorative Arts. Fluent in Italian. **Syracuse University** Syracuse, New York Emphasis on Liberal and Fine Arts with related courses in advertising and marketing.

LAWRENCE BURTON, Ph.D.
Clinical Psychologist
123 White Road
Westchester, NY 10000
(914) 222-2222

Objectives: Counselor/Teacher in College Setting
Psychologist in Clinical Setting

HIGHLIGHTS OF QUALIFICATIONS

- Licensed clinical psychologist; 30 years professional experience as college counselor
- Strong practical and theoretical foundation in variety of therapeutic modalities
- First-hand experience with multi-cultural differences as they relate to
counseling, therapy, and teaching environments
- Excellent planning, organizational, communication and administrative skills
- Energetic, innovative, dedicated, adaptable, intuitive problem solver
- Conversant in Spanish

PROFESSIONAL EXPERIENCE

College Counseling and Teaching
- Counseled a wide range of individual multi-cultural students regarding personal, social,
and academic difficulties interfering with success in college
  - Assisted students in planning for meaningful realistic career choices.
  - Devised academic strategies which included referral to college and
community resources
  - Collaborated with teaching faculty in tracking and providing intervention to
maximize academic success.
- Created and implemented syllabus for group counseling with students on academic
probation which enabled group members to explore and rectify roots of problems
- Developed and implemented innovative programs for counselors to use in their daily work
including mentoring and transfer student orientation programs
- Coordinated, supervised, and administrated a unit staff of eighteen counselors
- Taught freshmen orientation and development courses, as well as introductory psychology
and adjustment problems of aging.

Psychotherapy and Psychological Testing
- Provided individual psychotherapy for adolescents and adults for the past 25 years, using
a psychodynamic approach
- Conducted goal-oriented couples counseling
- Provided psychodiagnostic testing for adolescents and adults, including over 100 OVR
evaluations.

123

College and university faculty. *Linsey Levine; Chappaqua, NY*

Like many college professors, this one does more than "just" teach classes. He is both a professor and counselor and he does "extra curricular" activities related to his training

Lawrence Burton, Ph.D.   Page 2

EMPLOYMENT HISTORY

Professor/Counselor	The City College, CUNY	1966-present
Dept. of Special Programs	New York, NY	
Psychotherapist	Westchester, NY	1970-present
Private Practice		
Staff Psychologist	Manhattanville College	1972-1977
	Purchase, NY	
Staff Psychologist	Westchester County Dept. of	1968-1972
	Mental Health, Yonkers, NY	
Lecturer	Bronx Community College	1967-1968
	Bronx, NY	
Psychotherapist	Mental Health Consultation Center	1965-1968
	West Nyack, NY	
Staff Clinical Psychologist	V.A. Hospital	1964-1966
	Montrose, NY	

RECENT PUBLICATIONS

Burton, L., "Success Rate of Transfer Students Enrolled in a Program for the Underprepared at a Senior College": <u>Journal of College Student Development</u>:11, 56-60,1993

Backner, B.L., and Burton, L., "A Survey of Disadvantaged Students Attitudes Toward a Special College Program": <u>Journal of Human Resources</u>: V.2, 1992.

PROFESSIONAL ORGANIZATIONS

American Psychological Association
Westchester County Psychological Association

EDUCATION

State University of NY at Buffalo, Buffalo, NY
Ph.D., Clinical Psychology, 1964
Brooklyn College, Brooklyn, NY
B.S. Psychology, 1958
NY State Certification Exam Passed, 1965

To show this kind of flexibility makes him more desirable to an employer

Anthonee DuBois

162 Oxford Avenue, Reno, NV 89501
775.893.9479
ADfit@yahoo.com

This person's resume downplays his entrepreneurship somewhat, to be sure it does not hinder his attempts to gain employment that matches his passion — fitness education.

Fitness Specialist

**A hands-on professional / goal-oriented strategist
whose confidence, perseverance and vision promote success.**

GOAL: An opportunity to serve as a **Youth / Athletic Director**
employing my abilities to improve and motivate the physical fitness / rehabilitation of individuals.

GENERAL QUALIFICATIONS

Recognize client's needs and set goals.
Utilize initiative, achievement and independent judgment.
Set and meet high performance standards.
Give detailed attention to schedules, deadlines, budgets and quality results.
Possess a track record for creativity and innovation.

PROFESSIONAL FITNESS EXPERTISE

Twenty years' progressive experience and responsibility with documented success in the areas of health / fitness

▸▸ Successfully develop, initiate, and coordinate individual and group exercise programs.
▸▸ Demonstrate correct and safe use of exercise equipment and routines.
▸▸ Observe participants during exercise sessions for signs of physical stress; compensate pace.
▸▸ Conduct group and independent aerobic, strength and flexibility sessions.
▸▸ Supervise other instructors.

MAJOR PROJECT: "ANTHONEE'S KIDS"

Developed franchised program implemented nationally in public / private schools

▸▸ Innovative fitness education program for improving overall health of high-risk children.
▸▸ Encourage positive lifestyle choices to offset school violence and nutrition problems.
▸▸ Detailed curriculum designed for infusion into school districts nationwide.
▸▸ Utilize behavior-style profiling and customized physical fitness equipment for children.

SPECIALIZED TRAINING

Certifications: Strength & Conditioning / CPR / Athletic Trainer / American Red Cross
A.C.S.M. Exercise Specialist / Respiratory Technician

EXPERIENCE

DuBois & Associates, LLC	*Owner / Personal Trainer*	Barstow, NV
Reno Health & Rehabilitation	*Co-owner / Personal Trainer*	Reno, NV
Tower Fitness Industries	*Fitness Consultant / Wellness Center Program Director*	Las Vegas, NV
Reno Medical Center	*Respiratory Therapy Technician* (American Red Cross Certified)	Reno, NV

BODYBUILDING / WEIGHTLIFTING CHAMPIONSHIPS

1999	Western Power Lifting	*2nd Place*	1997	Beast of the Southeast Deadlift	*2nd Place*
1998	Northeastern Power Lifting	*2nd Place*	1996	Nevada Strongest Man (lightwt)	*2nd Place*
1998	State Bodybuilding	*5th Place*	1995	Mid-Pacific Strongman (middlewt)	*1st Place*
1997	State Bodybuilding	*2nd Place*	1991	Northeastern Texas Bodybuilding	*3rd Place*

Gym Design / Layout

Kansas City Royals
St. Joseph's Hospital
J.T.O. Corporation
McDonald Rehabilitation
World Gyms
Gold's Gyms
Federal Correctional Institute

Equipped / Set Up Gyms

Washington Redskins
Ford Motor Company
Phoenix Cardinals
Greenville Wellness Center
University of Missouri
Texas State University
Police and Fire Departments

124

Fitness specialist. *Jane Roqueplot, CBC; Sharon, PA*

Michelle's strong educational credentials are presented first. Note the crayon bullets—originally colored to add an element of creativity and fun.

MICHELLE T. WIDELY

College Avenue | Bangor, ME 04401 | (555) 555-5555

OBJECTIVE: PRESCHOOL / NURSERY SCHOOL TEACHER

EDUCATION:

UNIVERSITY OF MAINE, Farmington, ME (May 1996)
Associate in Arts, Early Childhood Education
Completed five Special Education elective courses including Educating Exceptional Children.

BANGOR HIGH SCHOOL, Bangor, ME (1993 Graduate)
Child Care and Nursery School Program, Bangor Regional Vocational Center (1992-1993)

Awards: Nursery School Program Student of the Year (1993)
Child Care Program Student of the Year (1992)
National Vocational Technical Honor Society (1993)
Recognition Award for service to Bangor Head Start Program (1993)

Achievements: Member of class which organized first grant-sponsored Nursery School at the Vocational Center. Interviewed prospective parents, ordered equipment and supplies, set-up room, performed research/paperwork.

CAPABILITIES:

- Encourage "whole child" development through facilitation of child-guided activities
- Plan and teach individual/group activities including circle time
- Research and develop variety of lessons with art, math, science, and self-care themes
- Communicate openly with parents, children, fellow teachers and supervisors

EXPERIENCE:

Preschool Teacher CHILDREN ARE GREAT PRESCHOOL, Bangor, ME (5/96-present)
Supervise activities of children ages 2-6 providing choices and guidance when needed; organize and teach special projects and conduct circle time; assist with lunches and field trips; interact extensively with parents and children.

Student Teacher CHILDREN'S PRESCHOOL, Bangor, ME (9/95-5/96)

Service Clerk THE FOOD BANK, Brewer, ME (1994-96, part-time)

Teacher's Helper MOM'S DAY CARE, Brewer, ME (Summer 1992, f/t)
Assisted director with routine activities for children ages 1½ to 7.

Volunteer HEAD START, Bangor, ME (1992-93)
Volunteered 3 mornings/week planning and teaching daily activities.

125

Preschool teacher. *Elizabeth M. Carey, CPRW; Waterville, ME*

Donna used this resume to get the head teacher's position at a corporate preschool facility, she since moved into a managerial role curriculum and preschool teachers (resume writer's comments).

DONNA L. GILBERT
55 North Main Street
Augusta, ME 55555
(550) 555-0050

overseeing the direction of eight

PHILOSOPHY AND ATTRIBUTES

Highly motivated and dedicated teaching professional with empathy and compassion toward young children and their individualized strengths and needs. Advocate for hands-on, student-centered learning which fosters an appreciation for multiculturalism and integrates a Whole Language approach. Possess an energetic, enthusiastic, and creative style; performance characterized as loyal and hard-working. Proficient in various computer software packages for Macintosh and IBM systems, including WordPerfect and Microsoft Works. Financed 100% of undergraduate education.

These key skills say much about her personality and are important to employers

EDUCATION

University of Maine • Orono, ME
- *Bachelor of Science* in Elementary Education; Concentration: Sociology (1991)

University of Massachusetts • Amherst, MA — Concentration: Liberal Arts (1986–88)

CERTIFICATION

- Maine Teacher Certification (K-6) — Infant and Child First Aid/CPR

PROFESSIONAL EXPERIENCE

Mountain Magic Children's Center • Waterville, ME   June 1990–Present
Preschool Teacher (promoted from Childcare/Assistant Preschool Teacher in 1994)
- Plan exciting, developmentally appropriate, child-focused activities for group of 10 children.
- Utilize thematic-based instruction, including implementation of such innovative, hands-on units as The Feeding and Caring of Ourselves (nutrition), We Grow as the Seasons Change (a year-long look incorporating science, weather, and human growth), and Our Gardens Teach Us (environment, commitment, and outdoor activities).
- Conduct annual parent conferences; provide individualized learning summaries based on observation of each child's progress.
- Maintain observation-based anecdotal records; developed and implemented a systematic program for evaluating student development and growth.
- Regularly attend workshops presented by NAEYC to ensure skills are fully up to date and professional education is ongoing.

Orono Nature Center • Orono, ME   Summers, 1993–Present
Summer Camp Naturalist
- Instruct summer camp four days per week to preschoolers (8–12 attendees); program emphasis is on protecting and understanding the wonders of nature. Thematic program includes focus on insects, trees, birds, and animals.
- Conduct programs on habitats, adaptations, and "KIDS CARE" at local schools, community centers, churches, and day care facilities.

Before/After School Program • Waterville, ME   Spring/Summer 1991
Assistant Program Director
- Initiated recreational opportunities for 25 school-age children, grades kindergarten through six.

STUDENT TEACHING EXPERIENCE

John Smith Preschool • Winslow, ME   Feb. 1991–May 1991
- Planned and implemented hands-on mathematics, science, and language arts units, gradually assuming all classroom teaching responsibilities in a classroom for 15 preschoolers.
- Developed age-appropriate, integrated units and lesson plans in introductory chemistry, multiplication, and poetry.

Winslow Elementary School • Winslow, ME   Fall 1989, 1990
- As kindergarten bilingual tutor, formulated creative learning techniques for non-English speaking students.

126

Preschool teacher. *Jan Melnik, CPRW, CCM; Durham, CT*

Sandy overcame the "babysitter" stigma that often follows day care workers by focusing on skill areas rather than employment...

SANDY SUE CLARK
1999 Wilmington Street
Wilmington, North Carolina 28000
(910) 555-0000

SUMMARY

Committed to quality in every task from personal interaction with co-workers and customers to any services provided to the company or customer.

Possess excellent interpersonal skills and have a strong commitment to customer service. Experienced in working with individuals of many backgrounds, cultures, and age groups.

Demonstrated ability as a supervisor with experience hiring, training, and motivating employees as well as conducting performance reviews.

Dependable and hard working employee.

Her responsibilities were very intensive in regulatory compliance and quality at this respected corporate child care center (resume writer's comments).

SKILLS AND ABILITIES

Customer Service and Sales:
- Arrange and conduct tours of facilities. Provide information regarding company policies and procedures and answer questions.
- More than four years experience in retail sales and customer service through full-time positions during college.

Supervision:
- Directly supervised up to 15 employees including all responsibility for ongoing training and performance reviews.
- Interview applicants and conduct orientation for new employees.

Policy and Regulation Compliance:
- Ensure teachers are in compliance with company policies and state regulations include OSHA and health regulations as well as regulations relating to center's certification with childcare agencies.
- Conduct monthly team meetings. Prepare agenda and materials. Present new company business and/or policies and answer questions the group may have.

Computer Skills:
- Computer skills include word processing and basic desktop publishing on IBM compatible PCs.

EDUCATION AND TRAINING

UNIVERSITY OF NORTH CAROLINA AT WILMINGTON   1991
Bachelor of Arts - Elementary Education
North Carolina Teaching Certificate - K-6
Infant & Child CPR Certified

EMPLOYMENT HISTORY

BIG KID'S DAY CARE CENTER, Wilmington, NC   1992 - Present
Assistant Director
Head Teacher - Infants and Toddlers
Infant Teacher

127

Preschool teacher/supervisor. *Sandy Adcox Saburn, CPRW; Charlotte, NC*

This resume's unique design and attractive graphics make a great first impression for this recent college graduate seeking a job as a kindergarten teacher.

Shelly Shane

555 Rt. 23, Summit, NJ 07901
908-918-5555
shelshane@world.net

EDUCATION

May 2002 Bachelor of Arts
Elementary Education
Stockton State College
Stockton, New Jersey

Dean's List, GPA 3.4

OBJECTIVE

A position as a **Kindergarten School Teacher** utilizing my proven abilities to create a motivational and stimulating learning environment.

CERTIFICATIONS

Education and
Special Education K–6
(New Jersey and New York)

Current Substitute Teacher K–12
(New Jersey)
Current First Aid and CPR

MY PRIMER OF SKILLS

- **Achieve** total educational involvement by developing rapport with students; **adapt** to individual learning styles and capabilities.
- **Brainstorm** for educational ideas to **benefit** my students; **believe** in holding students accountable for their actions.
- **Creative**, flexible approaches and **cooperative** learning activities; **caring** about each and every student.

MEMBERSHIPS

New Jersey Teachers' Association
National Child Care Association
New Jersey Child Care
  Association
Teachers' Club — President
  (Stockton State College)
Stockton Girl Scouts
  (Volunteer for 5 years)

EXPERIENCE

January 2002–present
Student Teacher K–2
Summit Elementary School
Summit, NJ

- Teach or team-teach six classes in math, reading, language arts and special education. Use thematic approach to all classes.

2001–present
Co-Lead/Lead Teacher
Extended Day Care Program
Stockton School District, NJ

- Manage before- and after-school care program for 160 students in grades K–6, with tutoring and enrichment programs.
- Teach summer enrichment classes to K–8th graders in science, drama, and arts.

2000 Summer
Program Coordinator
Stockton School District, NJ

- Oversaw and coordinated summer programs for five sites serving 600 students.
- Supervised five program site coordinators and 40+ enrichment class teachers.
- Troubleshot and served as liaison with the Director of Community Education and the Extended Day Program Coordinator.

128

School teacher: kindergarten. *Susan Guarneri, NCC, NCCC, LPC, CPRW, IJCTC, CCM, CEIP; Lawrenceville, NJ*

A recommendation from a credible source — a school principal — leads off this functional-style resume.

Eileen M. McFadden

(973) 548-9002 — PO Box 203, Morristown, NJ 07960 — eileenmac@hotmail.com

Eileen is an outstanding teacher who spends long hours preparing lessons and activities that foster individual talents and capabilities of her students — a seemingly overwhelming task with 35 children! I am constantly amazed at the progress of her children and their enthusiasm for learning. They love their teacher and really do their best in such a positive, nurturing atmosphere. — Principal, Moreford School

Experienced Elementary Educator
Early Childhood Specialist

Resourceful, caring teacher accomplished in assessing young children's abilities and needs to enhance literacy development and early language acquisition. Outstanding class management skills promote an inviting learning environment while maintaining discipline in the classroom.

Contributions

Her teaching experience is listed below without detail, while her contributions are grouped front-and-center for greatest impact.

✓ Conceive, produce and direct annual "Kindergarten Graduation" performance program. Received numerous kudos over the past 8 years from parents and faculty for perennially successful ceremony.
✓ Introduced Kindergarten Screening Program based on Brigance Program to identify and recommend appropriate placement of special needs and at-risk students.
✓ Create "Kindergarten Books" and "Reading Books" for each student to document progress throughout the year and apprise parents of continually evolving skills.
✓ Promote positive teacher-student-parent alliances by volunteering to assist with numerous extracurricular activities such as Drama Club, Latchkey Program and Field Day Games.

Education

Master of Science in Education and Bachelor of Arts in Psychology
William Paterson College, Paterson, NJ

Credentials

New Jersey State Certification — Elementary and Nursery
New York State Permanent Certification — N–6
New York City Teaching License

Selected In-Service Workshops

Attention Deficit Disorder, Emergent Literacy (2 years), Reporting Child Abuse, Reading Workshop (2 years), Agriculture in the Classroom
   Milltown High School, Milltown, NJ (1991–Present)

Math/Science Workshop (3 years), Computers in the Classroom, Math/Computer Workshop
   Morris County Community College, Morristown, NJ (Summers 1991–1997)

Teaching Experience

Moreford School, Milford, NY (1987–Present)
Kindergarten, 1991–Present... **Grade 1,** 1989–1991... **Pre-K,** 1987–1989

Frances Smith Elementary School, New York, NY (1980–1987)
Kindergarten and Grade 1

129

School teacher: kindergarten/elementary. *Meg Guiseppi, CPRW; Andover, NJ*

This resume was successful because it was eye-catching and hit the "hot buttons" in elementary education today.

CAROLE A. SAUNDERS

15 Bedford Lane • Concord, MA 01742 • 978-371-0224 • saundersc@verizon.net

ELEMENTARY CLASSROOM TEACHER

STRENGTHS:
Creative Lesson Planning • Motivating Students • Organization • Classroom Management

EDUCATION, CERTIFICATION AND COMPUTER SKILLS	**Bachelor of Science in Elementary Education,** Salem State College, 1998 **Coursework** (Selected): • Independent Study: Creating an Innovative Approach to Teaching • Language Arts • The Exceptional Child • Child Growth & Development • Curriculum Designs for Young Children • Mental Health Education in Schools • Creative Experience Curriculum • Foundations of Reading • Children's Literature **Certified Elementary School Teacher,** Grades 1–6, Commonwealth of MA **Professional Development:** Business Math, Principles of Supervision **Applications:** Microsoft Word, Excel, Quattro Pro, Harvard Graphics
TEACHING EXPERIENCE • **Individualized Instruction** • **Different Learning Styles** • **Team-Based Learning** • **Integrated Curricula** • **Hands-On Learning**	**Teacher, Grade 2,** Alcott School, Concord, MA, 2000–Present • Taught whole-class and small-group lessons in all subject areas. • Improved reading scores by an average of 1.3 grade levels on standardized tests. • Used formal and informal assessments and developed plans for skill improvement. • Worked with mainstreamed special-education students. • Prepared and taught units that integrated different learning modalities. • Developed a curriculum on dinosaurs emphasizing hands-on learning and the use of both gross and fine motor skills. • Presented a "Shaping Up with Geometry" unit that combined math and art skills. • Conceived and taught a self-discovery unit called "ME-Mobiles." **Teacher, Grade 4,** Willard School, Concord, MA, 1998–2001 • Taught lessons in language arts, math, science, social studies and art using whole-class, team-based and individualized methodologies. • Developed a hands-on approach to learning about famous historical figures that combined reading, social studies, and drama. • Led weeklong field trip to Nature's Classroom Program, Sandwich, MA. • Introduced computer technology into the classroom as part of a creative writing unit. Children produced their own "books" using word-processing and graphics software. • Developed tactile, auditory, and visual interactive lessons for teaching states and capitals.

Bullet items reflect "hot buttons" in elementary education.

130

School teacher: elementary. *Jean Cummings, MAT, CPRW, CEIP; Concord, MA*

This new graduate was getting ready to move to another state.

Jennifer S. Perkins

1829 First Avenue South, Ann Arbor, MI 48104
JennyP245@aol.com   734-555-0856

Personal Profile

Jennifer had unusual experience for someone so young, and this experience is emphasized throughout her resume.

- Committed to children and the belief that *everyone can learn.*
- Strive to create caring, nurturing, learning-filled environment.
- Adaptable and flexible to meet children's diverse needs.
- Exceptionally patient, especially with special-needs students.
- Highly motivated and energetic; held multiple jobs simultaneously while attending college full time.
- Strong academic preparation; graduated Magna Cum Laude from rigorous program.

Education

University of Michigan
Bachelor of Arts in Elementary Education (2002)
Magna Cum Laude
- Minors: Special Education and English

Certification

State of Michigan Provisional Certification
Endorsements:
- Elementary Education
- K–12 Emotionally Impaired

Her extensive hands-on experience in special education is highlighted, because it is atypical for a recent graduate.

Education-Related Experience

Student Teaching — *Chelsea Community Schools* • Chelsea, Michigan   2001–2002
- Semester-long **Regular Education** experience in 1st grade classroom at Pierce Elementary.
- Semester-long **Special Education** experience in 4th–6th grade Resource Room at Gates Elementary.

Field Work — *Shiawassee Intermediate School District* • Corunna, Michigan   1999–2001
- Over 50 hours of hands-on **classroom** experience for university methods classes including physical education, mathematics, reading, science, and social studies.

Additional Relevant Experience

Licensed Day Care Facility — *Discovery Center* • Ann Arbor, Michigan   1999–2002
- Worked as Day Care Provider at facility licensed for up to 59 children aged 6 weeks to 12 years.

In-Home Child Care   1996–2002
- Significant experience providing care to children in their homes during summers and after school (family names available on request). Responsible for planning activities, dropping off and picking up at school, and assisting with homework.
- Under direction of Washtenaw County Community Mental Health Department, provided day care for three autistic siblings in their own home. Planned activities and arranged field trips. Prepared meals. Performed personal care and assisted children with activities of daily living with the goal of increasing their functioning and independence.

Volunteer Experience

Camps   *Seasonal* 1995–2001
- Acted as counselor at end-of-the-year camp for 6th graders. Led students in outdoor activities and ensured their safety. *(Dexter Community Schools)*
- Volunteered at Spring Camp for physically and mentally disabled students. Assigned to supervise and provide direct care to 2 special needs children. *(Ann Arbor Community Schools)*

– References available on request –

131

School teacher: elementary. *Janet L. Beckstrom; Flint, MI*

After several years of self-employment, John decided to pursue New Jersey's alternate route (education degree not required) to become a secondary-level teacher.

JOHN HENSON

321 Cinder Court, Brick, NJ 08723
Home: 732-477-5172 • E-mail: jhenson@aol.com

TARGETED POSITION: TEACHER (9–12)

- Applied for New Jersey Certificate of Eligibility for teaching with late April/early May 2002 anticipated arrival.
- Possess a bachelor's degree in psychology and working towards a master's in counseling psychology.
- Experienced in training employees, tutoring college students, and coaching children of differing abilities.
- Enjoy interacting with children and very motivated to obtain a teaching opportunity.
- Student affiliate of the American Psychological Association (APA) & member of Psi Chi National Honor Society.

EDUCATION & TRAINING

Pending Master of Arts in Counseling Psychology, Rutgers State University, Newark, NJ • Began Fall 2001
Courses:

- Educating Exceptional Children in Inclusive Settings
- Counseling Processes
- Assessment In Counseling
- Advanced Statistics & Research Methods

Bachelor of Arts in Psychology, Rutgers State University, New Brunswick, NJ • 2001 Cum Laude Graduate
Senior Awards Night: Received one of two awards presented for outstanding performance in psychology
Senior Seminar 25-page paper: "The Effects of Extracurricular Activities Among School-Age Children"
Selected Courses:

- New Jersey Family Law
- Psychology of Learning
- Child Psychology
- Public Speaking
- Educational Psychology
- Multicultural Psychology
- Alcohol & Substance Abuse
- Adolescent Psychology

Associate of Arts in Liberal Arts, Brookdale Community College, Lincroft, NJ • 1998 Cum Laude Graduate

His related instructional experience as a coach and college tutor are emphasized here.

──(INSTRUCTIONAL EXPERIENCE

OCEAN COUNTY LITTLE LEAGUE ASSOCIATION, Lakewood, New Jersey — Fall 1999 & Spring 2000
Baseball Coach
Taught baseball fundamentals and strategies to a team of 8-year-old boys. Conducted weekly practices and coached weekly games. Promoted a fun learning environment with the successful results of placing 2nd in the fall and 1st in the spring for overall team performance.

BROOKDALE COMMUNITY COLLEGE, Lincroft, New Jersey — 1994 to 1996
Volunteer Tutor (part-time)
As member of the national honor society Phi Theta Kappa, volunteered to provide assistance with remedial algebra and statistics on a walk-in basis in a campus classroom. Tutored college students for various lengths of time from one-time homework assistance to repeated help with the courses.

WORK HISTORY)

His non-teaching experience was included to show work ethic, ability to work independently, and training background. All are transferable skills for teaching.

LAKEWOOD HEATING & AIR CONDITIONING, Lakewood, NJ — 1995 to Present (concurrent with college)
Owner/Operator
Conducted on-the-job instructional training for new hires. Interviewed, hired, and supervised two helpers. Interacted with public to provide HVAC installations and repairs. Performed needs assessments and troubleshooting. Resolved customer problems.

JERSEY SHORE HEATING & AIR CONDITIONING, Lakewood, New Jersey — 1989 to 1995
Supervisor • 1993–1995 // **Mechanic** • 1991–1993 // **Helper** • 1989–1991
Supervised mechanics, helpers, and subcontractors. Worked independently with little supervision. Responded to customer and employee questions. Coordinated projects and provided continual on-the-job training to employees.

132

School teacher: secondary. *Carol Rossi, CPRW; Brick, NJ*

Robert Valencia

404 Fortsolanga Lane
Bayshore, NY 11706
(631) 382-2425
robvalencia@juno.com

Overview

Patient, understanding, and firm *Special Education Teacher* who enjoys enhancing the quality education of high-risk students. Employ a unique balance of humor, empathy, and stability in the classroom.

Summary of Qualifications

- Develop innovative classroom instruction consistent with educational plans and treatment goals. Integrate knowledge of New York State special education laws, rules, and regulations into lesson plans.

- Sensitive to students' backgrounds, interests, and handicaps. Fluent in Spanish and American Sign Language.

- Effectively manage behavior of students to create a safe physical and emotional classroom environment.

Education

Master of Science in Special Education, Dowling College, Oakdale, NY, 1995

Special Education Certification and New York State Certification, 1995

Bachelor of Science, Biology, State University of New York, Stony Brook, NY, 1993

Professional Employment

Special Education Teacher, Pine Street Middle School, West Islip, NY, 1995 to Present

Teach various populations including students with ADD, mental retardation, visual impairment, deafness and hearing impairment, developmental and learning disabilities, and those who are physically, emotionally, and behaviorally challenged.

[handwritten note: Subheadings are used to increase the visibility of important achievements.]

Classroom Management and Presentation

- Provide a clear, consistent structure for the classroom that ensures that the academic, social, and emotional needs of each student are met within the guidelines of the Individualized Educational Program.

- Assess students' abilities and implement creative lesson plans to motivate student learning. Highly successful teaching techniques include visual articulation, photography for language use and awareness, personal picture diaries to aid students in recognizing basic concepts through symbols, and positive reinforcement programs.

- Incorporate the latest technology in the teaching process, including computers with synthesized speech, interactive educational software programs, and audiotapes.

- Integrate academic subjects with daily activities education; recommend integration/inclusion of students in mainstream education.

Interpersonal Skills

- Cooperate in a multidisciplinary team that includes parents, social workers, school psychologists, occupational and physical therapists, and school administrators.

- Review and present each student's IEP to parents, administrators, and classroom teachers.

Affiliation

New York State Special Education Teacher Association

133

Special education teacher. *Linda Matias, JCTC, CEIP; Smithtown, NY*

This special-education teacher was concerned about the almost 3-year gap in her employment history. However, during that time, she had worked as a full-time volunteer for a human services organization for children, further refining her skills in social work.

Carla T. Burke

212 Meadowlark Lane • Morristown, NJ 07960
Phone: (908) 984-9776 • E-mail: ctb@cohn.edu

Professional Profile

Special Educator with 12 years of classroom experience in the areas of Severe Learning Disabilities and Emotional & Behavioral Disorders. Effective communicator with solid writing, speaking and presenting skills. Able to remain calm and maintain an objective viewpoint under duress. Expert organizer and team facilitator able to work and interact with individuals from diverse social and cultural backgrounds. Able to achieve short- and long-term goals established in the classroom.

Highlights of Qualifications:
Individualized Education Programs • Evaluation & Assessment • Advocate Case Management
Supervision & Training • Counseling • Diagnostic Testing & Task Analysis • Research

Experience

Cohn Child Development Center, Menlo Park, NJ   1/99 – Present

- Implemented IEPs for the developmentally disabled and autistic students.
- Supervised and mentored Special Ed. student teachers and trained them to accomplish IEP goals.
- Worked with the developmentally delayed to help mainstream students into conventional settings.

The School For Exceptional Children, Staten Island, NY   9/92 – 12/96

- Acted as social worker implementing therapies and teaching home-based programs for parents.
- Promoted order and discipline within classroom by introducing a wide variety of teaching aids and innovative incentives.
- Customized and integrated strategies to teach a range of mentally disabled students from 3–6 years of age.

UCP of New York State, Brooklyn, NY   9/86 – 6/92

- Developed and established IEPs for moderately to severely handicapped adults.
- Worked closely with physical and occupational therapists on basic cognitive and developmental therapies for infants and toddlers to achieve milestones.

Education and Certifications

MS, Special Education, Harper College, Staten Island, NY, 1986
BS, Elementary Education and Special Education, Harper College, Staten Island, NY, 1982
NJ State Certification for Teacher of the Handicapped
NY State Certification for Teacher of the Handicapped

Volunteer Work

This section was included to explain her employment gap & to show her passion for helping children.

Worked as a full-time volunteer for New York Child Care and Welfare, New York, NY, 1996 – 1998

Professional Affiliations

National Association of Teachers of Special Education.

134

Special education teacher. *Elona Harkins; Westfield, NJ*

Unlike most legal resumes, design and type give this one a less-formal look. Notice the lack of dates. This makes it impossible to determine his age.

JOSEPH DONS, ATTORNEY AT LAW

25 West Main Street ◆ East Alton, Illinois 62024
Home (618) 555-5000 ◆ Cell (618) 355-5555 ◆ jd@simmonsanddons.com

Licensed in Illinois, Missouri, and Georgia

EDUCATION

Juris Doctor
Southern Illinois University ◆ Edwardsville, Illinois
Moot Court...Mock Trial...Christian Legal Society

Bachelor of Science, Political Science
Southern Methodist University ◆ Dallas, Texas
Student Body President...Dean's College...Dean's List...Student Senator...
Who's Who Among College and University Students...Scholastic All-American

EXPERIENCE

The Simmons & Dons Firm, P.C., East Alton, Illinois
A professional corporation and taw firm specializing in

Wills & Trusts	Estate Planning
Probate	General Practice
General Litigation & Appeals	Nonprofit Corporations
Small-Business Affairs	Ecclesiastical Agencies

Dale A. Allison, Jr. & Associates, St. Louis, Missouri
Leaders in legal representation for churches, evangelistic associations, ministries, and Christian schools. Provided legal support involving litigation, governmental compliance, asset management, and organizational structure.

Tax Fraud	RICO
Pastoral Compensation	Sexual Harassment
Church Real Estate Withdrawal	IRS Audits

Clark/Bardes, Inc., Dallas, Texas
Used corporate-owned life Insurance (COLI) to fund projects and cooperate planning. Lobbied state legislatures to pass COLI laws. Clients included American Airlines, Dial Corporation, and Wrigley Corporation.

OTHER

◆ U.S. Army Combat Engineer, Expert Rifle/Grenade Division

More information could be provided in an interview.

135

Lawyer. *John A. Suarez, CPRW; O'Fallon, IL*

FRANCINE NUMANN, ESQ

144 Bankbert Court • Robbins, New Jersey 00000
(555) 555-5555

SUMMARY of QUALIFICATIONS:

A highly dedicated professional with a successful career and the capacity to contribute to the development of a progressive organization. Demonstrated strengths include the capacity to analyze large volumes of complex information, strong interpersonal skills with the ability to interface with individuals at all levels and strong follow up skills.

AREAS of EXPERTISE:

**GENERAL NEGLIGENCE • MEDICAL MALPRACTICE • LITIGATION
AUTOMOBILE NEGLIGENCE • PRODUCTS LIABILITY**

PROFESSIONAL AFFILIATIONS:

BROTHERS INSURANCE (formerly American Reliance Insurance Company)   Lawrenceview, NJ
Staff Attorney   *1990 - Present*
- Serve as in-house counsel handling liability claims with a caseload of 100 files concurrently.
- Examine complaints, analyze legality of suits and prepare/file answers/pleadings on behalf of clients.
- Prepare and participate in all phases of pre-trial discovery.
- Organize materials required for defense of negligence suits.
- Evaluate pending suits, review settlement demands and negotiate settlements.
- Participate in jury and non-jury trials.

Selected Achievements:
- ◆ *Consistently achieve a high success rate in obtaining dismissals of automobile negligence suits for failure to meet verbal threshold.*
- ◆ *Specifically requested by the Claims Department to handle verbal threshold cases.*

REISEMAN, MATTIA & SHARP   Roseland and Wall Township, NJ
A law firm specializing in insurance defense litigation, automobile negligence, medical malpractice defense and product liability defense.
Associate   *1986 - 1990*
- Assisted partners in all phases of pre-trial discovery, including drafting/filing pleadings and reviewing legality of suits.
- Prepared for and participated in jury and non-jury trials.

Selected Achievement:
- ◆ *Successfully obtained a high rate in suit dismissals for failure to meet the statute of limitations.*

(continued...)

136

Lawyer. *Alesia Benedict, CPRW, JCTC; Rochelle Park, NJ*

FRANCINE NUMANN, ESQ. (555) 555-5555 **Page Two**

PROFESSIONAL AFFILIATIONS continued...

THE HONORABLE B. THOMAS LEAHY, J.S.C./THE HONORABLE BERNARD RUDD, J.S.C.
SUPERIOR COURT of NEW JERSEY Newark, NJ
Law Clerk *1985 - 1986*
- Assisted Family Court and Special Civil Part judges in daily court activities including motions and trials.
- Researched case law and assisted in drafting legal opinions.
- Assisted in the drafting of three legal opinions selected for publication in N.J. Super.

HOSPITAL of the UNIVERSITY of PENNSYLVANIA, Legal Department Philadelphia, PA
Legal Intern *1984 - 1985*
- Assisted legal counsel in drafting hospital policies and contracts.
- Assessed merit and monetary value of medical malpractice suits.

EDUCATIONAL BACKGROUND:

Rutgers School of Law • Camden, NJ
Juris Doctor

S.U.N.Y. at Binghamton • Binghamton, NY
Bachelor of Arts • History

BAR ADMISSIONS:

New Jersey • New York

MEMBERSHIPS:

New Jersey State Bar Association
Mercer County Bar Association
American Bar Association

References and Writing Samples furnished upon request

A clean format that includes good statements of what she can accomplish

Ms. Ramirez's issues included the fact that she had had a couple short-term jobs. Also, she worked for the government and had her own private practice but had little experience as a corporate counsel.

DOLORES RAMIREZ, J.D.

931 Corea del Rio
Cincinnati, OH 45237

Email: dramirez@msn.com

Home/Office: (513) 781-0254
Cellular: (513) 353-3604

Summary

Versatile corporate legal professional with diverse experience as in-house counsel to Fortune 500 corporations and general counsel to government, commercial businesses, and nonprofit organizations. Known for creativity, resourcefulness, innovation, and timely completion of major projects. Highly skilled negotiator with a reputation for consistently achieving win-win scenarios. Private practice experience includes corporate transactional, administrative, civil and criminal litigation, trial and appellate practice, and public sector law.

Competencies

To downplay her relative lack of experience as a corporate counsel, a lot of space was used to highlight competencies

- Corporate transactional support

- Investment Management Agreements
- Intellectual Property Agreements

- Complex contract creation and negotiation

- Due Diligence and Executive Summaries of the same
- Memoranda of Understanding

- Joint Venture Agreements

- Nondisclosure Agreements

- Confidentiality Agreements

- Vendor and supplier contracts

- Outsourcing contract negotiations

- Administrative and Regulatory Order review

- Uniform Commercial Code (UCC) Articles 2, 2A, 3, 4, 4A, 5, 8, 9

- Code of Federal Regulations (CFR)

- Federal Energy Regulatory Commission (FERC) rulings and bulletins

- Securities and Exchange Commission (SEC) rulings and bulletins pertaining to public utilities
- Residential, Commercial and Community Development planning policy

- Nonprofit corporation formation, acquisition of tax exempt status, governance and policy

- Civil and commercial litigation, trial and appellate practice

- Bankruptcy (Chapters 7, 11. and 13)

- Recruiting, hiring, and training

- Community Development Block Grant (CDBG) packages

- Criminal defense

- Breach of Contract and collection cases

- Wills, Trusts, and Estates

- Personal Injury defense

- Civil Rights cases

Practice

PAN AMERICAN ELECTRIC POWER & UTILITIES – Cincinnati, OH
Nation's eighth-largest electric utility with 38 power plants serving 4.9 million customers in 11 states, Australia, Brazil, China, Mexico, the Philippines, and the UK. Employs 26,376 people and yields $13.6 billion.

Senior Counsel, Corporate Development (11/2000 – Present)
Provide general corporate transactional support, advice, and counsel to unregulated wholesale and retail marketing departments. Create/negotiate contracts, nondisclosure agreements, and other documents related to sale of power to industrial, commercial, and residential users. Review/negotiate all vendor/supplier contracts, joint ventures, and management agreements. Key member of team performing due diligence for construction/purchase of cogeneration plants.

Lead teams that negotiate numerous multiyear transactions valued up to $400 million. Negotiate outsourcing contracts for Mutual Energy Service Company's (a division of Pan American Electric Power) billing/statement printing, lock-box agreement, third-party bill payment/collection agreement, and other service-center contracts. Secure and directly manage assistance from outside counsel for projects undertaken by the unregulated retail marketing and business development units.

137

Corporate counsel. *Janice Worthington, MA, CPRW, JCTC, CEIP; Columbus, OH*

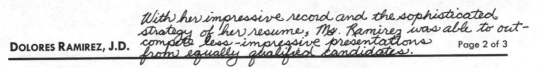

With her impressive record and the sophisticated strategy of her resume, Ms. Ramirez was able to out-compete less-impressive presentations from equally qualified candidates.

DOLORES RAMIREZ, J.D.   Page 2 of 3

Report to Senior Vice Presidents of wholesale marketing and retail residential marketing departments, providing all requisite legal support (contract negotiation/drafting/review, creation of nondisclosure agreements, negotiation/ review of intellectual property agreements, administrative/regulatory order review). Research and keep unregulated marketing units informed of legal ramifications of bulletins and rulings from FERC, SEC, CFR, and UCC.

Contributions:

- Crafted and negotiated multiyear master investment-management agreements, with ten separate national and international investment management firms, for placement of PAEP's $2+ billion ERISA Pension Trust Fund into Index and Fixed-Income Investment portfolios.

- Created and negotiated a multiyear, seven-figure bill and invoice master agreement to print and distribute 3+ million monthly utility bills, statements, and marketing materials.

- Negotiated and successfully resolved securities fraud matter that named PAEP as a defendant.

- Crafted and negotiated multiyear, $5 million call-center master agreement (with the telemarketing division of a Fortune 500 communications conglomerate) that allowed customers to receive accurate and timely answers to questions regarding utility bills and statements.

- Designed, structured, and negotiated a multiyear, $5+ million agreement involving U.S. Bureau of Fish and Wildlife to reforest 10,000 acres with hardwood trees that, over the next 70 years, will reduce atmospheric emissions of carbon dioxide and greenhouse gases.

- Served as in-house counsel for negotiations to construct a $400 million cogeneration facility for a Fortune 500 international chemical company.

CITY/COUNTY OF PHILADELPHIA – Philadelphia, PA
Nation's fifth-largest municipal corporation providing governmental services to 3.5 million people in the tristate region of eastern Pennsylvania, southern New Jersey, and Delaware.

Divisional Deputy City Solicitor (02/2000 – 08/2000)
Served as General Counsel to Director of Office of Housing and Community Development (OHCD). Provided legal review, analysis, and oversight to the director, who was tasked to allocate $70 million in federal Community Development Block Grant monies leveraged to fund $250+ million of infrastructure rebuilding/replacement, low to moderate housing, and community development projects.

Supervised Deputy City Solicitor, Assistant City Solicitor, a paralegal, and two support personnel in reviewing, amending, and certifying proposed funding contracts of up to $50 million. Served as legal advisor to city's Trade Representative, advising project managers regarding compliance with Housing and Urban Development (HUD) regulations, on expenditures of $200+ million in federal funds for commercial and industrial development.

Reviewed, coordinated, and amended all CDBG-proposed commercial and industrial project funding. Also advised the Director of Public Affairs on the text of publications, brochures, flyers, and other printed materials sent out by OHCD. Served as the in-house counsel to the Vacant Property Review Committee, tasked with selling/donating liened/abandoned property, and advised the committee on the legality of such conveyances.

Contributions:

- Saved city $9 million in funding by mediating and resolving three-year-old dispute with HUD, preventing a threatened cutoff or retroactive denial of previously spent monies for a $47 million commercial development. Dispute centered on whether the project qualified as a Community Redevelopment Project under federal guidelines.

- Played instrumental role in moving toward resolution of a $3 million intercity agency dispute between school district and various agencies. Negotiated with Mayor's Office, Revenue Commissioner, city's Redevelopment Authority, City of Philadelphia School District, and City Solicitor's Tax Division.

LAW OFFICE OF DOLORES RAMIREZ , P.C. – Pittsburgh, PA
General practice firm handling bankruptcy, civil litigation, business negotiations, criminal defense, and probate matters. Employed one full-time attorney, three associate attorneys, two paralegals, and five support personnel.

Owner/Principal (1989 – 2000)
Oversaw all business-related expenses with full financial and budgetary responsibility for a mid six-figure organization. Recruited, hired, trained and supervised support personnel and associate attorneys. As firm's principal "rain-maker" solicited, represented, and retained client base of several hundred. Represented Fortune 500 companies such as IBM and

MCI in addition to entrepreneurs of small and mid-sized businesses. Practice concentrated on bankruptcy, criminal defense, business negotiations, civil and commercial litigation and trial, property damage disputes, and mortgage foreclosure cases.

Took hundreds of depositions, argued thousands of motions, prepared hundreds of Requests for Production of Documents, issued hundreds of Request for Admissions, negotiated/settled over 200 cases, and was involved in more than 100 trials. Participated in/handled at least a dozen Chapter 11 cases, more than 250 Chapter 13 cases, and over 50 Chapter 7 cases. Defended before juries over 100 times for crimes ranging from theft to vehicular homicide.

Contributions:

- Settled, on behalf of plaintiffs, five-year $400,000+ negligent construction civil action against subdivision developer, City of Pittsburgh, the city's Redevelopment Authority, and two banks, for inadequate preparation of soil and foundation that resulted in partial or full collapse of three houses and irreparable damage to five other houses.

- Oversaw building of $147 million, state-of-the-art penal facility as member of Allegheny County Prison Board.

- As General Counsel to Sickle Cell Society, negotiated six-figure funding contracts for the society with the Pennsylvania Department of Health.

- Represented Allegheny County in carrying out its responsibility under a Consent Decree assuring that low- to moderate-income people could live in desegregated, affordable housing. Helped ensure $30 million the plaintiffs would receive over seven years would be allocated and spent in accord with HUD regulations.

- Settled $400,000 federal claim against bankrupt client for $40,000.

- Advised Hampton Township Council on $50+ million in residential and commercial development as member of Township's Planning Commission.

Professional Profile

Academic:
Duquesne University School of Law — Pittsburgh, PA
Doctor of Jurisprudence

University of Detroit — Detroit, MI
Bachelor of Business Administration/Finance
Honors: *Blue Key Honor Society*
Dean's Award for Exceptional Performance

Admissions:
U.S. Supreme Court; U.S. Court of Appeals, Third Circuit; U.S. District Court for the Eastern District of Pennsylvania; U.S. District Court for the Western District of Pennsylvania

Supreme Court and all subordinate Courts of the Commonwealth of Pennsylvania
Supreme Court of Ohio, *Corporate Status until August, 2003*

Affiliations:
American Bar Association
Association of Corporate Counsel of America
Cincinnati Bar Association
National Bar Association (Life Member)
National Institute of Trial Advocacy
Pennsylvania Bar Association
Philadelphia Bar Association
Alpha Kappa Psi Business and Professional Fraternity (Life Member)

Community Service:
Former Member and General Counsel, Sickle Cell Society of Southwestern PA
Former Member, Allegheny County Prison Board
Former Member, Hampton Township Planning Commission
Former Member and General Counsel to Board of Directors, Operation Better Block, Inc.
Former Special Counsel to the Allegheny County, PA Board of County Commissioners
Former Judge, Appellate Moot Court, University of Pittsburgh Law School

Justice "Dean" was applying for adjunct faculty positions so did not need detailed descriptions about his court work. I minimized the narrative and listed one "bulleted" statement to show consistent performance throughout his career.

(Resume writer's comments)

JUSTICE MARTIN DEAN

5555 Brockton Way
Houston, Texas 55555
Chambers: (555) 555-5555
Residence: (555) 555-5555

EDUCATION

J.D.   **UNIVERSITY OF TEXAS COLLEGE OF LAW**
- Graduated first in class (1976)
- President of Student Body Association senior year

B.A.   **SOUTHERN METHODIST UNIVERSITY**
- Graduated Magna Cum Laude with Degree in Speech Communication (1972)

LEGAL EXPERIENCE

1988-Present   **SUPERIOR COURT JUDGE**
County of Houston (appointed by Governor Ann Richards)

Preside over civil, criminal, family law, and probate matters. Arbitrate disputes; advise counsel, jury, litigants, and court personnel; establish rules of procedure; examine evidence for admissibility; sentence defendants according to state or federal statutes.

- Presided over high-profile homicide case which drew national media attention.

1986-1988   **MUNICIPAL COURT JUDGE**
County of Houston (appointed by Governor Ann Richards)

- Served as Presiding Court Judge for Juvenile Division.

1976-1986   **DEPUTY DISTRICT ATTORNEY**
Houston County District Attorney's Office

- Promoted to Lead Attorney, Career Criminal Unit (1982-1986).

1976   **ADMITTED to the Texas State Bar**

- Passed Bar Exam on first attempt.

TEACHING EXPERIENCE

1987-1994   **ADJUNCT PROFESSOR**
University of Texas, Houston

- Planned and presented instruction in the following areas: Business Law; Paralegalism; Real Estate Principles; and a General Law course for the Peace Officer Standards and Training (POST) Academy.

MILITARY SERVICE

1970-1976   **FIGHTER PILOT**
Air National Guard 178th Fighter Interceptor Squadron

138

Lawyer/law teacher. *Susan Britton Whitcomb, CPRW; Fresno, CA*

EVELYN R. JENKINS

98A Forrest Avenue, Melville, New York 11750 ◆ (631) 555-3029

PARALEGAL

Experienced, Certified Paralegal with excellent office management and client relations skills seeking a position within a corporate legal department where a working knowledge of legal terminology, general law, and legal proceedings pertaining to the following case types will be fully utilized and expanded:

Civil Litigation…Corporate Law…Wills & Estates…Negligence…Matrimonial and Mediation… Personal Injury…Real Estate…Malpractice…Family Court…Bankruptcy…Criminal

This comprehensive introduction showcases Evelyn's solid knowledge, experience, and educational qualifications.

Detail-oriented with excellent research, investigative, and reporting skills.
Exercise independent judgment and decision-making abilities and a high level of confidentiality.
Uphold the ethical standards of the legal profession.

◆ ◆ ◆

Windows 98, Word Perfect 8.0, LEXIS/NEXIS, MATLAW, McKinley's, DAKCS
Time Slips / Time Reporter, Forms of Bankruptcy (FOB)

PROFESSIONAL EXPERIENCE

Paralegal, Nevins & Associates, Melville, New York   8/99 – present
- Report directly to four attorneys with broad-ranged responsibilities that encompass the timely and complex preparation of cases from discovery to trial phase.
- Coordinate multifaceted office functions encompassing court calendar management, retainment of court reporters, and scheduling of conference rooms for deposition proceedings.
- Liaison between attorneys, clients, healthcare providers, insurance carriers, law firms, and government agencies.
- Ensure open lines of communication and satisfaction of deadlines through execution of dated correspondence.
- Perform computerized and law library research to obtain and gather case-relevant data and materials.
- Prepare content-specific case files for attorneys reflecting supporting forms, documentation, and photographs to use during client presentations, and index/cross reference network database information.

Legal Assistant, Funds Recovery, Inc., Levittown, New York   2/94 – 8/99
- Collaborated with Collections, Medical Billing, and Finance departments to obtain documentation pertaining to the status of more than 50 weekly referred collections cases forwarded to the Legal Department.
- Carefully sourced and selected nationally based bonded attorneys utilizing the American Lawyers Quarterly, Commercial Bar Directory, National Directory List, and Columbia Directory List; determined the appropriate choice upon obtainment and review of résumés, copies of insurance policies, and court filing fees.
- Integrated traditional investigative methods and DAKCS database system to gather account histories and case-sensitive documentation for attorneys including credit bureau reports, court affidavits, judgments, skip-tracing records, bankruptcy notices, banking statements, proof of assets, and trial letters.
- Maintained ongoing communications with attorneys and clients from point of referral/discovery to trial phase, facilitating and expediting case settlements that awarded clients a minimum of 80% in recovered funds.

Evelyn used this resume only once and landed a position at double her former salary!

EDUCATION

Certificate of Completion, Paralegal Studies Program, 1998
LONG ISLAND UNIVERSITY at C.W. POST, Brookville, New York
Approved by the American Bar Association

139

Paralegal. *Ann Baehr, CPRW; Long Island, NY*

This resume was designed to help Beverly get a promotion to a higher-level Flavor Chemist position with more management responsibilities.

She got the position she wanted!

Beverly Martindale

222 Fleming Drive, Princeton, NJ 08540
(609) 924–5555 • Email: Bemar52@optonline.net

Flavor / Food Chemist

Beverly's resume reflects her strong, outgoing personality as well as her experience in the industry.

CAREER PROFILE

- ☑ Well-qualified and technically proficient Flavor Chemist with 10+ years' experience in the food and beverage technology industry.
- ☑ Strong ability in conducting analyses, project management and problem solving.
- ☑ Highly motivated and dependable in achieving set goals; up-to-date computer skills.
- ☑ Communicate and collaborate well with project scientists on task teams.

PROFESSIONAL EXPERIENCE

1989 – present FlavorCore, Inc., Princeton, NJ

Flavor Chemist (1991 – present)
- Create and duplicate cost-effective Natural, N/A and Artificial flavors for 10–15 core multinational beverage accounts for FlavorCore USA and worldwide affiliates.
- Gained extensive experience in add-back juice systems for the citrus industry for this international company, ranked in the top 5 in the flavor industry.
- Pro-active in identifying and obtaining new and unique flavor raw materials from other divisions and companies and ensuring that they meet company quality standards.
- Worked abroad in Switzerland (six months) and Brazil (three months), creating unique flavors for Latin American and European markets.
- Trained and supervised two bench-top technicians to ensure accuracy and efficiency.

Beverage Food Technologist (1989 – 1991)
- Gained industry experience in beverage product development and formulation.
- Identified new flavor and product trends leading to new concept promotions.
- Delivered monthly presentations to client accounts on new product development.
- Trained, supervised and evaluated five entry-level technicians to successfully complete assigned independent projects. Technicians promoted to higher-level assignments.

1988 Summer Food Science Technologist (Co-op Student), Agro-Brands, Spring Green, WI
1988 January Laboratory Externship, Kraft Corporation, Madison, WI

EDUCATION & COMPUTER SKILLS

B.S., Food Science, University of Wisconsin, Madison, WI (1989)
Continuing professional-development training in time management, salesmanship, public speaking and presentation skills.

Windows 2000	Microsoft Office 2000	Microsoft Excel 2000	Quicken
Windows 98	Microsoft Word 2000	Lotus 1-2-3	Internet Explorer

PROFESSIONAL ASSOCIATIONS

Society of Flavor Chemists, Certified Member
Institute of Food Technologists, Professional Member
American Chemical Society, Member

Beverly's versatility, combined with her in-depth industry background made her a highly attractive candidate.

140

Agricultural and food scientist. *Susan Guarneri, NCC, NCCC, LPC, CPRW, IJCTC, CCM, CEIP; Lawrenceville, NJ*

This agricultural scientist was interested in relocating to another state and working in a university or government agency related to agriculture.

DONALD A. BURROWS
3477 Granby Road
Monson, MA 01034
(413) 357-7889 • burrowsda@aol.com

CAREER PROFILE

Agricultural/Food Scientist with expertise in farm management, research and teaching in university and agribusiness environments. Demonstrated successes in contributing to efficient, productive and profitable farm operations.

EDUCATION

Master of Science in Animal Sciences, University of Maine, Orono, ME   1991
- Concentration in ruminant nutrition with additional course work in sustainable agriculture
- Teaching Assistant – Taught laboratory classes in ruminant physiology and livestock production systems.

Teacher Certification in Agricultural Education, University of Connecticut, Storrs, CT   1982

Bachelor of Science in General Agriculture, School of Agriculture, University of Vermont, Brattleboro, VT   1981
- Major in Animal Sciences and minor in Agricultural Economics

PROFESSIONAL EXPERIENCE

Summarizes his skills, experience, and primary accomplishments in each position. This goes beyond what is typically included in a curriculum vitae, which is the standard format for academic positions.

UNIVERSITY OF MASSACHUSETTS, Amherst, MA   1990–present
Farm Manager & Instructor

Report to the Board of Directors in operating the farm according to commercial business requirements as well as to the Dean of the agricultural science department. Develop curriculum, teach agricultural/food science courses and supervise department instructors. Accomplishments:
- **Reclaimed 14 acres of very marginal land and put it into production; results yielded 4.5 tons per acre from first-year crop.**

RURAL LAND DEVELOPMENT CO., Monson, MA   1986–1990
Livestock Extension Officer

Coordinated farming activities at a rural agricultural cooperative. Assisted farmers in optimizing holdings for profitable production of dairy, beef, pork and poultry as well as in practicing sound land/soil conservation techniques. Accomplishments:
- **Persuaded small dairy farmers to practice sustainable techniques that directly caused a 5% to 12% increase in milk output within a year.**

ANIMAL SCIENCE RESEARCH CENTER, Orono, ME   1989–1991
Research Assistant

Designed, analyzed and reported on nutritive and reproductive trials using lambs, heifers and lactating cows at a regional livestock research operation affiliated with the University of Maine. Conducted research on alternative protein feed sources for ruminants. Executed variety trials with several different forage species. Accomplishments:
- **Implemented a comprehensive vaccination regime for Dorset ewes and lambs, Holstein heifers and calves, and Jersey cows, resulting in a 16% reduction in mortality rate in the first year.**

CRESENT FARMS (200-head registered Holstein dairy operation), Brattleboro, VT   1981–1986
Manager

Scope of responsibilities encompassed milking, managing herd health, calf care, milking parlor maintenance, record keeping and monitoring all herds, including dry and heifer herds. Accomplishments:
- **Compiled and fed new least-cost ration that replaced 10% of commercial grain mix with local farm by-products, resulting in a 12% increase in milk production within 15 months and 10% reduction in feed cost.**
- **Implemented heat-detection techniques that significantly improved herd reproductive efficiency.**

Mr. Burrows landed the new position he had targeted.

141

Agricultural and food scientist. *Louise Garver, MA, JCTC, CMP, CPRW; Enfield, CT*

after his father sold the family funeral home, John wanted to transition his mortician experience into scientific research.

JOHN A. HELTON

2001 Cove River Lane • Rossford, Ohio 43460
419-666-6224
E-mail: helton1999@aol.com

SCIENTIFIC RESEARCH / TESTING / DEVELOPMENT

Well-qualified and technically proficient professional with strong academic qualifications in the area of science and laboratory facilitation. Organized and take-charge with exceptional follow-through abilities and detail orientation; capable of planning projects from concept to successful completion. Analytical problem solver, with demonstrated ability to efficiently prioritize a broad range of responsibilities to achieve a maximum level of effectiveness. Expertise in legal documentation, compliance standards, and the logistical management of human remains. Seeking opportunity to transition skills to the area of scientific research, testing and development. Computer proficient utilizing Windows and MSOffice Suite. Areas of strength include:

Customer Relationship Management • Embalming • Operations Management • Scheduling • Facilitation
Project Management • Detailed Documentation • Compliance Standards • Quality Assurance

EDUCATION

Bachelor of Science • Pre-Medical, University of Toledo, Toledo, Ohio • 1992
(Microbiology, chemistry, physics, anatomy, physiology, biochemical Pharmacology, prevention and control of diseases)

Participated in Medicinal Chemistry Research program with Master's and Ph.D. candidates involving synthesizing a contrast agent to pinpoint cancerous tumors in the kidney

Diploma from the Cincinnati College of Mortuary Science, Cincinnati, Ohio • 1984
Lourdes College, Sylvania, Ohio • Coursework in Pre-Nursing
Owens Community College, Perrysburg, Ohio • Business Statistics Coursework

CAREER HISTORY

HELTON – COOK FUNERAL HOME, Toledo, Ohio • 1980 – Present
Mortician

Family-owned and -operated business

Trained, licensed and practicing embalmer providing daily operations management expertise to ensure detailed coordination of arrangements and logistics for funeral services. Interview family members or appointed individual to make arrangements; coordinate arrangements with clergy; and establish arrangements for final disposition or shipment of remains. Maintain sanitary and preservative process through which bodies are prepared for interment. Complete detailed records such as embalming reports and legal documentation, adhering to OSHA compliance standards.

- Encourage employees to increase awareness and pay closer attention to details while academically challenging them to increase knowledge, improve skills and foster compassion toward customers.
- Cut waste by streamlining operations, improving bottom-line cost to customers.
- Play pivotal role in increasing overall business and profitability through relationship-building, honesty and quality of work exhibited over the years.

FLOWER HOSPITAL, Sylvania, Ohio • Summer of 1999
Patient Care Technician

Assisted RNs in managing individual patient care and patient charting. Performed assessments of patients' vitals, glucose testing, urinary catheterization, and the setup of oxygen and life support monitors and traction apparatus per physician instructions. Inventoried and restocked patient resuscitation cart. Fostered excellent relations with interdisciplinary team comprising doctors, nurses and other healthcare professionals.

- Increased level of confidence and knowledge of clinical procedures and built cooperative working relationships with professionals and patients.

THE UNIVERSITY OF TOLEDO, Toledo, Ohio • 1995
Chemistry Lab Instructor

142

Biological and medical scientist. *Deborah S. James, CPRW; Rossford, OH*

Now that Dr. Avery was at a senior-management level, his resume needed to focus on his management and scientific accomplishments rather than on all the technical details of his previous positions.

Thomas M. Avery, Ph.D.

111 Nassau Street, Princeton, NJ 08540
(609) 924-5555 Home • (609) 882-5555 Business • tomavery@att.net

Senior Executive – Environmental Management

CAREER PROFILE

Versatile senior-level Environmental Management professional with 20 years of diversified experience overseeing energy projects, including permitting 20+ waste-to-energy plants as well as solid waste facilities, biogas, geothermal, coal, oil, and gas power plants. Extensive experience negotiating with regulatory agencies worldwide, coordinating staff and meeting compliance standards. Technical expertise includes computer simulation modeling, statistical analysis, technical writing, environmental report writing, and expert testimony.

PROFESSIONAL EXPERIENCE

ENVIRONMENTAL CONCERNS, INC., (ECI) Trenton, NJ　　　　　　　　1985 – present
Executive Vice President of Permitting and Compliance
Oversee environmental impact assessments, including planning and compliance requirements, for multimillion-dollar capital projects worldwide. Serve as liaison with national, federal, state, and local regulatory agencies. Supervise 40 environmental professionals. Promoted from Project Manager to senior-level environmental management positions.

Accomplishments:

- Achieved an outstanding track record of obtaining permits and meeting licensing requirements on time and under budget for diverse energy projects including a combined cycle plant, biogas facilities, wood burners, coal plant, and geothermal plant.

- Reduced noncompliant events by more than 60% in less than five years. Invigorated Environmental Compliance Department's reputation; now highly regarded by clients, government agencies and professional colleagues alike.

- Increased profits of operational energy facilities through innovative technical improvements involving the maintenance of air pollution control equipment.

- Pioneered professional staff development, providing opportunities for environmental professionals to specialize in different disciplines (legal, operations, engineering).

- Collaborated with the Technical Committee of the Board of Directors to determine strategic investment decisions. Contributed comprehensive recommendations regarding the impact of international regulatory requirements on strategic planning.

- Spearheaded R&D committee challenged with meeting tighter environmental requirements. Succeeded in enhancing existing air pollution control equipment while simultaneously keeping costs under control.

- Created an Environmental Mission Statement, adopted by the Board of Directors, that was subsequently implemented company wide.

- Improved the compliance history of the company and significantly reduced penalties through the creation and implementation of cost-effective environmental audit procedures.

- Continued -

143

Environmental/atmospheric scientist. *Susan Guarneri, NCC, NCCC, LPC, CPRW, IJCTC, CCM, CEIP; Lawrenceville, NJ*

Thomas used this resume as the basis of discussion at his annual review—and he got the promotion he sought.

Thomas M. Avery, Ph.D.   Page 2
(609) 924–5555 Home • (609) 882-5555 Business • tomavery@att.net

---

MASON CARUTHERS JEFFRIES & MALLOY, INC. (MCJ&M), New York, NY   1980 – 1985
Project Manager
- Oversaw and directed environmental impact studies for major capital projects in 10 states throughout the U.S. Diverse projects involved air emissions and pollutants investigations for highway construction, energy plants, and a landfill, as well as emergency evacuation plans for a nuclear facility.

- Provided environmental expertise for real-estate development projects in Manhattan. Wrote proposals and prepared environmental reports to fulfill licensing requirements.

NATIONAL INSTITUTE OF SPACE STUDIES (NISS), New York, NY   1979 – 1980
Scientific Consultant
- Designed and developed mathematical program simulating the turbulent boundary layer. Developed carbon dioxide predictions and earth's warming trends analyses.

IMPACT ENGINEERING PARTNERSHIP, New York, NY   1978 – 1980
Environmental Consulting Engineer
- Team member involved in environmental impact assessments for proposed and existing power facilities in coastal and continental locations within the U.S.

- Collaborated in the design of air-quality and water-quality field measurement programs. Developed and utilized dispersion models.

- Conducted quality control analysis, processing, and interpretation of on-site meteorological and air quality data.

- Prepared environmental impact reports, as well as evaluations of and specifications for standard meteorological instrumentation.

NATIONAL INSTITUTE FOR SPACE STUDIES (NISS), New York, NY   1975 – 1978
Atmospheric Scientist
- Participated in the development of a general circulation model. Focused on the programming of a fluid model of the surface conditions (land and ocean) on earth.

- Applied the statistically validated model to air / sea interactive problems, investigating the complex turbulent transfer of heat and momentum fluxes at the surface. Gained an understanding of the long-range transport of air pollutants and precipitation.

STATE UNIVERSITY OF NEW YORK, Plattsburgh, NY   1975 – 1978
Adjunct Assistant Professor of Physics

EDUCATION
Ph.D., Atmospheric Science, State University of New York, Plattsburgh, NY
M.S., Atmospheric & Environmental Science, State University of New York, Plattsburgh, NY
B.A., Applied Mathematics, City University of New York, New York, NY

Ongoing Professional Development in Environmental and Atmospheric Studies, Team Building, Project Management, and Leadership.

Publications List Available Upon Request) *a list of publications was created as an optional page three.*

Michael T. Washington

75 Main Street, Coventry, RI 04444
(401) 555-5555
mtwashington@yahoo.com

Professional Profile

Skilled project and business manager with specific experience in the chemicals industry and a strong track record of improved processes, successful product development and introduction, and effective management of both laboratory and production staff.

Creative problem-solver who applies technical skills and business/finance knowledge to achieve improved research and production results. Able to manage multiple projects simultaneously. Productive in both individual contributor and team environments. Excellent communication and relationship-building skills.

Achievements

) — This good-sized "Achievements" section pulls out significant accomplishments while overall responsibilities are described under each position.

- Developed procedures for superior pigments with sales potential of $5 million annually. Prepared cost and expense analyses and contributed to planning process for taking product to market.

- Simplified production method of major dye product, creating a more stable product at lower cost.

- Identified problems and made recommendations in $4 million renovation of distillation facility that resulted in significantly improved plant efficiency.

- Managed project to improve production lagging up to 8 weeks behind delivery dates. Efforts resulted in timely delivery dates and improved customer service.

- Thoroughly trained lab and production personnel; achieved skilled staff able to react to and solve routine problems as well as successfully handle challenges such as new product introductions.

Professional Experience

overall responsibilities (

2000–2002   **Plant Chemist,** Pigments • QUALITY INDUSTRIAL PIGMENTS, INC., Coventry, RI

In response to corporate mandate, set up SPC/SQC programs, supervised and trained operators, and achieved quality and yield improvements and productivity increases.

1993–2000   **Research Chemist,** Azo Pigments • HOECHST-CELANESE CORP., Coventry, RI

Developed and scaled up new procedures. Achieved cost reduction for existing products. Acquired U.S. patents for pigment compositions for water-base systems. Communicated extensively with marketing and sales to determine customer needs and prepare custom applications. Coordinated with safety, health, and production departments to ensure safe product production; contributed expert knowledge of material toxicology. Wrote operating procedures and contributed to preparation for ISO 9000 certification.

1989–1993   **Senior Color Chemist,** Acrylic Sheet Division • ARTISTIC COLORS, Pawtucket, RI

Set up and managed SPC and QC programs. Assured quality control by improving pigment dispersions, developing a quantitative flocculation test, and developing new specifications and test methods for incoming pigments.

1983–1986   **Product Development Chemist** • TRIO SCIENCE & CHEMICALS, Providence, RI

Responsible for development, scale up and troubleshooting of manufacturing procedures and processing techniques. Prepared cost/price estimates in product research and development. Designed equipment and wrote manufacturing procedures. Supervised 7-person production staff. Worked directly with customers and assured development of products to meet their needs.

Education

MBA Finance, BOSTON COLLEGE, Chestnut Hill, MA
BS Chemistry, WORCESTER POLYTECHNIC INSTITUTE, Worcester, MA
Continuing Education: Qualpro SPC training, Dale Carnegie training, Toastmasters International
Computer Training/Proficiency, Lotus 1-2-3, Excel, word processing, Windows, DOS

144

Chemist. *Louise M. Kursmark, CPRW, JCTC, CEIP, CCM; Cincinnati, OH*

A good example of a resume that can be easily scanned into an electronic database — *and searched by keywords by employers*

PAUL F. RYAN
2 Isabel Court
Nanuet, New York 10954
(914) 425-3166

Environmental Geologist/Project Manager Diversified experience managing environmental remediation projects. Expert in planning remedial investigations, conducting negotiations with regulatory agencies, coordination of PRP groups, development of feasibility studies and implementation of remedial actions.

PROFESSIONAL EXPERIENCE

1991 To Present — **PROJECT ENVIRONMENTAL GEOLOGIST** <u>TEXACO INC.</u>, Beacon, NY
- Manage $87 million Superfund site
  - Negotiate Consent Decrees, schedules, and remedial action objectives with US EPA
  - Direct and monitor daily operations of project
  - Negotiate compliance standards with EPA and Department of Natural Resources
  - Evaluate and retain environmental consulting firms and contractors
- Manage projects and participate in PRP groups for over 20 waste sites nationwide
  - Provide technical assistance
  - Strategic planning
  - Budget forecasting

1988 To 1991 — **GEOLOGIST** <u>JAMES C. ANDERSON ASSOCIATES, Inc.</u>, Mount Laurel, NJ
- Oversaw construction of 60 acre double composite landfill liner system
- Managed numerous soils and groundwater remediation projects
- Analyzed data and prepared hydrogeologic reports for various sites
- Provided geotechnical evaluations of clays and geosynthetics for landfill applications
- Managed investigative and sampling programs at various municipal and uncontrolled landfills

1986 To 1988 — **GEOLOGIST** <u>NUS CORPORATION</u>, Wayne, PA
- Conducted US EPA mandated investigations of active and abandoned hazardous waste sites
- Implemented investigative activities in accordance with CERCLA and RCRA regulations

1986 — **FIELD TECHNICIAN/GEOLOGIST** <u>GROUNDWATER TECHNOLOGY, INC.</u>, Chadds Ford, PA
- Installed, maintained, and augmented groundwater remediation systems
- Performed analytical sample acquisition

EDUCATION
Bachelor of Science, Environmental Geology, State University of New York, Cortland, NY (1986)
Graduate Division, Drexel University, Philadelphia, PA

LICENSE/CERTIFICATION
Registered Geologist in Tennessee and Delaware
Hazardous Waste Investigation 40 Hour Course - 1910.120E (1986); Re-certified Annually

CAREER DEVELOPMENT SEMINARS
Underground Storage Tank Management / Groundwater Modeling (National Groundwater Association)
Technical Project Management (American Management Association)
Negotiation Skills / Financial Management / Presentation Skills / Microsoft Project / RCRA Regulations
DNAPL Seminar (University of Waterloo)

PAPERS/PRESENTATIONS
"Why Prompt Investigative /Remedial Actions are Necessary at an Identified Subsurface Release" September 1995

145

Environmental geologist. *Marian K. Kozlowski, MBA; Poughkeepsie, NY*

JAMES A. VANDOLEN

1821 Maxine Blvd. ★ Jackson, Michigan
(517) 555-0944
planetarydude@earthlink.net

PROFILE

[handwritten: This section highlights his public "persona" for this high-visibility position.]

- ★ Knowledgeable astronomy educator with longstanding interest in the field.
- ★ Over 18 years of planetarium administration and operations experience.
- ★ Professional demeanor and dynamic personality well suited to public interaction.
- ★ Creative and innovative, eager to adapt a variety of unique talents toward new challenges.
- ★ Respected by peers and the public.
- ★ Extensive experience involving public relations, marketing, and presentations.
- ★ Experienced in conceptualizing, planning, promoting, and executing multifaceted projects.

KEY PROFESSIONAL ACCOMPLISHMENTS

[handwritten: James had no experience with the specific high-tech equipment where he was applying. So, this section describes his years of experience without specifying equipment type.]

- ★ Created, produced, and programmed planetarium shows covering a variety of astronomy-related and special-interest topics.
- ★ Prepared and presented seminars and workshops on topics relating to astronomy.
- ★ Interacted with media during special events; responded to public and media inquiries regarding astronomy and the space program.
- ★ Developed and implemented contemporary programming formats for public and educational group audiences resulting in increased popularity and attendance.
- ★ Generated monthly star map/sky events publication.
- ★ Presented planetarium programs to individuals and groups of all ages.
- ★ Installed and upgraded computerized automation system hardware and software.
- ★ Maintained planetarium equipment and performed ongoing troubleshooting.
- ★ Hired, trained, and supervised up to 50 full- and part-time staff members.
- ★ Initiated promotional efforts and materials to increase name recognition and awareness of facilities.
- ★ Developed, monitored, and implemented program budgets.
- ★ Experienced in Windows and Macintosh computer environments.
- ★ Originated and instituted annual museum membership program.

EMPLOYMENT HISTORY

FORD SPACE THEATRE—Jackson Public Schools ★ Jackson. MI 1990–Present
    Producer/Assistant Director

GALAXY PLANETARIUM/SCIENCE MUSEUM,—Hope College ★ Kalamazoo, MI 1981–1990
    Acting Associate Director for Development/Planetarium Director
    Coordinator of Visitor Programs/Planetarium Director
    Assistant Coordinator of Visitor Programs/Planetarium Director

EDUCATION

WESTERN MICHIGAN UNIVERSITY ★ Kalamazoo, MI 1988–1990
    Master's-level coursework
THE UNIVERSITY OF MICHIGAN ★ Ann Arbor, MI 1981
    Bachelor of Science—Astronomy

AFFILIATIONS

- ★ Great Lakes Planetarium Association
    Awarded the rank of *Fellow*
    State Meeting Chairperson (1997–1990)
    Michigan State Chairperson (1985–1995)

- ★ International Planetarium Society

- ★ Michigan Museum Association

[handwritten: James got the job over 20 others! (Resume writer's comments)]

Astronomer. *Janet L. Beckstrom; Flint, MI*

Meredith Salyers

(203) 555-2455   244 Stony Brook Drive, Branford, CT 06405   msalyers@juno.com

---

MARKETING / MARKETING RESEARCH / PROJECT LEADERSHIP
- Marketing/research strengths in analyzing data and reaching meaningful conclusions.
- A track record of accomplishments in program management and team leadership.
- Proven ability to work effectively in crisis and pressure situations.

PROFESSIONAL EXPERIENCE

Marketing Research Assistant • MAR-COM ASSOCIATES, Hamden, CT   June 2001-July 2002

Contributed to research, analysis and recommendations designed to guide clients in the selection of effective marketing strategies.
- Analyzed consumer response data to determine strengths and weaknesses of new product concepts; made appropriate recommendations based on findings.
- Utilized proprietary software and applications to forecast components of consumer volume for potential new products based on consumer response data and proposed marketing plans.
- Responded to project-specific and general client questions and requests on a daily basis.

As a member of the company's Information Services Task Force, contributed to the initial planning for a computer-networked intra-company resource base.

Marketing Intern • ELM CITY ADVERTISING, New Haven, CT   September 2000-March 2001

Conducted detailed market research for new and existing advertising accounts. Studied feasibility of new advertising and sales promotion programs.
- Prepared reconciliation analysis detailing fulfillment of media buys and effectiveness of media options. Interacted extensively with the client, a radio media buyer, serving as the company's primary liaison on this research project.

To position Meredith for a higher-level role, her volunteer experience is included to demonstrate her leadership skills.

LEADERSHIP EXPERIENCE

Disaster Team Member • AMERICAN RED CROSS, New Haven County, CT   2000-Present

Respond to local emergencies providing relief to victims of natural and manmade disasters. Conduct damage assessments of property to determine habitability. Provide comfort and counseling to those affected by community disasters.
- Passed through a competitive selection process designed to ensure that team members possess leadership skills and are able to respond appropriately in crisis situations. Received training in essential skills including CPR, First Aid, and Disaster Services.

EDUCATION

This detailed "Education" section is appropriate for this recent graduate. It also spotlights additional leadership qualifications.

B.A. in Economics, 2001 • QUINNIPIAC COLLEGE, Hamden, CT

Minors in Business Administration and Legal Studies.
Coursework in Marketing, Econometrics, Accounting, Finance, Income and Employment Theory, Government Regulation, Business Law, Economics of Law and Constitutional Law.
- Dean's List
- Selected as Teaching Assistant for Seminar in Law & Society, 2000; facilitated group discussion on current legal issues among freshman students through case study.
- Peer Advisor, 1999-2001
- Treasurer and Chair for Spring Carnival, 2001
- Captain, Intramural Soccer, 1999-2001

147

Marketing research analyst. *Louise M. Kursmark, CPRW, JCTC, CEIP, CCM; Cincinnati, OH*

Curriculum Vita
Marion E. Appleby, Ph.D.

555 Main Street
Jonesburg, IL 55555
(505) 505-5050

Education

Boston University, Ph.D., 1979 — Clinical Psychology, APA approved
Boston University, M.A., 1976 — Psychology
Wesleyan University, B.A., 1973 — Psychology

Clinical Experience

Private Practice
Director of Appleby Psychological Associates   1983–Present
Jonesburg, Illinois
  Provide psychotherapy, psychological evaluation, and consultation to a diverse patient
  population as well as manage seven full-time psychologists, four consultants, and support staff.

Post-Doctorate Intern
New York Child Guidance Clinic, Family Therapy Training   Summer 1983

Associate Director and Director of Training
Affiliated Mental Health Services   1981–83
Newton, Massachusetts
  Responsible for managing six programs in a 85-staff comprehensive community mental health
  center.

Director of Training, Consultation and Education Coordinator, Staff Psychologist
The Mental Health Clinic of Boston   1979–81
Brookline, Massachusetts
  Responsible for providing staff training, community consultation, psychotherapy to children
  and families, coordinating psychology internship program, and personnel selection for four
  municipal police departments.

Staff Clinical Psychologist
Tri-Town Mental Health Center   1978–79
Wakefield/Reading, Massachusetts

Clinical Psychology Intern
Boston Psychiatric Hospital   1977–78
Boston, Massachusetts

Teaching Experience

  Lecturer, Graduate Psychology Department, Northwestern University — 1983–Present
  Adjunct Professor, Graduate Counseling Department, Boston University — 1980–83
  Teaching Fellow, Psychology Department, Boston University — 1976–77

148

Psychologist. *Jan Melnik, CPRW, CCM; Durham, CT*

I prepared a typical traditional "curriculum vita" on pure white parchment paper for this client.

Marion E. Appleby, Ph.D.

Vita Page Two

Workshops

Have presented over 75 workshops on a range of mental health topics to various groups and agencies including hospitals, clinics, chambers of commerce, school systems, police departments, attorneys, business groups, and medical staffs.

Research Interests

Selected Papers and Presentations

Appleby, M.E. Imitation of resistance to temptation in male children. Paper presented at Northeastern Psychological Association, Boston, MA, May 1979. (Master's Thesis).

Appleby, M.E. The process of description and perception of stigmatized and non-stigmatized persons. Paper presented at National Psychological Association, New York, NY, March 1981.

Appleby, M.E. and Smith, L.S. Alcohol and Drug Services to a Rural Community. Paper presented at Annual National Alcohol and Drug Abuse Conference, Chicago, IL, September 1983.

Appleby, M.E. Psychotherapeutic Applications of the MMPI: Beyond Assessment, Feedback and Outcome Evaluation. Paper presented at the 21st Symposium on Recent Developments in the Uses of the MMPI, Washington, D.C., March 1989.

Appleby, M.E. The MMPI and its Specific Use as a Therapeutic Tool in Marital Therapy. Paper presented at the 22nd Symposium on Recent Developments in the Uses of the MMPI, Boston, MA, May 1990.

Appleby, M.E. Assessment of Marital Strength and its Use in Couples' Psychotherapy, presented to the Illinois Psychological Association, Chicago, IL, May 1993.

Professional Affiliations

American Psychological Association — Division 12

Illinois Psychological Association

National Register of Psychologists

Association for the Advancement of Psychology

Licensed Psychologist, State of Illinois

Affiliate Medical Staff, Illinois State Psychiatric Hospital, Chicago, Illinois

Affiliate Medical Staff, City Hospital, Chicago, Illinois

Slightly atypical is the inclusion of some key identifying information regarding responsibilities in several key positions.

This client operates a successful psychological practice and has effectively used this vita to secure a variety of high-level consulting arrangements with national organizations.

(Resume writer's comments)

Since not all city planners have professional certification, this information is included twice in Lena's resume.

LENA GRIFFIN, AICP

1900 West Eighth Street • Cincinnati, Ohio 45202 • (513) 352-9999 • griffinaicp1@yahoo.com

reference to certification ——— (

CERTIFIED PLANNER

Community Development • Grant Proposals • AutoCAD • Negotiator • Conflict Resolution

Visionary leader that correctly interprets goals, beliefs, and cultural settings of communities providing them comprehensive plans to achieving objectives. Utilize common-sense approaches in solving problems resulting in saved time and capital. Experienced in communicating with all levels of government and private sector through written and verbal presentations. Possess excellent research and data-forecasting skills.

CAREER HIGHLIGHTS) *This section showcases special projects that might be lost if included under job descriptions.*

Successfully gained **90%** approval from city council for proposal detailing plans revitalizing the historical Germantown Metro Area in Cincinnati, Ohio. Secured economic growth in community by increasing the number of small-business owners in the area by **52%**. Special projects included performing feasibility studies for construction of new sports arenas and residential dwellings in the downtown area as well as cataloging historical buildings in the Metro area.

Led negotiations on South Woods Windstone Terrace Development Project in Columbus, Ohio. Project consisted of implementing community redevelopment plans and scheduling public meetings to inform Windstone residents of 2-year renovation plan. Provided detailed information of all project phases and answered all questions and concerns. Submitted final proposal to South Woods Area Commission Board of Directors with recommendations on areas of compromise.

Awarded **$2 million** in funding from grant proposals submitted for the following projects: Columbus Park Open Space Project, Germantown Metro Area Revitalization Study, South Woods Redevelopment Housing Plan.

PROFESSIONAL HISTORY

B.R.I.D.G.E. Planners Group, Cincinnati, Ohio   1997-Present
City Planner 4
- Serve as liaison for Hamilton County City Planning Department; prepare proposals for city's downtown revitalization projects.
- Implemented *"We Care"* program for small-business owners to receive assistance in completing forms for financial aid, zoning clearances, and writing business plans; provided service to over **300** participants within 6 months.

South Woods Area Commission, Columbus, Ohio   1994-1996
Zoning Officer
- Researched zoning status for property inquiries.
- Decided individual zoning request changes on case-by-case basis.

EDUCATION
Master of City & Regional Planning, The Ohio State University, Columbus, Ohio, 1994
Bachelor of Arts, Political Science, University of Cincinnati, Cincinnati, Ohio, 1992

reference to certification ——— (

CERTIFICATION/MEMBERSHIPS
Certified Planner, American Institute of Certified Planners, 1994
Member, Columbus Zoning Board, 1994

COMPUTER SKILLS
AutoCAD 2000 Lite, Solid Edge Software by Unigraphics, Microsoft Office Suite, Internet

149

Urban planner. *Leah Brantley, CEIP; Cincinnati, OH*

What is unusual about this chiropractor is that he had a 10-year history in business management in another industry before he followed his passion into chiropractic services.

MICHAEL SHIELDS, D.C.

1147 Beacon St., Unit 111
Boston, MA 02110

617-599-6255
michael@shields.org

Dr. Shields highlighted his diverse experience in this section to demonstrate that he had the skills to manage a chiropractic practice.

Chiropractor

- Over 20 years' combined health-care and business experience with an extensive teaching, clinical, and management record of achievement.
- Health-care experience includes 1500+ patient visits and 5+ years in hospital settings.
- Teaching experience involves medical students and undergraduates.
- Teaching assistant in physiotherapy, microbiology, clinical pathology (Northwestern)
- Certified first responder for emergency medical and scene management; CPR certified; specialist in extremity dysfunction, injury, and treatment

EDUCATION & PROFESSIONAL DEVELOPMENT

NORTHWESTERN COLLEGE OF CHIROPRACTIC, Bloomington, MN   1995–1998
- Doctor of Chiropractic, Magna Cum Laude
- Valedictorian
- Dean's List, Wolfe Scholarship, National Board of Chiropractic Examiners Scholarship

UNIVERSITY OF MASSACHUSETTS, Lowell, MA   1991–1994
- Graduate and undergraduate course work in Biochemistry and Computer Science

RIPON COLLEGE, Ripon, WI   1977–1981
- BA, Biology & Chemistry (double major)
- Honors: National Biology Honor Society, Dean's List

CLINICAL & TEACHING EXPERIENCE

SHIELDS CHIROPRACTIC CLINIC, Boston, MA   1999–present
Owner & Chiropractor
A family-centered practice with a focus on wellness, nutrition, and patient education and an emphasis on spinal health and extremity dysfunction. Case management and treatment of a general population; individual, group, and community health presentations. **Led rapidly growing practice to a four-fold increase in patient visits in Year 2; surpassed that total in the first quarter of Year 3.**

NORTHWESTERN COLLEGE OF CHIROPRACTIC, Bloomington, MN   1997–1998
Supervisor, Student Health Center (Clinical Externship, 1998)
Oversaw case management of 68 interns and their patients as well as the treatment of a student population with regard to general health.
Wolfe Harris Center for Clinical Studies (Clinical Internship, 1998)
Case management and treatment of a primarily pediatric and obstetrics population with an emphasis on extremity dysfunction.
Wolfe Harris Center for Clinical Studies (Clinical Internship, 1997–98)
Case management and treatment of a general patient population with emphasis on spinal dysfunction.

EDGEWATER HOSPITAL, Chicago, IL   1987–1990
Research and Clinical Microbiologist
Clinical microbiology and serology of patient specimens. Research on Herpes staining techniques. Taught autopsy techniques and continuing education with regard to sexually transmitted diseases and microbiology to medical residents. Assisted in the training of a new laboratory technologist.

TEWKSBURY HOSPITAL, Tewksbury, MA   1982–1987
Laboratory Technician
Hematology, Urinalysis, Chemistry, and Microbiology department. Assisted with autopsies.

AFFILIATIONS

American Chiropractic Association   Massachusetts Chiropractic Society

150

Chiropractor. *Bernice Antifonario, MA; Tewksbury, MA*

Dr. Martin wanted to sell his dental practice and work in a consulting or management capacity with a corporation involved in dental products and services.

ROBERT MARTIN, D.D.S.

477 Covington Avenue
Bloomfield, CT 06002

(860) 243-0590

rmartin@yahoo.com

This section highlights his expertise in the profession, his recognition as a pioneer, and his consulting experience.

PROFESSIONAL SUMMARY

Expertise in all areas of dentistry combines with equally strong qualifications in business planning, development and management to enhance productivity and profitability.

Recognized internationally as a pioneer in the implementation of leading-edge techniques with a specialization in restorative and periodontal dentistry.

Distinguished career encompasses consulting, teaching and leadership roles with a major medical center as well as national and state professional associations in the dental field.

SPECIAL AWARDS & LICENSURE

Fellow of the Academy of General Dentistry
Master Candidate of the Academy of General Dentistry
State of Connecticut License in Dentistry

SELECTED ACHIEVEMENTS

♦ Grew dental practice to a profitable business through effective business planning, cost controls, consistent service excellence and referral-based marketing.
♦ Achieved reputation for innovation and expertise in the dental profession as one of first to implement state-of-the-art, non-surgical periodontal techniques.
♦ Elected President of the Connecticut Academy of General Dentistry and spearheaded the development and implementation of innovative programs that improved profitability.
♦ Honored as "Dentist of the Year" by the American Dental Association for contributions and dedication to the field of dentistry.
♦ Invited to join Connecticut State Board of Dentistry as consultant and provide expertise on program development and consumer relations.
♦ Fostered a motivating work environment and promoted open communications, resulting in high performance and staff retention.

MANAGEMENT EXPERIENCE

HARTFORD DENTAL GROUP • Hartford, CT
President (1970–present)

Established and built highly successful business providing comprehensive dental services to several thousand patients. Acquired 3 private practices and led office through steady growth. Recruited and managed team of professional and support personnel. Provided ongoing staff training and development, leading to peak productivity, exceptional patient relations and continual referrals.

CONSULTING & TEACHING EXPERIENCE

CONNECTICUT BOARD OF DENTISTRY • Hartford, CT
Consultant (1984–present)

Selected as consultant to the statewide organization in the design and implementation of educational, consumer relations and other programs.

151

Dentist. *Louise Garver, MA, JCTC, CMP, CPRW; Enfield, CT*

ROBERT MARTIN, D.D.S. – Page 2

UNIVERSITY OF CONNECTICUT SCHOOL OF DENTISTRY • Hartford, CT
Instructor (1990–present)

Revamped and expanded the curriculum. Teach operative dentistry and other courses in the School of Dentistry.

NEW YORK MEDICAL CENTER • New York, NY
Consultant (1999–present)

Consultant to medical center's pain management program for patients suffering from TMJ disorder.

EDUCATIONAL CREDENTIALS

Doctor of Dental Science
University of Connecticut School of Dentistry • Hartford, CT
Graduated with high honors

Continuing Education

Successfully completed over 1000 hours of continuing education, earning graduate credits in all areas of general dentistry and practice management including:

TM Disorders	Tooth Colored Restorations	Soft Tissue Surgery
Implants	Overlay Dentures	Endodontics Esthetics
Ceramic Restorations	Oral Pathology	Orthodontics
Auxiliary Utilization	Pharmacotherapeutics	Fixed Prosthodontics
Dental Materials	Dental Jurisprudence	Operative Dentistry
Table Clinics	Partial Dentures	Radiology
Treatment Planning	Clinical Diagnosis	Surgical Endodontics
Oral & Maxillofacial Surgery	Removable Prosthetics	Financial Management
Practice Management	Periodontics	Patient Education
	Patient Insurance Programs	

AFFILIATIONS

American Dental Association
Connecticut Dental Association
Academy of General Dentistry
Connecticut Dental Research Group

This resume piqued the interest of several employers, and Dr. Martin accepted a management position in product development and marketing.

Jane N. Larske, OD

2192 NW Rosethorn Drive #741
Hillsboro, OR 97124

503.444.0082
janenlarske@att.net

Profile

- ✧ Optometrist with full scope of optometry experience: contact lens, ocular pathology, primary care, and co-management with Ophthalmologists.
- ✧ Enthusiastic about all areas of optometry.
- ✧ Warm, caring personality with a contagious enthusiasm that expands patient base.
- ✧ Midwestern work ethic; worked since age of 16.

Education

PACIFIC UNIVERSITY COLLEGE OF OPTOMETRY (PUCO), Forest Grove, OR
Doctor of Optometry, 2000
B.S., Vision Science, 1997

Optometric Thesis: Statistical Analysis of Refractive and Ocular Prevalences in Children
- Beta Sigma Kappa International Optometric Honor Society
- Amigos Optometry Club
- American Optometric Student Association

ST. CLOUD STATE UNIVERSITY, St. Cloud, MN
Biological Science Major, 1993–96
- Dean's List; awarded scholarships
- Biology Club, *President* and *Photographer*
- Pre-Optometry Club, *Treasurer*
- Biology Department Work-Study Program

Using this resume, Dr. Larske was hired upon graduation!

Licensure and Affiliations

Active license in Colorado, Oregon, and Washington
Member, American Optometric Association and Oregon Optometric Association

Professional Experience

PORTLAND HEALTHCARE, Portland, OR, 2000–Present
- Provide primary care to all age groups.
- Diagnose and treat ocular pathology.
- Serve as one of very few contact lens doctors at Portland Healthcare.
- Respected for having exceptional rapport with colleagues and ophthalmologists.
- Frequently commended by patients for providing friendly and caring service.

TARGET OPTICAL, Salem, OR, 2000–Present (part-time, weekends)
- Provide primary care and contact lens care for diverse age and ethnic groups.

Preceptorships

PORTLAND HEALTHCARE, Portland, OR, 1/00–4/00
- Provided primary eye care to all ages in HMO setting.
- Examined large volume of patients daily.
- Utilized medical records program, EpicCare, in a paperless office.
- Diagnosed ocular complications.

Dr. Larske was a new graduate, so her preceptorships are included to show that her experience extended to a variety of settings and skills.

152

Optometrist. *Mary Laske, MS, CPRW; Fargo, ND*

Jane N. Larske, OD — Page 2   503.444.0082

Preceptorships, continued

INNOVIS HOSPITAL, Portland, OR, 9/99–12/99

- Gained experience in geriatric optometry and learned how to interpret visual fields.
- Diagnosed ocular complications resulting from systemic diseases.
- Worked with cosmetic and therapeutic contact lenses.
- Assisted with maintenance of patients' prosthetic eye care.
- Selected, fitted, adjusted, sorted, and repaired spectacles.

SHAWNEE INDIAN RESERVATION, Portland, OR, 9/99–12/99

- Provided eye care to all age groups from infants to adults; screened preschoolers.
- Gained experience in primary care, contact lenses, ocular diseases, visual fields interpretation, and anterior and posterior ocular photography.

PACIFIC UNIVERSITY COLLEGE OF OPTOMETRY, 5/99–8/99
Family Vision Center, Forest Grove and Portland, OR

- Performed comprehensive primary care and pediatric optometric examinations, including contact lens follow-ups, evaluations, checks, and fittings, as well as ocular pathology follow-ups, evaluations, and treatment.
- Examined patients requiring language translators.
- Evaluated and treated low-vision patients.
- Designed and implemented vision therapy programs.
- Selected, fitted, adjusted, sorted, and repaired spectacles.
- Gave case presentations.

Related Experience

AMIGOS OPTOMETRY CLUB, PUCO, Forest Grove, OR, 1998
Volunteer

- Traveled to Romania to examine eyes and dispense glasses to children in orphanages.
- Provided eye screenings to the locally underprivileged.

JOHNSON OPTICAL, Portland, OR, 1998
Optician

- Sold, adjusted, and repaired zyl and metal frame glasses in an upscale retail store. Interacted with diverse personalities, cultures, and professional levels.

Continuing Education (not an exhaustive list)

- Classifications of the Glaucomas, Glaucoma Surgery, Angle Closure Glaucoma, Congenital Glaucoma, Laser Therapy in Glaucoma, Newest Glaucoma Drugs Available (6 hrs), 9/01
- Retinal Pathophysiology with Case Studies (6 hrs), 8/01
- Visual Examination of Computer Users (2 hrs), 8/01
- Solution-related Keratitis and Non-Keratitis (1 hr), 6/01
- A Systemic Approach to Disease Diagnosis (1 hr), 9/00
- Cerebrovascular Disorders: TIA to Stroke in 90 Days (1 hr), 9/00
- The Diabetes Horizon: Primary Eye/Vision Care in 2005 (1 hr), 9/00
- Non-Refractive Laser Procedures (1 hr), 9/00
- Non-Ophthalmic Systemic Medications in Optometry (2 hrs), 9/00
- Use and Abuse of Steroids (2 hrs), 9/00
- Oops — How Not to Treat Red Eyes (2 hrs), 9/00

SEYED M. YAZDANFAR, M.D.
60 Reservoir Avenue — Abington, PA 19041 — 215-659-2012 — dryaz@hotmail.com

OBJECTIVE

A career in cardiology combining academic pursuits, research, and clinical practice.

EDUCATION AND LICENSURE

M.D., Isfahan University of Medical Sciences, Iran   1992
Graduated in top 10% of class.

Pennsylvania Training License (MT-044823-T)
Permanent License to Practice Medicine, Iran
ECFMG Certification   1998

[handwritten annotation: Doctors trained in other countries are required to undergo intensive retraining and practice before being granted a U.S. medical license. The "Experience" section below shows Dr. Yazdanfar's progression from primary care in Iran to internal-medicine resident — and hopefully to cardiac specialist in the U.S.]

EXPERIENCE

Pennsylvania State Hospital, Philadelphia, PA   6/00 to Present

Internal Medicine Resident / PGY-2 (6/01 to Present) — Participate in a series of rotations: ICU/CCU, ER, ambulatory care, ID, nephrology, and cardiology. Manage patients in conjunction with attending physicians. Supervise interns. *Received excellent rating from peer-review evaluations.*

Internal Medicine Intern / PGY-1 (6/00 to 6/01) — Completed three rotations in ICU/CCU, cardiology, ER, and ambulatory care. Conducted research as well. *Scored the highest in the class, in the 94th percentile nationally, on in-service exam.*

Frankford Memorial Hospital, Philadelphia, PA   6/99 to 6/00

Transitional Year Resident — Completed rotations through medicine, general surgery, ICU/CCU, ER, cardiology, neurology, and hematology/oncology. *Ranked third out of 49 interns.*

San Jose Hospital, Baytown, TX   5/98 to 6/99

Medical Assistant — Supported a family practitioner, neurologist, and pulmonary/critical care specialist. Performed initial patient examinations, took H&Ps, made evaluations, and held consultations with physicians regarding treatment.

Seyed M. Yazdanfar, M.D., Shahriar, Iran   8/94 to 6/97

Primary Care Physician — Owned and operated a private general practice with top reputation in the area for quality care and patient service. Supervised licensed medical staff and administrators.

RESEARCH

Pennsylvania State Hospital, Philadelphia, PA. Participated in a retrospective multicenter study to compare and evaluate protected and unprotected stenting.   2001

Houston Central Hospital, Houston, TX. Provided research assistance compiling background data for a prospective study on internal cardioversion and arterial fibrillation.   1997

ARTICLE

Bruce D. Wasserman and **Seyed M. Yazdanfar**. "One-Year Outcomes of Unprotected and Protected Left Main Stenting in the Current Era." Submitted to <u>Cardiology Americana</u>, 2001.

153

Cardiologist. *Jewel Bracy DeMaio, CPRW, CEIP; Royersford, PA*

Dr. Fredericks is also involved in health-care management, so the format of this resume combines elements of a traditional medical curriculum vitae with components of any effective resume.

Sam Fredericks, MD, FACC

DocSam@hotmail.com
82 Ball Road, Wayne, NJ 07470

973-633-4809 tel
973-633-2656 fax

This summary is one of the usual components of an effective resume.

SUMMARY OF QUALIFICATIONS

Medical Director. 16 years' direct experience in the creative leadership of continuing and long-term health-care organizations. Clinical abilities complemented by management and administration skills. Demonstrated track record of delivering quality, cost-effective medical care through competencies in strategic analysis, problem solving, decision making, teaching, quality assurance/improvement, audit tool development, and utilization of computer technology.

EDUCATION

Fellowship, Cardiology—Columbia Presbyterian Medical Center, New York, NY   1981–1983

Residency, Internal Medicine—Columbia Presbyterian Medical Center, New York, NY   1978–1981

Doctor of Medicine—Cornell University Medical College, New York, NY   1978

Bachelor of Arts (Summa Cum Laude)—New York University, New York, NY   1974

BOARD CERTIFICATION & MEDICAL LICENSURE

Board Certified in Cardiovascular Disease   November 1984

Diplomate of the American Board of Internal Medicine   September 1981

New York State Medical License   August 1979

Diplomate of the National Board of Medical Examiners   July 1979

PROFESSIONAL POSITIONS & APPOINTMENTS

Founding Partner, Vice President, and Corporate Medical Director   1985–Present
Madison Avenue Health Care Management, New York, NY
Now serving 50 facilities in New York State.

- Selected as Medical Director for Clara Barton Health Center (900-bed facility) with challenge of converting state and federal regulation violations into a sound medical model. Success led to extended services and referrals to perform turnarounds for additional facilities.
- Increased revenues by expanding to provide guidelines and protocols to ensure compliance; medical services through a contingent workforce; an on-call program for night, weekend, and holiday coverage; and administrative/billing services.
- Innovated focused audit tools — for admissions, discharge to hospital, antibiotic usage, and diabetes management — to promote early identification and analysis of specific issues. Worked closely with Quality Improvement staff to develop effective tools and to oversee the program.
- Managed development of computer information systems to coordinate physician schedules and follow-up care.

The lists of achievements here and on the second page are another one of the usual components of an effective resume.

154

Medical director. *Kirsten Dixson, JCTC, CPRW, CEIP; Bronxville, NY*

Sam Fredericks, MD, FACC

Madison Avenue Health Care Management (continued)

- Demonstrated ongoing commitment to staff development by mentoring nurse practitioners, speaking on clinical topics to physicians and nurses, and distributing relevant literature.
- Served as Medical Director for select clients:

Whitestone Extended Care Facility, Bronx, NY (2000–Present)
- Reduced pharmacy bill by $5000 in the first month without compromising care.

Lincoln Extended Care Center, Long Island City, NY (1999–Present)
- Cut pharmacy bill by 20% and the use of certain drugs such as "H2 Blockers" by 50%. Comprehensive review of patient charts disclosed no indication of prescriptions.

Cloisters Geriatric Center, Bronx, NY (1992–Present)

Martin Luther King, Jr., Rehabilitation & Nursing Center, Bronx, NY (1991–Present)

Clara Barton Health Center, New York, NY (1985–Present)

Clinical Assistant Physician (Cardiology)
Columbia Presbyterian Medical Center, New York, NY

1983–Present

Samuel Fredericks, MD, FACC
Private Practice affiliated with Columbia Presbyterian Medical Center, New York, NY

1984–1993

- Provided office cardiology and internal medical care, including noninvasive cardiac testing (echocardiograms, stress tests, and Holter monitoring).

TEACHING

Clinical Instructor of Medicine, **Columbia Presbyterian Medical Center**   1983–Present

- Taught physical diagnosis course several months per year for 13 years.
- Serve as teaching attending for medical house staff on the medical units.

Guest Instructor, **Cornell Medical School**   1991-2000

- Instructed visiting public health students on medicine in nursing facilities.

CURRENT PROFESSIONAL & SOCIETY MEMBERSHIPS

Fellow, American College of Cardiology

New York Medical Directors Association

Alpha Omega Alpha Honor Society

Patricia R. Ayensu, DVM

230 Johnson Circle • Lanham, MD 20706 • (301) 886-8932 • PAyensuDVM@earthlink.net

SUMMARY

Recent DVM graduate with solid education and clinical experience in small-animal medicine — an effective communicator who enjoys working with people and animals.

- Well-developed listening and analysis skills.
- Understanding of the positive effect of client education on animal health.
- Strong interest in preventive medicine.

Dr. Ayensu is a newly qualified veterinarian, so her education is presented first.

EDUCATION

Doctor of Veterinary Medicine, 2002   North Carolina State University, Raleigh, NC
Fourth-year clinical curriculum provided experience with:

- Preventive medicine
- Client relations
- Large and small animals
- Dentistry
- Early spay/neuter
- Diagnostic procedures

Her relevant experience is listed after her education.

PROFESSIONAL EXPERIENCE

externship

Extern, January to May 2002   Brookside Veterinary Hospital, Lanham, MD

- Obtained patient histories and completed physical exams.
- Administered vaccinations and medications.
- Prepped animals for surgery and assisted with surgical procedures.
- Obtained diagnostic samples including blood, urine, skin scrapings, and aspirates.
- Treated and followed patients in critical care situations such as diabetic coma.
- Explained patient diagnoses and treatments to clients.

paid positions

Anesthesia Assistant, 2000 to 2001   North Carolina State Veterinary Teaching Hospital, Raleigh, NC

- Maintained, inspected, and cleaned anesthesia equipment.
- Ordered medications and anesthesia supplies.
- As needed, intubated and catheterized patients in preparation for surgery.
- Gained working knowledge of commonly used anesthetic agents.

Veterinary Technician, 1995 to 1998   Mobile Veterinary Services, Lexington Park, MD

- Accompanied veterinarian to visit animals at clients' homes or stables.
- Administered injections and oral medications under veterinarian's supervision.
- Assisted with surgeries and monitored post-surgical patients.
- Educated clients about animal nutrition, behavior, and wellness care.
- Ordered medications and supplies.
- Collected lab samples and prepared them for transportation to testing facilities.
- Telephoned clients for follow-up reports and appointment confirmations.

volunteer position

Animal Care Volunteer, 1992 to 1994   Silverwoods Veterinary Clinic, San Diego, CA

- Provided basic care to animals in kennel.
- Assisted with various medical procedures and restraint of animals.
- Conducted tests for heartworms, Feline Leukemia, and FIV.
- Assisted with radiographs.

Previous professional experience was in Human Resources and Training. Progressed through a series of increasingly responsible positions, demonstrating abilities in problem solving, training-program development, data analysis, efficiency improvement, and employee supervision.

PROFESSIONAL AFFILIATIONS

American Veterinary Medical Association (Student Chapter)

155

Veterinarian. *Rima Bogardus, CPRW; Cary, NC*

The greatest challenge in preparing this resume was culling the most-important information from a career spanning more than fifteen years.

HELEN C. NEMHEIN, R.D.

helen-RD@juno.com   305 14TH Avenue, Belmar, NJ 08751   (732) 681-2663

DIETETIC SERVICES MANAGEMENT

Registered dietician with 17 years of professional experience, including 10 years in long-term care. Clinical proficiencies complemented by business management abilities. Interested, empathetic, hands-on administrative style that motivates both individual and team performance, enhances patient quality of life, and increases bottom line profits. Familiar with OBRA survey procedures; actively participate in both state and federal inspections. Extensive experience in nutrition care plan formulation, laboratory screening evaluations, and the MDS process.

CAREER HISTORY ACCOMPLISHMENTS

LEISURE CHATEAU CARE CENTER, Lakewood, NJ; 1993–2002
A 242-bed, long-term-care facility that features two kitchens in accordance with religious mandates for the separation of dairy and meat.
Director of Dietetic Services / Registered Dietician
Responsible for the clinical care of residents, encompassing food service management, dietary recommendations, nutritional assessments, documentation and care plan formulation, and budgetary oversight for a half-million dollars. Reported directly to the facility administrator.

- ❑ Evoked increased resident satisfaction and improved patient eating habits by liberalizing restrictive diets. Achieved a 60% reduction in pressure wounds six months after instituting a Wound Care Committee and a vitamin / mineral intervention protocol.

- ❑ Captured $540,000 in annual facility revenues by accelerating the fee-billing process for Medicare patients requiring enteral support via timely completion of Certificates of Medical Needs (CMNs).

- ❑ Assessed and determined patients in need of TPN and enteral support programs. Recommended appropriate products, administered programs, monitored and evaluated patient progress.

- ❑ Saved facility $73,000 per year through strategic inventory-management techniques and by implementing direct purchasing of tube feeding and supplements. Transitioned facility in eliminating billing-company brokers and vendor sourced to attain a competitive pricing structure.

- ❑ Instituted a nourishment program that cut supplement costs by 30% and created a weight-loss and dehydration tracking program that culminated in a highly successful nourishment / rehydration program.

- ❑ Coordinated and taught Nursing Assistant Certification classes, eliminating the need for outside consultants, and conducted interdepartmental staff education inservices.

- ❑ Achieved zero clinical nutrition citations on all state, OBRA and federal surveys.

- ❑ Spearheaded monthly Food Committee meetings, attended Resident Council meetings, and provided monthly reports at Quality Assurance meetings.

- ❑ Hired, directed and monitored staff, with accountability for overseeing two kitchens in preparing meals that met both dietetic guidelines and Glatt Kosher mandates. Ensured regulatory standards by monitoring test tray temperatures and performing periodic sanitation checks.

156

Dietician. *Nina Ebert, CPRW; Toms River, NJ*

This resume helped Helen land a job at a renowned New York City hospital!

LEISURE CHATEAU CARE CENTER
Director of Dietetic Services / Registered Dietician, continued

- ❑ Active member of the Interdisciplinary Care Team, providing dietary recommendations for all residents, including coma, dialysis, Huntington's Chorea, and AIDs patients. Ordered consults as needed. Collaborated with speech therapist to identify patients' swallowing problems and implement rehabilitation program.

- ❑ Functioned as liaison between residents, doctors, and families. Organized special-event dinner functions for residents and families.

APPLEGARTH CARE CENTER, Hightstown, NJ; 1993–1994
Consultant / Registered Dietician
Evaluated individual patient needs, established nutritional care plans, and instituted a weight-loss and dehydration tracking program that resulted in the facility's premier nourishment/rehydration program.

THE HOMESTEAD, Stamford, CT; 1990–1993
Director of Dietetics
Challenged to reduce waste, succeeded in deflating cost on a per-patient basis, capturing $30,000 in facility revenues in six weeks. Rewrote menus to utilize existing inventory and implemented an ongoing waste-reduction program. Reduced patient per-day costs, capturing $81,000 in annual savings.

PERMANENT WEIGHT CONTROL CENTER, Greenwich, CT; 1986–1990
Owner / Manager
With full P&L responsibility, built company from start-up into a solid revenue generator through extensive clinical skills and aggressive sales, public relations, print and electronic advertising, and networking efforts. Developed marketing plan and business strategy, closing 95% of sales, developing a customer base of 500, and achieving $260,000 in annual sales volume (with a gross profit margin of 23%). Coordinated course curriculum and provided weekly behavior-modification classes.

BURDETTE-TOMLIN MEMORIAL HOSPITAL, Cape May, NJ; 1984–1986
Dietician / Consultant
Directed nutritional care in an acute-care setting with emphasis on surgical, critical care and cardiac areas. Participated in medical and discharge planning. Led National Nutrition Month activities: Wrote press releases, developed a nutrition hotline, and was a featured guest speaker on a local television show. Conducted a lecture series on "Nutrition and Aging" for a civic organization.

EDUCATION

B.S., Clinical Dietetics, UNIVERSITY OF CONNECTICUT, Storrs, CT
Completed an accelerated program, Coordinated Undergraduate Program (CUP) in clinical dietetics.

PROFESSIONAL AFFILIATIONS

New Jersey Dietetic Association
American Dietetic Association

Consulting Nutritionist In Private Practice
Gerontological Nutritionist

Since Cheryl had held the same job title with three employers since 1987, all of her jobs and achievements are grouped to avoid redundancy.

Cheryl Ruiz
**Two Hundred Maine Road
Huntington, NY 11743
(631) 382-2425
crz@aol.com**

OCCUPATIONAL THERAPIST

Innovative health-care provider with 14 years' experience with the following populations:

- Cerebral Palsy
- Head Trauma
- Sensory Integration
- ADD
- HIV
- Neurological Disorders
- Metabolic Disorders
- Juvenile Arthritis
- Orthopedic Conditions
- Developmental Delays
- Chromosomal Disorders
- Burn Victims

Demonstrate strong performance in the areas of communications, problem solving, and organization. Licensed to practice in New York State. Certified by the American Occupational Therapy Association.

PROFESSIONAL EXPERIENCE

Evaluate children's abilities, recommend and provide therapeutic services. Incorporate imagination in adapting activities to stimulate client needs. Perform evaluations of home safety in preparation for discharge. Create a healing, safe, and nurturing environment.

three jobs, three employers, same job title

Occupational Therapist, JumpStart Park Therapy, New York, NY, 1995–Present
Occupational Therapist, New Beginnings, Hauppauge, NY, 1992–1995
Occupational Therapist, Crosley Health Associates, Smithtown, NY, 1987–1992

achievements in all three jobs

- Planned and directed administrative and operational activities of the O.T. Department. Supervised a cohesive team which includes 3 occupational therapy aides and 2 certified occupational therapy assistants.

- Function as a member of an interdisciplinary team, encouraging parental involvement by providing training and education.

- Working knowledge of the latest equipment and modalities, including e-stim, ultrasound, and short wave diathermy equipment.

- Work cooperatively with social workers, psychologists, doctors, and other health-care team members to maintain a progressive healing environment.

- Implement and modify treatment programs based on patients' needs, maintain accurate documentation on patient progress.

- Provide specialized post-surgical wound care, burn therapy, and scar management as well as splinting.

EDUCATION

B.S., Occupational Therapy, New York University, New York, New York, 1987
    Licensed and Certified, New York State, 1987

A.A., Liberal Arts, Nassau Community College, Garden City, New York, 1981

LANGUAGES

Fluent in Spanish and Italian. Knowledge of Portuguese.

AFFILIATIONS

American Occupational Therapy Association
New York State Occupational Therapy Association

157

Occupational therapist. *Linda Matias, JCTC, CEIP; Smithtown, NY*

This resume uses a centered key word list...

JANE A. BROWN

100 Park Avenue • Ridgewood, New Jersey 07555 • (201) 333-3333

Highly qualified Licensed Pharmacist/Consultant with strong background in retail and institutional pharmacy services.... Experienced in working with geriatric patients in residential care.... Recognized for excellent counseling and client interface skills.... *Areas of expertise include:*

Key word list ⎰ Drug Utilization & Regimen Review / Third Party Systems / OBRA Regulations ⎱ Medication Counseling / High Volume Prescription Dispensing / IV Admixtures

EDUCATION/PROFESSIONAL:
New York College of Pharmacy and Science, Bronx, New York - <u>B.S. Degree in Pharmacy</u>
- New Jersey State Board of Pharmacy License
- New York State Board of Pharmacy License
- New Jersey Consultant Pharmacist (Eligible 10/96)
- Lambda Kappa Sigma Professional Fraternity

The profile statement communicates her professional title immediately in bold...

CAREER EXPERIENCE:
MAIN STREET PHARMACY, Ridgewood, New Jersey   1985-Present

Pharmacist
Staff pharmacist in fast-paced retail and institutional pharmacy dispensing up to 900 prescriptions daily. Perform compounding, physician detailing and in-services for nursing homes and residential facilities.

- Consult with medical professionals including both private physicians and institutional staff. Respond to inquiries regarding drug interactions and make recommendations for proper dosing and drug regimens. Credited with preventing medication errors.

- Counsel with clients about medication usage. Assist clients to set up schedules and administer their prescriptions safely.

- Troubleshoot medical problems for clients. Research information contacting drug companies for current data when necessary. Recommended changes resulted in patients' improved well being.

- Conduct in-service training for institutional nurses and staff such as *Administration of Eye Drops & Patches* and *Proper Administration of Oral Medication.*

- Set up medication systems (Multiple Fill Cards) for assisted living residences. Train staff in use.

- Monitor compliance with state and insurance regulations. Initiated record keeping system for compounding medications to meet requirements.

Pharmacy Technician
- Gained valuable experience in interpreting and filling prescriptions. Performed extensive compounding and assisted in consulting with clients and medical professionals.

INTERNSHIPS:
Presbyterian Hospital, New York, New York
Graduate Hospital, Philadelphia, Pennsylvania
Village Pharmacy, Fair Lawn, New Jersey
Squib Pharmaceuticals, Princeton, New Jersey

Education and professional certifications are high-profiled since they are critical for advancement (resume writer's comments).

AFFILIATIONS:
American Pharmaceutical Association   New Jersey Pharmaceutical Association
Bergen County Pharmaceutical Association   Professional Compounding Centers of America

158

Pharmacist. *Vivian Belen, NCRW, CPRW, JCTC; Fair Lawn, NJ*

This distinctive resume highlighted Susan's extensive, multifaceted career in pharmacy and positioned her for relocation to another state.

SUSAN M. MATTHEWS

907 Simon Avenue • Sanford, ME 09728 • (207) 436-0956 • smm@email.net

PROFESSIONAL PROFILE

REGISTERED PHARMACIST
Institutional & Community Pharmacy Services • Long-Term Care Administration

Highly qualified pharmacist with a 19+ years of experience blending pharmacy services with management, administrative, and consulting experience in retail and institutional settings. Demonstrated versatility in adapting to ever-increasing complexity in the healthcare industry. Strengths include:

- Pharmacy Operations Management
- Long-Term Care Pharmacy Services
- Senior-Care Consultant Pharmacy Services
- Healthcare Administration
- Retail Pharmacy Services
- Multidisciplinary Collaboration

Empathetic and intuitive in client interactions; elicit trust and build strong customer relations. Committed to providing quality pharmaceutical care as an essential link in disease management; poised and confident as a contributing member of the healthcare team. Flexible in quickly mastering new technologies and information systems.

EXPERIENCE HIGHLIGHTS

AAA Pharmacy, Sanford, ME   **1999–Present**

COMMUNITY PHARMACIST

- Serve as pharmacist in a fast-paced retail pharmacy. Interpret, compound, and dispense prescriptions. Oversee 5 pharmacy technicians.
- Interface with physicians and other caregivers to render pharmaceutical care and collaborate in multidisciplinary disease-management efforts.
- Maintain accurate patient and third-party billing records on the proprietary pharmacy computer system.
- Counsel clients on medication usage; troubleshoot, investigate, and respond to drug-interaction inquiries.

Sanford Nursing & Geriatric Center Pharmacy, Sanford, ME   **1986–1999**

OWNER-OPERATOR / PHARMACIST MANAGER / CONSULTANT PHARMACIST

- Founded and managed this institutional pharmacy. Provided 16 years of exclusive, 24x7 on-site pharmacy services for two skilled nursing facilities; serviced a client base of more than 300 residents.
- Managed all aspects of pharmacy operation including A/P and A/R, third-party billing, records maintenance, reporting, inventory, and purchasing. Ensured compliance with federal and state regulations and third-party agreements.
- Evaluated needs of the facilities; recommended, selected, and implemented effective drug distribution and control systems. Planned, organized, directed, and monitored all aspects of pharmaceutical service.
- Formulated and implemented drug administration policies and procedures and established efficient systems for precise medical record-keeping.
- Consulted on a daily basis with medical professionals and institutional staff to provide drug information and manage resident drug regimens.
- Conducted in-service training programs for licensed staff to enhance pharmaceutical services program effectiveness.
- Chaired the Pharmaceutical Services and Infection Control Committees.

159

Pharmacist. *Michelle Dumas, CPRW, NCRW, CCM, JCTC, CEIP; Somersworth, NH*

SUSAN M. MATTHEWS

Page 2

**EXPERIENCE
HIGHLIGHTS
CONTINUED**

Seacoast Convalescent & Rehabilitation Center, Portsmouth, NH   **1983–1986**

NURSING HOME ADMINISTRATOR

- Launched and directed all operations of this newly established 120-bed skilled nursing facility while simultaneously managing the Sanford Nursing & Geriatric Center Pharmacy.
- Participated in constructing all policies and procedures and instituted cost-effective programs and administrative systems; maintained high levels of quality service while improving financial performance.
- Hired and managed team of 130 healthcare, administrative support, and maintenance personnel. Selected and trained replacement Nursing Home Administrator.

Portsmouth Medical Center, Portsmouth, NH   **1982–1983**

ASSISTANT DIRECTOR OF PHARMACY SERVICES (1982–1983)
STAFF PHARMACIST (1982)

- Promoted to Assistant Director after just 5 months of employment with this 180-bed non-profit community hospital.
- Supervised a 10-person staff and planned, organized, and directed administrative functions and professional pharmacy services.
- Managed drug distribution and dispensing activities. Provided drug information to medical staff, conducted in-service training programs for licensed staff.
- Prepared and monitored IV admixtures and chemotherapy solutions.
- Played integral role in the development of comprehensive oncology services.

**EDUCATION &
CREDENTIALS**

B.S., PHARMACY, summa cum laude, GPA: 3.9 (1982)
Temple University, School of Pharmacy, Philadelphia, PA

- Beta Lambda Chapter President of Rho Chi (national honor society)
- Member, Rho Pi Phi (pharmaceutical fraternity)

A.S., APPLIED SCIENCE, pre-pharmacy concentration (1979)
Northampton County Area Community College, Bethlehem, PA

PROFESSIONAL LICENSURE

- Licensed Pharmacist, Maine and New Hampshire
- Licensed Nursing Home Administrator, New Hampshire

**PROFESSIONAL
AFFILIATIONS**

Maine Pharmaceutical Association (MPA)
New Hampshire Pharmaceutical Association (NHPA)
American Society of Consultant Pharmacists (ASCP)

Shelley A. James, PTA

15 Buttonwood Road
Lewiston, Maine 04240

Telephone: (207) 785-5555

Email: SAJames@aol.com

Credentialed Physical Therapy Assistant

- ◆ Orthotic training with stroke patients.
- ◆ Prosthetic training with amputee patients, BK and AK.
- ◆ Modalities including E-STEM for wound healing and pain management, hot and cold packs, and CPM for total knee replacements.
- ◆ Knowledge and experience with total hip replacement, ORIF, and total knee replacement.
- ◆ Establishing appropriate home exercise programs.
- ◆ Seating and positioning in wheelchair with paraplegic, stroke, and general debilitation.

Education

Her weight-training achievements are included because they relate to the field of physical therapy.

Associate of Science, Physical Therapy Assistant
— Canyon Hills Technical College, Fairfield, Maine   1997
Additional Training/Certifications
— Certified Weight Trainer (1999); completed International Weightlifting Association Weight Training Course
— Completed National Cognitive & Skills Evaluations (1999)
— American Heart Association for Healthcare Providers Program (1988)

PTA Training

Including this section was a good way to add weight to Shelley's relatively limited experience.

Clearwater Rehabilitation & Nursing Center, Yarmouth, Maine   (May 5–June 20, 1997)
— Rehab/CVA and other Neurological/Neuromuscular Disorders
— Multiple Trauma/MVA, Chronic Pain, and General Reconditioning
Mid-State Medical Center, Thayer Unit, Waterville, Maine   (January 1–February 16, 1996)
— Acute, Orthopedic Care, Amputation and Joint Replacement
Maine Coast Memorial Hospital, York, Maine   (May 22–June 23, 1995)
— Outpatient, Orthopedic, Pediatric and Aquatic Therapy
Clover Living Center, Ellsworth, Maine   (April 19–May 20, 1995)
— Sub Acute, Chronic Obstructive Pulmonary Disorder

Professional Clinical Experience

Physical Therapy Assistant, Physical Therapy Associates, Lewiston, Maine   **August 1997–Present**
Provide physical therapy services to sub-acute, chronic, and long-term-care patients at three PTA-owned skilled nursing facilities: Gleason Rehabilitation & Living Center, Oak Park Rehabilitation & Living Center, and Englewood Rehabilitation & Living Center.

Position Highlights

- ◆ Collaborate with Physical Therapist and implement treatment programs according to patient's plan of care.
- ◆ Participate in Medicare meetings with the team to discuss status of skilled patients; knowledgeable in Medicare Prospective Payment Service (PPS).
- ◆ Attend Interdisciplinary meetings with patients and family members to set up plans for patient's return home.
- ◆ Provide home-treatment sessions to increase safety and improve outcomes after discharge.
- ◆ Perform outpatient therapy services.

In-Service Staff Educator

This heading under her current position highlights the added value she brings to the organization.

- ◆ Wound Care Prevention & Training with Positioning in Bed and Wheelchair
- ◆ Restraint Reduction with Patients with Dementia & Alzheimer's Disease
- ◆ Gait Belt Training to Increase Patient Safety and Decrease Injury
- ◆ Back School Training to Decrease the Risk of Back Injury in the Workplace

Physical Therapist Assistant (Grades K–5)   **August 2000–June 2001**
— Presque Isle Elementary School, Presque Isle, Maine

160

Physical therapy assistant. *Rolande L. LaPointe, CPC, CIPC, CPRW, IJCTC, CCM; Lewiston, ME*

Job-fair recruiters love this format!
It is easily read in 30-60 seconds
and packs a lot of punch.

215 Hampton Road
Findlay, OH 45840
(419) 348-0203
jiglehart@yahoo.com

JILL IGLEHART

OBJECTIVE

To obtain a position in PHYSICAL THERAPY where my skills and education will make a positive difference as an individual or as a team member.

SUMMARY of QUALIFICATIONS

Many of the responsibilities in this field are the same from job to job, so they do not need to be listed under each employer. Instead, they are presented in this summary.

\\ **Interpersonal skills** achieved by successfully communicating with physicians, patients, professors, co-workers, visitors, hospital personnel, and other agencies.

\\ **Problem-solving skills** gleaned by determining and providing individualized care and rehab to patients with neurological, orthopedic, and generalized diagnoses in home and clinical settings, and by visualizing and preparing short- and long-term goals with functional outcomes to maximize patient independence level.

\\ **Leadership skills** displayed by developing and directing programs related to stress management, substance abuse awareness, assertiveness training, and self-esteem to provide additional patient support.

\\ **Organizational skills** as evidenced by the ability to manage and prioritize tasks in a fast-paced environment; co-organized EMU Reach Out "Run for the Homeless."

PROFESSIONAL EXPERIENCE

1/99 – PRESENT	**PRIVATE RESIDENCE,** Findlay, OH *Home Health Aide*
9/99 – PRESENT	**RAINBOW REHABILITATION CENTER,** Findlay, OH *Physical Therapist — Traumatic Brain Injury*
6/99 – 1/01	**EVERGREEN CARE & HEALTH CENTER,** Medina, OH *Certified Nursing Assistant*

This resume depicts a well-rounded, intelligent, multi-tasking individual who can contribute a great deal to any physical therapy setting.

CLINICAL/PRE-CLINICAL EXPERIENCE

3/99 – 6/99	**ST. FRANCIS MERCY MEDICAL CENTER,** Toledo, OH *Physical Dysfunction, Inpatient Acute Care Setting*
1/99 – 3/99	**BLANCHARD VALLEY HOSPITAL,** Taylor, MI *Psychosocial Dysfunction, Inpatient Psychiatric Hospital*
9/98 – 12/98	**HERITAGE HOME SERVICES,** Howell, MI *Physical Therapist in Home-Based Community Setting*
6/98 – 9/98	**INTENSIVE PSYCHIATRIC COMMUNITY CARE,** Ypsilanti, MI *Intensive Clinical Case Management, Department of Veterans' Affairs*

EDUCATION

EASTERN MICHIGAN UNIVERSITY, Ypsilanti, MI
Master *of* Physical Therapy, 2001   GPA: 3.8

BOWLING GREEN STATE UNIVERSITY, Bowling Green, OH
Bachelor *of* Arts *in* Psychology, 1998   GPA: 3.5

PROFESSIONAL AFFILIATIONS *and* ACTIVITIES

American Physical Therapy Association, APTA Membership Committee
Ohio Physical Therapy Association, Boston Marathon (Pre- and Post-Event)
Special Olympics Co-Chair, Big Brother/Big Sister, Pathways for the Future

ADDITIONAL SKILLS

- First Aid • NeuroDevelopmental Techniques • CPR • MMT
- OSHA Bloodborne Pathogens • ADL • Adaptive Equipment
- Prefabricated Splinting • Spanish • Microsoft Word & Windows 2000

161

Physical therapist. *Sharon Pierce-Williams, MEd, CPRW; Findlay, OH*

Salina has no paid experience as a P.A. but offers a strong nursing background in acute care and employee health programs. The combination functional format with chronological work summary gives a strong overview of her experiences. Subcategories add the "human" touch to her clinical skills (resume writer's comments).

SALINA PIEDRA, P.A.

555 North Wickendale Drive
Selma, Alabama 55555
(555) 555-5555

PROFESSIONAL GOAL

Physician Assistant in a healthcare setting where my comprehensive clinical training and 20+ years of broad-based nursing experience will be of value.

QUALIFICATIONS

♦ **P.A. Clinical Training:** Over 1,600 hours of advanced clinical training in the role of Physician Assistant with emphasis on caring for patients of all ages from infant to geriatric, eliciting complete patient history and physical, and effectively managing and treating common acute illness and stable chronic illness.

♦ **Professional Skills:** Excellent professional judgment and documentation skills. Noted by supervisors for making well thought out decisions and utilizing consultants appropriately. Convey a sincere concern for patient's physical and emotional well-being. Excellent performance history in highly-structured managed care environments.

♦ **Prior Clinical Experience:** Well-rounded nursing experience, primarily with Foundation Medical Center, in capacities as Emergency Room Nurse, Wellness Center Nurse, Employee Health Nurse, Pre-Op/Post-Op/Recovery Nurse, Telemetry Nurse, Medical/Surgical Staff Nurse, and Oncology Staff Nurse.

♦ **Related Experiences:** Performed annual employee physicals. Assessed and treated work-related injuries. Made referrals. Provided preventative health education. Counseled individuals regarding health assessment results and lifestyle changes. Served on Emergency Department QA and Peer Review committees.

♦ **Teaching Experience:** Precepted nurse interns on medical-surgical floors (cited for my unusual patience and helpfulness). Taught nurses instructional methods for conducting pre-op classes and advising diabetic patients. Assisted in teaching EMT classes for Yellowstone National Park medics.

PROFESSIONAL EXPERIENCE

Emergency Nurse/Employee Health Nurse/Wellness Center Nurse -- Foundation Medical Center	1984-Present
Clinical and Emergency Nurse -- Yellowstone National Park	1983-1984
Telemetry Nurse/Staff Nurse -- Foundation Medical Center	1975-1982

EDUCATION, CERTIFICATION

Physician Assistant Certification -- University of California, School of Medicine	9/96
Bachelor of Science Degree, Nursing -- California State University, Long Beach	1975
Associate of Arts Degree, Liberal Arts / Minor in Child Development -- Long Beach City College	1971
Registered Nurse License (#RN 55555)	1975-Present
Advanced Cardiac Life Support	1981-Present
Certified Emergency Nurse	1985-Present
Mobile Intensive Care Nurse	1989-Present

AFFILIATIONS

California Coalition of Nurse Practitioners (CCNP); National Nurses Association (NNA)

References Upon Request

162

Physician assistant. *Susan Britton Whitcomb, CPRW; Fresno, CA*

This job seeker did not immediately go into her field after earning her degree...

RECREATIONAL RUTH
1982 GOPHER DRIVE ■ SACRAMENTO, CA 99959 ■ (777) 555-1212

PROFILE

- ▸ Diverse experience in the field includes therapeutic recreation services applied in psychiatric, rehabilitation, and preschool settings. Knowledgeable in documentation of case progress from initial assessment interviews to discharge summaries.

- ▸ Approach to therapeutic recreation is characterized by enthusiasm and a strong commitment to the field as an evolving profession.

- ▸ Skilled in working with all age groups; particular strengths interacting with children.

- ▸ Proven organization and time management skills utilized to achieve goals for the client, team, and myself.

RELEVANT EXPERIENCE

CALIFORNIA SCHOOL DISTRICT, Sacramento, CA
Diagnostician
Administer and score battery of academic tests to children in ten elementary, middle and high schools who have been identified for possible placement in the Exceptional Children program. Assist psychologists with written behavioral observations and parent interviews.

Work Site Specialist
Prepared mentally handicapped high school students for employment utilizing a variety of training techniques. Trained employers in supervision encouraging a successful transition from teaching program to independent employment. Assessed and documented student performance through interviews with parents, teachers, and employers.

LOS ANGELES REGIONAL MEDICAL CENTER, Los Angeles, CA
Earthquake Rehabilitation Hospital & The Pines (psychiatric facility)
Therapeutic Recreation Specialist
Filled in for staff Therapeutic Recreation Specialists on leave. Provided programs on exercise, leisure education, horticulture, pottery, needlework, woodwork, as well as community outings for patients. Conducted initial assessment interviews, counseled patients and documented their progress, participated in treatment team meetings, wrote treatment plans, and prepared discharge summaries.

Earthquake Rehabilitation Hospital
Volunteer

CALIFORNIAN DEVELOPMENT CENTER, Los Angeles, CA
Therapeutic Preschool Teacher
Designed and implemented a new program for developmentally delayed preschoolers. Adapted class activities to the changing needs of both mainstreamed, normally-developing students and delayed students. Promoted mainstreaming concept to parents, other professionals, and the community.

163

Recreation therapist. *Sandy Adcox Saburn, CPRW; Charlotte, NC*

Family matters and a stint in real estate "distracted" her from her profession...

RECREATIONAL RUTH
■ PAGE TWO ■

RELEVANT EXPERIENCE (CONTINUED)

WESTERN HEALTH CENTER, Sacramento, CA
Support Teacher
Programmed and led activities for classroom of students ages three to six with behavioral disorders. Taught movement class incorporating physical education and play therapy. Designed and led weekly workshop series for parents and day care providers on topics that included self-esteem, communication, and discipline.

CALIFORNIA RECREATIONAL DEPARTMENT, Sacramento, CA
Camp Director
Camp Counselor
Performed duties of camp counselor for groups of children, both with and without disabilities. Responsible for pre-camp planning, including design of program structure, distribution of registration materials, purchasing supplies, and hiring and training 19 employees. Developed camp manual.

CALIFORNIA MEMORIAL HOSPITAL IN HOLLYWOOD
Intern
Full time internship position on acute psychiatric unit. Documented initial assessments, treatment team plans, and discharge summaries for fifteen adolescents and adults. Planned and led individual and group programs on stress management, relaxation therapy, exercise, horticulture, games, and leisure education. Facilitated patient meeting to plan weekly community outings.

EDUCATION

UNIVERSITY OF SOUTHERN CALIFORNIA
Teacher Certification in Special Education (all but Student Teaching)

Bachelor of Arts in Parks and Recreation
Option in Therapeutic Recreation

CERTIFICATION

Certified as a Therapeutic Recreation Specialist
Administered by the National Council for Therapeutic Recreation

Her resume emphasizes relevant experience and leaves out dates to grab the reader's attention.

PROFESSIONAL AFFILIATIONS

▸ American Therapeutic Recreation Association

▸ Californian Therapeutic Recreation Association

▸ Californian Recreation and Parks Society

Questions on matters of dates and other experience are left to the interview (resume writer's comments).

REFERENCES

Provided upon request

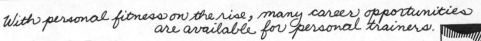

With personal fitness on the rise, many career opportunities are available for personal trainers.

Julia S. Pratt, Personal Fitness Trainer

110 Sundown Road — St. Paul, MN 55101 — 651.555.8988 — bodyrefined@usbell.com

SPECIALIZING IN ... FITNESS & HEALTH MANAGEMENT/FITNESS TRAINING AND MODELING

PROFILE

Self-motivated leader dedicated to helping others improve themselves through fitness. In +10 years as a Trainer, **Coach, Athlete, Referee, and EMS and Law Enforcement Professional,** have gained **extensive experience in the** creation, implementation, and supervision of wellness/fitness programs. Adaptable to all ages and degrees of ability.

FITNESS CREDENTIALS & SPECIALTIES

- ⅄ Certified Personal Fitness Trainer, International Fitness Professional Association, #17805, expiration 10/04.
- ⅄ Certified Kari Smythe Trainer, The K-Smythe Total Workout®, K-Smythe, Inc.
- ⅄ K-Smythe Rehabilitative Exercise Specialist: Knees, Hips, Lower Back, and Shoulders.
- ⅄ Mommy Fitness® Prenatal Exercise Specialist.

CAREER HIGHLIGHTS

PERSONAL FITNESS, WELLNESS & ATHLETICS

- **Assistant to Kari Smythe,** K-Smythe, Inc., K-Smythe Total Workout® Retreats, California, 1998–present
  - Lead attendees through introduction to a program that literally reshapes the body as it resets the metabolism to burn fat at a faster rate. Program incorporates an internal, CRT™ System for the skin.
- **Fitness & Wellness Instructor,** White Bear Lake Community Education, 2000–present
  - **Lead 4 classes:** K-Smythe Total Workout®, K-Smythe Total Workout® Introduction, Personal Profiles wellness and nutrition, and Beauty Secrets Shared in the Model Industry.
- **7th & 8th Grade Girls Volleyball Coach,** Meadowbrook Middle School, Golden Valley, MN, 1989–1999
- **Volleyball Referee,** YMCA, Golden Valley High School, and Volleyball Tournaments, 3 years

MODELING

- **Runway Model,** K-Smythe Website and marketing materials, 2000–present
- **Robert Adamo Photo Shoot Model,** 1999–present; **Runway Model,** MTM/Mall, 2000–present

LAW ENFORCEMENT

- **Police School Liaison Officer/Juvenile Detention Center Administrator/Deputy Sheriff,** Hennepin County Sheriff's Department, Minneapolis, MN, 1995–2001
- **Police Officer,** Plymouth Police Department, Plymouth, MN, 1994

EMERGENCY MEDICAL SERVICES

- **Emergency Medical Technician/First Responder,** St. Cloud State University, St. Cloud, MN, 1990–1994

EDUCATION, TRAINING & OTHER CREDENTIALS

- **B.A. in Physical Education & Sports Science/Criminal Justice Studies** (dual majors), St. Cloud State University, 1994
- **Graduate,** John Casablanca's Modeling & Acting Center, Minneapolis, MN, 2000
- **Certified First Responder,** Minnesota Emergency Medical Services Regulatory Board, #516782, exp. 6/03
- **Minnesota P.O.S.T. Licensed Peace Officer,** #14712

AFFILIATIONS

Better Body Basics®, K-Smythe, Inc., MTM Modeling Agency, National Association of School Resource Officers, Minnesota Peace Officers Association, Minnesota Juvenile Officers Association, South West Metro Gang Task Force

LIFESTYLE & COMMUNITY PRESENCE

- KARE 11 Health Fair Volunteer.
- Wayzata (Plymouth, Minnesota) High School "Athlete of the Year."
- Avid **"active and balanced lifestyle"** enthusiast. Bodybuilding, weightlifting, aerobics, volleyball, softball, rollerblading, hiking, biking, basketball, football, camping, canoeing. Eat sensibly. Take pride in appearance. Also enjoy family time, cooking, computers, and project multitasking!
- More than 5 years' experience as a public speaker/instructor for fitness, CPR, safety topics, DARE, and more.

This resume packs a lot of information into an entertaining format.

164

Personal physical trainer. *Barb Poole, CPRW, CRW; St. Cloud, MN*

A creative one-page resume that displays the power of testimonials taken from reference letters.

Melanie Stone, CRNA

1555 Main Street • Charleston, WV 25302 • (304) 555-5555

"... exhibits high degree of intelligence and readily grasps new concepts ... has an affable charm ... interacts well with patients, colleagues ... even in the most stressful of situations."

James Austin, MD
General Anesthesia Services
Charleston, WV

"... reliable and responsible team player ... willingly shares the workload ... level headed and competent in an emergency ... proficient and knowledgeable in anesthetic skills and techniques."

Barb Parrott, CRNA
CAMC-Memorial Division
Charleston, WV

"...an excellent anesthetist who remains calm under pressure ... highest integrity ... exhibits excellent leadership ... has been a tremendous asset to our organization."

Lee Ann Johnson, CRNA, BA
Instructor, CAMC School of
Nurse Anesthesia
Charleston, WV

"... a very responsible employee ... always volunteering for additional assignments ... prompt and punctual ... has a positive attitude ... a valuable asset to our staff."

Tamy L. Sarab, Charge CRNA
CAMC-Memorial Division
Charleston, WV

Professional Profile

- Certified Registered Nurse Anesthetist
- Bachelor's degree and four years CRNA experience
- Clinical instructor with over 1,000 hours experience
- Outstanding clinical expertise and proficiency
- Attend weekly continuing education meetings
- Excellent problem solver who works well under pressure
- Reputation as a team player with superb people skills
- Upbeat, personable, and highly energetic

Licensure & Professional Affiliations

- Certified Registered Nurse Anesthetist, Certificate #2250
- Registered Professional Nurse, License #022200
- Member, American Association of Nurse Anesthetists
- Member, West Virginia Association of Nurse Anesthetists
- Professionally involved with local Women's Health Center

Professional Experience

CHARLESTON AREA MEDICAL CENTER—MEMORIAL DIVISION
Charleston, West Virginia   1986-Present
- **CRNA - Cardiovascular Center** - 1991-Present
  Surgeries include arterial bypasses, hearts, amputations, gallbladders, mastectomies, biopsies, major orthopedics
- **RN - Medical Surgical** - 1986-1989
  RN and charge nurse duties on a 40-bed med/surg unit, included adolescent ward and peritoneal dialysis

Education

- **Certificate of Anesthesia**, Charleston Area Medical Center School of Anesthesia, Charleston, WV, 1991
  - Received Josephine A. Reier Memorial Scholarship Award
- **Associate Degree in Nursing**, University of Charleston School of Health Sciences, Charleston, WV, 1985
  - Received Nursing Student Achievement Award
- **Bachelor of Fine Arts Degree, *magna cum laude*,** Arizona State University, Tempe, Arizona, 1979

A very powerful technique!

165

Registered nurse. Barbie Dallmann, CPRW; Charleston, WV

Placing heads in the left column separated by a line, make for a crisp and readable resume

Maria Eléna Navarro, CRTT
127 Pine Street, Unit D
Morris Plains, NJ 55555

(000) 000-0000

OBJECTIVE	***Respiratory therapist*** in a hospital where previous experience in clinical settings such as ICU, CCU, and NICU would be put to use and valued.

EDUCATION	County College of Morris, Randolph, NJ
	  Completed AMA approved certificate program in Respiratory Therapy, 1992
	
	William Paterson College, Wayne, NJ
	  Associates in Applied Science, Allied Health, 1988

TECHNICAL SKILLS	***Equipment:*** MA-1, Puritan-Bennett 7200, and Bear series ventilator initiation and management, including transport, set up and maintenance. ***Treatment Modalities:*** Under the direction of a physician, perform gas, aerosol and humidity therapies; intermittant positive pressure breathing (IPPB); chest physiotherapy; cardiopulmonary rehabilitation. ***Techniques:*** Endotrachael intubation/extubation; administration of medical gases, drugs, treatments and tests as prescribed by an authorized physician; drawing and interpretation of arterial blood gases; airway management; bedside spirometry for checking pulmonary functioning and recording patient progress; quality control checks for optimal equipment performance of respiratory equipment. ***Patient Interaction:*** Implementation of patient care plans and follow-up treatment on patients of all ages, newborn through geriatric; instruction of patients on use of liquid oxygen, concentrators, c-paps, bipaps and apnea monitors as well as use, care and troubleshooting of their ventilators; direct responsibility for the management of respiratory compromised patients; assistance to crisis team in the administration of basic life support in code situations.
WORK EXPERIENCE	3/95 to Present **Respiratory Technician** HomeCare Agency, Rockaway, NJ 2/93 to 3/95 and currently on per diem basis **Respiratory Therapist** Memorial Hospital, Morristown, NJ 1/92 to 2/93 **Respiratory Technician** Wayne General Hospital, Wayne, NJ 10/90 to 12/91 **Telemetry Technician** Cardiologics, Inc., Glenridge, NJ 8/87 to 10/90 **Telemetry Technician/Nurses Assistant** Beth Israel Hospital, Passaic, NJ
LANGUAGES	Bilingual fluency in English and Spanish

This approach allows her to emphasize her key skills and keep the work experience section short

a plus in some healthcare settings

166

Respiratory therapist. *Melanie Noonan, CPS; West Paterson, NJ*

Client has strong work history, thus the chronological format. Profile stresses "experienced" and "qualified" rather than objective-type sentence.

Impact statements under employment indicate her ability to go above and beyond. Other entries emphasize experience, stressing exposure to various hospital departments.

Anna Maria Delario

5555 East Middlesex Way
Fontana, California 55555
(555) 555-5555

❖❖❖

PROFILE, OBJECTIVE

Experienced Respiratory Therapist -- Qualified for licensed respiratory therapist positions with an organization that will benefit from my 16+ years' experience in home health care and acute care environments.

EDUCATION, CERTIFICATION

Registered Respiratory Therapist -- National Board of Respiratory Care
Respiratory Care Practitioner -- State of California
Exemptee Certificate -- State Board of Pharmacy for Medical Device Retailer
Bachelor of Science Degree, Respiratory Therapy -- California State University, Long Beach (1980)

PROFESSIONAL EXPERIENCE

SOUTHERN CALIFORNIA MEDICAL CENTER, Los Angeles, California   3/89-Present

Staff Lead Respiratory Therapist: Administer respiratory therapy care and life support to cardiopulmonary patients including management of home oxygen, nasal CPAP, apnea monitors, pulmonary aides, and home ventilators. Provide technical support and troubleshooting of ventilator devices and other apparatus. Conduct follow-up patient visits. *Contributions / Accomplishments:*

 ❖ Established clinical protocols in preparation for successful JCAHO survey.

 ❖ Initiated and conducted education series for patients, families, medical support staff, and other nursing agencies.

 ❖ Assumed additional administrative responsibilities (order intake, insurance verifications, purchasing, inventory).

VISTA MEDICAL CENTER, Fontana, California   11/84-2/89

Staff Therapist: Performed respiratory therapist functions similar to those listed above.

 ❖ Gained extensive ER and surgery intensive care experience, as well as ICU, CCU, NICU, PICU, and burn center experience in a regional trauma center.

TRAVELING THERAPIST CORPS (medical traveling organization)   1/83-11/84

Tuscany Medical Center, Neonatal and Pediatric ICU's, Tuscany, Mississippi:

 ❖ Held broad decision-making responsibility under progressive protocol system. Drew and ran CBGs and ABGs via arterial stick and through UAC and arterial lines. Administered aerosol therapy, IPPB, and CPT.

Saint Luke's Hospital and Medical Center, Chicago, Illinois:

 ❖ As Staff Therapist, duties included IPPB, aerosol therapy, CPT, incentive spirometry, and critical care work in units.

This section gives a picture of her values and commitment and leaves a great

ADDITIONAL EXPERIENCE

Served as volunteer Respiratory Therapist on multi-disciplinary medical teams which conducted outreaches to under-served populations in Mexico, Venezuela, and Cambodia.

lasting impression

❖❖❖ *(resume writer's comments).*

167

Respiratory therapist. *Susan Britton Whitcomb, CPRW; Fresno, CA*

Beth uses this resume both as a marketing piece for contract work and for part-time work elsewhere.

The graphic is also on her business cards and letterhead.

Beth Martin
CCC-S

—

555 First Street
Charleston, WV 25314

—

(304) 555-7777

The bubbles are significant...

One hundred years from now it will not matter what my bank account was, the sort of house I lived in, or the kind of car I drove, but the world may be different because I was important in the life of a child.
—Anonymous

Blowing bubbles is commonly used to help children with speech problems (resume writer's comments).

— Professional Overview —

o Bachelor's degree in speech pathology and master's degree in communication disorders with three years' therapy experience
o ASHA Clinical Competency Certification in Speech Pathology
o West Virginia Licensed Speech Pathologist
o Experience with all ages, specializing in birth to age 3
o Outstanding assessment skills and therapeutic techniques
o Organized, flexible, and easygoing with an ability to quickly develop a good rapport and put clients—especially children—at ease
o Faithful researcher with good documentation practices

— Education —

o **Master of Arts Degree in Communication Disorders**, Marshall University, Huntington, West Virginia, 1989
o **Bachelor of Arts Degree in Speech Pathology**, Marshall University, Huntington, West Virginia, 1986
o **Continuing Education**:
   ✳ Sensory Input and Swallowing Therapy, Jeri A Logemann, Ph.D.
   ✳ Facilitating Vocal/Verbal Expression, Pamela Marshalla, MA, CCC-S
   ✳ Attention Deficits in Children & Adults, Catherine Christie, Ph.D.

— Professional Experience —

o **Speech Language Pathologist** (contract; part time)   1990-Present
Home Health Services, Inc., Morgantown, WV
   ✳ Work with early intervention B-3 out-patients in Ripley and Spencer
   ✳ Cases include pervasive development disorders, premature births, and phonological disorders
o **Speech Language Pathologist** (part time)   1990-1996
Watson's Nursing & Rehabilitation Center, Parkersburg, WV
   ✳ Worked with geriatric population with swallowing disorders
   ✳ Cases included post-CVA, aphasia, dysarthria, and adult apraxia
   ✳ Assisted in conducting modified barium swallows
o **Speech Language Pathologist** (itinerant; part time)   1987-1990
Indiana County Schools, Indiana, WV
   ✳ Worked with children K-12 in four schools in Indiana County
   ✳ Cases involved various aspects of communication disorders and articulation therapy
o **Rehabilitation Therapy Aide**   1981-1987
Charleston Area Medical Center, Charleston, WV
   ✳ Worked with speech therapists while learning all aspects of the interdisciplinary team approach to rehabilitation

— Memberships —

o American Speech Language Hearing Association
   ✳ Carry $3 million in ASHA Professional Liability Insurance
o West Virginia Speech Language Hearing Association
   ✳ Chair of the Speech Pathology Affairs Committee

168

Speech pathologist. *Barbie Dallmann, CPRW; Charleston, WV*

PATTY PATHOLOGIST
1521 Market Street
Wilmington, North Carolina 28405
Home: (000) 111-2222
Work: (000) 333-4444

PROFILE

Highly competent and energetic professional with demonstrated experience in developing and leading a TBI program. Experienced inservice provider. Experienced and well-qualified Speech-Language Pathologist adept in dealing with sensitive populations as part of an interdisciplinary team. Possess exceptional organization and time-management skills. Outstanding oral and written communication skills.

EDUCATION

Master of Arts in Speech-Language Pathology 1984
Bachelor of Science in Speech-Language Pathology 1983
Florida State University, Tallahassee, FL

PROFESSIONAL EXPERIENCE

Atlantic Hospital, University Medical Center, Wilmington, NC
Clinical Coordinator, Traumatic Brain Injury Program 1994 to Present
Accomplishments:
Integral part of team that designed all policies and procedures for this new facility prior to accepting the first patient. Participated in screening, interviewing, and hiring to develop staff. Instrumental in preparing for accreditation and special needs certification. Under my leadership, TBI program was under budget and over revenue with a higher than anticipated patient census.

Responsibilities:
Direct brain injury program for inpatient, day treatment, and outpatient services. Directly supervise 10 member interdisciplinary clinical staff, develop and implement program-related policies and procedures, and develop and manage annual program budget. Member of Quality Improvement Team. Clinical duties include evaluation and treatment of patients within the brain injury program, as well as assessment of swallowing disorders via modified barium swallow x-ray studies for all rehabilitation patients as needed.

Washington Memorial Rehabilitation Hospital, Washington, DC
Level III Speech-Language Pathologist, Head Injury Unit 1992 to 1994
Provided inpatient and outpatient services to neurologically-impaired adults and children including diagnostic and therapeutic treatment for speech and language, cognitive, and swallowing disorders. Supervised students, assisted with program development, and coordinated the unit's quality improvement activities.

Jellystone Hospital, Yogi, VA
Speech Pathology Supervisor 1990 to 1992
Supervisory and clinical duties associated with treatment of rehabilitation patients in an inpatient rehabilitation unit. Supervised department staff, budget planning, as well as diagnosis and treatment of patients. Caseload consisted primarily of adolescents and adults recovering from strokes and head injuries, with strong emphasis on swallowing disorders.

New Hanover County Schools, Wilmington, NC
Speech-Language Pathologist 1986 to 1990
Computer-assisted diagnostic and speech therapy services to children from pre-kindergarten through sixth grade.

This very competent professional has extensive accomplishments in her field . . .

169

Speech pathologist. *Sandy Adcox Saburn, CPRW; Charlotte, NC*

Patty Pathologist   **Page 2**

EXPERIENCE **(continued)**	*Rehabilitation Hospital of North Carolina*, Raleigh, NC 1986 to 1990 **Speech-Language Pathologist** Contract speech pathology services to nursing homes and home health patients, ranging from pediatrics to the geriatric population. Assisted with filing and follow-up appeals for Medicare and insurance claims.

Center for Communication Disorders, Palo Alto, NM
1985
Speech-Language Pathologist
United Way Agency providing speech-language services to children and adults with emphasis on language delay, aphasia, and articulation.

Center for Rehabilitation and Special Education, Charlotte, NC
1984 to 1985
Speech-Language Pathologist
Diagnostic and speech-language therapy services to mentally, emotionally, physically, and multi-handicapped students, ages 5 to 21, in a county-wide school program.

CERTIFICATIONS

Certificate of Clinical Competence in Speech-Language Pathology
American Speech-Language-Hearing Association, July 1985

North Carolina Licensure in Speech-Language Pathology, August 1994

RECENT
CONTINUING
EDUCATION

Interaction Management Series (15 month program)

The Art and Science of Rehabilitation Management Today: Surviving The Challenges

FIM Certification Workshop

1995 Carolinas Brain Injury Symposium

CARF 101: How to Prepare for a CARF Survey in Comprehensive Inpatient-Acute and Subacute Settings, Spinal Cord Injury and Traumatic Brain Injury

Dysphagia and Long Term Care

Communication Disorders after Brain Injury - Second Annual Conference

INSERVICE
TOPICS

Multiple presentations of these topics to students, peers, patients and family members, rehab therapists, physicians, and nurses:
- Working with Dysphagic Patients
- Communication with the Traumatic Brain Injury Patient
- Using Videoflouroscopy to Assess Swallowing Disorders
- Augmentative Communication with the Aphasic Patient
- The Quality Improvement Process in the Rehab Setting
- Developing a Patient/Family Education Process
- Support Needs for Families of the TBI Patient

PROFESSIONAL
ORGANIZATIONS

- Coastal Brain Injury Support Group, Group Facilitator
- Community Advisory Committee
- American Speech-Language-Hearing Association
- National Brain Injury Association
- Brain Injury Association of North Carolina - Member of Annual Symposium Planning Committee

This resume was condensed from five pages and well-received by hiring authorities (resume writer's comments).

"Profile" and "Professional Experience" sections emphasize Amanda's ability to handle a heavy patient load while remaining personable and producing accurate test results, which are highly desirable qualities in healthcare technicians.

Amanda C. Jackson, CCT, RDCS

785 Bentwood Drive
Willowick, OH 44095

(440) 906-4431
acjackson@aol.com

PROFILE

Amiable, caring **Echocardiography Technician** with over 10 years' experience • Recognized for reliability and accuracy • Proven ability to develop positive rapport with patients who have a variety of needs, conditions, and backgrounds • Strong mechanical troubleshooting skills • Able to win patient confidence and cooperation • Computer proficient

PROFESSIONAL EXPERIENCE

Echo Technician   1993–present
Advanced Cardiology Services, Cleveland, OH
Cardiac Diagnostic Center consists of 4 labs and supports 25 physicians.
Echo lab is accredited by ICAEL.

- Perform echocardiograms, stress echoes, Holter monitoring, Holter scanning, thallium stress tests, Cardiolite studies, and pacemaker evaluations. Excellent working knowledge of Agilent 5500 and HP 2000 cardiac ultrasound machines.
- Conduct diagnostic testing on an average of 20 patients per day without compromising accuracy or compassion.
- Developed a reputation as a strong troubleshooter. Often assist co-workers who are having technical problems with equipment.
- Research products, manage inventory, and order medical supplies for 2 labs. Purchase cardiac medications for all 4 labs. Saved facility thousands of dollars per year through wise selection of products.

EKG/Stress Technician   1990–1993
Mt. Sinai Hospital, Dayton, OH

- Conducted EKGs, stress tests, thallium stress tests, and Holter scanning in various units of the hospital.
- Developed a reputation for quality and compassion. Was encouraged by cardiologists to apply for position at Advanced Cardiology Services.

EKG/Stress Technician   1988–1990
Cardiovascular Consultants, Philadelphia, PA

- Conducted EKGs, stress tests, and Holter scanning.
- Managed heavy patient load. Became proficient at multitasking with 10 physicians in the office every day.
- Trained new employees.

CREDENTIALS

Registered Diagnostic Cardiac Sonographer (RDCS)   1999
Certified Cardiographic Technician (CCT)   1990
BCLS Certified
Currently pursuing ACLS Certification

EDUCATION

Technical Workshop in Cardiac Ultrasound   1991
Owen-Brown, Dallas, TX

Cardiography certificate GPA 3.9   1989
Pennsylvania School of Health Technology, Philadelphia, PA

PROFESSIONAL AFFILIATIONS

Society of Diagnostic Medical Sonographers
American Society of Echocardiography

COMMUNITY INVOLVEMENT

Nursing home volunteer
Nursing home ombudsman (Ohio program)

170

Cardiovascular technician. *Rima Bogardus, CRPW; Cary, NC*

Her company was acquired by another and had two name changes prior. She originally listed her positions separately, giving the impression of job-hopping...

DONNA WARREN, M.T., ASCP

555 West Zenith Avenue
Conejo, California 55555

Home: (555) 555-5555
Work: (555) 555-5555

Listing employers in parantheses rids this misperception (resume writer's comments).

PROFESSION

Experienced Clinical Laboratory Technologist with 20+ year career in hospital, reference laboratory, and blood center settings. Generalist skills include:

- Blood Banking
- Coagulation
- Serology
- Microbiology
- RIA Special Chemistry
- Chemistry
- Hematology
- Urinalysis
- Immunology

EDUCATION, LICENSURE

STANFORD UNIVERSITY

B.A., Biology (1974)

LICENSURE

California Clinical Laboratory Technologist (1980)

PROFESSIONAL EXPERIENCE

METROPOLITAN MEDICAL CENTER, Long Beach, California
(formerly HEALTH LABORATORIES)

9/92-Present
6/76-9/92

Licensed Clinical Laboratory Technologist (9/92-Present)
(Department of Newborn Screen and Prenatal Tests Laboratory)

▶ Perform newborn screen laboratory tests required by the State of California Department of Health Services to detect genetic diseases of newborns, including phenylketonuria, galactosemia, hypothyroidism and hemoglobinopathies. Perform prenatal laboratory testing for alpha-fetoprotein in maternal serum. Maintain equipment and resolve instrumentation problems. Direct the activities of laboratory assistants as needed.

Licensed Clinical Laboratory Technologist (6/89-8/92)

▶ Performed generalist functions, with experience in all areas of the clinical laboratory (immunohematology, serology, chemistry, special chemistry, coagulation, urinalysis, hematology, microbiology, radioimmunoassay, toxicology). Monitored laboratory equipment (daily maintenance, quality control, calibration, correction of malfunctions). Assisted with rotation and inventory control of supplies. Solved technical problems using moderate degree of independent judgment with minimal supervision.

Department Head of Radioimmunoassay (1984-1989)

▶ Performed all radioimmunoassay (RIA) tests. Maintained quality control records for all assays. Documented assay and radioimmunoassay procedures and maintained safety manual for College of American Pathologist inspection. Evaluated and set-up new RIA assays. Scheduled monthly workload. Instructed student trainees in laboratory procedures. Analyzed and evaluated capital expenditures for new instrumentation and negotiated purchases. Maintained and controlled operating supplies.

171

Clinical laboratory technologist. *Susan Britton Whitcomb, CPRW; Fresno, CA*

DONNA WARREN, M.T., ASCP

Page Two

I opted for two pages given her well-rounded experience and extensive involvement in industry-related affiliation and corporate committees (resume writer's comments).

PROFESSIONAL EXPERIENCE

HEALTH LABORATORIES, continued

Prior Assignments

▶ Radioimmunoassay Specialist Technologist (1981-1984)
Clinical Laboratory Technologist (1980-1981)
Clinical Laboratory Temporary Technologist (1979)
Clinical Laboratory Technologist Trainee (1978)
Laboratory Assistant, Madera Community Hospital (1976-1977)

SO-CAL BLOOD CENTER, Long Beach, California   4/90-2/93

Per Diem Clinical Laboratory Technologist

▶ Performed laboratory work in the following technical areas: bacteriology, chemistry, hematology, and serology.

ADDITIONAL PROFESSIONAL ACTIVITIES

HEALTH LABORATORIES

- Secretary of Quality Assurance Committee
- Safety Committee Member
- Radiation Safety Officer
- Organized and planned activities for National Medical Laboratory Week, holiday festivities, and annual corporate barbecue.

PROFESSIONAL AFFILIATIONS

CALIFORNIA ASSOCIATION FOR MEDICAL LABORATORY TECHNOLOGY (CAMLT)

- Fresno Chapter, CAMLT
- Executive Committee Member
- Past Newsletter Editor, *Erythro-Sights*
- Delegate to CAMLT Annual Convention
- Sergeant at Arms, CAMLT Annual Convention
- Nominations Committee, CAMLT Annual Convention
- Secretary and Membership Chairperson
- Volunteer, Community Awareness Program

References Upon Request

Emily had "uneventful" positions in doctor's offices where "old school" was the norm. But she liked this, as her strongest asset is in client relations, not state-of-the-art technology (resume writer's comments).

EMILY V. DAVIS

2993 Raven's Nest Drive ❖ Wilmington, NC 28412 ❖ (000) 123-4567

PROFILE

Eight years experience as a dental hygienist. Career is highlighted by many long-term clients and track record of excellent feedback from patients. Special skills with teenagers and apprehensive patients.

Efficient in use of patient time. Stay on schedule.

Administrative skills include use of office computer systems.

Flexible. Fit in well with many types of office environments.

EXPERIENCE

Dental Hygienist:

Since these job tasks are all similar and understood by employers, there is no need to provide details

- Daniel Dentist, DDS
  Wilmington, NC — 1996 to Present

- Evan Bigtooth, DDS, PA
  Wilmington, NC — 1995 to 1996

- Wally Wash, DDS
  Wilmington, NC — 1991 to 1995

- Handy Tool, DDS
  Wilmington, NC — 1991 to 1993

- Tooth & Yell Family Dental Care
  Wilmington, NC — 1989 to 1991

- Dennis Drill, DDS
  Wilmington, NC — 1989 to 1990

EDUCATION

A.A.S. - Dental Hygiene — 1988
Cape Fear Community College
Wilmington, NC

REFERENCES

Available upon request

172

Dental hygienist. *Sandy Adcox Saburn, CPRW; Charlotte, NC*

Natalie worked for several dentists doing the same thing, so the "Experience" is tailored to eliminate duplication. The vertical layout gives visual distinction. I added the "human" element

5555 North Glenn, #555
Gloucester, Nevada 55555
(209) 439-9581

NATALIE F. JENSEN, R.D.H.

to complete the picture for the closing. (resume writer's comments).

OBJECTIVE: Continued career growth as a Registered Dental Hygienist within a progressive dental practice whose emphasis is on periodontal therapy and preventative dentistry.

SPECIALTY PROCEDURES:

- ★ Local Anesthesia
- ★ Nitrous Oxide
- ★ Coronal Polish
- ★ Endodontics
- ★ Pedodontics

- ★ Gingival Curettage
- ★ Periodontal Therapy
- ★ Orthodontics
- ★ Periodontics
- ★ Radiology

LICENSURE: **California State Board of Dental Examiners** (License Number 55555)

EXPERIENCE: **Registered Dental Hygienist:** Perform a full range of RDH responsibilities, including FMS, BW, prophylaxis, scaling, root planing, local anesthesia, nitrous oxide, OHI, and periodontal charting. Excellent record with former and present employers:

Keenan Wynn, D.D.S., Gloucester, Nevada	7/94-Present
Angela Berrins, D.D.S., Gloucester, Nevada	2/93-6/94
Warren Minnis, D.D.S., Gloucester, Nevada	9/91-1/93

EDUCATION: GLOUCESTER CITY COLLEGE, Gloucester, Nevada

- ★ **Associate of Science Degree, Dental Hygiene** (1991)
- ★ **Advanced Training** in Periodontal Therapy (scaling and root planing)

AWARDS: **Clinical Award** -- Selected by instructors as top graduate with exceptional clinical skills. Award is given jointly by the Glouster Dental Society, the County Dental Society, the Waxahachie Dental Society, and the Gloucester Dental Foundation.

Special Honors -- Chosen by Dental Hygiene graduating students for demonstration of leadership and clinical skills.

AFFILIATIONS: American Dental Hygienists Association; Nevada Dental Hygienists Association; Gloucester Dental Hygienists Association (Vice President)

VOLUNTEER:

- ★ Provided public health information as Dental Hygiene Representative at City High School's Health Fair.
- ★ Informed students of Dental Hygiene career opportunities at Gloucester College's Career Day.
- ★ Presented lecture series on dental hygiene to elementary school children and senior citizens in connection with "All Smiles" and "Target Group" programs respectively.
- ★ Assisted in organizing the first annual National Dental Hygiene Week at Gloucester City College.

REFERENCES: Provided upon request.

An excellent way to include positive comments from former employers

Selected comments from performance evaluations: "it is critical to the health and prosperity of my practice that staff *care* about our patients -- Natalie is exemplary in her rapport with patients which stems from her belief in, and appreciation for, the uniqueness and worth of every individual, whether young or old."

173

Dental hygienist. *Susan Britton Whitcomb, CPRW; Fresno, CA*

Jenna Morton
5445 Sunningdale Drive
Los Angeles, California 55679
(555) 989-0000
jennamorton@hotmail.com

Profile

Essential adaptive skills

Manual dexterity...excellent vision...writing skills...aptitude for working with electronic equipment...and the ability to work with patients and health personnel.

Education, Specialized Training, and Credentials

Specialized training is a job requirement, so credentials are listed first.

California State Medical Licensing Board
- Registered Electroneurodiagnostic Technologist, 1997
- L.P.N. License, 1994

Vocational Technical School of California
- Electronics and Instrumentation, Associate Degree, 1997
- L.P.N. Diploma, 1994

Union General Hospital
- Evoked Potential Testing Program
- Nerve Conduction Testing Program

Professional Experience

L.A. Cardiovascular Services, Inc.   June 1997 to Present

Electroneurodiagnostic Technologist. Skilled in the use of an electroencephalograph (EEG) machine to record electrical impulses transmitted by the brain and the nervous system. Assist physicians in diagnosing brain tumors, strokes, toxic/metabolic disorders, epilepsy, and sleep disorders. Also measure the effects of infectious diseases on the brain, determine whether an individual with mental or behavior problems has an organic impairment such as Alzheimer's Disease, as well as determine "cerebral" death and assess the possibility of a recovery from a coma.

Union General Hospital   January 1994 to May 1997

Licensed Practical Nurse. Cared for the sick, injured, convalescing, and handicapped under the direction of physicians and registered nurses. Took vital signs, treated bedsores, prepared and gave injections, applied dressing, and more. Also observed patients and reported adverse reactions to medications or treatments.
On-the-job training in using an electroencephalograph machine to look for changes in the patient's neurologic, cardiac, and respiratory status. Also took patients' medical histories and chose the appropriate combination of instrument controls and electrodes to correct for mechanical or electrical interference that came from somewhere other than the brain.

Affiliations and Memberships

America Health Care Association
American Society of Electroneurodiagnostic Technologists, Inc.
National Association for Practical Nurse Education and Service, Inc.
American Board of Registration of Electroencephalographic Technologists

A conventional chronological format.

174

Electroneurodiagnostic technologist. *Thelma Silvola; Indianapolis, IN*

Tammy was an RN/Paramedic with a large, high-volume metropolitan ambulance division. She thoroughly enjoyed her work, but was on the edge of job burnout.

TAMMY R. WALDEN, R.N.

276 Pit Greene Road
Hartsville, TN 37022 · walden615@hotmail.com · Home (615) 655-3772 · Pager (615) 291-2078

Professional Summary

Highly skilled **EMERGENCY HEALTHCARE PROFESSIONAL** with ten years' practical experience in both hospital and field environments. Interact effectively with patients and colleagues in stressful, unpredictable situations. Exhibit strong leadership abilities as Acting District Chief for Ambulance Division and as hospital Charge Nurse. Maintain high personal standards of professionalism, keeping current on medications, treatments, and changing technology.

To support her qualifications for transferring into a management or teaching role within the department, her resume stresses her previous leadership responsibilities and her medical training.

Education and Certification

BACHELOR OF SCIENCE IN NURSING — 2000
Belmont University — Nashville, TN

REGISTERED NURSE — 1997 — Hold current Tennessee RN license
State University of New York (SUNY) Regents College — Albany

Advanced Cardiac Life Support (ACLS)
Basic Trauma Life Support (BTLS)
Trauma Nurse Core Course (TNCC)

Work Experience

PARAMEDIC / REGISTERED NURSE .... 1996 – Present
Nashville Metropolitan Fire Department/Ambulance Division — Nashville, Tennessee

Respond to 911 emergency medical calls. Make critical decisions regarding the nature and extent of injury or illness and transport to medical facility. Monitor critically ill patients during hospital-to-hospital transfers. Acquired significant management experience as Acting District Chief supervising paramedics and EMTs.

CHARGE NURSE .... 1994 – 1996
Trousdale Medical Center — Hartsville, Tennessee

Night-shift Charge Nurse duties in a 30-bed county hospital, including ER, medical, and surgical units. Supervised LPNs, CNAs, and technicians. Prioritized and managed patient load, including triage, patient assessment, diagnostic procedures, nursing care and treatments, and patient education.

PARAMEDIC / EMERGENCY MEDICAL TECHNICIAN .... 1993 – 1994
Sumner County Ambulance Service — Portland, Tennessee

EMERGENCY MEDICAL TECHNICIAN .... 1991 – 1993
Metropolitan Ambulance Service — Nashville, Tennessee

Professional Affiliation

American Association for Critical Care Nurses (AACN) — Member since 1998

175

Paramedic/nurse. *Carolyn Braden, CPRW; Hendersonville, TN*

On track to obtain her RN, this LPN wanted to move to a larger facility that would allow her to smoothly transition to an RN position once qualified.

Angela Martina, LPN

67-45 Maple Drive, Farmingdale, NY 11735
(631) 949-4786 • amlpn23@yahoo.com

Patient advocate; uphold the highest standards of nursing care

- Experienced, with excellent patient care and leadership skills.
- Currently enrolled in Registered Nurse Program.
- Keen observation, communication, and intervention skills.
- Adapt easily to change of environment and work schedule.

Since her patient-care experience had focused on geriatric patients, the use of artwork alongside a concise summary of her qualifications conveys at a glance her value, while making a somewhat serious resume much warmer.

Nursing Experience

Licensed Practical Nurse / Shift Leader, Seniors Center, Hauppauge, NY   3/95 – present
Licensed Practical Nurse, St. Mary's, Jamaica, NY   10/93 – 2/95

◈ Responsible for the care of 40 geriatric patients through the direct supervision of four CNAs encompassing:

– dispensing of medications	– oxygen therapy	– tracheostomy care
– vital signs	– wound care	– nasopharengeal and oral suctioning
– intravenous therapy	– application of dressings	– insertion of catheters

◈ Administer controlled narcotics, assuming full responsibility for possession of keys.
◈ Enforce regulations requiring the witnessed counting and charting of medications during change of shift.
◈ Develop and implement nursing care plans, and supervise patients' admission and discharge procedures.
◈ Oversee direct patient-care requirements within the Nursing Rehabilitation and Ambulatory Program.
◈ Liaison between patients, nurses, and physicians to address problems needing immediate/long-term resolution.
◈ Educate CNAs on the prevention of transmitted infectious bacteria.
◈ Ensure open lines of communication and accurate charting procedures; update computerized patient data.
◈ Facilitate a creative and safe environment with diversified and stimulating recreational activities.
◈ Assist staff nurses with initial assessment of patients upon admission.
◈ Report changes in patients' conditions and other matters of concern requiring prompt attention.
◈ Train and supervise personnel in all areas of patient care and daily procedures.

Education

Currently enrolled in Registered Nurse Program
Certificate of Completion, Licensed Practical Nursing Program, 1993
ST. JOHN'S COLLEGE, Jamaica, NY

Licenses & Certifications

New York State Licensed Practical Nurse, 1993

176

Licensed practical nurse. *Ann Baehr, CPRW; Long Island, NY*

This person had worked in hospitals and larger medical centers but wanted to start her own business working on a contractual basis.

Mary Alice Carroll, R.R.A., C.C.S.

1934 Westminster Drive • Iowa City, IA 52240 • 319-555-6988 • maclady@mail.com

GOAL
Contractual reimbursement position in a group practice or medical center.

EDUCATION

These two sections emphasize her broad knowledge and extensive certifications.

HANSON COLLEGE • Cedar Rapids, Iowa
Bachelor of Applied Science — Health Information Management • 1995
- Course work in medical, legal, and computer information systems, strategic planning, and management.

Associate of Applied Science — Health Information Technology • 1990
- Course work in medical record systems, coding and classification systems.

CERTIFICATIONS
▶ **Certified Coding Specialist-Physician based** (CCS-P) — 1999
▶ **Registered Record Administrator** (R.R.A.) — 1996
▶ **Certified Coding Specialist** (C.C.S.) — 1996
▶ **Accredited Record Technician** (A.R.T.) — 1991

EMPLOYMENT HISTORY

UNIVERSITY OF IOWA HOSPITALS • Iowa City, Iowa
Reimbursement Manager • 1999–Present
- Oversee coding and reimbursement procedures for professional services delivered to in- and outpatients.
- Assign ICD-9-CM and CPT codes for procedures and professional services.
- Review E/M codes to ensure documentation requirements/teaching physician regulations are met.
- Ensure adherence to Medicaid/Medicare and managed care reimbursement/billing requirements.

BUTTERWORTH HOSPITAL • Des Moines, Iowa
PRN Medical Record Coder • 1997–1999
- Utilized 3M system to assign ICD-9-CM and CPT-4 codes and DRG assignments.

MEMORIAL HOSPITAL • Waterloo, Iowa
Medical Record Coder • 1995–1996
- Performed duties as described above using Procoder system.

CUSTER REGIONAL MEDICAL CENTER • Davenport, Iowa
Medical Record Coder • 1993–1995
- Performed duties as described above utilizing 3M system.
Medical Record Clerk I • 1992–1993
- Assembled and analyzed patient records; managed physicians incomplete room; performed data entry and filing.
Patient Registration Clerk • 1991–1992
- Performed emergency-room patient registration and admission procedures.

SKILLS
▶ Expertise in coding, JCAHO requirements, billing requirements in physician offices.
▶ Over seven years of experience in hospital Health Information Management department.
▶ Excellent communication and interpersonal skills; comfortable interacting with physicians, insurance companies, and patients.

177

Health information technician. *Janet L. Beckstrom; Flint, MI*

Elizabeth's compact resume presents experience to support her job objective, plus her many other skills.

ELIZABETH J. LEMING
456 Main Street
Milford, MI 484381

810-555-7623

PROFILE

Skilled transcriptionist with expertise in adapting to the diversity of those who are dictating. Knowledgeable about office procedures. Experienced receptionist who interacts well with others. Professional, pleasant demeanor.

HIGHLIGHTS OF EXPERIENCE

These are the "extra" skills that increase her flexibility

- ☐ Accurately and efficiently transcribe the dictation of patient records, requests for medical records, and correspondence in hospital and private practice settings.
- ☐ Acted as receptionist and scheduled appointments.
- ☐ Collected payments.
- ☐ Prepared invoices and shipping orders utilizing computerized system.
- ☐ Provided general secretarial support including typing, filing, and acting as receptionist.

SUMMARY OF SKILLS

- ☐ Keyboarding speed 75-80 words per minute with high degree of accuracy
- ☐ Medical and general transcription utilizing Dictaphone
- ☐ Medical terminology and medical office procedures
- ☐ Multi-line telephone system
- ☐ Standard office equipment (computer, electric typewriter, facsimile, copier)
- ☐ Popular DOS and Windows applications including:
  - Microsoft Word
  - Microsoft Excel
  - Microsoft PowerPoint
  - WordPerfect
  - Sunquest
  - Medical Manager
  - Lyrix

EMPLOYMENT HISTORY

Metropolitan Medical Center • Pontiac, MI
Medical Records Transcriptionist (1995-Present)

Physician's Osteopathic Hospital • Flint, MI
Medical Receptionist/Transcriptionist (1994-1995)

Family Practice Associates • Holly, MI
Medical Transcriptionist (1993-1994)

Plymouth Manufacturing Co.
Receptionist (1990-1994)

EDUCATIONAL BACKGROUND

Baker College • Flint, MI
Medical Transcription Certification (1993)
General Coursework - English, social sciences, general sciences

Delta College • University Center, MI
Accredited Record Technician program (1992-1993)

References available on request.

178

Medical transcriptionist. *Janet L. Beckstrom; Flint, MI*

MARTIN YRACEBORO, ARRT(N)(R), CNMT, CRT

5555 North Portsmouth Avenue
Longview, California 55555
(555) 555-5555

Because credentials are essential for working in this job, he lists them first

QUALIFICATIONS

Experienced **NUCLEAR MEDICINE TECHNOLOGIST** with 15 years in hospital and freestanding imaging facilities . . . additional experience as Radiological Technologist. Prior background in health care marketing, education, and clinical research. Credentials include:

- ◉ American Registry of Radiologic Technologists, #055555, (R) 1969, (N) 1987

- ◉ Certified Technologist, Nuclear Medicine, State of California, #RHN 555, 1989

- ◉ Certified Radiological Technologist, State of California, #55555-5555, 1985

PROFESSIONAL EXPERIENCE

IMAGING CENTER, Longview, California   3/91-Present

Nuclear Medicine Technologist II/Lead Technologist

Established start-up operating procedures for Nuclear Medicine Department, including protocol, scheduling, record keeping, computer systems, ordering, and procedures for handling, storage, and decay of radiopharmaceuticals. Performed full scope of planar, flow studies, and SPECT imaging procedures. Interviewed and made hiring recommendations for Nuclear Medicine Technologist.

Contributions:

- Researched and advised physicians regarding selection of upgraded equipment.

- Customized computer applications to automate protocol writing process.

- Received excellent bi-annual audit reviews for record keeping compliance.

- Awarded Employee of the Year. Received outstanding performance evaluations annually.

- Assumed additional responsibility for ordering of supplies for entire facility.

Staff Radiological Technologist   3/90-3/91

- Initially employed with Imaging Center's parent company, Saint Luke's Medical Center, as Staff Radiological Technologist. Performed routine radiological procedures.

- Contracted with Veteran's Administration Hospital to manage Nuclear Medicine Department on pre-arranged temporary assignment.

Martin's work history includes nuclear medicine, research/teaching, then back to nuclear medicine . . .

179

Nuclear medicine technologist. *Susan Britton Whitcomb, CPRW; Fresno, CA*

I reformatted his five-page resume with a summary for his first and second career phases and created a more traditional job listing for his most recent and relevant experience (resume writer's comments).

MARTIN YRACEBORO, ARRT(N)(R), CNMT, CRT
Page Two

PROFESSIONAL EXPERIENCE (cont.)

1984-1990	Seven years' experience in the field of blood cell separation. Involvement extended to: supervision of **clinical trials,** including report writing and collaboration on publication of research; **technical functions** (blood cell collection and plasma exchange procedures); and **marketing** and **educational presentations** on use of blood cell separators to hospital nursing staff on a national scale.

- **Clinical Research Coordinator** (1988-1990)
  Boster Labs, Inc., Manheim, Michigan

- **Apheresis Technician, Satellite Operations** (1986-1988)
  American Red Cross, Denver, Colorado

- **Marketing Product Specialist** (1984-1986)
  Blood Bank Products Corporation, Boston, Massachusetts

1974-1984	Initial professional experience as Nuclear Medicine Technologist and Radiologic Technologist. Performed full range of procedures. Advanced to hold departmental administrative responsibilities: management of Nuclear Medicine Department; scheduling and supervision of technologists and support staff; inventory control; and budget tracking.

- **Chief Nuclear Medicine Technologist** (1980-1984)
  Radiology and Nuclear Medicine Technologist (1979-1984)
  Valley Community Hospital, Valley View, California

- **Radiology and Nuclear Medicine Technologist** (1974-1979)
  Denver Metropolitan Hospital, Denver, Colorado

EDUCATION

Graduate, Valley View Community Hospital School of Radiological Technology, 1967-1969
Certified CPR and First Aid Instructor, American Red Cross
Continuing Education requirements met through attendance at local, regional, and national meetings conferences, and seminars.

AFFILIATIONS

Society of Nuclear Medicine, Technologist Section, since 1987
Sierra Valley Society of Nuclear Medicine, since 1989

ADDITIONAL DATA

Abstracts, publications, oral presentations, and references provided upon request.

Kelly had a great deal of experience and wonderful communication skills.

Kelly Smith

37 142nd Street ▪ Flushing, NY 11358 ▪ (718) 933-3321 ▪ ksmith@aol.com

Highly organized and experienced Licensed Optician with strong background in exceeding sales goals and providing exemplary customer service

Her resume is designed to highlight her many talents and show the results of her actions at work.

SUMMARY OF QUALIFICATIONS

- Demonstrate excellent presentation and communication skills, both verbal and written.
- Specialize in team building, improving business and increasing sales and profits.
- Able to take command of difficult projects and effectively resolve problems.
- Relate well to people on all levels of business and management.
- Work well independently, as well as part of team.
- Excel under pressure. Willing to "go the extra mile."
- Quick and effective mastery of new skills and information.
- Proficient with computers, including Microsoft Office, Internet and various POS programs.

PROFESSIONAL EXPERIENCE

OPTI-SIZE, INC., Kew Gardens, NY   1999 – Present
Store Manager
- Promoted from Optician in 2000 as a result of high sales performance and customer feedback.
- Interview, schedule and manage staff for million-dollar retail location.
- Develop marketing strategies and promotions to increase sales.
- Implement sales techniques to improve business.
- Design store and window displays, increasing public interest and attracting new clients.
- Market new products and evaluate product performance, effectively addressing customers' needs.
- Effectively resolve customer-service conflicts, maintaining strong and positive client relations.
- Oversaw operations of additional retail location in Queens, New York, enforcing company policies and procedures, as well as ensuring high-quality service and products to customers.

EYEWEAR IMAGES, Long Island, NY   1998 – 1999
Optician
- Assisted customers in choosing eyewear appropriate for their prescriptions and lifestyle.
- Measured patient pupilary distance and fitted eyeglasses on customers.
- Trained patients on insertion, removal and care of contact lenses, ensuring safety and health of patients' eyes.
- Verified prescriptions and performed quality-control checks on incoming eyeglass orders from outside laboratory.
- Updated client files and maintained computer system, including sales and data entry, as well as performing daily, weekly and monthly closing procedures.
- Developed and maintained strong customer relations.

EYE GLASS WORLD, New Hyde Park, NY   1993 – 1998
Optician/Buyer
- Originated eyeglass frame inventory system and supervised product pricing and store layout.
- Responsible for all eyeglass frame, lens and accessory vendor, purchasing and inventory decisions for million-dollar retail outlet.
- Sold frames, lens options and contact lenses to meet individual needs of clients, ensuring increased business and customer satisfaction.
- Designed store and window displays, highlighting new and "hot" products to increase customer interest and sales.
- Performed laboratory duties, including blocking, edging, polishing and coating lenses, as well as assembling eyeglasses.
- Developed strong customer relations, significantly contributing to store growth and increased repeat business. Successfully resolved customer service issues.

Kelly had not earned her dispensing license until 1998 but had been an apprentice for several years prior. The date of her license was simply left out, so her lack of "licensed" years would not affect her negatively.

EDUCATION & LICENSES

Bachelor of Arts in English, Queens College, Queens, NY
Graduated Cum Laude

New York State Licensed Ophthalmic Dispenser

She received job offers within a couple of weeks!

180

Optician, dispensing. *Michelle Kennedy, CPRW; Port Washington, NY*

Margaret Edwards

The challenge in preparing Margaret's resume was to show her related skills and experience even though she has never worked as a pharmacy technician.

29 Maplebridge Road
Catskill, NY 12415
518-943-3654
margarete@aol.com

Objective ~ To obtain employment as a **Pharmacy Technician** by offering current certification and excellent customer service skills

Qualifications) ~ *This section focuses attention on her transferable skills gained in previous jobs.*

- ~ Recently earned Pharmacy Technician Certificate.
- ~ Ensure customer satisfaction by providing quick, pleasant and effective service.
- ~ Diagnose problems by using listening skills; recommend solutions.
- ~ Assemble planograms to enhance visual appearance and increase sales.
- ~ Trained in the observation and confrontation of shoplifters.
- ~ Fluent in both English and Spanish.

Education

➢ **Pharmacy Technician Certificate** ~ January 2001
Binghamton University; Binghamton, NY

➢ **High School Diploma** ~ Catskill High School; Catskill, NY

Employment History

Detailer ~ October 1999–November 2001
Prime Auto Parts; Binghamton, NY

➢ Promoted from driver to detailer after 6 months by proving energy and commitment to the company.
➢ Operated office equipment and searched for parts by order number, part description, automobile make and model or VIN number.
➢ Managed the multiple phone line and maintained an organized store.
➢ Developed and implemented the New Staff Training program.
➢ Counted inventory and compared to corporate on-hand figures to determine supply need.

Cashier / Stocker ~ February 1999–October 1999
Edna's Café; Binghamton, NY

➢ Prepared menu items, served customers and maintained a clean facility.
➢ Independently assured product stock remained full.

Cashier / Stocker ~ October 1998–February 1999
CVS Pharmacy; Catskill, NY

➢ Ensured customers received all promotions, discounts and sales applicable to them.
➢ Oversaw alarm verification logging.

181

Pharmacy technician. *Andrea J. Howard, MSEd; Albany, NY*

PAUL D. MARTIN

3918 Park Avenue • New York, New York 10010 • (212) 826-8452
pdmartin@hotmail.com

PROFILE

(handwritten note: This section contains an Objective Statement that clearly identifies this as a transitional resume.)

Articulate, self-motivated individual, with progressively responsible pharmacy support experience, eagerly seeking to *transition into challenging position with opportunity to utilize pharmaceutical and medical knowledge.* Focused on results; will contribute to team goals or work independently with little guidance. Proven public relations and team leadership achievements. Maintain cooperative relationships with management, clients and colleagues at all levels. Flexibility to learn new assignments and excel in their implementation. Welcome challenges.

PROFESSIONAL EXPERIENCE

APP • New York, NY   5/01 to Present
($22MM National Pharmaceutical Distribution House • 30 Employees)
Pharmacy Technician
Assist supervising pharmacist to meet state compliance for documentation of controlled-substance prescriptions. Provide customer service and troubleshoot inquiries and problems.
- Maintain internal budget control guidelines required for reordering and maintaining inventory.
- Source new and existing suppliers for price and delivery; advise management of negotiations.
- Maintain patient control log of pharmaceutical usage to ensure physician-prescribed compliance.
- Train and supervise new hires for technical product requirements, pharmacy control and reordering skills to maintain adequate inventories to satisfy target market requirements — i.e., Transplant and HIV patients throughout U.S.
  ~ *Implemented procedures to control overnight shipping requirement – resulting in $25,000 annual savings.*

(handwritten note: Italic font used to highlight this significant savings accomplishment.)

B.J.K., INC. • Poughkeepsie, NY   5/00 to 10/00
($10MM Wholesale Pharmaceutical House)
Computer Technician
Provided data entry for filling and monitoring prescriptions for nursing homes, hospitals, group homes and additional applications.

R.X. EXPRESS • Staten Island, NY   9/98 to 5/00
($8MM Pharmacy & Drug Store)
Pharmacy Technician
Assisted pharmacist in the preparation of medications, patient medication counseling, and inventory control. Provided customer service and performed cashier functions.

EDUCATION

Briarcliffe College, Bethpage, NY — **Bachelor of Business Administration in Management, 2003**
Concentration: Information Technology

Nassau Community College, Uniondale, NY — **Liberal Arts Program, 2000**

CERTIFICATIONS

Certified Pharmacy Technician (CPhT)

COMPUTER SKILLS

MS Word/PowerPoint/Outlook • Windows 98 • Technically based programs • Internet

182

Pharmacy technician. *Donna Farrise; Hauppauge, NY*

GENE TRENT, RT(R) CRT

1445 S. DOBSON ROAD, #305
TEMPE, ARIZONA 85202
602-699-9393
GENEXRAY@AOL.COM

PROFESSIONAL PROFILE	More than 15 years of professional experience in RADIOLOGIC TECHNOLOGY, holding positions demanding quality-conscious attention to detail. Abilities include but are not limited to

This section provides a thorough listing of what he can do.

Radiologic examinations	Department management
Quality assurance	Staff supervision
X-ray film development	Training & evaluation
Equipment operation	Scheduling work assignments
Patient relations	Budget compliance
Physician liaison	Procedure development

- Well-organized, with the effective prioritization skills necessary to complete assignments in a timely and professional manner.
- Strong leadership skills with a proactive approach; instrumental in creating an effective, efficient team offering optimum quality diagnostic procedures.
- Demonstrated concern for patient well-being, developing innovative methods as needed to secure required diagnostic examinations.
- Flexible and cooperative; ready to accept additional responsibilities and promote team effort in achieving goals.
- Communicate clearly and concisely in both oral and written form. Maintain productive relations with patients, physicians, and other professionals.
- Firmly committed to the radiology profession; participate in on-going education to maintain knowledge of advances and current technology.

EDUCATION	Graduate, School of Radiologic Technology Children's Hospital of Los Angeles (California)

These sections make a clear presentation of his credentials.

LICENSURE	1987: AART #147886 1987: State of California #RHT - 61556 1990: State of Arizona #77-CRT-7574

CAREER HIGHLIGHTS	**DEPARTMENT MANAGEMENT & SUPERVISION**

This is a more chronological listing of his work, related skills, and accomplishments.

- Supervise and manage 10 to 14 multi-modality professional and support staff. Management and supervisory responsibility for active second-shift department operation during primary manager's absences (approximately 40% to 50% of the time).
- Involved in staff development and decision-making relating to employee job performance evaluation, quality, and training.
- Develop procedures and policies; implement and maintain safety and hospital protocols, policies, and procedures; provide training and orientation to new technologists and support staff to ensure personnel meet required standards.

SCHEDULING & BUDGETING

- Control payroll expenditures through careful preparation of work schedules to ensure appropriate coverage without costly over-staffing; release redundant staff when not needed to reduce overhead.

(Continued)

- Involved in budget development and budget compliance, with input on expenditures for equipment purchases and supplies as well as personnel costs.

183

Radiologic technologist. *Brooke Andrews, CPRW; Chandler, AZ*

TECHNICAL SKILLS

- Demonstrated expertise in the use of state-of-the-art radiologic and related equipment performing efficiently both independently and as part of a team.
- Developed new CPT4 codes in compliance with Federal regulations.
- Instrumental in development of new CT scanner protocols and procedures and trained operators at new installation site.
- Experience in hospital environments of various sizes, from 25-bed to 750-bed facilities, resulted in ability to secure radiologic data on patients in unusual or life-threatening situations. Considered above-average professional by peers.
- Extensive Level I trauma experience.
- Use of PC and/or mainframe computer for patient tracking, billing, folder maintenance, diagnostic data, and more.

QUALITY ASSURANCE & TROUBLESHOOTING

- Personally check all film to ensure that it meets high quality standards.
- Use problem-solving skills to resolve personnel issues and patient concerns and handle emergency situations.
- Work directly with administration to assist in team-building efforts.

listing of jobs held

1993–PRESENT AND 1990–1992   **Samaritan Health Service**   Arizona
Excellent job performance and commitment to quality health assessment resulted in re-hire and advancements, involving transfers to several facilities within the Samaritan Health Service organization.

Samaritan Medical Center   Mesa, Arizona
SENIOR RADIOLOGIC TECHNOLOGIST

Page Samaritan Hospital   Page, Arizona
CT—RADIOLOGIC TECHNOLOGIST

Havasu Samaritan Regional Hospital   Lake Havasu City, Arizona
CT—RADIOLOGIC TECHNOLOGIST

Samaritan Medical Center   Phoenix, Arizona
RADIOLOGIC TECHNOLOGIST

1992–1993   **Scottsdale Memorial Hospital**   Scottsdale, Arizona
RADIOLOGY TECHNOLOGIST—SHIFT COORDINATOR
Performed all functions normally associated with the position, including operation of general radiology and portable x-ray equipment, developing film, replenishing chemicals, and resolving patient-relations issues.
Additionally, coordinated shift operations involving scheduling and supervision of staff and troubleshooting.

While this resume does include a listing of jobs held, this approach is much more effective than a traditional chronological listing of jobs.

SYLVIA P. PRIMKIN
404 North 22nd Avenue
Sarasota, Florida 32933
(407) 867-5309

OBJECTIVE

To secure a position as a Certified Surgical Technician.

CREDENTIALS

- National Certification as a Surgical Technologist #000000 by the Liaison Council of Certification for the Surgical Technologist
- Extensive experience in Operating Room procedures
- Ability to communicate a calming influence to patients in distress
- Accomplished and comfortable with all ages from pediatrics to geriatrics.
- Outstanding quality control, double and triple-checking chart documentation for surgery prep

PROFESSIONAL PROFILE

Certified Surgical Technician - 1989 to Present
Surgical Technician - 1984 to 1989
ELLIS HOSPITAL, Sarasota, Florida
- Performed scrub nurse duties for this 500 bed, 11 operating room trauma center, assisting with operations and circulation.
- Prepared instruments, and maintaining count of instruments and swabs.
- Set up operating rooms.
- Provided patients with pre-operative consultations.

Licensed Practical Nurse - 1980 to 1989
DEVEREUX NURSING CENTER, Venice, Florida
- On emergency call three nights each week for this nursing home.
- Performed all scrub and circulation responsibilities.

EDUCATION

Pharmacology Review Course
NEW COLLEGE, Sarasota, Florida

Geriatric Course Certificate, 9 months
WUESTHOFF CLINICAL SCIENCES, Space City, Florida

Operating Room Course Certificate, 12 months
UNIVERSITY OF SOUTH FLORIDA, Tampa, Florida

Associate of Science in Nursing, 2 years
UNIVERSITY OF SOUTH FLORIDA, Tampa, Florida

Older workers should emphasize more recent jobs and avoid dates that show age. This resume uses these techniques well since Sylvia's education was 20 to 30 years ago.

184

Surgical technologist. *Laura A. DeCarlo, CPRW, ICCC; Melbourne, FL*

Service Occupations

Resumes at a Glance

Building and Grounds Clearing and Maintenance Occupations

Food Preparation and Serving Related Occupations

Healthcare Support Occupations

Personal Care and Service Occupations

Protective Service Occupations

Summary of key strengths — effective customer interaction and demonstrated success supervising multiple teams of workers throughout a large facility and/or at numerous sites.

WALTER WILLIAMS

E-mail: Willy99@yahoo.com

522 Oregon Street　　　　　Webster, NY 14580　　　　　585-895-1122

EXECUTIVE HOUSEKEEPER / INSTITUTIONAL CLEANING & MAINTENANCE

Management professional with experience directing daily cleaning and routine maintenance activities in health care and hospitality settings as well as Fortune 500 industrial organizations. Outstanding team-leadership and motivation skills, combined with superb customer-relations capabilities. Demonstrated P/L success supervising multiple teams in large manufacturing complexes and multiple commercial sites. Accountability for multimillion-dollar budgets and wide ranging health and safety issues.

WORK EXPERIENCE

Walter's diverse experience covers health care, hospitality, and industrial facilities.

PAUL MANAGEMENT, LTD., Syracuse, NY　　　　　1999–Present
(Management firm operating Rochester Ritz Carlton Hotel)

Executive Housekeeper
Direct housekeeping operations for 375-room luxury hotel.

- Ensure that hotel guest rooms and public areas meet superior cleanliness standards.
- Manage staffing and scheduling; control costs to meet/exceed budgetary goals.
- Train, supervise, and evaluate housekeeping staff; advance employee development programs.
- Collaborate with fellow department heads and General Manager to ensure objectives are met.
- Establish a safe and secure environment for guests and employees.
- Promote Guest Satisfaction initiatives consistent with hotel mission statement.
- Participate on Management Team to develop and implement operational plans.

METRO BUILDING SERVICES, Rochester, NY　　　　　1997–1999

Resident Manager
Managed Xerox Park Building Services/Janitorial with full charge for 15 million square feet.

- Directed activities of 110 employees, including seven supervisors across A & B shifts. Determined personnel requirements. Hired employees and supervised training.
- Administered budgets up to $1.5M for 52 buildings. Monitored and authorized accounts payable.
- Interacted with building managers and customers to identify and meet specific requirements.
- Responsible for all special projects and demand work.
- Purchased supplies and equipment.
- Facilitated team needs and team-building for each supervisor.
- Participated on team to develop and document company-wide policies and procedures.
- Served on Q1, ISO-9002 team.

FACILITIES SERVICE SYSTEMS (FSS), Rochester, NY　　　　　1995–1997

Supervisor of Building Services
Managed building services for various corporations throughout Rochester. Assignments included:
General Motors — 1,750,000 square feet with 59 union employees.
Eastman Kodak — 2,200,000 square feet and 32 FSS employees.

- Monitored budget and maintained expenses within established parameters.
- Interfaced with building managers and senior management to ensure compliance with building specifications based on contract.
- Managed and directed employees. Maintained employee records.
- As a member of the Training Committee, identified and implemented training requirements.
- Managed facilitation of special building projects.
- Trained self-directed work teams.

185

Executive housekeeper. *Arnold G. Boldt, CPRW, JCTC; Rochester, NY*

WALTER WILLIAMS E-mail: Willy99@yahoo.com

WORK EXPERIENCE (Continued)

ONTARIO BEACH SENIOR LIVING CENTER, Rochester, NY 1993–1995
   <u>Director of Environmental Services</u>
   Managed laundry, housekeeping, purchasing and services for a 239-bed facility.
   - Purchased all housekeeping, linen and chemical supplies.
   - Oversaw 57 employees. Hired, trained, delegated assignments and evaluated performance.
   - Maintained housekeeping and laundry records related to budget, payroll and personnel. Responsible for two million pounds of linen per year.
   - Responsible for hazardous and infectious waste control and ongoing testing for pH, rust and residue chlorine in laundry supply for resident safety.
   - Oversaw overall cleanliness of facility, maintaining New York State standards.
   - Responded to and resolved resident/family concerns regarding laundry or housekeeping.
   - Maintained washers, dryers, floor buffers, Bonnett and dry-method extraction carpet shampooers, auto scrubbers and tow motors.

METHODIST SENIOR COMMUNITY, Rochester, NY 1988–1992
   <u>Housekeeping Superintendent</u>
   - Managed three shifts of fifteen employees. Coordinated scheduling. Submitted yearly performance reports and made wage recommendations.
   - Managed employees in Community Service Sentencing Program. Assigned responsibilities to program participants, monitored work, and submitted written reports to courts.
   - Controlled inventory for all paper goods and cleaning products.
   - Filled in for Maintenance Manager in his absence.

PROFESSIONAL DEVELOPMENT/TRAINING

Regularly attend courses, workshops and seminars to keep current and for personal development.
   OSHA Trainer (40-hour training course) 1997
   Tow Motor Licensed Operator 1996
   Self-directed Work Team Training 1996
   OSHA Bloodborne Pathogen Training 1993
   Third Class Stationary Engineers Course 1991
   Master Series Carpet Care Technician School 1989
   General Electric Lighting Institute 1986

EDUCATION

   Brighton Business Institute (Continuing Education); Rochester, NY
   Major: Business Management. Minor: Computer Science.

   Villa Buena College (Continuing Education); Contra Vista, CA
   Major: Criminal Justice. Minor: Security Administration.

PERSONAL

   Basketball Coach — Catholic Youth Organization 1987–1996
   Managed a fund raising campaign that resulted in $18K for international basketball tournament involving a ten-day trip to France with a high school team.

References available upon request.

Kevin used this resume to apply for a position in golf-course management and groundskeeping in the east. He was offered and accepted the position!

KEVIN HARTLEY

3203 West Loop 289 #155
Lubbock, Texas 79407

806.793.4242
khartley@aol.com

PROFESSIONAL QUALIFICATIONS

Fifteen years' experience in the turf grass industry with ten years' experience in golf course management, maintenance, and design. Proven expertise in management of finances and personnel. Strong interpersonal and communication skills. Adaptable to ever-changing situations. Excellent time-management and organizational skills. Formal education includes an Associate Degree in Applied Science in Golf Course Technology, Landscape Maintenance, Greenhouse Operations, and Golf Shop Operations.

- Over 7 years' management experience for a city-owned, 9-hole golf course.
- Maintained farm operation of $400,000 to $500,000 in sparse times by reducing costs.
- Selected, trained, and supervised 2 to 15 employees.
- Managed budgets from $120,000 to $500,000.
- Trained others to complete detail-oriented tasks in a timely manner.
- Successfully designed, implemented, and coordinated golf course and landscape projects.

CAREER SUMMARY: *) His work experience was not with prestigious courses but was solid and was coupled with job-specific training.*

Club Manager, Superintendent, and Assistant Superintendent
Island Oakes Golf Club, Idalou, Texas

1993 to present

Started as Assistant Superintendent; promoted within 1 year to Superintendent and then in the last two years advanced to Club Manager for a city-owned golf course. As personnel were trimmed from seven to three employees, assumed additional responsibilities including budgeting, preparing accounting records, purchasing, maintaining golf course, selecting personnel, training, and supervising inside sales at the pro shop.

- Supervised and spearheaded the golf course operation through numerous personnel reductions.
- Performed and/or supervised all club and golf course operations.
- Developed valuable communication skills, strong public relations abilities, and excellent rapport with people.
- Created a pleasant golfing atmosphere.
- Solicited public donations with a 20% increase in the second year.
- Formed liaisons with city, county, and state organizations.

Partner
Course Design, Snyder, Texas

1990 to 1993

One of three partners in the development and implementation of a firm specializing in golf course design/construction and irrigation design/installation. Solicited, bid, and completed the work. Developed the business to $125,000 annually. Projects completed:

- Designed and laid out 9-hole addition, Yoakum County Golf Course, Plains, Texas.
- Designed and renovated putting green and driving range tee box, Greentree Country Club, Midland, Texas.

186

Groundskeeper. *Lynn Hughes, MA, CPRW, CEIP; Lubbock, TX*

KEVIN HARTLEY

PAGE TWO

CAREER SUMMARY (CONTINUED):

- Designed and constructed retaining wall around lake, Greentree Country Club, Midland, Texas.
- Designed and laid out renovation of 9 greens at Levelland Country Club, Levelland, Texas.

Owner
Lawnscapes of Lubbock, Lubbock, Texas   1985 to 1989

Established a design, installation, and maintenance company for lawns and landscapes. Started the business with no customers and built it to over 220 clients.

- Hired, trained, and supervised five 3-person crews.
- Developed strong customer loyalty by providing exceptional service.

Owner/Operator
Hartley Farms, Farwell, Texas   1976 to 1985

Operated and owned family farm of 960 acres. Hired, trained, and supervised four full-time employees. Farmed corn, cotton, and wheat on land irrigated by 6 pivot circles. Teamed with an attorney brother, an accountant brother, and father to run the operation for 9 years.

- Successfully managed the $400,000 to $500,000 annual budget.
- Worked with the Agriculture Stabilization Conservation Service.

EDUCATION:

Associate Degree in Applied Science, Western Texas College, Snyder, Texas   1992
Earned degrees in the following:

- **Golf Course Technology**
- **Landscape Maintenance**   ) *job-specific training*
- **Greenhouse Operations**
- **Golf Shop Operations**

General Business (earned junior standing), Texas Tech University, Lubbock, Texas   1976

PROFESSIONAL AFFILIATIONS:

Member of West Texas Golf Course Superintendent's Association
Member of Golf Course Superintendent's Association of America
Former member of the Farwell Jaycees
Past member of the Plains Cotton Co-op Association

References Available Upon Request

Bill W. Hixson

2504 Cardinal Court
Arlington, TX 76018

(682) 555-0302
billhixson@choice.net

PROFILE

Management professional with expertise in the pest-control industry and a track record of leading **professional, profitable, customer-focused service businesses.** Track record of **turnaround management** through close attention to **financial management, operating procedures,** and **customer service.**

PROFESSIONAL EXPERIENCE

PEST ARREST — Arlington, TX   2000–2002

Real Estate Inspector

- Launched and managed business providing termite inspection services to the real estate industry.

- Built successful business within niche industry by forging relationships with major real estate agencies.

- Negotiated profitable sale of the business to a national franchise.

ORKIN EXTERMINATING — Dallas, TX   1988–2000

Branch Manager, 1998–2000

- Took over underperforming branch and improved sales revenue, profitability, morale, accountability, and communication. Improved hiring and training.

- Reduced customer "allowance" for nonperformed services from 25% to zero. Doubled number of routes.

Service Manager, 1995–1998

- Restored relationship with key client by eliminating backlog and providing responsive customer service.

- Delivered 50% profit margins by increasing production during primary service season.

Sales, 1988–1995

EDUCATION

B.S. Business Management: Texas A&M University, 1985

Concentration in Marketing including numerous graduate-level marketing courses.

PROFESSIONAL AFFILIATIONS

National Pest Control Association

Texas Pest Control Association

National Pest Management Association

A straightforward resume for a man who had held several service and management positions in the pest-control industry.

187

Pest controller. *Louise M. Kursmark, CPRW, JCTC, CEIP, CCM; Cincinnati, OH*

MICHELE LASSEAU

555 S. Benchside Dr. Tempe, AZ 55555 [555] 000-0000
topchef@earthlink.net

SUMMARY OF QUALIFICATIONS

- ∝ Over 15 years experience as Executive/Corporate Chef/Consultant.
- ∝ Experienced culinary instructor at Scottsdale Culinary Institute.
- ∝ Developed recipes/menus restaurant concepts.
- ∝ Catered simultaneous functions for up to 250,000 people.
- ∝ Provided Executive Chef services/catering for Super Bowl XXXVI.
- ∝ Opened new properties employing seafood/Northern Italian Bistro concepts.
- ∝ Traveled throughout the Eastern U.S. to establish services at hotel properties.
- ∝ Designed/developed culinary classes for school/retail outlet.
- ∝ Consulted with owners on opening new stores.
- ∝ Controlled costs/inventory/labor.
- ∝ Interviewed/hired/trained/supervised/evaluated employees.
- ∝ Prepared food service for numerous venues from parking lot events to Black Tie affairs.
- ∝ Excellent communication skills...creative...innovative...team leader...dedicated...organized...detail oriented...decision maker...problem solver....

EDUCATION

CULINARY INSTITUTE OF AMERICA—Hyde Park, NY
AOS Degree

UNIVERSITY OF GEORGIA EXTENSION PROGRAM—Atlanta, GA
Module Teaching Techniques: Completed 30 Modules
Additional Course Work in Nutrition

Lack of dates gives no indication of age.

Externships:
- ∝ Hugo's West Hyatt Regency Hotel—Atlanta, GA
- ∝ Alfredo's Restaurant—Myrtle Beach Hilton, SC
- ∝ Top of the Crown Restaurant, Crown Center Hotel, Kansas City, MO

188

Chef. *Fran Holsinger; Tempe, AZ*

This resume presents a professional, sophisticated appearance that is appropriate for the job.

Michelle Lasseau, page 2

PROFESSIONAL HIGHLIGHTS

EXECUTIVE CHEF

- ∝ Facilitated food/beverage service for NFL Arizona Cardinals/ASU football games.
- ∝ Directed food/beverage service for University Club/Gammage Theater/Sun Dome Theater/ASU Athletic Department: football/men's and women's basketball/baseball training tables.
- ∝ Wrote/costed menus for 5,000 spectators/game.
- ∝ Catered special functions.
- ∝ Supervised 70 employees.
- ∝ Functioned as Corporate Chef; conceptualized/set up 15 different restaurants/hotel operations throughout the Eastern U.S.
- ∝ Served as personal chef for CEO of Eastman-Kodak.
- ∝ Opened new properties with seafood/Fedora concept:
  Chequers Bar & Grill—Atlanta
  Devon Seafood Grill—Washington, D.C. and Houston
  Bristol Bar & Grill—Minneapolis
  Fedora Cafe—Miami and Tyson's Corner, VA

INSTRUCTOR

- ∝ Taught Basic/intermediate/Advanced Classical Cuisine.
- ∝ Provided personalized approach through small classes.
- ∝ Developed/planned curricula.
- ∝ Created culinary program for new training school.
- ∝ Set up/instructed classes for retail kitchen outlet.
- ∝ Furnished services for Scottsdale Culinary Institutes enterprises: L'Ecole restaurant/banquet/catered events/saucier.

EMPLOYERS

ART INSTITUTE OF PHOENIX—Phoenix, AZ
Chef/Instructor, 2000 to Present

FINE HOST CORPORATION—Tempe, AZ
Executive Chef, 1999 to 2000

SCOTTSDALE CULINARY INSTITUTE—Scottsdale, AZ
Chef/instructor, 1992 to 1999

B. F. SAUL—Chevy Chase, MD
GILBERT/ROBINSON—Kansas City, MO
Corporate Chef, 1991 to 1992/1990 to 1992

AWARDS

CULINARY ART SHOWS:
- ∝ Tucson, 2002
- ∝ South Carolina, 2001
- ∝ Atlanta, 2000
- ∝ Houston 1999
- ∝ New York 1998

Carla Rossini

55555 Bedford Drive
Camarillo, California 93010
Tel: (805) 555-1111
E-Mail: chefxtrodnry@yahoo.com

professional profile

CERTIFIED EXECUTIVE CHEF — American Culinary Federation (ACF)
- Over 10 years' food preparation and kitchen management experience ranging from high-volume buffet (2000+ meals per day), to hotel, to intimate bistro settings
- California School of Culinary Arts "Le Cordon Bleu" graduate
- Continuing education in contemporary cuisine through Culinary Institute of America (CIA)
- Management expertise includes cost- and quality-control metrics, food-service management, dining-room service and supervision, beverage management, and management information systems (MIS/PC)
- Culinary proficiency in tableside cooking, baking / pastry / patisserie, charcuterie, cold buffet preparation, nutritional / dietary cooking, menu development, global cuisine (Classical, Nouvelle, American, Pacific Rim, Middle East, Latin), presentation, and environmental design
- Multilingual (English, Spanish, Italian) — Team Builder — Thrive in a high-energy environment

influences

- Mary Sue Milliken/Susan Feniger *(for their passionate seasonings)*
- Iron Chef Masaharu Morimoto *(for his food artistry and spontaneity)*
- Wolfgang Puck *(for his marketing genius and interior design)*
- Julia Child *(who brought classical cuisine into all our homes via TV)*

professional experience

EXECUTIVE CHEF (1998–PRESENT), L'AUGBERGINE RESTAURANT, CAMARILLO, CA
[Provençal and Mediterranean cuisine with a French country inn theme]
Collaborate with owner, sommelier, pastry and sous chefs on introduction of one new item weekly. Monitor market/vendor prices for ticket adjustment. Implement customer-driven improvements within cost constraints.
- Created a steady "happy hour" following by writing a press release describing our cold table (tapas, antjitos, hors-d'oeuvres) as "fast food for the seasoned palate."
- Planted a vegetable garden to ensure a ready supply of the freshest herbs and seasonal vegetables. The garden also increased the ambiance of the patio dining area.
- Added 4 outdoor natural gas heaters: Installation costs were recouped within 2 months of installation. Clientele doubled during traditionally slower winter months.

recent inventions

- *Tartare of belly tuna with Thai chili-infused pine nut oil*
- *Curaçao-lime sorbet*

ROOM SERVICE CHEF (HEAD) & KITCHEN MANAGER (1996–1998), RADISSON RESORT HOTEL, OXNARD, CA *[1,000+ room hotel and spa]*
Demonstrated versatility in delivering on-demand, 24/7, VIP and unusual orders from ingredients on hand. Streamlined kitchen procedures and supply usage in terms of product quality, efficiency, and economy. Directed and trained 20–30 food service employees in food preparation, presentation, and sanitation.
- Implemented an Excel first in/first out (FIFO) system to insure ingredient freshness.
- Introduced a Pacific Rim menu that resulted in 25% jump in patronage by Asian customers.
- Promoted to Head Room Service Chef & Kitchen Manager from Assistant in 1996.

FOOD SERVICE MANAGER (1990–1995), FURR'S CAFETERIA, OXNARD, CALIFORNIA
Supervisor for over 50 employees in a public cafeteria/buffet serving up to 2000 diners daily. Oversaw and trained food-service workers in food preparation, area sanitation, and personal hygiene. Scheduled work shifts. Assessed employee performance and resolved work-related problems. Controlled expenditures (e.g., food, supplies, utilities, and salaries) for conformance with corporate financial parameters. Ensured all activities reflected well on the company standards.
- Raised establishment's County sanitation rating from B to A within first 3 months on board.
- Instituted a local employee incentive award in the form of a paid day off for the employee of the quarter.

professional training

CALIFORNIA SCHOOL OF CULINARY ARTS, PASADENA, CA (1995–1996)
- Le Cordon Bleu Culinary Arts Program — Graduate

THE CULINARY INSTITUTE OF AMERICA (CIA) AT GREYSTONE, ST. HELENA, CA
- Continuing Education toward the American Culinary Federation (ACF) Master Chef Certificate expected 2003

The creative format of this resume met the challenge of showcasing this chef's superb education, creativity, and accomplishments.

189

Chef. *Roleta Fowler, CPRW, CEIP; Fillmore, CA*

Milton had never had a resume. This one—his first—reveals layer upon layer of accomplishments.

MILTON B. KERZNER

405 Spruce Street, Point Pleasant, NJ 08742 ❖ (732) 899-1456 ❖ mkerzner@gbsias.com

SENIOR OPERATING AND MANAGEMENT PROFESSIONAL / EXECUTIVE CHEF
Consistently successful in maximizing sales, service, satisfaction, and bottom-line profits.

Creative, entrepreneurial, and visionary business leader with 20 years of senior operating and general management experience. Combine cross-functional expertise in strategic planning, business development, operations management, and technology implementation to transition upscale food and beverage facilities into top-flight establishments. Create successful business ventures to meet innovative market-niche demands.

Award-winning chef with a dynamic career reflecting expertise in delivering solid and sustainable financial gains in start-up and turnaround businesses. Deliver multimillion-dollar revenues through profit-and-loss management, human resource training and administration, facilities management and maintenance, purchasing and inventory management, multi-site operations management, customer service and guest relations, food and labor cost controls, promotions and special events, public relations and media affairs, and productivity and efficiency improvements.

Dynamic negotiation, presentation, and customer-management skills. Skilled problem solver and decision maker, with a reputation throughout the tristate area for industry and operations expertise.

PROFESSIONAL EXPERIENCE
ANTHONY'S BRIELLE HOUSE, Brielle, NJ (1990–Present)
Fast-track promotions through a series of increasingly responsible management positions. Advanced rapidly based on consistent increases in facility revenues and customer satisfaction. Key to facility enjoying YTD gross sales that increased daily for seven consecutive years.

Executive Chef / General Manager
Full P&L responsibility for the strategic planning, financial affairs, and overall operations of this upscale restaurant. Scope of responsibility is diverse and includes operating and capital budgeting, regulatory compliance, purchasing, human resources, facilities management, food and beverage operations, sales and retail operations, and customer services.

- ❖ Redesigned back-of-the-house operations, implemented incentives to support customer service objectives, and delivered reductions in operating costs.
- ❖ Expanded service programs to include special promotions, such as wine flights and food pairings.
- ❖ Transitioned facility from a single-cuisine northern Italian restaurant to include Asian-infusion techniques, as well as American Regional and eclectic specialties.
- ❖ Increased wine sales by 20 percent.
- ❖ Implemented stringent labor-cost controls.
- ❖ Achieved / surpassed all food and beverage revenue objectives.
- ❖ Integrated point-of-sale computer system into financial and record-keeping process.
- ❖ Streamlined administrative infrastructure, integrated similar functions, reduced staffing requirements, incorporated spot purchasing, and effected dramatic annual cost savings.
- ❖ Captured revenues with effective vendor negotiations and contract administration.
- ❖ Designed promotional and marketing communications to improve customer retention.
- ❖ Created unique menu items and service standards that drove strong gains in customer service throughout front-of-the-house operations.

190

Chef. *Nina Ebert, CPRW; Toms River, NJ*

Milton B. Kerzner ❖ Page 2 ❖ (732) 899-1456 ❖ mkerzner@gbsias.com

SIZZLING STEAKS, East Rutherford, NJ (1988–1990)
Executive Chef / General Manager

- ❖ Sales and service responsibility for 500 dinners nightly.
- ❖ Despite highly competitive arena of casual dining facilities, succeeded in driving lunch sale revenues.

YOUR PERSONAL CHEF, INC., Clifton, NJ (1986–1988)
Owner / Founder

- ❖ Challenged to increase club sales within this upscale off-premise personal catering company servicing upper-echelon individuals and large-scale events throughout Bergen County.

R and R MANAGEMENT COMPANY, INC., East Rutherford, NJ (1982–1986)
Fast track promotions through a series of highly responsible positions in facilities owned by R and R Management as **Landmark II Executive Chef,** East Rutherford, NJ (8/85–10/86), **Riggers and Razzles General Manager / Executive Manager,** Seaside Heights, NJ (2/85–8/85), **Landmark II Off-Premise Catering Executive Chef / Sales Associate,** East Rutherford, NJ (9/84–2/85), **Riggers and Razzles Executive Chef,** Seaside Heights, NJ (3/83–9/84), and **Harpers Assistant General Manager,** Union, NJ (8/82–2/83)

- ❖ Restructured menu pricing and improved profit on the average ticket.
- ❖ Standardized portion-control procedures to reduce escalating costs.
- ❖ Administered million-dollar food budgets.
- ❖ Dramatically increased annual menu and liquor sales.
- ❖ Instituted cocktail hour buffets, early-bird dinners, theme menus, and promotional events that increased sales and exceeded projections.

THE WALDORF–ASTORIA HOTEL, New York, NY (1981–1982)
First Commis to Commis De Tournant

- ❖ At 19 years old, the youngest person to hold this position, achieved within three months of hire.
- ❖ Cooked for banquets of up to 1,400 patrons.
- ❖ Worked throughout one main kitchen, four restaurant kitchens, and three catering kitchens, and fulfilled "cooked to order" room-service requests.
- ❖ Served foreign and domestic dignitaries, heads of state, and many renowned individuals.

EDUCATION
JOHNSON AND WALES UNIVERSITY, Providence, RI
Associate of Science, Culinary Arts, May 1981 (3.7 GPA)
Accomplished two-year program in an accelerated 12-month program.

HONORS / AWARDS
International Food Service Executive Chef Award
Statler Hilton Award

CERTIFICATION
Sanitation and Supervision

Milton's ultimate goal was to be rehired by the Waldorf-Astoria — and he was!

OTHER INFORMATION
TV News 12 New Jersey Featured Guest — 1999 and 2001 (Tape available for review)

This resume shows a combination of business achievements and creative food preparation — both of which are essential for a successful food-service operation.

Antonio Ramirez

11 Crescent Drive, Totowa, NJ 07422 ◆ (908) 844-7788

Executive Sous Chef

Large-Facility Banquet Catering — Multi-Event Management
Staff Training & Development — Innovative Preparation and Presentation

High-performance, resourceful professional with 15+ years' food preparation and kitchen staff management experience. Award-winning career distinguished by diverse cooking experiences, gained by shoulder-to-shoulder association with noted international and local chefs. In-depth knowledge of basic technique including seafood, meat and pastry preparation. Highly qualified for Executive Chef with large-scale catering operation. Fluent in English and Spanish. Recognized for:

◆ Fusing eclectic international ingredients to create fresh, appealing cuisine blendings.

◆ Establishing and demanding first-class service and food-quality standards.

◆ Improving productivity and boosting profits through management of ethnically mixed staffs.

Professional Experience

Brentwood House, Far Hills, NJ   1993–present
Family-owned dual operation of on- and off-site banquet catering hall, regarded statewide as a premier facility, and of smoked salmon factory, nationally distributed and rated #1 by Food and Wine magazine.

Fast-tracked through **Salmon Fillet Master** to **Manager/Production Chief** and **Garde Manger Chef**. Selected for **Executive Sous Chef** within first year, based upon talent and performance. Scope of responsibility includes food preparation and staff management for up to 350 weddings per year, 10 annual non-profit agency fundraisers, numerous trade shows, seminars, holiday parties and business meetings. Challenged with concurrent responsibility for elegant Sunday brunches, serving up to 1,200 meals over 6-hour period. Delegate kitchen assignments for 5 chefs and prep staff of 10.

example of a business achievement

◆ Boosted Sunday brunch profit by 89% within 6 months by introducing well-received variations on standard fare.

◆ Invited to prepare special dishes at annual James Beard Culinary Awards in NYC (1995, 1996, 1997 and 1998).

example of creative food preparation

◆ Organized prestigious annual *Wild Game Dinner,* building creative menus from locally supplied goods for internationally renowned chefs.

◆ Created several new smoked-salmon specialties that immediately went into production for nationwide distribution.

◆ Introduced several popular dishes, such as *Sauteed Chicken Ramirez,* which is served at all wedding cocktail hours.

◆ Cater to clientele's specific requirements by preparing dietary-sensitive menus.

◆ Earned numerous awards for restaurant including *1998 Gold Plate Award* and *1998 Restaurateur of the Year.* Featured in many newspaper and magazine articles.

◆ First-time recipient of restaurant's Recognition Award for exemplary creativity, planning and team leadership along with *Perfect Attendance Award* (five years).

Previous experience (1979 to 1993) includes chef and wholesale/retail sales at several New York City restaurants, world-famous fish market and upscale gourmet-food store.

191

Sous chef. *Meg Guiseppi, CPRW; Andover, NJ*

CHARLES A. SMYTH
412 Main Street
New York, New York 10019
(212) 555-6908

Food Service Manager combining knowledge acquired through educational training with extensive background in food service, staff management, contract negotiations, vendor selection, budget administration, and security/loss control.

A victim of corporate "downsizing," Charles had changed careers from inventory control manager to food service manager (resume writer's comments).

QUALIFICATION HIGHLIGHTS

all based on his recent experience in food service

- American Culinary Foundation certified in:
  - Management Ethics and Team Supervision
  - Nutritional Food Preparation and Menu Planning
  - Controlling Food Cost
  - Serving Safe Food and Sanitation Regulations

- Catering director for private sportsmen's club special events
  - Organize food service of annual fund raiser for 300 members and family
  - Oversee all kitchen operations; handle merchandising, ordering, and purchasing

- Coordinate parties and events for approximately 5000 people
  - Solicit and review vendor bids, conduct contract negations, submit recommendations to senior management
  - Administer $300,000 annual budget ($70,000 earmarked for special events)

- Act as liaison between corporation and contractors
  - Oversee Marriott Food Service deliveries to three satellite sites

- Provide performance evaluations of internal and external personnel to human resources
  - Address personnel problems

- Security and loss prevention:
  - Monitor premises, perform surveillance watch to detect internal theft and espionage
  - Manage shipping/receiving staff and contracted security force

EMPLOYMENT HISTORY

Assistant Chef	Catalano's Pasta Garden, Hopewell Junction, NY	1996-Present
Assistant to Chef	Plum Tomato Restaurant, Hopewell Junction, NY	1995
Catering Director	Whortlekill Sportsmen's Club, Hopewell Junction, NY	1985-Present
Senior Administrative Specialist	IBM Corporation, Yorktown, NY	1985-1995
Senior Security Officer	"	"

EDUCATION/SPECIALIZED TRAINING
Culinary Institute of America, Hyde Park, NY
American Culinary Foundation Certification Program

His previous career is not described since it is not relevant now.

1995

CERTIFICATION
Department of Transportation Hazardous Material Transportation
American Red Cross CPR and First Aid

192

Food and beverage service. *Marian K. Kozlowski, MBA; Poughkeepsie, NY*

*The border design adds visual
interest to this resume*

Courtney A. Bellany

Greenwood Rd., Box 1790, Murietta, CA 92467, (555) 357-9752

Overview: Flexible and competent Dental Assistant with experience in 4-handed dentistry, radiology and front office duties. Excels in patient relations/ education areas while respecting time constraints. Documented record of initiative and commitment to a team approach in all situations.

*A simple but effective
review of what she can do*

Qualifications:

- State of California Dental Radiology License and CPR Certified

- Experienced in 4-handed dentistry—taking impressions, pouring models, making temporary crowns, and assisting dentists with extractions, fillings, dentures, and sealants

- Skilled in completing patient medical histories (including some BPs and charting) and taking dental x-rays

- Front office skills include appointment scheduling, insurance billing, filing, computerized patient billing, and telephone/personal communications

Education/Professional Development:

Degree: Dental Assistant
Murrieta Valley Technical College, Murrieta, CA
1992 Graduate; Dean's List

Conferences: Yankee Dental Conference, Boston, Massachusetts
Dentures, Nutrition, and Midwest Handpiece workshops

Seminars: Emergencies in the Dental Office, Composite Bonding, Credit Management and OSHA seminars/lectures

Related Employment:

Dental Assistant	Cathy Hoover, D.D.S., Murrieta, CA	3/94 - present
Dental Assistant	Fred Smith, D.D.S., Open Beach, CA	4/92 - 3/93

193

Dental assistant. *Elizabeth M. Carey, CPRW; Waterville, ME*

Jennifer gained most of her dental skills in school and while externing, so she wisely emphasizes her skills and experience in the most effective way.

JENNIFER R. CROMLEY
2987 Main Street
Davison, Michigan 48423

810-555-3379

DENTAL ASSISTANT

SUMMARY OF SKILLS

- Adult and pediatric dentistry
- 4-handed dentistry
- Surgical assisting
- Endodontics including placement of rubber dams
- Fabrication and placement of temporary restorations

- Orthodontics
- Bone grafting
- Tissue-free grafting
- Extractions
- Impressions
- Radiographs
- Use of Goretex

- Placement of sealants
- Amalgams
- Bridges
- Dentures
- Occlusal guards
- Lab work

ADDITIONAL EXPERIENCE

- Consult with patients to explain procedures and provide postoperative instructions.
- Generate patient treatment plans; prepare general practitioner reports at doctor's direction.
- Take and record the medical and dental histories of patients.
- Maintain understanding of current OSHA regulations and sterilization procedures.
- Oversee cleanliness of operatories and instruments; ensure supplies are ordered and stocked.
- Interact with patients to develop trust and make them comfortable; calm distressed patients.
- Maintain contact with patients through use of call book.
- Schedule appointments; promptly rebook canceled appointments.
- Utilize computerized system to bill patients and insurance companies; process payments.
- Quote fees to patients and assist them in making payment arrangements.
- Reconcile cash drawer and prepare bank deposits.

CERTIFICATIONS

- **C.D.A.** - Certified Dental Assistant
- **R.D.A.** - Registered Dental Assistant

EDUCATION

Delta College • University Center, MI   1995
Associate of Applied Science with Honors
Dental Assisting Certification

PROFESSIONAL EXPERIENCE

Robert Short, D.D.S., Periodontist - Short Dental Group • Burton, MI	1995-Present
Mary Ann Roberts, D.D.S., Periodontist • Flint, MI	1995
John Stone, D.D.S. [Externship] • Burton, MI	1995
Richard Anderson, D.D.S. [Externship] • Grand Blanc, MI	1995

AFFILIATIONS

- American Dental Assistant Association
- Genesee District Dental Assistant Association

COMMUNITY INVOLVEMENT

- Volunteer - Humane Society of Genesee County

References available on request.

194

Dental assistant. *Janet L. Beckstrom; Flint, MI*

MARIANNE HIGGINS DOYLE

8400 Industrial Parkway
Plain City, Indiana 00000
(000) 000-0000

OBJECTIVE

Medical Assistant/Technologist position for a private practice.

PROFESSIONAL EXPERIENCE

Patient Service Technician/Unit Clerk   1989 - Present
COMMUNITY HOSPITAL, Coronary Care Unit, Columbus, Indiana

- Order lab work and x-rays
- Prioritize patient daily care according to acuity and scheduled patient procedures
- Assist patients with A.M. care, take vital signs, prep for procedures, draw blood and obtain specimens
- Maintain and set-up patient rooms
- Perform preventive maintenance on emergency equipment
- Assist with patient and family education
- Assist R.N. with sterile and non sterile dressing changes
- Perform EKGs
- Trained in Phlebotomy
- Utilize PC to enter and retrieve patient data
- Answer multi-line phone, operate fax and copy machine

Office Assistant   (6-month part-time position) 1995
HERBERT FOX, M. D., Columbus, Indiana

- Answered phone, scheduled patients
- Greeted patients
- Updated patient charts

With no formal education or credentials as a medical assistant, Marianne wisely emphasizes her related work and training experience.

EDUCATION

In-house training programs, <u>Community Hospital</u>
EKG, 1998
Phlebotomy, 1998
Tech Class, 1992
Unit Clerk Class, 1990
Nursing Assistant Class, 1989
CPR Certified, since 1989

<u>Columbus State Community College</u>
Computer training: Word Perfect I, Certificate 1995

<u>The Ohio State University</u>
Major: Pre-veterinarian, 1989-1990

195

Medical assistant. *Susan D. Higgins, CPRW; Plain City, OH*

David E. Pierson
(812) 882-4542

1309 Scott Street
Vincennes, Indiana 47591

All are adaptive skills of great importance in his desired job

PROFILE

{
- O Open, honest, and self-motivated.
- O Gain tremendous satisfaction from meeting patient's needs and seeing positive results from quality care.
- O Dependable, trustworthy and adaptable, a quality team member.

EDUCATION

Associate Degree in Nursing (May 1995). *Vincennes University.*
Vincennes, Indiana. Licensure in July 1995. GPA 3.575
B. S. Degree in Agriculture Finance. *Purdue University.*
West Lafayette, Indiana: 1987

SEMINARS

HIV/AIDS Seminar (6 hours). *Indiana State University.*
Sponsored by Riverfront Home Health, Inc. Linton, Indiana: 1994
Attended monthly inservice seminars on various current topics involving patient care.

EXPERIENCE

1993 - Present

Certified Home Health Aide. *Riverfront Home Health, Inc.*
Vincennes, Indiana.
Apply nursing skills toward quality patient care. Complete records and attend meetings as required. Train new personnel on existing cases. Appointed to Quality Improvement Committee to assist in meeting Joint Commission accreditation.

- O Adaptable, able to discern needs of patient and provide appropriate care.
- O Encourage active mental and physical involvement of clients.
- O Establish rapport and respects privacy of clients and family members.
- O Dedicated to the personal integrity of all clients, going the extra mile to see that dignity of client is preserved in the home environment as long as possible.

196

Nursing and psychiatric aide. *Colleen S. Jaracz; Vincennes, IN*

David is a good example of someone who had a four-year degree but went back to school to get a two-year degree in order to change careers.

David E. Pierson

(Page 2)

1991-1992	**Certified Nursing Assistant**. *Willow Manor Convalescent Center, Inc.* Vincennes, Indiana. Provided hygiene, feeding, and other personal care to dependent residents in long-term care setting. Worked primarily on the skilled care unit. Employee of the month, July 1992.

○ Enjoyed the challenge of organizing and coordinating quality patient care to consistently achieve the most benefits possible - continued throughout the limited time constraints of the position.

1991-1992	**Representative**. *Marketing and Management Company*. Evansville, Indiana. Set up individual retirement accounts and insurance sales.

1988-1991	**Assistant Manager**. *American General Finance Company*. Vincennes, Indiana. Supervise employees and performed office manager duties as necessary. Knowledgeable in insurance sales, loans, collections, and the public relations aspect of the business.

COMMUNITY ACTIVITIES

President in charge of membership development and Rose Day. *Vincennes Lions Club*. Provides eye glasses for families who cannot afford them.

HONORS

National Dean's List: 1993.
Recipient of the Gregory Kimmel Memorial Scholarship for Nursing: 1993.

REFERENCES

References furnished upon request.

Nellie Mercy, C.O.T.A.

Certified Occupational Therapy Assistant

2300 N. 700 E.
Anytown, Indiana 46121
(317) 259-4360

Expertise: Rehab Specialist

Two bulleted columns

Strengths:

- Rehab equipment sales
- Excellent organizational skills
- Exceptional memory
- Effect good judgment decisions
- Thorough assessment of patient needs

- Strong clinical background
- Attention to detail
- Experienced communicator
- Genuine patient advocate
- Skilled leader

Experience

Notice the variety of type and format to vary the look and increase readability

Only Care Services, Inc., Indianapolis, Indiana   5/88-Present

REHAB EQUIPMENT SPECIALIST: — *CAPS*

Leader in developing Rehab Division for Onlycare Services, Inc. Opened Indianapolis Division (1990) and expanded to $1.2 million Indiana territory (1995). Manage customer service representative, and create new business with hospitals and medical facilities. *Bold face*

Team with physicians and therapists to ascertain proper rehab medical equipment. Evaluate and measure customers for wheelchairs and seating. Design custom seating orthotics; oversee fabrication. Deliver equipment to clients and ensure proper fitting. Write letters of medical necessity to secure funding, and communicate with case managers to clarify equipment need. Generate billing and assist with inventory control.

- Conduct wheelchair clinics in several facilities throughout Indiana.
- Frequent guest lecturer at University of Indianapolis.
- Train and educate occupational/physical therapists and insurance case managers. *Bullets*
- Extensive clinical assessment to create solutions for patients' needs.

State Home Health Services, Indianapolis, Indiana   118/190   7/87-7/88

REHAB SPECIALIST: Marketing of customized wheelchair seating devices. Supervised design technicians and customer service representative; in charge of quality control.

- Assisted in development of a growth-adjustable seating system.
- Expanded territory by 200%.

Using specific numbers to support a results orientation is important

197

Occupational therapy assistant. *Carole E. Pefley, CPRW; Indianapolis, IN*

a second page of a two-page resume should fill the page, as this one does. You can do this by adding more details and white space.

Nellie Mercy, C.O.T.A.

-2-

Rehab Engineering and Repair, Inc., Danville, Indiana   10/85-7/87

REHAB SPECIALIST: Marketing of customized wheelchair seating devices. In charge of financial management; made major business decisions to facilitate ongoing growth and development.

- Increased business by 400%.
- Co-owner, 5/86; sold business to State Home Health Services.

Union Hospital of Indiana, Inc. Indianapolis, Indiana   11/80-10/85

CERTIFIED OCCUPATIONAL THERAPY ASSISTANT:
- Developed customized seating program.
- Primary therapist for Muscular Dystrophy Association Clinic; implemented Saturday treatment program.

Education

Associate Degree, Occupational Therapy; Indiana University, Indianapolis, Indiana; 1979.

Certifications

- Certified Seating Specialist, University of Tennessee.
- LaBac Certification
- Pindot, Jay, Roho, Avanti, Silhouette, and Cozy Craft Seating Certification

Specialized Training

- Customer-Oriented Selling
- Hearst Power and Manual School
- Franklin Time Management Seminar
- Nero Developmental Treatment Conference, Indianapolis, Indiana
- Treatment of Spinal Cord Patients, Rehab Institute of Chicago

Professional Organizations

- National Registry of Rehab Technology Suppliers
- American Occupational Therapy Association
- United Cerebral Palsy Association
- Muscular Dystrophy Association

Since she has relevant training and work experience, Robin uses a Chronological Resume to best present her move up a career ladder.

ROBIN A. PTA

910 Yellow Brick Dr. Oz, KS 00000 **(913) 555-5768**

OBJECTIVE: To contribute my skills and knowledge in Physical Therapy by continuing my career as a Physical Therapist Assistant in a challenging, team-oriented environment.

PROFILE:

Putting Key accomplishments up front gets them noticed

- ◆ **Direct Care Provider of the Quarter**
- ◆ **Three-time recipient of the Star Therapist Award by three different facilities.**
- ◆ **Team player experienced with working with other rehabilitative disciplines to incorporate patients' functional activities.**
- ◆ **Highly organized individual with excellent time-management skills and strong work ethics.**

EXPERIENCE:
1993–Present

PHYSICAL THERAPIST ASSISTANT *WIZCARE, INC., LION'S DEN, PA.* Currently work as float between 13 facilities in the Kansas City and surrounding areas. Provide patients with therapeutic exercise, and transfer and mobility training, using modalities such as ultrasound, gait training equipment, and hot and cold packs. Also provide wound care with sharp debridement. Supervise two Restorative Aides.

- ◆ Train as many as 50 staff members at a time on certain rehabilitative aspects of patient care, such as proper body mechanics, proper wheelchair positioning, use of gait belts, and infection control.
- ◆ Teach patients' family members how to assist the patients without hindering independence and self-confidence.
- ◆ Teach patients how to be functional in their living environments and make suggestions for changes in the home to increase independence.
- ◆ Document patients' daily progress for Medicare, insurance and medical records, as well as reassess plans of care and make treatment suggestions with Registered Physical Therapist.

1991–1993

INSTRUCTOR, LIFETIME FITNESS CENTER *HOME COUNTY COMMUNITY COLLEGE, HOME PARK, KS.* Conducted general education seminars on wellness. Developed lesson plans and class materials. Supervised two student employees.

- ◆ Taught approximately 45 people about better wellness, including the importance of fitness and nutrition.
- ◆ Explained and demonstrated the proper use of various pieces of exercise equipment.

1990–1991

PHYSICAL THERAPIST TECHNICIAN *ADVANCED PHYSICAL THERAPY, DOROTHY, IN.* Assisted Physical Therapist with patients before, during and after treatment, using exercise and modalities such as electrical stimulation and hot and cold packs.

- ◆ Implemented patient exercise programs using weight machines, thera-bands and various stretching routines.
- ◆ Instructed pool therapy.

1987–1990

PHYSICAL THERAPIST TECHNICIAN *PHYSICAL MEDICINE ASSOCIATES, SCARECROW, IN.* Gained hands-on training while assisting Physical Therapists. Along with mentioned modalities, also used weights, bicycles, treadmills and whirlpool baths.

- ◆ Assisted with orthotic braces.

EDUCATION: ASSOCIATES DEGREE IN PHYSICAL THERAPIST ASSISTANT; North Valley Community College; May, 1993.
BACHELOR OF SCIENCE DEGREE IN EXERCISE PHYSIOLOGY; Ball State University; May, 1987.

198

Physical therapy assistant. *Kristie Cook, CPRW; Olathe, KS*

This resume reflects an entry-level person willing to work part time or volunteer to gain experience in her chosen field...

MARIA CARDOZA

555 Courtney Boulevard
Boston, MA 55555

Home: (555) 555-5555
Work: (555) 555-5555

PROFESSIONAL GOALS

Long-term goal reflects commitment to continued career growth...

Immediate: Secure a Physical Therapy Aide position providing exposure to evaluation, treatment, and discharge planning for a variety of patient populations.

Long-Term: Pursue a Masters Degree in Physical Therapy and obtain designation as a Registered Physical Therapist.

PROFESSIONAL SUMMARY

Physical Therapy Aide	Foundation Medical Care, Boston, Massachusetts	(part-time)	2/96-Pres.
Physical Therapy Volunteer	Orthopedic Services, Cambridge, Massachusetts	(part-time)	12/95-Pres.
Physical Therapy Volunteer	St. Francis Hospital, Boston, Massachusetts		1/95-12/95
Physical Therapy Aide	Physical Performance Center, Boston, Massachusetts		10/93-1/95

PHYSICAL THERAPY EXPERIENCE

♦ Over three years' experience as Physical Therapy Aide and Physical Therapy Volunteer in a variety of environments including acute medical (orthopedic, neurological, cancer, cardiac, and burn units), cardiac rehabilitation, outpatient rehabilitation, outpatient orthopedic, sports medicine, and hydrotherapy settings.

♦ Under supervision of Registered Physical Therapist, assisted with treatment, monitoring, and documentation. Populations represented a variety of geriatric orthopedic, neurological impairment, and adolescent/adult sports injuries. Attended interdisciplinary team evaluation meetings, treatment sessions, and family conferences.

♦ Familiar with various physical therapy technologies and modality equipment. Under supervision, prepared patients for hot/cold packs, ultrasound, electrical stimulation, cervical or pelvic traction, and other modalities. Interpreted and implemented exercise lists to sustain recovery from a variety of impairments and disabilities.

♦ Assisted in other clinic areas as needed: regulated chemical balance for hydrotherapy, purchased clinical supplies, input patient data on computer (familiar with Microsoft Word, WordPerfect, and basic programming).

Maria had very little paid experience so I combined volunteer and paid experiences in summary paragraphs above. The teaching assistant position helps overcome lack of science degree

EDUCATION

BOSTON UNIVERSITY, Boston, Massachusetts

Bachelor of Arts Degree in Sociology (1996)
Completed a number of pre-med requisites.

UNIVERSITY ACTIVITIES

Teaching Assistant: Performed cadaver dissections for Human Anatomy Laboratory and instructed undergraduate students in class material.

Intramural Sports: Active participant in flag football, co-ed softball, tournament tennis, and soccer.

References Upon Request

199

Physical therapy aide. *Susan Britton Whitcomb, CPRW; Fresno, CA*

Packed with details, the design and short statements keep this resume readable and effective.

Michele Gibson

842 N. Main ▪ Menasha, Wisconsin 54952 ▪ (414) 784-8752

Licensed Cosmetologist, State of Wisconsin

Summary of Attributes
- Enthusiastic professional with outstanding customer relation skills; upbeat, friendly, and genuinely care about providing satisfactory service.
- Strong sales techniques; consistently increase volume through additional product purchases.
- Carefully listen to clients to correctly address their needs/desires.
- Good business management aptitude; knowledgeable in all aspects of salon operation.
- Excellent technical skills evidenced through extemely loyal clientele and high referral rate.

Experience

The Ultimate Salon, Appleton, Wisconsin
Independent Hair Stylist/Make-Up Artist   1994-Present
- Provide full range of services including precision hair cuts, permanent waving, color, and styling.
- Conduct one-on-one make-up consultations, providing hands-on instruction, individualized color selection, and written guidelines.
- Manage all aspects of business including inventory control, bookkeeping, price determination, and marketing.

Accomplishments:
- Conceptualized and publish a quarterly client newsletter which contributed to an increase in client base, as well as product sales.
- Specialize in creating unique images for bridal clients incorporating various ornamentations into hair styles.
- Researched and introduced a private label make-up line.

A New You Salon, Menasha, Wisconsin
Hair Stylist/Make-Up Artist   1991-1994
- Performed hair stylist duties including cuts, styles, color, and permanent waves. Functioned as an apprentice, 1991-1993.
- Lead Make-Up Artist for special occasions and one-on-one demonstrations.

Accomplishments:
- Achieved retail sales of 31% compared to national average of 15%, 1993.
- Orchestrated salon-wide Cut-A-Thon to benefit United Cerebral Palsy, including public relations, donation solicitation, and raffle organization. Tripled donations over previous year.
- Coordinated complimentary seminar to educate clients on new hair trends, products, and the benefits of various salon services.

Education

Northeast Wisconsin Technical College, Green Bay, Wisconsin   1993
Certificate of Completion; Cosmetology Training (included 400 hours of classroom instruction and 3,600 hours of on-the-floor supervised training)

Industry Involvement

Redken Symposium, Las Vegas, Nevada, January 1996
Redken Regional Seminar, Schaumburg, Illinois, 1994
- Assisted national and regional platform artists.
Aerial Hair Show, Stevens Point, Wisconsin, 1994
- Applied stage and runway make-up for models.

These state-ments reinforce Michele's strong business skills

200

Barber/cosmetologist. *Kathy Keshemberg, NCRW; Appleton, WI*

Fonts and graphics were carefully chosen to create a stylish resume for applying for jobs in upscale Los Angeles hair salons.

LaTonya Jefferson
500 Maple Street, Apt. 103
Kansas City, Missouri 64134
(816) 555-1212
LaTonyaJefferson@email.com

LaTonya's resume was a hit with everyone who saw it!

HAIR STYLIST / COSMETOLOGIST

Accomplished professional dedicated to enhancing client appearance in areas of universal hair care. Proven skills in execution of perfect hair-coloring techniques. Builder of "totally satisfied" customer relationships. Peer mentor and public educator in all facets of cosmetology. Licensed in Kansas and Missouri. PC-competent in MS Word, Excel and the Internet. World traveler fluent in Spanish and French.

EXPERIENCE

HAIR COLOR SPECIALIST, Spectacular Salon and Day Spa, Mission, KS *(6/99 to Present)*
Serve 18 clients per day from diverse cultural backgrounds. Participate in hair-show demonstrations.

➢ Acknowledged for highest level of salon retail sales among 10 stylists.

➢ Achieved rank of Head Colorist after only two-year employment period.

ASSISTANT MAKEUP ARTIST, Monique's Boutique Fashion Show, Kansas City, MO *(9/99)*

➢ Performed makeup and color services for 30 models in this annual event.

EDUCATION

INSTRUCTOR TRAINING, Superior School of Hair Styling, Leawood, KS *(1999 to 2000)*

➢ Completed 300 of the 350 hours required for certification.

CERTIFICATE OF COMPLETION, Midwest College of Cosmetology, Blue Springs, MO *(7/98)*

➢ Pivot Point Curriculum

➢ Sales Woman of the Month — awarded seven times

➢ Perfect Attendance

➢ Selected courses: Hair Chemistry; Advanced Color; Production Makeup Artist

PROFESSIONAL TRAINING, Heartland College of Beauty Arts, Kansas City, MO *(1995 to 1996)*

➢ Outstanding Work Award — received three times

➢ Selected courses: Ethnic Hair Care; Hair Weaving and Extensions; Hair Color

She recently landed the job of her dreams and moved west.

201

Hair stylist/cosmetologist. *Meg Montford, CCM, CPRW; Kansas City, MO*

This resume was very effective for Stacey, despite the fact that she had no experience as a flight attendant.

STACEY HERD

3382 Collier Road
Acampo, California 95220
home: (209) 334-9685   cell: (209) 327-2673
(luv2fly@msn.com)

The airline she applied to was impressed by her resume and commented positively on the e-mail address, which she created for this position.

FLIGHT ATTENDANT

KEY QUALIFICATIONS

Her qualifications include solid people skills and the ability to handle stress.

- Over 6 years of successful experience in customer service and customer response operations.
- Strong desire to work in a fun-filled, high-energy, customer-focused environment, or contribute to making it that way.
- Excellent people skills and understanding of human behavior, combined with coursework in General Psychology.
- Proven ability to adjust to changing situations; utilize good judgment during unexpected emergency situations.
- Genuine team player committed to positive performance and efficient operations.
- Demonstrate leadership and problem-solving ... meeting day-to-day challenges, juggling multiple responsibilities.
- Build relationships with customers through attention to detail and providing service and solutions.

RELATED EXPERIENCE

EQUESTRIAN SERVICES, Acampo, CA
Manager/Business Owner (1996 to Present)
Successfully maintain overall operations of active equestrian business. Assist trainers and support staff. Acquire confidence and customer satisfaction of a highly professional customer base.

- Establish outstanding customer relationships, acquiring a business reputation for strengths in service quality, customer needs assessment, and knowledge.
- Investigate, listen, and problem-solve customer complaints to mutual satisfaction.
- Track expenditures within budget; maintain inventory and billing functions.

STALLION STATION, Porterville, CA
Office Manager (January 2000 to July 2000)   Supervisor: Jeff Davis, Business Owner
As Office Manager, significantly improved accuracy and timeliness of A/R, monthly billing, purchasing, and inventory.

- Served effectively as team player in a team of 10.
- Member of the customer service team charged with entire customer relationship management for 300+ customer base.
- Performed data, file management, and order fulfillment functions.

UNION BANK, Stockton, CA
Merchant Teller (1995 to 2000)   Supervisor: Donna Schmidt, Vice President

- Organized and coordinated multiple tasks including cash transactions, balancing, and customer service.
- Named "Employee of the Month"... maintained high standards for job performance and initiated work process improvements when necessary.

HONORS & AWARDS

Recipient of 6 awards for outstanding efforts and performance in improving productivity and increasing sales.

EDUCATION

San Joaquin Delta College, Stockton, CA —Dean's List
- Undergraduate Studies in General Psychology (45 Units): Principles of Sociology, Social Psychology, Human Behavior, Child Development, Abnormal Psychology, General Psychology
Graduate, Johnson High School, Sacramento, CA

She was hired within two weeks!

Flight attendant. *Anita Radosevich, CPRW, JCTC, CEIP; Lodi, CA*

Each item in the Summary is very important to most employers. Emphasizing these attributes <u>will</u> give Susan an edge over other applicants.

Susan J. Cascade

1872 West Main Street
Appleton, Wisconsin 54914
(414) 830-7878

Summary of Attributes

- Excellent communication and interpersonal skills; demonstrate a compassionate and caring approach to patient care and assistance with activities of daily living.
- Enjoy providing care and assisting people to make them comfortable; particularly sensitive to the needs of elderly clients.
- Complete assignments with limited supervision.
- Excellent attendance record; always punctual.
- Accurately record information, paying close attention to details.
- Certified in C.P.R.

Experience

Homecare Specialists, Neenah, Wisconsin   1994-Present
Home Health Aide
- Assist clients in their homes with a variety of duties including meal preparation, daily living tasks, and housekeeping.
- Administer medications and carry out medical treatments as instructed by Registered Nurse.
- Participate in exercise and ambulation programs.

Bethel Home, Oshkosh, Wisconsin   1992-1994
Nursing Assistant
- Provided patient care, monitored and recorded vital signs, maintained patient charts, assisted with daily living skills, and administered range of motion therapy.

Education

Fox Valley Technical College, Appleton, Wisconsin
Certified Nursing Assistant   1992

Additional Training: CPR certified, July 1993

Oshkosh North High School, Oshkosh, Wisconsin; Diploma   1990

203

Home health and personal care aide. *Kathy Keshemberg, NCRW;*
Appleton, WI

Sheila Thompson

HOUSEHOLD MANAGER / PERSONAL ASSISTANT
DISCREET ⟍ RELIABLE ⟍ PROFESSIONAL ⟍ TRUSTWORTHY ⟍ RESPONSIBLE

⟍ Diversified Household Professional offering over 12 years' experience in the domestic field.

⟍ Extensive educational background within the household arena including: support supervision, meal preparation, entertaining, floral arrangements and selections, shopping, account management, schedule arrangement, travel and appointments, and CPR/First Aid certification.

⟍ Knowledgeable and adept in all facets of household implementation.

⟍ Strong management and supervisory skills; strengths in delegation, coordination, organization, and follow-up on required tasks.

⟍ Flexible and adaptable; work well with others and capable of handling multi-level tasks simultaneously.

⟍ Conversational Spanish skills.

⟍ Willing to travel and relocate if necessary.

EDUCATION

Well-regarded training program she completed after graduating from college

STARKEY INTERNATIONAL INSTITUTE FOR HOUSEHOLD MANAGEMENT, Denver, CO
Certificate program in Household Management   1999

UNIVERSITY OF COLORADO, Boulder, CO
Bachelor of Science in Business Administration   1995

PROFESSIONAL EXPERIENCE

After graduating from college, Sheila realized she wanted to work as a personal assistant to a busy film executive or celebrity. She took progressively responsible positions to gain experience before going after her dream job.

PERSONAL ASSISTANT/HOUSEHOLD MANAGER, Los Angeles, CA   **1999–2002**

⟍ Assisted with all household management tasks including shopping and errands, bill paying, filing and recordkeeping, light housekeeping, laundry and dry cleaning, gardening, pool and yard care supervision, car maintenance scheduling and supervision, party planning, floral arrangements, meal preparation and service. Supervised part-time (3 days per week) housekeeper.

⟍ Selected and coordinated furnishings, bedding, towels, accessories, and decorations for three bedrooms and two bathrooms.

⟍ Managed household move from 7000-sq.-ft. suburban residence to small city condominium. Supervised packing and moving. Coordinated auction of furniture and household goods.

⟍ Supervised and coordinated numerous contractors involved in home remodeling and decoration. Responsible for quality checks, follow-up, and communication with construction contractors and decorators.

HOUSEKEEPER, San Mateo, CA   **June–November 1999**

⟍ Managed scheduling and completion of all housecleaning duties for 10,000-sq.-ft. home.

⟍ Cared for extensive wardrobe.

⟍ Communicated with vendors and coordinated all required work.

NANNY/HOUSEKEEPER, Boulder, CO   **1992–1995**

⟍ Provided child care; prepared meals and snacks.

⟍ Handled household cleaning, laundry, grocery shopping, and related errands.

Employer Names and References (Written and Verbal) Gladly Provided upon Request

2543 Flora Boulevard, Apt. 7B, Los Angeles, CA 90026 ⟍ (213) 555-0945 ⟍ sheilathompson@juno.com

204

Private household worker. *Louise M. Kursmark, CPRW, JCTC, CEIP, CCM; Cincinnati, OH*

Mark is marginally mentally handicapped. He needed a resume that showed his potential as a contributing member of an employer's team (resume writer's comments).

Mark L. Rogers
3499 N. Klein Road
Bay City, Michigan 48706

517-555-8341

STRENGTHS	❏ Strongly motivated to perform. ❏ Anxious to use current skills and to learn more. ❏ Upbeat attitude and ability to get along with others.
EXPERIENCE	BAY VALLEY HUMANE SOCIETY • Bay City, MI **Kennel Aide** 1996-Present • Assisted staff with feeding animals. • Cleaned and disinfected kennels; performed light cleaning of facility. • Worked with animal crematorium. DR. MICHAEL CLARK, DVM • Flint, MI **Animal Caretaker** 1994-1996 • Fed and bathed animals. • Maintained cleanliness of animal areas. • Assisted doctor as requested. ST. VINCENT DEPAUL THRIFT CENTER • Flint, MI **Moving Helper** 1992-1994 • Removed donated furniture and appliances from contributors' homes; unloaded at facility. • Performed light janitorial functions in office area and restrooms. GOODWILL INDUSTRIES • Saginaw, MI **Janitor / Light Industrial Worker** 1988-1992 • Participated in on-the-job training (cleaning, light industrial). • Cleaned carpets, restrooms, walls and floors. • Operated drill press
EDUCATION	NORTH CENTRAL HIGH SCHOOL • Flint, MI **Graduated** 1986
REFERENCES	Available on request.

205

Animal caretaker. *Janet L. Beckstrom; Flint, MI*

Wendy was very proud of and very involved in activities relating to her cultural heritage. Since her background was an integral part of her, an employer would need to recognize this...

WENDY D. STONE

4430 Draper Rd.
Davison, Michigan 48423

810-555-9806
Tribal Affiliation: Member of Ojibwa Nation

PROFILE

Capable, people-oriented support provider with wide-ranging skills adaptable to a variety of applications. Compassionate animal care provider.

PROFESSIONAL EXPERIENCE SUMMARY

Veterinary/Medical Office Administration

- Assist doctor in patient treatment including surgical procedures, ice/heat packs, injections, and routine health examinations.
- Greet owners/patients and schedule appointments.
- Maintain familiarity with veterinary and medical terminology.
- Ensure efficient operation and provide friendly service in reception area.
- Respond to telephone calls and handle accordingly; screen calls for doctor.
- Utilize customized computer applications to process payments and manage patient records.
- Self-taught physiology; developed floor and water aerobics programs for all ages and levels of fitness, including rehabilitative programs.

PERSONAL SUMMARY

Heritage and Cultural Expertise

- Calm, compassionate personality well suited to interaction with humans and animals.
- Semi-fluent in Ojibwa language.
- Experienced in sharing culture with non-native people in presentations and dance demonstrations to schools, colleges and other groups.
- Dedicated to role of language, cultural and spiritual teacher of native children.
- Follower of traditional teachings regarding respect for elders and sanctity of life.
- Accomplished artist of beadwork, pottery and weaving; reputation among community for beadwork creations.
- Participant of Pow Wows across the state; served as Head Dancer when requested.

EMPLOYMENT HISTORY

Eastside Veterinary Clinic • Davison, MI
Veterinary Assistant/Front Desk Receptionist

1993-Present

Swanson Veterinary Clinic • Davison, MI
Veterinarian's Assistant/Front Desk Receptionist

1985-1993

Bay Golf Club • Bay City, MI
Certified Aerobics Instructor

1980-1985

Additional experience in Chiropractic Medicine

TRAINING AND EDUCATION

Midland Indian Center - Student of Ojibwa language under instructor Amy Morgan
Ainsworth High School - Graduate

References available on request.

She hoped to land a job in a tribal office, but her resume is suited to mainstream employment as well (resume writer's comments).

206

Veterinary assistant. *Janet L. Beckstrom; Flint, MI*

Geraldine A. Tompkins

44 Starr Lane
Great Falls, NJ 55555   (000) 000-0000

CAREER GOAL: **Director of Activities** in a long term care facility.

PROFILE:

- Ten years experience in the planning and evaluation of therapeutic or recreational activities geared to the individual needs of the elderly, including Alzheimer's patients.
- Supportive, understanding and helpful to peers, subordinates and residents.
- Talent for clear and comprehensive report writing as well as effective oral communications in all interpersonal matters.
- Strongly motivated to continually learn and implement new developments in the field to bring about real, practical results in people's lives.
- Recognized for exceptional volume and quality of work, displaying good judgment under stressful conditions.

EDUCATION: **B.S. Health Education/Community Health**, *cum laude*, 1987
Columbia University, New York, NY

CERTIFICATIONS: **SENIOR FITNESS INSTRUCTOR**, 1987
Passaic County Department of Parks, Recreational and Cultural Affairs

ACTIVITY DIRECTOR CERTIFIED BY NCCAP, 1993
Met state qualifications through attendance at numerous adult education seminars which included: Activities with Meaning, Creative Movement, Validation Therapy, Activity Documentation, and Dementia

MEMBERSHIPS: NATIONAL ASSOCIATION OF ACTIVITY PROFESSIONALS
NEW JERSEY ASSOCIATION OF ACTIVITY PROFESSIONALS

PROFESSIONAL EXPERIENCE:

Organizes skills under major headings

Activities Planning

- Worked with elderly residents of varying physical, mental and emotional capabilities to minimize their symptoms and improve their well being.
- Contributed input during weekly interdisciplinary meetings with team comprised of health care and social services professionals to develop specific goals for each of over 180 residents.
- Based on patient diagnosis, personal interaction or staff reports, designed activity regimens which included exercises, dancing, choral participation, crafts, games, special events, group discussions or relaxation techniques.
- Implemented programs by degree of need to help each resident improve physical strength and coordination, build confidence and self esteem, manage stress and express feelings in positive ways.

Assessment

- Wrote 50-60% of all resident evaluations from an activities standpoint.
- In conjunction with interdisciplinary team, assessed care plans quarterly or sooner if needed, to adapt to individuals' status changes in psycho-social, cognitive or physical abilities.
- Provided input on development of new interdepartmental assessment forms which improved quality of data and ultimate results.
- Conducted complete reviews every six months.

... Continued

207

Recreation worker. *Melanie Noonan, CPS; West Paterson, NJ*

Geraldine A. Tompkins   Page 2

Administration
- Maintained up-to-date files on all residents. Continually prepared for unplanned inspections by State Department of Health.
- Planned, prioritized and organized several ongoing programs simultaneously.
- Recruited and supervised a large staff of aides and activity specialists.
- In earlier positions, wrote Recreation Department policies and procedures, developed monthly calendar/newsletter of events, and filled in for Activities Director during vacations and absences.

Special Projects and Achievements
- In current position, assumed charge of volunteer services program, increasing participation over the last year from 5 to 52.
  - ... Conducted recruitment through selective mailings to clubs and churches, postings on public bulletin boards, and presentations to women's groups, which generated an enthusiastic response.
  - ... Compiled an orientation and training manual, and worked with volunteers one-on-one or in groups.
  - ... Assured consistency of procedures, with particular attention to safety, infection control, and sensitivity training.
- Upgraded activities/events calendar to include a "beauty boutique" which became an immediate hit with the women residents, serving to enhance their self esteem. Successfully cold called to solicit a $3,000 donation of cosmetic products from a direct distributor.
- Initiated a weekly supervised "walking club" for Alzheimer's residents, which has helped to channel some of their restlessness, thereby cutting down on their aimless wandering and the possibility of injuries from falls.
- At recent State Department of Health inspection, was especially complimented during exit meeting for maintaining an exemplary model of a deficiency free department.

RELEVANT EMPLOYMENT:

1988–Date   FALLSVIEW MANOR NURSING HOME, Great Falls, NJ

         Director of Activities (Since 1/94)
         Assistant Director of Activities (6/90–1/94)
         Activity Specialist (9/88–6/90)

1986–1987   MOUNT PLEASANT ADULT DAY CARE CENTER, North Bergen, NJ

         Recreation Assistant (6/86–9/86; 12/86–11/87)
         Acting Recreation Director (9/86–11/86)
         Student Intern—Recreation Assistant (1/86–6/86)

A thorough resume with sections that emphasize her many credentials, skills, and accomplishments

Peter M. Quinn

7509 Maple Drive
East Haven, Connecticut 06555
(203) 555-5555   peterquinn@snetco.net

Summary

Qualified and certified **Law Enforcement Officer** with two years' experience with the New Haven County Sheriff's Department.

- Graduate of Connecticut Police Officer Training; certified 1999.
- Proven ability to deal effectively with prisoners, establishing respect for authority while treating individuals fairly.
- Thorough, hard working, disciplined, and reliable, with a serious attitude and a career commitment to law enforcement.

These sections emphasize Peter's objective to become a police officer.

Professional Experience

NEW HAVEN COUNTY SHERIFF'S DEPARTMENT   January 2000–Present
Deputy Sheriff/Corrections Officer • County Correctional Facility

Maintain inmate control over 100-plus prisoners in a dormitory-style jail. Supervise inmate behavior and respond to infractions. Count and lead prisoners to meals and recreation. Maintain detailed hourly logs and records of inmate transfers and other activities. Transport felons to higher security jails. Assume responsibility in other areas of the jail on an occasional basis.

- Developed skills in dealing with individuals of all types.
- Gained experience in effectively handling tense situations.
- Consistently achieved excellent performance evaluations.
- Member of Sheriff's Power Lifting Team; hold an American record in bench press.

Other Experience

RYDER'S, New Haven, CT   1998–1999
Doorman/Bouncer

GRANT ASSOCIATES, New Haven, CT   1997–1998
Field Representative

Negotiated and sold the services of a collection firm to business clients such as mortgage companies, doctors, and other health-care providers.

Education

Connecticut Police Officer Training and Certification (1999), CONNECTICUT POLICE OFFICERS ACADEMY, Storrs, CT

Criminal Justice Degree Program (1998–Present), QUINNIPIAC COLLEGE, Hamden, CT

Graduate (1996), NORTH HAVEN HIGH SCHOOL, North Haven, CT
- Member of Wrestling Team

208

Correctional officer. *Louise M. Kursmark, CPRW, JCTC, CEIP, CCM; Cincinnati, OH*

Lee Stephens

1111 North Hill Street ♦ Radcliff, Kentucky 40100 ♦ (502) 351-0000

Objective

Corrections Rehabilitation Counselor

Summary of Qualifications

- Master's degree in Counseling. Bachelor of Science degrees in Criminal Justice and Psychology.
- Over 20 years of experience in corrections.
- Excellent interpersonal skills with staff and inmate population and sensitive to their problems and counseling needs. A proven team-player who works well with people and can be counted on in any type of situation.

Professional Experience

FEDERAL CORRECTION FACILITY ♦ Any City, USA
Deputy Education Director & Operations Officer ♦ Mar 92 - Present

- Counseled inmates and correlated day-to-day administrative operations for this facility which provided vocational training and educational classes to prisoners. As Custody Control Administrator, handled all disciplinary problems; maintained a roster of all day and evening students/inmates and instituted a system to monitor student's progress and course completion. Developed and established a program to provide evening college classes. Coordinated with local universities to contract instructors.
- As Assistant Test Control Officer, administered and graded GED, DANTE, and ASIP tests. Awarded high school diploma, college semester hours, or certified students in vocational areas such as auto mechanics. Occasionally escorted prisoners into the city to take tests that could not be provided by any other means.
- Supervised six subordinate administrative employees. Acted as liaison to ten contracted teachers and resolved problems.
- Coordinated and established an inmate barber shop which resulted in an annual savings of $10,000.
- Consistently received commendable / outstanding ratings during security and safety inspections.
- Selected to attend Correctional Management Training which was usually reserved for prison wardens and correctional administrators.
- Coordinated and implemented educational programs for inmates to return them to civilian life with better employment skills.

FEDERAL CORRECTION FACILITY ♦ Any City, USA
Correctional Counselor ♦ Jul 86 - Mar 92

- As Counselor, had a case-load of approximately 150 inmates; counseled each inmate at least twice a month and provided advice concerning their personal problems. Counseled and advised families, arranged visits, and occasionally assisted spouses find lodging near the facility.
- Escorted and closely supervised inmates who were allowed to return home during times of family emergencies or death. Sat on Disciplinary Board and Parole Board and made recommendations for clemency, parole, etc., based upon thorough knowledge of each case. Issued medications and maintained an accurate, detailed record of medications which were dispensed. Served on the Classification Board; after careful review of records, made recommendations for custody-level of new arrivals and determined appropriate work assignments.

The vertical and horizontal rules, bold subheads, bullets, and arrows give a professional and clear presentation of his abilities

209

Correctional officer. *Connie S. Stevens; Radcliff, KY*

Lee Stephens

STATE CORRECTION FACILITY • Any City, USA
Chief of Employment Branch • Dec 80 - Jul 86
➡ Supervised 11 staff personnel and evaluated their performance. Provided employee training, guidance, and counseling.
➡ Managed the office responsible for providing work details to the community. Inmate details included such tasks as mowing grass, providing office-building maintenance, shop work, and routine repairs.
➡ Counseled and evaluated approximately 130 inmates. Ensured that prisoners' surroundings were secure at all times. Monitored their activities and assigned employment details based on the inmate's background and custody level. Assigned guards to escort prisoners.
➡ Attended weekly staff meetings with superiors and made recommendations. Attended semi-monthly in-service training sessions on various topics including riot control, apprehension planning and practice exercises, use of gas masks, and survival training.

REGIONAL CORRECTION FACILITY • Any City, USA
Chief of Prisoners' Service & Supervision Branch • May 76 - Dec 80
➡ As Chief of Prisoners Service Branch, supervised 25 employees. Assigned duties and evaluated job performance. Provided employee training and counseling. Managed the administration office, prisoner property and funds section, supply room, mail room, and probation and parole sections. Supervised all aspects of prisoner's processing into and out of the Regional Correction Facility.
➡ As Chief of Supervision Branch, supervised and managed the guard force consisting of 110 personnel. Awarded *Best Safety Program* twice in one year.
➡ Devised, developed, and implemented the Vocational Employment Training Program for minimum custody inmates. Work site supervisors provided inmates with on-the-job training in such areas as carpentry and plumbing. At the end of the program, inmates were given certificates to be used for future employment stating they had received vocational training in particular areas.
➡ Developed, staffed, and implemented an Escort Section which increased security and provided excellent inmate accountability. Supervised three guards whose responsibilities included scheduling appointments and escorting prisoners to medical and legal appointments.

Education

UNIVERSITY OF KENTUCKY • Lexington, KY
Master of Arts in **Counseling** • May 83

EASTERN KENTUCKY UNIVERSITY • Richmond, KY
Bachelor of Science in **Criminal Justice** • May 74
Bachelor of Science in **Psychology** • May 74

Addendum containing information on additional training courses is available upon request

This resume could also fit into other categories such as "counselors" or "education administrators," but I included it among "protective service occupations" to show the diversity of jobs available in various industries.

Dorian's resume, written as he separated from the military successfully translated his diverse military experience onto one page...

DORIAN M. PETERSON

33335 N.W. Massachusetts Drive
Simpkins, SC 33323
(407) 555-1212

this update also was successful...

OBJECTIVE

To secure a position as a Firefighter with the opportunity for advancement and increasing responsibilities.

CERTIFICATIONS

- South Carolina Fire Officer I
- South Carolina & National Registry EMT
- NFPA Fire Inspector I
- South Carolina Fire Standards
- NFPA Firefighter II
- NFPA Apparatus Driver / Operator PUMPER
- Interspiro Breathing Apparatus Service Tech

- U.S. Air Force Fire Rescue
- Confined Space Rescue Training
- NFPA Fire Instructor I
- U.S. Air Force Fire Protection Specialist
- NFPA Airport Firefighter
- NFPA Apparatus Driver / Operator ARFF
- U.S. Air Force Contingency Firefighting

QUALIFICATIONS

- Able to perform duties at a Firefighter II and Fire Officer I level, to include Crash / Fire / Rescue, and Hazardous Materials operations.
- Proficient in the use and operations of specialized power/hand tools used in rescue operations.
- Performs dispatch communications.
- Wide scope of experience in Emergency Services.

PROFESSIONAL PROFILE

Fire Protection Specialist -
- Structural / Crash firefighter
- Dispatcher
- Trainer of new incoming Firefighters.

- Driver/operator
- Substitute crew chief as needed
- Experienced in Municipal Depart.

Crash / Rescue / Firefighter - (part-time)
- Fire protection for Joint-Stars aircraft
- Fire Fighter/EMT

- Driver/operator

AWARDS AND HONORS

- Southwest Asia Service Medal for Saudi Arabia
- Below the Zone promotion granted 6 months early due to outstanding productivity
- U.S. Air Force Good Conduct Medal and U.S. Air Force Achievement Award

EDUCATION AND TRAINING

he delivered one resume and got the firefighter job! (resume writer's comments).

- U.S. Air Force Fire Protection Academy
- U.S. Air Force Fire Rescue School
- South Carolina Fire College
- Commons Community College
- Community College of the Air Force
- Associate of Science degree in Fire Science
- Trained on numerous aircraft, structural, motor vehicle, hazardous materials and marine emergency exercises

WORK HISTORY

2/95-Present **Firefighter/EMT** - City of Geneboro Fire and Emergency Services, SC
12/91-2/95 **Fire Protection Specialist** - U.S. Air Force, Dulles AFB, SC
11/93-Present **Crash/Rescue/Firefighter** - Norton Inc., Geneboro, SC

210

Fire fighter. *Laura A. DeCarlo, CPRW, ICCC; Melbourne, FL*

Donald used this resume to apply for Fire Chief in a very small community with many complicated political barriers for outside candidates to overcome.

He secured an interview three days after submitting his resume.

Donald Osborne, Jr.
3340 Mount Pleasant Road
Lexington, Kentucky 40508
Residence (859) 759-2219 · Mobile (859) 516-2000
chief@aol.com

FIRE CHIEF / OPERATIONS SPECIALIST / CONSULTANT
Delivering substantive gains in efficiency and safety since 1975.

A highly effective liaison and manager able to engender enthusiasm and purpose, offering more than 26 years of experience as a firefighter (since 1975), professional firefighter (since 1982), and Chief Officer (since 1987). Extensive executive experience as a motivator, coordinator, and catalyst, able to focus the efforts of diverse groups onto common goals. Committed to providing innovative protection programs that reflect the values, diversity, aspirations, and priorities of the communities they serve. Effective combination of interpersonal, analytical, and organizational qualifications with strengths in:

- Policy Design, Development & Direction
- Design of Policy & Procedures
- Grant Writing, Fund Raising & Development
- Leadership of Volunteer & Support Members
- Accurate Needs / Assets Assessment

- Coordination with Existing Organizations
- Budget Preparation & Administration
- Public Speaking & Community Outreach
- Federal / State Regulatory Compliance
- Team Building, Training & Management

PROFESSIONAL EXPERIENCE

Fire Chief — Training Officer
Nicholasville Fire Department, Nicholasville, KY (Volunteer 1999 - Present)

Challenge: To provide consistently high-quality fire service for the community and region of approximately 5,000 citizens within a volunteer organization of 30 members and an annual budget of $400K.

Recruited to serve by the city selection committee. Scope of responsibility is broad and includes first-line supervision of 29, direction of all fireground activities and emergency scenes, safety of all firefighters, and the protection of life and property. Maintain equipment and provide ongoing training for all department members. Additionally responsible for updating training records and reporting all department activity to the State of Kentucky, thereby ensuring continued legislative compliance.

- Developed and implemented an extensive firefighter training program resulting in improved standards, 10 new certifications, and recognition from city officials and professionals throughout Fayette, Garrard, and Mercer Counties.
- Conceived and created an effective, first-time Operations Manual designed to standardize guidelines for procedures and safety. The manual has been requested for use as a model by departments nationwide.
- Proven ability to develop and maintain productive relationships and partnerships with public board members, local citizens, and governmental and community regulators.

Director of Operations
Blue Grass Airport, Lexington, KY (1982 – 1999)

Challenge: With a staff of 70, administrate annual operating budget of $4 million and construction projects averaging in excess of $10 million while maintaining smooth daily operations, providing direction at all emergency and accident scenes, and coordinating fire, police, and EMT activities.

- Demonstrated ability to effectively handle safety, rescue, and recovery initiatives at accident scenes of large proportion and complex nature.

211

Fire chief. *Debbie Ellis, CPRW; Danville, KY*

Donald Osborne, Jr.   **Page Two**

PROFESSIONAL EXPERIENCE, Continued

- Combined and streamlined Fire, Police, and EMS departments establishing consistency of standards, policies, and procedures. Result: $100K annual cost reduction and significant, sustainable gains in efficiency and productivity.
- The newly created departmental design was recognized as the state's standard and has been used as a model for domestic and international airport administrators across the U.S. and in Canada.
- Secured federal and state grant funding to plan and build a state-of-the-art, $5 million firefighter training facility to serve the entire southeastern region of the U.S.
- Received recognition for this facility's success in the form of the FAA South Region's *Airport Manager of the Year* award.
- Also with federal and state grant funding, developed plans and completed two major airport renovation projects worth in excess of $12.5 million.
- Selected to chair the compliance committee for the Americans With Disabilities Act responsible for completing airport modifications required by the new legislation.

EDUCATION AND CONTINUING SPECIAL TRAINING

Louisiana State University – Batten Rouge, Louisiana
Degree awarded as Firefighter I

Special training coursework completed: *FDIC, Rapid Intervention Training Development, Basic Firefighter Training Program Development, Underwater Rescue, Firefighter Survival & Rescue, EMT Training, Hazardous Materials Training, Arson Investigation, Aircraft Crash & Rescue Training, Urban & Rural Firefighter Training, Fire Service Instruction Training, Command Decision and Incident Training, Anti-Terrorism DOT Training, Crisis Management, Public Information & Media Training.*

CERTIFICATIONS AND LICENSURE

Professional Firefighter
Certified Volunteer Firefighter
EMT
State Fire Instructor Levels I and II
Dive Master, Master Scuba Diver & Rescue Diver Certifications

PROFESSIONAL MEMBERSHIPS

National Association of EMT's
American Association of Trauma Specialists
Professional Association of Dive Instructors
National Association of Fire Service Instructors
Past President, Central Kentucky Fire Fighters Association
Past President, Kentucky Aviation Association
National Fire Chief Association
Fayette County Fire Department Rescue Squad

--- Supporting documentation and excellent professional referrals available on request ---

The functional style works well here to avoid repetition of duties.

ROBERT SMITH

❖

1235 Main Street, Berkeley, California 94703
robtsmith@netzero.com
(510) 684-5624

Experienced security guard available for a challenging opportunity utilizing my expertise in loss prevention, administration, and customer service.

Highlights qualifications in three key areas.

Areas of Expertise

Security ───────────────────────────────────

Committed to establishing a secure and safe environment for both staff and customers.

◆ Observe buildings for property damage and security breaches. Screen visitors for proper identification. Prepare work space for next shift of workers; responsibly open and close office while taking security measures.

◆ Monitor vehicles to prevent illegal parking. Maintain records of vehicles cited for parking violations. Arrange ground transportation for customers.

Customer Service ──────────────────────────

Dedicated to offering friendly, professional, and resourceful customer service to diverse groups of people in a timely manner.

◆ Quick to answer customer questions and complaints; repeatedly solicit customer feedback, all to ensure high-quality service.

◆ Experience selling products and services directly to customers over the phone and in person.

Administration ────────────────────────────

Execute indispensable clerical support for busy management teams.

◆ Skilled in answering multi-line phones and routing calls to appropriate party with expedience and ease.

◆ Accurately completed reports of daily income after handling cash transactions.

Work Experience

1992–2002	**Security Manager**	ABC Security — Berkeley, CA
1987–1992	**Security Guard**	Burns Security — Oakland, CA
1980–1987	**Night Manager**	Kmart — El Cerrito, CA

❖ ❖ ❖

212

Security guard. *Leatha Jones, CPRW, CEIP; Orinda, CA*

Allen's resume brings all his experience together into a strong, cohesive presentation.

Allen Michaels

1290 River Walk Dr. ◆ Ocean City, MD 21045
(410) 884.5555 ◆ Email: allen@hotmail.com

SECURITY GUARD

Physical ◆ Industrial ◆ Facility ◆ Personal

EDUCATION

AA Degree in Business, Howard Community College, Maryland
February 2002

Self-defense Courses, Ocean City PD
1994 to Present

EXPERIENCE

University of Maryland Physics Laboratory, Baltimore, Maryland   1998 to Present
Security Officer (DoD Contractor, SECRET Clearance)

- ◆ Manage two large security databases for 20,000 personnel (input and access information).
- ◆ Control the movement of property and personnel into and out of the facility. Verify government clearances and determine entry rights.
- ◆ Observe facilities for security violations.
- ◆ Respond to and investigate incidents and accidents; draft detailed reports.
- ◆ Escort visitors.
- ◆ Manage emergency calls and dispatch fire, police, or medical assistance as required.

Independent Contractor   1994 to Present
Personal Protective Services & Trainer

- ◆ Accept independent contracts to protect individuals. Drive personal vehicles and monitor the activities of clients. Ensure that clients are not disturbed, harassed, or otherwise bothered in public locations.
- ◆ Install personal home security systems.
- ◆ Conduct one-to-one classes in self-defense techniques including the use of deadly force and such weapons/aids as pepper spray.

U.S. Army, Italy and Macedonia) *Allen transitioned successfully from military to civilian* 1994 to 1998
Security Guard *security operations.*

- ◆ Managed security requirements for a base: Controlled entry to and exit from restricted-access areas. Searched individuals, vehicles, and materials. Escorted authorized personnel.
- ◆ Effectively moved an arms room to the field. Inventoried, moved, and re-set up hundreds of line items of weapons worth over $5M. Operated and maintained 2.5-ton vehicles.
- ◆ Received recognition for superior performance of guard duty during the salvaging of Secretary Don White's plane in Macedonia.

213

Security guard. *Diane Burns, CPRW, IJCTC, CCM, CEIP; Columbia, MD*

Richard A. Stevens

123 Whiteoak Drive ◆ Martin, Kentucky 40100 ◆ (502) 555-1111

OBJECTIVE

A law enforcement position in which professional background and commitment to excellence will be effectively utilized

SUMMARY OF QUALIFICATIONS

- Graduate of Department of Criminal Justice Police Academy. Certified in SWAT/SRT. Certified sniper.
- Associate degree with major course of study in Law Enforcement.
- Excellent leadership skills. Reliable. Detail-oriented. Believe in operating "by the book".

PROFESSIONAL EXPERIENCE

Martin Police Department ◆ Martin, KY   1986 - Present
Police Officer
- Spearheaded a successful undercover drug investigation lasting eight months and involving six other officers. Commended by the Governor and received a special citation from the President of the United States.
- Lead SWAT team operations.
- Assisted and aided citizens in emergency situations, and responded to citizen complaints.
- Provided patrol for the city. Discouraged theft, arson, and vandalism by patrolling business and residential areas during night time hours. Arrested/detained persons violating the law. Monitored traffic.
- Received *The Marksmanship in Gold* for excellent marksmanship from the German Army Liaison Staff at Fort Knox, Kentucky.

RELEVANT MILITARY EXPERIENCE

It relates, so it should be included.

Marine Corps Reserves ◆ Desert Storm   1990 - 1991
Tank Commander/Tank Platoon Sergeant
- Participated in Desert Storm. Supervised a 20-man tank platoon. Received Navy Achievement Medal and Navy Commendation Medal from the Secretary of the Navy.

Marine Corps (active duty)   1980 - 1984
Steadily progressed in level of responsibility from Private to Platoon Sergeant
- Supervised a 24-man team. Participated in Security Operation in Beirut, Lebanon. Participated in the Evacuation Operation of noncombatants, United States, and foreign nationals from Beirut and Juniyah, Lebanon. Participated in Operation Urgent Fury, liberation of Islands of Grenada and Carriacou and further evacuation of United States and foreign nationals.

EDUCATION

- *Eastern Kentucky University* ◆ Associate in Science ◆ 1986 ◆ Major: Law Enforcement

CERTIFICATIONS, SPECIAL SKILLS, & TRAINING

- *Special Weapons & Tactics & Special Reaction Team (SWAT/SRT)* ◆ Law Enforcement Activity ◆ 1988
- Graduate of *Basic Police Science* ◆ 1986 ◆ Department of Criminal Justice
- *Additional training, certifications, awards, and commendations are listed on Addendum*

PROFESSIONAL MEMBERSHIPS

- Fraternal Order of Police ◆ Lodge Number 93

214

Police/detective. *Connie S. Stevens; Radcliff, KY*

The introduction summarizes Carl's leadership abilities and his 25-year career and shows that he is qualified to assume a police chief's position in a smaller community.

Carl Standish

257 Mile View Road
Durham, CT 06422
Home (860) 555-0245 — Work (203) 555-3974 X17 — cstandish@msn.com

Law Enforcement Leader
Community Police Programs — Crime Prevention & Resolution — Officer Development & Supervision — Interagency Cooperation

Twenty-five year career in law enforcement, primarily involved in leading the investigation and resolution of homicides, child abuse cases, and other major and high-profile crimes. Graduate of Southern Police Institute Administrative Officers Course. Deep knowledge of law enforcement issues, agencies, and key players in New Haven County and Southern New England. Strong record of effective police work. Key skills and strengths include:

Leadership
Investigative Management
Organization and Process Development
Staff Development
Multiagency Collaboration

Experience

NEW HAVEN POLICE DEPARTMENT, 1977–Present
Detective Sergeant, 1988–Present

Lead a unit of 14 detectives and supervise the investigation of all deaths and child abuse cases in the city. Assign cases, review progress, lend expertise, and personally participate in all major, high-profile, and homicide investigations. Prepare case reports and collaborate with coroner, prosecutor, and multiple city, county, state, and federal agencies to bring cases to successful conclusion.

Represent the Police Department to the community and media. Communicate appropriately with victims' family members during difficult and emotional times.

- Over 16 years, maintained 95% closure rate on homicides.
- Gained reputation for active, results-focused collaboration with multiple agencies. Use leadership skills to overcome traditional bureaucratic barriers and inspire groups and individuals to cooperate to attain common goals.
- Effectively supervised detective staff, building professional abilities and developing for advancement.
- Created structured protocols and organizational routines that contribute to tight investigative procedure.
- Overhauled the detective unit record-keeping processes and systems, creating impeccable records that hold up in court and provide useful data for both current and prior crime investigations.
- In high-stress environment, successfully maintain focus on evidence and procedure to build solid cases.

Patrol Sergeant, 1985–1988

Supervised 25 to 30 patrol officers providing police services to residents of New Haven.

Detective, 1979–1982

Assigned to the Juvenile Squad with the primary responsibility of child abuse investigation.

- Instrumental in 4-year multiagency effort that led to the creation of a Child Advocacy Center at Yale-New Haven Hospital to serve young victims of physical and sexual abuse.

Uniform Patrol Officer, 1977–1979

215

Police supervisor. *Louise M. Kursmark, CPRW, JCTC, CEIP, CCM; Cincinnati, OH*

Carl Standish   Page 2

Experience, continued

FINNEY MANUFACTURING, New Haven, CT, 1989–Present
Police Consultant

As liaison between Finney's corporate security and local law enforcement, provide expertise and assistance in any police-related matters affecting the company, its employees, and contractors at its 1000-employee West Haven Research Laboratory and 800-employee Branford logistics center. Consulting contract continually renewed since 1989.

Education and Professional Development

1985	Southern Police Institute Administrative Officers Course	University of Louisville, Louisville, KY
1973	Peace Officer Training	Connecticut Police Academy, Orange, CT
1978–1983	Undergraduate Studies: Social Science (90 credit hours)	Southern Connecticut State University, New Haven, CT
	Business Administration (54 credit hours)	Quinnipiac College, Hamden, CT

This additional training is notable and important.

Additional Law Enforcement Training

2001	Racial Profiling	Northeastern University College of Criminal Justice, Boston, MA
1994	Training for Trainers	Southern Connecticut Police Institute
1994	Homicide Investigation	Southern Connecticut Police Institute
1991	Interview and Interrogation	John E. Reid and Associates
1991, 1987	National Serial Murder Conference	MAGLOCLEN
1990	Interrogation Techniques	Southern Connecticut Police Institute
1988	Child Sexual Exploitation	Southern Connecticut Police Institute
1984	PR24 Police Baton Course	National Traffic Institute
1984	Horizontal Gaze Nystagmus	National Traffic Institute
1984	Traffic Management	National Traffic Institute
1983	Interview and Investigation	Southern Connecticut Police Institute
1982	First Line Supervision	Southern Connecticut Police Institute
1980	Investigative Skills	Southern Connecticut Police Institute
1979	K55 Radar Training	Southern Connecticut Police Institute
1978	Model Rules	Southern Connecticut Police Institute

Military

UNITED STATES MARINE CORPS, 1970–1974
Sergeant

- Involved in Military Supply Administration.
- Thirteen-month tour of duty in Vietnam, 1970–1971.

As a police veteran, Ken's resume does a good job of presenting his experience in "civilian" terms appropriate for his objective.

KENNETH QUINN
141 Mount Joy Road
Milford, New Jersey 08848
(908) 995-9841

OBJECTIVE

To continue my career in the area of **Corporate Security**.

SUMMARY OF QUALIFICATIONS

Broad-based experience in areas including:

all useful corporate skills

⇒ Managerial and Leadership Training
⇒ Psychophysiological Detection of Deception Examinations (Polygraphs)
⇒ Narcotics Investigation
⇒ Method of Instruction Training
⇒ Interviewing and Interrogation
⇒ Verbal and Non-Verbal Body Language
⇒ Fraud and Theft Investigations
⇒ Security and Shrinkage Control

EXPERIENCE

WOODBRIDGE TOWNSHIP POLICE DEPARTMENT, Woodbridge, NJ — 1971-Present
Ranked as one of the largest police departments in the State of New Jersey

Executive Officer, Criminal Investigation Division	1994-Present
Lieutenant Commander, Internal Affairs Unit	1992-1994
Executive Officer, Criminal Investigation Division	1990-1992
Sergeant, Radio Patrol Division	1986-1990
Detective, First Class	1974-1986
Patrolman, Radio Patrol Division	1971-1974

a brief history with details to follow

PROFESSIONAL ACCOMPLISHMENTS

- **Forensic Psychophysiological Detection of Deception**

  Certified as a Forensic Psychophysiologist in 1991. Graduated from Maryland Institute of Criminal Justice, FBI Academy School of Polygraph, and the Department of Defense Polygraph Institute.

  Conduct issue testing including suspects, victims, witnesses, and informants. Wrote department policies for polygraph procedures; oversee all quality control related to Polygraph Testing. Instruct municipal prosecutors in the art and science of Polygraph. Chosen to conduct homicide testing for Middlesex County Prosecutor's Office.

216

Private detective and investigator. *Beverly Baskin, MA, NCC, CPRW; Marlboro, NJ*

To counter his lack of formal education, two additional pages listed his many continuing education programs.

Professional Accomplishments (continued)

Experience arranged into groups

- **Executive Officer, Criminal Investigation Division**

  Overall command of 41 investigative personnel. Researched Division effectiveness and structure. Reorganized all components of the Division to operate more effectively and efficiently.

- **Internal Affairs**

  Chosen as the first full-time Internal Affairs Commander. Supervised Sergeant; received complaints against police; investigated problems and reported directly to the Chief of Police. Prepared cases for hearings and criminal case reports. Testified against police officers in court, resulting in their removal from office. Created all administrative forms; computerized the department, and adopted unit procedures.

- **Training**

  Obtained Police Teaching Certifications in 1990 from the State of New Jersey. Instructed all members of the Woodbridge Police Department in various aspects of police work including search and seizure, arrests, executed search warrants, use of excessive force, and patrol procedures.

- **Narcotics Investigations and Weapons**

  Served as an Undercover Narcotics Detective for purchasing of drugs, weapons, and prostitution. Assigned to Middlesex County Narcotics Strike Force.

- **Security and Shrinkage Control**

  In charge of parking lot security police, Woodbridge Center Mall. Hand picked off-duty police officers to patrol parking areas for the protection of the shopping public and to apprehend law violators, including those committing shoplifting and theft. Trained officers and store personnel in the detection of shoplifters.

MILITARY SERVICE

Active duty with the United States Marine Corps which included one tour of duty in Viet Nam with the infantry as a machinegunner, team leader and squad leader. Received an Honorable Discharge as a Lance Corporal.

MEMBERSHIPS

New Jersey Narcotic Enforcement Officer's Association; Police Benevolent Association; American Legion; Veterans of Foreign Wars; Marine Corps League; New Jersey Police Honor Legion; American Red Cross Underwater Recovery Team; American Polygraph Association, New Jersey Polygraphists.

This individual is applying for security positions at a senior level to include guard services and risk management.

MICHAEL B. SMITHSON

9701 Bay Shore Drive * Ocean City, MD 20145
410.555.1234 (h) * mbsmith@aol.com

CORPORATE SECURITY & RISK MANAGEMENT

EXECUTIVE PROFILE

Strong leader with a consistent record of achievement throughout a 21-year career in security services management and operations. Gained a reputation in the national security arena as an innovative leader—challenging and changing Cold-War policies, while embracing new and more efficient technologies.

Establish strong, large, and productive networks of influence with government and industry leaders, allowing significant influence of national policy and leverage of scarce resources. Demonstrated ability to plan, modernize, and create comprehensive security strategies, programs, and policies.

Direct personnel administration requirements, training, and professional development. Identify, hire, and supervise talented teams of security professionals. Execute budgets. Review, revise, and implement Presidential directives. Compose Congressional correspondence. Confident and eloquent public speaker.

- **Investigative Management**
- **Budget & Policy Formulation**
- **Hold a TS/SCI/SAP Clearance**
- **Embrace Technology and E-Business**
- **Design Technical & Operational Corporate Security Programs**
- **Develop & Implement Security Measures, Training Programs & Internal Policy Regulations**

PROFESSIONAL EXPERIENCE

DIRECTOR, SECURITY MANAGEMENT OFFICE
Vega Corporation, Washington D.C.   1990 to Present

- Direct asset protection programs for all Vega centers (14 nationally) including every security discipline: Personnel, Physical, Industrial, Counterintelligence/Counterterrorism and Information Security. Expertly guide security operations ensuring the safety of the general public (millions) who visit Vega facilities annually and direct security requirements for employees and contractors. Oversee operations through center managers.

- Articulated a vision for the security program that includes key milestones and performance goals, incorporates close working relationships with customers, and embraces new technologies including supporting and adopting ISO quality processes and cutting-edge computer resources.

- Review and ensure that proper and effective policies, training programs, resourcing, and oversight are in place for security officers including armed and uniformed guard forces. Formulate policy for the use of deadly force and other vital security operational issues. Design and analyze metrics to monitor the health of all programs. Evaluate center security managers and ensure that security managers are well informed and proactive.

- Serve as advisor to the director on matters regarding security. Represent the corporation's interests before industry, special-interest groups, labor groups, other federal agencies, state and local governments, and the American public through external task forces, working groups, public hearings, and meetings.

217

Corporate security specialist. *Diane Burns, CPRW, IJCTC, CCM, CEIP; Columbia, MD*

Michael B. Smithson, Page 2
_____

CHIEF, CORPORATE SECURITY
Northrop Corporation, Hawthorne, CA   **1981 to 1990**

* Promoted from Policy Analyst, Industrial Security Specialist, and Case Controller. Left as one of the three most highly decorated employees in the department's history.

- Managed industrial security oversight for Special Access Programs (SAP). Reengineered the role of the industrial security program, resulting in a new, secure, high-quality, customer-responsive service that attracted new customers. Collaborated with industry and government on the creation of company-wide Industrial Security Program policy.

- Fostered and cemented a close working relationship with the FBI regarding counterintelligence investigations and operations involving industry. Participated in classified roles in several high-profile industrial espionage investigations.

- Lectured thousands of cleared contractors around the country on security and intelligence issues. Served as a guest lecturer at the CIA Academy and the Federal Security Institute.

- Managed and conducted hundreds of highly complex and sensitive personnel security investigations regarding criminal and security issues/violations. Maintained a keen ability to elicit information and apply technical procedures to draw accurate conclusions for critical investigations.

- Audited and assessed the effectiveness of security programs and recommended corrective actions. Conducted and reported audits and inspections of cleared facilities nationwide.

EDUCATION & PROFESSIONAL DEVELOPMENT

Stanford University
- Non-degree program for senior security officials in government and industry, 1995

University of Southern California (USC)
- Bachelor of Science in Psychology, 1979

A short listing…
- Corporate Security Training Academy for Executives
- ISO 9000 Quality Training
- FBI Citizens Academy
- Security Management, Education Program Management & Leadership Training

PROFESSIONAL ACTIVITIES & MEMBERSHIPS

- National Association of Chiefs of Police
- Industrial Security Program Policy Advisory Committee
- Extranet for Security Professionals
- National Security Policy Board Forum
- American Society of Industrial Security

Sales and Related Occupations

Resumes at a Glance

Cashiers

Counter and Rental Clerks

Demonstrators, Product Promoters, and Models

Insurance Sales Agents

Real Estate Brokers and Sales Agents

Retail Salespersons

Sales Representatives, Wholesale and Manufacturing

Sales Worker Supervisors

Securities, Commodities, and Financial Services Sales Agents

Travel Agents

Nancy Wilkerson

This individual was seeking a higher-paid job in customer service with the same company.

Cashier / Customer Service / Warehouse

The functional format was selected to make the most of Nancy's limited experience as a cashier.

5523 East 42nd Street Apt. A
Oakland, CA 94606
(510) 484-2345
nancywilk@hotmail.com

Customer-driven Assistant helping companies build and sustain a loyal customer base. Committed to assisting management in providing impeccable service and products. Dedicated to offering friendly, professional, and resourceful service in a timely manner to diverse customer base.

Strengths and Abilities

Customer Care / Cashier
- Accurately handle cash transactions and balance cash drawer with efficiency.
- Quick to answer customer questions and complaints; repeatedly solicit customer feedback, all to ensure high-quality service.
- Train new employees in product knowledge, customer service, and operation of cash registers.

Warehouse
- With careful detail, conduct inventory of total stock and perform inventory restocking.
- Able to meticulously sort cargo for quality control. Strictly adhere to company policies for disposing damaged goods.
- Capable of retrieving requested merchandise and loading on forklift.
- Cooperatively and efficiently work to store and remove merchandise, ensuring proper storage and safe handling.

Work Experience

Taco Bell — Hayward, CA
Cashier   1997 – 2002
Worked as cashier for drive-through and restaurant counter. Accurately took orders and registered payments, returning correct change. Restocked food and performed other tasks as needed.

Additional Information and Excellent References Available Upon Request

218

Cashier. *Leatha Jones, CPRW, CEIP; Orinda, CA*

Juan needed a resume to secure a position in another state, where he was relocating to be near his children.

JUAN D. BUSCATO

125 South Valley Road • Hendersonville, Tennessee 37075

Home (615) 826-2179 • E-mail JDBus@hotmail.com

KEY QUALIFICATIONS

Thorough knowledge of the **PLUMBING SUPPLY INDUSTRY** acquired through 15 years of experience in wholesale plumbing supply, showroom, and general hardware environments. Strong record of providing a high level of customer service resulting in increased sales and customer loyalty. Actively promote products and services by maximizing selling opportunities.

Juan worked in management for several years but did not care for the stress, so he moved into counter sales for this wholesale supply house.

PROFESSIONAL EXPERIENCE

SALES ASSOCIATE
Steinhaus Supply Company, Inc. — Nashville, Tennessee   1995 – Present

- Counter sales of plumbing fixtures and supplies primarily to plumbers and plumbing contractors for high-volume wholesaler.
- Provide professional assistance to walk-in customers and pull orders from the warehouse.
- Started in 3,000-sq. ft. showroom, working one-on-one with customers to select plumbing fixtures and products appropriate to their decor and budget.

MANAGER / PLUMBING DEPARTMENT
Home Improvement Warehouse — Nashville, Tennessee   1993 – 1995

- Promoted from Sales Associate to manage all aspects of this location's largest department selling all major brands of plumbing supplies and fixtures.
- Oversaw department sales, customer assistance, merchandising, product displays, and inventory. Supervised, scheduled, and trained eight employees.
- Conducted numerous "How-To" clinics to instruct customers in basic plumbing improvements and repairs.

STORE MANAGER
True Value Hardware — Mt. Juliet, Tennessee   1990 – 1993

- Oversaw performance of all store operations, including staffing, merchandising, inventory, and customer service.
- Hired, trained, and supervised five employees.

ASSISTANT MANAGER
Ace Hardware — Lebanon, Tennessee   1987 – 1990

- Assisted store manager with all day-to-day activities of independent hardware store, such as customer service, ordering store merchandise, and employee scheduling.

PROFESSIONAL TRAINING

Eljer Plumbingware, Inc., Showroom Training, 1997
Sales Strategies, Customer Service, and Motivational Training, 1994 – 1995

This resume reflects Juan's solid history working in the hardware industry.

219

Counter clerk. *Carolyn Braden, CPRW; Hendersonville, TN*

Using this resume, Merrilee immediately received two new promotion & spokesmodeling assignments. She subsequently took a full-time promotional job for a major automotive leasing company, staging golf tournaments and other promotional activities to support the company's marketing efforts.

Merrilee L. Jackson

385 Spring Trail
Seattle, Washington 98990
Cellular: 213-554-1788
E-mail: merrilee@seattle.rr.com

Objective

Seeking a position that will capitalize upon my record of developing promotions, generating outside
sales, and making presentations and demonstrations before large groups.

Summary of Qualifications

❖ Superior interpersonal skills, both written and oral, combined with the ability to
establish rapport quickly and easily among diverse groups. Excellent listening
skills; poised in large and fast-paced environments.

❖ Excellent credentials in the design and implementation of retail promotions within
the restaurant and hospitality industries; possess a well-developed portfolio of
managerial relationships.

❖ Strong multitasking abilities with a good record of success in fast-paced
environments; solid administrative and account-management skills.

This section briefly describes who she worked for and makes passing reference to the major accounts she serviced.

Modeling / Promotional Highlights

Promotions — <u>HUSKY ENTERPRISES</u> — Seattle, WA   12/99–Present
(Promoters of Bacardi and Asahi products in the Seattle / Tacoma area.)
Oversee the implementation of retail promotions designed to increase market share and awareness
for Bacardi's new Tropico products and Asahi beer. Engage patrons of host restaurants and
entertainment facilities, establish rapport, and utilize various suggestive-selling techniques to
encourage the sampling of new beverages.

❖ Regularly increase sales of targeted products by an average of 200% (three to five
cases) on event nights.

❖ Continuously requested by bar owners and managers.

Spokesmodel / Promotions — <u>GORMAN PROMOTIONS</u> — Seattle, WA   02/98–11/99
Effectively accomplished numerous independent promotions, with accounts including Starburst,
Kamora Coffee, and Australia's Tangleridge and Banrock wines, for various distributors.

❖ Produced substantial increases in product awareness and sales; enjoyed positive
residual sales increases after the event.

Model — <u>CARLSON MARKETING</u> — Miami, FL   Spring 1998
Model/hostess for the 1998 North American Auto Show in Detroit, in which Carlson managed the
introduction and world premier of the VW Beetle. Correctly directed press inquiries to appropriate
product-knowledge specialists; coordinated promotion events, including virtual-reality NASCAR events;
generated or distributed press releases; and provided crowd-control functions when necessary.

Fragrance Model — <u>CHANEL</u> — Seattle, WA   Fall 1997
Managed the new line "Allure" perfume launch, during the Christmas Season, at major chain
department stores (Nordstrom and Macy's) throughout the SeaTac area.

Assignment Roster Upon Request

This page served as a "teaser" to a companion second page that was an exhaustive list of every assignment she had ever accepted.

220

Demonstrator, product promoter, and model. *William G. Murdock, CPRW;
Dallas, TX*

Althea used this resume to apply to modeling schools.

Althea Sivertson

Poised and Inspirational Model

For this high school student just breaking into the field of modeling, design and uniqueness were extremely important to catch the reader's attention. The design reflects her personality.

Physical Statistics	Height:	5'10"		Hair:	Blonde
	Weight:	115 lbs.		Eyes:	Blue
	Measurements:	34-24-34			

Training

Focus on Teens, Clark Modeling School, Jamestown, ND
Photo Movement I, James Anderson, Jamestown, ND
Runway Modeling, James Anderson, Jamestown, ND
Promotional Modeling, James Anderson, Fargo, ND
Professionalism, James Anderson, Fargo, ND
Modeling Invitational, Minneapolis, MN
Modeling Seminar, Moorhead, MN

Modeling Experience

Runway
KVLY TV, Bridal Showcase (3 years)
Marshall Fields, Back-To-School
Matrix, Hair Expo
Dayton's, Women's Showcase
Hair Success, Women's Showcase

Mannequin
Dayton's
The Buckle
Vanity
JC Penney
Vanity, Women's Showcase

Print

The Forum (newspaper), Abraham Nelson
Virtual Closet (website fashion), Video Arts Studio
Laconian (Lincoln HS yearbook)
Photo Testing, James Anderson
Photo Testing, Abbott Bonnet
Photo Testing, Mac Taxdalen
Photo Testing, Abdul Tangen
Photo Testing, Ali Ludden
Photo Testing, William Taylor

Promotional

Pretzel Maker, Minneapolis and Moorhead, MN

Skills

Ballet ❖ Basketball ❖ Hockey ❖ Track ❖ Rollerskating

30 Monte Carlo Drive ❖ Jamestown, ND 58401
701-222-2444 ❖ althea@hotmail.com

This resume was designed to fit within an 8 x 10" frame, rather than on standard 8½ x 11" paper, so it could be pasted on the back of her 8 x 10" photograph.

221

Model. *Mary Laske, MS, CPRW; Fargo, ND*

Although very successful in insurance sales, Bradley wanted to move into another industry.

BRADLEY J. EDWARDS

352 Redwood Court
Hendersonville, TN 37075

BradEdw@aol.com

Home: (615) 824-4326
Cellular: (615) 969-7221

AREAS OF EXPERTISE

Sales • Sales Management • Contract Negotiations
Client Relations • Business Management • Marketing

Key Qualifications

) This section focuses on his overall sales abilities.

- Top-producing **Sales Professional** with highly successful career in insurance sales/business management plus additional experience in operations management.
- Highly focused, with the ability to consistently achieve sales objectives through strong account management and commitment to customer satisfaction.
- Build lasting business relationships through performance and credibility. Develop positive rapport with people at all levels of responsibility.

Professional Experience

) This section showcases his sales and operations management experience.

NEIGHBORHOOD OFFICE AGENT .... 1994 – Present
Providence Insurance Agency • Hendersonville, TN

Established and developed successful insurance agency from the ground up. Handle initial claims for all lines, including home, auto, auto financing, life, health, extended care, and extended warranties. Manage five-figure operating budget; negotiate terms for office space; hire, train, and supervise office staff.

- Prospected and acquired account base of over 1,500 clients through referrals, networking, advertising, and community involvement.
- Impressive record of regional and national sales honors, including *National Champion, Honor Ring, Quality Agency Award,* and *Most Profitable Agent in Territory* (Nashville to Memphis).
- First agent in Nashville district to achieve perfect score (100%) on Life exam.

MANAGING PARTNER / FARM OPERATIONS MANAGER .... 1982 – 1994
J & E Farms • Plains, GA

Oversaw all aspects of management, administration, and operation of modern, 5,000-acre row-crop farm (peanuts, corn, soybeans, and wheat). Managed annual operating budget of $2 million. Ensured planting was done according to rotation schedule.

- Supervised 10–12 full-time and 60–70 seasonal employees.
- Negotiated purchase prices for chemicals, fertilizers, and irrigation equipment; also terms and prices for land leases.

Education and Professional Training

Degree Program: BUSINESS ADMINISTRATION • Belmont University, Nashville, TN

LUTC License • Comprehensive 16-week training course • 1995

Ongoing professional training provided by Providence in the following key areas:
Sales . . . Customer Satisfaction . . . New Products . . . Sensitivity . . . PC Applications.

222

Insurance sales agent. *Carolyn Braden, CPRW; Hendersonville, TN*

John C. Zienert
3874 Sycamore Lane ▪ Neenah, Wisconsin 54956 ▪ (414) 729-4718

Dynamic, motivated professional with a proven track record in business management. Well-rounded background in sales and marketing, staff training, and account development. Accomplished teacher and leader.

Summary of Attributes

- Excellent communication and interpersonal skills; easily develop a positive rapport with clients, staff, and peers.
- Strong organizational and time management abilities.
- Patient and effective teacher with strong leadership traits.
- Creatively develop and implement sales and marketing strategies.

Experience

After 30 successful years in insurance, John wanted a position as a regional trainer. His resume stresses his teaching experience and in-depth knowledge of insurance sales management (resume writer's comments).

XYZ Insurance Companies   1975-Present
Agency Manager (1987-Present)
Orchestrate operational and management aspects of branch office.
- Manage sales, customer service, and claims functions.
- Develop and implement business and marketing plans.
- Generate and oversee annual budget
- Screen, hire, and train support staff.

Senior Account Agent (1984-1987)
- Managed sales and customer service functions.
- Trained new personnel.

Account Agent (1982-1984)
- Accounted for receipts, applications, and general business forms.

Sales Representative (1975-1982)

Accomplishments:
- Retained 92% of client base and continued to grow agency while company decreased their book of business by 25% (1991-1994).
- Consistently increased sales and maintained profitability each year.
- Demonstrated ability to attain sales production, retention ratio, loss ratio, and production levels necessary for the following awards:
  - Quality Agency Award   – Conference of Champions
  - Honor Ring (five times)   – Regional Vice President Award
- Selected to serve on various company strategy, competitive, and product enhancement forums, as well as various communication committees.

Eau Claire School District, Eau Claire, Wisconsin
Teacher and Principal   1970-1975
- Managed an elementary school with an enrollment of 230 students and a professional staff of 18. Prepared operating budget, oversaw physical building maintenance, developed curriculum, resolved disciplinary issues, administered school policies, and acted as liaison between School Board, staff, parents and the community.
- Taught sixth grade Math.
- Served as Athletic Director, coaching girls basketball, boys basketball, football, track, and baseball.

Education

Bachelor of Science   1970
University of Wisconsin-Madison

LUTC   1978-1979

223

Insurance agency manager/trainer. *Kathy Keshemberg, NCRW; Appleton, WI* *a compact presentation that displays a lot of good information on a one-page format.*

DANETTE INGRAMS, CRS, GRI
1050 Cokeberry
Houston, Texas 77256
(713) 580-4689

PROFESSIONAL SUMMARY:	**REAL ESTATE PROFESSIONAL**

Dynamic Top-Producing Real Estate professional with 18 years experience building, developing and leading high caliber sales and marketing divisions in competitive, fast-paced real estate environments. Outstanding presentation, negotiation and leadership qualifications. Areas of expertise include:

- ★ New Product Development
- ★ Sales Recruitment and Training
- ★ Presentations and Negotiations
- ★ Market Appraisals and Evaluations
- ★ Financing and Banking Relationships

- ★ Marketing and Sales Strategies
- ★ Client Relationship Management
- ★ Promotional Advertising
- ★ Residential and Commercial Sales
- ★ New Business Development

PROFESSIONAL HIGHLIGHTS:

- Developed and implemented sales and marketing programs for 350 lot subdivision (Fairview Park) and 200 lot subdivision (Mission Hills Country Club). Created all advertising vehicles for both properties; assisted builders in the layout and design of floor plans; conducted neighborhood surveys and advised builders on preferred standard features, architectural design, decorative and color schemes. Designed and coordinated furnishings for model homes.
- Established/managed REMAX sales office in Odessa, Texas. Recruited, trained and motivated seventeen sales agents. Successfully grew business from zero base to $25 million annual sales within 18 months.

AWARDS AND DISTINCTIONS:

Received Odessa Board of Realtors' Multi-Million Dollar Sales Award for thirteen consecutive years.
Attained National Remax International President's Club status in 1986.
Repeatedly qualified for the National Multi-Million Dollar Club Award.

CERTIFICATIONS AND LICENSES:

Certified Residential Specialist (CRS)
Graduate, Realtors Institute (GRI)
Texas Real Estate Brokers License 1980

PROFESSIONAL AFFILIATIONS:

National Association of Realtors
Montgomery County Association of Realtors
Texas Association of Realtors
Houston Association of Realtors
Montgomery County Chamber of Commerce
International Toastmasters Club
Greater Houston CRS Chapter

LECTURER:

Odessa College, Odessa, Texas
Real Estate Brokerage Management

PROFESSIONAL EXPERIENCE:

REMAX SPRING - WOODLANDS, The Woodlands, TX — 1993 - Present
Real Estate Broker/Associate

REMAX OF ODESSA, Odessa, TX — 1986 - 1993
Real Estate Broker/Owner

CARRIAGE COMPANY, San Antonio, TX — 1983 - 1986
Real Estate Broker
- Achieved top 5% of all salespersons (30) for three consecutive years.

ADOBE REALTORS, Albuquerque, NM — 1978 - 1983
Sales Associate
- Achieved top 3% of all salespersons (20) for five consecutive years.

224

Real estate agent and broker. *Cheryl Ann Harland, CPRW, JCTC; The Woodlands, TX*

This list contains terms that are unique and important to retailing. It also lists Andrea's more general sales and management skills.

Andrea J. Ruiz
4793 Hopewell Avenue
Meriden, CT 06450
(203) 555-1010 • ajruiz@aol.com

Qualifications Summary

Accomplished and motivated **Senior Retail Sales Associate** with 5+ years' exemplary experience and performance track record characterized by continued advancement into positions of increased visibility.

- Expert organizational skills, highly effective assessment and analytical skills, and key strategic planning ability.
- Broad range of operational experience includes sales, marketing, merchandising, sales analysis, public/vendor relations, markdowns, inventory control, and shrinkage.
- Strong leadership skills and ability to train new staff.
- PC skills include Windows, Excel, and Microsoft Word; bilingual (fluent in English and Spanish).

Core Competencies

- Dynamic Assortment-Building and Planning
- Quick Problem-Solving
- Accomplishment, Goal-Oriented Approach
- Merchandising Presentation Expertise
- Expert Negotiation Ability
- Key Decision-Making Skills
- Vendor Relation Skills
- Savvy Assessment Skills

Professional Experience

1999–Present   **J.C. PENNEY** • Trumbull, CT
Senior Sales Associate *(promotion, 3/2000–Present)*
- Handle retail sales of Men's Sportswear; coordinate wardrobes and provide professional advice.
- Achieved "Selling Star for the Month" award, three consecutive months.
- Recipient of customer commendation letter and award pins recognizing exemplary customer service.
- Consistently exceed monthly goal for opening new customer charge accounts.
- Collaborate with Merchandising Manager in revamping department, coordinating fashion shows, and increasing traffic/exposure.

Sales Associate *(5/1999–3/2000)*
- Top producer in both American Woman and Ladies' Accessories departments.

1996–1999   **LORD & TAYLOR** • West Hartford, CT
Sales Associate *(part-time during academic year; full-time summers/vacations)*
- Ranked top floater among part-time staff; adept in quickly learning new departments.
- Named among top 3 sales associates in each department (Girls' Sportswear, Children's, Men's, Ladies', Home Boutique).

Education   TRINITY COLLEGE • Hartford, CT
Bachelor of Art Degree, History *(1999)* — Concentrations: Design and Photography
- Recipient of Parson's award for outstanding leadership.

Continuing Professional Education includes successful completion of corporate training programs in such topical areas as leadership/supervision, communication skills, mentoring, merchandising, motivational skills, and teamwork.

225

Retail salesperson. *Jan Melnik, CPRW, CCM; Durham, CT*

MILLICENT JOHNSON

3145 Chicken Coop Road
Norfolk, Virginia 23501

804 . 465.3906

OBJECTIVE

To obtain a challenging position in Retail Sales Management with a dynamic corporation where I can use my energy and skills to develop, motivate and lead while encouraging employee productivity.

KEY QUALIFICATIONS

- More than seventeen years of successful experience in professional sales and marketing with ability to develop accounts and product promotion.
- Excellent verbal, and interpersonal skills. Relate easily at all levels of the decision making process. Work well as individual producer or team member in the achievement of sales objectives. Have a high aptitude for acquisition of new product sales and marketing technologies.
- Experience includes scheduling, budgeting, purchasing, distribution, inventory management, merchandising, personnel supervision and relations, and related aspects of business operations.
- A unique bilingual background, success in professional endeavors, ability to make effective decisions, and a blend of flexibility, high energy and maturity.

PROFESSIONAL EXPERIENCE

MANUFACTURER'S REPRESENTATIVE/DISTRICT MANAGER.
Accounts included Cosmetic and Perfume Manufacturers, Ready-to-Wear and related lines • Hired to explore and develop territory • Able to manage a large staff, and a variety of retail sales accounts including the military • Take inventory and write orders.

CORPORATE TRAINER. Bachrach's Department Store, North Carolina and Virginia.
Corporate, Sales, and Motivational Trainer for a variety of retail outlets • Taught management and employees how to do their jobs successfully • Held training sessions in intimate apparel, and shoe workshops.

ACCOUNT EXECUTIVE. Bachrach's Department Store, North Carolina and Virginia.
Consistent success in surpassing business goals • Able to meet all deadlines and exceed quotas • Designed and successfully implemented creative marketing programs including sales strategies, advertising, and public relations functions • Managed simultaneous projects in store chain to establish uniformity in all locations • Monitored consumer trends and improved company image • Compiled sales figures for analytic reports and outlined future sales projections • Ability to recruit and motivate sales staff • Encouraged staff development and conducted product training sessions • Positive attitude with buyers, account managers, and store management • Solid manager, team builder, and motivator.

ACCOUNT COORDINATOR. XYZ COSMETICS, INC., New York, New York.
Sell-through covered 42 accounts in New York, New Jersey and Delaware • Motivated, positioned, and promoted new products • Conducted training seminars • Developed a sales training program for new personnel and in-service employees • Increased sales figures from $538,000 to $1,550,200.

226

Retail sales supervisor/manager. *Anne G. Kramer; Virginia Beach, VA*

MILLICENT JOHNSON

Page 2

ACCOUNT EXECUTIVE. ABC Company, New York, New York.
Fully responsible for sell-in and sell-through involving 50 accounts • Responsible for a variety of budgets including special events, and sales projections in the greater New York, New Jersey and Delaware area • Set up training schedules for freelance artists and product promotions • Coordinated special events • Hired and trained freelance personnel and consultants • Handled administrative communications and reports • Performed in-service training of counter personnel • Scheduled and assigned freelance artists for product promotion • Responsible for stock to sales planning, product merchandising, and projections on volume.

EDUCATION

TOMPKINS COUNTY COMMUNITY COLLEGE, Ithaca, New York.
Business Administration.
UNIVERSITY of PARIS, Paris, France.
Fashion design, Beauty culture and Business management. Speak fluent French

SEMINARS:
TIME MANAGEMENT, Cortland, New York
QUARTERLY MARKETING/FINANCIAL SEMINARS, ABC Company, New York, New York.
TEAM MANAGEMENT, Bachrach's Department Store, North Carolina and Virginia.
SEMINARS INTERNATIONAL, "Working With Almost Anybody."

Since Millicent does not have a degree, her education is presented last. She is a dynamic and successful individual and those strengths are emphasized throughout her resume.

After a successful career in retail sales, Mary moved into management. Her resume helped her land several interviews.

MARY LANDISHE

2735 Patriot Lane
Laurel, MD 21045

410.555.1234
mary@yahoo.com

~ Retail Sales Management ~
~ Finance & Business ~

Team Leader	**Trainer**	**Coordinator**
Personnel Administrator	**Customer Service First**	**Business Operations**

- *Assemble, train, and motivate talented teams—effectively building consensus.*
- *Skilled and respected team leader. Create quality, 'customer service first' environments.*
- *Progressive record of accomplishment for analyzing/dissecting in-place operations, identifying problems, determining solutions, and reworking processes. Designed unique marketing promotions.*
- *Cost-effective manager with wise understanding of resource utilization/allocation. Consistently exceed sales goals.*

~ EXPERIENCE ~

Hecht's, Baltimore, MD   **1997 to Present**

DEPARTMENT MANAGER
* *Supervise up to 45 personnel during peak seasons in a high-volume department selling clothing. Draft and post schedules, train and develop employees, manage merchandising, generate business, coordinate displays, and oversee cash operations. Supervise one co-manager and two assistant managers. Hired as a co-manager and promoted to manager within four months.*

- Effectively manage a $3M annual retail store department in a prominent mall. Interview, hire and train new sales associates. Manage payroll reports; determine and meet sales goals.
- Successfully implemented sales promotions and proper training of sales associates increasing sales from $2.5M to $3.2M in less than one year—moving the store from 19% loss to +4%/profit.
- Review weekly, monthly, quarterly and annual numbers/sales and determine methods to grow numbers. Compare prior years' numbers to current numbers to create strategic plans for increases.
- Recognized by the sales team as a fair manager, able to work well with anyone. Strong delegator. Keep the team pumped up without monetary incentives.
- Manage cash register operations with an annual cash flow of $3M+. Balance bank deposits and daily sales. Speak to the representatives of the bank on a weekly basis.

The Brand Shoe Outlet, Columbia Mall, Columbia, MD   **1994 to 1997**

ASSISTANT STORE MANAGER
* *Supervised a staff of 10 associates selling shoes and footwear accessories with an annual volume of $700K. Oversight for all sales-floor activities.*

- Opened and closed the store, prepared/reviewed payroll reports and sales goals. Managed customer service. Designed displays and maintained an organized sales area.

~ EDUCATION & PROFESSIONAL DEVELOPMENT ~

Bachelor of Science in Business Management, University of Maryland, 1997

Situational Leadership, Blanchard
Attended a number of in-house conferences (Leadership, Retail Operations, and Managing People).

227

Retail sales supervisor/manager. *Diane Burns, CPRW, IJCTC, CCM, CEIP; Columbia, MD*

This individual was the casualty of a business shutdown.

JANE KINGSTON

22 Pinegreen Avenue • Ormond Beach, Florida 32174
(904) 412-7842 • jkingston@fl.rr.com

CAREER PROFILE

Retail Sales Manager with 15 years of progressive experience in all phases of retail operations. Consistently successful in achieving profit and loss, sales plans, productivity, budget, inventory, and shortage goals. A high-energy, results-oriented leader with excellent interpersonal, presentation, and communication skills. Exceptional staff development, training, and motivational skills. Persuasive sales and customer service skills.

Information included here describes Jane's contributions to the company during her brief tenure – in spite of its closing.

PROFESSIONAL EXPERIENCE

UPTONS DEPARTMENT STORES, INC.   1998 to Present

Store Manager

Manage all phases of daily operations for Orlando store generating $8 million in annual revenues. Accountable for profit and loss, sales plan and payroll quotas, and $3 million inventory. Responsibilities include accounting, operations management, merchandising, staffing, security, and facility maintenance. Report directly to Regional Sales Director.

- Chosen for "New Store Opening Team" responsible for the launching of two new locations.
- Selected to facilitate a Leadership Development Program providing off-site training for Merchandise Team Managers throughout the Central Florida region.
- Consistently achieved or exceeded payroll productivity quotas.
- Exceeded sales plan by 3% in 1999, 6% in 2000, and 7% in 2001.
- Developed and promoted three team members to mid-managers.
- Awarded Florida's Leading Achiever Award three consecutive years.
- Awarded Top Credit Solicitor three consecutive years for opening Uptons' charge accounts.

BURDINES DEPARTMENT STORE   1984 to 1998

This information about her previous job was designed to demonstrate her stability and longevity and to show that she had been promoted through a series of increasingly responsible positions.

Instrumental in opening the new Burdines store in the Seminole Town Center. Earned promotions through a series of management positions based on superior performance, excellent leadership, and innovative strategies.

Divisional Sales Manager

Responsible for achieving statistical objectives in relation to sales, profit, and selling productivity for $24 million store.

- Maintained stock levels and merchandising for the entire store.
- Managed, trained, and developed 10 direct-report sales managers.
- Developed ongoing relationships with supervisors and central organization for responsive store support.

228

Retail sales supervisor/manager. *Beverly Harvey, CPRW, JCTC, CCM; Pierson, FL*

JANE KINGSTON

PROFESSIONAL EXPERIENCE (Continued)

- Worked with buying office in planning, quantity projections, and implementation of all physical inventories.
- Maintained high level of customer service.
- Assisted in the development of selling tools to train and develop a professional selling staff responsible for driving credit for store.
- Ensured implementation of merchandise prototype through visual support and merchandise context. Oversaw all aspects of operational functions such as sale set up, merchandise processing, and product placement.
- Won recognition for increasing sales of home store by $1 million, 1994–1995.

Director of Selling Service

Managed all selling service activities for 10 sales managers and 84 selling associates.

- Oversaw training and development programs for developing managers and associates.

Director of Loss Prevention / Operations Manager

Responsible for overseeing the shortage committee and executing physical inventory and shortage audits for the entire store.

- Consistently met all budget quotas and shortage goals.
- Managed the cash office, customer service, and all receiving and maintenance.
- Received "Burdines Conch Award" for slashing inventory shortages.

Group Selling Service Manager

Full responsibility for a $2 million business unit.

- Utilized innovative merchandising and management techniques to generate sales volume.
- Maintained inventory/shortage, merchandising, and floor design/layout.
- Managed staff training, development, and evaluation for superior customer service.

EDUCATION / PROFESSIONAL DEVELOPMENT

B.S., Marketing, University of Central Florida, Orlando, Florida — 1983

Burdines Training — Extensive training in all phases of operations and management

Dale Carnegie Course

Michael Yakobian — Sales Training

JOHN H. GUSTAVSEN

12 Frye Road
South Berwick, ME 03908
207.555.1010 • jhgus65@aol.com

SUMMARY

- **Highly Motivated Manufacturers' Sales Representative** with successful account-development and -management experience. Background reflects consistent achievement of sales objectives—from effective cold-calling techniques to strategies for establishing and retaining strong customer base.
- Resourceful sales professional with keen marketing/sales acumen. Polished skills in account cultivation and management as well as all facets of sales cycle from cold-calling through successful closure.

PROFESSIONAL EXPERIENCE

The names of well-known clients are included to show that John has the ability to sell to large, high-profile companies and to show that he has a good network of contacts in the industry that will carry over to his new position.

JOHNSON EQUIPMENT • Waterville, ME
Senior Sales Manufacturers' Representative *(1997–Present)*

- Manage territory comprising Vermont, New Hampshire, and Maine, including strategic accounts; function as liaison on all quality issues between manufacturers and clients.
- Successfully represent broad range of products in 15 lines across the metal-casting and metal-working industry.
- Instrumental in targeting, developing, turning around, and/or retaining such key accounts as A.W. Chesterton, HP Medical Electronics/Royal Phillips Medical Electronics, Siemens Medical, and Teradyne.
- Extensive experience in account cultivation, development, and management across a sales cycle of typically up to 12 months; successfully closed sales ranging from $10K to $100K with several orders in excess of $1 million.
- Partner extensively with clients in new-product development, consulting, and research and development projects.

Key Accomplishments ... *To avoid confusion with the extensive job activities listed above, his key accomplishments have their own sub-heading to make them stand out.*

- Highly effective in successfully managing territories characterized by changing boundaries; challenged to open/penetrate new states/regions.
- Consistently exceeded quota within 1 year of being deployed to new territories; provided strong account management with a track record of producing sustainable results.
- Achieved gross sales results in excess of $7 million.
- Represent client companies at 3–4 trade shows annually; facilitate training seminars.
- Awarded *Chicago White Metal (CWM) Diecasting's* **2001 Winner Top Sales**.
- Earned *CWM 2000* **First Place Sales Honors** ($3,500 award plus 4-day vacation).

EDUCATION   **University of Maine** • Orono, ME   1997   B.S. Social Sciences

PROFESSIONAL DEVELOPMENT

- Dale Carnegie Courses
- Leadership Forum
- Risk-Taking Professional Development

- Managing Customer Service
- Team-Building: New Results
- Sales Administration

- Managing Diversity
- Consumer Behavior
- Influence Forum

229

Manufacturers' sales representative. *Jan Melnik, CPRW, CCM; Durham, CT*

After many years running a daycare center, Christina wanted back in the workforce. But she hated the first job she took and was ready to leave. Since she had extensive training and transferable skills, I listed her present job. Her cover letter explained the rest (resume writer's comments).

CHRISTINA V. SUMMERS
8400 Industrial Parkway
Plain City, Ohio 00000
(614) 000-0000

PROFILE

Over ten years diverse experience successfully interacting with management, technicians, sales representatives and customers to effectively solve problems. Possess strong communication skills leading to excellent rapport with customers in retaining their confidence and their business.

EDUCATION

Bachelor of Arts, Political Science *(in progress)*
THE OHIO STATE UNIVERSITY

PROFESIONAL EXPERIENCE

DIRECTORY ADVERTISING COMPANY
Advertising Department, Columbus, Ohio   August 1998 - Present
Sales Representative
Customer Service

- Sell yellow page advertising to a specific geographical customer base.
- Research and perform needs assessment used to evaluate and promote a business' product(s) or service(s).
- Designed programs to meet customer needs. During first month on the job, 50% of customers contacted upgraded their advertising.
- Attended three-week intensive sales training seminar in Dallas, Texas for product knowledge, computer knowledge, and presentation skills. Received IST Sales Training Certificate.

HOME DAYCARE SERVICES, Columbus, Ohio   1990 - 1998
Owner, Operator

- Coordinated the sales and duties of child care services for discretionary parents.
- Planned organized activities to enhance child development and achieve parents highest expectations and trust.

TROPICAL TANNING SALON, Heath, Ohio   1989 - 1990
Manager

- Consistently met or exceeded sales goals established by company.
- Designed successful scripts and campaigns which increased clientele significantly.
- Hired, trained and managed staff of up to eight employees.
- Coordinated scheduling of entire operation.
- Wrote and compiled first employee's handbook.

"The most important single ingredient in the formula of success is knowing how to get along with people."
— Theodore Roosevelt

TELEMARKETING GROUP, Lancaster, Ohio   1986 - 1989
Telemarketer

- Possessed enterprise in obtaining new customers.
- Proficient in following company sales presentation system and increased sales.
- Earned four "Outstanding Sales Performance" awards.

230

Services sales representative. *Susan D. Higgins, CPRW; Plain City, OH*

Chandra Fox

1 Pomeroy Road, North Reading, MA 01867 • (978) 555-8345 • cthefox@hotmail.com

EXPERTISE	**Mass Media Sales**
	Strategic sales professional with a track record of accelerating sales, building strong client relationships, and creating focused marketing programs that meet clients' objectives and deliver results — frequently exceeding projections and generating additional sales opportunities.
EXPERIENCE	**Account Executive,** WAVZ-102 Radio, Manchester, NH, 1998–2002
	Built solid account base from the ground up — **increased billings every year** by focusing on account management and direct account development.
	Assessed clients' marketing needs and created integrated marketing/advertising programs; assisted key accounts with ad production.
	Developed strong skills in preparing professional proposals and presenting to clients at all levels including senior executives.

Sales Results

- President's Club winner for exceeding annual sales goals.
- Increased sales 32% second year, 22% third year; on track to exceed fourth-year goal.
- Doubled sales with a key account through strategic marketing planning.
- Grew sales from zero to $150K for a local agency; started with one account and brought all accounts into program by year two.
- Developed synergistic relationships with sales reps from other media, collaborating to create integrated sales and marketing campaigns that best fit clients' needs.

Marketing

- Developed creative promotion to invigorate attendance figures for a popular weekend attraction; increased attendance 7% in first weekend and motivated business owner to double length of advertising campaign.
- Conceived marketing concept and campaign for a new sports event, a race to benefit charity; generated advertising revenue of $40K for one-day event; achieved participation 40% above sponsor's projections.
- Created marketing program tie-in with two key accounts designed to build traffic and visibility for both; proposal well received by clients and planned for implementation in spring/summer 2002.

[handwritten note: Organizing her experience under these separate headings ensures that her accomplishments are not lost in a lengthy list of bullet points.]

Assistant Program Director (Internship), WBZ-TV, Boston, MA, January–June 1997
Marketed program offerings to syndicators; assisted Program Director with program selections; analyzed ratings and developed strategies to improve them.

EDUCATION	Bachelor of Arts in Electronic Media, 1997
	University of Massachusetts at Lowell

Honors & Activities

- Dean's List
- Elected to leadership positions in Alpha Lambda Pi sorority: Outside Events Chair (organizing, coordinating, and managing alumni events); Steward (supervising food preparation staff, purchasing food, managing budget and payroll); and Vice President (managing team of 10 officers and serving as liaison to university Greek council).

VOLUNTEER	Media liaison and in-kind gift solicitor for Special Olympics.

[handwritten note: Chandra intended to tap into her strong sorority network for job leads, so her resume lists the leadership roles she held in this organization while she was in college.]

231

Services sales representative. *Louise M. Kursmark, CPRW, JCTC, CEIP, CCM; Cincinnati, OH*

MICHAEL HEGARTY
(520) 541-3845
1542 BROWN STREET, TUCSON, AZ 85719
MICHAELHEGARTY@HOTMAIL.COM

PROFESSIONAL OBJECTIVE
Sales Management that emphasizes achievement in volume, profit, and development of personnel.

PROFESSIONAL EXPERIENCE

COCA-COLA ENTERPRISES, Tucson Branch   August 1996 – Present
DISTRIBUTION SUPERVISOR (August 2000 – Present)
ACCOUNT MANAGER (February 1999 – August 2000)
COLD-DRINK ACCOUNT MANAGER (August 1996 – February 1999)

- *As Distribution Supervisor,* manage all areas of distribution including expense control, fleet, safety, labor flexing, hiring, and training of employees.
- Interface extensively with sales force on standards, opportunities within venues, and improving customer relationships.
- Work with warehouse manager and employees to improve overall efficiencies.
- Assisted in executing 50,000-case volume in Wal-Mart of Tucson.
- Initiated and executed policies to increase cases per hour over prior (YTD through August) for sideload and bulk delivery as well as merchandising.

- *As Account Manager,* managed over 50 accounts, ranging from supermarkets, mass merchandisers, independent superettes, convenience stores, and virtually all cold-drink channel accounts.
- Built relationships with key managers, controlled inventory, managed space, and developed promotional marketing activities.
- Placed equipment in cold-drink accounts (30 placements – 4th quarter, 1999).
- Closed exclusive contract with Tucson School District, won Elway School District food-service bid, and beat competition in two new large independent fountain accounts, Hudson's Classic Grill and Hereford & Hops.

- *As Cold -Drink Account Manager,* managed all aspects of assigned territory from the Chandler Branch, including full service, regular cold drink, wholesale, tele-sales, fountain, and equipment.
- Exceeded budgeted volume and gross profit for territory, Fiscal 1998.

[handwritten annotation, left: This table was designed to rapidly attract the attention of prospective employers.]

[handwritten annotation, right: The table is effective because numbers are critical in the sales industry and are central to the planning that a beverage distribution company uses to successfully move its product.]

OPERATING RESULTS	VOLUME CHANGE	GP / CASE	± GP/ PRIOR
Full Service	+ 9.01%	$6.98	+ $.33
Regular Cold Drink	+ 17.44%	$3.78	+ $.30
Wholesale	-1.05%	$2.86	+ $.31

"Mike's effort enabled us to turn in the best cold-drink numbers in the entire division in 1998." – Performance Review

EDUCATION

ARIZONA STATE UNIVERSITY, Phoenix, AZ
MASTER – BUSINESS ADMINISTRATION, DECEMBER 1995; GPA 3.4
BACHELOR OF SCIENCE – BUSINESS ADMINISTRATION, May 1996; BUSINESS GPA 3.5

232

Products sales representative. *Julie Walraven; Wausau, WI*

CAROL M. JACOB

4 Baywood Blvd.
Brick, NJ 08723

cmjacob@yahoo.com

Res.: (732) 477-5172
Cell: (732) 600-7896

SALES MANAGER / ACCOUNTS MANAGER

Driven sales and management professional with proven track record of increasing sales, expanding services, and improving systems. Successful background in regional as well as national management of customer accounts and field personnel. Assertive and very customer oriented with excellent interpersonal skills. Computer literate in Windows, e-mail, the Internet, and internal company programs including Delta System, Soft-Pac System, and Excel Front-Load Calculator used for customer tracking and price setting. Willing to relocate. Highly skilled in:

- New Business Development
- Key Account Management
- Public Speaking/Presentations
- Revenue Growth
- Problem Resolution
- Account Retention
- Sales Team Support
- Team Building/Motivation
- Personnel Training

CAREER HIGHLIGHTS

- Recruited from Jersey Shore by United to open and manage a new Lakewood Office. Oversaw acquisition of new customers and built revenues to $150,000 per *month* in the new Ocean County territory.
- Increased United's sales to levels requiring additional truck purchases plus the hiring of more sales representatives and drivers, Neptune site.
- Overhauled commission plans at both United and Jersey Shore to provide clearer structure and accountability.
- Increased United's and Jersey Shore's annual revenues for commercial and residential accounts by implementing a monthly program requiring sales reps to add on or expand services for existing customers.
- Developed and instituted new service for Jersey Shore producing additional revenues of $150,000 annually.
- Exploded Jersey Shore's recycling sales with a 200% increase in annual revenues, 1990–1991.
- Won *every* monthly sales bonus for highest producing sales representative, Jersey Shore Waste, 1989–1994.

SALES MANAGEMENT PROFICIENCIES

Operations & Budget Management
- Managed $90,000 sales budget for United and $168,000 sales budget for Jersey Shore.
- Set annual/biannual price increases and instituted corporate-mandated price increases.
- Analyzed daily call logs and sales numbers for compliance with targeted sales quotas.
- Signed off on all sales contracts including new sales, seasonal start-ups, cancellations, and service changes.
- Oversaw processing of orders faxed in by sales reps and verified acquisition of appropriate deposits.
- Reviewed monthly collections reports for delinquent companies whose services should be interrupted.
- Prepared weekly sales statistics and approved monthly commissions for the sales staff.

Account Management
- Wined and dined key personnel nationally to maintain major accounts or acquire new ones.
- Improved account retention by interacting with dissatisfied customers and producing viable solutions.
- Conducted in-services for groups of 10–100 at customer locations to provide training in legal requirements and procedures for appropriate sorting/recycling, Jersey Shore Waste & United Disposal.

Personnel Management
- Hired and managed 3–10 sales representatives nationwide. Terminated employees when warranted.
- Conducted monthly sales meetings with sales staff and completed annual performance reviews.
- Provided support to field sales representatives and approved commission schedules.
- Motivated sales personnel through incentives including special lunches and half-days off with pay.

Carol did not want to be pigeonholed in the waste-disposal industry, so the first page of her resume highlights her strong sales and management accomplishments with only brief mention of her employers.

Page 1 of 2

233

Sales manager. *Carol Rossi, CPRW; Brick, NJ*

CAROL M. JACOB (732) 477-5172 • cmjacob@yahoo.com   **Page 2 of 2**

This section lists specific employers, but they are not emphasized because they appear on the second page.

SALES EXPERIENCE

UNITED DISPOSAL COMPANY, Lakewood, New Jersey — 1996 to 2002
Solid waste and recycling company servicing residential, commercial, and industrial customers. Subsidiary of publicly traded National Services since 1999 buyout.

> **Sales Manager** • Neptune 1997–2002: Ocean & Monmouth County Territories
> **Sales Manager** • Lakewood 1996–1997: Ocean County Territory
> Supervised activities of three sales representatives in Ocean and Monmouth Counties. Oversaw approximately 8,000 residential and 6,000 commercial accounts.

JERSEY SHORE WASTE SERVICES, INC., Lakewood, New Jersey — 1989 to 1996
Medical waste disposal and parking-lot sweeping services for commercial clientele.

> **Sales Manager** • January 1994-March 1996
> **Sales Representative** • July 1989-January 1994
> Supervised 8 sales representatives across 5 counties. Managed 15,000 commercial accounts in Ocean and Monmouth Counties, as well as 5,000 commercial accounts in Mercer, Burlington, and Camden Counties.

EARLY CAREER
Sales career includes additional experience as national sales manager, regional sales manager, and sales representative for Hollywood Wardrobe, Inc. (now closed), in Lakewood, New Jersey. Managed 10 national sales representatives and traveled heavily across the U.S. to entertain potential as well as existing clients.

EDUCATION & TRAINING

Sales Seminars • Conducted by National Services (United Division Company) • Annually since 1999

Comprehensive Sales Training (Berkeley Learning System: tape and video program) • May 2000–May 2001

Sales Management/Sales Training Conferences • National Services • Oct. 1999, Sept. 2000, Nov. 2001

Sociology & Psychology College Courses (3 years) • Georgian Court College, Lakewood, New Jersey

James is a young, vital go-getter whose career really took off when he discovered a small company with a fledgling product he felt had great potential. He prepared this resume while looking for his next challenge.

JAMES HENDERSON

60 Gilbert Road
Tiburon, CA 94920

Mobile: (413) 511 4247
E-mail: james@naturalfire.com.au

Residence: (415) 989 3655
Business: (415) 967 3525

His resume draws attention away from his youth and focuses on his key skills & all his significant accomplishments.

SENIOR EXECUTIVE
SALES • MARKETING • BRAND/PRODUCT MANAGEMENT • START-UPS • MATURE MARKETS
Finalist: Young Entrepreneur of the Year 2000. Finalist: Import Replacements Products Award

Consummate executive, change agent and entrepreneur. Key influencer driving outstanding revenue growth and market-share gains that transformed a start-up venture to the largest "natural oil" healthcare product company in Asia exporting to Australia and the US. Personal center of influence boasts network of accomplished leaders and innovators across diverse corporate cultures. **Professional strengths include:**

Business Development	Database Management	International Sales
Brand & Market Positioning	Customer Service Development	Multi-Channel Distribution
Product Design & Development	Brand Management	Revenue Growth
Product Launch	Competitive Market Intelligence	High-Impact Presentations
Strategic Sales & Marketing Planning	Business Mentoring	Sales Force Leadership

Technology: MS Office, MS FrontPage, Internet, E-mail, HTML, Windows 2000, Network Design, Database Design.

Resourceful • Competitive • Innovative • Tenacious • Pioneering • Positive • Assertive

---

EDUCATION

Bachelor of Science, Business Administration (Marketing)
John Carroll University, Cleveland, OH

BUSINESS EXPERIENCE

NATURAL FIRE, Tiburon, CA 1997–Current
Manufacturer, distributor and marketer of medicated natural-care products blended with natural aromatherapy oils. From a start-up in 1997, the company has experienced explosive growth, gaining chain-store distributorships across Asia and growing a large network of 300+ people, exporting successfully to Australia and the US.

Brand/Product/Marketing Director
Budget: $800K. Report to: Shareholders/Investors. Staff: 5 Sales, Accounting, Reception, Warehousing.
Launched business from start-up throughout each phase of its impressive growth, exploiting niche market for pure blended healthcare products in the Australian, Asian, and American markets. Strategically drove all infrastructure and operational business development enhancements, pursued and negotiated lucrative partnerships and distributorships, developed successful multimedia branding/sales campaigns, trained sales force, created performance and management measuring systems, and spearheaded complete range of differentiated sales and point-of-sale materials.

- Captured 95% of total sales for natural oils in Asia among intense competition; wooed large percentages of lucrative arthritic and skin-condition markets from major pharmaceutical companies.
- Drove fundamental branding decision to maximize impact by targeting lucrative therapeutic market.
- Won clients including Faulding Healthcare, Mediderm Laboratories, Groway (Malaysia), Kmart, and more. Grew internal VIP customer base of 10,000 direct clients.
- Successfully grew and launched 6 new products into Australian and overseas markets, managing all channel relationships from front-end customers through distributors and wholesalers.
- Personally negotiated $1 million x 5 year product supply contract with Malaysian company.
- Influenced the design of all product packaging, formulation, size, price, and product positioning, transforming from bare-bottle presentation to cost-effective, innovative packaging instrumental in propelling the Natural Oil product to No. 1 position.
- Conducted highly successful integrated multimedia PR campaigns that gained favorable coverage in leading magazines and newspapers. Designed multimedia campaign, sample sachet giveaways, free information booklets, POS "shelf talkers," window displays, web site, and billboards.
- Gained TGA approval on medicated range — the only company of its type worldwide.

James Henderson   Page 1   Confidential

234

Product/brand manager. *Gayle Howard, CPRW, CRW, CCM; Melbourne, Australia*

BUSINESS EXPERIENCE
Continued

FAXES INTERNATIONAL, Tiburon, CA 1996–1997
World leader specializing in hardware and software manufacturing – faxes, photocopiers and printers.

Account Manager
Budget: $60K month. Reported to: Sales Manager.
Achieved and exceeded sales expectations consistently from the first month of commencement for high-end photocopier machines targeting medium and large companies. Quickly recognized by management for exceptionally strong closing talents that captured several elusive sales "on the boiler" for extended periods, frequently accomplishing sales 40% over budget. Won business from competitors and retained client loyalty, building strong and continuing relationships.

NORFOLK DATA, Tiburon, CA 1991–1992
Computerized network and communication solutions provider.

Computer Sales/Network Design & Planning
Distinguished by peers for quick ability to assess customer's needs and find rapid solutions. Acknowledged by management as "Top Salesperson" each year, winning acclaim for designing innovative strategies to generate leads and capture new accounts through a series of diverse and carefully researched sales approaches.

NATCOMP TECHNOLOGY, Sydney, Australia 1990–1991

Salesperson/Store Manager
Promoted in recognition of leadership talents and proven expertise in winning retail sales.

ADVANCED TRAINING/MEMBERSHIPS

Member, Marketing Institute

Brad Cooper's Business Development • Aussie Host Customer Service • Maximizing Investments
Computer Software Proficiency Course (Microsoft Office, Internet web design and management)

REFERENCES

Available upon request

"Work smart, work hard, dream, and believe in yourself."
James Henderson 2002

Using this resume, James was successful in achieving a national brand-management role.

James Henderson   Page 2   Confidential

Experienced in sales but open to other opportunities, Mark's resume does not include a specific job objective

MARK K. DANIELS

1234 Hickory Lake Drive
Big City, Tennessee 00000

Days: (000) 000-0000
Evenings: (000) 000-0000

SUMMARY OF QUALIFICATIONS:

- Academic background includes B.A. in Marketing from Southern Christian University
- Strengthen and manage the sales and marketing efforts for equipment financing and commercial lending
- Effectively deal with senior level corporate, banking, and finance executives in developing tailored financing packages
- Strong interpersonal, communication, and leadership abilities developed through organizational skills, constant negotiation, and attention to detail

EDUCATION:

B.A. MARKETING ♦ May 1990 ♦ 3.7/4.0 GPA
Southern Christian University ♦ Major City, Tennessee

EMPLOYMENT HISTORY:

AMERICAN BANK OF COMMERCE ♦ Big City, Tennessee
Leasing Officer/Marketing Representative ♦ October 1992 - Present

- Market ABC's Leasing Program to equipment vendors within bank's trade area to solicit new business opportunities
- Review and approve applications for equipment lease financing
- Communicate with established vendors to maintain solid working relationships
- Maintain positive performance of personal loan portfolio through new loan growth and constant monitoring of present loans

NATIONAL LEASE PLANS, INC. ♦ Capital City, Tennessee
Lease Sales Representative/Manager ♦ June 1990 - September 1992

- Marketed lease financing programs to area equipment vendors and companies involved in equipment sales/purchasing
- Maintained positive relationships with area lenders and other funding sources and presented various lease transactions to lenders
- Managed all major accounting functions and financial analyses for company

SOUTHERN CHRISTIAN UNIVERSITY ♦ Major City, Tennessee
Market Research ♦ Fall 1989

- Participated in market research project for Information Management Systems
- Assisted in conducting focus group of corporate officers of area companies
- Coordinated writing and presenting final report for results and recommendations

COMPUTER SKILLS:

Proficient in: Lotus 1-2-3 ♦ WordPerfect ♦ dBase III ♦ Pagemaker ♦ Microsoft Word ♦ Excel

REFERENCES & ADDITIONAL INFORMATION AVAILABLE UPON REQUEST

235

Investment sales representative. *Carolyn Braden, CPRW; Hendersonville, TN*

This resume was used to position Jane for a role as liaison between money managers and high net worth accounts.

Jane Roadman

2360 432d Ave. East, Unit 301
Seattle, WA 98112

(206) 444-2222

Roadman@msn.com

INVESTMENT EXECUTIVE
Building profitable, long-term relationships between
high-profile investors and strategic investment partners in diversified markets.

---

although not a top-producing sales person, Jane had very loyal clients, industry knowledge, and the respect of other people in the industry. These qualities are highlighted here, since they are key qualities for a relationship manager.

✓ Results-oriented investment executive and relationship manager: 11 years' progressive experience in consultative sales, retail brokerage and client management services.

✓ Enterprising problem solver, leader and idea champion, perennially closing business and meeting goals for new investment ventures and products.

✓ Consistently rank in top tier for account development, averaging a 90% closing rate.

✓ Respected advisor to a loyal clientele, building referrals and account longevity through relationship building and outstanding service. Ethical, respected community leader.

✓ Skilled at translating client investment objectives into effective portfolio strategies. Solid knowledge of the securities industry, capital markets, and portfolio management, including goal setting; strategy development; asset allocation; risk and style analysis; trust, estate and tax planning.

LICENSES AND REGISTRATIONS

Series 7 ▪ Series 63 ▪ Series 65 ▪ Insurance License — Life and Disability

---

PROFESSIONAL EXPERIENCE

Assistant Vice President, Investments — Piper Jaffrey, Seattle, WA   1997–present

Direct portfolio strategy and asset placement for 300+ accounts, managing relationships with high-net-worth individuals, foundations, business owners and professionals. Serve long-time accounts:

✓ **Maintain a 98% client retention status** through volatile and declining markets.
✓ **Transferred 85% of clients** upon promotion to Piper Jaffrey.
✓ **Close 75% of new revenues** from accounts secured through client referrals.

Assess client portfolios quarterly, evaluating holdings and investment managers, performance, risk/reward analysis, and investment style relative to goals/objectives.

✓ **Grew revenues 50%** by expanding strategic partnerships in new and existing accounts.

Investment Executive — FirstBank Investments Inc., Seattle, WA   1990–1997

Built and retained a book of 600 clients, despite multiple intercompany transfers. Monitored profit, loss and sales growth for a startup investment operation, serving 7 bank branches. Trained staff.
Valued as a problem solver: Frequently relocated to troubleshoot falling revenues at failing branches.
Forged strong alliances with bank branch department managers, building credibility for new venture.

✓ **Top Producer 1993–1999.** Increased production 40% annually by servicing clients/referrals.
✓ **Grew assets 300%**, driving $13 million to $37 million in 36 months, FY 1996–1999.

EDUCATION / CREDENTIALS

Bachelor of Arts, Speech Communications. University of Washington, 1990

Notary, State of Washington.

236

Securities, commodities, and financial services sales representative.
Alice Hanson, CPRW; Seattle, WA

Marc Zimmer

(845) 499-8928 Mobile
marczimmer@yahoo.com
PO Box 825, Nyack, NY 10960

This individual's resume is organized into several sections to account for all of his specific financial services knowledge and his licenses. Note headings on left side of page.

FINANCIAL CONSULTANT

- 8 years' experience building partnerships to maximize revenues.
- Demonstrated track record of business development through competencies in Consultative Sales, Presentations, Customer Service, Decision Making, Marketing, Sales Closing, Negotiating, Account Management.
- Trainer of staff and colleagues in both formal and informal programs.
- Proficient in Windows applications for word processing, spreadsheets, e-mail, database management, and Internet research.

CORPORATE FINANCIAL SERVICES EXPERTISE

Financial Planning, Corporate Stock Plans, Employee Stock Options, Cashless Exercise, Retirement Advisory Services, Directed Share Programs, Group Retirement and Insurance Planning, Tax Efficiencies of Financial Planning (NQs vs. ISOs), Non-Qualified Deferred Compensation, Restricted Stock Sales, Cash Management, 401(k)s, Estates & Trusts

LICENSES

NASD Series 6, 7, 63, 65
Life & Health Insurance—NY, AZ, CA, CT, IL, MA, NC, NH, NJ, PA

PROFESSIONAL EXPERIENCE

SECOND VICE PRESIDENT, Charles Schwab, New York, NY—1995–Present
Manage corporate and private global accounts representing $150 million in assets. Report to Senior Vice President. Oversee five sales staff. Started as a sales assistant and earned promotions based on sales track record.

- Increased sales 150% in 18 months by winning five major accounts and applying cross-selling techniques.
- Increased market share 40+% during tenure.
- Won Triple Crown (most new accounts, top gross, top assets), Pace Setter, and Blue Chip awards.
- Initiated department's retail sales efforts and cultivated relationships with private clients who are senior executives of leading technology corporations.
- Designed a new product, PensionPlus, that uses actuary models to maximize return on pension payouts.
- Championed utilization of a Professional Referral System, bundling attorney, CPA, and broker services to add value.
- Forged the development of new markets in Europe and Australia.

REGISTERED REPRESENTATIVE, Equity Investments, Spring Valley, NY—1993–1994
Accountable for broker/dealer operations involving tax shelters for non-profit organizations. Developed relationships with key decision-makers (school superintendents, administrators, and union representatives). Interfaced with over four dozen individual investment and insurance companies considering financial product selection for individual client investment portfolios.

- Opened new, profit and non-profit, group markets for broker/dealer in tax shelters and financial/estate planning.
- Established firm's presence at conventions/conferences and pursued leads.
- Gained experience in custodial accounts, mutual funds, variable life and annuity contracts, life and health insurance, long-term care, disability, and unit investment trusts.

Marc was concerned about not having his bachelor's degree. However, since he was only two classes away from graduation, this information was included and used as a way of strengthening the "Education" section.

EDUCATION

Rutgers University, Camden, NJ (two classes short of BA)—1989–1992

MEMBERSHIPS

Member, National Association of Stock Plan Professionals (NASPP)—2000–Present
Volunteer Fireman, Rockland County, NY—1997–2000

237

Financial sales consultant. *Kirsten Dixson, JCTC, CPRW, CEIP; Bronxville, NY*

With strengths in business management, sales and marketing, and travel, Thomas is well-positioned for a variety of management opportunities (resume writer's comments).

Thomas J. Clifton

799 Broadway, Revere, Massachusetts 02151
(617) 555-5555 Home • (617) 555-5551 Business

SUMMARY

- Experienced business manager with specific expertise in the travel industry and strong skills in sales, marketing, and staff development.
- Entrepreneur who grew business from start-up to $3 million in annual sales through effective business planning, creative sales techniques, innovative marketing, and development of strong niche markets.
- Fluent in Spanish, French, and German.

Important for his industry

PROFESSIONAL EXPERIENCE
1987-Present

President, ADVENTURE TRAVEL, INC., Boston, Massachusetts
Partner/owner and lead agent of highly profitable travel agency.

Business Management

Emphasizes transferable business and management skills

- Analyzed market and re-focused business in response to market changes. Initially concentrated primarily on student travel; adapted to become corporate travel specialists and then to current area of specialization, South American travel, with emphasis on low cost and fast service. Established nationwide South American client base.
- Negotiated agreements with suppliers and vendors that resulted in significant benefits to the business, specifically: incentive income agreements with major carriers ($30,000 annual bonus income) and free automation and signing bonus upon selection of computer system vendor.
- Initiated use of and trained agency outside sales agents.
- Supervised accounting, tax return, and record-keeping activities.
- Selected and hired self-motivated sales staff and allowed them autonomy to resolve customer problems. Resulted in hard-working, customer-focused staff who required minimal day-to-day supervision.

Travel

- Lead agent personally generating over $1 million in sales annually as well as assisting with sales of outside sales agents. Focused on providing quality customer service which generated substantial referral business.
- Sabre proficient, Worldspan trained, and familiar with Apollo.
- Extensive personal travel knowledge both international and domestic.

Sales/Marketing

- Developed strong niche markets. Conceived and implemented marketing plans to acquire market share within chosen segments.
- Established name recognition and generated sales through a combination of sales and marketing techniques including cold calling, corporate account development, and judicious placement of advertising in Yellow Pages and niche market journals.
- Created and implemented promotions to spur sales including a bonus travel program for ministers of South American churches.

EDUCATION

BSBA / Finance, 1987, BABSON COLLEGE, Wellesley, Massachusetts
- Started travel business part-time by making commission sales to fellow students for an established travel agency.

PROFESSIONAL AFFILIATIONS

American Society of Travel Agents
Airline Reporting Corporation

238

Travel agent. *Louise M. Kursmark, CPRW, JCTC, CEIP, CCM; Cincinnati, OH*

Office and Administrative Support Occupations

Resumes at a Glance

Bradley was aiming for a senior operator position in his current company.

BRADLEY CUMMINGS
90 Parkway Road
Croton, NY 10566
(914) 772-9866
irwcu45@compuserv.com

Profile

These sections highlight his staff leadership and training experience and his technical expertise.

Technical Skills

Computer Operations Professional

- Skilled technical professional with 6 years of computer operations experience in mainframe systems, as well as leading and training staff.

- Desktop support includes installation and troubleshooting of PC hardware, operating systems and software applications.

- Recognized by management for dedication, strong service orientation and consistent record of quality performance.

Hardware/Operating Systems: IBM 3083 and ES/9000; IBM 3880 disk drives; IBM 3203 printers; IBM-PC compatibles; Windows 95, 97 and 2000.

Software: MVS, JES2, IDMS, CICS, PANVALET, TSO, DOS, MS Office (Word, Excel, PowerPoint, Access).

Programming Languages: JCL, COBOL.

Experience

His resume presents a very well-rounded picture of his capabilities.

HARTWELL INDUSTRIES, White Plains, NY   1990–present
Computer Operator (1998–present)

Promoted to computer operator in Information Systems with oversight of 3 other operators on IBM ES/9000 mainframe system, using MVS, JES2, IDMS, CICS, PANVALET and TSO. Generate timely reports to all departments; perform daily and weekly system backups.

➤ Provide first-level technical support to internal users and monitor hardware to ensure effective operations.

➤ Selected to lead a continuous improvement team to enhance computer operations efficiency.

➤ Train and develop new operators in system procedures and processes.

➤ Support users on PC hardware, operating systems (Windows 2000) and software (MS Office products) installation and troubleshooting.

Tape Librarian (1990–1998)

Performed all tape library functions to support daily computer operations in a timely manner.

➤ Monitored and filed tape media for mid-range operations; scanned tapes for vaulting.

➤ Assisted with disaster recovery and media handling for backup/recovery operations.

➤ Maintained up-to-date documentation of tape and library operations.

➤ Supported customer requests for off-site storage or other needs.

Education

A.S. in Computer Technology/Programming, 1995
Dutchess Community College, Poughkeepsie, NY

Bradley faced a very competitive interview process, but he landed the job even though another person had more years of experience.

239

Computer operator. *Louise Garver, MA, JCTC, CMP, CPRW; Enfield, CT*

MELISSA WRAYFORD

3667 Belltree Ct., Silver Spring, MD 20906 • Home: 301-933-1717 • Work: 301-890-9995 • mwrayford@erols.com

SUMMARY PROFILE

COMPUTER OPERATOR AND MEDIA SPECIALIST with strong aptitude for new technology. Responsible, technology-focused candidate with firsthand knowledge of Sun, Unisys, and IBM media-management systems. Ten years proven experience with media management, document retrieval, imaging, emergency tape backup, and computer-control console operation. Currently seeking a computer/operations help-desk position, progressing into LAN management. Top Secret Clearance (TK/SI).

DEMONSTRATED STRENGTHS

- Computer Control Console Operator
- Tape Library Inventory Management
- Data Integrity & Backup Operations
- DS/S Media Mounting/Dismounting
- D2C Tape Purging & Shipping

- Workload Monitoring & Scheduling
- Document Retrieval & Management
- Imaging & Scanning Operations
- Job Request Production Runs
- Equipment & Program Troubleshooting

PROFESSIONAL HISTORY

CORPORATE IMAGING CENTER (CIC) — Silver Spring, MD   **Aug 1989 to Present**

Media Specialist (Nov 1997 to Present)
Maintain inventory and manage library of approximately 20,000 D2C data tape cartridges.

- Monitor computer terminal for master tracking. Based on Volume Server calls for tapes, retrieve and load data tower with up to six tapes for end-user access.
- Inventory and organize returned D2Cs by shelf location number. Also create new tapes and clean and migrate D2C tapes in the system.
- Purge data-tape cartridges from the system, in preparation for loan to outside operations.
- Use SUN computer terminal, E-MASS Data Tower, and CD1200A Tape Cleaning Machine to perform media-management operations.
- Issue regular status reports on DS/S media-support and media-vault statistics, including inventory and usage totals.

Computer Operator/Computer Assistant (Nov 1991 to Oct 1997)
Operated A-12 Unisys Control Console to monitor and control mainframe computer and all peripherals while in production. Isolated and corrected any problems caused by programs or equipment that impacted the overall computer system.

- Monitored tape and disk library entries to ensure data integrity and availability of back-up files for data recovery. Worked with cartridges and large-reel tapes.
- During system failures, performed system start-up and restart procedures, using the control console or individual equipment controllers.
- Monitored workload, scheduled production, and controlled inventoried and archived files. Shipped and received files electronically using established online operations procedures.
- Programmed ad-hoc job request production runs. Input computer instructions to allow portion processing, hardcopy extraction and report writing.
- Executed regular weekly and monthly job request production runs. Reviewed new and recurring production runs for completeness and accuracy.

240

Computer operator. *Helen Oliff; Reston, VA*

MELISSA WRAYFORD, Page Two

Tape Library Technician (Aug 1990 to Nov 1991)
Maintained large-reel tape library inventory and controlled tape circulation.

- Updated database to reflect scheduled tape use, using a terminal served by a Unisys mainframe.
- Used a variety of imaging and scanning equipment to image documents.
- Retrieved document images and imagery-related data for production personnel. Ensured adherence to security regulations for document retrieval and access.

Administrative Support Specialist (Aug 1989 to Jul 1990)
Prepared Personnel Action forms, travel orders, training requests, and other forms. Screened calls for the Division Chief and processed personnel time and attendance.

- For three months, administratively supported three Nuclear Regulatory Commission attorneys.
- Achieved promotion to Tape Library Technician based on aptitude and technical interest.

SHIPPING RESEARCH & DEVELOPMENT CENTER — Rockville, MD　　　**Dec 1987 to Aug 1989**

Administrative Support Specialist
Prepared classified reports for six engineers at this military-focused R&D center. Provided additional administrative support as required.

CONTINUOUS EDUCATION & TRAINING

SELF-DIRECTED TRAINING
USDA Graduate School — Washington, DC　　　**1999 to Present**
Courses completed: LAN Concepts, Communications, and Telecommunications
Courses in progress: Introduction to Computer Technology, Introduction to Computer Programming for Structured Problem-Solving, MS-Office 97, and Windows 95

PG Community College — Largo, MD　　　**1997**
Introduction to Personal Computers

ON-THE-JOB TRAINING
CIC Training — Silver Spring, MD　　　**1989 to 1994**
Excel 3.0, Word 6.0, Intro to dBase III Plus, AS-400 Operations, Developing Listening and Memory Skills, and Listening Skill Dynamics

OTHER TRAINING
Norfolk State University — Norfolk, VA　　　**1986 to 1987**
Sociology, English, and Business Math

AWARDS

Exceptional Service Award (CIC)	1997
Team Special Act Award (CIC)	1996
Highly Successful Award (CIC)	1994
Outstanding Performance Award (CIC)	1993

This resume incorporates Maria's military background into her employment background.

Maria Z. Abueño
55 Broad View Terrace, Lawrenceville, NJ 08648
(609) 771-5555 — mariazee@tierra.net

Career Summary
- ☑ Proven achiever with strong **secretarial and data entry** skills; type 70 wpm.
- ☑ **Computer skills**: Windows, MS Word, Excel, WordPerfect, Lotus 1-2-3, AS/400, Jalan, Amaps 3000, and Promis Gavel. Experienced using Sony Transcriber and Dictaphone B1-35.
- ☑ Strong organization, time management and interpreting (Spanish) abilities.

Employment

1992 – 2002

Word Processing Operator: Training Department
Middle County Prosecutor's Office, Trenton, NJ

Her many accomplishments (bullet items) showcase the fact that she is strong in multitasking, organization, detail orientation, and follow-through.

- Ensured smooth administration of training programs' logistics, documentation and operations in a fast-paced office, enrolling law enforcement agency members and Prosecutor's Office staff in schools, conferences and in-service training programs.
- Maintained workflow operations with no loss of continuity despite tenfold increase of training programs to include the Prosecutor's Office Training Program and the Chiefs of Police Coordinated Training Program with thousands of recorded training hours.
- Assisted Training Director in the preparation of numerous training documents including budgets, rosters/schedules/calendars, catalogs, correspondence and reports.
- Arranged and coordinated logistics for off-site training programs and served as liaison to 12 Chiefs of Police, coordinating training schedules and troubleshooting problems.
- Created a new monthly and annual training recording system, tracking and recording training hours/schedules for attendees: 11,000 training hours, 900 attendees (1998).
- Initiated streamlined office procedures to increase efficiency and effectiveness, accommodating 400% increase in workload and reduction in secretarial staff.
- Transcribed tapes, took statements, interpreted and word-processed large volume of diverse legal documents for 11 detectives, three officers and two attorneys.

1991

Teacher's Aide, Hispanic Resources and Services, Broad Hills, DE
- Tutored adults in English as a Second Language; prepared / presented daily classes.

1989 – 1991

Invoice Processor / Quality Control Clerk, Dennison Clothing, Inc., Dennison, DE
- Processed hundreds of invoices daily for this manufacturer and distributor of women's clothing. Revised computer records of invoices to correct data-entry errors.

Military

1991 – 1999

Automated Logistics Specialist – Phase I and II
U.S. Marine Corps Reserves, Company X 555th SBM, Newport, DE
- Operated Materials Controlling System and the INFORM 1 system (computer databases) to process documents between customer units and sources of supply.
- Established / managed warehouse activities, inventory and survey data processing.
- Trained and supervised four automated specialists in the computer-based systems.

1989 – 1990

Food Service Specialist, U.S. Marine Corps Reserves, Newport, DE
- Primary cook: prepared and served full meals for 100. Supervised two kitchen aides.

Education

- 1989 Diploma, Computer Literacy and Life Skills / Job Readiness
  Hispanic Resources and Services, Broad Hills, DE
- 1988 University of Sao Paolo, Communications courses (1 year), Sao Paolo, Brazil
- Diploma, Secretary / Accounting, Commerce High School, Sao Paolo, Brazil

Maria moved to San Antonio to be closer to her family and took a job with the federal government – at a GS level higher than she anticipated.

241

Word processor/data entry keyer. *Susan Guarneri, NCC, NCCC, LPC, CPRW, IJCTC, CCM, CEIP; Lawrenceville, NJ*

This format presented her many years with the same employer better than a chronological arrangement.

Laura Kresnicki
1917 Topsail Drive
Boynton Beach, FL 55555
(000) 000-0000

—Objective—

To handle Medicare billing for a hospital, medical office,
convalescent center or nursing home.

—Summary of Competencies—

Medicare Knowledge:

- ▶ Eight years experience with all aspects of Medicare outpatient billing; also some exposure to inpatient billing procedures.
- ▶ On-line computer systems for electronic teleprocessing and by disk to CMC in Chicago.
- ▶ Adjustments to keyed data that was rejected due to erroneous codes.
- ▶ UB-92 billing, recently converted from UB-82.
- ▶ Coordination with commercial billing in cases where Medicare is either primary or secondary payer.
- ▶ Submission of hard copy billing with explanation of questionable items or late charges.
- ▶ Investigation of fraud, complaints, or reasons for refunds.
- ▶ Continuous updating on all changes affecting billable charges.
- ▶ Representation of hospital at Medicare seminars three to four times a year.

Professional Qualifications:

- ▶ Committed to increasing revenues through timely, accurate and thorough billing practices.
- ▶ Excellent rapport with management, coworkers and patients, with particular concern for the elderly.
- ▶ Commended for perfect record of professional conduct, high productivity, and ability to learn quickly with little guidance.

—Experience—

a good way to present multiple jobs with the same employer

1986 – Present   COLUMBUS HOSPITAL, JENSEN BEACH, FL

Lead Billing Clerk (Since 1989)
Outpatient Medicare Biller (1987-89)
Commercial Biller (1986-87)

- ▶ As only Medicare biller for this 226-bed facility, accounted for 48% of all revenues despite non-participation in Blue Cross/Blue Shield provisions.
- ▶ Processed an average of 50-60 bills per day, later increasing in volume due to layoff of assistant biller.
- ▶ Advanced to second in command in department employing six other clerks (cut down from ten due to budget reductions).
- ▶ Filled in during supervisor's absence and fully supported department's goals.
- ▶ Trained and delegated responsibilities to a multicultural staff which consisted of file clerks, commercial billers, and office volunteers.
- ▶ Provided written documentation to management on any staff violations or abuses of privileges requiring disciplinary action.
- ▶ Overcame ongoing internal problems with computer, which then allowed for recovery from Medicare of previously unbilled backcharges.

Prior Background:

1980 – 1986   Break from career to raise a family.
1976 – 1980   Clerical position reporting to division manager at United Parcel Service, Secaucus, NJ

—Education—

Completed three semesters at Bloomfield College, Bloomfield, NJ
Major: Personnel Management.

Attended numerous Medicare seminars to learn of the latest changes.

242

Billing clerk. *Melanie Noonan, CPS; West Paterson, NJ*

Organizing her skills into major groupings under the summary allows Mary to better present her strengths.

Mary S. Johnson

4833 Lancaster Lane • Port Huron, MI 48444 • (810) 555-0254

PROFILE

Over 20 years of comprehensive experience in office management and bookkeeping. Strong leader who motivates others. Exceptionally well organized and resourceful with wide range of skills. Ability to flourish in pressure-filled environment. Computer literate.

SUMMARY OF EXPERIENCE and ACCOMPLISHMENTS

Bookkeeping
- Thorough understanding of all aspects of general ledger accounting (manual and computerized systems) through financial statements.
- Monitor and reconcile five bank accounts generating 2500-3500 checks per month.
- Track accounts receivable and accounts payable for approximately 500 vendors.
- Perform collections on personal and commercial delinquent accounts.
- *Instigated design of computerized check-writing system to increase efficiency.*
- *Designed and implemented program to minimize delinquent accounts receivable.*

Managerial
- Hire, train, schedule and supervise sales, accounting/clerical and technical employees.
- Represent employer in communication with vendors, customers and official representatives.
- Identify and solve problems as they occur.
- *Designed new route schedule to maximize time and reduce fuel consumption.*

Customer Service and Marketing
- Receive and process customer requests for information and quotations.
- Respond to and resolve customer complaints.
- Maintain customer records utilizing computerized systems.
- *Developed and implemented customer-friendly programs; tripled customer base in five years without expanding territory.*
- *Initiated program utilizing telephone inquiries to increase sales; resulted in converting 35% of inquiries into new sales.*
- *Developed promotional program utilizing existing accounts; added 160 new accounts within six months.*
- *Increased commercial accounts by 30%.*

This format allows for a short job listing

EMPLOYMENT HISTORY

Office Manager/Bookkeeper	Food Brokers, Inc. - Rochester, MI	1991-Present
Bookkeeper	Kline's - Ann Arbor, MI	1990-1991
Secretary/Marketing Specialist	All State Insurance - Novi, MI	1988-1990
Assistant Manager/Bookkeeper	Clarkville Sanitation - Clarkville, MI	1983-1988
Assistant Manager/Bookkeeper	Johnson's Party Shoppe - Port Huron, MI	1979-1983

EDUCATION and TRAINING

Business Management and **Accounting** coursework
Delta College and Washtenaw Community College   Ongoing

COMMUNITY INVOLVEMENT

"Rainbow Program" - Facilitator for elementary school children dealing with loss from death or divorce.
Port Huron Business Association - Former member and committee leader.

• Notary Public •
References available on request

243

Bookkeeping, accounting, and auditing clerk. *Janet L. Beckstrom; Flint, MI*

This longtime homemaker returned to school...

MARY A. HOMEMAKER

5555 East Main Circle	Elmira, NY 55555	(555) 111-0000

The functional format highlights qualifications (in pyramid layout)

OBJECTIVE
Clerical/Bookkeeping/Office Support position.

and skills are grouped in four categories (resume writer's comments).

SUMMARY OF QUALIFICATIONS
Outstanding math skills; enjoy working with figures.
Knowledge of clerical details, record and file maintenance.
Strong background in all aspects of customer service and support.
Excellent organizational, planning, interpersonal and communication skills.

SKILLS AND ABILITIES

Bookkeeping:
- Responsible for all accounts receivable and payable functions as auditor for hotel operation.
- Prepared daily, monthly and yearly balance sheets for auditing purposes.
- Oversaw daily cash control, prepared bank and credit card deposits.
- Collected payments for customer billing and posted to general ledger.

Clerical:
- Posted all room, tax, valet, long distance and restaurant charges to house guests' individual accounts.
- Prepared comprehensive housekeeping report for Head Housekeeper.
- Utilized computer to schedule reservations around the world for guests.

Customer Service:
- Handled customer inquiries and complaints in a professional manner.
- Adept at handling confrontational situations, resolving them appropriately.
- Communicated with guests and customers via switchboard operation.

Management:
- Scheduled, trained and supervised staff arriving for daily shift.
- Supervised and oversaw security of building, including physical plant.
- Oversaw all hotel operations and guest relations as management staff.

EXPERIENCE

Clerk/Bookkeeper	Elmira Conference Center	Elmira, New York
Desk Clerk	Happy Town Hotel	Elmira, New York
Secretary/Production Clerk	Elmira Manufacturing Company	Elmira, New York
Job Cost Clerk	Binghamton Mailing (Mail Order Dept)	Binghamton, New York

EDUCATION/TRAINING

Business Administration Program - Purdue University Extension, Purdue, New York
Associates Degree, Secretarial Science - Elmira Technical College, Elmira, New York
Graduate - Anywhere High School, Anywhere, New York

ACTIVITIES/INTERESTS

Volunteer: Travel & Tourism (Information Center), Anywhere County Chamber of Commerce;
   Anywhere Soup Kitchen, Anywhere, New York
Past Instructor of Quilting Program, James Human Resource Center, James, New York
Past Girl Scout Leader

REFERENCES AVAILABLE UPON REQUEST

244

Bookkeeping clerk. *Betty Geller, CPRW; Elmira, NY*

Katrina was an office/billing clerk who wanted to return to her prior occupation as a Payroll clerk.

KATRINA LARSON

7889 Forester Avenue • Huntington Beach, CA 92647 • (714) 847-3362 • katlarson@juno.com

A functional-style resume with an objective is used so her payroll experience leads and is emphasized to prospective employers.

OBJECTIVE: Payroll Clerk

SUMMARY OF QUALIFICATIONS

- Well organized and detail oriented with experience in payroll, office support, data entry and billing. Computer skills include MS Word, Excel and various proprietary software programs.

- Self-motivated employee who performs diligently to accomplish business goals. Able to learn new skills quickly and effectively.

- Adept in customer relations with the ability to handle and resolve issues. Team-oriented; thrive in fast-paced environments. Record of dependability.

EXPERIENCE

Payroll / Billing

- ◆ Maintaining up-to-date payroll data and records, including entering changes in exemptions, insurance coverage, savings deductions, job title and department transfers.
- ◆ Compiling summaries of earnings, taxes, deductions, leave, disability and nontaxable wages for report preparation.
- ◆ Calculating employee federal and state income and social security taxes and employer's social security, unemployment and workers' compensation payments.
- ◆ Researching and resolving payroll discrepancies in a timely manner.
- ◆ Maintaining accurate customer billing information and preparing invoices in an efficient, timely manner.

Reception / Customer Service

- ◆ Greeting visitors; answering busy multiline telephone systems; screening and transferring calls while handling general inquiries.
- ◆ Addressing customer concerns, researching and resolving problems to ensure service satisfaction; extensive interface with all levels of internal personnel.

Administrative Support

- ◆ Performing diverse administrative duties such as word-processing correspondence, creating presentations and maintaining confidential files/records.
- ◆ Scheduling and coordinating meetings and appointments; ordering department supplies.

EMPLOYMENT HISTORY

This resume was very effective for her and successfully averted the issue of noncurrent payroll experience.

) — *This section is placed at the end, so the fact that her current position is not in payroll becomes less important.*

SULLIVAN CORP., Huntington Beach, CA
Office/Billing Clerk (1996–present)

JENSEN INC., Long Beach, CA
Payroll Clerk (1994–1996)

FINLANDIA INC., Long Beach, CA
Payroll Clerk (1992–1994)

WARNER PACKAGING, Westfield, MA
Receptionist/Accounting Clerk (1989–1992)

EDUCATION

Accounting courses — Fullerton Community College, Fullerton, CA

245

Payroll clerk. *Louise Garver, MA, JCTC, CMP, CPRW; Enfield, CT*

Patricia has strong credentials and a solid financial background, clearly presented here.

PATRICIA A. EVANS

1234 Devon Drive
Norfolk, VA 23500
804-456-3456

OBJECTIVE

To obtain a position as a Bank Teller where I can be responsible for serving the public directly, use my education and skills for mutual benefit, and where there is an opportunity for development, responsibility, and advancement.

EXPERIENCE

First American Bank of Virginia, Norfolk, Virginia
Customer Service Representative

- Varied banking experience includes customer assistance, selection of proper accounts and reconciling bank statements.
- Qualified to sell, renew, and redeem certificates of deposit, savings bonds, and travelers checks.
- Capable of handling rental and billing of safe deposit boxes, filing loan papers, signature cards, reports, and correspondence.

Bank Teller

- Meet the standards of bonding companies to handle large sums of money.
- Qualified to perform routine bank transactions including deposits and withdrawals of cash and negotiable instruments from savings and checking accounts.
- Able to receive cash/checks and verify amounts and endorsements. Accurately account for transactions on days end settlement sheet.
- Have the ability to determine the current value of foreign currency in U.S. dollars and cash foreign checks in accordance with bank policy.
- Trained to record transactions into computer and fulfill day-to-day responsibilities.
  1985 to present.

FIRST VIRGINIA BANK OF TIDEWATER, Norfolk, Virginia
Customer Inquiry Clerk

- Assisted customers in resolving problems with checking and savings accounts.
- Handled telephone inquiries concerning references for checking accounts and installment loans. 1982

EDUCATION

Virginia Polytechnic Institute and State University, Blackburg, Virginia
Bachelor of Science in Finance, 1985

246

Bank teller. *Danitza Grimes; Nashville, TN*

During a 5-year career with a credit organization, Carole had some great accomplishments, most notably in the area of improving operational processes. Her areas of expertise are highlighted in the "Value Offered" section.

CAROLE MORGAN-LOWE

2525 Kiesewetter Drive, Loveland, OH 45140
(513) 555-0050 • morganlowe@cinci.rr.com

VALUE OFFERED

Credit Authorization Expertise: Five years' experience in credit approval marked by steady advancement and record of accomplishments in training, team leadership, fraud prevention, and problem resolution.

Process Improvement: Increased efficiency, reduced staff time, eliminated fraud, and drastically cut numbers of problem calls by analyzing and improving operational processes.

Training: Trained new associates in all facets of credit authorization; earned consistently excellent training evaluations.

Personal Attributes: Rapidly productive in new positions and new environments. Dedicated to continuous learning and performance improvement. Focused and capable under pressure and time constraints.

EXPERIENCE AND ACCOMPLISHMENTS

FACS GROUP, Mason, Ohio (Credit services facility for Federated Department Stores)   1997–2002
Lead Associate, Credit Authorization Unit, 1999–2002

Promoted to manage call center of 8 to 20 associates involved in opening new accounts, granting credit, and approving credit increases. Served as liaison to nationwide credit bureaus. Developed weekly, quarterly, biennial, and annual reports and statistical analyses of associate performance.

- Successfully met performance standards for call response time and customer satisfaction while contending with high staff turnover and supporting a rapidly growing organization.

- On own initiative, aggressively addressed fraudulent accounts. Analyzed account activity, identified trends, and developed process to identify potential fraud and shut down the account before a loss occurred.

- Eliminated 350,000 problem calls annually by analyzing nature and volume of calls, then developing a proactive reporting system to identify potential problem accounts before they resulted in calls to the call center.

- Dramatically improved the efficiency of management reporting processes. Created spreadsheets that automated numerous processes for multiple reporting requirements and saved at least 40 management hours monthly; spreadsheets adopted for use throughout the department.

- Personally handled all escalated customer calls, striving to maintain customer satisfaction while enforcing company policies and good credit practices.

Credit Authorization Trainer, 1998–1999

In a rapid-growth environment, trained new hires in credit fundamentals, credit authorization, and computer system use in fast-paced 6-week training courses.

- Averaged 2.8 (of maximum 3.0) on post-training student surveys for communication style, effectiveness of training methods, and classroom management.

Authorization Associate, 1997–1998

Assessed customer information and granted or denied credit extensions.

EDUCATION

University of Cincinnati: Completed 2 years toward B.S. in Business Administration.

247

Credit authorizer. *Louise M. Kursmark, CPRW, JCTC, CEIP, CCM; Cincinnati, OH*

Mary K. Doe

11850 W. McDonald Lane   Tempe, AZ 55555   (555) 000-0000   mkdcredit@cs.com

Professional Qualifications

✓ Over 10 years experience as Credit Manager for manufacturing concern doing $65+ million/year…

✓ Oversaw dealer base of 950 accounts including Puerto Rico/Canada…

✓ Assisted in company growth from $25 million to $65 million…

✓ Managed key accounts…traveled to dealer locations to examine/analyze financial documents/facilities/operations…

✓ Established criteria for credit approval…

✓ Evaluated/approved new accounts for credit limits up to $400,000…evaluated/recommended new accounts for approval of up to $2.5 million…determined credit terms…

✓ Set up/processed records for account base…

✓ Significantly reduced bad debt loss to .02%/.2% of sales for 1999…

✓ Wrote/implemented computerized credit approval system…streamlined paper flow 10–15%/reduced man hours 25%…

✓ Created improved computer systems/programs between A/R…Customer Service…Shipping, which reduced time/supplies…

✓ Assisted in securing guest speakers for Furniture Manufacturers Credit Association annual meetings: U.S. Appellate Court and Bankruptcy Judges…

✓ Provided contribution in lobbying in Washington. D.C. for Senate Bill 540 on bankruptcy reformation…

✓ Initiated/implemented/chaired Creditors' Rights Committee…

✓ Excellent communication skills…tenacious…organized…analytical…motivator…innovative… excellent negotiation skills…work well independently…able to establish rapport with all levels of management…

Education   ARIZONA STATE UNIVERSITY—Tempe, AZ
Major: Finance

PORTLAND STATE UNIVERSITY—Portland, OR
Major: Accounting/Management

Using check marks and brief statements is both different and effective.

This is a good way to present your education if you do not have an actual degree.

248

Credit manager. *Fran Holsinger; Tempe, AZ*

Mary K. Doe

Professional Highlights

WOODSTUFF MANUFACTURING, INC.—Phoenix, AZ
<u>**Credit Manager**</u>   1988 to Present

✓ Wrote Policy and Procedure manual...

✓ Handled conversion of dealer base from waterbed to conventional furniture industry...

✓ Approved all customer orders prior to shipping...

✓ Resolved customer issues/problems...

✓ Tracked/analyzed marginal accounts...

✓ Advised/worked with attorneys regarding legal issues...

✓ Secured marginal accounts by utilizing Purchase Money Security Agreements/initiated bank letters of credit...

✓ Maintained Day Sales Outstanding 5-10 days above optimum of 38 days...

✓ Made numerous suggestions, which reduced man hours by 160 hours annually...

✓ Determined collateral requirements for customers...Established/maintained network of industry financial relationships for the exchange of more extensive credit information to keep bad debt losses to a minimum...

✓ Prepared month-end reports for management...

✓ Assisted sales manager in hosting customer functions at trade shows...

Additional Training

✓ International Bank Letters of Credit   ✓ Office Management
✓ Bankruptcy and UCC Codes   ✓ Negotiating
✓ Financial Statement Analysis   ✓ Credit and Collections

Affiliations

✓ Furniture Manufacturers Credit Association:
   Membership Committee 1997; Created/Chaired Credit's Rights Committee 1998–2000

✓ Credit Managers Association of California/National Association of Credit Management

✓ Lyon's Mercantile & Dunn & Bradstreet

Awards

✓ Certificate of Merit for Community Service from   ✓ Credit Manager of the Year: 1989
   MCC

Sally Schenker

327 Delavan Avenue, #7A
Buffalo, New York 14202

(716) 831-9320
sschenker@itt.net

OBJECTIVE: Position utilizing solid experience, skills, and training in records
management, file maintenance, and data entry/retrieval.

SUMMARY:

Only her last three jobs are listed below under "Experience," but her previous experience is alluded to in this first bulleted item.

➤ Oversee records-creation and file-maintenance activities in such diverse
settings as engineering/technical, medical, legal, sales, banking, and
collegiate environments.
➤ Perform a variety of administrative and office duties, including word
processing, document preparation, data entry/retrieval, and records
management.
➤ Organize data, verify information, and maintain records.
➤ Check files for inconsistencies, accuracy, completeness, and status.
➤ Demonstrate a positive, efficient, and professional manner.
➤ Train new employees in company policies and procedures.

SKILLS: Typing 60+ wpm, Microsoft Windows, WordPerfect 8, data entry/retrieval,
medical records management, and Dictaphone.

EXPERIENCE:

She had no real accomplishments but did have nice solid experience in a rather uneventful job.

File Clerk/Records Management   1994–Present
ST. GREGORY'S MEDICAL CENTER, Buffalo, New York
Pull patient records and charge them out to appropriate clinics. Correctly tag
and sort files for all departments. Create new medical charts and coordinate
information contained in multiple files. Collect, sort, and file reports and
correspondence. Handle over 250 files a day.

Secretary   1993–1994
CRISTANTELLO EMPLOYMENT SERVICES, Amherst, New York
Assigned to University of Buffalo. Revised and updated employee manual.
Tabulated research results for Bioengineering Department and entered
information into campus-wide computer system.

Medical Records Secretary   1993
THE SELIGMAN CLINIC, Lynbrook, New York
Maintained medical records and ensured accuracy. Performed extensive
telephone work to collect information and update and complete files.

EDUCATION:

Her medical records training is included, but it is placed at the bottom of her resume since she did not want to be pigeonholed as just a medical file clerk.

SUNY Technical College, Pottsdam, New York
Certificate in Secretarial Science

Sally did not want to draw attention to her age (mid-50s), so her college date is omitted.

Professional development and training:
Introduction to Microsoft Windows, 1995
Understanding Coding and Medical Insurance Forms, 1993
Understanding the Medical Record, 1993
Medical Terminology, 1993

249

File clerk.   *Freddie Cheek, CPRW, CWDP; Amherst, NY*

Farrah's career was dedicated to guest services and she felt confident she had a solid background for a management position.

She needed a professional tool, and this is it (resume writer's comments).

FARRAH A. HEWETTSON

1234 Street
Any Town, MI 49001
(333) 333-3333

AREAS OF EXPERTISE

- ◇ 15+ Years Hotel Experience
- ◇ Efficiency in Registering Clients
- ◇ Guest Satisfaction

- ◇ Outstanding Communication Skills
- ◇ Client Relations
- ◇ Team Player

PROFESSIONAL EXPERIENCE

FRONT DESK CLERK / PBX OPERATOR
STORY CITY HOTEL   Story, MI, 11/1987 - Present
- ◇ Received, processed, and checked guests out of hotel facility
- ◇ Maintained good rapport with guests to assure comfortable stay and return of patrons

FRONT DESK CLERK
ROSE FLOWERS HOTEL   Story, MI, 7/85 - 11/87
- ◇ Worked extensively with family leisure groups on a daily basis
- ◇ Assisted in the set-up and serving of banquet occasions
- ◇ Coordinated activities with different departments of the facility

FRONT DESK CLERK / HOUSEKEEPING
PALETTA HOTEL RESORT   Story, MI, 6/83 - 7/85
- ◇ Promoted from Housekeeping to Front Desk Clerk in December 1983
- ◇ Greeted all clients in a highly professional manner

HOUSEKEEPING
USA SUITES HOTEL   Story, MI, 1/80 - 6/83
- ◇ Managed room inventory of 238 guest suites
- ◇ Effectively completed housekeeping tasks within allotted time
- ◇ Worked within a team environment

EDUCATION

WordPerfect Hands-on 13-Week Training Course
Computer USA Center, Story, MI, 1992

Graduate, Story High School, Story, MI

MEMBERSHIPS

National Hotel & Motel Association
Welcoming Committee
Social Fundraising Committee

American Hotel & Motel Association
Member

250

Hotel desk clerk. *Betty A. Callahan, PC, CPRW; Kalamazoo, MI*

This military-transition resume is careful to use civilian terms and to describe her experience in readily understandable terminology.

Mary N. James

Permanent Address
1265 Limber Avenue
Baltimore, MD 21201

410-884-5555
marynjames@aol.com

These top two sections contain no reference to military experience.

HUMAN RESOURCES GENERALIST
~ Administrative Operations ~

Excellent Written Skills
Word, PowerPoint, Excel, Access

Personnel Specialist
Poised Public Speaker

Customer Service
Files & Records Management

PROFESSIONAL HIGHLIGHTS

◇ Consistently successful in increasing customer satisfaction and maintaining precise and updated personnel records.
◇ Direct management of personnel actions for 3,100 individuals assigned to 150 geographically separated elements in 14 countries. Maintain critical files in a flawless manner.
◇ Rendered a 97% error-free rate in personnel actions, achieved through close attention to detail.
◇ Established and implemented a performance feedback-tracking system, significantly increasing on-time feedback from 70% to 100%, resulting in immediate feedback mentoring for over 100 personnel.

PROFESSIONAL EXPERIENCE

PERSONNEL SPECIALIST, Germany, United States Army, Secret Clearance   1997 to 2002
Oversight accountability for personnel actions supporting 3,100 individuals in 150 separate locations.
(1999 to Present)
- Advise senior management regarding personnel. Inspect personnel activities to ensure compliance with policies and directives. Expertly review in-place processes and determine solutions for streamlining effectiveness. Detect potential problems and apply preventive measures.
- Conduct succinct briefings outlining the provisions of personnel programs, assignment selection, promotions, separations, retirement, personal affairs, retention, classifications, training and career progression. Guide personnel through career decisions.
- Create, maintain, and audit personnel records. Update computerized personnel information.
- Provide sensitivity while assisting family members of deceased veterans on applying for benefits.

Meticulously managed personnel actions and administration requirements for 309 personnel.
(1997 to 1999)
- Administered health, immunization and dental programs.
- Guided customers through benefits and personal affairs programs, offering wise counsel. Directed the leave program and controlled in- and out-processing. Input data and maintained accurate records.
- Expertly monitored the Individualized Newcomers Orientation.

EDUCATION
AA in Human Resources Management, Central Texas College
(Dean's List)

AWARDS
Received several notable awards for professionalism and quality work performance.

~ Available for employment, Summer 2002 ~

251

Human resources clerk. *Diane Burns, CPRW, IJCTC, CCM, CEIP;*
Columbia, MD

William was looking for a growth assignment with a larger company.

William L. Dorland

He used this resume to get interviews, referrals, and eventually a job at a Fortune 500 computer company!

545 Beltline Drive, Elwin, North Carolina 27526
(919) 555-1896   dorlandpers@person.com

Professional Summary
Human resource clerk or generalist seeking growth-oriented company. Reputation for leadership and productivity improvements to existing administrative programs supporting the human resources area.

Qualifications and Skills
- Solid base of skills for human resources generalist position with direct and transferable skills from various personnel administration, project assistance and related human resource project assignments.
- Software: Microsoft Office Suite; Windows 95, 98, 2000; Oracle.
- Competent problem-solver who successfully will help managers develop, lead, and coordinate new human resources and recruiting initiatives to support business goals.
- Excellent written and verbal communication skills.
- Utilize and recognize ways to improve work-flow efficiency and schedules to increase productivity.

Resume reflects his network of contacts with Human Resources personnel dating back to his Disney World position. Also highlights his more-recent training courses.

- Human Resource Management
- Compensation Program Issues
- Recruiting Issues Knowledge
- Customer-focused Strategies
- Training Program Development
- Report Writing
- Basic Employment Law Knowledge

- Operations Resource Management
- Business Communications
- Work Flow Analysis/Improvements
- Scheduling/Planning Events
- Project/Key Intercompany Liaison
- Benefits Administration
- Liaison to HR Director

Education And Specialized Training
UNIVERSITY OF NEBRASKA
- Bachelor of Arts in Personnel Management with a concentration in Human Resources Operations, December 1996

PERSONNEL PRODUCTIVITY ACADEMY
- 9-week HR Generalist Certification, September 2001

WALT DISNEY WORLD COLLEGE PROGRAM
- Participated in and completed a comprehensive Human Resources Management Seminar. Certification, September 1996

Professional Experience
Human Resources Clerk (5/98–Present)   **PRODUCTIVITY PLACE, LLC., Raleigh, NC**
- Utilize various personnel programs and Oracle software to administer human resources functions.
- Current specialized program work includes customer service focus and efficiency focus while working with the Human Resources Director.
- Monitor daily work flow performance management program and recommend systematic changes to increase customer satisfaction and operations.
- Provide customer appointment assistance on issues including appointments, complaints, warranty codes, file history and research, work orders.
- Maintain and develop key relationships with all aspects of the company, including staff, management, sales, maintenance, etc.

Management Trainee (1/97–5/98)   **HERTZ RENT-A-CAR, Raleigh, NC**
- Trained in comprehensive vehicle leasing operations.
- Provided account service and follow-up.
- Established, managed and developed new accounts.
- Performed payment and collections duties including tracking and collecting accounts receivable.
- Solved customer problems by offering mutually beneficial options to maintain company reputation/image and continue relationship.
- Tracked expenditures and gross/net revenues daily; assisted with payroll activities.
- Improved customer contact and built customer relationships that helped "turn around" office.
- Maintained proper automobile maintenance and record-keeping on all vehicles.

252

Human resources clerk. *John M. O'Connor; Raleigh, NC*

This resume was written not for an active job search but for promotion within the same organization.

Maria J. Tomasino
796 Topeka Avenue, Austin, TX 75364
Home: 512.789.4146
Cell: 512.789.1875
Work: 512.789.9426
Email: mjtomasino2000@yahoo.com

Unemployment Compensation Specialist
Seasoned professional in all aspects of state Unemployment Compensation issues/procedures.

Mission
To share my professional expertise and years of dedicated experience to the TEXAS DEPARTMENT OF LABOR AND INDUSTRY for the **Office of Unemployment Compensation Service Centers.**

Bold accomplishment statements are used at the beginning of both the current and previous employment sections.

Current Employment and Achievements
TEXAS ONE-STOP CENTERS, Austin, TX
Western Texas Area Coordinator
(1999 to Present)

Supervised opening of 28 centers in 1999 with 20⁺ future openings

- Successfully implement *Workforce Investment Act* policies via elected officials, youth councils and partners.
- Thoroughly research and identify regional employment opportunities and needs.
- Isolate and utilize best existing state programs for use in One-Stop system.
- Travel extensively to assist in strategic planning sessions / problem solving for entire system.
- Clearly communicate ideas and solutions to colleagues.
- Deliver concise presentations to organizations / employers extolling advantages of One-Stop program.
- Recipient of "United Way Gold Award" in 1999.
- Received *Team Pride* award from TX Deputy Secretary of Labor and Industry, January 2000.

Profile of Previous Employment
TEXAS DEPARTMENT OF LABOR AND INDUSTRY
(1971 to 1999)

Instrumental in Aground-up@ development of services for point-of-contact programs and centers to resolve challenging social service problems resulting from unemployment

One-Stop Area Coordinator for Eastern Region (Job Center Field Operations — Beaumont, TX Regional Office)
Job Center Manager (County Job Center — Dallas, TX)
Dislocated Worker Representative for Eastern Region (Dislocated Worker Unit, Beaumont, TX)
Unemployment Compensation Supervisor / Claims Examiner / Interviewer (San Antonio, TX)

- Extensively networked with community organizations to make Job Center programs more visible
- Acted as interoffice liaison, maintaining detailed communications, reinforcing understanding of policies
- Responsible for comprehensive Job Center employee performance evaluations and weekly status reports
- Provided guidance for employers in need of assistance
- Creatively designed committees to function as public relations vehicles for services
- Researched details of area job openings and employer needs resulting in hiring increase through Job Center
- Educated job seekers on employment requirements to ensure excellent performance on hire
- Directed assistance to businesses undergoing downsizing or closing
- Advised students on career choices; secure opportunities to provide work experience
- Assisted UNITED STATES DEPARTMENT OF LABOR in quality appraisals for Virginia, Maryland, Washington, D.C.

Page 1

253

Eligibility interviewer. *Jane Roqueplot, CBC; Sharon, PA*

Maria J. Tomasino, continued

Education

TEXAS SCHOOL OF BUSINESS
Austin, TX
Diploma: Business Administration

TEXAS STATE UNIVERSITY
Laredo, TX
Diploma: Leadership Development

Military

U.S. ARMY RESERVE SCHOOL

Achievements:
~Sergeant First Class (E-7, Non-commissioned), Trainer of enlisted personnel
~*Department of the Army Achievement Medal*
~*Outstanding Student Award*

Certifications:
~Instructor Training Course
~Supply Specialist Course
~Basic and Advanced Non-Commissioned Officers School

Computer Equipment / Software

IBM-Workpad-C3, IBM Thinkpad
Microsoft Windows NT, Internet Explorer, Outlook, Excel, PowerPoint; WordPerfect; Internet

Community Involvement / Affiliations

Board of Directors:
~Smith County Economic Development Corporation
~Smith County School-to-Work Initiative
~Western Valley Urban League
~Community YMCA
~IUIV — Tyler, TX
~Dallas / Fort Worth Girl Scouts

Memberships:
~Women in Business Network (Founding group / chapter for Smith County)
~Leadership Smith County
~Dallas Rotary #89
~National Association of Business and Professional Women
~National Association for the Advancement of Colored People (NAACP)
~Women in State Government Alumni

SARAH G. RADER

19 Thompson Boulevard • Springfield, MA 01101
413.515.2020 • sarahrader@yahoo.com

PROFESSIONAL SUMMARY

- Skilled professional with background characterized by key skill development in areas of research, reference, and cataloging, complemented by overall written and verbal communications strengths.
- Possess effective project management skills and excellent organizational and administration abilities.
- Able to simultaneously manage multiple responsibilities and deadlines; methodical and tenacious approach with keen attention to detail.
- Resourceful, dedicated team player; fluent in Italian; reading proficiency in French and Spanish.
- Technology expertise includes Microsoft Word/Excel and Internet.
- Industry-specific knowledge includes SIRSI, OCLC bibliographic records, AAACR2, Library of Congress Classification Schedules, DIALOG, Lexis-Nexis, and Factiva.

PROFESSIONAL EXPERIENCE

2000–Present *Circulation Assistant* • **JONES FREE MEMORIAL LIBRARY** • West Springfield, MA
- Manage main circulation desk of community library; augment staff by serving as sole adult reference resource on weekends; expert in using interlibrary loan program.
- Provide instruction one-on-one to patrons in use of technological resources; teach skills used in effectively using the Internet, accessing databases, and using search engines.
- Initiated development of a classic film series planned for implementation in winter 2001–2002; researched and proposed comprehensive list for initial collection of classic films; will be authoring program highlights and film reviews for publication.

1999–2000 *Library Assistant* • **EDGARTOWN MIDDLE SCHOOL** • Edgartown, MA
- Served as key resource to educators and students; researched and prepared materials on various subjects for classroom instructional purposes.
- Coached students in methods of conducting thorough research, from accessing Internet resources effectively to using periodicals, reference texts, and a wide range of print materials to supplement traditional sources; acted as technological resource in using computers.
- Assisted school librarian with circulation, inventory, and book processing.

EDUCATION

UNIVERSITY OF MASSACHUSETTS
- Master of Library Studies (2001)

YALE COLLEGE
- Bachelor of Arts Degree, English (1999)

AFFILIATIONS

AMERICAN LIBRARY ASSOCIATION, Member
SPECIAL LIBRARIES ASSOCIATION, Member

After two years as a library and circulation assistant, Sarah had completed her Master of Library Science degree and was eager for a position in a larger public or university library.

254

Library assistant. *Jan Melnik, CPRW, CCM; Durham, CT*

MARIE L. VANUCCI

515 Paterson Street
Port Jervis, NY 12555

(845) 988-1205
MLVan@yahoo.com

OFFICE SUPPORT — ADMINISTRATION — ORDER ENTRY & MANAGEMENT

Solid background in administrative support and assisting executives with daily priorities. History of devoting extra time and effort to enhance the success of every project. Dependable, efficient, resourceful.

Despite a constant turnover of temporary employees, Marie was able to keep her department running smoothly and get all orders out to customers on time.

- **Deadline-driven with standout organizational skill** — juggling multiple projects and calmly facing hectic schedules with determination and an infectious positive attitude.
- **Intuitive communicator and team contributor** — cross-functioning to improve productivity and meet market demands. Build rapport with co-workers at all levels to strengthen team efforts.
- **Office support strengths** — comprehensive secretarial skills with excellent keyboarding and steno ability. Familiar with MS Word and Fed Ex Power Ship.

PROFESSIONAL EXPERIENCE AND ACHIEVEMENTS

ELITE FRAGRANCES, Port Jervis, NY   1976 to Present
(Manufacturer of fragrances and flavors for major cosmetics firms and fragrance houses.)

Order Manager (1980 to Present) / **Secretary to President** (1976 to 1980)

Process and expedite high volume of complex purchase orders in a fast-paced, demanding environment. Forward pre-shipment and co-shipment samples when requested by customers. Thorough understanding of export documentation procedures. Follow strict regulations in preparing documentation to ship hazardous materials. *HAZMAT Certified, Export Documentation.*

ORDER MANAGEMENT

- Outstanding record of meeting shipment deadlines throughout history with company.
- Completed and shipped out one months worth of orders in two weeks to compensate for 2-week holiday closing and impending inventory accounting.
- Improved productivity by developing processes to speed repetitive tasks.
- Commended by brokers for thorough documentation and speed in completing orders.

DEDICATION & ACCURACY

- Maintain near perfect accuracy rate in preparing documentation and orders, despite working with partially non-computerized system.
- Earned reputation for arriving early each day and remaining until all work is done. *"Marie is the heart of this company, she has high standards and continually sets a great example for all of us to follow."* — Peter Kane, CEO
- Used to handling increased workload to accommodate critical project demands.

TEAM COLLABORATION

Skills that made her indispensable.

- Contributed to initial planning and development of shipping department. Cross-trained to learn entire operation in its infancy.
- Instrumental in the success of satellite production facility in Mexico. Prepared appropriate documentation to expediently move high volume of raw materials through customs to destination. *"Marie has been a great part of our achievement in Mexico. We owe her, most of all, for the growth of this affiliate."* — Pio Esposito, President, Mexican affiliate
- Bolstered department through frequent turnovers in management. Remained a steadying influence through turnovers in seasonal and temporary backup.
- Able to move orders quickly by developing good rapport and close working relationships with Production Supervisor, QC Supervisor, shipping clerks and freight forwarders.

255

Order clerk. *Meg Guiseppi, CPRW; Andover, NJ*

Specialty paper helped Cathy's resume stand out during her job search. With much competition in office support services, a well written resume in an eye-catching format can move an applicant's resume to the top of the stack (resume writer's comments)

Cathy Bralley
1145 Bedford Road • St. Albans, WV 25177 • (304) 555-0929

▼ Business Administration ✆ Receptionist

Summary of Qualifications
- Proficient with media relations, public contact, organization, and program administration
- Experienced in purchasing, travel planning, time sheet processing, and job tracking
- Computer experience includes Word Perfect, Lotus 1-2-3, Reflex 2.0, and Excel
- Managed 30 line phone system and received all visitors for high profile brokerage firm
- Comprehensive knowledge of a wide range of office equipment, including copiers, faxes, shredders, calculators, typewriters, postal meters, blue line machines, etc.
- Punctual, accurate, and highly professional in both personal appearance and demeanor

Employment History

WEST VIRGINIA DEPARTMENT OF EDUCATION, Charleston, West Virginia   **1996 to present**
Secretary III - School Community Relations
- Coordinate statewide media and public relations efforts; interact directly with public
- Process purchasing requests and coordinate section needs within the department
- Computerized and organized the office, including mailing lists of more than 5,000

RHÔNE POULENC, Nitro, West Virginia   **1987 to 1994**
Advanced Clerk
- Tracked 700+ construction, maintenance, and repair projects, preparing regular progress reports and notifying management of time-sensitive priorities
- Maintained 99% input accuracy rate and consistently met all deadlines
- Acted as liaison between project engineers and plant workers
- Processed all contractor invoices, confirming rates and verifying work completion
- Input data and calculated timesheets for up to 75 department personnel
- Organized United Way Campaign activities, including auctions, raffles, and picnics

SMITH BARNEY SHEARSON, Charleston, West Virginia   **1985 to 1987**
Front Desk Receptionist
- Answered and directed up to 50 calls an hour, including accurate message relaying
- Greeted and personally interacted with up to 35 clients daily
- High degree of security and confidentiality; bonding required
- Sorted and distributed incoming mail and processed outgoing mail
- General office tasks, including typing, photocopying, faxing, etc.

McJUNKIN, Charleston, WV; Marietta, Ohio; Houston, Texas   **1979 to 1982**
Sales and Customer Service Representative
- Assigned to high volume accounts, including DuPont, Shell Oil, and Union Carbide, where providing exceptional customer service was mandatory
- Processed and followed up on all orders for pipes, valves, fittings, etc.
- High level of interpersonal communication and public relations skills required

Volunteer Activities
- Patient volunteer, Hospice of Kanawha Valley, 1995-present
- Board Member, Putnam County Animal Shelter, 1987-1990

Education
- Georgia State University, Atlanta, Georgia, 1969-1972

256

Receptionist. *Barbie Dallmann, CPRW; Charleston, WV*

Patricia faced some difficult challenges. At age 55, she had only 18 months of work experience in her life. Her husband had been medically discharged from his long-time employment, so Patricia

PATRICIA F. RILEY

needed to supplement the family income.

1549 Meadow Road
Yakima, Washington 98900
509-882-4115
patriciariley@yahoo.com

OBJECTIVE

Seeking a position in the travel industry or in administration where my travel training and strong customer service skills can be further developed.

SUMMARY OF QUALIFICATIONS

Profile:

Excellent Customer Service	Office Machinery	Document Management
Suggestive Selling Skills	Itinerary Planning	Personal Care

Training: **Diploma**
SABRE TRAINING CENTERS — Seattle / Tacoma Airport

PROFESSIONAL HISTORY

04/02–   CAMPBELL TRAVEL — Yakima, Washington
10/02   **Travel Consultant**
Booked commercial and leisure air and cruise travel. Analyzed airline schedules to optimize scheduling. Made presentations in person and by phone to the public.

) She was laid off from this position after the events of September 11, 2001.

> ➤ Excellent training and experience in booking rental cars, hotels and plane flights.
> ➤ Utilized experiences gained at Coastal Adventures to make presentations on a wide portfolio of cruises.
> ➤ Used a variety of business machines — copiers, faxes and email.

01/00–   COASTAL ADVENTURES — Yakima, Washington
04/02   **Cruise Specialist**
Analyzed customer needs and desires and made recommendations for a variety of cruises and cruise packages on some of the world's leading cruise ships.

> ➤ Interacted with airline and cruise vendors to determine suitability and scheduling.
> ➤ Made presentations concerning flight and cruise availability and dates; booked business, made reservations and generated a number of repeat customers.
> ➤ Personally booked a one-sale eight-cabin cruise on Scandinavian Sea; sold an 18-day excursion in Switzerland to a cruise customer.

This informa-tion is included to supplement her work experience. It was hard work, and she did get paid for some of it.

(1988–
1998

STELLA BLANCHE / VALLEY HOME HEALTH SERVICES — Wapato, Washington
Personal Assistant
Provided in-home semi-skilled care to a family member, gaining in-depth expertise in the treatment and progression of two neurological diseases: Myasthenia Gravis and Parkinson's.

> ➤ Assisted in physical therapy and rehabilitation.
> ➤ Administered medications and maintained charts and records.
> ➤ Provided personal care and assisted with transportation to and from medical centers, including the Mayo Clinic in Rochester, New York.

Patricia took a job in a call center — at the wage she desired — until she can return to travel.

Travel clerk. *William G. Murdock, CPRW; Dallas, TX*

The combination format allowed us to keep this resume at one page. This format also presents a strong overview of her qualifications without presenting too much detailed information.

JENEANNE BRYERS

404-32 Wilson Circle, Brentwood, NY 11717 • (516) 544-0006 • worldlylady@aol.com

CORPORATE RESERVATIONIST / TRAVEL AGENT

Travel Consulting & Reservations
Customer Service/Client Relations
Staff Training & Supervision
Computerized Systems Operations

Corporate Sales Management
Key Account Development
Flight Schedule Coordination
Ramp Service / Airport Security

– Offer 20+ years of cross-functional sales and customer service experience throughout the travel industry in corporate call centers, major airports, and private travel agency environments.
– Provide complex travel consultation with a demonstrated knowledge of domestic/international travel.
– Supervise ramp and flight service operations, with heightened awareness of security risks and focus on intercepting suspicious activity, in full compliance with federal guidelines and regulations.
– Maintain an excellent track record for effectively managing and growing corporate accounts.
– Provide general staff supervision and advanced agent-training on computerized systems operations.
– Demonstrate exceptional research, time-management, and problem-resolution skills.
– Effectively communicate with people of all ages and cultural origins; fluent in English and native French.

PROFESSIONAL EXPERIENCE — *Overview*

- Supervising broad areas of corporate travel including air/bus/cruise travel and hotel reservations, coordination of U.S. and European group tours, e-ticketing, and boarding-pass processing.
- Acting as a liaison between customers and airline/airport personnel to provide timely information concerning flight schedules, close-outs, stand-bys, connections, payments, ticket exchanges, and refunds.
- Training and motivating call-center staffs of 25–30; monitoring and troubleshooting telemarketing techniques.
- Establishing, growing, and maintaining corporate accounts, significantly exceeding monthly sales quotas.
- Planning and coordinating promotional campaigns for air- and land-based European vacations.
- Monitoring inventory control records and preparing sales analysis reports for management review.
- Ensuring on-time performance of aircraft; directing and training ramp/flight service personnel in all areas of fueling, cargo cleaning, loading/unloading baggage, air freight, mail handling, and food/beverage.
- Investigating damage to aircrafts to ensure the safe and cost-efficient operation of scheduled flights, maintaining timely log reports, and processing daily freight-activity documentation.

WORK HISTORY

Corporate Reservation Agent, WORLDWIDE TOURS, Huntington, NY	1996 – present
Reservationist/Sales Agent, WORLD TRAVEL CORP., Fairview, NY	1991 – 1996
Tour Operator, JET SET VACATIONS, New York, NY	1986 – 1991
Lead Agent / Flight Service Scheduler, WORLD AIRWAYS, Jamaica, NY	1982 – 1986
Ramp Supervisor, GUIDED TOURS, Jamaica, NY	1980 – 1982

TRAVEL SYSTEMS

PARS, SABRE, DCS, Panamac, System One, Amadeus, and Atoll

EDUCATION

A.A.S., Business Management, 1995
Manhattanville College, Purchase, NY

258

Travel agent. *Ann Baehr, CPRW; Long Island, NY*

An appropriate resume for the job; it is simple and includes good design elements.

Shawn Manaker
459 Sherman Oaks Drive
Indianapolis, IN 46227
(317) 555-9980

Objective

To obtain a position as a Messenger in a bicycle
delivery company while continuing my education

Summary of Qualifications

+ Top-Rated Cyclist in 1995 Messenger Olympics
+ Extensive bicycle maintenance knowledge
+ Extremely proficient in map reading

Related Experience

Speedy Delivery Service   January, 1995 to present
First-Call Team Leader. Responsible for entire downtown delivery locations.

Rapid Delivery Company   1993 - 1994
Messenger. Began as the 1- and 2-day delivery messenger, promoted to downtown
rush deliveries within two months.

Other Experience

1990   Harrison's Hardware   1991   Mr. C's Grocery   1992   Club T's
       Stock Clerk (PT)   *Stock Clerk (PT)*   *Dishwasher (PT)*

Education

Indiana University   September, 1994 - present
Bachelor of Liberal Arts (expected in 1998)

Hartley High School   Graduated 1993

References Available

Messenger. *Thelma Silvola; Indianapolis, IN*

While a dispatcher, Paul has many other management and mechanical skills.

This resume helps him keep his options open.

PAUL LANDER
P.O. Box 1024
Peekskill, NY 10566
(914) 736-3981

OBJECTIVE

A position in municipal/state maintenance which will fully utilize my technical skills, organizational abilities, and experience.

PROFILE

This resume was revised for a specific opening in a government agency

- Motivated, detail oriented maintenance professional with proven follow through abilities.
- Significant exposure to maintenance and repair of Air Conditioning/Ventilation systems.
- Possess hands-on experience in wiring and switch installations.
- Familiar with local Electrical Codes.
- Able to read blueprints and wiring lay-out diagrams.
- Hands-on experience in repair/replace furnace oil pumps and other heating systems.
- Effective supervision skills; successful at delegating responsibility.
- Possess exceptional problem resolution skills; work well under pressure.

EXPERIENCE
December 1993 -
Present

NEW YORK STATE DEPARTMENT OF TRANSPORTATION, Somers, NY
Highway Maintenance/Dispatcher
- Respond to resident complaints; directing repair crews to proper location so as to effect repair.
- Oversee fuel and salt inventories.
- Maintain attendance log for staff of 40 maintenance workers.
- Developed, recommended and implemented procedure to expedite submission and processing of truck reports resulting in a *savings of more than 12.5%.*
- Liaise with engineering staff regarding current construction projects.
- Organize and maintain tracking system for work orders.

June 1992 -
December 1993

LAKEVILLE INDUSTRIES, Mohegan Lake, NY
Driver's Helper/Warehouse Assistant
- Filled orders from inventory based upon job requirements.
- Delivered kitchen counters and cabinets.

June 1990 -
June 1992

P L CONSTRUCTION & LANDSCAPING, Peekskill, NY
Owner/Operator
- Remodeled private homes including: electrical installations; dry wall installations; painting; tile floor installations; masonry; and roof repair.
- Provided landscaping services: lawn mowing; shrub trimming; planting of flowers and shrubs; and small tree removal.

EDUCATION

NORTHERN WESTCHESTER/PUTNAM TECHNICAL CENTER, 1987 - 1990
Yorktown Heights, NY
Received training and was awarded certificates in the following programs:
- *Construction Electricity*
- *Electrician's Helper*
- *Heating - Ventilation and Air Conditioning*

YORKTOWN HIGH SCHOOL, Yorktown Heights, NY   Graduated: 1990

REFERENCES

Available upon request.

260

Dispatcher. *Mark D. Berkowitz, NCCC, CPRW; Yorktown Heights, NY*

With three young children, Matt wanted a job enabling him to spend more time a home than his truck driving job.

MATTHEW R. PARSONS
3067 Crestview Avenue ◆ Rogerston, Illinois 63067
(800) 555-1212

OBJECTIVE	Position in the transportation industry as **Safety Supervisor**, **Dispatcher** or **Operator**.
PROFILE	◆ Over 15 years professional experience in the transportation field.
	◆ Familiar with industry operating procedures and policies. Understand the importance of each department in maintaining efficiency and productivity.
	◆ Accident-free professional driving record, CDL Class A License (T–X).
	◆ Knowledge of transportation routes in midwest area.
	◆ Hard-working and self-motivated, doing what it takes to get the job done.

EXPERIENCE

The functional format allows him to present his skills more effectively

Delivery Operations:

◆ Skilled in the operation of tractor, flatbed, dump and straight trailers, tankers and dry vans. Experienced in bulk transportation of hazardous liquids, building materials, grain, livestock and various freight.

◆ Very knowledgable in D.O.T. regulations. Special expertise in flammable and hazardous materials.

◆ Accuracy and compliancy of log books commended by safety director.

◆ Emphasis on projecting a good company image in customer relations. Professional and friendly manner; committed to delivering the best possible service.

Problem Solving:

◆ Work well with dispatcher, mechanics and office personnel to identify and solve problems before they affect customer service.

◆ Heads-up troubleshooter. Able to find solutions to delivery problems (*incorrect directions, order discrepancies, equipment malfunction, etc.*) and communicate action taken with office staff or customer.

◆ Mechanically minded. Identify and handle small repairs on the road. Diagnosis skills respected by staff mechanics.

Related Training:

Paperwork Documentation	Equipment Use	Hazardous Materials Certification

WORK HISTORY

Operator

Moore Cartage Company ◆ Morristown, Illinois	1985 – Present
Harvard-Dempster Block Company ◆ Hanover, Illinois	1984 – 1985
Cooper Cartage Company ◆ Hanover, Illinois	1979 – 1984

References Available Upon Request

The resume worked — he got the office job he wanted (resume writer's comments).

261

Dispatcher. *Robin Folsom; Rockford, IL*

Andrew wanted a promotion, so I emphasized items important to his employer. We listed his church involvement because his company is family-oriented and this would be a plus (resume writer's comments).

ANDREW P. HOLDEN
4307 Maplewood Dr.
Vassar, Michigan 48768   (517) 555-6756

This powerful statement about his personality and ability to contribute would impress most employers.

PROFESSIONAL SUMMARY

Highly motivated, focused, and goal-oriented. Familiar with all aspects of warehouse and inventory control operations through hands-on experience in positions of increasing responsibility. Strong communication skills demonstrated on a daily basis. Decisive and respected. Committed to mutually beneficial company and personal ideals. Ready and eager to meet new challenges.

HIGHLIGHTS OF RESPONSIBILITIES

Notice all the skill verbs he uses

- Empower and motivate employees by creating desirable working atmosphere where employee feedback is encouraged.
- Train employees in many aspects of warehouse operations.
- Recruited to participate in Future Planning Committee.
- Contributed to creation of *Receiving Operations Manual*.
- Manage operations in receiving dock; anticipate needs and demands, troubleshoot as necessary.
- Coordinate inter-company shipments.
- Monitor inventory control utilizing company-developed computer system.

EMPLOYMENT HISTORY

MEYER FOODS • Port Huron, MI   1988-Present
     Lead Man - Receiving Dock
     Receiving Dock Checker
     Lead Man - Turret Drivers
     Turret Driver
     Merge Operations
     Selector

FORD HOSPITAL • Plymouth, MI   1984-1988
     Storekeeper - Head of Receiving for Dietary Department

EDUCATION and TRAINING

MANAGEMENT TRAINING I & II (Meyer Foods)   1995-1996

DALE CARNEGIE COURSE   1995

KIRKWOOD COMMUNITY COLLEGE • Bayville, MI   1986-1987
     Business and general coursework

ACHIEVEMENTS *) — a useful category to include here*

- Received *Highest Award for Achievement* from the Dale Carnegie course.
- Awarded Meyer Food's *Outstanding Warehouse Production Award*.

COMMUNITY INVOLVEMENT

- Annually participate in *World's Largest Garage Sale* which benefits American Tuberous Sclerosis Foundation.
- Serve as *Deacon* and active member of Vassar Community Church.

References available on request.

262

Shipping, receiving, and traffic clerk. *Janet L. Beckstrom; Flint, MI*

Tomas C. Martinez
(973) 727-4423

77 South Street, Parsippany, New Jersey 07454
Email: tommar@yahoo.com

Retail Receiving Management
Inventory Control... Backlog Reduction... First-Class Customer Service

High-performance 10-year career supervising loading dock and warehouse operations for a major national department-store chain. Impressive record of assuming responsibilities of Receiving Manager.

Strengths

Standout organizational and logistical planning... innate ability to see the whole picture to improve inventory flow and reduce warehouse backlogs.

Excellent communicator and team mentor... well liked by diverse co-workers, able to boost damaged morale, motivate and lead by example.

Customer-driven professional... courteously provide superior service quality. Gifted in diffusing complaints to encourage loyal customers.

Conscientious, hard worker... flexible in responding to ever-changing and ever-hectic workplace and corporate demands. Considerable physical stamina with history of taking on added responsibility to expedite merchandise to floor.

Computer Experience: MS Word. Confident in learning and using new technology.

Professional Experience

From the time he began working at the department store, he had assumed the role of receiving manager many times but had been overlooked for promotion the several times the job had come open. This led him to believe he had nothing to offer!

Stock Leader — Dock Supervisor   1991 to Present
JC PENNEY, Middletown, NY

Rapidly progressed to Stock Expediter in 6 months, then to acting **Receiving Manager.** Diverse responsibilities include unloading, processing, and delivering merchandise to departments; retrieving used equipment; retrieving/rearranging display apparatus; assisting with floor moves; and maintaining clean back-of-house area. Track loading-dock supplies and report shortages to manager. Provide customer service in directing shoppers to departments and assisting with carry outs.
Requested by Operations Manager to train new hires (not in job description).

Reduced 8-month merchandise backlog within 2 months after Christmas season 2000, despite high staff turnover. Reduced potentially high return-to-vendor expense.

Completely reorganized receiving dock, compact room and processing room, allowing for more available storage space and better flow.

Assumed increased work load to compensate for continual staffing cuts and high turnover rate caused by corporate merger.

Usually the last one out, staying after store closing to process late deliveries and avoid clutter for early next-day shoppers.

Earned reputation for being the "go to" person when the job has to be done quickly and correctly. Complete most tasks in half the time of others.

Respected for rapidly responding to customer carry-out pages, satisfying customer and returning quickly to receiving duties.

Previous experience (1985 to 1988) includes Mail Room Clerk and Golf Club Greens Staff.

Education

By highlighting his accomplishments, he was able to land a position as receiving manager with a more upscale department chain!

93 credits toward **B.S., Political Science**
Fairleigh Dickinson University, Madison, NJ, 1991 to 1993
A.A., Humanities and Social Science
St. Johns College, Morristown, NJ, 1991

Stock clerk. *Meg Guiseppi, CPRW; Andover, NJ*

Mary includes no job objective which allows her the flexibility to consider various jobs.

Mary Smith
766 Hilliard Drive, 2E
Trent, NY 88970
(906) 456-8900

She emphasizes her adaptive skills first {

Profile

Considered an accurate, dependable employee.....enjoy working with people and utilizing direct telephone contact.....ability to learn new procedures and new office technology quickly and efficiently.

Summary

Increasing responsibilities in areas such as

Credit Investigation   Accounts Receivable
Secretarial Duties   Collections

Experience

1987 - Present   *Eastern Community Exports*, Dayton, NY
                        (Major distributor of Diamond Back bicycles, exercise equipment, etc.)

Credit Assistant

File Clerk

The computer disk icon is a nice touch

- Responsible for preparation of credit applications and credit memo applications. Report directly to the regional credit manager.
- Customer contact when credit is denied, credit discrepancies, and reconciliation's.
- Request bank and trade references for new and existing accounts. Responsible for reporting to TRW's and D & B reports.
- Assist Credit Manager
- Maintain a log and prepare credit claims
- Computer knowledge, business writing, and client interaction

Education

Graduate, Allentown High School
Major: Business

Excellent references furnished upon request.

264

Office clerk, general. *Beverly Baskin, MA, NCC, CPRW; Marlboro, NJ*

Valerie was concerned that she would be considered only for an accounts receivable position, so the goal was to emphasize her range of qualifications at a glance.

Valerie M. Arlington

91 South Street, Bay Shore, NY 11706 • (631) 297-0054 • vmaadm12@earthlink.net

ACCOUNTING AND ADMINISTRATIVE ASSISTANT

Accounts receivable, bookkeeping, credit & collections, customer service, client relations, sales support

Manage a diversity of routine functions and projects in a fast-paced, computerized corporate environment.
Possess strong analytical skills and detail orientation. Able to produce high-quality work on deadline.
Demonstrate excellent communication, organizational, time management, and problem solving skills.
Exercise independent judgment, decision-making abilities, and a high level of confidentiality.

Windows; WordPerfect, MS Word/Excel, Quicken, Peachtree Accounting, Lotus Notes, Internet

PROFESSIONAL EXPERIENCE

Accounts Receivable Supervisor, AVIATION AIRLINES (AA) Havington Station, NY   9/99–present
A division of Keller International, leading accounts receivable/payable firm for the Airline Industry

- Joined this Division at the point of inception as accounts receivable clerk and was rapidly promoted after five months to current role responsible for managing departmental functions and a staff of four clerks.
- Direct the timely and accurate processing of more than five million dollars in monthly receivables for Aviation Airlines, Keller's primary account from an extensive portfolio of major airline companies.
- Engineered departmental systems and procedures and successfully trained in excess of 40 employees.
- Communicate with AA personnel by phone, correspondence, and PC network on the status of accounts.
- Handle General Ledger postings and daily reconciliations and screen large volumes of mail for checks.
- Update, track, and monitor account status; execute letters and notices; generate monthly reports.

Customer Service Representative/Sales Associate, ACCURATE TYPE, Collins, NY   9/97–9/99

- As an integral team member of a worldwide leading fonts manufacturer/distributor, acted as liaison between management, sales force, and a broad customer base in all areas of product sales and problem resolution.
- Researched product availability to ensure the fulfillment of special requests and standard orders from an in-house inventory of more than 15,000 fonts; followed through with proposal preparation.
- Prepared and processed Internet-based, e-mail, postal mail, telephone, and fax orders from individuals and corporate accounts; approved, process and tallied credit cards and personal/commercial check purchases.
- Trained others in all areas of sales techniques, software management, and general office procedures.

Collections Representative, Litigation Department, HASTINGS BANK, Harrington, NY   2/95–9/97

- Reviewed delinquent accounts to determine the qualification for establishing or avoiding a lawsuit based on billing disputes, health issues, life crises, and a broad range of other financial considerations.
- Resolved difficult collection issues through means of direct client contact and cooperation with external collection agencies in an effort to resolve outstanding delinquencies.
- Established computerized methods of payment; mailed schedules of payment plans and summonses.
- Performed extensive data research on customers utilizing credit bureaus, banks, DMV, and other resources.

EDUCATION

Associate in Applied Science, Business Administration/Accounting, Suffolk Community College   1995

Excellent References Provided upon Request

This tab-binder format clearly communicates her broad areas of experience.

Valerie used this resume to land interviews for administrative assistant, full-charge bookkeeper, and contracts administrator in the airline industry and government sectors.

Office clerk, general. *Ann Baehr, CPRW; Long Island, NY*

Janet M. Mirren

428 Main Street • Elmira, NY 00000 • (000) 000-5555 • janmarie1212@hotmail.com

OBJECTIVE

Position in Office Support / Customer Service

CAREER PROFILE

) — Functional profile and skills sections avoid redundancy in job descriptions. (resume writer's comments)

- Proven administrative, secretarial, and general office experience.
- Strong background in all aspects of customer service and support.
- Knowledge of computers: Microsoft Word, PageMaker, FileMaker and others.
- Outstanding typing skills (85 WPM); proficient in use of office equipment.
- Efficient and good natured; excellent reputation with all former employers.

SKILLS AND ABILITIES

- Provided administrative and secretarial support in various office environments.
- Provided secretarial support for Assistant Vice President as well as task groups and committees.
- Responsible for the organization and efficient processing of bulk mailings to customers.
- Utilized efficient and courteous customer service in both retail and business settings.
- Processed orders; entered and retrieved data using both PCs and mainframe computers.
- Facilitated spreadsheet and database management for Assistant VP of Marketing/Public Affairs.
- Coordinated provision of communications materials for all segments of the medical center.
- Gained exposure to all aspects of sales, marketing, promotion, and public relations activities.
- Maintained accurate, up-to-date, comprehensive, and confidential files and records.
- Opened and routed mail to appropriate departments within the company.
- Coordinated and managed multiple priorities and projects on a timely basis.
- Answered busy telephones, directed and routed calls, and scheduled appointments.

WORK HISTORY

1997–Present	General Office Clerk	Elmira Power Company, Elmira, NY
1993–1997	Receptionist/Clerk	James Company, Elmira, NY
1992–1993	Office Assistant	Temporary Services, Elmira, NY
1990–1992	Secretary	Elmira Health Services, Elmira, NY
1984–1990	Receptionist/Typist	Elmira Paper Company, Elmira, NY
1980–1983	Customer Service Clerk	Precision Company, Elmira, NY

Janet has no work history gaps suggesting a chronological resume, but looks closer.

EDUCATION

Elmira Community College, Elmira, NY
A.A.S., Secretarial Science• 1989

Precision Company, Elmira, NY
Various Customer Service Seminars

Elmira Health Services, Elmira, NY
Attended various Secretarial Seminars
Obtained JET Proofreading Certificate

266

Office clerk, general. *Betty Geller, CPRW; Elmira, NY*

The interesting mail-related icons help give this resume a good appearance.

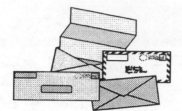

Marilyn Mason
3456 Newberry Lane
Franklin, Indiana 46143
(317) 555-1234

<u>Objective</u>)– *For an upgrade in position with her current employer, Uncle Sam*

To obtain the position of Mail Clerk I in the Central Mail Processing Center

<u>Related Experience</u>

U.S. Postal Service
1993 – present

Mail Clerk II. Responsibilities include operation of the optical character readers and bar code sorters as well as other duties as assigned.

Mail Handler. Responsibilities included unloading sacks of incoming mail; separating letters, parcel post, magazines, and newspapers; and transporting these to the proper sorting and processing areas. Occasionally loading mail into automated letter sorting machines, performing postage canceling operations, and rewraping packages damaged in processing.

<u>Other Work Experience</u>

Lance Carter Inc.
1991–1992

Order Clerk. Responsibilities included receiving catalog orders by phone, fax, and incoming mail, keying orders into computer, and confirming orders.

Fast Food King
1990 – 1991

Fry Cook. Responsible for preparation of full menu during lunch rush crowd.

<u>Affiliations</u>

American Postal Workers Union
National Postal Mail Handlers Association

267

Postal clerk and mail carrier. *Thelma Silvola; Indianapolis, IN*

Grace's resume conveyed the skills and background of a secretary/receptionist. Challenging her to look deeper, the information began to flow.

GRACE A. MWARINGEN

Grace was thrilled to see her background and skills projected in a concise, clear, professional manner (resume writer's comments).

1234 Street
Any Town, MI 49001
(333) 333-3333

COMPUTER SUMMARY

- ◊ Microsoft Word
- ◊ Microsoft Office
- ◊ Excel
- ◊ dBase

- ◊ IBM PC
- ◊ Microsoft Windows
- ◊ Microsoft Access
- ◊ PageMaker

PROFESSIONAL HIGHLIGHTS

STORM CITY PRODUCTS
Stenographer III

October 1991 - Present
Story, MI

- ◊ Promoted in recognition for high quality performance in 1993
- ◊ Designed Stenography Performance Reporting Packet for utilization on a company-wide basis and serve as Stenographer Manager until completion
- ◊ Document all verbal conversations during organizational meetings
- ◊ Coordinate diversified activities required for efficient job performance

MIDDLE ASSOCIATES, INC.
Stenographer II

1989 - 1991
Story, MI

- ◊ Worked within a team environment throughout SW Michigan in serving clients
- ◊ Established strong rapport and repetutation with client base for efficient, accurate work
- ◊ Recognized for outstanding time management and organizational skills at annual organizational meeting

SSRT STENOGRAPHERS
Stenographer I

1987 - 1989
Story, MI

- ◊ Gained tremendous insight and knowledge on applications and efficiency techniques as applied to the responsibilities of stenographer
- ◊ Assisted fellow stenographers within a team environment

EDUCATION

Are You Listening?
Stenography Association of SW Michigan
Detroit, MI • 1996

Total Office Efficiency - All Aspects [Training Seminar]
Stenography Association of SW Michigan
Detroit, MI • 1994

Associate of Science Degree in Stenograhy
Kristopher Community College
Story, MI • 1987

268

Stenographer. *Betty A. Callahan, PC, CPRW; Kalamazoo, MI*

Linda was unsure about future career goals, so "Professional Strengths" emphasizes general skills that could transfer to any support or administrative function (resume writer's comments).

LINDA J. JONES

101 Thomas Court   **Tulsa, Oklahoma 70000**   **(918) 000-0000**

PROFESSIONAL STRENGTHS

Excellent people skills; enjoy assisting clients from all socioeconomic levels; comfortable dealing with media. Thrive as team player and coordinator of special events and programs. Self-starter who meets program deadlines and requirements while performing multiple tasks. Proficient at handling all support staff functions. Computer skills: Wordperfect 5.1, File Express, Print Shop Deluxe, specialized test scanning programs.

PROFESSIONAL EXPERIENCE

VOCATIONAL-TECHNICAL SCHOOL, Tulsa, Oklahoma   **1994 - Present**
Student Services Secretary/Assessment Facilitator
- Sign up clients for assessment; administer, electronically grade and record tests. Provide information concerning enrollment, financial aid and assessment.
- Maintain student records and reports per state and district requirements. Assist with compiling statistical reports. Notify students of absences and implement excessive absence procedures.
- Answer phones; generate and file correspondence.
- Special accomplishments include organizing in-house seminar on suicide; as member of Safety Committee, ordering safety films for in-house viewing.

Secretary, Single Parent/Displaced Homemakers/Single Pregnant Women Program (SP/DH/SPW) and Student Services
- Assisted clients and maintained program database per rules of U.S. Department of Education.
- Composed correspondence and handled bulk mailing of newsletter. Oversaw program library.
- Represented school at health fairs; assisted organizing campus career fair. Managed campus clothes closet.

CRISIS CENTER, Tulsa, Oklahoma   **1992 - 1993**
Volunteer Coordinator
- Recruited, trained and scheduled volunteer staff in six different programs: Crisis Line; Sexual Assault Advocates; Kids Group; Sunshine Squad; Office Volunteers; Donation Distribution Center.
- Organized and directed community awareness special events: recruited panelists, speakers, and other participants; handled publicity with print media and community organizations and businesses.
- Coordinated content and publishing of quarterly newsletter.
- Provided crisis intervention over telephone and face to face.

INSTITUTE FOR PETROLEUM AND ENERGY RESEARCH, Tulsa, Oklahoma
Secretary and Property Specialist   **1985 - 1990**
- Conducted complete inventory of equipment and set up inventory plan and files.
- Tracked company contracts and proposals (approximately 500 outstanding at any time); handled Department of Energy reports; expedited purchase orders; filed; assisted with property sales.

EDUCATION & TRAINING

Associate of Arts degree, concentrating in Behavioral Science, Secretarial Science, and Journalism. Tulsa College, Tulsa, Oklahoma, 1982.

Ongoing computer training courses.

Most of her work has been in "helping" positions

COMMUNITY INVOLVEMENT

Member, Board of Directors, Tulsa County Association for Mental Health.
Certified child caregiver with the Cooperative Disaster Childcare Organization.
Deacon and member of Administrative Board, First Christian Church, Tulsa, Oklahoma.

REFERENCES AVAILABLE UPON REQUEST

269

Secretary. *Laura C. Karlak, CPRW; Bartlesville, OK*

With experience as a receptionist, Sandy now wants a position with more responsibility.

SANDY A. SECRETARY
5509 Third Avenue
Kinkaid, NJ 00000
(555) 555-5555

a good review of her transferable skills and credentials

OBJECTIVE: Secretarial Position

SUMMARY OF QUALIFICATIONS
- 5 years of office support experience in diversified environments.
- Graduate of the Drexel Institute of Business Administration.
- Demonstrated planning and organizational skills.
- Able to work in a fast-paced setting, under tight deadlines.
- Excellent phone manner; relate well with clients.
- Extremely dependable, conscientious, and detail-oriented.
- Computer knowledge: WordPerfect 5.1, dBase III Plus, VP Planner, Lotus 1-2-3

EDUCATION
Graduate, Office Technology Program, The Drexel School of Business Administration, Hilton, NJ, 1992

OFFICE SKILLS

- Typing/Word Processing, 60 wpm	- Appointment Scheduling	- Desktop Publishing
- Record Keeping/File Maintenance	- Speedwriting, 80 wpm	- Cash Management
- Multi-Line Phone Systems	- Medical/Legal Terminology	- Transcription
- Database Management/Spreadsheets	- Travel Planning	- Billing

Work-related skills

OFFICE ADMINISTRATION AND PLANNING
- Coordinated with travel agency to book business trips for Damian Management Company employees.
- Organized and coordinated business meetings and holiday parties for up to 40 people.
- Ordered office supplies and maintained inventory.
- Maintained Pitney Bowes postage machine and generated end-of-day status reports; distributed incoming mail and processed outgoing mail.

RECORD KEEPING, CASH MANAGEMENT, AND CORRESPONDENCE
- Maintained information on employee sick days/late time for payroll records.
- Opened and closed real estate and litigation files; prepared legal documents; typed police discoveries.
- Documented monetary transactions at lawyer's office and handled billing; performed cash and credit transactions for physical therapy practice.

TELEPHONE AND COMMUNICATION SKILLS
- Skillfully managed busy 20-line phone system, with 55 extensions, for environmental subcontracting company; provided information and routed calls.
- Elicited information from utility clients wishing to participate in energy conservation programs; entered data into computer.
- Handled incoming calls at law office; scheduled/confirmed appointments; took detailed messages.
- Scheduled and confirmed medical appointments; responded to patients' inquiries.

WORK HISTORY

Office Assistant/Receptionist	The Damian Management Co., Kinkaid, NJ	1992 - Present
Secretary	Lance Owens, Esquire/Prosecutor, Elcron, NJ	1992
Receptionist	Craigston Physical Therapy, Parlton, NJ	1990 - 1991

Organizing experience into clusters allows for better emphasis

Secretary. *Rhoda Kopy, CPRW; Toms River, NJ*

270

Box used to draw attention to special strengths that would be important during the screening and selection process.

JANICE A. ASHLEY

516 Lawson Street
Lodi, California 95240
janice-ashley@juno.com
(209) 334-2223

> **Experienced Administrative Assistant with strengths in:**
> ✔ **Support** — office management, reception, file management, new office start-up, correspondence, client interface.
> ✔ **Technology** — computer software and Internet (QuickBooks Pro, MS Works, MS Word, MS Excel), typing (50+ wpm), office equipment, online banking, multi-line phones.
> ✔ **Terminology** — business language and medical terminology.

KEY QUALIFICATIONS

✔ Readily accept new challenges and highly conscientious in the planning, follow-through, and organization of new projects.
✔ Easily establish rapport and interact well with management, staff, and clients.
✔ Hardworking individual who always strives to do the best job possible.
✔ Exceptional initiative and resourcefulness; organized in performing work assignments.
✔ Retrieve and manipulate data (numeric, alpha) quickly and accurately.

CAREER HIGHLIGHTS

Janice was a homemaker seeking to return to the work force, so her family business experience is included.

ASHLEY CONSTRUCTION, Palo Alto, California   11/00–Present
Office Support

relevant qualifications

• Paired good business sense with computer skills to start up and transition DeJong Construction business office from Palo to Lodi, California.
• Set up business phones, online banking, billing, and invoicing utilizing QuickBooks Pro.
• Initiated the design of company's Website to accelerate revenue and market penetration.

VALLEY ELEMENTARY SCHOOL, Lodi, California   1996–2000
Volunteer

• Participated in a variety of school activities — assisted teachers with arts and crafts in the classroom, field trips, copying, and errands as well as PTA fund-raising initiatives.

THE DBM (Database Management Group), Palo Alto, California   1995–1996
Customer Service Representative

• Conducted surveys to establish database of major corporations (Microsoft, Toshiba, Nokia, Instead, Sony).
• Managed multiple tasks for a high-volume call center; answered multi-line phone system, entered data for warranties, and scheduled appointments. Worked in a team environment.

COMMUNITY COLLEGES, Palo Alto, California   1993–1995
REGIONAL OCCUPATIONAL PROGRAM (ROP)
Student/Internship — Kaiser Permanente, Nursing Assistant/Acute Nursing

• Mastered new concepts quickly and developed solid medical office and clerical skills.

DP INDEX, Palo Alto, California   1992–1994
Research Assistant (seasonal)

• Streamlined workflow for this database management company including phone communications and research; entered data to update information (current names, addresses, contacts).

DAVID S. CARLICK ADVERTISING, Palo Alto, California (3 years)   Previous
Office Manager/Receptionist

• Developed relationships with clients, prepared correspondence, and managed files.
• Tackled projects that improved efficiency and exceeded performance criteria, winning manager's confidence and earning promotion to Office Manager.

EDUCATION AND TRAINING

• Foothill and DeAnza Community Colleges, Palo Alto, California
  Undergraduate Studies: Psychology, American History, and Medical Terminology
• Regional Occupational Program (ROP), Certified Nursing Assistant (6 months)

Administrative assistant. *Anita Radosevich, CPRW, JCTC, CEIP; Lodi, CA*

To avoid repetition, one "Accomplishments and Experiences" section at the top covers all her jobs.

JUDY FITZSIMMONS
4533 Oak Street * Louisville, KY 40207 * 502-555-8882 * judy@envision-resumes.com

EXECUTIVE ADMINISTRATIVE ASSISTANT

The format used here saves space, makes the resume easier to read, and puts the information the hiring manager needs to see right up front.

Accomplishments and Experiences

- Provided executive administrative and secretarial support to upper-level management including Senior Vice Presidents and Chief Operating Officers.
- Reduced expenditures on office supplies 20% by researching suppliers and buying in bulk.
- Increased office productivity by developing a more efficient filing and record-keeping system.
- Used desktop-publishing skills to design marketing materials in-house, saving the company over $2000 in design fees for one project alone.
- Organized and arranged domestic and international travel arrangements for executives and other office personnel.
- Successfully handled meeting scheduling, coordination, and planning.
- Prepared spreadsheets, PowerPoint presentations, and word-processing documents.
- Answered multi-line telephone courteously and efficiently while simultaneously performing other job responsibilities.
- Performed Internet and library research. Compiled and analyzed results. Designed graphs and tables and other visual aids for presenting results.
- Handled confidential information with discretion and respect.
- Outstanding typing skills (74 WPM); proficient in use of office equipment, digital cameras, scanning equipment, and imaging applications.
- Efficient and good natured; excellent reputation with all former employers.

Work History
) List of specific job titles and dates.

EXECUTIVE ADMINISTRATIVE ASSISTANT	Action Corporation Louisville, KY	1999 to Present
EXECUTIVE ADMINISTRATIVE ASSISTANT	Sullivan Management Systems Frankfort, KY	1996 to 1999
ADMINISTRATIVE ASSISTANT	The Breckinridge Group Frankfort, KY	1990 to 1996
SECRETARY	Jefferson Science Institute Lexington, KY	1985 to 1990

Computer Knowledge

- Microsoft Word
- Excel
- PowerPoint
- Access
- Lotus Email and Organizer
- Outlook
- WordPerfect
- Internet

Education and Training

Bachelor of Science in Business Administration; 1985 — University of Kentucky
Sales and Customer Relations Training; 1998 — Sales Institute of Indiana

272

Executive administrative assistant. *Amy Whitmer, CPRW; Louisville, KY*

Farming, Fishing, and Forestry Occupations

Resumes at a Glance

Fishers and Fishing Vessel Operators

Forest, Conservation, and Logging Workers

This person's goal was to demonstrate that he could be much more valuable than a "hook, line, and sinker." He could also lead and manage people.

Lawrence C. Williams

28 Summer Street ● Philadelphia, PA 19144 ● (215) 771-5496 ● fishermanlarry@aol.com

Qualifications Summary

- Experienced commercial fisherman offering extensive job training as well as significant management background.
- Strengths encompass supervision, leadership, employee training, and client relations.
- Superior past performance in high-stress, tight-deadline conditions.
- Seasoned international traveler.

Employment

COURAGEOUS SEAFOODS, INC., Seattle, WA, 11/90 to Present

Commercial-fishing company operating a series of vessels in the Bering Sea and exporting catch to distributors internationally and domestically.

Deck Supervisor – Direct operations on board the decks of vessels in Kamchatka, Russia, and Dutch Harbor, Alaska, that have consistently ranked among the top five in the world in production levels.

- **Management / Leadership:** Supervise a crew of up to ten commercial fishermen. Rank third in the on-board chain of command.
- **Employee Training:** Provide job education on safety precautions pertaining to weather conditions, equipment use, and emergency management.
- **Client Relations:** Maintain direct communications with Russian and Japanese buyers to learn customer requirements and specifications and deliver high quality control.
- **Technical Skills:** Use and conduct on-board repairs of major, heavy equipment including a boom and a seven-ton-capacity crane.

U.S. MARINE CORPS, Camp Lejeune, NC (Honorable Discharge), 6/83 to 11/90

Corporal E-4 – Coordinated and distributed artillery fire and naval gun fire in support of up to 300 ground troops, or up to five units. Conducted land surveys and topographical assessments for staging a battery or platoon unit.

- **Supervision:** Directed a lance corporal, private first class, and private.
- **Data Management:** Manipulated numerical data accurately to execute the science of artillery: computed target distances, altitude, velocity, and projectile ranges. Justified computation methods to superior officers.

Education

Diploma, Philadelphia Preparatory College, Philadelphia, PA — 1983

273

Fisher and fishing vessel operator. *Jewel Bracy DeMaio, CPRW, CEIP; Royersford, PA*

MARK COOKSON

257-B St. Paul Street, Brookline, MA 02445 • 617-242-0942 H • 617-600-4390 M • mcookson@hotmail.com

Focus: Environmental Auditor • Environmental Officer • Flora & Fauna Technician

Mark was a recent graduate, so he did not have a great deal of paid experience other than short-term retail positions through school.

SUMMARY

Mark had been actively involved in volunteerism, so that experience is shown on the first page of his resume.

Master's-qualified environmentalist — passionate, proactive and unbiased. Simultaneous employment and promotion to leadership roles during university studies emphasizes intense personal drive and commitment. Hands-on community projects and team-based assignments underscore tireless dedication towards environmental issues. Uniquely poised for first step in full-time environmental career.

KEY CREDENTIALS

— For ease of reading, the information in this section is grouped under headings.

Advanced Knowledge of:

- ✓ Flora & Fauna Conservation
- ✓ Habitat Management
- ✓ Land for Wildlife Schemes
- ✓ Management Plan Design & Implementation
- ✓ Waste Management/Auditing
- ✓ Feral Animal Control
- ✓ Community Awareness & Education

- ✓ Conservation Programs
- ✓ Environmental Act Legislation
- ✓ Land Use Planning
- ✓ Sustainable Development
- ✓ Survey Administration & Analysis
- ✓ Strategic Conservation Planning
- ✓ Pest Control/Weed Eradication

Profile:

- ✓ Comprehensive understanding of biological, socio-economic, political and legal issues affecting conservation; keen to create/execute strategies and analyze data that forms the basis for influencing change.

- ✓ Interact well with colleagues, general public, councils, special interest groups, committees, and government agencies; handle all communications with discretion and professionalism.

- ✓ Robust leader and cheerful motivator; create powerful, committed environments for others that reward personal growth and achievement. Frequently complimented by management and clients for enthusiastic, "upbeat" attitude to the most challenging and demanding tasks.

- ✓ Natural talent to effectively build relationships that consistently meet the immediate and long-term needs of customers, management, and team members.

- ✓ Lifelong learner; keen willingness to engage in the learning process to maximize relevance across diverse industries, people and career tasks.

Technology:

- ✓ Windows 95/98; Microsoft Office Suite 2000 (Word, PowerPoint, Excel, Outlook); Adobe Acrobat, Internet and email.

QUALIFICATIONS & TRAINING

Master of Science (Natural Resource Management), *Boston University*	2001
Certificate in Environmental Management, *Audubon Institute*	1999
Bachelor of Science (Marine Biology), *Northeastern University*	1998

Mark Cookson   Page 1   Confidential

274

Conservation scientist. *Gayle Howard, CPRW, CRW, CCM; Melbourne, Australia*

COMMUNITY/ENVIRONMENTAL ACTIVITIES

- Feral animal-control and weed-eradication program team member, Brookline Parks Department. Conceived strategies for further conservation initiatives.

- Audited compliance to waste management processes for the City of Brookline. Interviewed business owners on waste practices; completed, administered, audited, and tabulated surveys.

- Cited in City of New Bedford's Waste Audit Report, for recommendations and findings in collaborative student survey auditing the area's waste disposal activities.

- Team member in native tree-planting project on Nantucket for Reforest America.

- Traveled extensively throughout New England participating in annual Clean Up America programs for CoastClean.

EMPLOYMENT EXPERIENCES

Sales Assistant, *Hardware Warehouse*　　　　　　　　　　　　　　　Nov 95-Present
Part-time senior assistant's role for the Boston area's No.1 hardware retailer.

Track record of achievement in team leadership role. Mentor and supervise less-experienced team members, enforce staff compliance to stringent safety procedures, and juggle the multitude of challenges posed by customers in a high-volume retail environment.

Monitor stock to meet peak customer demands, negotiate favorable ordering and value-added services from supplier's representatives, design water-irrigation systems for domestic usage, and collaborate with coordinators and departmental managers to maximize service delivery.

Forklift Driver / Warehouse Worker, *Simon Transport Networks*　　　　Nov 94-Feb 95
Leading freight and goods distributor.

100% accident-free record as self-taught forklift driver; developed strong competencies in warehouse operations, order picking, and stock distribution. Resolved customer concerns on damaged and unavailable items, responded to telephone enquiries, checked invoices against deliveries, and maintained workplace cleanliness.

PROFESSIONAL ASSOCIATIONS

Member, Audubon Foundation　　　　　　　　　　　　　　　　　　　1998-Present

PERSONAL

Open Water Diver's License. Leisure interests include surfing, snowboarding, mountain bike riding, scuba diving, fishing, stock markets and property development.

REFERENCES

Available Upon Request.

Janice wanted to capitalize on her six years of experience, which included a great deal of field work, to find a management role in a larger organization

Janice Parrington

12 Oak Street, Apt. #2
Chelmsford, MA 01824

978-740-1504
janiceparrington@aol.com

Environmental Consultant with effective combination of scientific knowledge, field experience, and project management skills.

Profile

- Strong presentation and interpersonal skills, with the ability to communicate effectively with clients, public officials, and a broad range of technical experts.
- Experience in both public and private sectors involving land planning, conservation, and wetlands permitting on federal, state, and local levels.
- Extensive experience with field investigations, research, analysis, and documentation on both small and large projects.

Selected Projects

- Investigated over 70 sites in two states proposed for construction of cellular phone towers, conducting wetland delineations and researching sites for the presence of endangered species, floodplain zones, and historic and archeological resources.
- Conducted extensive wetland delineation on a 90-acre parcel using federal, state, and local delineation criteria, investigating 5 wetland resource areas for vernal pool species.
- Designed a 10,000-SF wetland-replication area on a town landfill site to mitigate for a resource area filled during landfill capping activities.
- Prepared and submitted successful state vernal-pool certification applications on behalf of local Conservation Commissions, based on field investigations.

Permit Application Preparations

- Notice of Intent
- Request for Determination of Applicability
- 401 Water Quality Certification
- Ch. 91 Waterways License

- CZM Consistency Statement
- MEPA Environmental Notification Form
- ACOE Section 10 & 404 Permit
- NPDES Permit

PROFESSIONAL EXPERIENCE

GOODHUE ENVIRONMENTAL CONSULTANTS, Reading, MA   1997–Present
Project Manager – Wetland Scientist

Assist clients with investigation of wetlands issues and guide the permitting process in accordance with local, state, and federal regulations. Represent individuals, commercial and residential developers, and the Town of Andover as their environmental consultant of record for third-party reviews. Investigate and determine freshwater and coastal wetland delineations.

Full project control: cost estimates, evaluation of proposals, budget management, contract management, billing, invoicing, and collections. Work closely with company engineering and survey divisions to facilitate progress. Provide assistance with land planning, project design (including wetlands replication/restoration where required), and revisions as ordered by controlling authorities.

Prepare applications in accordance with zoning, planning, and conservation board requirements and present proposals at hearings and appeals.

Janice's resume was designed to reflect her significant wetlands experience, with related educational and certification credentials.

275

Conservation scientist. *Bernice Antifonario, MA; Tewksbury, MA*

Janice Parrington   Page 2 of 2   978-740-1504

(Experience, continued)

COLER & COLLINS, INC., Hanover, MA   **1996–1997**
Wetland Scientist

Worked on large projects, including extensive roadway construction development. Investigated and certified vernal pool habitats. Determined wetland delineations and prepared wildlife habitat assessments. Prepared local, state, and federal permits and represented clients at hearings.

TOWN OF HAVERHILL, Haverhill, MA   **1994–1996**
TOWN OF NORTH ANDOVER, North Andover, MA   **1995–1996**
Conservation Administrator/Associate

Administration and enforcement of by-laws and state regulations for the protection of wetlands. Conducted site inspections and reviewed wetland delineations. Assisted developers and the general public in the filing process and participated at Conservation Commission hearings, offering technical explanations and recommendations.

EDUCATION, TRAINING & CERTIFICATION

) Educational and certification credentials.

University of New Hampshire, Durham, NH
- B.S., Environmental Conservation, with a minor in Resource Economics, 1994
- Wetland Delineator Certification Program, U.S. Army Corps of Engineers, 1996

University of Massachusetts, Amherst, MA
- Graduate Studies Program in Hydric Soils, 1999

State of Massachusetts
- Certified Wetland Scientist

Memberships
- Society of Wetland Scientists
- Association of Massachusetts Wetland Scientists
- Massachusetts Association of Conservation Commissions

John's goal was to transition into a consulting position that would allow him greater freedom in his work.

JOHN STEELE

1021 Lake Drive
Clearlake, California 95424

(707) 362-4142
jsteele@lakenet.net

FORESTRY CONSULTANT

Professional Forestry Consultant specializing in all areas of timber harvesting encompassing log procurement, planning and supervision, appraisals, bid practices, and contract negotiations. Comprehensive experience in Timber Harvest Plan (THP) preparation and timberland road location layout. Ability to handle high-stress operations while maintaining positive attitude.

Proven Areas of Expertise

The resume's combination format and this keyword section define his specific areas of expertise.

> • Hazard Ranking • EPA Projects • Remedial Investigations • Remedial Action Planning
> • Multimedia Contaminant Assessments • Landfill Investigations • Health & Safety
> • Sampling & Analysis Planning • Asbestos & Lead-Based Paint Surveys • AST/UST Systems
> • Air Quality Assessments • Compliance Audits • Habitat Improvement • Expert Testimony
> • Watershed Management • Waste Minimization • Feasibility Studies • Emergency Response

PROFESSIONAL ACHIEVEMENTS

Management

☑ Successfully managed clients' properties as consulting forester in marketing, timber harvesting, planting, and tax preparation.

☑ As area forester, supervised 12 unlicensed foresters and provided timber resources for 3 sawmills.

Log Procurement

☑ Controlled log mill test runs and assured consistent lumber-recovery appraisal values.

☑ Procured logs from Santa Barbara to Trinity Counties for up to 6 sawmills.

☑ Conducted timber cruises, assessed timber values, and predicted harvest costs while providing wood resources for sawmills.

Negotiations

☑ Negotiated extensively with logging, road building, and planting contractors to achieve landowner goals at reduced costs.

Timber Harvest Plans

☑ Prepared timely THPs in all North Coast counties and achieved high approval rate.

☑ Produced record number of THP plans for Coastal California.

☑ Ensured compliance with state regulations and permits addressing timber harvests.

276

Forestry consultant. *Nancy Karvonen, CPRW, CCM, IJCTC, CEIP; Orland, CA*

JOHN STEELE   Page 2

PROFESSIONAL ACCOMPLISHMENTS (Continued)

Supervision/Training

☑ Organized and supervised timber harvest operations for small-area timber owners.

☑ As forester and logging superintendent, supervised up to 15 contract loggers.

☑ Instituted strong safety focus through employee empowerment, resulting in impressive record of no major lost-time contractor accidents.

EMPLOYMENT HISTORY

1986–Present   *Louisiana-Pacific Corporation*, Petaluma, California

Area Forester	2000–Present
Mill Forester (3 sawmills)	1989–2000
Log Procurement Forester (6 sawmills)	1986–1989

Write timber harvest plans, plan log flow, and follow up on harvests. Supervise forestry technicians during planting and harvest seasons.

Prior Experience

Consulting Licensed Forester, *John Steele Forestry Services*, Clearlake, California

Compiled timber harvest plans and supervised timber harvest for landowners in Northwestern California Redwood Region.

Log Procurement Forester, *Masonite Corporation*, Petaluma, California

Procured logs for Western Woodlands Division. Purchased and harvested redwood timber for 2 sawmills.

Forester/Logging Superintendent, *Vista Lumber Company*, Fort Bragg, California

Supervised logging operations on 90,000-acre Lighthouse Ranch.

EDUCATION

Bachelor of Science, Chico State University, School of Forestry, Chico, California

SPECIALIZED TRAINING

☑ Archeological Training for Resource Professionals

☑ Arc View Computer

AFFILIATIONS

☑ California Licensed Foresters Association (CLFA), Member

☑ Chico State Alumni Association, Member

RELATED ACTIVITIES

Mountaineering and Travel

By distributing this resume to networking contacts, John secured a consultation project within the first week!

Construction Trades and Related Workers

Resumes at a Glance

Boilermakers

Brickmasons, Blockmasons, and Stonemasons

Carpenters

Carpet, Floor, and Tile Installers and Finishers

Cement Masons, Concrete Finishers, Segmental Pavers, and Terrazzo Workers

Construction and Building Inspectors

Drywall Installers, Ceiling Tile Installers, and Tapers

Electricians

Elevator Installers and Repairers

Glaziers

Hazardous Materials Removal Workers

Painters and Paperhangers

Pipelayers, Plumbers, Pipefitters, and Steamfitters

This is a straightforward chronological resume that successfully combines related civilian and military experience.

R. Jon Sheldon
25826 Castle Way • Brighton, MI 48116
810.555.1985 • flipfore@captiva.com

JOURNEYMAN BOILERMAKER

Experienced Journeyman – Accumulated more than 39,000 hours to date.

EMPLOYMENT HISTORY

LOCAL 780
Boilermaker, 1989–present
Consistent union employee; Foreman/General Foreman on numerous projects.
- Knowledge of estimating processes and procedures.
- Constructed/repaired projects including black liquor boilers, fossil-fueled boilers, nuclear power plants, air pollution devices including precipitators and bag houses, holding tanks, heat exchangers, condensers, piping, smoke stacks, blast furnaces, and oil refineries.
- Skills include blueprint reading, oxygen-acetylene cutting, arc-gauging, metal fabrication, high rigging, and welding.
- Proficient with MIG, TIG, and 7018, 8018, 9018, 5P, and Jet rods in all positions.
- Certified high-pressure tube welder; also certified in stainless steel and Inconel.

UNITED STATES ARMY
Sergeant — Electronic Technician, 1985–89
Held top secret/sensitive compartmented information clearance. Completed one year in Korea gathering intelligence; reviewed by the KCIA, CIA, NSA, and the Joint Chiefs of Staff.
- Diagnosed unusual and complex malfunctions in tactical and airborne intercept systems, electronic countermeasures, and direction-finding equipment.
- Performed technical inspections on electronic warfare equipment, modules, subassemblies, and circuit cards.
- Performed duties as the noncommissioned officer in charge of the electronic maintenance shop at the Military Intelligence Company, 1st Special Forces Group (Airborne).
- Provided technical guidance to lower-grade personnel in accomplishment of their duties.
- Recipient of Army Commendation Medal for Meritorious service in warlike conditions; Army Achievement Medal with Oak Leaf Cluster; Good Conduct Medal; Overseas Ribbon.

EDUCATION

LAWRENCE TECHNOLOGICAL UNIVERSITY; Southfield, Michigan
Qualified for Academic Scholarship in **Bachelor of Engineering** program

SCHOOLCRAFT COLLEGE; Livonia, Michigan
Associate In Science Degree — Summa Cum Laude (3.8/4.0 GPA), 1998

UNITED STATES ARMY
Honor Graduate in Electronic Warfare Curriculum — Intelligence Center
NCO Academy — Primary Leadership Development Course
Distinguished Honor Graduate — 1st Special Forces Recondo Course
Parachutist Certification — Airborne School

277

Boilermaker (journeyman). *Lorie Lebert, CPRW, JCTC; Novi, MI*

A clean design that uses "white space" for visual appeal.

Bryan Miles
8870 South Hampton Ave.
Lafayette, Mississippi 67758
(412) 555-6789 (leave message)
(412) 555-6790 (digital pager)
brythebrickguy@missnet.com

Summary of Qualifications

Over 10 years of experience.
Primary focus on new construction.
Complete knowledge of all types of raw materials.

Experience

J.F. Steel Mills International   June 1997 to present

Refractory Mason
Specialized in installing firebrick and refractory file in high-temperature boilers, furnaces, cupolas, ladles, and soaking pits primarily in industrial buildings.

America's Home Builder   August 1995 to May 1997

Bricklayer
Primarily worked on single-family one- and two-story homes. Duties performed varied in complexity from laying a simple masonry walkway to building walls, floors, partitions, fireplaces, chimneys, and other structures with brick, precast masonry panels, concrete block, and other masonry materials.

Hanson Builders   July 1992 to July 1994

Hod Carrier

Assisted bricklayers by bringing brick and other materials, mixing mortar, and setting up and moving scaffolding.

Memberships

National Bricklayers Association
Steel Workers Union of America

Bricklayer and mason. *Thelma Silvola; Indianapolis, IN*

A well-written resume where every point supports his job objective.

Michael Dillan
25 M Street
Pertherly, New Jersey 08256
(888) 258-6663
ifihadahammer@hotmail.com

Objective

To obtain a **carpentry** position in the **building and maintenance industry** that will utilize my experience in residential and commercial construction.

Summary

Broad-based experience in areas including
- Carpentry/framing/construction
- Cost estimating
- Blueprint drawing and design
- Interior and exterior finishing

Profile

Conscientious, responsible worker who gets the job done in a timely manner, pays close attention to detail and technical specifications, and possesses the ability to supervise all aspects of construction and maintenance, with excellent communication skills with both management and tradespeople.

Good emphasis on his adaptive skills.

Experience

Bulleted items present his many skills in various trades.

1997–Present

CJA Remodeling, Jacobs, NJ
Carpenter
- Work on new residential and commercial buildings.
- Provide accurate cost estimates.
- Interpret blueprints to specification.
- Frame and install siding and roofing materials.
- Install cabinets in bathrooms and kitchens.
- Complete installations throughout the building and handle all maintenance of completed projects.

1996–1997

J. G. Carpentry, Piscataway, NJ
Carpenter
- Constructed and maintained residential construction sites.
- Installed all doors and windows.
- Installed sheet rock and countertops throughout the buildings.
- Completed custom ceilings.
- In charge of maintenance after construction.

1995–1997

Carpentry Workers International, Penthington, NJ
Carpenter• Local 835
- Worked as a carpenter apprentice.
- Installed cabinets.

Education

Diploma, Mountaintown County Vocational Technical High School, 1989
Special Courses:
- Carpentry and Cabinet Making
- Architectural and Mechanical Drawing and Drafting
- Cost Estimation

Emphasizes related courses.

Awards

- National Builders Association, First Place, 1988 and 1989
- Honorary Excellence Award, New Jersey Builders' Association, 1989
- Mountaintown County Carpentry Exhibition, Second Place, 1988–1989

279

Carpenter. *Beverly Baskin, MA, NCC, CPRW; Marlboro, NJ*

JOHN P. MORGAN
2323 FROZEN PATH ROAD
BALTIMORE, MD 00000
(555) 555-5555

SUMMARY OF QUALIFICATIONS

PROJECT / PRODUCTION / CREW MANAGEMENT

Over 10 years experience directing multi-site flooring installation projects for commercial and residential construction. Well-qualified in estimating materials/labor planning, specifications/change orders, field supervision, problem resolution and inspections.

Consistently successful in bringing in projects to meet time, budget and quality objectives. Outstanding technical skills complement strong planning, organizational and communication abilities. Effective in developing cooperative working relationships with general contractors, corporate management personnel and customers.

EXPERIENCE

Production Manager
BEST FLOOR COVERING. Baltimore, MD   1992 to Present

Supervised carpet installation for two major builders with new residential construction projects throughout Maryland. Managed several concurrent projects with field crews of up to 15. Expedited materials, conducted inspections and resolved all field site problems or customer service issues. Served as the liaison with corporate management and customer project managers.

- Received numerous letters of appreciation from Tuttle Homes, Best Floor Covering's key customer.
- Promoted from Service Technician to Production Manager.

Senior Installer - Top Crew
CARPET HEAVEN, Baltimore, MD   1987 - 1992

Completed carpet installation projects for residential, builder and commercial customers. Responsible for performing work to meet specifications while meeting strict time and quality of work objectives.

- Trained newly hired or less experienced installers.

John, a very experienced carpet installer, moved into a management job in the same company.

280

Carpet installer. *Dede Penick; Indianapolis, IN*

Jason's boss recommended he have a professional resume. After seeing his resume for the first time, Jason was very surprised and motivated to present himself confidently to a potential employer (resume writer's comments).

JASON H. CHESTERFIELD

9900 Robinhood Way
Lawrenceville, GA 30245
(000) 000-0000

Areas of Expertise

- Complete Knowledge of Concrete - Sand Base Composition, Exotic Metals, & All Types of Raw Materials and Long-Term Effects Based Upon Usage
- Troubleshoot Existing Problems
- Liaison Between Masons & Management
- Team Coordination of Final Product
- Select, Place, & Monitor Mason Crews

Experience

Concrete Mason
Concrete International

Story, MI
1985 - Present

- Designed fixtures and masonry processes for military bases on a nation-wide basis, as well as commercial aircraft sites
- Concrete applications of all configurations
- Complete knowledge of all types of bases - the application of concrete to different base structures, especially being sensitive to unstable applications
- Continually updated knowledge of concrete and terrazzo to maintain quality control

Concrete Mason
Concrete USA

Story, MI
1979 - 1985

- Set forms to meet desired pitch and depth through proper alignment
- Utilized shovels and special tools to spread and work concrete into forms
- Gained a strong foundation of the principles and applications of concrete
- Fulfilled Apprenticeship program

Education

Apprenticeship Program
Concrete USA, Story, MI, 1988

Specialized Training - Seminars
Shop Mathematics
Blueprint Reading
Mechanical Drawing
Safety On The Job
Layout Work
Cost Estimating
Creative Design
Terrazzo Specialties

Memberships

Story County Cement Association
Home Builders Association of Story County
Associated General Contractors of America

281

Concrete mason. *Betty A. Callahan, PC, CPRW; Kalamazoo, MI*

ANTHONY L. CONSULTANT

1111 S. James Ave.   Danville, OH 36897   (125) 555-5555

This strong opening presents his key skills and abilities

PROFILE

Extensive experience in the planning, development, and management of construction/maintenance operations with a record of consistent achievement in improving quality, accountability, and efficiency. Proven ability to train, motivate and supervise staff. Innate knowledge of the construction process. Proficient at managing simultaneous projects and successfully meeting deadlines. Special expertise:

- Problem Solving
- Program Development
- Employee Training

- Motivational Management
- Goal Setting
- Coordination of Multiple Projects

PROFESSIONAL EXPERIENCE

Utility Construction Inspector
EMPLOYEE MANAGEMENT, Anywhere, OH   3/95 - Present

Anywhere-based employment firm supplying personnel to area businesses. Hired as Anywhere Electric Company's representative. Manage and coordinate operations for the construction of substations. Directly responsible for quality control, reports, and final documentation.

- Oversaw three-month construction of substation for Ballyhoo Station, Anywhere's new housing development. Project involved coordinating activities of six contractors. Directly responsible for the finished product.
- Coordinated activities of four contractors in the construction of three substations in the Anywhere area; Lake John, Kane, and Arthur. Involved coordination of activities of four contractors. Supervised project from inception to completion and final quality control check.

Supervisor
ANYWHERE ELECTRIC COMPANY, Anywhere, OH   11/67 - 1/95

An excellent statement to make

Started as a laborer and progressed to Supervisor within nine years. Learned essential skills for successful management of personnel. Oversaw and managed construction and maintenance of three power plants and facilities in surrounding areas. Directly responsible for up to 19-person crews. Coordinated layout and design, communicated with engineers and key plant personnel; procured material, supervised personnel and performed final quality inspections. Managed budget process and financial expenditures.

- Directed monthly safety meetings; responsible for meeting OSHA requirements
- Taught CPR; qualified instructor
- Implemented program for in-house precast concrete operation that resulted in major savings
- Instrumental in identifying, documenting, and testing for mastery of skills needed for journeyman certification
- Certified Professional Manager
- Implemented programs for continuous employee training
- Created in-house refractory crew

Use of numbers here provides specific responsibilities

Utility construction inspector. *Carol Heider, CPRW; Tampa, FL*

ANTHONY L. CONSULTANT   Page Two

EDUCATION/TRAINING
Community College, Anywhere, OH
Major: Construction Technologies

University of Buffalo, NY
Major: Mechanical Engineering
Varsity Football and Wrestling

Attended 40+ in-house Leadership/Management classes and seminars

This does not state he has a degree — a good approach for those who attended but did not graduate college

ACTIVITIES
Consultant Management Association (CMA)
- President, 1992-1993
- Member of the Year, 1986 & 1991
- Member of the Quarter (five times)
Paint Your Heart Out
United Way
- Committee Chairman
Mayor's Alliance
Self-Reliance (wheelchair ramp building)
Youth Football League (12 years)
- Athletic Director, Coach and Founder
Johnson High School
- Assistant Wrestling Coach

His activities are either job related or support his leadership skills

GEORGE INSPECTOR, JR.
707 SOUTH ROOFTOP LANE ✳ TREMONT, MICHIGAN 48812 ✳ 616-555-5555 ✳ EYEINSPECT@JUNO.NET

Emphasizes important adaptive skills first.

PROFILE

Professionalism

* Highly experienced and detail-minded construction inspector with a broad base of knowledge in all aspects of construction.
* Reputable qualities include courtesy to the public and responding to inquiries on a timely basis with a friendly, pleasant disposition and helpful attitude.
* Noted for cooperation, fairness, and respect toward all levels of management, lenders, coworkers, government officials, and customers.

Organization

* Complete reports in an efficient and timely manner by developing and following an appointment schedule.
* Knowledgeable in maintaining records and submitting all necessary government inspection forms for all departments including FMHA, HUD, FHA, and Fannie Mae.
* Prepare construction activity reports on progress, review bids, pay estimates, read plans and specifications, and assist in preparing construction appraisals to meet all state and local business building safety codes.

Expertise

* Perform on-site inspection during all phases of construction projects including commercial, single- and multi-family developments, water towers, plants, and wastewater treatment facilities, migrant camps, fire stations, and other community facilities.
* Coordinate and act as liaison between various government officials, departments, private contractors and engineers, and lending institutions.
* Ensure adherence to plans and specifications and an acceptable level of workmanship.
* Make recommendations on appropriate actions for problems with existing and new construction projects, resolving differences and approving minor design changes not involving additional cost or alteration of basic design.
* Check materials, work methods, safety measures, installation of electric and plumbing hardware, and all other aspects of projects to determine contract compliance.

PROFESSIONAL EXPERIENCE

Construction Inspector Farmers Home Administration USDA, Grant, Michigan	7/1992–Present
Construction Inspector City of Houston, Houston, Texas	5/1984–7/1992
Salesman Boise Cascade, Houston, Texas	6/1987–5/1990
Field Engineer Townsend and Bottom Inc., St. Clair, Michigan	5/1981–4/1984
Surveyor's Assistant Dunn Construction Engineering, Inc., Port Huron, Michigan	1/1981–5/1981

Note that this resume does not include educational credentials as this person's strength.

283

Construction inspector. *Patricia L. Nieboer, CPS, CPRW; Fremont, MI*

Richard A. Stevens
1111 North Hill Street ◆ Any City, USA 12345 ◆ (123) 555-1111

SUMMARY

- More than 20 years of management and supervisory experience. Bachelor's degree in Business Administration.
- Highly motivated, positive thinker with the ability to motivate people to accomplish desired goals and meet deadlines. Excellent team building skills.
- Strong background in task analysis, project design, and development.
- Effective communication skills. Work well with people. Good coordinating and planning abilities.

HIGHLIGHTS OF WORK EXPERIENCE

Administration & Management

- As Office Manager, supervised and managed 7 subordinate junior managers and 46 employees. As Training Manager, supervised 16 instructors. Assigned duties and evaluated work performance.
- Developed and implemented an incentive awards program to motivate, recognize, and reward employees and to emphasize team building and increase productivity.
- Created an atmosphere that inspired employees to strive for excellence.
- Provided professional and personal counseling.
- Supervised all administrative operations including employee and company training requirements, taskings, and suspense dates. Coordinated and organized the employee training program.

Training Management & Development

- As Project Officer, analyzed the tasks, designed a training program, and developed simulated scenarios to train drivers to safely and efficiently operate heavy equipment. Acted as expert technical advisor to General Electric executives. Recommended design improvements to create more believable ambient light changes and sounds to closer simulate the actual equipment, operating environment, and conditions under which the equipment would be functioning. All proposals were adopted. Edited and condensed existing material, coordinated, and wrote a training manual.
- Developed curriculum, lesson plans, and training strategies. Coordinated with other agencies in the development of training materials, visuals, and film.
- Administered tests and conducted reviews on various skills including effective communications, cardiac-pulmonary resuscitation, and use of safety equipment to 120 students a day.

Property Management

- Met with approximately 8 to 12 residents daily and always provided excellent customer service. Handled problems quickly and efficiently.
- Inspected rental houses, property, grounds, and landscaping for deficiencies. Closely monitored all details and called in repair requests or work orders when necessary. Wrote condition reports to summarize the current state of the property.
- Condensed the standard three page condition report into one page by eliminating duplicated

284

Housing inspector. *Connie S. Stevens; Radcliff, KY*

Richard A. Stevens

and unnecessary information and saved the organization $7,000 a year in wasted man-hours and paper.

➤ When a resident moved, inspected the house, compared findings to the last condition report, determined if repairs were a result of "fair wear and tear" or neglect on the part of the occupant, and, if required, prepared paperwork to charge the resident for repairs. Used specialized computer software to enter information into a database.

Sales Management

➤ Expanded the territory in a two hundred mile radius by contacting prospects through target marketing. Recruited and trained other agents. Analyzed sales quotas, then established goals and personal sales strategies. Attended classes on motivation, positive thinking, and sales techniques.

➤ Received the Eagle Award for exceeding all goals and requirements. Maintained client files; ensured information was always current and easy to retrieve. Used specialized computer program to run quotes, design policies, and make mutual fund and dividend projections.

EDUCATION

McKENDREE COLLEGE ◆ Radcliff, KY
Bachelor of Science in **Business Administration** ◆ Degree Conferred 1996

ADDITIONAL TRAINING

Task Analysis, Design, and Development Course ◆ 1990
Advanced Leadership and Management Course ◆ 1984
Basic Leadership Course ◆ 1977

WORK HISTORY

DIRECTORATE OF PUBLIC WORKS ◆ Any Fort, USA   Dec 93 - Present
Housing Inspector (Federal Civil Service)

METROPOLITAN LIFE ◆ Any City, USA   May 92 - Dec 93
Account Representative

U.S. ARMY   May 72 - May 92
Retired First Sergeant ◆ Held positions of increasing levels of authority primarily in **Training Development / Implementation** and **Administration**

A good example of how a veteran can present his substantial military experience in "civilian" terms. The lack of a job objective allows him to consider many jobs.

Karl used his resume to promote his skills and back-ground to a major building company in the metro-politan area (resume writer's comments).

KARL SMITH

1234 Street
Any Town, MI 49001
(333) 333-3333

DRYWALL

Areas of Building Knowledge

- Drywall
- Plumbing
- Window & Door Replacement
- Custom Laminate Work
- Roofing

- Electrical
- Carpentry
- Ceramic Tile
- Wood Floors
- Siding

Licensure

Builder License #3333333333
State of Michigan • Lansing, MI • Since 1981

Experience

DRYWALLER
DEALLELTON BUILDERS • Story, MI • 1989 - Present
PROFILE & HIGHLIGHTS
- Specialize in Kitchen & Bath remodeling
- Coordinate drywall phases of refurbishing projects for commercial and residential clients
- Establish deadlines and time charts with building specialties [electrical, plumbing, etc.] to accomplish tasks in a timely manner within required sequence
- Monitor individual quality workmanship during drywall phases of completion
- Establish positive rapport with clients to insure satisfaction and repetitive business

DRYWALLER APPRENTICE
INTERNATIONAL DESIGN & CREATION • Story, MI • 1983 - 1990
- Worked directly with established Drywaller in learning and applying techniques and skills required of drywall phase in finishing new home interiors
- Performed extensive remodeling to existing homes to meet client specifications under the direct guidance of Drywaller
- Gained a solid base of appreciation and understanding of the intricacies and timing involved in final completion of building jobs

Education

Story Valley Community College
Curriculum Emphasis: Carpentry & Drywall Applications
Story Valley, MI • 1982 - 1983

References Available Upon Request

285

Drywall installer and finisher. *Betty A. Callahan, PC, CPRW; Kalamazoo, MI*

Glen Brown
2404 West Dove Street
Jackson, NJ 01022
(606) 555-3489

Glen is an electrician who is now interested in sales, so he emphasizes his skills for the sales position he wants.

Unique Qualifications

Over eight years of increasing responsibilities in areas including:

Electrical Contracting	Customer Relations	Technical Liaison Work
Blueprint/Specifications	Planning/Scheduling	Marketing

Sales Experience

1997–Present   **Capitol Electric, Inc.**   *Sales Representative*

Sell lighting and electrical service contracts; also retrofitting installations. Provide technical support on commercial and industrial projects.

Technical Experience

1994–Present   **Nationwide Electrical Workers**   *Union Electrician*

Worked on commercial and industrial projects, power distribution, instrumentation, programmable controllers, and DCS equipment.

Education and Training

Completed four years of Apprenticeship Training through the Nationwide Electrical Workers/Department of Labor.

Completed the following Dale Carnegie Courses:
- Effective Speaking and Human Resources
- Dale Carnegie Sales Course (chosen to lead several classes; became a Graduate Assistant, 1994)

Graduate, Baytown High School, College Preparatory Course

New Jersey Licensed Realtor

286

Electrician. *Beverly Baskin, MA, NCC, CPRW; Marlboro, NJ*

Raymond wanted to get back into elevator installation after a few years as a crane mechanic. The results of his resume were quite effective – he landed the position he wanted!

RAYMOND FINNEGAN

887 Ballinger Road
Westfield, MA 01085
(413) 562-0789 • rayfin@aol.com

His specialized skills and license are mentioned here.

QUALIFICATIONS

Licensed Elevator Mechanic with specialized skills in hydraulics, motor controls, wiring controls, rigging, electrical print reading, solid-state computers and print boards.

> Experienced in troubleshooting, repair, installation and testing of electro-mechanical systems, including pumps, drives and reducers.
> Contributor in self-directed, high performance team environment with proven ability to complete multiple projects in a timely, efficient manner.
> Skilled in welding (steel, aluminum and industrial equipment), pipefitting, millwrighting and machining. Strong mathematical, organizational and time management skills.

CURRENT EMPLOYMENT

His experience is categorized under two headings to draw attention to his elevator service background.

BAYSTATE ELECTRO-MECHANICS, Springfield, MA
Overhead Crane Mechanic (1998-present)

- Perform on-site service calls on overhead cranes for customers in the chemical, power and paper industries.
- Diverse responsibilities include repairing, troubleshooting, removal, installation and testing of electro-mechanical equipment to ensure safe operations.
- Repair and install chemical processes and related equipment such as pumps, drives and reducers.

ELEVATOR SERVICE EXPERIENCE

VANGUARD ELEVATORS, Springfield, MA
Elevator Mechanic (1990–1998)

- Performed all aspects of elevator installations from set-up to alignment of brackets, rails and car to setting up motors on tractions and wiring the elevators.
- Serviced contracts for elevator equipment at major area companies: American Technologies, Payne & Company, Montgomery Corp., Dover Enterprises and others.

INTERNATIONAL UNION OF OPERATING ENGINEERS, West Springfield, MA
Hoisting Engineer (1986–1990)

- Operated and maintained heavy equipment, including backhoes, cranes, bulldozers and rollers.

Additional Experience: Service Manager, MARLAND PROPERTIES, Chicopee, MA
Supervised staff of 9 in all aspects of property maintenance for 300 residential units. Ensured that repairs were completed in timely, cost-effective manner while maintaining quality standards. Prepared and maintained up-to-date documentation on all repairs performed *(1984-1986)*.

EDUCATION

Massachusetts Technical Community College, Westfield, MA
Electronics courses

International Union of Elevator Constructors' School, Springfield, MA
Completed training in: Elevator Mechanics, Electronics, Hydraulics, Motor Controls, Electrical Theory

287

Elevator mechanic. *Louise Garver, MA, JCTC, CMP, CPRW; Enfield, CT*

Ahmed was very experienced in the field but had been caught in a company downsize.

AHMED P. NELSON
254 Baywood Boulevard, Brick, NJ 08723
Home: 732-477-5172 • E-mail: anelson@aol.com • Cell: 732-452-5164

ENVIRONMENTAL MANAGEMENT
Emergency Response Incident Command/Hazardous Materials Spill Control/Waste Remediation

Award-winning background of emergency response, treatment, recycling, and disposal of hazardous and non-hazardous materials in complete compliance with strict state and federal regulations. Strong track record of reducing operational expenses and increasing system efficiencies. Skilled with pH monitors, atomic absorption spectrophotometers, and ion exchange towers. Computer literate in Word, Works, Windows, e-mail, and the Internet. Developed proficiencies in the following areas:

- Materials Identification/Classification
- Cost Reductions/Profit Growth
- Inventory Ordering & Control
- Process Improvements
- Environmental Regulations
- Equipment Maintenance
- Treatment Plan Formulations
- Hazardous Material Clean-Ups
- Personnel Training & Leadership

CURRENT CERTIFICATIONS

- Level 5 On-Scene Incident Commander by New Jersey State Office of Emergency Management
- Level 3 Hazardous Materials Technician by New Jersey State Office of Emergency Management
- Class C Haz-Mat Response by New Jersey State Office of Emergency Management
- Hazardous Toxic Waste Manager from Response Technologies (EPA Contractors)
- Hazardous Materials Transportation from Response Technologies (EPA Contractors)
- Forklift Safety/Forklift Operator by Caterpillar Inc.

ENVIRONMENTAL MANAGEMENT EXPERIENCE

NATIONAL CHEMICAL PRODUCTS CORPORATION, Trenton, New Jersey — 1993–Present
Multibillion-dollar international metal-plating and maintenance-products producer for the electronics industry.

Environmental/Waste Control Manager, Water Waste Treatment Department • 1996–Present
Supervisor • 1994–1996 // **Lead Man** • 1993–1994

Supervise 4 personnel. Identify and classify wastes from 11 departments as nonhazardous or hazardous according to DEP and EPA standards. Formulate and implement treatment programs for non-hazardous wastes. Arrange for disposal and proper handling of hazardous materials. Enforce company-wide compliance with environmental protection regulations. Manage $30,000–$40,000 in raw-materials inventory. Conduct daily inspections of waste-storage area. Act as hazardous-spill response-team leader. Maintain current knowledge of hazardous-material regulations by monitoring the EPA Web site, reading professional newsletters and reviewing EPA notifications. Prepare year-end financial and departmental summary reports.

Spill Control Management
- Headed off hazardous cooling oil blowing out of a damaged pipe and running toward railroad tracks. Initiated rapid clean-up, prevented local shut-down of railroad service and avoided involvement of the EPA, New Jersey Transit and local fire department (July 2000).
- Stemmed in-house 3,000-gallon methane/sulphonic-acid spill caused by a forklift and guided spill-control team to complete clean-up within 3 hours (Aug. 1999).

Page 1 of 2

288

Hazardous materials removal manager. *Carol Rossi, CPRW; Brick, NJ*

ENVIRONMENTAL MANAGEMENT EXPERIENCE

NATIONAL CHEMICAL PRODUCTS CORPORATION continued...

Environmental/Waste Control Manager (continued)

Recycling/Waste Treatment Management
- Authored waste-remediation guidelines and procedures manual at management request. Carried by company executives overseas and implemented in new Philippine plant, 2001.
- Cut hazardous nickel waste recycling costs by $600 per bag (an annual cost savings of $15,600) by pinpointing the one hazardous waste getting into the nickel waste, providing a separate collection system for the hazardous material, and reclassifying the nickel waste as nonhazardous, thus reducing paperwork and eliminating the need for special haulers, 2001.
- Reduced raw materials expenses 45% and cut treatment times 1.5 days after implementing a new state-of-the-art sulfur-based waste treatment program, 1999.

Audits & Awards
- Consistently pass on-site inspections by the EPA (quarterly), the local sewerage commission (5x/year) and the local fire department (annually).
- Earned certificate of achievement and a bronze plaque from the local sewerage commission for 100% compliance with discharge regulations, 1997, 1998, 1999, 2000.
- Honored every year since 1997 by the World Resources Organization for implementing a highly effective nickel recycling program.

Career includes additional operator and foreman/yard supervisor experience with Amcs Oil Corporation in Trenton, New Jersey (now closed). Treated/recycled oil and arranged for transportation of hazardous materials. Supervised 3–5 operators. Assisted crew of 11 with public utility company's transformer accident in Cherry Hill and cleaned up PCP-contaminated oil within 8 hours.

EDUCATION & STATE TRAINING

College Education
- Bachelor of Science in Criminal Justice, Rutgers State University, New Brunswick, New Jersey

State Training
- EPA Hazardous Waste Reduction & Recycling Assessment
- Hazardous Waste Regulations Compliance
- Resource Conservation & Recovery Act Training
- EPA Waste Minimization
- Hazardous Waste Generator
- First Responder

Ahmed's abilities in hazardous-materials management in both a plant environment and in hazardous-spill situations were emphasized throughout the resume to broaden the job opportunities for which he could apply.

Her artistic and creative talents are displayed in this resume and support her skill statements. This resume is used to help her gain new clients.

Angelina Newson
456 Party Time Lane
Beech Grove, CA 69580
(607) 555-1234

Objective

To personalize your home or
office decor with stylish wallpapering ideas

Unique Qualifications

Dozens of satisfied clients
Over ten years wallpapering experience
First Place in the State Decorators Exhibit, 1995 and 1996

Recent Experience

Dr. Rachel McCleash   January, 1996
Redecorated office space including wall papering and window treatments.
Also, consulted on office furnishings and wall treatments.

State Office Building   September, 1995
Senator Jonathon Parker
Senator Patricia Mulligan
House Representative Douglas Fargo
House Representative Janice Moore

Updated meeting offices as well as individual office space with innovative
wall papering. Each office personalized to distinctive preferences.

Mr. & Mrs. John Miller   July, 1995
Supplied wall paper samples, accessories catalogs, and furnishing catalogs
while working with the client to make their home reflect personal style and
taste. Wall papered entire home and assisted in the placement of accessories.

Specialized Training

Herron School of Art   Diploma
     Special Courses: Color Enhancement, Texture/Textiles

289

Painter and paperhanger. *Thelma Silvola; Indianapolis, IN*

Presenting the facts with little narrative is an appropriate approach for this experienced and credentialed trades worker.

Rodney Jones
21 Ballmer Avenue
Sahton, Ohio 55768
(709) 475-8869

Objective

To continue my career as a Plumber working in all phases of plumbing and heating

Summary of Qualifications

Experience in the following areas:

- ✤ Hospitals
- ✤ Institutions
- ✤ Single and Multi-Family Housing
- ✤ Hotels

Quickly demonstrates his wide experience base

License

Plumber License, State of New York,   1996 - Present

Employment

Rod's Plumbing and Heating   1996 - Present
Plumber. Work with residential and commercial projects

Axtec Plumbing Supplies   1990 - 1995
Plumber Apprentice. Completed five years of apprenticeship plus on-the-job
training/repiping in new and old buildings.

Education

Graduate, New Uttech High School, Brooklyn, New York
Plumbers Apprentice School, New York, NY

References available

An essential certification, it is prominently listed

290

Plumber. *Beverly Baskin, MA, NCC, CPRW; Marlboro, NJ*

Installation, Maintenance, and Repair Occupations

Resumes at a Glance

Nabila's recent computer training, along with his natural troubleshooting abilities, had put him in high demand with the store's customers. His reason for putting together this resume was to try to get a promotion to supervisor— and he got it!

NABILA ASWANI
17 Greene Street, Rockaway, NJ 07866
973-957-5555 Home ▪ Naswani@aol.com

CAREER TARGET:
Entry-level Computer Services Support / Computer Technician / Help Desk

HIGHLIGHTS OF QUALIFICATIONS
☑ One year successful computer diagnosis and repair experience combined with up-to-date training in computer technical support services.
☑ Proven ability to troubleshoot and repair computer hardware and software problems.
☑ Skilled in telephone communications — patient, personable and receptive.
☑ Strong organization skills. Efficient and self-motivated team player.

TECHNICAL SKILLS
Windows NT / 98…MS Office 2000…MS Access 2000…LAN…Novell Netware…
Yes I Can Database…Visual Basic…Oracle…Internet Explorer.

EDUCATION
2000 Certificate — Visual Basic, SQL, Oracle: ComputerSoft Technology, Parsippany, NJ
1998 BA, Political Science: Samuel Morris College, Morristown, NJ
Worked full-time while attending classes and completing degree requirements.

PROFESSIONAL EXPERIENCE
2000 – present **Computer Technician** (on-the-job training), Computer Stores, Inc., Rockaway, NJ
- Provide technical service and repair work on computer hardware, such as hard drives, disk drives, printers, controller cards and network interface cards, as well as software installation, upgrades and configuration for small businesses.
- Accurately interpret customers' problems and offer the best solution via telephone hot-line support and in person to retail-store customers.
- Educate customers in the proper running and maintenance of hardware devices and software programs, optimizing their performance and troubleshooting capabilities.

1999 – present **Courier,** Rockaway Packet, Rockaway, NJ
- Coordinate and deliver time-sensitive legal documents from 20 Rockaway-area law firms to New Jersey courthouses and airports, scheduling deliveries for maximum efficiency and timeliness.
- Maintain frequent contact with customers to quickly identify and solve delivery problems, ensuring that all delivery dates are met.

1994 – 1998 **Supervisor,** Secure Payments Central, Haddon Heights, NJ
- Provided protection services at the security command center, as well as 5 outside locations, troubleshooting emergencies and handling fire drills and evacuations.
- Supervised 23 security guards at 6 locations and trained new security guards.

Willing to travel and relocate within the tristate area.

291

Computer repairer. *Susan Guarneri, NCC, NCCC, LPC, CPRW, IJCTC, CCM, CEIP; Lawrenceville, NJ*

This says it all!

Electrical service technician with solid experience!

Donald Williams
200 W. 12th St. (317) 642-0000
Anderson, IN 46016

Objective:

Seeking to secure a position where I can best utilize my training and background as an electrical service technician.

Professional Experience:

Lineman with Anderson Light & Power Dept. Current employment since 1990. Responsible for operation of line and bucket trucks, pole setting and climbing, <u>working primary and secondary voltages, transformers, and wire pulling</u>, both overhead and underground, and trouble shooting.

Delivery driver for Ruan Transport (Marsh Supermarkets), 1989-90. Delivery driver for food and produce.

Transport for Carter Industrial Services, Anderson, IN. 1987-89. Responsible for transporting GM auto parts and equipment from one plant to another.

General construction for M.K. Betts Engineering & Contracting, 1985-87. General construction crew responsible for projects such as: street construction, building construction, & related projects. Supervisor for Martin Luther King project.

Solid experience in electrical service technical applications

Hard worker, team-oriented.

Reliable, capable, fast learner.

Great attitude.

Education & Training:

● Successfully completed Electronics Tech program at ITT Technical Institute, Indianapolis, 1985. Maintained better than a 3.0 GPA in a course of study which included: fundamental analog components and circuits, digital & microprocessors, specialized test equipment, oscilloscopes, multimeters, logic probes, logic pulsers and microprocessor test fixtures. Technician's logbook maintained to document trouble shooting experience.

● Purdue University, Anderson Campus, studied electrical engineering. 3.0 GPA. 1985-87.

● Ivy Tech, Anderson, IN. Refresher courses in algebra/geometry as part of in-house apprenticeship program with Anderson Light & Power. 1990-92.

Electronics repairer, commercial and industrial equipment. *Jon Shafer; Anderson, IN*

Doug wants to stay with his current employer but move into supervision.

Doug Roberts
99 West Lowland Road
Atantice, New Jersey 07897
(888) 258-7895
witchita@prodigy.net

OBJECTIVE: To continue my career in the position of lineman for Jersey P&L Corporation.

SUMMARY: Broad-based experience in areas including:

Here and elsewhere, he emphasizes his supervisory skills.

- Union, company, and public safety enforcement
- Overhead construction and installation
- Forestry and tree services
- Supervision of employees; high work standards and performance levels
- Use and maintenance of numerous types of equipment
- Public relations functions

TRAINING AND
CERTIFICATION:
- Completed apprenticeship training program at the Madison Training Center, Metuchen, New Jersey (through PSENG).
- Passed first-line supervisor test.

EMPLOYMENT:

1993 to Present

Much of this experience is transferable to a new job.

IOU & M METRO DIVISION, CLIFEY, NJ
GRADE I LINEMAN
Initially hired as an apprentice lineman; promoted to grade I. Currently responsible for following through on all safety and all construction on overhead lines and equipment.

Train new apprentices; complete all jobs on a timely basis. In charge of vehicles and related equipment. Use my technical and mechanical skills and my extensive background in electricity.

Acquired a vast amount of knowledge and skill relating to construction and maintenance of overhead outside planned facilities. Responsible for setting and guying poles, installation of distribution transformers, installation of lightning and surge protection, fuses, switches, and protective grounds.

Developed an understanding of electrical principles and their application to electrical construction and maintenance work. Adhere to high safety standards and performance levels.

1984 to 1993

SAWS-R-US OF AMERICA, MONARY, NJ
PRESIDENT AND OWNER, RKD TREE SERVICE
Directed the day-to-day activities of the business including working with local municipalities, State Government, Rutters Forestry Division, and New Jersey State Tree Specialists. Obtained several nationwide contracts.

Hired and trained 100 technical employees. Supervised the employees concerning safety standards and company rules. Major contracts included Central Park, New York City, Monuth County, Mercee County, Cammy County, and Union Bay County.

Performed accounting and budgeting functions. Responsible for payroll. Monitored expenditures to improve the maintenance of equipment. In charge of all advertising and all public relations.

293

Cable television installer. *Beverly Baskin, MA, NCC, CPRW; Marlboro, NJ*

HERBERT NASH, JR.
19 Dorothy Place
Lynbrook, New York 14218
(716) 775-2224
cable.advantage@adelphia.net

SUMMARY

Over 12 years' experience in the operation of a cable television installation business, utilizing solid skills in customer service, staff supervision, and business development.

STRENGTHS

Technical Instruction   Installation and Repair
Needs Assessment   Product Sales
Customer Relations   Staff Development

EXPERIENCE
1988–Present

Herb really had only one related job — as a self-employed installer.

Cable Television Installer
Independent Contractor, Lynbrook, New York

Many aspects of his job are identified to give an overall picture of his competencies.

- Provide residential cable television installation throughout Upstate New York and Northern Pennsylvania.
- Supervise activities of four installers, with responsibility for recruiting, hiring, training, monitoring, and evaluating personnel.
- Perform hard-line wiring and splicing on exterior and in-home cable.
- Replace outdated cable boxes and inadequate connections with state-of-the-art equipment.
- Oversee purchase, repair, and distribution of equipment.
- Sell additional services and premium channels.
- Assist and train customers in proper equipment operation.
- Handle payments by cash, check, and credit card.
- Maintain daily logs and schedule installation and repair appointments.

Achievements

His achievements are spaced in a way that draws attention to them.

➢ Enhanced customer satisfaction and reduced number of call-backs by providing thorough and responsive service.

➢ Successfully resolved customer problems and increased consumer approval rating by 32%.

➢ Increased sale of premium packages and generated more than $60,000 in annual additional revenues for cable service provider.

➢ Completed Qualified Installer Program.

EDUCATION

Erie Community College, Williamsville, New York
Two years of study in Liberal Arts.

REFERENCES

Furnished upon request.

294

Telecommunications installer. *Freddie Cheek, CPRW, CWDP; Amherst, NY*

When David sent this resume to a competitor, he was immediately interviewed and hired!

DAVID A. STARKEY

86 Muldoon Street
Croton, NY 10520
(914) 271-4647
das320@aol.com

QUALIFICATIONS SUMMARY

Experienced telecommunications equipment service technician with expertise in installation, programming, troubleshooting, diagnosing and repair. Extensive technical and product knowledge, combined with superior skills in building and maintaining positive customer relationships, results in 100% service satisfaction. Adept in managing multiple projects, completed on time and accurately. Computer proficiency includes utilizing the Internet.

TECHNICAL TRAINING & PROFICIENCY

- Meridian 1 PBX System — Entire product line with extensive experience on Option 11 and 61
- Norstar PBX System
- Customer Control Management Information Systems (CCMIS)
- Business Communication Management System (BCM) – Voice over Internet Protocol
- Norstar Application Module — Voice Mail System

EXPERIENCE

NETWORKS CORPORATION   New York, NY
Installation Technician   1990–present

Progressed to senior-level installation technician in the Customer Care Division of a global leader in the telecommunications equipment industry that provides telephony and network solutions. Service single to multi-site enterprises in diverse industries throughout northern New Jersey area. Scope of responsibilities includes:

- Managing multiple small to large installation projects, efficiently planning each project step from reviewing customers' product needs to physical site/layout.

- Installing, programming, cross connecting, equipment testing and repair of Meridian 1 PBX and Norstar KSU systems at customer sites. Perform moves/adds/changes as well as software and hardware upgrades.

- Supervising outside subcontractors as needed on various installation projects to perform inside wiring and other functions.

- Providing product training and systems troubleshooting, maintenance, repair and service support to customers either on-site or remote via computer/telephone.

- Preparing accurate, complete documentation for each project or work order.

Awards: 7-time winner of company's annual Star Award for performance and service excellence.

PRIOR EXPERIENCE

Communications Equipment Repair, U.S. Coast Guard, San Diego, CA (4 years; honorable discharge).

EDUCATION

Associate of Science in Business
Westchester Community College, White Plains, NY

Additional: Comprehensive training on entire Nortel product line.

The interviewer told David, "This is the most concise, yet descriptive, resume we received. It clearly showed us what you are capable of."

295

Telecom (telephone) installer and repairer. *Louise Garver, MA, JCTC, CMP, CPRW; Enfield, CT*

Walter was concerned that I not make him look "too" good. Even with his technical experience, he hadn't developed a lot of confidence...

WALTER ROBERTS
P.O. Box 1234
Hawthorne, Nevada 00000

555-555-5555

QUALIFICATION SUMMARY

More than five years experience in most phases of domestic and foreign automobile maintenance and repair.

TOOLS/ EQUIPMENT

Hand Tools	Gauges	Test Meters
Vacuum Tester	Pressure Tester	Voltmeter
Hydraulic Jack	Drill Press	Lathe
Chassis Aligner	Acetylene Torch	Misc. Power Tools

EXPERIENCE

- ☐ Perform tune-ups: remove and replace or adjust spark plugs, points, coil/alternator.
- ☐ Replace defective chassis parts: shock absorbers, ball joint suspension, brake shoes, and wheel bearings.
- ☐ Inspect, test and repair cooling systems.
- ☐ Repair and overhaul brake systems, replacing brake shoe units or attaching new brake linings. Repair and replace leaky brake cylinders.
- ☐ Repair and adjust carburetors: test needle valves, repair or replace defective parts, reassemble carburetor and gas filter and install.
- ☐ Align wheels, axles, frames, torsion bars, and steering mechanisms. Straighten axles and steering rods. Adjust shims, tie rods, and joining pins to align wheels.
- ☐ Remove, repair, and replace transmission and clutch assemblies.
- ☐ Rebuild domestic and imported engines.

WORK HISTORY

1991 - Present	Mike's Auto Service	Hawthorn, Nevada
1994 - 1996	Auto Experts	Hawthorn, Nevada

EDUCATION

1991 - 1993	Desert Sands Vocational Skills Center
	Automotive Technology
	CAD Training
	Computer Programming
1993	Sierra High School (Graduate), Hawthorn, Nevada

Without doing anything "fancy," I showed him that he did have concrete skills and experience (resume writer's comments).

Lineman. *Lonnie L. Swanson, CPRW; Poulsbo, WA*

Most of James' resume presents his technical skills, but he also includes a few extra skills and accomplishments that others could not offer.

JAMES B. ENGINE
5 Fixit Road
Machinery, State 02222
(860) 211-1111

SUMMARY OF QUALIFICATIONS

◆ 8 years experience as jet engine mechanic.
◆ Varied jobs in build and tear down of modules and small components.
◆ Performed troubleshooting of any problem within the assembly of the product.

RELEVANT EXPERIENCE & ACCOMPLISHMENTS

1991-present   **Industrial Jet Engine Mechanic**   TURBINE ENGINE EXPERTS
City, State

Overhaul repair facility for industrial jet engines: GG3, GG4A and GG4C engines.
- Perform complete tear down of engine modules and components, including inlet cases, low and high compressor, low and high turbine; exhaust cases, diffuser cases, intermediate cases; carbon seals and bearing assembly.
- Assemble and static balance high and low compressor disk and blades, high and low turbine disk and blades. Secure locks on compressor disks and riveting turbine disks.
- Assemble and inspect engine modules and small components, including diffuser cases, intermediate cases, exhaust cases, carbon seal assembly, inlet cases and bearing assembly.
- Complete engine assembly and addtest equipment for testing at test cell.

1987-1991   **Jet Engine Assembler Mechanic**   PRATT & WHITNEY
City, State

- As team member, developed new methodology for engine assembly, resulting in <u>60% improved efficien</u>cy.
- <u>Trained emplo</u>yees on proper assembly techniques.

"Extra" Skills!

- Reworked defective parts after completion and inspection of module.
- Tested equipment for oil flow and performed analysis to determine source of problem(s).
- Used precise measuring tools to ensure that equipment met blueprint requirements.
- Assembled and performed tear down as required on modules and small components, including augmentors, afterburners, bearing assemblies, carbon seals, and horizontal build.
- Assembled diffuser, intermediate and outer duct cases with fuel controls, pumps and manifolds; oil coolers; various tube assemblies; electrical harnesses and controls.

1986-1987   **Assistant Manager**   CHEVROLET CAR DEALERSHIP
City, State

Maintained inventory, ordered parts, and provided customer assistance.

1985-1986   **Parts Counter Person**   FORD CAR DEALERSHIP
City, State

Sold parts to body shop repair facilities and to the public.

EDUCATION & TRAINING

U. S. Navy, 4 years as Jet Engine Mechanic.

Coursework includes:
Theory of Turbines and Compressors (U. S. Navy); Engine Technology (Pratt & Whitney);
Hall & Hall Computer Systems.

Town High School, Town, State, G.E.D.

297

Aircraft (jet engine) mechanic. *Annemarie Pawlina; Coventry, CT*

Michael worked as an auto painter/refinisher in an auto body shop.

Michael R. Brebeuf

1217 Holiday Court, #2
Tonawanda, New York 14150

(716) 656-5571
mrbrebeuf@aol.com

OBJECTIVE: Auto Painter/Refinisher

CERTIFICATION: **PPG Certified Refinisher Technician**

WORK TRAITS:

Michael's work traits are highlighted because his best assets seemed to be his excellent work ethic and his reliability.

- ⊘ Work well with supervisors, co-workers, and customers.
- ⊘ Utilize excellent organizational and time management skills.
- ⊘ Learn quickly and adapt easily to new situations.
- ⊘ Handle multiple tasks and assignments with efficiency.
- ⊘ Demonstrate solid attendance record.
- ⊘ Take pride in record of hard work and productivity.
- ⊘ Exhibit excellent attention to detail.
- ⊘ Work efficiently in a fast-paced environment.
- ⊘ Maintain safe and accident-free work area.

EXPERIENCE:

1996-Present

His work experience was unremarkable—no real accomplishments or special skills, so this information follows "Work Traits."

Auto Painter
CRANE'S COLLISION, INC., Brockport, New York

Perform full range of activities for the painting and refinishing of automobiles, vans, sport utility vehicles, motorcycles, and light trucks. Receive estimates and plan work schedule. Prepare work area and tape vehicles. Utilize computer to exactly match color and tint of paint. Apply protective, anti-corrosion coating and primer. Apply and blend paint. Clear-coat and finish vehicle to customer's specification and satisfaction.

1993-1996

Auto Painter
FRONTIER AUTO BODY, Buffalo, New York

1989-1993

Painter's Prep
MAYNARD FORD, Amherst, New York

EDUCATION:

PPG Refinish Training Course, Syracuse, New York
Diploma in Advanced Refinish Systems - 1993

Hewlett Senior High School, Cheektowaga, New York
Graduated — 1989 — Major in Automotive Body Shop

COMMUNITY: Volunteer with area Boy Scouts

INTERESTS: Mountain biking, archery, snowmobiling and radio-controlled cars

REFERENCES: Furnished upon request.

This personal information is included to give the employer a sense of who Michael is.

298

Automotive body painter/refinisher. *Freddie Cheek, CPRW, CWDP; Amherst, NY*

Barry Wallace

30065 Daisy Hills Drive
Terrace Canyon, California 91383

661-251-5469
bwallace@attnet.net

EXPERIENCED AUTO SHOP FOREMAN, domestic and foreign cars, with 20+ years of experience in the auto repair industry. Strong combination of business management and technical skills. Expertise in business startup and development, operations management, customer service, staff supervision, employee relations, and cash management. Committed to quality workmanship and ethical conduct.

Extensive hands-on experience performing and supervising minor, major, and mobile maintenance for commercial vehicles. Outstanding troubleshooting ability and a proven track record for high levels of customer satisfaction, quality assurance, cost savings, productivity, and overall vehicle readiness. A skilled training instructor with expertise in parts management and interpretation of vehicle system schematics.

- Up-to-date knowledge of auto industry trends, high-tech equipment, and environmental regulations (OSHA, HAZMAT). Conscientious application of policies and procedures, minute-detail oriented.
- Quick learner while dealing with new concepts, systems, and procedures.
- Thoroughly familiar with staff certification and training requirements.
- Scrupulous, fiercely loyal, dedicated, career committed.
- Profit conscious manager with successful experience in marketing and new business development.
- Knowledge of MS Word, Internet, Reynolds & Reynolds (software related to industry—parts tracking, estimating, billing, and shop operations).

Technical Proficiency/Certifications

These are extremely important and, in and of themselves, are a very strong qualifier.

- ASE Certified Master Auto Technician
- ASE L1
- Lifetime Master Technician (among top 15 winners of top 75 technicians in U.S. and Canada)
- EPA Refrigerant Handling Certification
- Current California Emissions-Control Certification

Professional Experience

SHOP FOREMAN
Crescent, Altadena, CA

1997–2002

Manage all aspects of high-quality, high-volume production shop. Oversee general auto and major collision repairs on late-model vehicles from economy cars to $100,000+ luxury sedans. Complete warranty work and paint projects; restore cars to pre-accident condition. Concurrently function as quality-control manager.

Supervise a staff of eight technicians. Scope of responsibility includes staffing; client relations; maintenance of tools, equipment, and inventory; estimating; parts ordering; troubleshooting; and cash management.

Exceptional supervisor—motivate personnel to increase efficiency, quality of service, and productivity. Hire, assist trainees, set up schools, write performance reviews, and terminate. Equitable with everyone. Administer injury-prevention program; conduct safety meetings. Perform all operations neatly and in strict compliance with all safety and environmental standards.

Accomplishments:
- Raised vehicle turnaround time to new levels of efficiency.
- Center point for sales and service departments for all computer and technical information.
- Selected to recruit graduate technicians in Florida (May 2000).
- Authored evaluation packet.
- Established solid business relationships with numerous vendors.
- Independently attend trade shows; established nationwide resource.
- Numerous customer commendations.

These are set apart so they are not overlooked.

299

Automotive shop foreman. *Myriam-Rose Kohn, CPRW, JCTC, CCM, CEIP; Valencia, CA*

Barry Wallace

JAGUAR MASTER TECHNICIAN   1989–1997
Topiak, Monterey Hills, CA

> Top-producing technician with a major focus on quality control. Repaired exceptionally problematic vehicles often referred by Jaguar district manager. Interacted with clients to ascertain their needs and ensure their satisfaction. Organized work flow to maximize productivity. Related with insurance companies.

> Developed extensive knowledge of urethane paint systems, including computerized mixing to produce customized colors, as well as a good working knowledge of all modern techniques and equipment including downdraft spray booths, filters, lights, and oil- or gas-fired burners. Expertise in precise color matching and blending in exact quantities needed to avoid waste.

> Able to establish beneficial relationships with jobbers and regional suppliers to support shop's needs quickly and efficiently. Passed all drug testing and bonding.

> Served on CSI (Customer Service Committee). Volunteered once a week for 2 years. Clarified unclear complaints and maintained customer satisfaction by educating customers in operations/use of vehicles.

BRITISH CAR MASTER TECHNICIAN   1985–1989
Trenton Motor Cars, Monterey Hills, CA

> Diagnosed, repaired, and maintained Jaguar, Aston-Martin, Rolls Royce, and a variety of modern and vintage exotic cars. Assisted owner/manager with daily operations as well as with fabrication of unavailable components.

PRIOR TO 1985
Associate Service Manager, Honda Of Redding
Owner/Operator, Future Engine Caretakers

Professional Affiliation

Jaguar Master Technician Guild Member

Education and Continual Training

Service Manager Training   Jaguar Training
Service Advisor Training   Rolls Royce Training
Business Management Training

Courses in premed and computer science, Armhurst College, Armhurst, NJ

The smaller print is still readable and includes many positive skills that support a higher-paying management job.

SAM D. FINCH

27-A Burton Road
Raleigh, NC 55555

(000) 000-0000

Objective: To manage painting operations for an auto body shop needing to increase efficiency and profitability in this area without jeopardizing quality.

Strengths & Skills:

- Extensive knowledge of urethane paint systems, including computerized mixing to produce customized colors.
- Expertise in precise color matching and blending in exact quantities needed to avoid waste.
- Good working knowledge of all modern techniques and equipment including downdraft spray booths, filters, lights, and oil or gas fired burners.
- Able to establish beneficial relationships with jobbers and regional suppliers of Sikkens, Spies-Hecker, Glasurit, DuPont and PPG paint lines to support shops' needs quickly and efficiently.
- Perform all painting operations neatly and in strict compliance with all safety and environmental standards.
- Self-motivated and productive in a heavy volume environment.
- Passed all drug testing and bonding requirements.

Related Experience:

1994 - Present **Auto Body Painter** — Triangle Buick & Mazda, Clayton, NC (Body shop sales of $1 million in 1994)
- Work alone at night on a commission basis, producing an average of 100-140 paint/labor billable hours a week.
- Entrusted with full responsibility for physical building security at end of shift.

1992 - 1994 **Auto Body Painting Subcontractor** (self-employed)
- Classic Auto Restoration, Cary, NC
- George's Auto Body, Durham, NC
- Wilson Collision Works, Raleigh, NC

1989 - 1990 **Auto Body Painter** — Square Deal Toyota, Roxbury, NJ

1986 - 1989 **Auto Body Painter** advancing to **Lead Painter** — Olafsen Auto Restoration, Dover, NJ

Other Employment:

1991 **Over-the-Road Truck Driver** (self-employed)

1986 **Administrative Assistant** — Commercial Mortgage Co., Pequannock, NJ

Military Experience:

1986 - 1990 **United Stated Navy** — Active duty at San Diego Naval Amphibious Base, Coronado, CA
- STG "A" Service School — Received training in surface sonar (submarine tracking), explosive ordnance disposal and marine mammal systems.
- Assigned to hazardous material control unit with responsibility for the proper storage of caustic and corrosive materials and coordination of Material Safety Data Sheets (MSDS).

Education:

1994 PPG Paint School — Refinish Training Course

1985 - 1986 County College of Morris, Randolph, NJ — Math and business courses.

1984 Morris County Vo-Tech, Adult Night School — Auto Body Repair course with on-the-job training at Olafsen Auto Restoration.

Additional Credentials:

- ASE Certified — Recertified in 1994.
- Class "A" Commercial Driver's License with hazardous materials endorsement.

300

Automotive mechanic and service technician. *Melanie Noonan, CPS; West Paterson, NJ*

This concise, dynamic resume has been very successful for John. Each time he faxes it to someone, he gets called for an interview within minutes!

JOHN C. TAYLER

Phone: 801-892-6299 • Pager: 801-892-6380 • 2463 Elm Avenue, Salt Lake City, UT 84109 • JCTayler@hotmail.com

The reader can see immediately how qualified John is within the industry.

ASE CERTIFIED MASTER TECHNICIAN
STATE INSPECTIONS CERTIFIED / COUNTY EMISSIONS CERTIFIED

Master Technician with 20+ years' experience in all phases of Automotive Technology. Proven leader in the industry possessing **expert diagnostic ability.** Proficient in **heavy equipment repair.** Highly motivated team player dedicated to producing outstanding results and increased profitability.

SPECIALIZED TRAINING

- ❑ **Advanced Automotive Climate Control,** Auto Parts Plus — 2001
- ❑ **Advanced Automotive Tune-up and Electrical Troubleshooting,** Federal Mogul/Champion — 2000
- ❑ **Advanced Hydrostatic Drive Diagnostics and Repair,** Bombardier Recreational Product — 2000
- ❑ **Advanced Applied Emissions Technical Training,** Salt Lake Community College — 1995
- ❑ **Utah Safety Inspection Training,** SLC Emissions Testing — 1995
- ❑ **ASE Certifications,** Salt Lake Community College — 1994

AUTOMOTIVE TECHNICAL EXPERTISE

- ❑ Full Service Automotive Excellence, providing **Bumper-to-Bumper Expert Diagnostics and Repair.**

- ❑ Specializing in major and minor repair for **ALL MAKES and MODELS:**
  Japanese, European and Domestic vehicles, 4x4s, Trucks, RVs, Dump Trucks, Caterpillars, Tractors, Tractor-Trailers, Snow Cats, Diesel, and other heavy equipment.

- ❑ Brakes — Clutches — Water Pumps — P/S Pumps — Rack & Pinion Steering — Shocks & Struts
- ❑ Front-end Work — 4 x 4 Front-end Work — Precision Engine Rebuilding — Engine Overhaul
- ❑ Cooling and Heating Systems — Batteries — Mufflers — Carburetors — CV Joints — Differentials
- ❑ Radiators — Alternators — Starters — Fuel Injection Systems — Wiring Repair and Replacement

PROFESSIONAL EXPERIENCE

- ❑ Tayler Mobile Automotive, **Owner/Manager,** present
- ❑ McNeil's Automotive, **Lead Automotive Technician,** 1996–present
- ❑ Snowbird Ski Resort, **Lead Heavy Line Technician,** 1992–1996
- ❑ Marathon Automotive, **Lead Automotive Technician,** 1991–1992
- ❑ Courtesy Car Company, **Service Manager,** 1985–1991
- ❑ Kmart (presently Penske Automotive), **Acting Service Manager,** 1980–1985

301

Automotive mechanic and service technician. *Diana C. LeGere; Salt Lake City, UT*

DAVID M. JOHN

111 E. South
Candlewood, OK 000000
(000) 000-0000

JOB TARGET ◇ AUTOMOTIVE TECHNICIAN

QUALIFICATIONS & STRENGTHS

- ◇ MDS
- ◇ DRB III
- ◇ Diversified Automotive Knowledge

- ◇ Diagnostic Abilities
- ◇ Technical Electrical Training
- ◇ Strong Work Ethics

CERTIFICATION

Engine Repair
Automatic Trans/Transaxle
Manual Drive Train & Axles
Suspension & Steering
Brakes
Electrical Systems
Heating & Air Conditioning
Engine Performance
Refrigerant Recovery & Recycling

All sections display his mechanical repair skills. The format succinctly presents his substantial experience.

PROFESSIONAL EXPERIENCE

GALLERY AUTOMOTIVE   USA
MASTER JOURNEYMAN AUTOMOTIVE TECHNICIAN   1978 - Present
- ◇ Proven ability to successfully perform diagnostic analysis, verification, and complete repair of automotive technology including:

Driveability	*Suspensions*
Electrical	*Air Conditioning 134R*
Anti-Lock Brakes	*Air Bag Systems*
Transmissions	*Complete Car Maintenance*

- ◇ CSI Conscious
  Contribute to promoting dealership's standards of performance
- ◇ Provide professional customer service regarding automotive repairs, including taking road tests with customers for the purpose of duplicating troubleshooting
- ◇ Selected as 1st technician for new products development and training

JOURNEYMAN AUTOMOTIVE TECHNICIAN   1978 - Present
AUTOMOTIVE TECHNICIAN   1976 - 1977

EXCELLENT AUTOMOTIVE   USA
JOURNEYMAN   1973 - 1976

EDUCATION

Community College, Community, OK
  Emphasis on Automotive Transmission & English Classes
Private Pilot's License, Planemasters of Dupage
Community High School, Community, OK, Graduate

REFERENCES AVAILABLE UPON REQUEST

302

Automotive mechanic. *Betty A. Callahan, PC, CPRW; Kalamazoo, MI*

DAVID M. JOHN_____

SPECIALIZED TRAINING

TOTAL TRAINING HOURS - 1981 - 1995

NEW CAR OVERVIEW

GROUP	SUBJECT	TOTAL HOURS
L.H.	OVERVIEW	24
NEON	OVERVIEW	16
CIRRUS	OVERVIEW	16
MINI VAN	OVERVIEW	24

GROUP	SUBJECT	TOTAL HOURS
5	BRAKES	8
9	ENGINE REPAIR	40
8	ELECTRICAL	24
14	FUEL & EMISSIONS	32
18	DRIVABILITY	24
21	AUTO TRANSMISSION	60
21	MITSUBISHI TRANSMISSION	16
23	BODY	16
24	AIR CONDITIONING	8
26	MAINTENANCE	8

GROUP	SUBJECT	TOTAL HOURS
G.M.	SPECIALIZED ELECTRONIC TRAINING	64

An impressive table indicating the total number of hours spent on each subject.

Because of a recently diagnosed physical condition, Scott needed to find a job that was less physically demanding.

SCOTT C. WATSON

4123 JUMBLE HILL ROAD – MADISON, TENNESSEE 37115

HOME: (615) 316-4468
EMAIL: MOTORPRO@AOL.COM

He wanted to stay in the same field, so decided to pursue a position as a Regional Technical Advisor for one of the premier manufacturers.

Highly skilled technical professional with 18 years' experience in the *service, repair, and warranty coverage of high-performance recreation vehicles.* Outstanding troubleshooting ability combined with high levels of customer satisfaction, quality assurance, productivity, and overall vehicle service. A skilled training instructor with expertise in *exhaust gas analysis, fuel injection, and electronics.* Proficient with *LightSpeed* software. Hands-on experience and professional training with the following premier manufacturers:

Motorcycles.................Yamaha, Suzuki, Excelsior Henderson, Kawasaki, BMW.

Watercraft ....Polaris, Yamaha, Sea Doo.

ATVs ....Bombardier, Yamaha, Suzuki.

Scott's resume clearly showcases his expertise!

WORK EXPERIENCE

SERVICE MANAGER 1991–Present
Mid-Tenn Motor Sports *(Member of Lemco Dealer Training Network)*—Lebanon, Tennessee

Oversee and coordinate service operations for dealership specializing in sales, service, and parts for Suzuki, Yamaha, Polaris, and Sea Doo products. Implement manufacturers' warranty recalls and safety modifications. Maintain detailed documentation records and follow through with customer to ensure vehicle is brought in for service. Serve as liaison between customer and manufacturer in resolving warranty coverage issues. Perform data entry for all warranty claims and follow through with entire claims process, from initial claim through final resolution. Hire, train, and supervise two Set-up Technicians, two Service Writers, and five Technicians.

- Receive positive feedback from both customers and manufacturers regarding all aspects of customer service.
- Deliver consistent annual growth in gross and net profits.
- Handpicked by Sea Doo to visit select dealerships to observe and evaluate customer/dealer interaction and report on problems or disputes.

TECHNICIAN... 1983–1991
Miller's Suzuki—Hermitage, Tennessee

Directed the set-up, repair, and maintenance for Metro Nashville Police Department's fleet of 36 Suzuki motorcycles.

- Modified vehicles with emergency and communications equipment required for police service.

PROFESSIONAL & TECHNICAL TRAINING

- **Excelsior Henderson Manufacturer Training School**—1999

- **Motorcycle Mechanics Institute (MMI)**—1998
Bombardier Basic & Advanced Electrical Training

- **Polaris Industries**—1996
Master Service Dealer Training (MSD)

- **Kawasaki High Performance Training**—1984

- **Yamaha Motor Corporation**—1983, 1984
Engine Exhaust Gas Analysis
Engine Power Plants 1 & 2

- **American Motorcycle School (AMS)**—1983
Motorcycle Mechanics Certificat

303

Motorcycle, boat, and small-engine mechanic. *Carolyn Braden, CPRW; Hendersonville, TN*

The chronological format of this resume shows that Mitchell has a good, solid work background in an industry where there is a lot of turnover.

MITCHELL P. MACKAY

148 Park ◆ Livonia, MI 48154 ◆ 734.444.7777 ◆ mitmac25@aol.com

SERVICE / REPAIR
Vending Industry

A highly experienced vending professional with a vast array of experience working effectively with clients, peers and management. A natural leader, with great interpersonal skills, who is dedicated and dependable.

STRENGTHS AND ABILITIES

- Troubleshooting
- Oral & Written Communication
- Maintenance Compliance
- Decision Making
- Training
- Record Keeping
- Customer Relations
- Organization
- Cash Management

WORK HISTORY

CONSOLIDATED VENDORS CORPORATION, Wixom, MI   1999–Present
ROUTE DRIVER

Assigned a specific region, with 20–22 customers that are each serviced three to five times per week. Responsibilities include filling and maintaining machines, giving good customer service, troubleshooting problems and servicing machines, as needed. Also, responsible for handling cash and maintaining records.

- Saved some customer accounts, so they wouldn't go elsewhere, by providing excellent customer service.
- Maintain great rapport with manager, coworkers and customers.
- Added new accounts to workload, while effectively maintaining existing accounts.

AMGROUP, Wixom, MI   1996–1999
ROUTE DRIVER

Stocked machines and assisted customers in facilities where vending machines were located. Prepared requisitions for food and drink supplies. Cleaned machines and maintained an orderly eating area.

- Trained new drivers on the tasks required to be an effective route driver. Training lasted approximately two weeks and all phases of the job were included. Also, trained drivers on repair of machines.
- Assigned extra responsibilities because management knew they would be handled correctly and that the job would get done.

MODERN VENDING, Royal Oak, MI   1991–1996
ROUTE DRIVER

Serviced assigned customers, handling extra responsibilities and providing excellent service.

MERCY HOSPITAL, Detroit, MI   1988–1991
COURIER

Responsibilities included picking up and delivering X-rays, EKGs, small medical supplies, etc., between clinics, doctors' offices and the hospital. Also, made bank deposits for the company.

EDUCATION

Schoolcraft College, Livonia, MI — completed various *Liberal Arts* classes

304

Vending machine servicer. *Joyce Fortier, MBA, CPRW, JCTC, CCM; Novi, MI*

With more than 20 years in the Air Force, Kelly avoids indicating his age by stating "over 13 years..."

KELLY P. ROTHLEY

403 Rio Rasta Road
Chicago, IL 33303
(407) 555-1212

AREAS OF EXPERTISE:

He uses civilian terms throughout

- Over 13 years experience in the installation, troubleshooting and repair of Heating, Air Conditioning, Ventilation, and Refrigeration Systems.
- Experienced in operation and maintenance of Chilled Water Systems up to 250 tons and Heating Systems including high temperature hot water, low pressure and high pressure steam boilers, and gas fire furnaces.
- EPA Certified to handle and recover refrigerants since August 1992.
- Safety Oriented with Hazardous Materials training.

ACHIEVEMENTS & ATTRIBUTES:

- Maintain zero error tolerances; successfully maintained over 150 commercial systems with no loss of business operations.
- Extremely resourceful; while working in remote locations, maintained portable refrigeration and air conditioning units with not readily available replacement parts.
- Respond immediately to emergency situations and handle pressure with ease; in emergency situation for Air Force Technical Applications Center chilled water systems, reacted efficiently causing no down time for all computer centers.
- Successful time management and supervisory skills; as crew foreman, completed the installation of 235 ton chiller which included all new water lines and cooling tower two weeks ahead of schedule.
- Received Air Force Commendations and Medals for performing Above and Beyond the Call of Duty in the areas of air condition, heating, ventilation, and refrigeration systems installation and repair.

EDUCATION AND TRAINING:

Associate of Science Degree in Air Conditioning/Heating
Valencia State College, Orlando, Florida

Air Conditioning, Heating, and Controls Courses
MacDill Air Force Base Training Facility, Tampa, Florida

EXPERIENCE:

UNITED STATES AIR FORCE, Various locations - 1983 to Present
Air Conditioning, Ventilation, Refrigeration, and Chilled Water Systems Repair, Maintenance and Installation

REFERENCES:

Available upon request.

The "Achievements" section links his substantial expertise to concrete accomplishments (resume writer's comments).

305

Heating, air conditioning, ventilation, and refrigeration mechanic and installer. *Laura A. DeCarlo, CPRW, ICCC; Melbourne, FL*

He includes good quotes from a previous supervisor

Joseph A. Bluecollar
Rt. 1 Box 5E
Shade, Ohio 45776
(614) 696-0000

" *... a top paid, top rated* **building technician** *for GTE with a superb attendance record.* "

" *... excellent working knowledge of carpentry, electrical and plumbing areas.* "

" *... produces excellent results and meets all schedules and time limits.* "

" *... highly skilled, highly trained individual who is always striving to improve himself .* " *

OBJECTIVE

Seeking a position in building maintenance or HVAC/Refrigeration which will utilize my extensive experience and training in these areas.

SKILLS ANALYSIS

- Over eight years experience as building technician
- Extensive experience and training in HVAC/Refrigeration
- Highly knowledgeable in all areas of building maintenance
- Supervisory experience; ability to motivate employees to work at peak efficiency levels
- Experience in installation of uninterrupted power source for large computer systems
- Experience with Sleeve Units to 700 ton chillers–Liebert A/C

RELATED EXPERIENCE

Building Technician - GENERAL TELEPHONE COMPANY	1988-present
Maintenance/HVAC Repair - CENTRAL OHIO COAL COMPANY	1982-1988
Owner - BLUECOLLAR REFRIGERATION & HEATING	1980-1982
Maintenance Supervisor - SOUTHERN OHIO COAL COMPANY	1973-1982
Production Supervisor - LOCKHEED AIRCRAFT	1967-1973
Diesel & Gas Mechanic Welder - U.S. ARMY	1964-1967

TRAINING & CERTIFICATION

Universal Technician Certification No. 277423951 - Refrigerant Transition & Recovery

Commercial Trades Institute - Training in HVAC & Refrigeration

Excellent References Provided Upon Request

*Excerpts from Performance Evaluations & Letter of Recommendation by Al Supervisor, Coord. of Bldg. Administration, GTE

306

Heating, air conditioning, ventilation, and refrigeration mechanic and installer. *Melissa L. Kasler, CPRW; Athens, OH*

This is a concise, well-written resume where everything supports his job objective.

Justin Meyers
100 North State Street
Marion, South Carolina 27658
(512) 555-4567
justintime@hotmail.com

Objective

Troubleshooting and repair of electronic home entertainment equipment.

Summary of Qualifications

Over 10 years of experience repairing home entertainment equipment, including extensive knowledge of

- Televisions
- Radios
- Video cameras
- Video games

- VCRs/DVD players
- Stereos
- Microwaves
- Home security systems

Experience

Electronic Pros, Inc.   1999–Present
Electronic Technician. Main responsibility is to troubleshoot and repair equipment or replace parts as needed. I also deal with clients directly and handle all customer complaints. Extensive knowledge of most electronic home entertainment equipment.

Office Machine Repair, Inc.   1996–1998
Service Technician. Service and repair of calculators and other small office equipment.

Manny's Office Equipment   1993–1995
In-House Sales/Service Technician. Sold small office equipment and provided limited service agreements.

Education

Indiana Vocational-Technical College, Terre Haute, Indiana
Associate Degree in Electronic Equipment Repair, 1993

T.C. Howe High School, Indianapolis, Indiana
Diploma, 1991

307

Home appliance repairer. *Thelma Silvola; Indianapolis, IN*

Tom's original resume focused more on where he had worked, rather than his area of expertise and continued education.

THOMAS X. PIOYUUM

By changing the format and content, employers initially concentrate

1234 Street
Any Town, MI 49001
(333) 333-3333

on his qualifications in the industry (resume writer's comments).

◆ APPLIANCE REPAIR TECHNICIAN ◆

QUALIFICATIONS

- Highly Knowledgeable on Diversified Name-Brand Manufacturers Including Sears • Whirlpool • Maytag • General Electric • Proctor Silex • Toastmaster
- Developed Reputation for Providing Prompt, Courteous Service to Clients
- Analyze, Determine, and Rectify Original or Problem
- Gain Solid Informational Base through Product Knowledge
- Communicate Effectively with Client on Options for Optimum Product Usage

EXPERIENCE

APPLIANCE REPAIR SERVICE
Technician

Story, MI
1996 - Present

HANSON REPAIR SERVICE
Technician

Story, MI
1987 - 1996

REPAIRS USA
Technician

Story, MI
1984 - 1987

PRONTO REPAIRS SERVICE
Technician

Story, MI
1981 - 1984

BBST REPAIRS
Technician

Story, MI
1980 - 1981

EDUCATION

REPAIR INSTITUTE OF SW MICHIGAN

Story, MI

<u>Specialized Curriculum:</u>

Small Appliances	Computer Applications in Appliance Repairs
Troubleshooting	Analysis & Solutions of Electrical Equipment
Electricity I, II & III	Fire Hazards & Maintenance of Equipment
Switches, Relays & Solenoids	Relay Activities & Sequence Charts
Wiring Diagrams	Motors & Capacitors

308

Home appliance repairer. *Betty A. Callahan, PC, CPRW; Kalamazoo, MI*

William has both a broad range of skills and in-depth knowledge of repairing and maintaining industrial equipment, electronic instrumentation, and professional audio equipment.

WILLIAM ROGERS

12 Rochester Street　　　　　　Bergen, NY 14411

E-mail: BillR@rochester.rr.com

585-494-2226

A conscious effort was made to pepper the resume with key words that would be meaningful to an industrial audience, such as CAD, EDM, & CNC.

ELECTRICAL ENGINEERING TECHNICIAN

- Strong troubleshooting skills, as well as machine and instrumentation control programming experience.
- Exceptional ability to identify and implement innovative solutions to repair and maintenance problems.
- Ability to quickly identify and resolve problems, understand and address customer requirements.
- Expertise in professional and consumer audio, production, and business communications equipment.
- Capacity to reverse-engineer electronic systems to re-establish functionality of dated equipment.
- Knowledge of data migration and recovery, CAD applications, and rudimentary programming.

William felt that these reverse-engineering skills were a big plus. He often finds himself called upon to repair outdated equipment for which no documentation exists.

WORK EXPERIENCE

Consulting Technician, Self-Employed, Rochester, NY *(1991-Present)*
Work on various short-term and long-term projects for a variety of industrial, institutional, and business clients, including Automotive Electric, Inc., Rochester Film Company, Seneca Community College, and Music Makers' Boutique.

- Troubleshoot and repair quality-control testing equipment to the component level.
- Effect repairs to Electronic Discharge Machining (EDM) and CNC Three-Axis Mill equipment.
- Design appropriate tests and build test fixtures to test, repair, and burn-in industrial electronics.
- Conduct reverse engineering from circuit board to CAD drawings.
- Identify proprietary components via experimentation and online research.
- Write computer programs for implementation of test fixtures.
- Troubleshoot, repair, and maintain a variety of professional audio equipment.

Consulting Audio Technician, Crane School of Music, State University of New York at Potsdam, Potsdam, New York *(1982-1992)*

- Repaired and modified audio equipment and audio-related computer peripherals.
- Programmed and repaired audio-related computers.
- Wrote programs to facilitate interfaces.
- Debugged systems. Identified and cleared duplicate files.
- Conferred with musicians and other professionals to assess requirements and address technical needs.

EDUCATION

Associate of Applied Science, Electrical Engineering Technology *May 2002*
　Orleans Community College, Albion, NY
　GPA: 3.74

Bachelor of Science, Business Administration *1982*
　Mt. Pleasant University, Nashville, TN
　Concentration in Recording Engineering

　Rochester Institute of Technology, Rochester, NY
　Electrical Engineering Curriculum: Calculus, Digital Circuits, A/D Converters

PROFESSIONAL DEVELOPMENT

Ongoing independent study of current PC operating systems and applications, including Windows 2000, Windows ME, and Microsoft Office applications. Review of study materials for MCP and A+ Certifications.

State-of-the-Art Color Imaging and Desktop Video (Adobe PhotoShop & Premier).

Certificates from Roland, Fender, Philips Technical Training.

COMPUTER SKILLS

Programming (C, C++, Pascal, BASIC), Low-Level Source and Embedded Code Languages, Schematic CAD, Windows, MS Office, HTML, and Internet. Build and maintain PC platforms for personal use.

309

Industrial machinery repairer. *Arnold G. Boldt, CPRW, JCTC; Rochester, NY*

JEFFREY K. KNOWLES

1823 Lakeshore Road ■ South Orange, NJ 07079 ■ (973) 585-7835
jkknowles@optonline.net

Special qualifications are emphasized with bold type.

PROFILE

Telecommunications Specialist with an extensive 18-year background in all phases of **cable splicing for the largest U.S. communications provider.** Special talent for identifying, troubleshooting, repairing and maintaining aerial, underground, and buried copper and fiber-optic cable. Progressive experience in new construction, upgrade installations, and emergency cable failures. Read and interpret work prints, circuit diagrams, and plat books. Strong work ethic; will do what it takes to get the job done and meet deadlines. **Hazmat Certified. OSHA familiarity. Hook qualified. Member of Local 2245, Communication Workers of America (CWA).**

PROFESSIONAL EXPERIENCE

VERIZON COMMUNICATIONS, INC. • Newark, NJ   4/69 to Present
(Largest U.S Communications Provider • Formerly Bell Atlantic Corp.)
Cable Splicer
Locate, troubleshoot, and clear analog and digital cable problems and leaks in pressurized cable. Identify the conditioning of cable pairs for special circuits.

- Read and interpret service orders, circuit diagrams, plat book, blueprints, and schematics.
- Work on energized circuits to avoid interruption of service. Climb utility poles/towers, utilizing truck-mounted lift bucket. Descend into sewers/underground vaults to locate cables.
- Cut lead sheath from installed cable to gain access to defective cable connections.
- Test (trace/phase-out) each conductor to identify corresponding conductors in adjoining cable sections, according to electrical diagrams and specifications.
- Prevent incorrect connections between individual communication circuits and electric power circuits, using test lamp or bell system.
- Fireproof and insulate materials.

Accomplishments are set apart & italicized.

~ *Accountable for troubleshooting over 100 major cable failures and restoring service to over 1,500 customer subscriber lines per failure in the wake of Hurricanes Gloria and Bob; and performed major repairs through ice storms of 1976 and 1977.*
~ *Instrumental in completing Generic 5E7 project.*
~ *Recipient of numerous awards for safety and perfect attendance.*

TECHNICAL EQUIPMENT

Safety Equipment: Blowers / Explosive Meters / Cone & Signs / Ladders / Slings / Ladder Steps Block & Step Ladders ■ **Locating Equipment:** 965 Dynatel Cable Analyzer / Breakdown Set / Heath Kit / Buried Cable Locator / Sidekick Meter / Digital Multi-Meter ■ **Hand Tools:** Cable Dresser / Siemen Case & Flats Side Cutters / Dikes / Can Wrenches / Electric & Air Powered Tools

INDUSTRY EQUIPMENT & SERVICE

ISDNs / DSLs / Frame Relays / Enterprises / T3 & T1 / DDS II (DSO) / Trunks / DIDs / Centrex & Analog Lines / Superpaths / Pots / Flexpaths / Switchways / TKNAs / Muxes / Multi-Plexers / Alarms

PROFESSIONAL DEVELOPMENT COURSES

ALTEC AT-2000 / TELSTA – A-28C/A-28D / Defensive Driving (Distance Learning) / Code of Business Conduct / IFAS DO I&M NY / CMC 386 Overview / Telecommunications Act Training / Asbestos Safety Awareness for Outside Field Techs / CAT for Customer Services / HAZCOM-Generic/Job Specific / D.O.T Motor Carrier Safety Regulations / Area HAZCOM Manager Training / First Aid/CPR / Ribbon Optic Cable Splicing / Siecor Optical Cable Fusion Splicing / SLC-96

These three final sections of the resume contain many relevant keywords.

310

Line installer and repairer. *Donna Farrise; Hauppauge, NY*

James Smith

5555 Delivery Road
Elmira, New York 00000

Home: (600) 000-0000
Pager: (800) 000-0000

OBJECTIVE

Seeking a challenging position offering an opportunity to utilize and expand my mechanical and technical skills.

The Objective, Summary, and Education are listed first as James plans to get his four-year degree in construction management (resume writer's comments).

SUMMARY OF SKILLS

- Strong background in mechanical maintenance, building and grounds maintenance.
- Knowledge of building trades: carpentry, masonry, heating, plumbing and electrical.
- Dependable, hardworking, efficient, and highly reliable.
- Detail-oriented with a strong work ethic.

EDUCATION

Elmira Technical College, Elmira, New York
A.A.S. in Construction/Building Trades - June 1992
    Field of Study: House Framing I; Exterior Finish and Trim I; Bricklaying, Blocklaying and Finishing; Electrical and Plumbing Introduction; House Framing II and Basic Cabinetmaking; Roof Framing, Roof Finish; Exterior Finish and Trim II; Interior Finish.

Elmira High School, Elmira, New York
General Studies Diploma - June 1992

PROFESSIONAL EXPERIENCE

Elmira Greenhouses Inc., Elmira, New York   1992 - Present
Maintenance Technician
- Responsible for overall building and grounds maintenance, including repair and trouble-shooting of greenhouse equipment.
- Handle small engine repair, maintenance of heating systems (gas and coal boilers);some experience with air conditioning and refrigeration repair.
- Operate and maintain basic equipment, such as forklifts, loaders and dump trucks.
- Train and orient new employees.

Dominick's Family Restaurant, Elmira, New York   1991 - 1992
Dishwasher
- Part-time employment concurrent with high school attendance.

Self-Employed, Elmira, New York   Summer 1990
Lawn Care Specialist
- Responsible for all aspects of landscaping and lawn care maintenance. Maintained excellent customer relations.

- **References Available Upon Request -**

311

Maintenance mechanic, general utility. *Betty Geller, CPRW; Elmira, NY*

ROBERT W. STEWART

(319) 338-6141

4235 Anderson Avenue SE • Iowa City, Iowa 52240

TARGET

Seeking a pipefitter opportunity where related plumbing education and experience plus mechanical background will contribute to efficient building operations and workplace safety.

He includes his adaptive as well as job-related skills in this section

PROFILE

Hardworking, <u>motivated</u> and <u>safety-conscious</u> individual able to draw upon competencies in the following areas:

- Highly skilled in **pump repair** through education and hands-on experience with vein, open and close, rotor, and piston pumps.
- Excellent **mechanical ability**—skilled in <u>troubleshooting</u> and repairing industrial, automotive, and agricultural machines.
- Extensive **industrial systems repair/maintenance skills**—experienced in HVAC (including steam heat/ventilation), hydraulics, robotics, electronic process control,. and chilled water and vacuum systems troubleshooting and upkeep; repair fire protection systems.
- Solid **communication ability**—able to <u>work well with others</u> using a <u>team-oriented</u> approach to focus on and <u>solve problems</u>.

EXPERIENCE

UNITED TECHNOLOGIES AUTOMOTIVE, Iowa City, Iowa   **1979 to Present**
Manufacturer of injection molded products supplied to the automotive industry.
Maintenance Mechanic

- Perform building maintenance and alert superiors to unsafe conditions.
- Troubleshoot, repair and perform maintenance on a variety of systems including: heating, ventilation, robotics, hydraulics (injection molding machines), electronic process control on production equipment, and chilled water and vacuum systems.
- Test water samples for water quality and pH balance.

CRANE CORPORATION, Washington, Iowa   1978 to 1979
Manufacturer of valves sized 1/2" to 24".
Lathe Operator

- Set up and operated turret lathes to produce gate, globe, piston, butterfly and ball valves both open or closed stem, telescoping or nontelescoping.
- Assembled and tested product for quality.

a list of what he studied is more effective than simply noting that he attended

EDUCATION

KIRKWOOD COMMUNITY COLLEGE, Cedar Rapids, Iowa

- Hydraulics
- Plumbing for Commercial and Industrial Applications
- Hazardous Materials Awareness
- Fire Hose Handling
- Residential/Electrical Wiring
- Industrial/Electrical Wiring

- Cryogenics
- Basic Welding
- Life Fire Training
- Materials Science & Corrosion
- Self Contained Breathing Apparatus
- National Electrical Code Works
- Electronics I

RECEIVED TRAINING IN FIRST AID AND CPR THROUGH IOWA CITY FIRE DEPARTMENT

312

Maintenance mechanic (pipefitter). *Elizabeth Axnix-Lower, CPRW, JCTC; Iowa City, IA*

DANIEL RICKS
76 Marionette Drive
New Baden, Illinois 62265
(618) 555-2623

POWER PLANT TECHNICIAN/FOREMAN

- Extensive hands-on experience supervising the operation and maintenance of mobile and stationary power plant equipment ranging from 3kw to 1000kw. Strong knowledge of:

Boilers	HVAC systems
Diesel/Gasoline Engines	Turbines
Generators	Pumps
Condensers	Compressors
Waste Heat Recovery	Heavy Maintenance Vehicles
Process Controls	Electrical Distribution Systems

Note use of adaptive skill words

- Skilled at performing building maintenance involving carpentry, plumbing, electrical repair, and masonry.

- Effective at planning work projects, coordinating with other tradesman, and overseeing completion with attention to deadlines, detail and overall quality.

- A reliable and safety-conscious worker; missed fewer than five days of work in the last 20 years. Supervised and trained personnel on safe work practices.

an excellent detail to include

WORK HISTORY

Prairie Farms, Granite City, Illinois   1994-Present
MAINTENANCE MECHANIC

United States Air Force   1974-1994
POWER PLANT FOREMAN
POWER PRODUCTION SHOP SUPERVISOR
ELECTRICAL POWER PRODUCTION TECHNICIAN
POWER PLANT OPERATOR

He uses civilian job title equivalents

EDUCATION/SPECIALIZED TRAINING

- A.S. Degree coursework, Power Plant Technology, Belleville Area College
- EPA Hazardous Waste Training: Hazardous Waste Removal and Clean-up, Asbestos Removal, and Protective Equipment Usage
- Additional Military Training: Electrical Power Production Courses, Solid State Circuits, Battery Bank Maintenance

REFERENCES AVAILABLE UPON REQUEST

His work history is short giving only job titles

Maintenance mechanic (power plant). *John A. Suarez, CPRW; O'Fallon, IL*

313

FREDERICK SWEENEY

9631 Patterson • Oak Park, Michigan 48237
248.555.1329 (Home) • 248.555.3731 (Mobile) • sweeneyman@twmi.rr.com

CAREER PROFILE: MILLWRIGHT

Management

People management includes supervisory experience within union and nonunion environments; program/project management includes regulating, controlling, and documenting equipment, data, materials, and supplies.

Technical Skills

Ability to troubleshoot; determine problems and resolve issues with competence and efficiency; meet deadlines within reasonable demands.

Personal Attributes

Strong work ethic, good listening skills, dependable and reliable, work very well in pressure situations.

Computer Skills

MS Word, Excel, PowerPoint; Ami Pro, Lotus 1-2-3, Quicken, AutoCAD.

SUMMARY OF QUALIFICATIONS

- Computerized data-entry system including time scheduling, parts ordering, and cross-referencing of supply base.
- Developed efficient work systems, training programs, service plans.
- Proficient in areas of robotics, optical tool/laser alignment, automation.
- Excellent oral/written communication skills; project evaluation.
- Performed efficiently as liaison between vendor and company.

EMPLOYMENT HISTORY

CONSULTANT   Oak Park, Michigan
FREELANCE MILLWRIGHT, 1993–current

- Analyze support-personnel requirements; investigate resources; coach, train, and support in all areas as required.
- Detect and determine problems; make presentations to management; resolve issues as requested.

MILLWRIGHT — LOCAL 956   Warren, Michigan
JOURNEYMAN SUPERINTENDENT, 1985–93

- Assigned to positions requiring excellent knowledge, understanding, and proficiency in all phases of millwright applications.
- Delegated to assignments incorporating Robotics, Turbines, Conveyor Systems, and Nuclear Applications.

EDUCATION AND TRAINING

SCHOOLCRAFT COLLEGE   Livonia, Michigan
  A.A.S. DEGREE, 1987
  Concentration: Laser Technology
MILLWRIGHT INSTITUTE OF TECHNOLOGY   Detroit, Michigan
  CERTIFIED JOURNEYMAN, 1984
  Certified: Nuclear applications
OAKLAND COMMUNITY COLLEGE   Oakland Hills, Michigan
  Concentration: Mathematics and English

MEMBERSHIPS & COMMUNITY INVOLVEMENT

Knights of Columbus — Deputy Grand Knight (Vice President)
St. Michael's Men's Club — President
Phi Beta Kappa — Member (with 3.8+ GPA)
Children's Sports Program — Fundraiser (raised six-figure amounts for programs)

314

Millwright. *Lorie Lebert, CPRW, JCTC; Novi, MI*

ADDENDUM to Résumé for:

FREDERICK SWEENEY

ROBOTICS EXPERIENCE

Chrysler Corporation
- Jefferson Assembly
- Dodge City
- Sterling Heights
- Warren

Ford Motor Company
- Livonia Transmission
- Flatrock
- Woodhaven Stamping
- Ypsilanti
- Ann Arbor
- Wayne Assembly

General Motors
- Warren Tech Center
- Fleetwood Cadillac
- Detroit Truck Assembly

TURBINE EXPERIENCE

Detroit Edison
- Enrico Fermi II (5-year project, including HPSI, RCSI, and Main Turbines)
- Willes Power Plant
- Beacon Power Plant
- Monroe Power Plant
- St. Clair Power Plant
- Marysville Power Plant
- Hancock Station Reserve Power Plant

Ford Motor Company
- Rouge Power Plant
- Dynamometer/Wind Tunnel (experimental couplings)

Page two of this resume is presented as an Addendum, thereby keeping the resume itself to one page and avoiding a cluttered look caused by too much text.

Gray box headings provide visual interest.

The graphics lighten up this rather serious resume.

Bradley Swanson
1500 Trio Circle • St. Paul, MN 55113 • 612.555.3308 • Mobile 612.555.0090 • bswan@aol.com

MOBILE HEAVY-EQUIPMENT MECHANIC/MANAGER ... CONSTRUCTION & DEMOLITION EXPERTISE

PROFILE

Motivated and competent professional with 20 years of accrued union and nonunion experience — over 10 years as an Equipment Mobile Mechanic. Earned a reputation for dependability, integrity, and professionalism. Equally comfortable in the "trenches" or a management role.

HIRING ASSETS

The functional format avoids repetition of job duties for similar positions.

HANDS-ON & TECHNICAL

- **Operated/repaired excavating, demolition, and construction equipment**: scrapers/spreaders, backhoes, loaders, bulldozers, compactors, road graders, haul trucks, forklifts, lattice friction cranes, boom welders, and over-the-road trucks. Brands: Caterpillar, Komatsu, Hitachi, John Deere, and more.
- **Owned and operated a 1987 Ford LN8000 Service Truck**, with a 15,000-lb crane, 500-amp welder, 45-CRM air compressor, water and oil capacities, and all hand tools required.
- **Performed all repairs** — light field maintenance/repairs to major field and/or shop overhauls.
- **Performed extensive welding fabrication and repairs** – stick or MIG.
- **Subcontracted welding, fabricating, and equipment maintenance/repair** for a number of construction businesses throughout Minnesota.
- **Mobile mechanic on large housing-site development and water-reclamation projects** throughout southern California during the housing boom of the 80s.
- Worked on **Housing and Highway projects** in the Minnesota Metro area.
- **In-house shop mechanic** for PT Wymann, a **global excavation and mining corporation**.

MANAGEMENT & SUPERVISION

- **Supervised a California-based water-reclamation project**. Directed and supervised a crew of 3 and made daily decisions regarding repair.
- **Oversaw equipment-repair operations in Guam**. Managed a staff of 9, procured parts from Mainland suppliers, negotiated equipment repairs and payment within a global market (Korea, Japan, Australia, and Guam), prepared written job estimates for customers, and performed mechanical repairs.
- **Selected as Lease Mechanic (1 out of 50+ candidates) by Minnesota Local Union and Carvatt Companies to spearhead a nonexistent Maintenance Program**. Managed all facets of establishing this new area, now Carvatt Companies' Equipment & Truck Division. The division has grown from initial staff of 1 to 11 and is accountable for 440+ equipment units.

CAREER PATH

TTP ENTERPRISE — St. Paul, MN, 1998–present
Subcontractor Mobile/Equipment Mechanic
INTERNATIONAL UNION OF OPERATING ENGINEERS — Metro Area, MN, 1991–1998
Mobile Equipment Mechanic (seasonal)
PT WYMANN — Alexandria, MN, 1991
Shop Mechanic
INTERNATIONAL UNION OF OPERATING ENGINEERS — Southern CA, 1985–1988; 1989–1990
Master Mechanic/Mobile Crew Mechanic
U.S. NAVAL BASE — Mariana Islands, Guam, 1988
Equipment Repair Shop Foreman
U.S. MARINE CORPS — Camp Lejeune, NC, 1981–1985
Heavy-Equipment Mechanic

EDUCATION & TRAINING

- **Graduate, Heavy-Equipment Mechanic Engineer School,** U.S. Marine Corps.
- **Ongoing dealer training** regarding changing maintenance requirements and product knowledge.

315

Mobile heavy equipment mechanic. *Barb Poole, CPRW, CRW; St. Cloud, MN*

This client wanted to transition from military mechanics to the "real world" by displaying his versatility.

JOHN J. REYNOLDS

9640 Amador Court
North Beach, MD 20714

Residence: 301-923-5498
Cellular: 301-821-0592

Email: jrey87@aol.com

FOCUS AND EXPERTISE

Master mechanic with supervisory skills and 10 years of significant experience in electrical troubleshooting, hazardous-waste management, and engine maintenance.

- Hazardous-materials manager
- Universal CFC/HCFC refrigerant license
- Two years' supervisory experience
- Known for quality workmanship
- Highly regarded for technical expertise
- Work merited several promotions

ENDORSEMENTS

These are comments from his performance reviews.

- "Technically competent...top achiever...work consistently displays quality workmanship; experience is far superior to peers...A truly outstanding performer, consistently exhibited perfection in all technical aspects of the job...Unprecedented technical expertise..."
  Frank Mason, SSgt., USAF 33rd Maintenance Squadron
- "Skillful technician...Has a keen eye for detail..."
  James R. Marshall, SSgt., USAF 33rd Maintenance Squadron
- "Outstanding maintenance abilities...Demonstrated impressive work efforts...Grasps a broad scope of responsibilities associated with the job; but also managed the flight's hazardous material program, receiving an outstanding rating for the recent environmental compliance inspections."
  Thomas Jameson, Jr., MSgt., USAF 33rd Maintenance Squadron

PROFESSIONAL HIGHLIGHTS

1991 – present   United States Air Force, Lackland Air Force Base, California.
Aerospace Ground Equipment Craftsman

- Removed and replaced defective turbine components, preventing failure of $108,000 engine.
- Identified improperly installed resistor on the temperature gauge of faulty gas turbine compressor, saving the $500 cost of a new gauge.
- Removed and replaced diesel generator engine in 12 hours, setting new standard for peers.
- Monitored usage of all hazardous materials used in maintenance process to protect environment.
- Installed alternator kits on three diesel generator sets to extend battery life and enhance cold-weather startups.

EDUCATION

Community College, Lackland Air Force Base, California.
Degree Program: 56 credit hours towards **Associate of Applied Science.**
Included coursework on turbine generators, air compressors, hydraulic test stands, diesel generator sets, air conditioners, performance-oriented packaging, and technical order systems maintenance.

CERTIFICATION/LICENSURE

1996 – present   Hazardous materials manager
1997 – present   Universal CFC/HCFC refrigerant license

316

Mobile heavy equipment mechanic. *Sheila Adjahoe; Upper Marlboro, MD*

BOB MACKEY
2345A Westwood Blvd.
Huntington, Georgia 68799
(919) 555-9876
bigmack@aol.com

OBJECTIVE

Mobile Heavy Equipment Mechanic

CERTIFICATIONS

Certified Welder
CDL License (Pending)
Certified Mobile Heavy Equipment Mechanic/Category A, Class 4

) This important information is presented near the top of the resume.

SUMMARY OF QUALIFICATIONS

Extensive training on the repair and maintenance of the following:

Cranes	AT 400	RT 900
RT 58	RT 500	Scissor lift
RT 400	RT 600	Man lift
Overhead Industrial Crane	RT 745	Fork lift
(10 Ton and 20 Ton)		

) Specific list of what he can repair and maintain.

WORK EXPERIENCE

Willow Company
February 1999 to Present
Diesel Mechanic

Responsible for the repair and maintenance of all company-owned equipment.

Aces Service Industries
January 1997 to January 1998
Mechanic Assembler

Assembled cranes from frame to completion. Welded, wired, and lubricated equipment.
Started and performed troubleshooting procedure.

EDUCATION

Certificate in Mobile Heavy Equipment Mechanics
Lincoln Technical College

Recipient of **Outstanding Student Award** in the Maintenance, Repair, and Operation of
Construction Equipment Program.

317

Mobile heavy equipment mechanic. *Thelma Silvola; Indianapolis, IN*

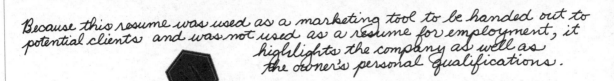

Because this resume was used as a marketing tool to be handed out to potential clients and was not used as a resume for employment, it highlights the company as well as the owner's personal qualifications.

FITZ-CO PRODUCTS, LTD
CUSTOM DRUM WORKS

Joseph Fitzgerald, Owner and Founder
PO Box 938, Schenectady, New York 12301-0938 • Office: 518-374-0251 • blankstare@mymailstation.com

MERGING OLD-TIME IDEAS WITH MODERN TECHNOLOGY
HAND-CRAFTED ACOUSTIC DRUMS
SATISFYING THE SOUNDS OF JAZZ, ROCK 'N ROLL, COUNTRY, AND ALTERNATIVE

COMPANY PROFILE

Custom International Drum Manufacturing and Repair company specializing in English makes such as Premier, Hayman and Ajax with emphasis on Custom Maple Snare drums. Highly skilled in all drum models from 1920s onward. Specializing in custom-crafted snare drums and drum sets – Keller shells and high-quality die-cast lugs. Satisfying drum fans worldwide with clients in US, Canada and Europe. Services include:

- *Maintenance / Repair / Customization*
- *Refinishing / Recutting*
- *Vintage & Modern Drums*
- *Professional Head Replacement*
- *Edging & Finishing*
- *Tuning*

"JOEY" FITZGERALD – MASTER CRAFTSMAN / TECHNICIAN
CREATING "ONE-OF-A-KIND" PRECISION DRUMS WITH A DISTINCTIVE ACOUSTICAL SIGNATURE

Accomplished drummer with 35 years' broad-spectrum experience playing and building all makes and models, including maintaining, repairing, and customizing vintage and modern drums. Expert in custom building and repair of rare and unique designs, specializing in British makes. *Keen musical "sixth sense"* – able to thump a raw cylinder and hear its potential sound before it's built. Musical competencies include:

DRUMS – GUITARS – BASS – KEYBOARDS – LYRICS – MUSICAL ARRANGEMENT – VOCALS

CAREER HIGHLIGHTS

- **Conceived, designed and launched production of the** *Fitz-Co Persuader Snare Drum,* which is the first model to feature custom machine parts made to the innovative Fitz-Co design.
- **Championed commission to build house drum for Arabellum Studios** – a 10-lug Persuader with all brass hoops dressed in an old art-deco finish called Charcoal Abalone.
- Regular **contributing author for** *Old Drummers Collective* of Sheffield, England, aka *UK Drum Bible.*
- **Wrote and recorded two 90-minute audio tutorials, "The Story Behind the Glory,"** with selected topics such as Buying Used Gear, Playing Attitudes, How to Overhaul a Drum Kit, and Buying New Gear.
- **Featured writer / drum expert in** *Not So Modern Drummer.*
- **Founder and director of Blank Stare Records.**
- **Drummer and Vocalist of the rock group, Panoramis.**

RECENT CUSTOM PROJECT

- Currently building Ludwig Super Classic clone using 40-year-old parts for Pete Isbell, "Ringo" in UK's best tribute band, "The Fab Beatles." Features the old Oyster Blue Pearl that Ringo Starr originally used in his 1966 tour.

318

Musical instrument repairer. *Diana C. LeGere; Salt Lake City, UT*

Production Occupations

Resumes at a Glance

Assemblers and Fabricators

Food Processing Occupations

Metal Workers and Plastic Workers

Plant and System Operators

Printing Occupations

Textile, Apparel, and Furnishings Occupations

Woodworkers

Other Production Occupations

Bradford's resume highlights his dependability, versatility, and leadership abilities. These are key competencies to emphasize as cell manufacturing and autonomous work groups become more prevalent.

BRADFORD JAMES

841 Maplewood Place   Rochester, NY 14671   585-244-6662

BradJames13@frontiernet.net

MANUFACTURING ASSEMBLER/TESTER

Offering successful experience, reinforced by strong technical aptitude and keen attention to detail, with abilities in the following:

Team Building	**Customer Relations**
Inventory Control	**Personnel Management**
Program Coordination	**Project Management**
Expediting/Procurement	**Scheduling**

- Motivated problem-solving team member who works well with others to deliver desired results on time and within budget parameters.
- Strong communication and interpersonal skills.

EMPLOYMENT EXPERIENCE

ASSEMBLER AND TESTER, Yellow Box Corporation, Chili, NY   1993–Present
- Assemble and test photocopier assemblies.
- Participated in a successful pilot program to launch digital network copier products, which involved digital manufacturing training.
- Participate on a team responsible for quality assurance.
- Implement Just-In-Time (JIT) procedures.

Selected for Y-Box Semi-Autonomous Work Group
- Participated in work group responsible for disassembly, cleaning and repair of products, and quality assurance.
- Led initiatives to enhance team motivation and promote continuous process improvements.

Awards and Achievements
- Recognized for 100% attendance record.
- Received Customer Hero Award (1998).
- Won Customer First Champion Award (5/98) for identifying and developing a process to resolve a problem to achieve significant savings and ensure launch target.

AREA MANAGER, Home Depot, South Queenstown, IL   1989–1992
- Responsible for all day-to-day operations from opening to closing of stores with regard to inventory, personnel, sales, and payroll.
- Planned inventory against sales predictions. Selected suppliers considering cost, performance, service, and lead time. Worked within designated budget parameters.
- Effectively utilized computer system to facilitate inventory tracking and order processing.
- Implemented JIT ordering strategies.
- Supervised up to 30 employees. Interviewed, hired, trained, scheduled, and delegated work assignments. Evaluated employee performance through a formal review process.
- Attended managers' strategy reviews to develop methods for achieving company goals.
- Managed organization to consistently perform within budget.

EDUCATION

B.S. IN INFORMATION SYSTEMS, S.U.N.Y. at Rochester, Rochester, NY   In Process
A.A. IN COMMUNICATIONS, Empire Junior College, Perinton, NY   1997

PROFESSIONAL DEVELOPMENT: Regularly attended company-offered courses, workshops, and seminars related to quality, Leadership Through Quality, electronics, team building, blueprint reading, precision measurements, injection molding, digital training, ESD training, and others to keep current in the industry and to enhance personal growth.

- Certificates in Basic Drawing Interpretation and Basic Electricity.

319

Assembler. *Arnold G. Boldt, CPRW, JCTC; Rochester, NY*

After many years as a butcher, Mark wanted to use his skills in a management position in the food-processing industry or as a food broker.

Mark J. Espinosa

12904 Range Road
Smiths Creek, Michigan 48074

313-555-4307
mjnosa@aol.com

Profile

➤ Comprehensive knowledge of retail—particularly meat department—operations, products, and trends.

➤ Respected manager with 20+ years of experience in grocery industry.

➤ Expertise in developing and retaining employees; demonstrated ability to turn around poorly performing workers.

➤ Eager to utilize extensive experience and hands-on knowledge to meet challenges in new setting.

Highlights of Experience

MANAGEMENT
- Manage day-to-day operations of meat department in the chain's highest-volume store.
- Independently negotiate special purchases with vendors.
- Selected by administrators to manage meat departments in other stores during the respective managers' absences.
- Build rapport with customers by being visible and approachable.
- Maintain departmental gross profit margins of 21–24%, approximately 1½–2% higher than meat departments in other stores within chain.

OPERATIONS
- Creatively merchandise cases and institute in-store specials to generate interest in high-profit or slow-moving products.
- Plan and implement periodic department resets.
- Generate orders; maintain appropriate levels of inventory to adequately cover projected sales and ensure timely turnover of perishable products.
- Conduct routine inventories to a high degree of accuracy.
- Process special orders; advise customers on product usage.
- Review and confirm accuracy of invoices before submitting for payment.

HUMAN RESOURCES
- Motivate employees to achieve and maintain high standards of sanitation, product handling, and customer service.
- Recruit, hire, train, and supervise trade employees.
- Utilize intuition and experience to identify and hire top-quality, productive workers.
- Monitor payroll budget and prepare employee schedules.

Employment History

BUECHE'S FOOD CENTER • Clio, Michigan
    Meat Department Manager
    Meat Cutter
    Apprentice Meat Cutter

1979–Present

UNITED STATES MARINE CORPS
    Sergeant (Rank E5) — Honorably discharged

1974–1979

Education

Completed **Leadership** and other relevant courses through the U.S. Marine Corps.

BAY CITY WESTERN HIGH SCHOOL • **Diploma**

320

Food processing: butcher and meat, poultry, and fish cutter. *Janet L. Beckstrom; Flint, MI*

MICHAEL SMITHERS

Plate Shop Production

5433 S.W. Lakeview Court, Lake Oswego, Oregon 97035   (503) 636-3055

This statement is very important to most employers in this field!

TECHNICAL SKILLS

Fully qualified journeyman with solid skills in plate shop production and press brake operations. Known for speed, accuracy and quality of work.

- Extensive experience in sheet metal production.
- Accustomed to working with various types of metal—aluminum, mild steel and hardened steel (16 gauge to 1/2").
- Able to read blueprints and schematics.
- Expertise in CNC programming.
- Capable of working with engineers and co-workers at all levels.

Indicates he is versatile

Able to operate, maintain and repair:

Pacific 500 ton press brake	Cincinnati 1000 ton press brake
Cincinnati 12' and 24' shears	Drill presses
Cincinnati 12' CNC control shear	Promecam 12' CNC press brake
Ironworkers	Wysong 16' shear
Hand grinders / hand tools	Roll press
Punches	Pacific 6" shear

EXPERIENCE

PEERLESS - Tualatin, Oregon   7/85-Present
Journeyman (Plate Shop)
Shear plates for various projects and manufacture custom parts from blueprints. Work with all types of metal, from thin aluminum to heavy steel plate. Utilize press brakes, shears and other types of shop equipment; perform routine maintenance and repair as needed.

ACKERMANN-SMITHERS TOOL & DIE GRINDING - Frankfurt, Germany   5/79-3/85
Partner / Maintenance Mechanic
After 20 months of on-the-job training, was accepted as partner in family-owned tool and die repair business. Helped build company into a respected, efficiently run business. Operated, maintained and repaired all equipment on the premises. Worked as sole operator after partner retired.

MERCEDES BENZ - Frankfurt, Germany   7/76-4/79
Mechanic
Responsible for routine maintenance on heavy trucks and buses.

UNITED STATES ARMY - Frankfurt, Germany   11/72-6/76
Mechanic
Repaired jeeps and various types of heavy construction equipment.

EDUCATION

General: Graduated from Frankfurt-American High School.

Technical: Completed comprehensive Mechanics Training School (U.S. Army); continuing education related to equipment operation and repair.

REFERENCES

Provided upon request.

321

Machinist and numerical control machine tool programmer. *Nancy Karvonen, CPRW, CCM, I JCTC, CEIP; Orland, CA*

This is a straightforward functional resume for a CNC operator with both general and automotive machinist experience.

DARRELL HAVERTY

243 Robinette Road
Portland, Tennessee 37148

Home: (615) 325-6431
Email: titansfan@hotmail.com

PROFILE

An experienced, career-committed **MACHINIST** with strong qualifications in computer numerically controlled (CNC) programming. Solid background in a high-precision job-shop environment. Creative, independent worker with strong mechanical and analytical skills. Enjoy contributing to a team effort and creating a productive work environment.

SUMMARY OF QUALIFICATIONS

Hands-on experience in the set-up and operation of general and automotive machinist equipment and tools. Working knowledge of precision measurement instruments, diagnostic equipment, and all types of hand and power tools.

General Machinist Skills
♦ Set up, program, and operate CNC lathes (DynaPath 20, Mori-Seiki SL-25, Anilam), manual lathes, Bridgeport EZ Path mills, and automatic and hand-held precision grinders.
♦ Perform precision measurements and layouts using a comparator.
♦ Specific experience in machining various grades of carbide, from submicron to coarse grains in a green (powder) state.
♦ Practical experience in reading blueprints, schematics, and technical layouts.

Automotive Machinist Skills
♦ Sound knowledge of basic automotive repair and maintenance.
♦ Understanding of electrical and mechanical automotive systems.
♦ Thorough knowledge of automotive replacement parts.

WORK EXPERIENCE

MACHINIST — **Vandenberg Engineering Company** — Hendersonville, TN   1997 to Present

CNC LATHE OPERATOR — **Tillwood Technologies** — Hendersonville, TN   1994 to 1997

PARTS DRIVER — **The Auto Parts Place** — Gallatin, TN   1992 to 1994

AUTOMOTIVE TECHNICIAN — **Premier Motor Cars** — Nashville, TN   1990 to 1991

AUTOMOTIVE TECHNICIAN — **Darrell Waltrip Honda** — Franklin, TN   1989 to 1990

EDUCATION AND TRAINING

Nashville State Technical Institute — Nashville, Tennessee
Engineering Graphics, Technical Writing — 1989 to 1990

Volunteer State Community College — Gallatin, Tennessee
Emphasis on Pre-Engineering — 1985 to 1988

322

Machinist. *Carolyn Braden, CPRW; Hendersonville, TN*

CHRISTOPHER RANDOLPH

633 Macedon Road • Wayne Center, New York 14599 • 315-825-3689 • crand@msn.net

SUMMARY: Skilled CNC Machinist with experience working to close tolerances while minimizing scrap and waste. Excellent track record of meeting deadlines and controlling costs. Ability to productively interact with co-workers at all levels. Exposure to ISO 9000 manufacturing environments.

TECHNICAL PROFICIENCIES:

It was important to name brands and models of equipment he has used, as well as various attachments & accessories.

Mills & Lathes:
— Kitimura; Okuma; Hardinge CHNC 111 SP; Fadal
— Cincinnati; Star; Harding; Conquest GT; Conquest T42 & T51
— Horizontal Boring Mill w/ 60" Travel
— Bar Feed; Haas

— Mazak 640M, M+32 with Mazatrol Controls Super Quick Turn 30; 15 M-Y Mark II; 15 MS Mark II

— Mori Seiki with MSC 501 18i & 16 Controls - ZL-25 MF-D6; SL-25 MF-T6
— Five Axis CNC Turning Center / FANUC Controls / Centerless Grinder
— CNC Programming from Blueprints to Finished Parts; Familiar with G Codes
— Mazak Laser Stamping; Amada Programming

His five jobs over the course of a 14-year period are viewed as a plus in some circles because they show he has experience in diverse environ-ments doing different kinds of work.

EXPERIENCE:

1999–Present **Machinist, Precision Manufacturing; Penfield, New York**
— Fabricate aircraft and aerospace parts.
— Set up and operate Conquest GT, Conquest T42 & T51 lathes, and Hardinge mill.

1996–1999 **Optical Machinist, Mag-Opt Corporation; Egypt, New York**
— Fabricated telescope tubes and parts.
— Cut stock and worked pieces from stock to finished parts.
— Programmed, set up, and operated manual and CNC mills and lathes.
— Employed ISO 9000 manufacturing standards.

1994–1996 **Machinist, Fab-X Industries; East Rochester, New York**
— Fabricated precision parts for Fortune 100 manufacturing firms using both manual and CNC mills and lathes.
— Set up and operated mills, lathes, and centerless grinders.

1991–1994 **Machinist, Micro-Tech Tool & Die; Scottsville, New York**
— Manufactured parts for copier and automotive industries.
— Programmed CNC machines from blueprints.
— Made dies and tooling.

1988–1991 **Machinist, Global Tool & Die; Gates, New York**
— Made parts from blueprints, fabricated prototypes, and built dies.
— Utilized manual lathes and Bridgeport mills.
— Made dies and tooling.

EDUCATION: **Lake Ontario Technical College; Webster, New York**
Pursuing **A.A.S.** in **Mechanical Engineering / Optical Engineering.**

SPECIAL SKILLS / TRAINING:

MasterCAM and SmartCAM Training (Legg-Donaldson Personnel).
Computer Literacy: DOS, Windows 95, WordPerfect, C+, CNC.
Livingston County BOCES CAD/CAM Training Course.
Canandaigua Tool and Machine Institute.

323

CNC machinist. *Arnold G. Boldt, CPRW, JCTC; Rochester, NY*

Detail is given regarding diverse job duties to show his versatility and experience.

The lack of an objective or summary is not a negative since the reader can instantly determine this person's expertise.

Joseph L. Lombardi
15 Grand Avenue
New Haven, CT 06514
(203) 555-0707
joelombardi@snetco.net

Professional Experience

Sikorsky Aircraft / United Technologies • Stratford, CT   1996–Present
Die Room Support Machinist, Class A   (5/99–Present)
- Operate manual vertical turret lathe (VTL), machining die details; utilize 62-inch table.
- Responsibilities include both set-up and operation of machine.
- Machine to blueprint and drawing specifications as well as verbal instructions.
- Train operators on VTL.
- Conduct inspection to high-tolerance aircraft specifications.
- Acquired set-up and operating experience on CNC controlled millers.

Tool Room Machinist, Class A   (10/96–5/99)
- Performed variety of machining responsibilities utilizing such equipment as:

  - engine lathes
  - OD and ID grinders
  - vertical millers
  - radial arm drill presses
  - surface grinders
  - horizontal millers
  - drill presses
  - honing machines

- Responsibilities included set-up and operation for tools and fixtures used in production.
- Trained peers in operation of standard equipment (lathes, surface grinders, and Bridgeport miller).

Norwalk Special Tool Company • Norwalk, CT   1995–96
Punch Press Operator
- Set up and operated both manual and automatic presses (up to 60-ton).
- Operated punch press to verify dies; stamped out parts as well.
- Responsible for first piece and in-process inspection and deburring operations; also responsible for troubleshooting and correcting problems with dies.

Wagner Products, Inc. • East Haven, CT   1993–95
Machinist
- Operated engine lathes, ID and OD grinders, surface grinder, and Bridgeport millers for manufacturer of molds for the injection mold industry.
- Learned operation of CNC vertical millers and machining centers (four-axis machines).
- Machined details from complex blueprints.

Education

Sikorsky Aircraft • Stratford, CT
- Completed three-year Tool Die and Gauge Training Program (in-house, 1999)

New England Technical School • New Britain, CT
- Successfully completed three-month Basic Machining Program (1993)

Vinal Regional Vocational Technical School • Middletown, CT (1993 graduate)

324

Metalworking machine operator. *Jan Melnik, CPRW, CCM; Durham, CT*

FERNANDO HERNANDEZ

8961 Lincoln Drive
Dansville, New York 14435

(585) 278-5067
E-mail: toolman@machinemail.net

SUMMARY

This information is included to draw attention to his State of New York credentials, which is uncommon among candidates at this level.

Certified Tool & Die Maker with experience in a variety of manufacturing environments. Proven ability to effectively support manufacturing operations through troubleshooting processes, developing and implementing solutions, and general repair and maintenance of dies and tooling. Self-starter with ability to work independently as well as function productively as part of a process engineering team. Extensive experience with lathes, mills, and grinders.

EXPERIENCE

1992–2002

South Monroe Machining, Inc.; West Rush, New York

Manufacturer of brass and steel hardware, including hinges, chain locks, and other metal stampings for construction industry.

- Built dies and fixtures from prints or verbal descriptions.
- Repaired and maintained production tooling, including set-up and trouble-shooting of punch presses.
- Modified old dies to meet new production requirements and process changes.
- Conferred with Process Engineers to identify and implement process improvements.

This heading was included to put the best spin possible on the company's closing.

Major Project: Documented processes and cataloged tooling in anticipation of company's sale to new owners. Assisted Manufacturing Engineers during transition to new manufacturing facility.

1987–1992

Royal Machine Tool & Die Corporation; Mendon, New York

Builder of manufacturing machines and tooling for Fortune 500 OEM firms, including Ford Motor Company, Kodak, and Bausch & Lomb.

- Built tooling and set up machines for pilot production.
- Assisted with installation of manufacturing lines in customer plants.
- Conducted first-piece inspections for Quality Control.
- Served as Acting Foreman, supervising up to 15 Tool Makers.
- Directed activities of Apprentice Tool Makers.

1985–1987

North American Metals Company (NAMCO); Greece, New York

Supplier of aluminum and steel cans to the beverage and food processing industries.

- Supported 24-hour, seven-day production operation.
- Troubleshot processes and developed solutions.
- Maintained and repaired carbide tooling.
- Performed internal/external grinding and welding to maintain tooling.

1983–1985

Richards Tool & Die Corporation; Rochester, New York

1981–1983

Ritter-Sybron; Rochester, New York

Additional experience as Production Machinist with small manufacturing firms.

EDUCATION

1980

New York State Certified Class A Toolmaker
Mechanics Institute of Rochester; Chili, New York

325

Tool and die maker. *Arnold G. Boldt, CPRW, JCTC; Rochester, NY*

The specific skill section and the "Certifications" section, combined with his obvious desire to enhance his abilities through education, stood out to hiring authorities.

LEONARD BAKER

10 Blackbird Lane • Bridgeville, Pennsylvania 16666

(412) 645-3219   **lbaker@hotmail.com**

MACHINIST • WELDER • FITTER

- Proficient and skilled in technical specialty. Recognized for dedicated work ethic and productivity. Capable of doing work that requires concentration, high degree of patience and attention to detail. Mechanically inclined. Able to work independently.
- Thrive in a team and deadline-oriented environment. Exceptional organizational skills; capable of prioritizing, scheduling and managing heavy workflow.
- Proficient in technical skills/machine operations/equipment processes, including:

specific skills

✓ MIG	✓ Fluxcore	✓ Computer Numeric Control
✓ TIG	✓ Submerged Arc	✓ Gantry Crane
✓ Stick	✓ Inner shield	✓ Tolerancing
✓ Pulse	✓ Drill Press	✓ Forklift Operator
✓ Aluminum	✓ Technical Math	✓ Machine Print Reading
✓ Blueprint Reading	✓ Applied Math	✓ Lathes and Milling Machines

PROFESSIONAL EXPERIENCE

His longevity in his current position and "Perfect Attendance" reference under "Education" show there is little risk to the employer in hiring this person.

WELDER A, Forker Industries — *Bridgetown, Pennsylvania*   *1988 – Present*
- Fit and weld boxcars with Fluxcore and Submerged Arc welding. Examine welds to ensure they meet specifications.
- Instrumental on shift that slashed project hours from 11 (by another shift) to 8, while maintaining quality of workmanship.

WELDER ASSEMBLER, Sun Engineering — *Walton, Texas*   *1987 – 1988*
- Used spray-arc welding equipment. Assembled dock levelers and functioned as a saw operator, forklift driver, truck driver and member of installation crew.

WELDER FITTER, Perfection Metal Products — *Hazen, Texas*   *1986 – 1987*
- Fitted and welded frames for the electronic industry using MIG and TIG welding. Recognized for outstanding workmanship by lead man.

LABORER, City of Wilding — *Wilding, Texas*   *1985 – 1986*
- Received commendation from mayor for exemplary service to the citizens of Wilding by working 96+ hours during a winter storm to repair water main leaks.

CERTIFICATIONS

- Arc Welding
- 1/8" LH
- Plumbing and Pipefitting Fundamentals
- Vertical Outside Corner
- Vertical, T-Butt Weld

- Flat, 3/8" Dia. Plug Weld
- AWS SMAW 3/8" Butt Weld
- Gas Metal Arc Welding, Advanced
- AWS D1
- 75-Fillet Vertical and Overhead Positions

- 7018 AWS Structural
- Code D1.1
- Flat and Vertical, Inside Corner Filler
- GMAW AWS D7.7
- 86 GMAW, Spray Arc Single V Groove w/ Backing 1G-Flat

EDUCATION

shows his desire to enhance his abilities

A.S., Machine Technology, November 2001
Dean's Certificates; 3.94 GPA; Perfect Attendance; Class President
Capitol School of Trades — *Weathersfield, Pennsylvania*

note reference to his perfect attendance

Welder, cutter, and welding machine operator. *Jane Roqueplot, CBC; Sharon, PA*

This entire resume is designed to show Brenden's value!

BRENDEN GALT

3336 Eastlawn • Wayne, MI 48126 • 734.555.0708 • Bregal@aol.com

WELDER / MILLWRIGHT / PIPEFITTER

HIGHLIGHTS OF QUALIFICATIONS

- Progressive experience of over 13 years in the welding and aerosol industry.
- Work well under pressure to meet deadlines.
- Excellent supervisory experience with up to 25 workers.
- Highly adaptable at learning and understanding new procedures and techniques.
- Assertive, a go-getter and pay attention to detail.

EXPERIENCE AND ACCOMPLISHMENTS

- Developed a marble sensor to ensure each aerosol can contained a marble.
- Designed the *"Galvin Pneumatic Filler"* for filling high-viscosity fluids.
- Produced a *"Single Head Filler"* — a pneumatically controlled, positive-displacement aerosol filler.
- Skillfully used a variety of hand and power tools to accomplish tasks.
- Managed all plant maintenance functions, drastically reducing down-time through careful scheduling of equipment and personnel.
- Built and maintained conveyors.
- Oversaw pneumatic control, making sure the atmosphere was explosion proof.
- Consulted with supervisors to resolve difficult installation and repair problems.
- Received a "Positive Suggestion Award" for a waste-reduction program.

EDUCATION / CERTIFICATIONS

Welding Classes: Technical Skills Institute, Taylor, MI

SMAW — AWS D1.1 certificate	Stick Welding - Structural Steel
GMAW — AWS D1.1 certificate	Mig Welding - Structural Steel
6G Pipe class	currently enrolled

Certification and Additional Training

OSHA (hazardous waste)	certification
Dynamics of Supervision	certification
Quality Improvement with Statistics	seminar
Electrical Seminar	certificate

All three of these sections are equally emphasized.

WORK HISTORY

1993 – present	Maintenance Manager	American Jetway, Wayne, MI
1993	Team Leader	Claire Manufacturing, Addison, IL
1991 – 1993	Maintenance Mechanic	Hydrolsol, Inc., Bridgeview, IL
1989 – 1991	Production Supervisor	U.S. Package, Wheeling, IL
1988 – 1989	Mechanic	Illinois Bronze, Lake Zurich, IL
1985 – 1988	Maintenance Technician	DupliColor Prod., Elk Grove, IL

327

Welder, millwright, and pipefitter. *Joyce Fortier, MBA, CPRW, JCTC, CCM; Novi, MI*

John H. Maddox

300 Green Road • Delmar, MD 00000 • (000) 000-0000

Senior level Health Care Engineer with extensive background in managing all phases of hospital plant operations. Five years experience as Director of Plant Operations at a major, 300,000 sq. ft., regional hospital complex.

Professional Experience

Aug 1996 to Present

WORCESTER HEALTH SYSTEMS, INC., DELMAR, MD
(Formerly Franklin Memorial Hospital and Fairlawn General Hospital)
Manager of Plant Operations/Franklin Memorial Hospital at Delmar, MD

1992 to Aug 1996

FRANKLIN MEMORIAL HOSPITAL AT DELMAR, MD
Director of Plant Operations/Hospital Safety Officer
Responsible for overall administration of all hospital plant operations including building systems (HVAC, electric, plumbing, boiler plant, etc), new construction, renovations, building and grounds maintenance, equipment maintenance and repair, security and safety.

His most recent and relevant experience gets the emphasis

• Planned and implemented budget reduction measures which resulted in savings of $243,000 in annual plant operating expense. Among other measures this included reductions in department personnel, implementing steps to reduce energy costs, and restructuring rates of rental properties.

• Drafted construction plans for Washington Pediatric Clinic. Reviewed and approved change orders for construction of Hambry Diagnostic Center.

• Designed and implemented staff cross training program between maintenance and environmental services personnel. Results were an improved level of patient care, greater operating efficiency and higher staff morale.

• Designed and implemented a mandatory in-service Safety Training Program for 1,400 hospital employees.

• Led team of workers to win first prize in a hospital wide competition designed to identify cost savings measures based on employee suggestions.

1991 to 1992   *Director of Plant Operations*
1986 to 1991   *Assistant Director of Plant Operations*
1984 to 1986   *Chief of Power Plant and Security*
1982 to 1984   *Chief Stationary Engineer*

Previous jobs with the same employer

1976 to 1982

FAIRLAWN GENERAL HOSPITAL, CAMBRIDGE, MD
Stationary Engineer

1975 to 1976

THE TOWN OF BISHOP, BISHOP, MD
Town Engineer

1974 to 1975

TECH-COM, BISHOP, MD
Chief Engineer

1973 to 1974

FIBERTECH, INC., CAMBRIDGE, MD
Quality Control Engineer

1971 to 1973

GRAYSON AUTOMOTIVE CO., JAMESTOWN, MD
Division Manager, Parts

1967 to 1970

UNITED STATES NAVY
Marine Propulsion

1965 to 1967

GRAYSON AUTOMOTIVE CO., JAMESTOWN, MD
Division Manager, Parts

328

Electronic power generating plant operator and power distributor and dispatcher. *Thomas E. Spann; Easton, MD*

Joe wanted to return to the petrochemical industry after leaving it to start a completely unrelated business (resume writer's comments)

JOE BLOE

P.O. Box 175 ♦ Bellville, Texas 77418 ♦ (409) 865-1130

PROFILE: **PETROCHEMICAL PROCESSOR**

Thirteen years experience in petrochemical processing, eleven years as a leader and trainer. Experience in utilities (boilerhouse), esterification and compound blending operations.

LICENSE: *Stationary Engineers License (Third Grade)*, City of Houston

COMMENDATIONS: Safety Performance Award - 10 years without incident
Several commendation letters from Department Managers on performance, teamwork, safety, and efficiency.

SPECIALIZED EQUIPMENT:

♦ *Slant tube Franklin Boilers (500 horsepower)*

♦ *"D" Design Murray Package Boiler (400 horsepower)*

♦ *Boiler Feedwater Softener*

♦ *Deaerator Tank*

♦ *Dual Pass impeller centrifugal pump (electric)*

♦ *Reciprocating pump (steam)*

♦ *Plate and frame filter press*

♦ *Peroxide Catalyst Feed System*

♦ *Reactor upset recovery system*

♦ *Stainless steel reactors with agitators*

♦ *Weigh Tanks (carbon and stainless steel)*

♦ *Overhead condenser, decanter, waste weigh tank (stainless steel)*

♦ *Thin Down Tanks (carbon and stainless steel)*

♦ *Blending Vats (up to 11,000 gallons capacity)*

♦ *Fork Lift; straddle buggy*

PROFESSIONAL EXPERIENCE:

SURETY BAIL BONDS, Bellville, Texas   1993 - Present
Owner
Founded bail bonding business serving clients in Austin, Waller, Washington and Fayette counties.

While this is his most recent work experience, it is given little space since it is not related to his objective.

329

Petrochemical processor.   *Cheryl Ann Harland, CPRW, JCTC;*
The Woodlands, TX

JOE BLOE   **PAGE TWO**

**PROFESSIONAL
EXPERIENCE:**
(Cont'd.)

EXXON CHEMICAL COMPANY, Houston, Texas   1979 - 1992
*Thirteen year career highlighted by a series of increasingly responsible positions within
several areas of petrochemical processing operations. Served as department representative
on Safe Operations Committee (SOC) and Operations Safety Committee (OSC)*

*His
previous
and
most
relevant
jobs are
given
the most
space*

Shift Leaderman Operator - Boilerhouse Unit   1987 - 1992
Scope of responsibility included monitoring Nitrogen tank and vaporizer, air compressors, air
dryers and compressor cooling tower. Sampled plant effluent and water treatment systems and
measured "Ph" for outside lab testing. Obtained extensive training in LOTO and gas
measurement procedures. Issued Hot, Cold and vessel Entry permits. Using gas detector,
measured level of flammables and oxygen present in work areas. Tracked all utility usage
through daily utility readings and conducted random checks of manufacturing areas to ensure
safety and operational compliances were met. Received Stationary Engineers License.

EXXON CHEMICAL COMPANY
Ester Unit Leader-Esterfication Unit   1982 - 1987
Completed two year leader unit training program. Responsible for total batch operations -
charged materials to reactors and conducted sampling of contents for QC specifications. Once
QC approved, cooled, thinned down, checked and pumped completed batch to bulk field
storage. Formulas produced included Phenolic Formaldehyde using p-tert Butyl phenol in
xylene breakdown, p-tert Amyl phenol/Formaldehyde and p-tert Nonyl phenol/Formaldehyde
in xylene or heavy aromatic Naptha breakdown, imadozolines, esterphosphates, organic salts
and complex esters. Co-wrote Ester Unit Training Manual.

Compound Blending Unit   1979 - 1982
Began training in an isolation suit with breathing apparatus and Scott Air Pack handling
dangerous chemicals. Strapped tanks, read strapping charts and conducted samplings.
Promoted to Operator Trainee responsible for blending and producing over 200 products using
operating directives.

**SPECIALIZED
TRAINING:**

Thousands of hours of specialized training through schooling and Exxon-sponsored
programs including:

★   1062 hours - A/C and Refrigeration
★   531 hours - Welding
★   Mission Control Ground School
★   Statistical Process Control (IQ)
★   Initiative for Quality
★   Fire Fighting & Safety Training

Henry's resume is organized to show that he is strong in all the many aspects of operating a water-treatment facility.

Henry J. Edwards

4281 Castle Road, Greece, NY 14499
585-924-2562   hjeh2o@email.net

SUMMARY

Licensed Water-Treatment Plant Operator with extensive experience maintaining and operating chemical-treatment, membrane-filtration, and sand-filtration systems. Repair and maintenance experience with treatment plants, wells, and distribution systems. Excellent laboratory sampling and testing skills.

EXPERIENCE

1996–Present   Village of Pultneyville Water Department; Pultneyville, New York
Water Treatment Plant Operator — IIA
Eight-million-gallon-per-day water-treatment facility.

❑ Monitor chemical treatment of water:
— Ensure Chlorine, Chlorine Dioxide, Fluoride, and Sodium Silicate levels are maintained.
— Calibrate pumps used to introduce treatment chemicals.

❑ Conduct laboratory tests of ground water and plant outflow:
— Take samples of water from various testing points in system.
— Perform bacteriological tests in certified lab setting.
— Test for inorganic factors (i.e., iron, calcium, chlorine).

❑ Participate in maintenance and repair of well pumps and distribution system:
— Clean and rebuild well pumps and distribution pumps.
— Perform scheduled maintenance on fire hydrants and water mains.
— Effect repairs to pump stations and pressure pits.

❑ Perform customer service/community affairs duties:
— Respond to consumer complaints/problems.
— Inspect water lines at construction sites for code compliance.
— Locate underground water lines at excavation sites.

Highlights his strength in the area of community affairs, which is important in a municipal setting.

1986–1995   Gulf Coast Water Cooperative; Sarasota, Florida
Lead Operator
Five-million-gallon-per-day membrane-filtration and one-million-gallon-per-day electrodialysis-treatment plants.

❑ Participated in the design and rebuild of entire treatment plant.
❑ Sampled water for organic testing; conducted inorganic testing.
❑ Developed and implemented maintenance programs.
❑ Ran tests and performed maintenance on membrane-filtration units.

1982–1986   United States Army; Fort Drum, New York
Water Treatment Specialist (Specialist 4)
Mobile membrane- and sand-filtration units providing potable water to military units operating in remote locations.

❑ Set up and operated filtration units in Grenada, Panama, and Turkey.
❑ Evaluated potential sources of water; sampled and tested surface water.
❑ Maintained fleet of 15 mobile filtration units.

LICENSES

Grade IIA Water Treatment Plant Operator (NYS — #05521)
Class A Water Treatment Plant Operator (Florida — #4946)

TRAINING & SPECIAL SKILLS

❑ Water Treatment Plant Operations — California State University at Sacramento
❑ Supervisory Management in Water & Waste Treatment — University of Michigan
❑ 57th Annual Short School, Water & Waste Treatment — University of Florida
❑ Advanced Water Treatment in Reverse Osmosis & Upflow Clarifiers — US Army
❑ AS/400 Computer Systems; System Control and Data Acquisition (SCADA)

330

Water and wastewater treatment plant operator. *Arnold G. Boldt, CPRW, JCTC; Rochester, NY*

Although this person is a supervisor, his hands-on experience is emphasized because it is highly valued in this industry. Even as a supervisor, he will probably have to set up and repair machines and be responsible for employee training.

JOHN MITCHELL

5831 Valley Drive, Huron, New York 14099
(716) 281-7425   jmitchell@coolmail.com

SUMMARY

Talented Bindery Manager possessing excellent supervisory skills and extensive hands-on experience with a wide range of bindery operations. Excellent track record of controlling labor costs, effectively scheduling production, and maintaining high quality and productivity standards.

PROFESSIONAL EXPERIENCE

Bindery Manager, Quicksilver Lithographers, Inc.; Buffalo, New York   **1995–Present**
Manage bindery operations for this fast-growing commercial printing firm serving Fortune 500 corporate accounts.

- Schedule production in coordination with pressroom and pre-press departments.
- Interact with vendors for outside bindery and finishing services.
- Hire, train, and supervise 20 employees covering two shifts.
- Prepare employee reviews and evaluate ongoing performance.
- Prepare impositions and approve press sheet layouts.
- Approve bindery work for accuracy and quality.
- Monitor labor costs, review job-cost reports, and participate in management team meetings.
- Direct maintenance and repair activities for all bindery equipment.
- Maintain hands-on knowledge of a wide array of bindery equipment:

— **Polar Cutters**	— **Stahl Folders**
— **Mueller-Martini Stitchers**	— **Baum Folders**
— **Heidelberg Letterpresses**	— **Haskins Folder/Gluer**
— **Label-Air Machine**	— **Slaughterbach Gluer (Fugitive Glue)**
— **Kugler Punches**	— **Macy Collators**
— **Scott Tab-Cutting Machine**	— **Scott Edge-Reinforcing Machine**

- **Accomplishments:**
  - *Managed the rapid growth of department as company sales increased by over 750% in five-year period. During this transition period, the company moved to new facilities, acquired numerous pieces of new equipment, and added substantially to production staff.*
  - *Spearheaded selection process for several new pieces of bindery equipment. Researched available equipment choices, including traveling to trade shows to observe demonstrations. Evaluated features and costs of competing pieces of equipment; made business case and purchase recommendations to senior management. Oversaw the installation and set-up of new equipment.*

Senior Bindery Operator, Occidental Publishing, Ltd.; Niagara Falls, New York   **1985–1995**
Set up and operated various bindery equipment. Served as group leader/supervisor for Production Aides and Junior Operators.

- Operated Side-Stitchers, Saddle-Stitchers, Perfect Binders, Drills, 3-Knife Trimmers, and Cutters.
- Collected time cards from production workers and ensured labor costs were accurately recorded.

Journeyman Operator, German Bindery Company; Hamburg, New York   **1982–1985**
Operated a variety of Case-Binding, Saddle-Stitching, and Perfect-Binding equipment.

Cutter Operator / Materials Handler, Seaway Printers; Massena, New York   **1981–1982**
Learned to operate Cutters, Folders, and Saddle-Stitchers. Coordinated flow of materials to maintain productivity.

TRAINING / SPECIAL SKILLS

Fred Pryor Seminars:	**Leadership Through Total Quality Management**
	How To Supervise People
	Conflict Management
Shop Floor:	**Labor and Materials Cost Tracking System**

331

Bindery worker. *Arnold G. Boldt, CPRW, JCTC; Rochester, NY*

This resume makes use of good graphic design but is not over-done since it is for a management job

RBS RICHARD B. STEIN

1931 Smith Street   **Peekskill, NY 10566**   **(914) 736-1997**
(914) 734-1996

OBJECTIVE

A management position in the print industry which will benefit from my technical expertise and strong leadership skills, utilizing my proven twenty plus year track record maximizing productivity and profitability.

PROFILE

- ☐ Versatile management professional with twenty plus year track record in the computer graphics industry; proven ability to manage multiple projects.
- ☐ Detail-oriented graphic artist with exceptional follow-through abilities and excellent management skills; able to plan and oversee projects from concept to successful final product.
- ☐ Demonstrated ability to efficiently prioritize a broad range of responsibilities in order to consistently meet deadlines. Effective in getting cooperation of staff.
- ☐ A resource person, problem solver, trouble shooter and creative turn-around manager. Proven ability in determining what the customer is doing wrong and minimizing expenditures.
- ☐ Demonstrated strength in resolving problems swiftly and independently.
- ☐ Possess comprehensive, diversified expertise in the print industry; knowledge of pricing, prep, and press.
- ☐ Strong computer skills; expertise in state of the art computerized graphics, scanning, layout, photo retouching and word processing programs.

AREAS OF EFFECTIVENESS

- ☐ Documented *consultative skills;* proven ability in suggesting methods to *increase project efficiency* and enhance esthetic quality.
- ☐ Proven customer service skills, achieved *high* levels of customer satisfaction *generating significant repeat business.*

Uses various bullets, indents, columns, and type styles

Management	✓ Production scheduling ✓ Oversee Production; estimate time and costs ✓ Produce imposition and lay-out dummies ✓ Monitor work flow; ensure efficiency
Training and Development	✓ Instruct prep people on methods to optimize variety of jobs
Electronic Stripping and Imposition	✓ Four color process ✓ Flat color creation
Scanner Work	✓ Optical character recognition, 4-color, duotone and B/W illustration

PROFESSIONAL EXPERIENCE

March 1994 - Present

MTM PRINTING, College Point, NY
Manager: Electronic Pre-press
- ◆ *Established electronic pre-press department* thereby *increasing billable in-house production by 31%.*
- ◆ Recommended software and hardware to enable in-house production of proofs and film for 4-color process printing.
- ◆ Set up network and trouble shoot conflicts.
- ◆ Train staff.

332

Prepress manager. *Mark D. Berkowitz, NCCC, CPRW; Yorktown Heights, NY*

April 1992- March 1994	**COLOR GRAPHIC PRESS,** Long Island City, NY **Manager: Graphic Services** ◆ Hired, trained and supervised staff of two. ◆ *Re-engineered work-flow* to take advantage of electronic image processing *resulting in a near doubling of revenues* from process color preparation work. ◆ Bought and *set up network* server using Novell Netware to *link PCs* and *MACs.*
June 1986 - July 1992	**ENHANCE-A-COLOR,** North White Plains, NY **Shift Supervisor: Color Correction/Re-toucher** ◆ Operated film setters and proprietary image manipulation systems for film out-put service. ◆ Implemented procedures which *increased production capacity by 71%.* ◆ Managed introduction of routines to process new customers' electronic files into plate-ready film. ◆ Analyzed and altered customer-supplied art work to achieve proper integration of parts into plate ready film.
October 1980 - June 1986	**XEROX CORPORATION,** Armonk, NY **Production Manager, Slide System Division** (sold October 1985 to MAGI Inc.) ◆ *Established successful profit center,* a service group designing and producing slide presentations on the MAGI slide system. ◆ *Managed production facility* with staff of 5 persons servicing country-wide customer base. ◆ *Instituted production and quality control procedures* and enlisted staffing to *effectively control a tripling of product volume.* ◆ *Provided continuity of management* during transfer of production facility from Xerox to MAGI after sale by Xerox to the system developer. ◆ *Supervised* and *documented* the commercial introduction of six new hard-copy products.
September 1979 - October 1980	**INTERACTIVE GRAPHICS, INC.,** Wayne, PA **Graphic Designer** Designed and produced slide presentations for major corporations on second generation computer graphics system, "Genigraphics."

EDUCATION

PARSONS SCHOOL OF DESIGN (THE NEW SCHOOL), New York, NY
Courses in color and design   1972 - 1973

COLUMBIA UNIVERSITY, New York, NY
Woodrow Wilson Fellow   1960 - 1961

ILLINOIS INSTITUTE OF TECHNOLOGY, Chicago, IL
Bachelor of Science   1960
Major: English
Minor: Graphics (Institute of Design)

REFERENCES   Available upon request.

Tamura's printing proficiencies and file-management skills are highlighted in the top third of the resume.

TAMURA YAMAGUCHI

400 Woodruff Lane
Oakwood, Kansas 66022

tyamaguchi@southernbell.net
(883) 109-9743

DIGITAL PRE-PRESS OPERATOR

PROFESSIONAL PROFILE

Talented print production specialist with impressive experience in digital imaging pre-press operations. Fast, accurate, and willing to work long hours to meet deadlines. Communicate with customers and vendors. Develop customer awareness of color and file format preparation.

printing proficiencies

SOFTWARE PACKAGES

- Illustrator
- Photoshop
- PageMaker
- FrameMaker
- QuarkXpress
- FileMaker Pro
- Acrobat Distiller and Exchange
- Preps
- Trapwise
- PressTouch
- PowerPoint Mac & PC

WORKFLOW

- Delta Workstation
- Scitex PS and PS Ripping

EQUIPMENT

- AgfaSelect Set 7000
- AgfaAvantra 44 Imagesetter
- Creo Platesetter and Lodum (CTP) Output

skills

FILE MANAGEMENT

- Manual Trapping
- Print Files to Disk
- Color Manipulation
- Troubleshooting Postscript and PDF Files
- Pre-Flight for Digital Imaging

VALUE OFFERED

Bulleted items in this section emphasize her accomplishments and her ability to assist customers in preparing their printing projects for best results.

Premier Printing, Inc., Oakwood, Kansas   2000–Present
Senior Desktop Operator
Produce complex metallic-on-metallic printing for one of state's largest sheetfed printing firms, serving software clients.

- Print Scitex workflow to Brisque Workstation, rip and trap, and impose files with Preps.
- Print ICF file to Brisque and output Iris 43 wide-digital Dylux or Iris4Print for Kodak approval.

Oakwood Printing Inc., Oakwood, Kansas   1999–2000
Desktop Operator
Accomplished digital pre-press operation for commercial printing firm.

- Reproduced jobs on Delta Workstation, ripped and trapped, imposed file with Signastation, and output with Epson Digital Dylux.
- Implemented Delta Workflow and directed to plate.

(Continued)

333

Prepress worker. *Nancy Karvonen, CPRW, CCM, IJCTC, CEIP; Orland, CA*

**VALUE
OFFERED
(CONTINUED)**

MidWest Lithographer, Oakwood, Kansas   1997–1999
Digital Imaging Technician/Lead

Led crew in digital pre-press for one of oldest printing companies in Kansas.

- Instrumental in setting up on-site processing team at Cisco.
- Completed and uploaded complex rush FTP website project in 3 hours. Instructed client on file preparation.

AMP Graphic Services, Kansas City, Kansas   1993–1997
Pre-Press Foreman

Oversaw 3 shifts for turnkey and fulfillment house utilizing web press. As qualified digital pre-press operator, prepared files for digital printing.

- Collected data and created 3000-record FileMaker Pro database for easy archival and retrieval of complete job histories including photos.
- Set company production record for 3-day turnaround of 8-book set of 50,000 prints to Europe. Worked crews in 3 shifts to finish 750 plates within 24 hours.
- Directed, trained, and evaluated desktop operator, stripper, proofer, and plater.
- Coordinated daily operations with pressroom foreman.
- Wrote and instituted detailed procedures in compliance with ISO Certification.

Advanced Publishing, Ltd., Tokyo, Japan   1986–1993
Production Manager/Photographer/Graphic Artist

Rapidly progressed from graphic artist to production manager for this fast-paced firm. Published monthly and weekly architectural publications within tight time frames.

- Supervised 9-person production team consisting of graphic designers, artists, and photographers.
- Produced business cards, letterhead, 4-color brochures, and flyers for commercial-art customers.
- Interacted with customers to correct errors and identify potential color and preparation problems.

**SPECIALIZED
TRAINING**

University of Wisconsin—Madison, Wisconsin
First Institute of Art & Design—Tokyo, Japan

- Graphic Arts   • Graphic Design   • Delta System   • Color Production
- Applescript   • Commercial Photography
- Fingerprint Press Device Calibration to Ensure Color Accuracy

Since Kathy has no formal education beyond high school, no education is included. Her resume emphasizes her management skills to keep that option open.

KATHY McWILLIAMS
10875 Barker Road
Greenville, North Carolina 47124
24-hour answering service: 225-243-9872
katemcw1013@earthlink.net

Objective

Responsible position in a full-service printing and bindery operation.

Summary

Over 13 years of experience in all phases of printing and bindery operations. Excellent attendance record and a stable work history. Willing to accept responsibility and have supervisory experience. Self-motivated, with a work history of superior production and performance. Good "people" skills and interested in learning new techniques.

Technical Skills

Over 13 years of experience in a variety of custom and high-volume printing operations. I can operate and maintain all standard printing and bindery equipment, including

- Stahl and O&M Folders
- Thermograph machines
- Heidelberg SORKZ
- Heidelberg KORD
- Solna 125 and 225
- Davidson 702 Perfector
- Plate making
- Polar & Challenger Papercutters
- Stitchers, drillers, and all bindery operations
- ATF 2217 Super Chief
- 1250 Multilith
- AB Dicks with T-51 head
- Stripping to 4-color process
- Camera experience

Related Skills

I have substantial work experience in the printing and bindery industries and am able to do most things needed, including:

- Repair most printing equipment, including total reconditioning.
- Certified forklift driver, familiar with warehouse operations.
- Have supervised as many as 12 press and bindery workers.
- Complete all necessary paperwork, including narrative report.
- Good customer contact and problem-solving skills.

These "extra" skills are listed separately.

Work Experience

Excellent references are available from

Shoney Newsweek	**Head Pressman/Foreman**	11/96 to Present
Minute Press	**Head Pressman**	11/89 to 11/96

This tells the reader that Kathy has a good work history.

334

Printing press operator. *Dede Penick; Indianapolis, IN*

John needed to show the "extras"—ways he saved his company money and improved operations—not buried

in a listing of job responsibilities. So, a separate "Accomplishments" section was added to his most recent position (resume writer's comments).

John L. Robertson
1411 Vine Street
Cincinnati, Ohio 45202
(513) 555-5555

SUMMARY

- Skilled press operator with a commitment to producing top-quality work through attention to detail, thorough planning, and sound knowledge of color printing operations.

- Expert in color matching, mixing, and production on the press.

- Strong communication skills and the ability to maintain positive professional relationships that lead to better planning and higher quality.

- Proven ability to analyze and adjust to varied equipment to achieve maximum output and quality.

PROFESSIONAL EXPERIENCE

QUEEN CITY PRINTING, INC., Cincinnati, Ohio   1982-Present

Commercial printer producing high-quality four-color business communications including brochures, catalogs, and magazines.

Web Pressman (1991-Present)

Maintain color and ink quality throughout the press run by diligent attention to detail and quality control. Monitor all production facets, including folding, compensation, registration, pagination, etc.

- Specialize in precise color mixing to achieve customer's desired output.

- Apply knowledge of individual presses to achieve maximum output and consistent quality.

- Thoroughly review specifications for upcoming job so that adequate planning and preparation can be made to ensure timely press operation.

- Troubleshoot print runs, monitoring for quality and conformance to specifications.

- Maintain open communication with MIC (Man in Charge, chief pressman) and Assistant Pressman to promote teamwork and ensure shared job knowledge.

- Coordinate computerized press operations to set appropriate color levels.

Accomplishments

- Analyzed operation of unique printing press and established appropriate settings that significantly reduced waste and increased production from 25,000 to 40,000 impressions per hour. Documented and explained findings to management.

- Recognized for ability to find errors and prevent them from contaminating the entire press run; contribute to company profitability by reducing waste in printing operations.

- Earned incentive compensation for hundreds of money-saving catches and ideas for efficient operations.

- Developed formal job description for Pressman position, at the request of management.

Assistant Pressman (1985-91)

Assisted in all phases of web press operation.

- Went beyond job parameters to initiate checking and pre-planning routine for upcoming jobs.

Packer (1982-85)

Performed printing-related tasks and learned the printing business.

- Promoted to Assistant Pressman based on initiative and demonstrated knowledge and ability.

335

Printing press operator. *Louise M. Kursmark, CPRW, JCTC, CEIP, CCM; Cincinnati, OH*

A resume with few words can be appropriate for a highly specialized job such as this one, but only if it is carefully crafted.

Garrison Newberg

14240 Newark Drive SE
Detroit, Michigan 49980
(810) 555-2555
garynew2020@worldnet.att.net

Objective

To secure a position as an Orthopedic Footwear Designer

Summary of Qualifications

Product development and control
Extensive Customer Relations Experience
International product and design knowledge

Experience

International Ortho-Wear, Inc.   1999–Present
Orthopedic Shoemaker

Responsible for the production of all orthopedic footwear in the European market as well as extensive interaction with manufacturers within the American shoe industry.

European Orthopedic Supplies, Inc.   1996–1998
Orthopedic Shoemaker Helper

Duties including attaching insoles to shoe lasts, affixing shoe uppers, and applying heals and outsoles. Fluent in Spanish and French. Experienced with international protocol.

Education

Michigan State University, BS

Affiliations

Pedorthic Footwear Association
Shoe Service Institute of America
International Orthopedic Association

336

Shoe and leather worker and repairer. *Thelma Silvola; Indianapolis, IN*

Brian left a highly stressful business career to be an upholsterer — a hobby he truly enjoyed...

BRIAN M. JEFFERSON

He didn't want his business background on his resume, but for the employer to

1234 Street
Any Town, MI 49001
(333) 333-3333

see his dedication and enjoyment at upholstering furniture (resume writer's comments).

Upholstery Knowledge

- 9+ Years Hands-On Experience in Upholstery
- Strong Educational Foundation in Upholstery
- Setup • Operation • Maintenance of Most Upholstery Tools & Equipment

- Cordwork • Trimwork
- High Integrity
- Computer Literate
- Experienced Instructor

Experience

UPHOLSTERY WORKS

Story, MI

Upholster

1988 - Present

- Dedicated to serving clients on an individualized basis in the upholstery of select furniture pieces from diversified eras of construction including:
  Client Relations • Product Selection • Estimation of Project [Time Involved and Monetary Services] • Intricate Steps to Complete Finished Product

Continuing Education

ASSOCIATE'S DEGREE
Story County College
Story, MI • 1988

Exceptional Customer Service
UPPS Seminars • 1996

The Exceptional Marketing & Sales Techniques
UPPS Seminars • 1995

Powerful Communication Skills for Upholsters
Story College Continuing Education Center • 1995

Community Involvement

Upholstery Association of Story County
Co-Chair • Public Relations Committee
Co-Chair • Program Committee
Committee Member • Public Relations

References Available Upon Request

337

Upholsterer. *Betty A. Callahan, PC, CPRW; Kalamazoo, MI*

This fun resume uses intricate bullets that reflect his artistic sensibilities. The bulleted items themselves describe some of the beautiful woodworking he has done.

GORDON L. SLOANE

75 Mountain Road ▪ Camden, ME 04843 ▪ (207) 230-4472 ▪ GLS30@aol.com

PROFILE

unusual bullet used throughout

▣ **FINE WOODWORKER.** Reputation as a meticulous woodworker with a high degree of integrity as a craftsman. More than twenty years' experience fabricating and building high-end projects including cabinetmaking, organ building, residential construction, and marine woodworking. Experienced, cost-conscious shop manager committed to product excellence and shop safety.

▣ Gifted with the ability to envision solutions to design and fabrication problems. Highly creative and analytical, with demonstrated ability to take projects from conception through to final installation. Skilled at breaking down large projects into component parts.

Inspired by a love of fine woodworking. Fascinated by new design and fabrication challenges.

WORK HISTORY

Mid-Coast Prehung Door, Rockport, ME   1990–Present
Shop Supervisor / Lead Woodworker

As lead man, perform all specialty work and supervise five woodworkers. Oversee maintenance and repair of machinery. Ensure safety. Plan for the efficient use of 1,440 square feet of shop space. Create custom mantles, doors, and stair treads.

▣ Trusted by owner to do the design work on the most challenging projects.

▣ Personally build all circular, curved, and elliptical work and create all inlay work.

▣ Built 600 linear feet of curved, raised paneling for a wainscot job that is featured on the back cover of *Builder Architect Magazine.*

▣ Fabricated a set of elliptical French doors.

▣ Built treads for two staircases, one with walnut inlay in white oak and the other with white oak inlay in walnut.

▣ Envisioned and built work aids to solve woodworking problems, saving time and labor costs.

▣ Researched newest tooling and made cost-effective purchases. Example: purchased a tool sharpener that avoided costs associated with outsourcing and subsequent downtime.

Milldam Building Corporation, Rockport, ME   1983–1990
Cabinetmaker

▣ Built all kitchens, built-in bookcases, and other cabinetry.

▣ Designed, built, and installed teak furniture and woodwork for a 67-foot yacht.

Milton Fine Organ Builders, Princeton Junction, NJ   1980–1983
Wood and Metal Worker

▣ Assisted in the building of electro-pneumatic organs. Jobs included soldering wires, woodworking, and finishing.

▣ Participated in an organ installation in Reading, PA.

▣ Fabricated circular iron stairs and railings.

338

Woodworker. *Jean Cummings, MAT, CPRW, CEIP; Concord, MA*

GORDON L. SLOANE   (207) 230-4472   Page 2

EDUCATION AND SKILLS

University of Rochester, Eliot College of Music, Rochester, NY   1980
Major: Organ Music

Courses included organ performance/design/appreciation/history, choral directing, voice, music theory, German language. Sang in the Chorale. Visited great organs located on the Eastern seaboard — played a favorite, the tracker-action organ built by C. B. Fisk, Inc., at Harvard University's Memorial Church.

Computer Skills

Microsoft Word. Internet research to identify and purchase state-of-the-art woodworking machinery and tools. Computer Courses: Basic Computing, Quicken, Internet.

Woodworking and Metalworking Skills

Draw blueprints by hand. Read architectural drawings. Knowledge of OSHA guidelines. Use wood lathes, shapers, molders, table saws, radial arm saws, planers, boring machines, miter saws, routers, metal lathes, surface grinders, milling machines, Blanchard grinders, vertical and horizontal band saws.

INTERESTS

- Building fine furniture, including tables and elaborate desks that have been given to children as family heirlooms. Have designed and fabricated built-in furniture for own home.
- Playing the organ.

This is a traditional chronological presentation of Suzanne's highly relevant skills, education, and experience.

Suzanne P. Michaels

19 Largo Street
Hopewell, NJ 08525
(609) 505-5055 / suzmich@earthlink.net

Summary of Qualifications

✓ This section includes all the important highlights.

- Qualified dental laboratory technician and hygienist with excellent clinical credentials as well as strong interpersonal and effective communication skills.
- Broad expertise fabricating orthodontic devices for customized treatment milieu.
- Philosophy centers on teaching patients skills that will enable excellence in dental care for the rest of their lives.
- Keen medical background with strong comfort level in anatomy, physiology, oral pathology, and surgery; radiology-qualified. Self-starter with highly focused and dedicated approach.
- New Jersey Licensure, Dental Hygienist (1998); Member, American Dental Hygienist Association.
- Proficient in WordPerfect and Microsoft Office Suite.

Education

RUTGERS UNIVERSITY — New Brunswick, NJ
Bachelor of Science Degree, Dental Hygiene (1998)
- Successfully completed all requirements for radiology
- Nominated for induction into Sigma Phi Alpha National Dental Hygiene Honor Society

Clinical Experience

DENNIS G. HERZOG, D.D.S./PRACTICE & LABORATORIES — Middletown, NJ   1998–Present
Laboratory Technician *(1999–Present)*
- Work exclusively fabricating all oral and orthodontic devices for variety of patient requirements in busy private practice and custom laboratory (support one dentist and eight hygienists).
- Trained in conducting computerized cosmetic imaging.
- Specialize in veneers, bonding, bleaching services, and laser treatments.

Dental Hygienist *(1998–99)*
- Highly competent in all phases of four-handed dentistry working in busy clinic/professional dental office.
- Expertise included dental hygiene examinations, charting of oral conditions, dental hygiene assessment, treatment planning and evaluation, complete prophylaxis, application of sealants, radiography, and patient education.

MEADOWLANDS DENTAL LABORATORIES — Bergen City, NJ   1997–98
Intern
- Complemented formal education with extensive internship experience; exposed to broad range of orthodontic fabrication processes as well as cosmetic and restorative dentistry.
- Contributed to community outreach programs; facilitated educational programs in senior citizen communities.

339

Dental laboratory technician. *Jan Melnik, CPRW, CCM; Durham, CT*

The challenge in preparing Renee's resume was to present her expertise as an OSHA inspector in a way that would be palatable to business.

RENEE ALANSON

Her previous resume was a laundry list of fines and legal actions she had helped facilitate! The goal of this resume was to make it easy for companies to understand how her skill set would benefit them in a safety or inspector role.

1115 Exfort Road
Raleigh, North Carolina 27612
(919) 342-6743
ralanson3234@toona.com

–CORPORATE SAFETY / INSPECTION COMPLIANCE OFFICER / SAFETY MANAGER–

Extensive background with Occupational Safety and Health. Excellent communication and presentation skills.
Able to develop strong business relations with the public and co-workers.

SKILLS SUMMARY

— OSHA Compliance Inspection Initiatives
— Hazard Recognition/Analysis/Documentation
— Community/External Business Collaborations
— Critical Relationship Management
— Multidisciplinary Training/Team Development
— Political Skill/Process Knowledge
— Liaison to Client Senior Management
— Safety Change Management
— Resource Assessment/Control

— Project Design/Implementation
— Post-inspection Activity Management
— Report Planning/Presentations
— Citation/Penalty Recommendations
— SOP/Precedent Interpretation
— Program Enforcement Activities
— Complex Issues Analysis
— Complete Hazard Documentation
— Policy/Procedure Development

SUMMARY OF QUALIFICATIONS

- *Compliance Officer with the Federal and State OSH program focused on ensuring compliance with occupational safety and health laws, rules and regulations to protect workers' safety and health in North Carolina workplaces.*

- *In-depth knowledge of and experience with compliance inspection procedures for nonexempt establishments across North Carolina. Proven skills in project research, documentation, case definition, planning and measuring of final success.*

- *A multi-tasking professional with extensive communication, presentation and liaison skills; successfully develop strong networks and positive rapport with the public and co-workers.*

- *Excellent communication skills, including the ability to plan, write and present arguments and recommendations on a variety of major program issues at the national level.*

- *Goal-oriented leader with demonstrated research, critical analysis and evaluation skills.*

- *Consistently display a progressive leadership-by-example attitude, working with integrity, initiative and a commitment to quality results. Outstanding ability to define corporate goals needed for successful project implementations, reallocate resources to achieve those goals and communicate goals to other team members, management and senior staff.*

SELECTED EDUCATION, TRAINING & LICENSURE

CHARLOTTE COLLEGE, Charlotte, NC: **Legal Program Studies (part-time)**
ST. LAWRENCE UNIVERSITY, Canton, NC: **Bachelor of Arts in Business Management & Economics, 1980**

SAFETY & OSHA PROFESSIONAL FOCUS:
— NCOSH Initial Compliance Course
— Lock-Out/Tag-Out Accident Investigation
— Health Standards for Safety Compliance Officers
— Fundamentals of Industrial Hygiene
— Legal Aspects & Investigative Techniques
— Interaction Management/Image and Communication

— Bloodborne Pathogens
— Safety Standards
— OSHA Confined Space
— Basic Accident Investigation
— Inspection Techniques & Legal Aspects
— Excavation Safety Workshop

340

Inspector. *John M. O'Connor; Raleigh, NC*

RENEE ALANSON

PROFESSIONAL EXPERIENCE

NORTH CAROLINA DEPARTMENT OF LABOR/SAFETY COMPLIANCE BUREAU, Raleigh, NC
OSHA Safety Compliance Officer, 1990 – Present

- Serve as a field operative for the OSH Division, ensuring compliance with occupational safety and health laws, rules and regulations to protect workers' safety and health in workplaces across North Carolina.
- Perform pre-inspection activities to prepare for actual compliance inspection.
- Conduct pre-occupancy inspections of migrant housing facilities. Coordinate efforts with the Safety Compliance Bureau and the Migrant Housing Bureau. Activities include:
  - *Scheduling the inspection with the grower and conducting opening discussions to explain the inspection's purpose.*
  - *Performing inspection in accordance with the requirements of the 1989 Migrant Housing Act of North Carolina and 1910.142 OSHA standards.*
  - *Completing environmental analysis to determine hazards that may be present.*
  - *Informing the grower of items to be corrected. Coordinating related issues, such as water and sewer provisions, with local health officials.*
- Conduct comprehensive inspections of non-exempt establishments involving the identification, analysis, and documentation of safety hazards. Issue corresponding citations and penalties for violations. Compliance inspection activities include but are not limited to the following:
  - *Conducting initial management conference with head company representatives to explain purpose of inspection.*
  - *Evaluating and recording the establishment's injury and illness reports.*
  - *Conducting the inspection to recognize potential hazards.*
  - *Documenting all data that are apparent violations of current standards through photographs, sketches, reports and employee interviews to determine whether safety hazards exist that are not readily apparent.*
  - *Making recommendations to correct hazards.*
  - *Conducting closing conference with employer and representatives.*
- Complete post-inspection activities, including:
  - *Writing narrative reports thoroughly describing findings, conclusions and recommendations.*
  - *If the inspection is contested, participating in pre-hearing conference with attorney, preparing conference report, and testifying at contestment hearings.*
- Fulfill administrative responsibilities of the department, division, and bureau.
- Provide ongoing professional support to the department and division regarding safety and health matters by performing training activities of OSH Division employees, training for new compliance officers, public speaking engagements, technical assistance to employers and review of related publications and publication drafts.
- Maintain the Field Information System of OSHA policies and procedures to be followed by compliance officers and OSH personnel in the performance of duties. Prepare specialty reports and maintain contact with trade associations and industry groups to enhance awareness of safety and health issues.
- Update and edit Industry Guides for the Education, Training and Technical Assistance Bureau.

NORTH CAROLINA DEPARTMENT OF LABOR/OSH COMPLIANCE, Raleigh, NC
OSH Reviewer, 1980 – 1990

- Provided technical information for questions regarding citation issues. Evaluated employers' hazard-abatement efforts. Determined Bureau response to employers' petitions for modification of abatement. Made recommendations to management concerning Bureau response.
- Reviewed compliance reports for proper interpretation, application and referencing of relevant state/federal standards.
- Coordinated initial hearing of appeal cases from employers taking exception to enforcement actions.
- Evaluated and prepared North Carolina Occupational Safety & Health Division case files for disclosure and evaluation.
- Coordinated the Division's response to contestments. Interpreted and applied standards; evaluated precedents.

Further Information Available Upon Request

By the time Charles finished college, he had accumulated a lot of experience as a jewelry bench worker.

He took his degree and experience to New York City, where he secured a development position in a good-sized firm.

CHARLES ASHER 746 8th Ave. #2C • New York, NY 10019 • 212-657-7786 • jeweler@msn.com

Experienced Jeweler with product development and design experience

PROFILE

- Significant experience in jewelry bench work, design, and fabrication, with a broad understanding of the industry from design to production
- Highly organized, with excellent interpersonal, communication, multi-tasking and problem solving skills used effectively in fast-paced production environments
- Strong design, conceptualization, and development abilities

EDUCATION

Rochester Institute Of Technology, Rochester, NY
School of Imaging Arts & Sciences — School for American Crafts

- BFA, Metalcrafts, 1998, conferred with High Honors, minor in Philosophy
- Four-year intensive hands-on program in metals design and fabrication
- Commencement speaker, School of Imaging Arts & Sciences

PROFESSIONAL EXPERIENCE

Zurich International, New York, NY **1999 – Present**
Merchandising Dept. — Product Development

Coordinate design and production with Zurich factories in New York, Israel, and the Dominican Republic as well as external suppliers. Use well-developed industry knowledge and experience to troubleshoot production issues. Maintain a constant flow of communication to ensure accurate and timely production. Work with account executives on custom orders and special needs for key customers.

Maintain accuracy of reporting tools and special-project rush list to coordinate product development from concept through final revisions. Develop technical drawings. Monitor and enable the timely, prioritized completion of models, molds, parts, chains, samples, and prototypes. Evaluate production samples.

Monitor the flow of product and samples between the vault, sample room, sample shop, and merchandising area. Maintain accuracy of electronic inventory system used to track product moving through development. Conduct regularly scheduled physical inventory, proactively controlling and organizing its status through the reduction of daily inventories.

Troubleshoot manufacturing issues in the Gold Line. Assist model makers, jewelers, and designers with production, facilitating development of new and revised line items.

Fashion Jewelry, Rochester, NY **1998 – 1999**
Bench Jeweler

Key jeweler in this 3-store operation. Completed jewelry repairs, mechanical watch repairs, restoration work, fabrication, setting, and custom work.

Recommended and implemented an apprentice/internship program to solve recruitment and retention problems. Developed criteria and interviewed candidates. Trained them in jewelry techniques and shop customs and practices. As a result, the business gained well-trained, reliable employees.

Contractor, Rochester, NY **1996 – 1999**
Freelance and Contract Services

Provided design, fabrication, and repair services to several Rochester jewelers.

Ameon Gems, Austinburg, OH **1990 – 1994**
Apprentice (part time)

Learned techniques of bench work at this extensive gem shop, working informally with the owner approximately two afternoons weekly. Developed a good working knowledge of gemology.

References and Portfolio Available

This version of Charles' resume was prepared soon after he took his New York job, so he would be ready for his next opportunity.

341

Jeweler and precious stone and metal worker. *Bernice Antifonario, MA; Tewksbury, MA*

This resume is appropriately creative in language & presentation.

GEORGE THOMAS MARTIN, G.I.A.

125 Prairie Lane ◆ Lafayette, LA 70501 ◆ h(337) 233-4121 ◆ w(337) 988-2522 ◆ email: gtm14@hotmail.com

MASTER STONE SETTER

GIA Diamond Certification ◆ 30 years of experience in every facet of jewelry manufacturing.
Jewelers of America Certified ◆ Senior Bench Jeweler — 5th in U.S. to Receive Distinction.
Experienced Stone Setting Trainer/Presenter ◆ Published Author

Platinum *record for training and retaining employees.*
Diamond *in the rough, with* **polished** *presentation skills.*
*Function as guide to others, providing multi-***faceted** *technical instruction.*
Facilitate **crystal** *ideas by providing artistic experiences within the tradition of jewelry manufacturing.*
Self-starting, dependable, passionate, and honest employee with a **four-carat** *work ethic.*
Career success aided by a **genuine** *sense of humor and* **sterling** *reputation.*
*Will "***weight***" for* **golden** *employment opportunity*

Work History

STULLER SETTINGS, INC., Lafayette, LA
Master Stone Setter and Trainer, 1991 to Present

◆ ◆ ◆ ◆

Supervise 62 setters for multimillion-dollar international company. Advise Model, Tool & Die, Metal Mold, and Stone department managers. Consult with Research and Development department on regular basis. Set most complex pieces of jewelry in company. Contribute technical articles on stone-setting issues for company newsletter.

Accomplishments:
* *Created "Complete Setting Department Training System" and "Have It Your Way" program for setting.*
* *Published book "Stone Setting" for Stuller Settings.*
* *Promoted from Diamond Stone Setter in 1992.*

LAFAYETTE REGIONAL VOCATIONAL TECHNICAL INSTITUTE, Lafayette, LA
Stone Setting Trainer, 1995 to Present

◆ ◆ ◆ ◆

Created Stone Setting curriculum for local region in effort to help fill community economic and educational gap. Facilitated employment opportunities for newly trained top students at Stuller Settings.

Prior Experience

TRI-GEM ◆ Diamond Setter
N.C. HAHN ◆ Diamond Setter
ZELL BROTHERS ◆ Head Diamond Setter
ASSOCIATE JEWELERS ◆ Diamond Setter
ACTIVE MANUFACTURING JEWELERS ◆ Diamond Setter / Inventory Control
MARGUILIS JEWELRY ◆ Retail Sales
MILLERS INTERNATIONAL ◆ Apprentice Diamond Setter
SILVER BY LANNING ◆ Turquoise Setter

This resume was effective in helping George land a top-level job with a West Coast jewelry maker.

Continuing Education

STULLER SETTING COURSES
Zenger Miller Teams ◆ Don Sutton Management Course ◆ Ron Rayes Management Course

342

Jeweler and precious stone and metal worker. *Laurie J. Roy, CRW, CPRW, CCM, CCA, MBA; Lafayette, LA*

After 18 months of successful employment, Victoria was downsized as the result of cutbacks in the semiconductor industry.

VICTORIA FRANKLIN

5712 Roosevelt Way
Seattle, Washington 99330
Phone: 206-503-7446
Email: Vfranklin@pacbell.net

MANUFACTURING / QUALITY CONTROL — SEMICONDUCTOR INDUSTRY

This section highlights her good process skills and visual skills.

SKILLS

Manufacturing Processes	Visual Inspection	Machine Calibration
Categorization	Records and Reports	Clean Environments

PROFESSIONAL HIGHLIGHTS

2001–2002 XEROX MANUFACTURING — Seattle, Washington
Manufacturing Specialist — Quality Control
Ensured ISO 2001 quality specifications were met for the wafer-fabrication process in manufacturing micro-processing chips for commercial use.

➤ Used high-gain electronic microscopes to determine the degree of severity for scratches manufacturing residue; cleaned and repaired when possible.
➤ Appointed team lead in the absence of the supervisor; ranked second in hourly production, completing between two and five discs containing 5,000 chips per disc.
➤ Promoted to FSI Cleaning in a clean-room environment during the last month of employment.

2000–2001 INTEL — Seattle, Washington
Manufacturing Specialist — Quality Control
Ensured quality standards in the wafer fabrication process were met for one of the nation's leading chip manufacturers.

➤ Visually inspected wafers, initially conducting electronic inspections of "boatloads" of completed wafers and subsequently inspecting visually for defects.
➤ Ensured machine calibration prior to the quality assurance processes.
➤ Completed 20 to 25 "boatloads" of wafers hourly, classifying defects according to severity and type.

1997–1999 SAFEWAY — Phoenix, Arizona
Front End Cashier (college employment)
Promoted to manage the front end cashier operations for Phoenix volume leader. Established a two-year record of excellent checkouts, staff training and customer service.

➤ Noted, in annual performance reviews, for the ability to memorize product codes.

EDUCATION

EVERGREEN COMMUNITY COLLEGE — Seattle, Washington
Associate of Science (program) — Biology
Completed 30 hours toward degree.

Victoria's resume shows that she would fit in nicely in any manufacturing environment.

343

Electronic semiconductor processor. *William G. Murdock, CPRW; Dallas, TX*

This resume is for an individual who was relocating. She had worked for the same organization for fifteen years.

This graphic adds some punch to skills and accomplishments that are fairly routine in Deborah's profession.

Deborah K. Rather

5452 Fossil Creek Blvd.
Haltom City, TX 76137
Phone: (915) 222-6666
debkrather@hotmail.com

Technical Skills

Topography

Biometry

Visual Fields

Angiography

Keratometer, Lensometer,
and Radiuscope Readings

Auto Refractor

Peropter

Laboratory Skills

Basic modification of rigid
gas-permeable and
soft/disposable contact
lenses

Clean, polish, sterilize and
disinfect patient and stock
contact lenses

The format of this resume suits Deborah's outgoing personality!

Profile

Energetic, personable management professional with 15 years of experience as **OPHTHALMIC ASSISTANT** and **DEPARTMENT MANAGER** providing support services and educational information about ocular health. Excellent customer service skills and dedication to providing 110% effort in every endeavor. Experience working with diverse age groups ranging from children to senior citizens.

Work History

McFarland Clinic, PC, Abilene, TX 1983–Present
MANAGER, CONTACT LENS DEPARTMENT (1998–PRESENT)

Member of three-person management team providing related services in support of four ophthalmologists and one optometrist at Abilene's largest physician-owned multi-specialty clinic.

- Manage contact lens services for over 2500 customers annually. Supervise one contact lens technician.
- Order, maintain, and price contact lens inventory and customer prescriptions. Hold full decision-making authority to purchase inventory from sales representatives.
- File and maintain contact lens records, insurance claims, and product invoices.
- Assist ophthalmologist on monthly satellite clinic appointments for cataract biometrics.

CONTACT LENS TECHNICIAN (1986–1998)

- Fitted all contact lens patients (50–75 per week). Carried out and evaluated vision and specific contact lens tests. Only professional qualified to provide A-Scans.
- Assisted doctor in providing post-operative services to 30 cataract and refractive surgery patients every Friday.
- Performed laboratory work such as cleaning and maintaining contact lenses.
- Maintained accurate updated records, monitored inventory, and administered patient care.

Education

Associate of Science, Ellsworth Community College,
Abilene, TX

344

Ophthalmic laboratory technician. *Marcy Johnson, CPRW, CEIP;*
Story City, IA

This young man wanted to advance his career even though he had just a few years of experience and only two years of college.

Charles Brown

Everything in his resume had to be written on the positive side.

5555 Cape Drive
Atlanta, Georgia 30024
Phone 404-777-4047
cbrown-atlanta@aol.com

Qualified and Resourceful Document Management/Imaging Specialist

**Scanning — Records Management
Technical Specifications — Technical Problem-Solving**

PROFESSIONAL EXPERIENCE

Dell Information Services, Atlanta, Georgia
Account Manager / Project Manager

June 1999–Present

Sales and Service Excellence
- ❑ Design, develop, and market Document Management/Imaging solutions to small and medium-sized companies, governments, and nonprofits in the southeast United States and the Caribbean.
- ❑ Demonstrate ability to identify and resolve problems with expediency.
- ❑ Prepare RFPs for clients needing to put out bids. Possess excellent presentation skills.
- ❑ Committed to excellent service and customer satisfaction.
- ❑ **Increased revenues from $110k to $450k during a one-year period.**

Technical Competency
- ❑ Translate customer needs into technical and workable solutions. Proposals include needs assessment, hardware configuration, and software recommendations.
- ❑ Prepare scanned documents that work with other peripherals for complete customization.
- ❑ Serve client at the highest level of professional competence and uphold the confidentiality of privileged information.
- ❑ Install LaserFiche software/imaging servers and scanners.
- ❑ Provide end-user training and technical support.
- ❑ Write instruction manuals and manage projects for all systems sold.
- ❑ Serve as Imaging Consultant for Southern Corporation, a key client.

EDUCATION

The City Institute, Pompton Lakes, New Jersey
Data Center Support
AS400, Windows 95/98/NT, Word/Excel, LaserFiche Document Management

1999–2001

United County College, United, New Jersey
A.A.S. Business

1997–1999

ORGANIZATIONS

Member, AIIM (Association of Information and Image Management)
Member, ARMA (Association of Record Managers and Administrators International)

Using this resume, Charles received an excellent position that doubled his base salary.

345

Photographic press worker. *Anne G. Kramer; Virginia Beach, VA*

Transportation and Material Moving Occupations

Resumes at a Glance

Daniel J. Rodriguez

2291 Bryce Lane • Lake Havasu City, AZ 86403 • (520) 855-3285 • drodriguez@mohaveweb.com

APD Rated Airline Pilot and Certified Flight Instructor with experience teaching aboard Boeing aircraft simulators.

PROFESSIONAL PROFILE

> This section includes important information that would not necessarily be expected and that would not easily fit the format of the rest of the resume.

Over 30 years' experience with United Airlines; rated on 12 different aircraft. Former B757 flight simulator instructor and B777 in-flight captain. Safety-conscious with excellent public speaking skills. Willing to commute to base of operation.

FLIGHT TIME

Total time:	22,000+	Instrument:	15,000
Pilot in Command:	10,047	Second in Command:	9,700
Flight Engineer:	840		

Pilot in Command by Aircraft		*Second in Command by Aircraft*	
B777	1,169	**MD-88**	1,180
B727	2,080	**B737**	2,503
B757/B767	4,158	**DC-9**	3,170
MD-88	820	**DC-8**	1,879
DC-9	840		

These sections provide information that would be expected on a pilot's resume.

EMPLOYMENT

UNITED AIRLINES   Chicago, IL

B777 International Captain	1999–2002
B767ER Line Check Airman	1996–1999
B757/B767 Captain	1991–1996
B757 Simulator Instructor	1985–1991
MD-88 Captain	1985
DC-9 Captain	1984
MD-88 First Officer	1979–1984
B727 First Officer	1976–1979
DC-8 and DC-9 First Officer	1970–1976
DC-8 Flight Engineer	1970

MILITARY TRAINING

UNITED STATES AIR FORCE
Lockheed P-3 Pilot   1964–1969

EDUCATION

UNITED STATES AIR FORCE ACADEMY, Colorado Springs, CO
B.S. Astronautical Engineering

COMPUTER SKILLS

Windows 98 and ME, Word, WordPerfect, Netscape, Outlook Express, Internet Explorer, Quicken

KEYWORDS

Airline Pilot, Flight Simulator Trainer, McDonnell Douglas, Lockheed, Learjet

346

Pilot. *Susan Geary, CRW, CPRW; San Diego, CA*

Juan was a police officer whose job was to fly a helicopter. This resume was written to help him secure a job in aviation management.

JUAN ALVAREZ

238 Ormond Drive
White House, TN 37188   JuanAlva@bellsouth.net

Home (615) 672-4509
Pager (615) 518-9611

PROFILE

Juan's resume emphasizes his "real-world" flight experience, to give him an edge over candidates with general management experience.

➢ Strong desire to obtain a position in **AVIATION MANAGEMENT** and apply leadership and management skills for a progressive, quality-driven aviation industry leader.

➢ In-depth understanding of aviation operations acquired through "real-world" flight experience and professional training. Able to fully convey this expertise to customers, sales reps, and corporate management.

➢ Graduate-level instruction in research and evaluation, data collection, statistical analysis, technical writing, and report preparation. Computer skills include Microsoft Word and Excel.

➢ Highly-developed organizational and time-management skills. Specific experience in managing duty schedules and assigning priorities.

ACADEMIC PREPARATION

MASTER OF SCIENCE IN PUBLIC SERVICE MANAGEMENT — Dean's List   2000
Cumberland University — Lebanon, Tennessee

BACHELOR OF SCIENCE IN CRIMINAL JUSTICE   1992
Middle Tennessee State University — Murfreesboro, Tennessee

PROFESSIONAL TRAINING

INITIAL ENTRY ROTOR WING TRAINING — US Army — Fort Knox, Kentucky
- Warrant Officer Basic Course — 1995
- Warrant Officer Candidate School — 1994

EXPERIENCE HIGHLIGHTS

POLICE PILOT   1996 – Present
Metro Nashville Police Department — Nashville, Tennessee
- Airborne law enforcement and aerial patrol. Provide backup support for officers on the ground, vice surveillance, and VIP escorts.
- FLIR and spotlight searches for manhunts, escapee tracking, and missing persons.

GUNSHIP PILOT (APACHE) — Currently on inactive status   1993 – Present
US Army Reserves — Fort Knox, Kentucky

FLIGHT RATINGS

Apache Qualified
Aircraft Single-Engine Land Rating

Commercial Helicopter
Instrument Helicopter

347

Pilot. *Carolyn Braden, CPRW; Hendersonville, TN*

The military airfield where Kenneth worked was shut down, so he decided to try his hand in the civilian sector.

Kenneth Rice

6401-1 Meade Loop
Fort Riley, KS 66442
Email: ricek@riley.army.mil

Home: (785) 784-9568

Work: (785) 239-4419

OBJECTIVE

A position as an air traffic coordinator that will effectively use my ATC training and experience to efficiently, expeditiously, and safely control aircraft operations.

SUMMARY OF QUALIFICATIONS

Sixteen years' experience supervising and providing air traffic control (ATC) service to military and civilian air traffic at various locations worldwide. Managed daily operations of tactical and fixed-base ATC facilities averaging 5,000 to 10,000 aircraft operations per month. Supervised and provided technical guidance for up to 15 personnel. Two years' experience as Training and Operations Manager of a 120-man organization. One year at an FAA ATC Tower facility.

AIR TRAFFIC CONTROL

Initiated and issued Air Traffic Control clearances, advisories, and control information to IFR, VFR, and SVFR military and civilian aircraft in all phases of flight. Applied FAA and/or Army Air Traffic Control rules and regulations. Processed flight-progress strips and flight-plan data. Coordinated terminal and enroute flight information with other ATC facilities. Provided assistance to emergency aircraft by issuing specific instructions and information regarding downed/disabled aircraft.

MANAGEMENT

Organized and planned activities of Air Traffic Control facilities and verified compliance with Army and FAA standards. Administered the implementation of the facility training program for rated and trainee controllers. Prepared and processed technical, personnel, and administrative reports of facility operations and other activities. Coordinated ATC operations with the FAA and other Army ATC facilities within the United States and overseas.

ADMINISTRATION

Compiled and processed technical data, training, and administrative reports for 120 personnel dispersed in four remote locations. Developed and established an office procedure that ensured the collection and delivery of information in a timely manner. Used a computer system to process and update personnel information and administrative data. Prepared reports and statistical data for upper-level management using PowerPoint, Word, and Excel.

SUPERVISION

Supervised and provided technical guidance to subordinates in the accomplishment of their ATC and other military duties. Supervised the assembly/disassembly, movement, and installation of tactical ATC equipment and related components. Monitored the use and filing of publications, logs, records, and duty performance of assigned controllers. Encouraged others to attend college classes after duty hours.

348

Air traffic controller. *James Walker, MS; Fort Riley, KS*

Kenneth Rice

TRAINING	Cross-trained personnel in job-related duties that resulted in reduced supervisory requirements and improved the overall operational efficiency of the facility. Conducted extensive on-the-job training of trainee controllers, thereby reducing training and qualification time. Administered work evaluations to ensure individual proficiency and currency of qualifications. Conducted and coordinated formal training sessions.
SECURITY	Compiled and maintained records and rosters of personnel authorized access to restricted and hazardous areas. Performed inventories and physical security inspections of sensitive areas and equipment to include weapons. Coordinated periodic inspections of the organization's assets with the local Military Police authorities. Prepared and processed sensitive items reports to upper-level management officials.

EMPLOYMENT HISTORY

- Air Traffic Control Supervisor, U.S. Army, Fort Riley, KS, July 1999–June 2002

- Training and Operations Manager, U.S. Army, Weisbaden, Germany, July 1997–June 1999

- Detachment Commander, U.S. Army, Weisbaden, Germany, July 1995–June 1997

- Air Traffic Control Manager, U.S. Army, Ansbach, Germany, August 1991–June 1995

- Air Traffic Control Manager, U.S. Army, Camp Casey, South Korea, August 1990–July 1991

- Air Traffic Control Supervisor, U.S. Army, Fort Stewart, GA, June 1986–July 1990

EDUCATION

- Certificate, Hazardous Waste Operations Course, 40 hours, U.S. Army, Fort Riley, KS, 2001

- Honor Graduate, Advanced ATC Management Course, 9 weeks, U.S. Army, Fort Rucker, AL, 1997

- Associate Degree, Professional Aeronautics, Embry-Riddle Aeronautical University, Fort Rucker, AL, 1997

- Certificate, Flight Operations Course, Correspondence, U.S. Army Institute for Professional Development, Fort Eustis, VA, 1993

- Certificate, Limited Weather Observer Course, 30 hours, FAA, David Wayne Hooks Airport, Spring, TX, 1990

- Commandant's List, ATC Operator Course, 13 weeks, U.S. Army, Fort Rucker, AL, 1986

Kenneth landed a civilian position monitoring vehicle speed and location for a large trucking firm — in essence, using the same skills to control traffic on the ground rather than in the air.

Constance S. Baker

The attention-getting format of this resume matches Constance's job performance.

99108 Woolery Lane
Dayton, OH 45415
Home: 937.251.9128
E-mail: c_baker@jitaweb.com

Summary ▶▶ ▶▶ ▶▶ ▶▶ ▶▶ ▶▶ ▶▶ ▼

MATERIAL HANDLER / SHIPPING & RECEIVING

Certified & Licensed Forklift Operator ~ Shipment Management ~ Union Negotiations ~ Hazmat Certified

Warehouse operations and procedures professional with strong material handling skills — storage, movement, loading / unloading, stock levels, container requirements, safety, and equipment / forklift operation. Network with cross-functional departments relating to shipment accuracy and JIT delivery. Well-focused shipping and receiving clerk, ensuring thorough records maintenance on incoming cargo, tracking internal order processing, and handling outbound client orders.

▼ ◀◀ ◀◀ ◀◀ ◀◀ ◀◀ ◀◀ ◀◀ ◀◀ Skills & Abilities

Scheduling	Facility Design	Quality Control
Vendor Relations	Cargo Loading / Unloading	Shipping / Receiving
Employee Relations	Process Automation	Safety Compliance
Records Management	Material Storage	Shipment Preparation

▼ ◀◀ ◀◀ ◀◀ ◀◀ ◀◀ ◀◀ ◀◀ ◀◀ Professional Experience

ROSE TECHNOLOGIES, ENGLEWOOD, OH
(A precision and technological company specializing in welding, stamping, and assembly.)

SHIPPING & RECEIVING CLERK, 1999–present
Move materials from within the warehouse and loading areas to commercial delivery trucks. Track all inventory (raw / finished materials) entering and leaving the building.

- **Achievements include** — Chosen as Head Shipping Clerk; Member of the Safety Committee; and hand-selected to become the Union Representative.

UNION REPRESENTATIVE, 1999–present
Mediate incidents between personnel and company representatives, avoiding legal action when possible. Participate in monthly meetings covering all issues at hand. Notify personnel of continuing business and new points of interest.

MATERIAL HANDLER, 1996–1999
Monitored stock levels for each operating station — inventory, purchasing, records maintenance, material handling, workflow optimization, and ergonomic efficiency.

LEAD PRESSROOM OPERATOR, 1995–1996
Entrusted with lead operator responsibilities within several months; met quotas, monitored machine performance, and assisted fellow operators. Machinery — feed presses, automatic and spot welders.

▼ ◀◀ ◀◀ ◀◀ ◀◀ ◀◀ ◀◀ ◀◀ ◀◀ Industrial Equipment & Licenses

License, Englewood Valley Forklift
License, MB Corporation Forklift
Equipment certified — Belt Loaders, MOD-Clerk, Forklift (stand-up and walk-behind), TOG, K-loader, and Hysters

349

Material moving equipment operator. *Teena Rose, CPRW, CEIP, CCM; Englewood, OH*

NATHAN MacINNIS

101 Augusta Court • Detroit, Michigan 48219
(313) 333-4455 • nmacinnis@net.com

After a career in the family business, Nathan decided to pursue his passion for driving.

OBJECTIVE: **BUS DRIVER**

PRIMARY QUALIFICATIONS

LARGE-VEHICLE EXPERIENCE:
➢ Over 600,000 safe miles of large-vehicle driving experience throughout North America
➢ More than 85% of experience with over-size loads

VEHICLE LICENSING:
➢ CDL license — Class A
➢ Trailer and Air Brake endorsements

CUSTOMER SERVICE:
➢ Outstanding interpersonal skills — friendly, courteous, professional
➢ 11+ years' customer service experience — expert at problem solving, conflict resolution, and satisfying the customer
➢ Extensive experience representing a professional corporate image while attending and hosting public relations events

FLEXIBILITY / ATTITUDE:
➢ Comfortable working non-standard hours and shifts
➢ Professional, dedicated, and hard-working with a sincere love for driving

CPR / FIRST AID:
➢ Current (St. Johns Ambulance)

DRIVING EXPERIENCE

His earlier experience is not included since it is not relevant to his current goals.

BLAYLOCK COMPANY INC. / BLAYLOCK FLAGPOLE CO., Detroit, Michigan
A world leader in the manufacture and installation of large-scale flag and banner poles and custom steel fabrication for the steel mill industry.

Driver / Traffic Operations   1985–1992, 1993–Present
In addition to sales, marketing, and customer service responsibilities, additionally required to transport materials and finished products to client locations throughout Canada and the U.S.
• Transported a variety of large and over-size loads to locations throughout North America, personally logging over 600,000 safe driving miles.
• Negotiated transport rates and arranged all permits, bridge approvals, escorting, loading, and delivery.

PORTWINE DELIVERY SERVICE, Detroit, Michigan
80-vehicle transport firm servicing the automotive assembly and sub-assembly industries.

Driver   1992
• Transported automotive assembly parts throughout U.S. (18-wheel tractor trailers, closed-door vans).
• Personally managed all loading, transport, and unloading.

PRIOR EXPERIENCE includes more than 10 years in Purchasing, Account Management, and Traffic Operations including extensive interaction with government / licensing officials.

EDUCATION

Operations Management (Honors), Centennial College, Scarborough, Ontario   1983

Bus driver. *Ross Macpherson, MA, CPRW, JCTC, CEIP, CJST; Pickering, Ontario*

There really are locomotive engineers and here is a resume for a real one (with changed name and other details, of course).

TOM L. HARRIS
594 Oak Drive • Adrian, Michigan 49221
(517) 459-1278

CAREER OBJECTIVE

Perform the duties of a locomotive engineer, using teaching skills to train and instruct others in the skills required to be a locomotive engineer.

← a valuable "extra" skill related to his formal education

PROFESSIONAL EXPERIENCE

S & E RAILROAD, Adrian, Michigan
Engineer   1991-Present
- Maintain and operate two GP9 locomotives.
- Maintain and operate trains carrying agricultural products.
- Have had an FRA field observation with no exceptions noted.
- Instructed student engineers on operation of diesel locomotives and train-handling techniques.

FLYNN RAILROAD, Saginaw, Michigan
Engineer   July 1984-Present
- Operate and maintain two steam powered and one diesel locomotives.
- Conduct classes in railroad rules and safety regulations.
- Worked with four engineer trainees in engineer training program in both book and running portions of the program.
- Train new firemen in the art of firing a steam locomotive.

Fireman   1980-1984
- Maintained proper water and fire levels.
- Prepared the locomotive for daily service by cleaning the grates and ash pan.
- Greased locomotive and rebuilt fire.
- Completed 250 hours of engineer training course.

LICENSURE

Locomotive Engineers License

ADDITIONAL WORK EXPERIENCE

CLAYTON COMMUNITY SCHOOLS, Clayton, Michigan
Instrumental Music Instructor   1980-Present
- Increased student enrollment from 100 students, grade 5-12 to 207 students.
- Replaced and upgraded both the music library and school owned instruments.
- Designed and extended bids for new band uniforms.
- Chairperson of the Policy Committee and Career and Employability Committee.
- Guided an Associate Teacher from Adrian College through the final requirements of music major degree.

EDUCATION

SOUTHERN MICHIGAN UNIVERSITY, Coldwater, Michigan
Masters in School Administration   1984-1986

MICHIGAN UNIVERSITY, Clinton, Michigan
Bachelor of Music Education   1980

References available upon request.

351

Locomotive engineer. *Christina M. Popa, CPRW; Adrian, MI*

An easy-to-read format and clear depiction of expertise make this an effective resume.

RONALD K. BILLINGS
1859 McCandlish Road
Grand Blanc, Michigan 48439

810-555-6954
otrguy@tir.com

PROFILE
- ❑ Hold current CDL-Class A with Hazmat endorsement.
- ❑ Skilled in all facets of safe and defensive truck driving.
- ❑ Ability to independently resolve problems as they arise.

HIGHLIGHTS OF EXPERIENCE
- ❑ Accurately maintain log book and appropriate documentation (bills of lading, permits, etc.) in orderly manner to comply with DOT, Customs and other governmental requirements.
- ❑ Perform troubleshooting and general maintenance of vehicle as needed.
- ❑ Communicate with dispatcher via computer data network.
- ❑ Regularly receive safety and performance bonus based on violation-free record since January 1995.
- ❑ Provide excellent customer relations as company representative.

EMPLOYMENT HISTORY

Information here reflects a successful transition from the military.

STP Transportation Services, Inc. • Lansing, Michigan
Professional Truck Driver (1993-Present)
- Travel over 125,000 miles annually across the continental United States and several Canadian provinces.
- Familiar with customs procedures and regulations.

Adventure Travels • Davison, Michigan
Bus Driver (1979-1980)
- Operated chartered coach for primarily regional excursions.

MILITARY EXPERIENCE

United States Air Force
Sergeant - E4 (1980-1991)
- Trained in aircraft maintenance.
- Received honorable discharge.

EDUCATION & TRAINING

Professional Roadranger Training Institute • Grand Ledge, Michigan
- CDL-Class A Driver Training Certification (1993)
- Michigan Center for Decision Driving Course Certification (1993)

United States Air Force
- Numerous training sessions relating to aircraft maintenance and other relevant topics (complete list available on request).

Grand Blanc High School • Grand Blanc, Michigan
- Graduate (1977)

ACHIEVEMENTS
- ❑ Received numerous Air Force commendations (complete list available on request).

COMMUNITY INVOLVEMENT
- ❑ Parent Volunteer - Central Elementary School
- ❑ Boy Scout Troop

References furnished on request

352

Truck driver. *Janet L. Beckstrom; Flint, MI*

LLOYD MINNES

minnes@pacbell.net

1280 Cactus Lane
Barstow, CA 96784
Tel: 555-786-2040

This headline format makes Lloyd's expertise and interests crystal clear.

Truck Driver / Transportation / Logistics

◇ **Vehicle Operations** ◇
◇ **Technical Authority** ◇ **Maintenance Programs** ◇ **Driver Trainer** ◇

SUMMARY

Combined experience and knowledge of all aspects of fleet and load management, vehicle operations, and driver training. Innovative problem solver. Managed maintenance-shop supply requirements. Maintained line items and conducted inventories for fuel and petroleum products. Conducted liaison with drivers, management, and contractors, ensuring working relations. Implemented emergency procedures.

KEY ACCOMPLISHMENTS

This box is an attractive way to highlight these important activities.

- Coordinated dispatching for 150 vehicles and drivers. Maintained a current status on all dispatched vehicles. Successfully passed an Inspector General's inspection.
- Assessed customer needs and analyzed services, monitoring the efficiency and utilization of the vehicles.
- Improved receipt, storage, and issue procedures for shop operations and supply requirements.
- Managed a crew responsible for refueling operations for up to 460 vehicles per day.
- Operated a Packard Bell computer for dispatching operations.
- Participated in resurrecting stagnant maintenance programs.

EMPLOYMENT

Transport Operator (CDL, Issued: 1993)
Managed dedicated lines. Inspected vehicles. Corrected vehicle deficiencies. Provided instructions on commitments, time, reporting point, cargo, route, and destination. Compiled time, mileage, and load data. Verified vehicle logbooks. Applied experience gained in military service to civilian transport operations.

- **Dubliner Enterprises Inc., Certified Trainer (effective 01/1999) and Driver, 1999 to Present**
  Equipment: Qual Comm. 48-state and regional operation. Train and evaluate new drivers. Maintain vehicles.

- **Minnes Transport, Owner/Operator, 1997 to 1999**
  Equipment: Landstar Ranger. 48-state operation. Trained drivers, dispatched vehicles, monitored loads and shipments, and prepared payroll. Owned and operated a truck. Dispatched three drivers. Employed a computer dispatching system. Directed load-management procedures.

- **Buckly Company, Driver, 1995 to 1997**
  Equipment: Reefer and Dry Van. 48-state operation, including 11 western states. Received three safety awards.

- **Simpson Transportation, Driver Trainer, Line Haul and Trailer Shuttle Driver, 1993 to 1995**
  Managed a seven-truck fleet.

353

Truck driver. *Diane Burns, CPRW, IJCTC, CCM, CEIP; Columbia, MD*

MILITARY SERVICE

- **United States Marine Corps, Reserves, Motor Transport Chief & Training Coordinator, 1993 to Present, El Toro Marine Base, CA**

- **United States Marine Corps, Tractor-Trailer Fuel-Tanker Driver Supervisor, 1991 to 1993 Marine Corps Air Ground Combat Center, Twenty-nine Palms, CA**
  Training Supervisor, Dispatcher, Refueling Operations Coordinator (Clearance: SECRET)

- **United States Marine Corps, Vehicle Inspection Supervisor, 1988 to 1991 Camp Lejeune, NC**
  Dispatcher for 150 vehicles, Driver's Trainer, Supervisor

RELEVANT ACTIVITIES AND ACHIEVEMENTS

Logistics/Dispatcher

- Technical authority on fuel, water, general supply planning, and operational requirements. Logistically coordinated the dispatching, repairs, refueling, and shipments of 150 trucks. Supervised, planned, and organized work operations to maximize efficiency and utilization of time, equipment, and personnel. Strictly enforced fire and safety regulations.

- Directed loading and unloading of cargo. Operated and supervised operation of loaded and empty vehicles through various terrain and weather patterns. Loaded and unloaded bulk liquid and fuels.

Driver's Trainer

- Presented instruction and trained personnel in the proper operation of vehicles and in maintenance techniques for troubleshooting and recovery operations. Conducted practical exercises for personnel preparing to deploy to Saudi Arabia in support of Operation Desert Shield/Storm; successfully trained them in motor transport skills.

Equipment Maintenance

- Expert mechanic. Operated vehicles for diagnostic and safety inspection purposes. Diagnosed and troubleshot malfunctions of commercial vehicle systems and components. Inspected vehicles before, during, and after operation. Completed maintenance forms, reports, and records.

Shop Operations

- Managed quality control of returned vehicles. Organized and controlled shop supply-room operations. Performed minor repairs of parts.

MILITARY EDUCATION

- Basic Truck School (Vehicle Operations)
- Motor Pool Operations School (Vehicle and Driver Management)
- Vehicle Recovery Course
- Motor Transport Chief School
  (Motor Pool Maintenance, Dispatch, Personnel Management & Training)
- Marine Corps Leadership Course
- Dispatch Procedures for Motor Transport
- Semi-trailer Refueler Operator Course

AWARDS

Received highly notable awards in motor transport operations for excellence in training and leadership and for superior knowledge of motor vehicles, dispatching, and refueler skills including the Meritorious Mast (x 3) and a Secretary of the Navy Commendation.

Charlie wanted to offer his insider

Knowledge of import/ export shipping to manufacturers looking for more global possibilities...

For visual → interest, I used a double border and diamond bullets suggesting waves...

Charles Kane

165 Pleasant Avenue
Bayonne, NJ 00000
(201) 555-5555

✦✦✦ CAREER FOCUS ✦✦✦

International marketing or **traffic management** position for a manufacturer, wholesale distributor or high volume retailer. Willing to travel and/or relocate.

✦✦✦ QUALIFICATIONS ✦✦✦

Import/Export Operations

✦ Knowledge of worldwide origination points for all types of goods and the movement process through multiple trade lanes, including the Far East, Europe, Middle East, South America and Canada.
✦ Experience with the operational documentation procedures and regulatory compliance required to clear shipments through United States Customs.

Pricing and Contract Negotiations

✦ Instrumental in negotiating mutually beneficial contracts for any type of material being shipped to the United States from foreign ports.
✦ Skilled in marketing cost effective, timely and hassle-free cargo movement services to and from distributors abroad, including the pricing of oversized shipments.
✦ Proven capability as intermediary to facilitate the opening of overseas markets for domestic manufacturers.

Customer Service Management

✦ Strongly committed to quality in every aspect of internal and external customer service.
✦ Expertise in managing both people and projects, with the vision to strategize the action steps needed to attain long and short term goals.
✦ Confident team leader, successful in developing and motivating a culturally diverse administrative staff to work cooperatively by promoting open lines of communication.
✦ Recognized for maintaining working relationships built on trust and respect with numerous industry contacts, thereby contributing to profitability in a highly competitive market.

Technical Liaison

✦ Interface with systems staff to provide information from a management standpoint for the development of advanced capabilities, most notably: customer activity tracking; follow-through on complaints and inquiries; and acceleration of response to sales leads.
✦ Familiarity with the various features of the Microsoft Office suite for Windows to create text and graphic materials for management presentations.

354

Water transportation manager. *Melanie Noonan, CPS; West Paterson, NJ*

I used a functional format to emphasize his transferable skills and showed his career progression and detailed his accomplishments on this page (resume writer's comments).

Charles Kane

Page 2

✦✦✦ EMPLOYMENT ✦✦✦

AQUATERRA CONTAINER LINES, INC., Port Newark, NJ   1988 to Date
U.S. headquarters of one of world's largest transoceanic shipping companies.

Career Progression

SENIOR MANAGER, CLIENT RELATIONS	1994 to Date
MANAGER, PAN AMERICAN MARKETS	1992 to 1993
MARKET ANALYST, EUROPEAN GROUP	1991 to 1992
MARKET ANALYST, HONG KONG/TAIWAN	1989 to 1991
PRICING AND DOCUMENTATION REPRESENTATIVE	1988 to 1989

Accountabilities and Accomplishments

✦ Monitored daily activity of high volume accounts that generated at least $1 million in revenue per year. Opened and personally oversaw import activities for leading manufacturers of toys, consumer electronics and athletic footwear.
  ▷ Marketed target accounts to be pursued by sales representatives.
  ▷ Developed all pricing from U.S. East Coast to Far East destinations.
  ▷ Prepared weekly management reports of sales activities in targeted areas, which also included recommendations to overcome operational weaknesses.
  ▷ Submitted proposals considered feasible to management for consideration and allocation of funds.
✦ Supervised the service center with staff of 17 engaged in receiving and shipping cargo, documentation, waybilling, assessing charges, and collecting fees for shipments. Set their goals, motivated them to exceed performance standards, and supported their career development.
  ▷ Received departmental recognition by the company as its benchmark work group for maintaining a high morale and low turnover rate.
  ▷ Established improvements in communications between corporate staff, service center and outside sales force, which corrected serious inconsistencies with information flow.
  ▷ Developed new procedures for tariff rate filings to circumvent the obstacles caused by non filed rates.
✦ Effected staffing changes brought about by company's reorganization from regional to centralized functions early in 1994.
  ▷ Headed the work group to facilitate the adoption of the AquaTerra Quality System, based on the Philip Crosby Quality Awareness Program.
  ▷ Trained over 50 employees in the various modules of the process.
  ▷ Organized a committee to recognize individual employee contributions.

✦✦✦ EDUCATION ✦✦✦

Fairleigh Dickinson University, Teaneck, NJ
B.S. in Business Management, May 1988

Job Opportunities in the Armed Forces

Resumes at a Glance

Military-to-civilian transitions

JOSEPH P. BAUMGARTER

9224 Lily Avenue J19C • Indianapolis, IN 46224 • (317) 290-5555 • baumj18@hotmail.com

A successful individual with proven talent in developing and implementing training programs seeks position in Human Resources.

To assist in his transition to a civilian HR position, his human-resources skills are positioned prominently here.

SUMMARY OF QUALIFICATIONS

➤ Over 20 years' experience in Human Resources Management.
➤ Generate ongoing bottom-line savings through the introduction of various cost-cutting programs.
➤ Continuously update knowledge relevant to EEO, OSHA, and Sexual Harassment policies.
➤ Confident, flexible, dependable; gifted with innate ability to develop loyal and cohesive staffs dedicated to tasks at hand.
➤ Established record of progressively responsible positions of trust; earned security clearance at the highest levels of government.
➤ Adept at problem identification, research analysis, and resolution.
➤ Impeccable leadership, communications, and project-management skills.

HUMAN RESOURCES EXPERIENCE

This information is positioned here so the importance of his distinguished military career is not lost.

• Direct, plan, and implement entire human resources and information-technology training programs.
• Responsible for the training of **3,000 soldiers** per year; successfully increased ratio of soldiers passing Infantry Training Program by **104%** for the last two consecutive years.
• Accountable for training division of **8,000 soldiers;** provided technical support and instruction.
• Improved, established, and maintained 450-computer network system.
• Oversaw purchasing budget of **$2.4 million** and computer training for **4,200-soldier brigade.**
• Saved division **$250,000** by upgrading computer software programs versus purchasing new system.
• Revised division's work calendar to promote organizational and time-management skills; edited document from 15 pages to a concise 4, allowing for simple location of assignments.

WORK HISTORY

United States Army   1982–2002
• Highest rank achieved: **Master Sergeant.**
• Completed training in areas of international diplomacy and protocol.

Recognition:
Purple Heart, Expert Infantry Badge, Combat Infantry Badge, Legion of Merit for 20 years of service; Meritorious Service Medals awarded for superb performance of duty.

EDUCATION

Bachelor of Arts, Computer Science, Indiana University, 1989

ADDITIONAL TRAINING

Sexual Harassment Policy Training, 1999
Consideration of Others Program, 1999
OSHA Safety Training, 1998
Advanced Leadership Program, 1997
Instructors Training Program, 1997

COMPUTER SKILLS

Completing Microsoft Certified Systems Engineer Course. A+ Certification.
Microsoft Office Suite, IBM Hardware, Microsoft NT, dBase.

LANGUAGES

Fluent in English and Spanish.

355

Military to human resources. *Leah Brantley, CEIP; Cincinnati, OH*

Upon leaving the Marine Corps, Mr. Finley knew only that he wanted some type of management position.

Patrick M. Finley

A functional format allowed him to emphasize his three distinct areas of management-level expertise without getting bogged down in military terminology.

Finley1243@msn.com

21 Madison Avenue, #4-G
New York, NY 10021
Phone: 212-357-2322

PROFILE

Experienced and proven leader with exemplary, verifiable 11-year record with United States Marine Corps. Progressed rapidly from rank of Second Lieutenant to Major. Highly successful in managing personnel under extreme pressure. Adept multitasker. Supervised maintenance and coordination of multimillion-dollar equipment. Methodical, using analytical and mathematical skills in advanced technical and financial calculations. Reputation among supervisors as a reliable, hard-working team player.

EXPERIENCE

three distinct areas of management-level expertise

MANAGEMENT

- Directed operations of four separate infantry companies and supporting units consisting of 600 military personnel.
- Supervised maintenance of 10 departments and 12 fighter jets during Operation Southern Watch; kept planes damage-free during entire operation.
- Provided direction and decisive team leadership in carrying out complex assignments, which required development of loyal and cohesive staff dedicated to the task at hand.
- Managed flight instructor training program for F/A-18 and T-34 fighter aircrafts.

OPERATIONS AND LOGISTICS

- Personally responsible for planning, executing, and controlling all aviation-related support for demanding military maneuvers during Operation Desert Fox.
- Extensive planning and coordination resulted in success of largest peacetime Marine Corps Helicopter Assault (California) comprising 5,000 military personnel in three different zones.
- Consistently received outstanding ratings for quality-assurance inspections.
- Developed and implemented daily scheduling plans for 180 military personnel's training flights.

TRAINING AND DEVELOPMENT

- Trained 100+ students annually in air-to-ground flight tactics; acted as counselor and mentor.
- Created flight training syllabus for F/A-18 Training Squadron.
- Directed survival training, flight instrument checks, and air-combat qualifications programs.
- Designed training goals and requirements for infantry battalion.

WORK HISTORY

UNITED STATES MARINE CORPS   June 1990–June 2001

- Air-to-Ground Program Manager
- T-34 Program Manager
- Assistant Operations Manager

- Quality Assurance Manager
- Combat Tactics Instructor
- Fleet F/A-18 Pilot

DEPLOYMENTS: Japan – Kuwait – Persian Gulf – Indian Ocean

MEDALS AWARDED: Navy Achievement Medal – National Defense Medal – Sea Service Deployment Medal (2) – Armed Forces Expeditionary Medal (2)

EDUCATION

BACHELOR'S DEGREE – 1990 – Psychology and Business Administration   SUNY, Albany

■ ■ ■

356

Military to management. *Ilona Vanderwoude; Riverdale, NY*

3
P·A·R·T

JIST Cards, Cover Letters, Thank-You Notes, and Other Job Search Correspondence

Major Topics in This Part

Introduction

In this section I discuss everything you need to know about other written correspondence that you can use along with your resume in a job search. In particular, you learn about my invention, the JIST Card, as well as cover letters, post-interview thank-you notes, and other job search correspondence.

JIST Cards®

JIST Cards are a powerful job search tool I developed many years ago. Think of a JIST Card as a mini-resume or a special business card. A JIST Card is unique because it is a far more useful and effective job search tool than a resume and provides more information and impact than a business card.

Cover Letters, Thank-You Notes, and Other Correspondence

During the course of your job search, you will probably send out several kinds of correspondence. The most common type is the cover letter. Resumes are often accompanied by cover letters, which provide details that there isn't room to include in the resume.

As with resumes, a big mistake people make with cover letters is using them in a passive job search as a replacement for direct contact with employers. Instead, I suggest that the best time to use a cover letter is *after* you have made some personal contact with a potential employer by phone or in person.

Job search books often overlook several other forms of written communication that people use during a job search. Thank-you notes, for example, can make a big difference if you use them well during your search for a job. This section covers these and other forms of written job search communication.

JIST Cards:
A Powerful, Unique Job Search Tool

The best way to understand the impact of a JIST Card is to look at and react to one. The following is a sample JIST Card. Before you look at it, try to imagine that you are an employer who hires or supervises people with skills similar to those presented in the card that follows. Simply react naturally, as yourself, when you read what follows.

John Kijek   Phone Message: (219) 232-9213
                                            Pager: (219) 637-6643

Position Desired: Auto mechanic

Skills: Over three years of work experience, including one year in a full-time auto mechanic's training program. Familiar with all hand tools and electronic diagnostic equipment. Can handle tune-ups and common repairs to brakes, exhaust systems, and electrical and mechanical systems. Am a fast worker, often completing jobs correctly in less-than-standard time. Have all tools required and can start work immediately.

Prefer full-time work, any shift.

Honest, reliable, good with people.

How Do Employers React to JIST Cards?

Don't get too analytical about this. Just note how you reacted as the JIST Card information was presented to you in your imagined role as an employer. With that mind-set, answer the following questions:

1.   Do you feel good about this person and how he presented himself?

2. Would you be willing to see him if you had a job opening?

3. If he asked, would you be willing to see him even if you did not have a job opening?

The odds are good that you reacted positively to the JIST Card you read. Most people can read a typical JIST Card in less than 30 seconds. Yet in that short period of time, most people react positively to what they read. It's amazing, but most people are willing to set up an interview with just 30 seconds of information. I know this because I constantly survey those who attend seminars I give, and over 95 percent react positively to their first JIST Card. In fact, most people who read one say they would interview such a person based on just this small amount of information.

A few people do react negatively to the JIST Card you just read, saying that it does not present enough information or that the person sounds *too* good. It's true that a JIST Card does not present much information. It certainly does not give enough information to hire someone—but neither does a resume, application, or any other job search tool I know of.

Six Things a JIST Card Does

My observation is that a JIST Card's brevity is one of its major advantages. It is the only job search tool I know of that does all of the following:

- Creates a positive first impression

- Provides specific details about what a job seeker can do

- Presents performance-related information in a memorable way

- Provides an effective tool for generating job leads and presenting information

- Predisposes most readers to consider giving the job seeker an interview

- Makes the reader more likely to read the information because he or she can do it in less than 30 seconds

Some Ways You Can Use JIST Cards

JIST Cards can help you get results in a way no other job search tool can. I have seen them posted on a grocery store bulletin board in Texas and displayed on a table at a salon in Southern California. I've even had friends tell me they've found them under their windshield wiper after going to a movie. But here are some of the best ways to use them:

- **Give them to friends and relatives.** The odds are good that the people who know you best can't describe what you can do as clearly as a JIST Card can. Give some cards to the people you know best and ask them to give them to others who might know of openings for someone with your skills. Friends and relatives are a major source of job leads, and you can quickly get hundreds of your cards into circulation this way. This expands your network and increases the results dramatically.

- **Use them as business cards.** Like a business card, you can give your JIST Card to almost anyone you meet while you are looking for a job. For example, a job seeker gave a handful of JIST Cards to her insurance agent, who put them in his waiting room where customers could see them. This resulted in several phone calls from employers and one job offer. This is an excellent way to equip your network contacts with a tool they can use to help you.

■ **Send them to employers before interviews.** Send an informal note thanking someone for setting up an interview with you, and enclose a JIST Card. It's just enough to catch an employer's interest.

■ **Enclose them with thank-you notes after interviews or phone contacts.** Sending an informal thank-you note is simply good manners. Enclosing a JIST Card is good sense. It's just one more way to tell the prospective employer about yourself and give him or her a tool for contacting you. This approach has often resulted in the person who sent the thank-you note getting the job over candidates with better credentials.

■ **Attach them to applications.** When you have to complete an application, attach a JIST Card so that the employer quickly gets a positive overall impression. It can't hurt.

■ **Attach them to your resumes.** Unlike a resume, a JIST Card can be read in under 30 seconds. It provides a clear and direct presentation of what you want and what you can do.

■ **Send them with e-mail.** Include them as part of your e-mail text to prospective employers or as an attachment to your resume file.

■ **Use them as the basis for a telephone presentation.** With just a few changes, you can easily adapt your JIST Card to use as a telephone script for obtaining interviews.

■ **Use them to help answer interview questions.** A well-prepared JIST Card includes a variety of information you can use to answer interview questions. For example, in response to the question "Why don't you tell me about yourself?" you could say, "You might want to know that I am a hard worker...." Or you can select almost any key skill, experience, or accomplishment statement from your JIST Card and use it as the basis for answering many interview questions.

In fact, even though the JIST Card is an effective job search tool, I believe its greatest value is the way it forces you to get to the essence of what you have to offer an employer. Completing one can foster a sense of identity and self-definition that comes through in an interview. I have seen it happen and know that it is true.

■ **Look for creative ways to use them.** People have found some very creative ways to use their JIST Cards, and I encourage you to do so as well. For example, consider what might happen if you got the alumni list from your high school or college and sent 10 JIST Cards to each person on that list along with a letter asking for help in your job search. Think about it.

Seven Reasons JIST Cards Work So Well

Over the years, I have been continually surprised at how well JIST Cards work, and I have some thoughts on why this is so:

1. **They are short.** Because it takes less than 30 seconds to read, a JIST Card typically holds the reader's complete attention without interruption. Resumes, letters, applications, and conversations cannot do this. And, because they are short, they are "polite" and to the point, so that few people react negatively to the presentation.

2. **They are clear.** A JIST Card quickly communicates what it is about. It gets to the point quickly and efficiently.

3. **They create a positive impression.** Although well-crafted resumes or applications can also create a positive impression, they take longer to do so and often provide details that can be interpreted negatively (such as not having a degree or enough experience). A well-crafted JIST Card includes nothing that could be interpreted negatively, and most readers are left with a positive (although admittedly general) first impression.

4. **They are easy to pass along.** Because of their size and brevity, JIST Cards are far more likely to be passed along to another person than a resume or application. For this reason, people in your network use them in ways that they don't use more traditional tools. JIST Cards generate job leads in the hidden job market more effectively than any other job search tool I know of. Put a hundred of them in the right hands and they get around in unexpected ways.

5. **They are hard to file.** Resumes and applications get put away, thrown away, or lost in a pile. JIST Cards are less likely to be handled that way because of their format. Their small size also makes them likely candidates to be put on a bulletin board or someplace where they are seen.

6. **They are memorable.** Although I have been teaching people about JIST Cards for many years, this is a very big country, and they are new to most employers. The novelty of the format is memorable in itself, but employers also remember the content of a well-crafted JIST Card, particularly when you include one in a thank-you note. It tends to help an employer remember (and be positively impressed by) one person over another.

7. **They present the essence of what an employer wants to know.** In a compact format, a typical JIST Card accomplishes some important things:

    - It introduces you by name.

    - It provides one or more ways to contact you.

    - It clearly states your job objective.

    - It summarizes your key credentials, including relevant training and experience.

    - It presents the most important skills you have to do the job, often including specific accomplishments to support them.

    - It details any extra flexibility, such as a willingness to relocate or work weekends (an optional section).

    - It closes with a summary of important adaptive skills, personality traits, or other characteristics that make you a good choice for the job you seek, without any negatives.

A JIST Card can't replace a resume; it's simply different. I think its power to help generate leads in the hidden job market is justification enough for its use.

Tips on Creating Your Own JIST Cards

There is no doubt that JIST Cards are effective tools in the job search. Employers respond positively to them, and you can use them in ways you can't use traditional resumes. But you might also find that they are more difficult to create than they appear. That's because they are sophisticated in their simplicity.

If you have not done your homework, JIST Cards can be very hard to write. For example, you need to have a clear idea of your job objective and the skills that best support it. You might first need to do some self-assessment activities and find more information to help you sort out your job objective, skills, and other matters. But if you need to get on with your job search right away, consider doing a basic JIST Card now, and a better one later.

To create a good JIST Card, you must know yourself very well, know what sort of job you are looking for, and be able to sort through all your personal information to find the few words that best describe your ability to do that job. *It is essential that every statement on your JIST Card be both accurate and true.* Copying someone else's just won't do.

Writing an effective JIST Card requires some time on your part. The tips that follow will help you create each section of the card. As you assemble your card, consider asking others for feedback before you create your final version.

The Anatomy of a JIST Card

Take a look at the pieces that make up this JIST Card:

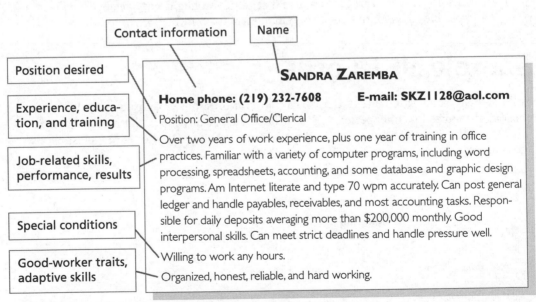

A JIST Card doesn't contain many details, but consider what Sandra Zaremba's card includes:

- **Identification.** Sandra's name is given.

- **Two ways to make contact.** Sandra lists two ways she can be reached: a home phone number and her e-mail address. Employers want to reach you quickly, so include at least two ways you can be contacted. Because employers usually won't write a letter, don't give your address. Instead, list two of these: a regular phone number, a cell phone number, a pager number, or an e-mail address. If you give a phone number, make sure the phone is answered professionally by a person, voice mail, or an answering machine!

- **Position.** Sandra includes a broad job objective. This will allow an employer to consider her for many jobs.

- **Length of experience.** Sandra lists her total length of work experience. Some of this experience was in part-time and volunteer jobs, something she can explain in an interview.

- **Related experience, education, and training.** Sandra lists her training along with her experience to give a longer total of work and training time. A person with more experience could use more detailed statements or separate sentences to emphasize more substantial education or training.

- **Job-related skills, performance, and results.** This section tells a little about what Sandra can do and how well she can do it. She describes important job-related skills for doing this work. Sandra mentions the key adaptive and transferable skills she learned or used in her work and other experiences. Note that she includes several numbers. The first is "70 wpm," which means she types quickly at 70 words per minute. She states that she was responsible for $200,000 of cash deposits each month. This tells employers that she can be trusted with substantial responsibility.

- **Special conditions.** Sandra mentions that she is willing to work any hours. This shows that she is flexible and willing to work.

- **Good-worker traits/adaptive skills.** Sandra lists her key adaptive skills and personality traits that would be important to an employer. And she does all of this on a 3-by-5 card! If you hadn't seen it, you might not have believed it was possible to do all this in such a small format—but there it is.

Sample JIST Cards

Following are some sample JIST Cards. They are for different jobs, from entry-level to those that require lots of experience. Study them and use any ideas that help you write your own JIST Card. Although you can type or even hand-write your cards, most people use a desktop computer and laser printer.

Jonathan McLaughlin
Answering machine: (509) 674-8736
Cell phone: (509) 541-0981

Objective: Electronics—installation, maintenance, and sales

Skills: Four years of work experience, plus two years of advanced training in electronics. AS degree in Electronics Engineering Technology. Managed a $500,000/year business while going to school full time, with grades in the top 25%. Familiar with all major electronics diagnostic and repair equipment. Hands-on experience with medical, consumer, communications, business, and industrial electronics equipment and applications. Good problem-solving and communication skills. Customer service oriented.

Willing to do what it takes to get the job done.

Self-motivated, dependable, learn quickly.

Jonathan is a new graduate from a two-year technical program. He was always interested in electronics, but worked in unrelated food service and construction jobs for three years after high school. He then got a job helping the owner of a TV and electronics repair shop. His job there was to answer phones, keep things clean, and other simple tasks. But he volunteered to fix things and the owner started to show him how to do more complex repairs—and encouraged him to go back to school. Jonathan worked at the electronics shop for three years and the owner let him schedule his work time so he could go to school, too. He eventually landed a job with a circuit board design and manufacturing company and now earns about three times what he had been earning.

Andrea Scott

Answering machine: (639) 298-9704
E-mail: andys@hotmail.com

Position Desired: Warehouse Management

Skills: Three years of experience plus two years of formal business coursework. Have supervised a staff as large as eight people and warehousing operations valued at over $4,000,000. Automated inventory operations resulting in an estimated annual savings of over $25,000. Working knowledge of accounting, computer systems, and advanced inventory management systems.

Will work any hours.

Responsible, hard working, and can solve problems.

Andy got her work experience in the military, where she was responsible for warehouse operations for an infantry unit. Her business education includes high school courses, military training, and some college-level courses she took while in the military. It was enough for her to land a job with Federal Express, where she now supervises 14 workers.

M A R I A   M A R Q U E Z

Home: (213) 432-8064 • Messages: (213) 437-9836

Position Desired: Hotel Management

Two years of experience in sales, catering, and food service in a 300-room hotel. Associate degree in Hotel Management, plus one year with the Boileau Culinary Institute. Doubled revenues from meetings and conferences and increased dining room and bar revenues by 44%. Have been commended for improving staff productivity and courtesy and received several promotions. I approach my work with effort, imagination, and creative problem-solving skills.

Enthusiastic, well-organized, detail-oriented.

Maria took some college courses at night while she worked at a local hotel. She did not start with a goal of hotel management, but ended up with a two-year degree in that field. She can't afford to go to school full time (she has family responsibilities), but wants to eventually get a four-year degree in business. She figures she can earn more money with her experience now and used this JIST Card to help her find a better job with the flexible schedule she needs to keep going to school.

Jafar Browning

Home: (846) 299-3643 • Pager: (846) 517-4525
E-mail: JMB0928@aol.com

Objective: Sales or business position requiring skills in problem solving, planning, organizing, and customer service

Skills: Two years of work experience plus coursework in business, sales methods, customer service, and business software. Promoted and received several bonuses for performance. Set record for largest single sale exceeding $130,000. Consistent record of getting results. Excellent communication skills. Familiar with database, word processing, and spreadsheet programs. Internet literate. Enjoy challenges and accept responsibility.

Willing to relocate.

Results-oriented, good problem-solving skills, energetic.

Jafar does not have formal education beyond high school but is smart and very good with people. He used these adaptive and transferable skills in sales, where he could earn good pay. He landed a position selling telecommunications services to businesses. His earnings have almost doubled from his previous job.

Lisa Marie Rhodes

E-mail: MLRhodes@earthlink.net
Phone: (424) 351-5935

Position desired: Internet startup or other Web-based business

Actively involved in intensive computer use and Web site development for more than four years. Familiar with all major software used in designing business-oriented Web sites, including graphics, interactive databases, credit card transactions, and security, firewall, virus, and other hacker-protection schemes. Excellent writing, grammar, and design skills. Did entire programming and design of a business-to-business e-commerce site and, over 12 months, grew it to annual sales of $620,000 before it went public.

Will consider contract work.

I work quickly and am persistent in finding solutions to complex problems.

Lisa is a recent high school graduate who learned most of her Web skills on her own. She did everything she says here by working at home on contract after school and in the summer. She wants to continue on to college and do Web design "on the side."

TOM ABLE

Cell phone at 872-924-6794 or e-mail at Tomable@juno.net

Job Objective: Responsible accounting or bookkeeping position

Skills: Four years of related work experience and training. Experienced with computerized accounting systems, spreadsheets, database programs, and report extraction programs. Practical experience in order entry, accounts payable, accounts receivable and collections, reconciling check and cash accounts, and posting to general ledger. Did full-service bookkeeping for a small business with sales of $900,000 and handled a variety of accounting functions in a large manufacturing company.

Can work any hours.

Well-organized, problem solver, willing to relocate.

Tom is a high school graduate who took business courses in school and learned the rest on the job. He took several temporary accounting positions until one of them was offered to him as a full-time position. He accepted and has had several promotions since.

JOHN HAROLD

Home: (619) 433-0040

E-mail: jh@eastern.com

Objective: Responsible Business Management Position

Skills: Over 7 years of management experience plus a degree in Business. Managed budgets as large as $5 million. Experienced in cost control and reduction, cutting more than 20% of overhead while sales increased almost 30%. Good organizer and problem-solver. Excellent communication skills.

Prefer responsible position in a medium-to-large business.

Cope well with deadline pressure, seek challenge, flexible.

John has lots of experience and great credentials. He accepted a job running a small window-manufacturing company that is now growing rapidly.

The JIST Card Worksheet

This worksheet provides instructions to help you write your own JIST Card. Read the instructions carefully, and then complete each section of the worksheet as well as you can. Later, you can use this worksheet to write your final JIST Card.

Your name _____

Tip: Keep this simple and professional. Don't use nicknames, middle names, or initials.

Contact information _____

Tips: Try to include two ways for an employer to contact you. Include a telephone number that will be answered all the time. Always include your area code. If you use an answering machine or voice mail, make sure it does not have a silly greeting. If the phone is at home, make sure anyone who might answer it knows how to take accurate messages. Include a cell phone or pager number if you have one. Including an e-mail address helps communicate that you are Internet literate.

Job objective _____

_____

Tips: Don't be too narrow in your job objective. Say "general office" rather than "receptionist" if you would consider a variety of office jobs. If you are specific in your job objective, try to avoid a narrow job title but give other details. For example, say "Management position in an insurance-related business" or "Working with children in a medical or educational setting."

Don't limit yourself to entry-level jobs if you have potential or interest in doing more. If you say "office manager" instead of "administrative assistant," you just might get a more responsible and higher-paying job. If you are not too sure of your ability to get a higher-paying job, it is still best to keep your options open if possible. Say "office manager or responsible secretarial position," for example.

Your Experience Statement

Writing your experience statement is a tricky matter for some people. I hope the following tips will help. The first set of tips will help you do the calculation that follows. Read those tips before adding up "your total experience."

Your total experience. Write years (or months, if you don't have much experience) in the spaces beside each question.

a. Total time paid work   _____

b. Total time volunteer work   + _____

c. Total time informal work   + _____

d. Total time related education
   or training   + _____

Your total experience   = _____

Tips for adding up your total experience. Take advantage of all the experience you have that supports your job objective. If you are changing careers, have been out of the work world for a while, or do not have much work experience, you will need to use other experiences to convince the employer you can do the job. Depending on your situation, you can include any or all of the following as part of your work experience:

- **Paid work.** You can list any work you were paid to do. The work does not have to be similar to the job you are looking for now. Baby-sitting and lawn-mowing jobs count. So does working at a fast-food place. If you worked part time, estimate the total number of hours you worked. Divide this total by 160 hours to get the number of months you worked. Of course, paid work that is directly related to your job objective is the best, if you have it.

- **Volunteer work.** You can include volunteer work as part of your total work experience. It counts, and you should list it if you don't have much paid work experience.

- **Informal work.** Include work you did at home or as an unpaid hobby. It is best if this work relates to the job, but it doesn't have to. For example, if you worked on cars at home and want to be an auto mechanic, there is an obvious connection. You may have experience working in the family business. This is real experience and, if it can help you to use it, do so.

- **Related education and training.** If you took courses in high school or college that relate to the job you want, you can count this as part of your total experience. You can also count any courses or training you received in the military, business or technical school, or anywhere else. If they relate in some way to the job you want, they can count.

Now, go back and complete the information under "Your total experience" on the previous page.

Tips for writing your experience statement. Because everyone has a different background, no single rule works. Here are some tips for writing your JIST Card experience statement:

- **If you have lots of work experience.** If some of this experience is not related to the job you want, you can leave it out. if you have 20 years of experience, say "over 15" or include just the experience that directly relates to the job you want. This keeps the employer from knowing how old you are. Your age is an advantage you will present in the interview!

- **If you don't have much paid work experience.** You need to include everything possible. If you have no paid work experience related to the job you now seek, emphasize your education, training, and other work. For example, "Nearly two years of experience, including one year of advanced training in office procedures." Remember to include the total of all paid and unpaid work as part of your experience! Include all those part-time jobs and volunteer jobs by writing "Over 18 months of total work experience."

- **If your experience is in another field.** Mention that you have "Four years of work experience" without saying in what field.

- **Other.** If you won promotions, raises, or have other special strengths, this is the time to say so. For example: "Over seven years of increasingly responsible work experience, including three years as a supervisor. Promoted twice."

(continues)

(continued)

Look over the sample JIST Cards for additional ideas, then write your own statement below.

Your experience statement _____

_____

_____

_____

_____

Your Education and Training Statement

Depending on your situation, you can combine your education and training with your experience. Several of the sample JIST Cards do this. Or you can list your education and training as a separate statement.

Don't mention your education or training if it doesn't help you. If you have a license, certification, or degree that supports your job objective, mention it here. For example: "Four years of experience plus two years of training leading to certification as an Emergency Medical Technician."

Look over the sample JIST Cards for more ideas and write your own education and training statement. If you want, you can revise your previous experience statement here to include your education and training.

Your education and training statement _____

_____

_____

_____

_____

Your Job-Related Skills Statement

In this section, you list the things you can do to support your job objective. If appropriate, mention job-related tools or equipment you can use. Use the language of the job to describe the more important things you can do.

Emphasize results. It is best to use some numbers to strengthen what you say. For example, instead of writing "can do word processing," state "accurately word-process 80 words per minute and am familiar with advanced graphic and formatting capabilities of Microsoft Word and PageMaker." It is too easy to overlook the importance of what you do. Add up the numbers of transactions you handled, the money you were responsible for, and the results you got. Here are a few examples:

- A person with fast-food experience might write, "Have handled over 50,000 customer contacts with total sales of over $250,000 quickly and accurately." While many think that a "lowly" job like those in fast food are not worthy ones, these jobs often require hard work, speed, and advanced skills. The figures are based on a five-day workweek, 200 customers a day for one year, and an average sale of $5. Impressive numbers, when presented in this way. You don't have to mention that this was done in a fast-food job.

■ Someone who ran a small store could say "Responsible for business with over $150,000 in sales per year. Increased sales by 35% within 18 months."

■ You could present a successful school fund-raising project as "Planned, trained, and supervised a staff of six on a special project. Exceeded income projections by 40%."

You should also include one or more of your transferable skills that are important for the job you want:

■ Someone with reception, customer service, or sales experience might add "Good appearance and pleasant telephone voice."

■ A warehouse manager might say "Well organized and efficient. Have reduced expenses by 20% while orders increased by 55%." It is certainly OK to give numbers to support these skills, too!

Think hard about your experiences and try to include numbers and results. Look over the sample JIST Cards for more examples of this and write your own statement below.

Your job-related skills statement _____

_____

_____

_____

Special Conditions or Preferred Working Conditions

This is an optional section. You can add just a few words—one or two lines at most—to let the employer know what you are willing to do. Do not limit your employment possibilities by saying "Will only work days" or "No travel wanted." It is better to not include this information than to state something negative.

Look at the sample JIST Cards for ideas. Then write your statement below.

Your preferred working conditions statement _____

_____

_____

Your Good-Worker Traits Statement

List three or four of your key adaptive skills. Choose skills that are most important in the job you are seeking. Be certain you do have them! Refer to page 26 in part 1 for your list of key adaptive skills. The sample JIST Cards also will give you ideas. Then list the skills you will include on your JIST Card.

Your good-worker traits statement _____

_____

_____

The Final Edit

To fit all this information on a 3-by-5-inch card, you will probably need to edit what you've written. Here are some tips to help you write the final version of your JIST Card:

- **Make every word count.** Get rid of anything that does not directly support your job objective.

- **Use short phrases.** You don't have to use complete sentences. Remember, every word has to count, so cut unnecessary words.

- **Add more information if your JIST Card is too short.** But add things only if they make your statements stronger.

- **Cut anything that is not a positive.** Get rid of anything that does not present you in a positive way.

- **Handwrite or print your content on a 3-by-5 card.** This will help you see whether you have included too much or too little information. Edit it again as needed to make it fit.

- **Read your JIST Card out loud.** This will help you to know how it sounds and may give you additional ideas to improve it.

- **Ask someone else to help you with the final version.** He or she may make some good suggestions, but make your own final decisions.

- **Check it one more time.** Make sure your final version does not have spelling, grammar, and other errors. One error can create a negative impression and undo all your hard work!

Tips to Produce and Reproduce Your JIST Card

Here are a few tips for getting your JIST Card produced in its final form:

- **You want to put lots of JIST Cards in circulation.** Although you can type or even handwrite individual JIST Cards, it is best to have them printed in quantities of at least 100 to 500.

- **If you have a computer and a high-quality printer, it is probably best to print your own JIST Cards.** If you don't have access to a computer and good printer, you can get this done at most print shops for a modest fee.

- **Be sure that no new errors were introduced in the final version.** Make sure that phone numbers, e-mail addresses, and other details are correct and that no new typographical errors have crept in.

- **You can fit five copies of the same JIST Card on one standard sheet of $8^1/_2$-by-11 paper.** Doing this allows you to copy or print multiple sheets in the most efficient way. Of course, you will need to cut the sheets down to the correct size of the individual cards. Good office-supply stores also have regular page-size sheets "micro-perforated" so that you can easily tear them into 3-by-5 cards. This enables you to do the cards on your own computer without having to cut the sheets yourself.

- **Use "light card stock," not paper, for your JIST Cards.** It is the same thickness used for a standard 3-by-5 card. Office-supply stores often carry it in a range of colors in standard 8½-by-11 paper that will work in most copy machines and laser printers.

- **I like off-white, ivory, or cream-color JIST Cards.** They give the cards a professional appearance. You can use other light pastel colors such as blue, gray, and others. For most purposes, I do not suggest pink, red, or green.

- **A good-quality photocopy machine can print copies of your JIST Cards.** Make sure that the copy quality is excellent and that it will handle light card stock without jamming.

- **Most good print shops also can print your JIST Cards (and resumes) on high-quality printing equipment.** They usually have a selection of card stock and paper. They may also have matching paper to give you a coordinated look for your resumes, JIST Cards, thank-you notes, and envelopes.

- **Look in the Yellow Pages for sources of printing and word processing.** Check under headings such as Printers, Resume Services, Typing Services, and Secretarial Services. Call in advance and ask for approximate prices for what you need to have done.

- **You will often save time and money by having your resume and JIST Cards prepared at the same time.** But do this only if writing your resume does not delay the start of your job search—and distribution of your JIST Cards.

Get Your JIST Card in Circulation

Once you have your JIST Card, use it! Give away hundreds freely because they will not help you get a job if they sit on your desk. The more JIST Cards you have in circulation, the more people know about you and your skills. Try them, they work.

Cover Letters, Thank-You Notes, and Other Job Search Correspondence

I n addition to resumes and JIST Cards, your job search will require you to create and use several other types of correspondence. The following sections give tips on how to use cover letters, thank-you notes, and other job search letters to your best advantage.

Writing and Using Cover Letters

It is not appropriate to send a resume to someone without an introductory letter or note attached to it. The traditional way to handle this is to send a letter along with your resume—known as a cover letter. Depending on the circumstances, the letter would explain your situation and ask the person who receives it for some specific action, consideration, or response. You would use this same basic approach if you were sending your resume over the Internet because your e-mail would take the place of your "cover letter."

Some job search books go into great detail on how to construct a "powerful" cover letter. Some even suggest that a cover letter can replace the resume entirely, providing similar information but specifically targeting the person who is receiving it. Although there is merit to these ideas, my objective here is to provide a simple, quick review of the basics of writing and using cover letters.

Although many situations require a formal cover letter, there are many others in which a simple note will do. See "Other Job Search Correspondence," later in this chapter, for additional information on notes.

Eight Guidelines for Writing Superior Cover Letters

No matter what the situation, virtually every good cover letter should follow these guidelines.

Write to Someone in Particular

Never send a cover letter to "To whom it may concern" or use some other impersonal opening. We all get enough junk mail; if you don't send your letter to someone by name, it *will* be treated as junk mail. When using the Internet, try to get a specific person's Web address to send your e-mail and resume to.

Make Absolutely NO Errors

A quick way to offend someone (or to make yourself look ignorant) is to misspell a name or use an incorrect title. If there is any question, call to verify the correct spelling of the name and other details before you send the letter. Review your letters carefully to be sure that they don't contain any typographical, grammatical, or other errors. This is also true with e-mail, where poor writing can quickly create a negative impression.

Personalize Your Content

Those computer-generated letters that automatically insert your name never fool me, and I find cover letters written this way a bit offensive. Although I know that some job search books recommend sending out lots of "broadcast letters" and e-mail to people you don't know, I suggest that doing so is a waste of time and money. If you can't personalize your correspondence in some way, don't send it. Find a way to tailor the information to the situation and the person who will be reading it.

Present a Good Appearance

Your contacts with prospective employers should always be professional. Buy good-quality stationery and matching envelopes. The standard $8^1/_2$-by-11 paper size is typically used, but you can also use the smaller "Monarch"-size paper with matching envelopes. Use only good-quality paper; I prefer a white, ivory, or light beige.

This is business correspondence, so don't write a cover letter by hand. A computer with high-quality printer is a must. If you are sending it as e-mail, take extra time to make sure it looks good.

Use an Appropriate Format

Any standard business correspondence format is acceptable. Look at the sample cover letters later in this chapter for ideas.

Provide a Friendly Opening

Begin your letter with a reminder of any prior contacts and the reason for your correspondence now. The examples will give you some ideas on how you can handle this.

Target Your Skills and Experiences

To do this well, you must know something about the organization or person with whom you are dealing. Present any relevant background information that may be of particular interest to the person.

Define the Next Step

Don't close your letter or e-mail without clearly identifying what you will do next. I do not recommend that you simply leave it up to employers to contact you because that really isn't their responsibility.

To Whom Do You Send a Cover Letter?

If you think about it, there are only two groups of people to whom you might send a resume and cover letter. They are

- People you know

- People you don't know

I know this sounds simplistic, but it's true. And this observation makes it easier to understand how you might handle a letter to each of these groups.

Writing a Cover Letter to Someone You Know

It is best if the person to whom you are writing has already met you. Written correspondence is less effective than personal contact, and it is always better to send a resume and cover letter to someone you have spoken to directly.

For example, it is far more effective to first call or e-mail someone than to simply send an unsolicited letter and resume. There are also the Yellow Pages, personal referrals, Internet directories, and so many other ways of making direct contact. So let's assume you have made some sort of personal contact before sending your resume. Within this assumption there are hundreds of variations, but here I'll review the most important ones and let you adapt them to your own situation.

Four Situations for Sending Cover Letters to People You Know

There are four situations in which you might send out a cover letter to someone you know. Each presents an approach that you can use in getting interviews. Getting interviews and job offers is the real task in the job search—not sending out resumes and cover letters. Look at the sample cover letters in the pages that follow and see how, in most cases, they assume that a personal contact was made *before* the resume was sent. The situations follow, along with an explanation of each.

Situation 1: An interview is scheduled and there is a specific job opening that interests you.

In this case, you have already arranged an interview for a job opening that interests you. The cover letter should provide details of your experience that relate to that job.

Situation 2: An interview is scheduled, but no specific job is available.

In this case you would send a letter before a scheduled interview with an employer who does not have a specific opening for you now but who might in the future. This is fertile ground for finding job leads where no one else is looking.

Situation 3: After an interview.

Many people overlook the importance of sending a letter *after* an interview. This is a time to say that you want the job (if that is the case, say so!) and to add any details of why you think you can do the job well.

Situation 4: No interview is scheduled yet.

There are times when you just can't arrange an interview before you send a resume and cover letter. In these cases, a good letter allows you to follow up more effectively.

Sample Cover Letters to People You Know

I've included a sample cover letter for each of the four situations involving people you know. Note that they use different formats and styles. Each letter addresses a different situation, and each incorporates all of the cover letter guidelines presented earlier.

Preinterview, for a Specific Job Opening

The writer called first and arranged an interview—the best approach by far. Note how this new graduate included a specific example of how he saved money for a business by changing its procedures. Although it is not clear, his experience dealing with lots of people was gained working as a waiter. Note also how he included skills such as "hard worker" and "dealing with deadline pressure."

Richard Swanson

113 S. Meridian Street
Greenwich, Connecticut 11721

March 10, 2003

Mr. William Hines
New England Power & Light Company
604 Waterway Blvd.
Darien, Connecticut 06820

Dear Mr. Hines:

I am following up on the brief chat we had today by phone. After getting the details of the position you have open, I am certain it is the kind of job I have been looking for. A copy of my resume is enclosed, providing more details of my background. I hope you have a chance to review it before we meet next week.

My special interest has long been in the large-volume order-processing systems that your organization has developed so well. While in school, I researched the flow of order-processing work for a large corporation as part of a class assignment. With some simple and inexpensive procedural changes I recommended, check-processing time was reduced by an average of three days. For the number of checks and dollars involved, this one change resulted in an estimated increase in interest revenues of over $35,000 per year. Details do count!

Although I have recently graduated from business school, I do have considerable experience for a person of my age. I have worked in a variety of jobs dealing with large numbers of people and deadline pressure. My studies have also been far more "hands-on" and practical than those of most schools, so I have a good working knowledge of current business systems and procedures. This includes a good understanding of various computer spreadsheet, word processing, and other business programs; the use of automation; and experience with cutting costs and increasing profits. I am also a hard worker and realize I will need to apply myself to get established in my career.

I am most interested in the position you have available and am excited about the potential it offers. I look forward to seeing you next week.

Sincerely,

Richard Swanson

Richard Swanson

Email: Rswan@energy.com

Preinterview, No Specific Job Opening

The writer of this letter first called and set up an interview as the result of someone else providing the employer's name. The writer explains why she is moving to the city and asks for help in making contacts there. Although there is no job opening here, she is wise in assuming that there might be one in the future. Even if this is not the case, she asks the employer to think of others who might have a position for someone with her skills. If the interview goes well and the employer gives her names of others to call, she is on her way to developing a good network of contacts.

ANNE MARIE FURN
616 Kings Way, Minneapolis, MN 54312
(612) 823-4593
annemariefurn@aol.com

February 10, 2004

Ms. Francine Cook
Park-Halsey Corporation
5413 Armstrong Drive
Minneapolis, Minnesota 54317

Dear Ms. Cook:

When Steve Marks suggested I call you, I had no idea you would be so helpful. I've already followed up with several of the suggestions you made and am now looking forward to meeting with you next Tuesday. The resume I've enclosed Is to give you a better sense of my qualifications. Perhaps it will help you think of other organizations with people who might be interested in my background.

The resume does not say why I've moved to Minneapolis, and you might find that of interest. My spouse and I visited the city several years ago and thought it was a good place to live. He has obtained a very good position here, and based on that, we decided it was time to commit ourselves to a move. As you can see from my work experience, I tend to stay on and move up in jobs, so I now want to more carefully research the job opportunities here before making a commitment. Your help in this task is greatly appreciated.

Feel free to contact me if you have any questions; otherwise, I look forward to meeting with you next Tuesday.

Sincerely,

Anne Marie Furn

Anne Marie Furn

After an Interview

This letter shows how you might follow up after an interview and make a pitch for solving a problem—even when no job formally exists. In this example, the writer suggests that she can use her skills to solve a specific problem she uncovered during her conversations with the employer. Although it never occurs to many job seekers to set up an interview where there doesn't appear to be an opening, many jobs are created in just these situations. I have often done it myself, just to accommodate a good person.

Sandra A. Kijeh

115 South Hawthorn Drive
Port Charlotte, Florida 81641
(941) 523-0942
sakijeh@juno.com

April 10, 2003

Christine Massey
Import Distributors, Inc.
417 East Main Street
Atlanta, Georgia 21649

Dear Ms. Massey:

I know you have a busy schedule, so I was pleasantly surprised when you arranged a time for me to see you. Although you don't have a position open now, your organization is just the sort of place I would like to work. As we discussed, I like to be busy with a variety of duties, and the active pace I saw at your company is what I seek.

Your ideas on increasing business sound creative enough to work. I've thought about the customer-service problem and would like to discuss with you a possible solution. It would involve the use of a simple system of color-coded files that would prioritize older correspondence to give them a priority status. The handling of complaints could also be speeded up through the use of simple form letters similar to those you mentioned. I have some thoughts on how this might be done, too. I will work out a draft of procedures and sample letters if you are interested. They can be done on the computers that your staff members already have and would not require any additional costs to implement.

Whether or not you have a position for me in the future, I appreciate the time you have given me. An extra copy of my resume is enclosed for your files—or to pass on to someone else. Let me know if you want to discuss the ideas I've presented. I will call you next week as you suggested to keep you informed of my progress.

Sincerely,

Sandra Kijeh

Sandra Kijeh

No Interview Is Scheduled

This letter explains why the writer is looking for a job and presents some information that is not normally included in a resume. Note that the writer obtained the employer's name from the membership list of a professional organization, an excellent source of job leads. Also note that the writer states that he will call again to arrange an appointment. Although this letter is assertive and might turn off some employers, many others would be impressed by his assertiveness and be willing to see him when he finally reaches them.

2435 Desert Sands Trail, Phoenix, AZ 27317
(602) 984-7843   cm2525@hotmail.com

January 5, 2003

Sarah Vernon
Vernon Clothing
8661 Parkway Blvd.
Phoenix, AZ 27312

Ms. Vernon,

As you may know, I phoned you several times over the past week while you were in meetings. I hope that you got the messages. Because I did not want to delay contacting you, I decided to write.

I got your name from the American Retail Clothing Association membership list. I am a member of this group and wanted to contact local members to ask their help in locating a suitable position. I realize that you probably don't have a position open now for someone with my skills, but I ask you to do two things on my behalf.

First, I ask that you consider seeing me at your convenience within the next few weeks. Although you might not have a position available for me, you might able to assist me in other ways. And, of course, I would appreciate any consideration for future openings.

Second, you might know of others who have job openings now or in the future. Although I realize that this is an unusual request and that you are quite busy, I do plan on staying in the retail clothing business in this area for some time and would appreciate any assistance you can give me in my search for a new job.

My resume is attached for your information, along with a card that summarizes my background. As you probably know, Allied Tailoring has closed, and I was one of those who stayed on to shut things down in an orderly way. In spite of their regrettable business failure, I was one of those who was responsible for Allied's enormous sales increases over the past decade, and I have substantial experience to bring to any growing retail clothing concern, such as I hear yours is. I will contact you next week and arrange a time that is good for us both. Please feel free to contact me at any time.

Sincerely,

Cornell Morley

Cornell Morley

Writing a Cover Letter to Someone You Don't Know

If it is not practical to directly contact a prospective employer by phone or some other method, it is acceptable to send a resume and cover letter. This approach makes sense in some situations, such as if you are moving to a distant location or responding to a "blind" ad that lists only a post office box number or e-mail address.

I don't recommend sending out "To Whom It May Concern" letters by the basketful. However, there are ways to modify this "shotgun" approach to be more effective. Try to find something you have in common with the person you are contacting. By mentioning this link, your letter becomes a very personal request for assistance. Look at the letters that follow for ideas.

Sample Cover Letters to People You Don't Know

I've included two sample cover letters addressed to employers the writers do not know. Note that both writers zeroed in on location as a common link.

Responding to an Ad

Responding to a want ad puts you in direct competition with the many others who read the same ad, so the odds are not good that this letter would get a response at all. The fact that the writer does not yet live in the area is another negative. Still, you should follow up on any legitimate lead you find. In this case, the position will likely be filled by someone who is available to interview right away. But there is always the chance that, with good follow-up, the writer will be considered if another position becomes available—or the employer might give him the names of others to contact.

John Andrews
12 Lake Street
Chicago, IL 60631
603-997-1045
johnandrews@yahoo.com

January 17, 2003

The Morning Sun
Box N4317
2 Early Drive
Toronto, Ontario R5C IS3

re: Receptionist/Bookkeeper Position

As I plan on relocating to Toronto, your advertisement for a
Receptionist/Bookkeeper caught my attention. Your ad stated that yours is a
small office, and that is precisely what I am looking for. I like dealing with
people and in a previous position had over 5,000 customer contacts a month.
With that experience, I have learned to handle things quickly and pleasantly.

The varied activities in a position combining bookkeeping and reception sound
very interesting. I have received formal training in accounting methods and am
familiar with accounts receivable, accounts payable, and general ledger posting.
I am also familiar with several computerized accounting programs and can
quickly learn any others you might be using.

My resume is enclosed for your consideration. Note that I went to school in
Toronto, and I plan on returning there soon to establish my career. Several of
my family members also live there, and I have provided their local phone
number should you wish to contact me. Please contact that number soon
because I plan on being in Toronto in the near future and would like to speak
with you about this or future positions with your company. I will call you in the
next few weeks to set up an appointment should I not hear from you before
then.

Thank you in advance for your consideration.

Sincerely,

John Andrews

John Andrews

A Long-Distance Letter

This is another example of a person conducting a long-distance job search using names from a professional association. This one also explains why the writer is leaving his old job and includes positive information regarding his references and skills that would not normally be found in a resume. The writer also asks for an interview even though there might not be any jobs open now, as well as for names of others to contact. Of course, the content for this and other cover letters can be adapted for use in an e-mail message.

John B. Goode
321 Smokie Way, Nashville, TN 31201
615.245.1945 — johnbgoode@nash.rr.com

July 10, 2002

Paul Resley
Operations Manager
Rollem Trucking Co.
1-70 Freeway Drive
Kansas City, MO 78401

Dear Mr. Resley:

I obtained your name from the membership directory of the Affiliated Trucking Association. I have been a member for over 10 years, and I am very active in the Southeast Region. The reason I am writing is to ask for your help. The firm I had been employed with has been bought by a larger corporation. The operations here have been disbanded, leaving me unemployed.

Although I like where I live, I know that finding a position at the level of responsibility I seek might require a move. As a center of the transportation business, your city is one of those that I have targeted for special attention.

A copy of my resume is enclosed. I'd like you to review it and consider where a person with my background would get a good reception in Kansas City. Perhaps you could think of a specific person for me to contact?

I have specialized in fast-growing organizations or ones that have experienced rapid change. My particular strength is in bringing things under control, then increasing profits. Although my resume does not state this, I have excellent references from my former employer and would have stayed if a similar position existed at their new location.

As a member of the association, I hope that you will provide some special attention to my request for assistance. Please call my answering service collect if you have any immediate leads. I plan on coming to Kansas City on a job-hunting trip within the next six weeks. Prior to then, I will call you for advice on whom I might contact for interviews. Even if they have no jobs open for me now, perhaps they will know of someone else who might!

Thanks in advance for your help.

Sincerely,

John B. Goode

John B. Goode
Treasurer, Southeast Region
Affiliated Trucking Association

E-mail Cover Letters—Short and Sweet

In many instances, you might be sending your cover letter and resume to a contact by e-mail rather than traditional mail. E-mail can be a highly effective tool in your job search. It speeds up your communication, lends an immediacy to your correspondence, and can send a message that you are technically savvy.

The primary difference between traditional and e-mail cover letters is that a letter sent by e-mail should be shorter. Your reader is likely to scan the letter quickly, then open and view your attached resume. Don't try to convey too much information in your cover letter. Get to the point.

Here is an example of an e-mail cover letter, sent to someone with whom you have already scheduled a meeting.

```
To: LMSmith@salescorp.com

From: jillthomas@yahoo.com

Re: Our Meeting on 8/20 - Territory Sales Position


Ms. Smith, thank you for agreeing to meet with me at 9 a.m. on August
20. I look forward to sharing my ideas for increasing sales in the East
Dallas territory, based on my track record of turning around
unprofitable territories for two prior employers.

Attached is a copy of my resume (MS Word format); I am also pasting the
text below in the event that it is more convenient for you.

I look forward to meeting you on the 20th. Should you have any
questions before then, please call at any time.

Sincerely,

Jill Thomas
```

The Thank-You Note: A Powerful Job Search Tool

Although resumes and cover letters get the attention, thank-you notes often get the results. That's right, sending thank-you notes is both polite and smart. They can help you make a positive impression with employers that more formal correspondence often can't.

So here are the basics of writing and using thank-you notes—those often overlooked but surprisingly effective job search tools.

Tips on When to Send Thank-You Notes—And Why

Thank-you notes have a social tradition that is more intimate and friendly than formal business correspondence. I think that's one of the reasons they work so well—people respond to those who show good manners and say "Thank you." Although a mailed paper thank-you note is often more effective, e-mailed thank-you notes also have their place, and the suggestions that follow can be adapted for that use. Here are some situations when you should use them, along with sample notes to show you how they're done.

Before an Interview

An informal note sent before an interview is often appropriate. You can simply thank someone for being willing to see you. You can also enclose a note with a copy of your resume, but if you do so, keep your note informal and friendly. Remember, this is supposed to be a sincere thanks for help and not an assertive business communication.

Enclose a JIST Card with your thank-you note. JIST Cards fit well into note-sized envelopes and they provide key information about you, as well as a phone number where you can be reached. They also list key skills and other credentials that will help you create a good impression. And, of course, the employer could always forward the card to someone else who might have a job opening for you.

Cynthia Adams,

Thanks so much for your willingness to see me next Wednesday at 9.00 A.M. I know that I am one of many who are interested in working with your organization and appreciate the opportunity to meet you and learn more about the position.

I've enclosed a card that presents the basics of my skills for this job and will bring a copy of my resume to the interview. Please call me if you have any questions at all.

Sincerely,

Bruce Dahlman

Bruce Dahlman

After an Interview

One of the best times to send a thank-you note is right after an interview. There are several reasons for this:

- Sending a note lets the employer know you have good follow-up skills, to say nothing of good manners.

- A thank-you note is another tool to keep your name before the employer at an important time.

- Should the employer have buried, passed along, or lost your resume and previous correspondence, the thank-you note (and an enclosed JIST Card) gives him or her a way to reach you.

For these reasons, I suggest that you send a thank-you note within 24 hours after the interview. Here is an example of such a note.

Dear Mr. O'Beel,

Thank you for the opportunity to interview for the position you have available in the production department. I want you to know that this is the sort of job that I have been looking for, and I am enthusiastic about the possibility of working for you.

I am not just saying this, either. I have been searching for just such a position and believe that I have both the experience and skills to fit nicely into your organization and be productive quickly.

Thanks again for the interview. I enjoyed the visit.

Sara Hall

Sara Hall

Send a thank-you note as soon as possible after an interview or other event. This is when you are fresh in the employer's mind and most likely to create a lasting good impression.

Whenever Anyone Helps You in Your Job Search

Send a thank-you note to anyone who helps you during your job search. This includes contacts who give you referrals, people who provide advice, or those who are simply supportive of you during your search for a new job. I suggest you routinely enclose one or more JIST Cards in these notes. The recipients can then give them to others who might be in a better position to help you. You just never know.

Debbie Childs
2234 Riverbed Avenue • Philadelphia, PA 17963
215-796-3456 • dchilds@philly.rr.com

October 31, 2002

Ms. Helen A. Colcord
Henderson & Associates, Inc.
1801 Washington Blvd., Suite 1201
Philadelphia, PA 17963

Dear Ms. Colcord:

Thank you for sharing your time with me so generously yesterday. I really appreciated talking to you about your career field.

The information you shared with me increased my desire to work in such an area. Your advice has already proven helpful, as I have an appointment to meet with Robert Hopper on Friday.

In case you think of someone else who might need a person like me, I'm enclosing another card summarizing my skills and experience.

Sincerely,

Debbie Childs

Debbie Childs

Tips for Writing Superior Thank-You Notes

The following tips will help you with the content and presentation of your thank-you notes.

Paper and Envelope

Use a good-quality note paper with matching envelope. Most stationery stores have thank-you note cards and envelopes in a variety of styles. Select a note that is simple and professional—avoid cute graphics and sayings. A simple "Thank You" on the front will do.

I suggest off-white and buff colors. You can also use a simple but excellent-quality stationery paper with matching envelopes, although I prefer the printed cards. If you are typing your notes, use the same paper and format as you did on your resume.

Typed vs. Handwritten vs. E-mail

Traditionally, thank-you notes are handwritten. If your handwriting is good, it is perfectly acceptable to write them. If not, or if your note is longer than a few sentences, it should be word processed—but thank-you notes should never appear formal. E-mail thank-you notes can also be reasonably effective, particularly because they can be delivered quickly. The best approach may be to consider an e-mail thank-you followed up by a mailed one.

Salutation

Unless you already know the person you are thanking, don't use her first name. Write "Dear Mrs. Smith" or "Ms. Smith" rather than the less formal "Dear Pam." Include the date.

The Note Itself

Keep it short and friendly. This is not the place to write, "The reason you should hire me is…." Remember, the note is a thank-you for what *they* did, not a hard-sell pitch for what *you* want.

As appropriate, be specific about when you will make contact again. If you plan to meet soon, send a note saying you look forward to the meeting and thanking the person for the appointment. And make sure you include something to remind the recipient of who you are; your name might not be enough to jog his or her memory.

Your Signature

Use your first and last name. Avoid initials—and make sure your signature is legible.

Send It Right Away

Write and send your note no later than 24 hours after you make your contact. Ideally, you should write it immediately after the contact, while the details are still fresh in your mind. Always send a note after an interview, even if things did not go well. It can't hurt, and it could help.

Enclose a JIST Card

Depending on the situation, a JIST Card is often the ideal enclosure to send with a thank-you note. It's small, soft-sell, and provides your phone number in case the person wants to reach you. It will remind the employer of you (should any jobs open up) and give him or her a tool to pass along to someone else. Make sure your thank-you notes and envelopes are big enough to hold an unfolded JIST Card.

Other Job Search Correspondence

There are several other kinds of correspondence you can send to people during the course of your job search. I've included some brief comments on a few of them in the following section.

Follow-Up Letters

You have already seen examples of letters and notes that follow an interview. In some cases, a longer or more detailed letter is appropriate. The objective in such a letter is either to provide additional information or to present a proposal. The Sandra Kijeh letter shown earlier is an example of a follow-up letter that suggests a specific proposal.

In some cases, you can submit a more comprehensive proposal that would essentially justify your job. If there is already a job opening available, you can submit an outline of what you would do if you were hired. And if there is not a job available, you can create a proposal that would create a job and tells what you would do to make it pay off for the employer.

In writing such a proposal, it is essential that you be specific in detailing what you would do and what results these actions would bring. For example, if you think you can increase sales, how will you do it and how much will they increase? It is not unusual for a job to be created as a result of this approach.

You can also use a follow-up letter to explain objections you encountered during the interview or present some new information about your background that you forgot to mention. Follow-up letters, like thank-you notes, will set you apart from others, because most job candidates do not write them.

Enclosures

You might want to include something along with other correspondence, such as an article you've clipped that is relevant to something you discussed at your interview. This is sometimes appropriate, although I advise against sending too much material unless it is asked for. And never send originals of anything unless you are willing to lose them. Assume, in all cases, that the employer will keep what you send.

Sticky Notes

You have surely seen and used those little notes that stick on papers, walls, and other things. These can be useful to point out specific items on attachments, to provide additional details, or simply to indicate who sent the materials.

Letters to People Who Help You in Your Network

As I mentioned before, you should send a note, e-mail, or letter to anyone who helps you in your job search. This includes people who simply give you the name of someone else to contact or who speak with you on the phone. Besides being good manners, it accomplishes three things:

- It gives them additional information about you through an enclosed resume and JIST Card.

- It helps to keep you in their mind.

- It gives them something (a resume or JIST Card) that they can pass along to others.

Although these advantages should look suspiciously like those I presented in the section on thank-you notes, it's worth repeating here. Anyone can become part of the network of people who help you in your job search. Staying in touch—and giving them tools such as JIST Cards—allows them to help you in ways that are difficult to know in advance.

A List of References

When an employer begins to look seriously at you, the person doing the hiring might want to contact your references as part of a final screening process. To make this easier, you should prepare a list of references in advance. This list should include the complete name, title, organization, address, e-mail, and phone number for each person. You should also include information about how each one knows you.

You should always ask potential references whether they will agree to serve as a reference. In some cases, you should take the time to prepare them by sending information on the types of jobs you are seeking, a current resume, and other details. If there is any question about whether someone will provide you with a positive reference, discuss it in advance so that you know what he or she is likely to say about you. If it is not positive, drop that person from your list.

Letters of Reference

In today's litigious climate, many organizations fear lawsuits as a result of giving out negative information about an ex-employee. For this reason, it is often difficult for a prospective employer to get meaningful information over the phone. This is one reason you should ask your previous employers and other references to write a letter you can submit to others if asked to do so. If the letters are positive, the advantages are clear. Even if a letter is negative, at least you will know in advance that there is a problem with that reference—and you will have the opportunity to call and negotiate what he or she will tell prospective employers. Of course, you should not volunteer a negative letter of reference.

Unsolicited Letters and E-mail Messages

Once more, I want to discourage you from sending unsolicited letters or e-mail messages requesting interviews or other assistance as your primary job search technique. Even though many job search books recommend sending out lots of unsolicited letters and resumes, the evidence is overwhelming that this does not work for most people. The exception is if your skills are very much in demand; but in most cases, you would still be better off to simply pick up the phone and ask for an interview.

However, sending a letter or e-mail to people with whom you share a common bond—such as fellow alumni or members of a professional group—can be reasonably effective. This is particularly true if you are looking for a job in another city or region and you ask them to help you by giving you names of contacts. Several of the sample cover letters provide examples of people using this very technique, and it can work, particularly if you follow up.

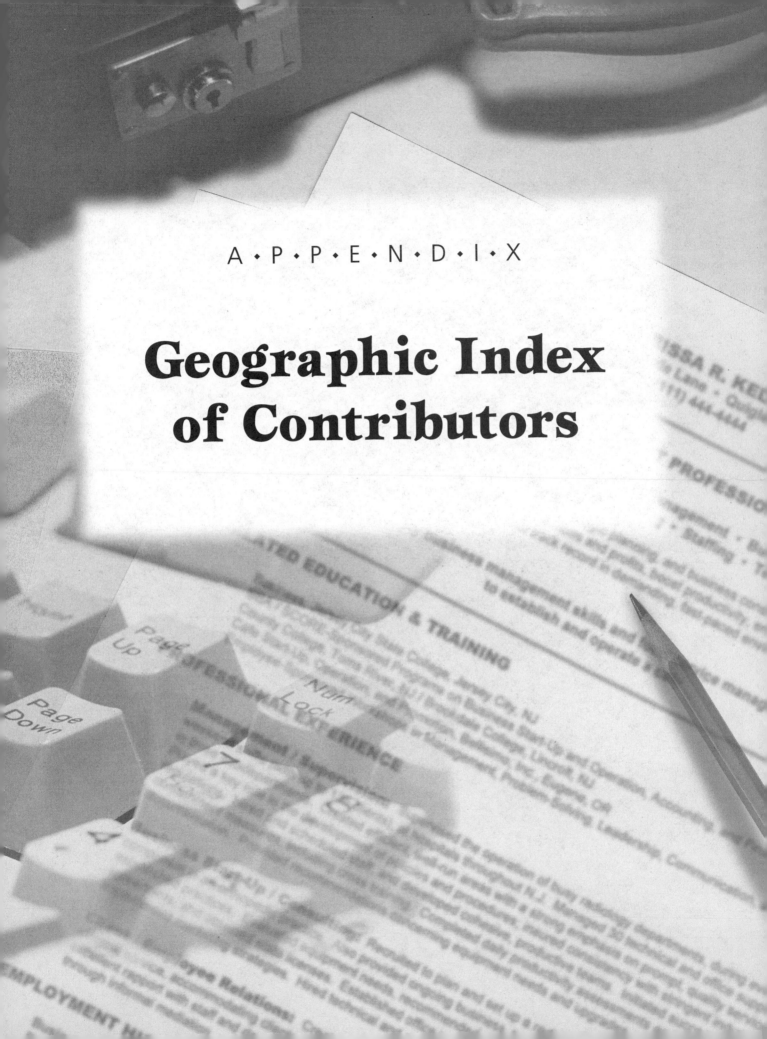

A·P·P·E·N·D·I·X

Geographic Index
of Contributors

Geographic Index of Contributors

The sample resumes in this book were written by professional resume and cover letter writers. If you need help with your resume and job search correspondence, you can use the following list to locate a career professional in your area.

United States

Alabama

Don Orlando, MBA, CPRW, IJCTC, CCM
President, The McLean Group
640 S. McDonough St.
Montgomery, AL 36104
Phone: (334) 264-2020
Fax: (334) 264-9227
E-mail: yourcareercoach@aol.com

Arizona

Brooke Andrews, CPRW
A New Beginning
521 N. Superstition Blvd.
Chandler, AZ 85226
Phone: (480) 786-1806
E-mail: Brooke@amug.org

Fran Holsinger
Career Profiles
4625 S. Wendler Dr., Ste. 111
Tempe, AZ 85282
Phone: (602) 748-1393
Fax: (602) 748-1394
fholsinger@aol.com

California

Roleta Fowler, CPRW, CEIP
Wordbusters Resume & Writing Services
Fillmore, CA 93015-1137
Phone: (805) 524-3493
Toll-free phone: (866) RESUME-0
E-mail: resumes@wbresumes.com or
wbresumes@yahoo.com
www.wbresumes.com

Susan Geary, CRW, CPRW
President, 1st Rate Resumes
4333 Copeland Ave.
San Diego, CA 92105-1207
Phone: (619) 280-2960
E-mail: sgeary@1stRateResumes.com
www.1stRateResumes.com

Leatha Jones, CPRW, CEIP
John F. Kennedy University
Career Development Center
12 Altarinda Rd.
Orinda, CA 94563
Phone: (925) 258-2568
E-mail: career@jfku.edu

Nancy Karvonen, CPRW, CCM, IJCTC, CEIP
Executive Director, A Better Word & Resume
4490 County Rd. HH
Orland, CA 95963
Phone: (209) 745-5107
Toll-free phone: (877) 973-7863
Fax: (209) 745-7114
E-mail: careers@aresumecoach.com
www.aresumecoach.com

Myriam-Rose Kohn, CPRW, JCTC, CCM, CEIP
President, JEDA Enterprises
27201 Tourney Rd., Ste. 201
Valencia, CA 91355-1857
Phone: (661) 253-0801
Toll-free phone: (800) 600-JEDA
Fax: (661) 253-0744
E-mail:
myriam-rose@jedaenterprises.com
www.jedaenterprises.com

Anita Radosevich, CPRW, JCTC, CEIP
President, Anita's Business & Career Services
315 W. Pine St., Ste. #5
Lodi, CA 95240
Phone: (209) 368-4444
Toll-free phone: (888) 247-3786
Fax: (209) 368-2834
E-mail: anita@abcresumes.com
www.abcresumes.com

Susan Britton Whitcomb, NCRW, CPRW, CCM
Alpha Omega Career Services
757 E. Hampton Way
Fresno, CA 93704
Phone: (559) 222-7474
Fax: (559) 227-0670
E-mail: coaching@mediaone.net
www.careerwriter.com

Connecticut

Louise Garver, MA, JCTC, CMP, CPRW
President, Career Directions, LLC
115 Elm St., Ste. 203
Enfield, CT 06082
Phone: (860) 623-9476
Toll-free phone: (888) 222-3731
Fax: (860) 623-9473
E-mail: TheCareerPro@aol.com
www.resumeimpact.com

Jan Melnik, CPRW, CCM
President, Absolute Advantage
P.O. Box 718
Durham, CT 06422
Phone: (860) 349-0256
Fax: (860) 349-1343
E-mail: CompSPJan@aol.com
www.janmelnik.com

Florida

Laura A. DeCarlo, CCM, CPRW, JCTC
President, A Competitive Edge Career Service
1665 Clover Circle
Melbourne, FL 32935
Toll-free phone: (800) 715-3442
Fax: (321) 752-7513
E-mail: getanedge@aol.com
www.acompetitiveedge.com

René Hart, CPRW
Executive Director, Resumes For Success!
5337 N. Socrum Loop Rd. #116
Lakeland, FL 33809
Phone: (863) 859-2439
Fax: (509) 277-0892
E-mail: renehart@resumesforsuccess.com
www.ResumesForSuccess.com

Beverly Harvey, CPRW, JCTC, CCM
President, Beverly Harvey Resume &
Career Service
P.O. Box 750
Pierson, FL 32180
Phone: (386) 749-3111
Fax: (386) 749-4881
E-mail: beverly@harveycareers.com
www.harveycareers.com

Carol Heider, CPRW
Heider's Secretarial Service, Inc.
10014 N. Dale Mabry, Ste. 101
Tampa, FL 33618
Phone: (831) 282-0011
hssheider@aol.com
browser.to/heidersresumecenter

Jean F. West, CPRW, JCTC
President, Impact Resume & Career Services
207 10th Ave.
Indian Rocks Beach, FL 33785
Toll-free phone: (888) 590-2534
Fax: (727) 593-7386
E-mail: resumes@tampabay.rr.com
www.impactresumes.com

Illinois

Sally McIntosh, NCRW, CPRW, JCTC
Advantage Resumes (of Illinois)
35 Westfair Dr.
Jacksonville, IL 62650
Phone: (217) 245-0752
Toll-free phone: (800) 485-9779
Fax: (217) 243-4451
E-mail: sally@reswriter.com
www.reswriter.com

Joellyn Wittenstein, CPRW
A1 Quality Resumes
2786 N. Buffalo Grove Rd., Unit 206
Buffalo Grove, IL 60004
Phone: (847) 255-1686
Fax: (847) 255-7224
E-mail: joellyn@interaccess.com

Indiana

Richard Lanham, MDiv, MA, MRE, CCM
General Manager/Senior Consultant,
R.L. Stevens & Associates, Inc.
8888 Keystone Crossing #950
Indianapolis, IN 46240
Phone: (317) 846-8888
Toll-free phone: (888) 806-7313
Fax: (317) 846-8949
E-mail: rlanham@rlstevens.com
www.interviewing.com

Carole E. Pefley, CPRW
TESS, Inc.
5661 Madison Avenue
Indianapolis, IN 46227
Phone: (317) 788-8377

Iowa

Marcy Johnson, CPRW, CEIP
President, First Impression Resume &
Job Readiness
11805 U.S. Hwy. 69
Story City, IA 50248
Phone: (515) 733-4998
Fax: (515) 733-4681
E-mail: firstimpression@prairieinet.net
www.resume-job-readiness.com

Kansas

Kristie Cook, CPRW
Absolutely Write
Olathe, KS
Phone: (913) 269-3519
E-mail: kriscook@absolutely-write.com
www.absolutely-write.com

James Walker, MS
Counselor—ACAP Center
Bldg. 210, Rm. 006, Custer Ave.
Fort Riley, KS 66442
Phone: (785) 239-2278
Fax: (785) 239-2251
E-mail: jwalker8199@yahoo.com

Kentucky

Debbie Ellis, CPRW
President, Phoenix Career Group
103 Patrick Henry Ct.
Danville, KY 40422
Toll-free phone: (800) 876-5506 inside U.S.
Toll-free fax: (888) 329-5409 inside U.S.
Phone or fax: (859) 236-4001 worldwide
E-mail: debbie@phoenixcareergroup.com
www.PhoenixCareerGroup.com

Andrea Peak, CPRW
3011 Boaires Ln.
Louisville, KY 40220
E-mail: andrea12@iglou.com

Amy Whitmer, CPRW
President, Envision Resume Services
P.O. Box 7523
Louisville, KY 40257
Phone or fax: (877) 808-3969
E-mail: amy@envision-resumes.com
www.envision-resumes.com

Louisiana

Laurie J. Roy, CRW, CPRW, CCM, CCA, JCTC
President, Professional Resume Writing &
Research Assn.
1106 Coolidge Blvd.
Lafayette, LA 70503
Toll-free phone: (800) 225-8688
Fax: (337) 233-1871
E-mail: laurie@prwra.com
www.prwra.com

Maine

Rolande L. LaPointe, CPC, CIPC, CPRW,
IJCTC, CCM
President, RO-LAN Associates, Inc.
725 Sabattus St.
Lewiston, ME 04240
Phone: (207) 784-1010
Fax: (207) 782-3446
E-mail: RLapointe@aol.com

Maryland

Sheila Adjahoe
Principal, The Adjahoe Group
Upper Marlboro, MD 20774
Phone: (301) 350-5137
Fax: (301) 324-7736
E-mail: sadjahoe@aol.com

Diane Burns, CPRW, IJCTC, CCM, CEIP
President, Career Marketing Techniques
5219 Thunder Hill Rd.
Columbia, MD 21045
Phone or fax: (410) 884-0213
E-mail: dianecprw@aol.com
www.polishedresumes.com

Massachusetts

Bernice Antifonario, MA
President, Antion Associates, Inc.
885 Main St. #10A
Tewksbury, MA 01876
Phone: (978) 858-0637
Fax: (978) 851-4528
E-mail: Bernice@antion-associates.com
www.antion-associates.com

Jean Cummings, MAT, CPRW, CEIP
President, A RESUME FOR TODAY
123 Minot Rd.
Concord, MA 01742
Phone: (978) 371-9266
Fax: (978) 964-0529
E-mail: jc@aresumefortoday.com
www.AResumeForToday.com

Michigan

Jennifer Nell Ayres
President, Nell Personal Advancement Resources
P.O. Box 2
Clarkston, MI 48347
Phone: (248) 969-9933
Fax: (248) 969-9935
E-mail: info@nellresources.com
www.nellresources.com

Janet L. Beckstrom
President, Word Crafter
1717 Montclair Ave.
Flint, MI 48503
Toll-free phone: (800) 351-9818
Phone or fax: (810) 232-9257
E-mail: wordcrafter@voyager.net

Joyce L. Fortier, MBA, CPRW, JCTC, CCM
President, Create Your Career
23871 W. Lebost
Novi, MI 48375
Phone: (248) 478-5662
Toll-free phone: (800) 793-9895
Fax: (248) 426-9974
E-mail: careerist@aol.com
www.careerist.com

Maria E. Hebda, CPRW
Managing Executive, Career Solutions, LLC
2216 Northfield
Trenton, MI 48183
Phone: (734) 676-9170
Toll-free phone: (877) 777-7242
Fax: (734) 676-9487
E-mail: careers@writingresumes.com
www.writingresumes.com

Lorie Lebert, CPRW, JCTC
President, Resumes For Results, LLC
P.O. Box 267
Novi, MI 48376
Phone: (248) 380-6101
Fax: (248) 380-0169
E-mail: Lorie@DoMyResume.com
www.DoMyResume.com

Minnesota

Beverley Drake, CPRW, CEIP, JCTC
CareerVision Resume and Job Search Systems
1816 Baihly Hills Dr. SW
Rochester, MN 55902
Phone: (507) 252-9825
E-mail: bdcprw@aol.com

Barb Poole, CPRW, CRW
President, Hire Imaging
1812 Red Fox Rd.
St. Cloud, MN 56301
Phone: (320) 253-0975
Fax: (320) 253-1790
E-mail: eink@astound.net

Missouri

Meg Montford, CCM, CPRW
President, Abilities Enhanced
P.O. Box 9667
Kansas City, MO 64134
Phone: (816) 767-1196
Fax: (801) 650-8529
E-mail: meg@abilitiesenhanced.com
www.abilitiesenhanced.com

Karen M. Silins, CRW, CCA
President, A + Career & Resume
9719 Woodland Ln.
Kansas City, MO 64131
Phone: (816) 942-3019
Fax: (816) 942-1505
E-mail: apluscareer@aol.com
www.careerandresume.com

New Hampshire

Michelle Dumas, CPRW, NCRW, CCM, JCTC, CEIP
President, Distinctive Documents
146 Blackwater Rd.
Somersworth, NH 03878
Toll-free phone: (800) 644-9694
Fax: (603) 947-2954
E-mail: resumes@distinctiveweb.com
www.distinctiveweb.com

New Jersey

Beverly Baskin, EdS, MA, NCCC, CPRW, LPC
BBCS Counseling Services
6 Alberta Dr.
Marlboro, NJ 07746
Toll-free phone: (800) 300-4079
Fax (732) 972-8846
E-mail: bbcs@att.net
www.baskincareer.com

Vivian Belen, NCRW, CPRW, JCTC
Managing Director, The Job Search Specialist
1102 Bellair Ave.
Fair Lawn, NJ 07410
Phone: (201) 797-2883
Fax: (201) 797-5566
E-mail: vivian@jobsearchspecialist.com
www.jobsearchspecialist.com

Alesia Benedict, CPRW, JCTC
Career Objectives
151 W. Passaic St.
Rochelle Park, NJ 07662
Phone: (201) 909-3772
Toll-free phone: (800) 206-5353
Fax: (201) 368-0411
Toll-free fax: (800) 206-5454
E-mail: Careerobj@aol.com
www.getinterviews.com

Nina Ebert, CPRW
President, A Word's Worth Resume & Writing Service
808 Lowell Ave.
Toms River, NJ 08753
Phone: (732) 349-2225
Fax: (609) 758-7799
E-mail: wrdswrth@gbsias.com
www.keytosuccessresumes.com

Susan Guarneri, NCC, NCCC, LPC, CPRW, IJCTC, CCM, CEIP
President, Guarneri Associates/Resumagic
1101 Lawrence Rd.
Lawrenceville, NJ 08648
Phone: (609) 771-1669
Fax: (609) 637-0449
E-mail: Resumagic@aol.com
www.resume-magic.com

Meg Guiseppi, CPRW
President, Resumes Plus
13 Perona Rd.
Andover, NJ 07821
Phone: (973) 726-0757
Fax: (973) 726-0121
E-mail: resumesplus@nac.net

Elona Harkins
President, Absolute Jobsearch Services
P.O. Box 2776
Westfield, NJ 07091
Phone: (908) 233-8910
Toll-free phone: (866) 233-8910
Fax: (908) 301-1234
E-mail: resumesplus@absolutejobsearch.com
www.absolutejobsearch.com

Fran Kelley, MA, CPRW, SPHR, JCTC
President, The Resume Works
71 Highwood Ave.
Waldwick, NJ 07463
Phone or fax: (201) 670-9643
E-mail: TwoFreeSpirits@worldnet.att.net
www.careermuse.com

Rhoda Kopy, CPRW
A Hire Image®
26 Main St., Ste. E
Toms River, NJ 08753
Phone: (732) 505-9515
Fax: (732) 505-3125
E-mail: ahi@infi.net
www.jobwinningresumes.com

Melanie A. Noonan, CPS
Peripheral Pro
560 Lackawanna Ave.
West Paterson, NJ 07424
Phone: (973) 785-3011
E-mail: PeriPro1@aol.com

Carol Rossi, CPRW
Computerized Documents
4 Baywood Blvd.
Brick, NJ 08723
Phone or fax: (732) 477-5172
Toll-free phone: (866) 477-5172
E-mail: info@powerfulresumes.com
www.powerfulresumes.com

Igor Shpudejko, CPRW, JCTC, MBA
President, Career Focus
1207 Sycamore Ln.
Mahwah, NJ 07430
Phone: (201) 825-2865
Fax: (201) 825-7711
E-mail: ishpudejko@aol.com
www.CareerInFocus.com

New York

Ann Baehr, CPRW
President, Best Resumes
Long Island, NY 11717
Phone: (631) 435-1879
Fax: (631) 435-3655
E-mail: resumesbest@earthlink.net
www.e-bestresumes.com

Barbara M. Beaulieu, CPRW
Academic Concepts
214 Second St.
Scotia, NY 12302
Phone: (518) 377-1080
E-mail: acresume@nycap.rr.com

Mark D. Berkowitz, NCCC, CPRW, CEIP
Career Development Resources
1312 Walter Rd.
Yorktown Heights, NY 10598
Phone: (914) 962-1548
Fax: (914) 962-0325
E-mail: Cardevres@aol.com

Arnold G. Boldt, CPRW, JCTC
Arnold-Smith Associates
625 Panorama Trail, Bldg. 2 #200
Rochester, NY 14625
Phone: (585) 383-0350
Fax: (585) 387-0516
E-mail: Arnie@ResumeSOS.com
www.ResumeSOS.com

(Ms.) Freddie Cheek, CPRW, CWDP
Cheek & Cristantello Career Connections
4511 Harlem Rd., Ste. 3
Amherst, NY 14226
Phone: (716) 839-3635
Fax: (716) 831-9320
E-mail: fscheek@adelphia.net
www.CheekandCristantello.com

Kirsten Dixson, JCTC, CPRW, CEIP
Principal, New Leaf Career Solutions
P.O. Box 991
Bronxville, NY 10708
Toll-free phone: (866) 639-5323
Toll-free fax: (888) 887-7166
E-mail: kdixson@newleafcareer.com
www.newleafcareer.com

Donna Farrise
President, Dynamic Resumes of Long Island, Inc.
300 Motor Pkwy., Ste. 200
Hauppauge, NY 11788
Phone: (631) 951-4120
Fax: (631) 952-1817
E-mail: donna@dynamicresumes.com
www.dynamicresumes.com

Betty Geller, NCRW, CPRW
President, Apple Resume and Career Services
456 W. Water St., Ste. 1
Elmira, NY 14905
Phone or fax: (607) 734-2090
E-mail: appleresumesvc@stny.rr.com
www.appleresumes.com

Andrea J. Howard, MSEd
Employment Counselor, NYS Department of Labor
175 Central Ave.
Albany, NY 12206
Phone: (518) 462-7600
E-mail: ah831254@aol.com

Michelle Kennedy, CPRW
President, Scribble Ink, Ltd.
P.O. Box 1375
Port Washington, NY 11050
Phone: (516) 767-7INK
E-mail: scribble_ink@hotmail.com

Linsey Levine
CareerCounsel
Chappaqua, NY
Phone: (914) 238-1065
E-mail: LinZlev@aol.com

Kim Little, JCTC
President, Fast Track Resumes
1281 Courtney Dr.
Victor, NY 14564
Phone: (716) 742-2467
Fax: (716) 742-1907
E-mail: info@fast-trackresumes.com
www.fast-trackresumes.com

Linda Matias, JCTC, CEIP
Executive Director, CareerStrides
34 E. Main St. #276
Smithtown, NY 11787
Phone or fax: (631) 382-2425
E-mail: careerstrides@bigfoot.com
www.careerstrides.com

Ilona Vanderwoude
The Vanderwoude Advantage
Riverdale, NY 10471
Phone: (914) 376-4217
Fax: (646) 349-2218
E-mail: info@YourResumeWriter.com

North Carolina

Rima Bogardus, CPRW
President, Career Support Services
P.O. Box 3035
Cary, NC 27519
Phone: (919) 380-3770
E-mail: rima@careersupportservices.com
www.careersupportservices.com

Karen McMahan, JCTC
President, Do-It-Write, Inc.
2530 Meridian Pkwy., 2nd Fl.
Durham, NC 27713
Phone: (919) 806-4690
Fax: (919) 806-4790
E-mail: kemcmahan@aol.com
www.do-it-write.com

John M. O'Connor
President, Career Pro Resumes
3301 Woman's Club Dr., Ste. 125
Raleigh, NC 27612-4812
Phone: (919) 787-2400
Fax: (919) 787-2411
E-mail: john@careerproresumes.com
www.careerproresumes.com

Deborah C. Sherrie, CPRW
Right Management Consultants
710 Jefferson Dr.
Charlotte, NC 28270
Phone: (704) 364-1441
Fax: (704) 365-8892
E-mail: dsherrie@bellsouth.net

North Dakota

Mary Laske, MS, CPRW
President, ExecPro
1713 Park Blvd.
Fargo, ND 58103
Phone: (701) 235-8007
Fax: (707) 760-3951
E-mail: execpro@att.net
www.execproresumes.com

Ohio

Leah Brantley, CEIP
President, Resumes That Work! Inc.
P.O. Box 9472
Cincinnati, OH 45209-9472
Toll-free phone or fax: (800) 949-4979
E-mail: brantleylg@aol.com

Melissa L. Kasler, CPRW
Resume Impressions
One N. Lancaster St.
Athens, OH 45701
Phone: (740) 592-3993
E-mail: resume@frognet.net

Louise Kursmark, CPRW, JCTC, CCM, CEIP
President, Best Impression Career Services, Inc.
Cincinnati, OH 45242
Toll-free phone: (888) 792-0030
Phone: (513) 792-0030
Fax: (513) 792-0961
E-mail: LK@yourbestimpression.com
www.yourbestimpression.com

Sharon Pierce-Williams, MEd, CPRW
President, TheResume.Doc
609 Lincolnshire Ln.
Findlay, OH 45840
Phone: (419) 422-0228
Fax: (419) 425-1185
E-mail: TheResumeDocSPW@aol.com

Teena Rose, CPRW, CEIP, CCM
President, Resume to Referral
P.O. Box 328
Englewood, OH 45322
Phone: (937) 264-3025
Fax: (937) 236-2059
E-mail: admin@resumetoreferral.com
www.resumebycprw.com

Janice Worthington, MA, CPRW, JCTC, CEIP
President, Worthington Career Services
6636 Belleshire St.
Columbus, OH 43229
Phone: (614) 890-1645
Toll-free phone: (877) 973-7863
Fax: (614) 523-3400
E-mail: janice@worthingtonresumes.com
www.worthingtonresumes.com

Oregon

Pat Kendall, NCRW, JCTC
Advanced Resume Concepts
18580 SW Rosa Rd.
Aloha, OR 97007
Phone: (503) 591-9143
Fax: (503) 642-2535
E-mail: reslady@aol.com
www.reslady.com

Pennsylvania

Jewel Bracy DeMaio, CPRW, CEIP
President, A Perfect Resume.com
340 Main St.
Royersford, PA 19468
Phone: (610) 327-8002
Toll-free phone: (800) 227-5131
Fax: (610) 327-8014
E-mail: mail@aperfectresume.com
www.aperfectresume.com

Jane Roqueplot, CBC
President, JaneCo's Sensible Solutions
194 N. Oakland Ave.
Sharon, PA 16146
Phone: (724) 342-0100
Toll-free phone: (888) 526-3267
Fax: (724) 346-5263
E-mail: info@janecos.com
www.janecos.com

Tennessee

Carolyn Braden, CPRW
President, Braden Resume Solutions
108 La Plaza Dr.
Hendersonville, TN 37075
Phone: (615) 822-3317
Fax: (615) 826-9611
E-mail: bradenresume@comcast.net

Texas

Cheryl Ann Harland, CPRW, JCTC
President, Resumes By Design
25227 Grogan's Mill Rd., Ste. 125
The Woodlands, TX 77380
Toll-free phone: (888) 213-1650
Fax: (281) 296-1601
E-mail: CAH@resumesbydesign.com
www.ResumesByDesign.com

Lynn Hughes, MA, CPRW, CEIP
A Resume and Career Service, Inc.
P.O. Box 6911
Lubbock, TX 79493
Phone: (806) 785-9800
Fax: (806) 785-2711
E-mail: lynn@aresumeservice.com
www.aresumeservice.com

William G. Murdock, CPRW
President, The Employment Coach
7770 Meadow Rd., Ste. 109
Dallas, TX 75230
Phone or fax: (214) 750-4781
E-mail: bmurdock@swbell.net

Utah

Diana C. LeGere
President, Executive Final Copy
P.O. Box 171311
Salt Lake City, UT 84117
Phone: (801) 550-5697
Toll-free phone: (866) 754-5465
Fax: (626) 602-8715
E-mail: executiveresumes@yahoo.com
www.executivefinalcopy.com

Virginia

Wendy S. Enelow, CPRW, JCTC, CCM
President, Career Masters Institute
119 Old Stable Rd.
Lynchburg, VA 24503
Phone: (434) 386-3100
Toll-free phone: (800) 881-9972
Fax: (434) 386-3200
E-mail: wendyenelow@cminstitute.com
www.cminstitute.com

Anne G. Kramer
President, Alpha Bits
4411 Trinity Ct.
Virginia Beach, VA 23455
Phone: (757) 464-1914
E-mail: akramer@kiscomputers.net

Helen Oliff
Turning Point
2307 Freetown Ct. #12C
Reston, VA 20191
Phone: (703) 716-0077
Fax: (703) 997-8651
E-mail: helen@turningpointnow.com
www.turningpointnow.com

Washington

Alice Hanson, CPRW
President, Aim Resumes
P.O. Box 75054
Seattle, WA 98125
Phone: (206) 527-3100
Fax: (206) 527-3101
E-mail: alice@aimresume.com
www.aimresume.com

Lonnie L. Swanson, CPRW, JCTC, CDF
A Career Advantage
21590 Clear Creek Rd. NW
Poulsbo, WA 98370
Phone: (360) 779-2877
E-mail: resumes@nwinet.com
www.TheResumePros.com

West Virginia

Barbie Dallmann, CPRW
Happy Fingers Word Processing & Resume Service
1205 Wilke Dr.
Charleston, WV 25314-1726
Phone: (304) 345-4495
Fax: (304) 343-2017
E-mail: BarbieDall@mindspring.com
www.HappyFingers.com

Wisconsin

Kathy Keshemberg, NCRW
A Career Advantage
P.O. Box 4010
Appleton, WI 54915
Phone: (920) 731-5167
E-mail: acareeradvantage@aol.com
www.acareeradvantage.com

Julie Walraven
President, Design Resumes
1202 Elm St.
Wausau, WI 54401
Phone: (715) 845-5664
Fax: (715) 845-8076
E-mail: design@dwave.net
www.designresumes.com

Australia

Gayle Howard, CPRW, CRW, CCM
Founder/Owner, Top Margin Resumes Online
7 Commerford Pl.
Chirnside Park, Melbourne 3116
Australia
Phone: + 61 3 9726 6694
Fax: + 61 3 9726 5316
E-mail: your.cv@bigpond.net.au
www.topmargin.com

Canada

Ross Macpherson, MA, CPRW, JCTC, CEIP, CJST
President, Career Quest
1586 Major Oaks Rd.
Pickering, Ontario L1X 2J6
Canada
Phone: (905) 426-8548
Fax: (905) 426-4274
E-mail: ross@yourcareerquest.com
www.yourcareerquest.com

Location Unknown

Betty A. Callahan, PC, CPRW

Elizabeth M. Carey, CPRW

Melanie Douthit

Jennie Dowden

Robin Folsom

Danitza Grimes, CPRW

Colleen S. Jaracz

Laura Karlak, CPRW

Marian K. Kozlowski, MBA

Carol Lawrence

David M. Newbold

Patricia L. Nieboer, CPS, CPRW

Annemarie Pawlina

Christina M. Popa, CPRW

Sandy Adcox Saburn, CPRW

Jon Shafer

Thomas E. Spann

Connie Stevens

John Suarez

Robert Thomason

Gary Watkins

Index

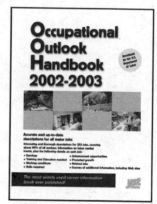
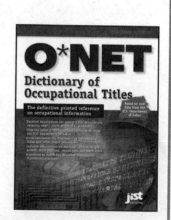

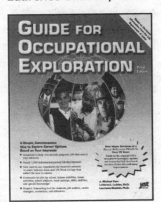